The Roots of Ancient India

Walter A. Fairservis, Jr.

THE
ROOTS
OF
ANCIENT
INDIA

Second Edition, Revised

The University of Chicago Press
Chicago and London

Library of Congress Cataloging in Publication Data

Fairservis, Walter Ashlin, 1921–
 The roots of ancient India.

 Bibliography: p.
 Includes index.
 1. India—Antiquities. 2. India—Civilization.
I. Title.
DS418.F24 1975   934   74–33510
ISBN 0–226–23429–0 pbk.

The University of Chicago Press, Chicago 60637
The University of Chicago Press, Ltd., London

International Standard Book Number: 0–226–23429–0
Library of Congress Catalog Card Number: 74–33510

To the Memory of
Bendapudi Subbarao
a true scholar of India
who died too soon
and to
Sir Aurel Stein
who opened
The Great Road

CONTENTS

III · THE PRELUDE TO SETTLED LIFE 82

IV · THE BEGINNING OF SETTLED LIFE 102

V · THE PRELUDE TO CIVILIZATION 166

VI · THE ORIGIN OF THE HARAPPAN CIVILIZATION 217

List of Illustrations

PLATES

FIGURES

MAPS

TABLES

Preface to the Revised Edition

THE ORIGINAL WRITING of this book was essentially complete toward the end of 1967. Since that time the pace of archaeological research in the subcontinent has been erratic, partially owing to the troubles between India and Pakistan and partially to the changes in the directorships of the departments of archaeology in both countries. More important, perhaps, is the fact that the generation which was trained by Sir Mortimer Wheeler in the 1940s has grown older and their place is gradually being taken over by a generation that never had the opportunity to study in the Wheeler school. It is a period of adjustment.

Archaeology itself has been shaken by the dynamism of the so-called new archaeology, which emphasizes the need to create testable models and to be unafraid of making assumptions which can in the end be proven false or true by those rational means which the scientist uses in analyzing natural phenomena. Among these means, quantitative approaches have become popular, for both computer and mathematical logic make possible the solution of numerous problems or the creation of methods by which problems can be posed. Quantitative methods generally have produced excellent results in the problem of absolute dating, in faunal and floral studies, and in the analysis of materials. In the intervening eight years since this book was first written, quantifying techniques have had an increasing role in subcontinental archaeology—although, with a few important exceptions, only in the analysis of nonartifactual materials.

In the summation of archaeological research between 1968 and 1974 (see Appendix K) the goals of present-day subcontinental archaeology can be readily ascertained. They are characterized by a broad program of survey and excavation aimed at constructing the outlines of a relative and absolute chronological framework which would eventually link up literary accounts to archaeological materials. Coupled with this is an ongoing effort to clarify or determine typological links, particularly to Western and Central Asia. These goals have placed emphasis on the determination of the stratigraphic position of artifact types, the discovery and enumeration of new sites by which to demonstrate cultural distribution, and the collection of C-14 dates. The recent field work has had considerable success in achieving these goals, even if only in part, and an increasingly respectable chronological scheme is emerging. However, whenever archaeologists gather on the subcontinent, there are always questions raised and theories set forth as to the character of these cultures which are being delineated in time and space. This has been true with regard to the Harappan civilization in particular and is increasingly so with non-Harappan cultures as well.

It is here, then, that little progress seems to have been made, for most subcontinental archaeologists lack a fundamental and valid methodology with which to interrelate all parts in defining that complexity known as "culture." The overwhelming number base their interpretative techniques on historical methods—methods which are particularly well suited to the comprehension of the factors which produce change in the gross sense (invasion, natural calamity, overpopulation, dynastic shift, technological innovation, etc.) but which fail to describe the complexity of relationships which characterize the culture when it was extant. These complexities not only depict a way of life but also provide evidence for the kinds of change characteristic of local cultural evolution (kinship organizations, inheritance patterns, sexual division of labor, micro-subsistence patterns, local polity, indigenous concepts of the supernatural, etc.); and since it is with that evolution that archaeologists most often deal, those working in the subcontinent ought not to be asking whether their evidences are demonstrative of the Aryan invasion or of the fall of the Harappans, but rather should be examining apparently unanswerable questions, such as what kind of evidence would one need to determine the presence of a caste system or what processes characterize intersettlement relationships above and beyond the simple economic.

In considerable contrast to the rather simplistic theoretical conclusions which characterize much of subcontinental archaeology, there is an ever-growing substantive and complex body of carefully gathered data and subsequent theory bearing upon Indo-Pakistan civilization which social anthropologists are obtaining. Based largely upon holistic studies of villages but in several notable cases on urban or Great Tradition Indo-Pakistan, this material forms a coherent and meaningful model for archaeologists. Particularly pertinent is the work of Robert Redfield, Milton Singer, McKim Marriott, and their colleagues. It is an outstanding example of a means by which archaeologists can come to grips with Indian civilization on its own terms and in the holistic manner required if a substantive reconstruction of India's "roots" is to take place. In my own case I find in this anthropological approach the theoretical concepts which I admitted that I lacked in 1967 and without which, as so many archaeologists do, I attempted to deal with the subcontinental past—with consequent difficulties in interpretation.

There is also a dictate which archaeologists and ethnologists must obey if anthropology is to maintain its essential coherence; they must recognize the commonality of their goals: the description and analysis of a cultural condition in time and space. Methodologies necessarily differ, but the goals are identical. Accordingly, we can set forth a testable model for Indo-Pakistan archaeology based upon Indo-Pakistan ethnology in the confidence that because there are identical purposes there ought to be substantive results. Whether or not these results will be proved correct or incorrect is a moot point at the moment. What does count is the creation of a framework which is based upon testable knowns in Indian civilization and not the often flimsy grounds upon which rest present interpretations of the Indian past.[1]

Robert Redfield (1941; also 1956) demonstrated that in parts of Middle America all communities in a given region, whether peasant, urban, or tribal, existed as interrelated parts of a whole separated only according to their degree of isolation from or contact with one another. None were in complete isolation. Redfield perceived that this continuum was a particular form of civilization, one which he referred to as primary or indigenous civilization; that is, a civilization which not only grew out of the indigenous folk-urban continuum but which maintained it as well. Primary civilization was distinguished from secondary on the basis that the latter civilization demonstrates discontinuity between the folk community and that of the urban. According to Redfield, two fundamental traditions are essential to this concept of civilization: a great tradition and a little tradition. "Great tradition" refers to the products of the total civilization: literature, intellectual achievements, fine art, music, political form; a "little tradition" is the local communities' folk culture—those special activities and products which are a small community's particularities. McKim Marriott, with special reference to India, describes as universalization and parochialization the processes which interrelate these traditions. Parochialization is the local transformation of elements of the great tradition which the latter's universalizing process communicates downward into the village community. Since primary civilization arises out of the multitude of little communities that make it up, it depends for its survival on a constant restatement of the binding elements of which it is constituted. The

[1] The following paragraphs contain my interpretation of the Redfield, Singer, Marriott, et al. concept in its special application to Indian archaeology. Admittedly my interpretation may differ in some details, but, as Singer has pointed out, in the case of the anthropologists' shift from the study of primitive cultures to that of civilization there has been sufficient progress to make some effort to shift the conceptual ideas of social anthropologists to the problems of archaeology—and nowhere is this so true as for the subcontinent (Singer 1972, pp. 251–252).

processes just referred to are thus dynamic or energizing factors in the life of the civilization.

Redfield, Marrott, Singer, Srinivas, and many other anthropologists describe each Indian village as a node in a network which connects the whole of Indian civilization. This general network is made up of a multitude of particular networks: kin, caste, religion, trade, authority, and so forth, along whose links pass the ideas, values, innovations, and traditions of the folk-urban complex. Thus each node in the network is subject to a certain kind of stimulus. In this context the process of urbanization may have originated in the selection of a given place in a pre-urban village network in response to a special demand, created by the complexity of interrelationships of the village societies, for a centralized activity. For example, recently Paul Wheatley, a prominent geographer, has set forth convincing evidence that the ceremonial center was a major step in the genesis of the urban center (Wheatley, 1971). Thus the critical node in the pre-urban village network could well have been a place of sacred allusion which grew as the result of common recognition of its sacredness and the consequent elaboration of ceremony.

Urban centers, with their complex interrelations and interdependencies of class, commerce, authority, and ideology, are marked by heterogeneity since they are the place where distant and disparate parts of the civilization's network interact. This heterogeneity is, of course, the principal reason for the genesis of new forms within the civilization—forms which transform both the urban and the village or folk order through the processes described above.

The term "tradition" refers to a time-culture relationship which describes the chronological placement of a culture trait, structure, or system and remarks on their continuity. It enables the present culture bearer to consider history as the source of a given cultural behavior used in the present. In primary civilization tradition preserves an older way of doing things and shapes the new to the essential style which characterizes the civilization as a whole. It is here that one might point out that urban traditions change more rapidly through time than do folk, or little, traditions. At any one point in time, however, the lateral image of a civilization is one which shows great diversity at the folk level and homogeneity at the urban level. Each little community expresses its own self style while the urban level is expressive of the universals in the civilization. The process of urbanization is then one in which there is a thrust toward the homogenization of the little community. In the case of primary civilization, homogenization becomes self-destructive, since it destroys the folk order basis which gave the civilization its genesis and maintains its creative energies. Thus primary civilization balances out its great and little traditions through the dual complementary processes of universalization and parochialization which can be seen as cyclic in character. This gives primary civilization a substantive flexibility to entertain the new while retaining its indigenous character.

Civilization can, however, absorb alien elements which upset these balances to the extent that it loses its identity. Foreign contacts which cause fundamental change of the core areas of a culture create a new form of civilization, one which is referred to by Redfield and Singer as secondary civilization. This kind of civilization is more successful in homogenizing the folk tradition to the point where the people of the little community become a peasantry which is then satellite for an ever-changing urban order. Singer has been particularly interested in India and the effect of its contact with European civilization: how much of the essential identity of Indian civilization is disappearing or changing because of Westernization?

The above description is of course, an oversimplification of a complex subject, yet it will serve in a demonstration of what might be done for the interpreter of archaeological evidence. Indian civilization can be said to have had three essential components: a great tradition intimately but not necessarily universally related to urban centers; a little tradition which rises out of villages; and a tribal tradition which is primarily that of non-Hinduized aboriginal peoples. In terms of a time order the tribal tradition may well have its origins in the Stone Age (see pp. 82–101, for example). Village India, on the other hand, appears to have grown out of the diffusion of settled life into the subcontinent, probably after 4000 B.C. (see pp. 102–66). A great tradition is certainly suggested by the Harappan civilization and was probably fully crystallized by 2300 B.C. In this context we are on reasonably sound chronological and distributional grounds for our estimate of the appearance of these components.

Since the essential premise for the genesis of a primary civilization is the presence of developed village communities, it is not difficult to envision the emergence of the Harappan civilization from those village networks (see pp. 232–239). The large urban centers which dramatize this civilization with their conformist appearance from site to site suggest that Wheatley's theory about the ceremonial center level in the evolution of urbanism has application here (see pp. 300–302). Recently Rafique Mughal set forth in his unpublished doctoral dissertation the idea that much of the material culture of villages identified in Baluchistan and adjoining areas of the "Greater Indus Valley" in a so-called pre-Harappan context was indeed identical to or proto-typical for objects in the material culture of the Harappan civilization. On this basis he has postulated an Early Harappan horizon to include the late developed village cultures which are pre-Harappan in the older context.[2] This idea is troublesome if the term "Early Harappan" is linked with the term "civilization," for, according to

[2] R. Mughal, 1970.

our model, primary civilization exists, when we have urban-folk continuum. The sharing of artifact types and styles through time even in generic terms does not demonstrate, per se, evolution toward civilization. Clearly, the evidence for a folk-urban continuum—that is, for the presence of great and little traditions—must be found if one is to confirm the presence of civilization. Thus our model gives precision to our archaeological goals.

The Harappan civilization may be called an indigenous civilization on the basis of what appears to be a folk-urban continuum (see p. 299, also pp. 263–273). But if we are to argue for its place at the foundation of Indian civilization, we are compelled by our model to detect both little and great traditions and the complementary processes of universalization and parochialization. The famous conformity of the Harappan civilization (pp. 300–302) suggests that the former process was present, but parochialization would be difficult to prove at present because of the lack of attention to little tradition sites. (It is hoped that new excavations at the small site of Allahdino, which were partially instituted for this purpose, will have some bearing on this problem.) It is of no small importance, however, that there is evidence that the end of the Harappan civilization came through a gradual transformation rather than through a catastrophe (pp. 302–311). On the basis of our model this might mean the little traditions survived and went their separate ways when the great traditions no longer made them cohesive. In all likelihood the little traditions coalesced regionally and created new great traditions or were affected by alien ones. Again, as in its genesis, the decline of a civilization ought to be evidenced by the presence or absence of given processes.

Tribal India tends to be an isolate either within or without Indian civilization, although this tendency has repeatedly broken down in the history of that civilization. Generally the recent evidence suggests that tribal people either moved away from contact with that civilization or were absorbed into it, though there are examples of the development of almost symbiotic relationships in the past. If little and great traditions are nonoperative in the tribal situation and most tribal cultures are self-contained, then there ought to be archaeological traces of tribal traditions.

It is a fact that as one moves forward in Indian history, the literary evidence becomes more and more abundant. When this is coupled with archaeological evidence, definitive pictures of the past should emerge. The fact that such pictures are few and far between is owing again to our failure to understand the workings of Indian civilization proper. The so-called Buddhist period is a good case in point. Marriott (1955, p. 207 ff.) describes what he calls residual categories. These are cultural materials within the traditions which apparently are stabilities which are neither parochialized or universalized and which help in identifying the particular tradition to which they belong. The emergence of Buddhism toward the close of the Vedic Age can be considered one consequence of urbanization in north India (see Epilogue). This urbanization does not appear to be of the kind postulated for primary civilization, for it appears to deny the folk order, and the literary accounts suggest an imposed coercive urban order non-Indian in character; that is, non-Indian if Indian civilization can be conceived to be of primary kind. Early Buddhism appears to be rooted in the little traditions of the time, traditions which in the secondary civilization were imperilled by an alien urban order. In this sense then, one might suggest that early Buddhism was an attempt to restore the folk-urban continuum. Such an attempt, however, could not take place without residual factors which survived the changes in traditions and the loss of processal balance. For archaeology the goal in unearthing remains of this time must include the identification of continuities in the little traditions as well as the great traditions. Wholesale excavation of Great Buddhist urban sites, monasteries, shrines, and so forth has marked the approach to this period. The evidence gathered remarks only on aspects of the great traditions and our archaeological impression of Buddhism in the subcontinent is in consequence largely a false one and for early Buddhism in particular almost nonexistent.

The phenomenon of two kinds of civilization present in the history of India raises questions as to which best describes Indian civilization itself. This is a subject of considerable interest to the archaeologist, for, as I remarked above, present tendencies are toward the definitions of contact with areas outside the subcontinent. The infusion of alien traits and people and the consequent disturbance of the primary civilization can be traced historically from the Aryan invasions to the conquests of Arab, Turk, and British. However, it appears that in time Indian civilization reasserted itself and absorbed secondary civilizations in a special and characteristic way. It is this apparently constant return to an indigenous primary civilized life which is a marker, as it were, of stabilizing continuities which may bend but never break. In tracing these archaeologically, as well as in the literary sources, there ought to be new strategies and methodologies created which take into full consideration the structures and processes that are vital parts of civilization. Such a model as the one briefly outlined here is an example of what great potential there is for better interpretations of the subcontinental human past than we have had hitherto. Of course, this is not the only possible model, but its holistic quality has a merit which will be hard to equal.[3]

1975

---

[3] It can be noted that S. C. Malik has already argued for this approach with a specific regard for Redfield's work (Malik, 1968).

ACKNOWLEDGMENTS

IT REMAINS TO EXPRESS MY THANKS to a number of people for help both in the research area and in the physical writing of this book. The bulk of the field work was carried out under the sponsorship of the Department of Anthropology of the American Museum of Natural History, New York, and I am particularly grateful to Dr. Harry L. Shapiro, chairman of the department, and to Dr. James Oliver, director of the museum. More recently the work has been co-sponsored by the Thomas Burke Memorial Washington State Museum of the University of Washington, Seattle. Both the administration of the College of Arts and Sciences and the staff of the museum have been most helpful in supporting the work.

A variety of funds have come from such as the Bollingen Foundation, the Wenner-Gren Foundation, the American Philosophical Society, and the National Science Foundation, which made possible important aspects of the field work.

In Pakistan I am especially indebted to F. A. Khan, Director of the Department of Archaeology, Government of Pakistan, for the opportunities to work in the field and for the free use of both the collections and the library of the department in Karachi and in Lahore. Much assistance was rendered by M. Rafique Mughul, of the Explorations Branch of the department.

In India opportunity to re-examine Stein's collections and others was readily granted by the then director-general of the Archaeological Survey of India, Shri A. Ghosh, and much help was received from his colleague, the present director-general, B. B. Lal. In Bombay, Moti Chandra was especially kind in permitting me access to important collections in the Prince of Wales Museum.

A number of individuals in one way or another have been most helpful to me overseas, including Dr. Robert Caldwell, Miss Helen Semmerling, and Mr. Russell Harris, officers of the State Department, and Dr. and Mrs. Sherman Minton, who provided me with a home and much encouragement.

I am particularly grateful to my student and now colleague, Mr. Gregory Possehl, for his many contributions, to Mrs. Thomas Beddall, who took over the horrendous task of typing the "damn thing," and to my wife, Jan, for undertaking the illustrations. The maps are by Mrs. Robert Free.

WALTER A. FAIRSERVIS, JR.

Introduction

IN THOSE FAR DAYS when the Buddha walked over the lands of the subcontinent he found on every hand the raw elements which compounded into the Faith and gave it meaning: the bodhi tree, the river Ganges, the milk bowl, the wide-eyed cow, the sun and its heat, the dust-haloed villages, the starkness of Indian death and the reality of Indian birth, the ultimate dignity of the village lady, the intensity of the male quarrel, the harmony of monsoon, growth, harvest, rebirth. Countless as the crystals of Himalayan snowfall were and are the fundamental pieces which are the essentials of the Indian environment. Indeed so far removed is this environment from the American's comprehension that most of us have been mere tourists in its presence, seeing without understanding.

A major factor in this phenomenon of the American and the subcontinent is the failure to recognize what is most basic to a true understanding. It is that on the subcontinent we are in the midst of an ancient civilization, still living, still vital, still of an importance to our world that is beyond price. Such terms as nation, republic, party, coalition, supply and demand, alignment, and the like, which all too often characterize American views of the peoples of the subcontinent, have small significance in the perspective of a living tradition already millennia old. Too often Americans think of those peoples in terms of pity for the condition of poverty and indeed of near famine under which so many of them live. Paradoxically, however, many Indians and Pakistanis have the same feelings for us. Our drab clothes, our rootlessness, our hypocrisies, our tensions and nervousness represent us as much as our machines, our ideals of freedom, and our enthusiasms. In contrast, when the priest or the old man tells the bereaved parents of the boy dead through malnutrition of the cycle of lives which is man's destiny and of the gods who move the actions of the world, he speaks with a voice given its tone of assurance by centuries of evolved tradition. Here tradition provides an answer and often a remedy. In such ways India has cared for its own. Because we seem to lack such concepts of harmonious relationship to nature, our world is poorly comprehended. We can examine it with microscopes, distill its materials in the laboratory, reshape the land with machines, but in the end we see only its form and fail to comprehend its living substance.

For thousands of years the sense that nature was a living presence ethical in quality, timeless in its vitality, all-knowing in its wisdom profoundly influenced the inhabitants of the South Asian subcontinent. What was originally a primitive animism evolved there into a magnificent code by which mortal man could live with his mortality and return again and again over the millennia to a reasonable relationship with himself and with nature. Ultimately the heartblood of Indian civilization is not the stoic acceptance of fate of which it is often accused by the West, but rather the full comprehension of fate so that it can be analyzed, measured, and used to support man's sense of security in his universe. The institutions, social and cultural, which arose are manifestations of this ultimate comprehension. Their viability is demonstrated in the resilience which finds no contradictions in the advent of Buddhism, Jainism, Islam, and Christianity or in the rise and fall of Maurya, Gupta, Mogul, or the English Raj. It seems that whoever reaches to Indian civilization comes away with more than he leaves.

In writing this book I have been all too aware that ultimately it bore upon the origin of the civilization of India itself. Certainly the earliest Stone Age is a necessary prelude to the middle Stone Age, and this in turn to the last Stone Age, and so on. Thus age by age, period by period, region by region, traits are born, grow, and change as they interweave with other traits and form the institutions, social behaviors, and cultural actions which together make up Indian civilization. The prehistorian dimly perceives these processes in his miserable collections of artifacts gathered from the earth by one means or another. Some of us prone to grasp too readily at mirages cast up by the touchstones of handaxes, old pottery, and ruined walls are led into a wilderness of speculation. Others too skeptical to see substance among the shadows simply count and recount our findings like the legendary Midas and are content. Still others strive with every means at hand to comprehend what clues we have and thus to resurrect the outlines of a teeming, long-dead world but somehow create shapelessness only. Withal, however, there is the sense of a complexity perhaps not found elsewhere in the world which ultimately makes us wary of stating an absolute where Indian civilization is concerned. For even today with all our perceptions sharpened by modern learning and in the presence of a living civilization we find our conclusions contradicted by the exception or the localization.

All this goes by way of pointing up, unnecessarily perhaps, the vulnerability of this writing. Much of what is described here is the result of field work carried out by the author and his colleagues, and thus the inordinate amount of emphasis on the Borderlands, where much of this research was carried on. A heavy percentage of what is described is derived from the work of others, much of it unseen in the original by this writer in spite of efforts to do so. In some cases the conclusions of others have unabashedly been built into the manuscript but hopefully in all cases with due acknowledgment. This is, of course, a necessary prerequisite for any who would write about subcontinental archaeology, for what evidence we do have is the result of years of devoted activity by many, some of whom have been led to sound ideas on the basis of this evidence which will probably stand well in spite of the growing store of new evidence. (In this regard so progressive are these researches that parts of this book will be out of date on publication!)

But the author's greatest vulnerability is rooted in his inability to perceive clearly a fundamental principle or a series of axioms with which to characterize the evidence. Consider what is presented: a review of the findings of archaeology on the South Asian subcontinent relating to the vast, essentially prehistoric, period before the Buddha. So vast is this prospect, so limited the research, so uncertain much of the evidence, so early in the history of these studies is the present that there is every reason to avoid the creation of theory. However, archaeology is a science using other sciences, and no matter how poor the evidence or at what stage the study, we are compelled for order's sake alone to formulate plausible reconstructions of the antique past. Thus here and there in the text are such reconstructions.

Though these are mere puppet shows compared to what will one day be revealed as the objects of ancient Indian civilization emerge from the earth, what we can show now is still provocative and worthy of attention. Essentially what is detailed in the chapters outlines a history which starts with the appearance, presumably from west and east, of the first men at least one quarter of a million years ago. Their artifacts suggest common origins with the early men of Europe, Africa, Java, and China. What follows is a long evolvement in the ice-free lands below the Himalayas during which an indigenous character is imparted to prehistoric life which was still receiving some outside influences, from the West especially. This phenomenon suggests a pattern which is to characterize cultural development for thousands of years: the diffusion and acceptance of new ideas and techniques from outside but with an apparent slowness of pace and an integration which changes their style so that we can recognize them as fully subcontinental whatever their origin.

The advent of West Asian food production, perhaps as early as the fifth millennium B.C., began that inexorable rise to civilization which was to culminate in the Harappan civilization in the Indus River Valley at the time, approximately, when Egypt's Old Kingdom was in its final decline and Sargon of Akkad was creating the first of the great Mesopotamian empires. This civilization remains enigmatic, still one of archaeology's greatest riddles. However, we are witness to its rise, climax, spread east and south, and its final decline. At a time when the Babylonian empire of Hammurabi's line was breaking up and Egypt was entering its imperial age, the Harappan civilization was merging into the Indian environment, perhaps to re-emerge in other forms. Again we are confronted with mysteries: the coming of rice cultivation, the tradition of strong cultural and human impulses from Central Asia, and the rise of Vedic India. The archaeological traces of these historical verities may be in our grasp, but we are still plagued with uncertainties. At last the dawn of historical Indian civilization in its Gangetic seat, and its equivalent in the Deccan, terminates the scope of the text.

Throughout this story it is evident that the Borderland country of the northwest, with its passes granting ease of access to the subcontinent, is the most important single geographic factor. Here was the contact zone which kept subcontinental cultures sensitive to the great innovations of the West. It has been possible to trace the advent of some prehistoric traits in the Borderlands, thus giving, hopefully, a chronological certainty to some of them. The accomplishment seems very limited, however, in consideration of the still unknown processes that turned these traits into aspects of Indian civilization. Nonetheless such small but concrete steps are being taken, and it is perhaps not too optimistic to expect that we will have secure demonstration of much that was involved in these great transformations as the research proceeds.

For certainly no countries are better served by their archaeologists than those of the subcontinent. Annually lakhs[1] of rupees are poured into programs of research, publication, and preservation which compare favorably with any in the world. The foreign scientists—British (especially), French, Italian, Swedish, and American—have made their contributions in the past, but now the devotion, hard work, and adroitness of subcontinental nationals ensures that much of ancient life will be resurrected as it should be to demonstrate the range and richness of ancient accomplishment.

In writing the book I have had opportunity not only to describe the evidences as they were available to me, but at the same time to speculate shamelessly about them. In some cases the reader will find contradictions in these speculations and in the efforts to theorize about this or that fact. This is perhaps in the nature of archaeological interpretation. One cannot expect to build great edifices of theory on archaeological evidence without also anticipating their collapse. What contradictions there are largely stem from the method of dealing with each situation as it comes and ulti-

---

[1] 1 lakh equals 100,000 rupees.

mately being unable to see what the collective aspect of all the cases together represents. Yet efforts are made to go beyond the mere artifact, and
on this stands or falls the merit of the work.

One needs patience and a degree of tolerance in reading books on
archaeology in spite of the initial aura of romance associated with the
profession. However, he who sticks to the task may find gratification and a
degree of satisfaction in sensing, as the author does, that archaeological
research on the subcontinent of India-Pakistan is on the verge of immense
and respectably clear prospects into time which will give greater meaning
to an important part of man's story.

The Physical Indian Foundation

THE PLETHORA OF WRITINGS on the Indo-Pakistan subcontinent that have arisen since World War II and which are aimed at throwing some light on the social, economic, and political aspects of the subject have generally one thing in common, a failure to come to grips with the physical world in which human activity is rooted. It is true that the monsoon, the seasons, the soils, and the general geographic features of a region are noted, but rare indeed is the study which attempts to envision the complex activities of man against the equally complex background of soil, geological history, temperature, rainfall, fauna and flora that constitutes the environment whose problems must be resolved if man is to flourish and that helps to imbue cultures with specific regional characteristics. This is nowhere so true as in Indo-Pakistan archaeology, where simplistic views as to the ancient physical environment have arisen in abundance. However, new instrumentation in archaeology plus greater understanding of various natural phenomena gained by both the physical and biological sciences have now made possible almost limitless opportunities to reconstruct past environments. Some of these newer data will be used in this book. Moreover it is the present environment which must be viewed as a first means of approaching its past.

It is strange that the great lessons taught by W. W. Hunter, among others in the nineteenth century, seem so easily to have been forgotten. Hunter was the original motivator and creator of the imperial gazetteers of India, from which derived those admirable series of provincial and district gazetteers which now, alas, are difficult to obtain. Hunter, aware of the historical reasons for present human events, was concerned that the British administration be well informed on all aspects of the lands they ruled. It was his claim that no administrator, whatever his role, should act out of ignorance. As an example he pointed up the signs which preceded the onset of famine in Bengal and how these had been ignored in the past. He saw such events as a complex interweaving of physical, political, and social conditions. These conditions were set forth with clarity in the gazetteers, and an enlightened administration saw fit to expand both their contents and their distribution, to the benefit of all concerned.

In this same sense archaeologists cannot interpret the past without a gazetteer of some kind where page by page the raw data which collectively constitute the various modern aspects of the regions under study are set forth. The modern environment, physical and cultural, is a point on a time continuum that connects past with present.

It is the awareness of such factors in the interpretation of man's history that is critical to scientific understanding. In this chapter are sketched in some of the aspects of the physical subcontinent which have to be considered to obtain that understanding.

✤ *The Method of Regional Zoning*

THE PHYSICAL PICTURE IS A VARIED ONE. It is habitual in science to arrange things into categories. One system of classification often used in archaeology is that of regional zoning—the demarcation of geographical bounds for a given phenomenon or group of phenomena, or, in other terms, the pole about which cultural elements cluster giving that situation its characteristic identity. Regionalization varies with the subject matter, and there is always grave danger that too literal an interpretation of regions will provide a misleading picture. It is clear, however, that regionalization developed for one criterion, as, for example, for climate, may not coincide with another, as, for example, with that developed for soils. This may be obvious, but it is often the case that the efficacy of regional classification makes one regional definition a catchall for other data not organic to it, and the resulting effect in interpretation is misleading. Nonetheless, provided the user is aware of some of these pitfalls, the regional method is an excellent way of handling physical evidence of the kind outlined below.

It is proposed, however, to outline several physical environmental criteria, all of which are important to an understanding of the past of the subcontinent, and which can be interrelated in the context of the chapters that follow. These are selected for their obvious importance to archaeology, but they are by no means the only criteria. Others will be referred to in context.

There is a classic physiographic division of the Indo-Pakistan subcontinent that separates it into three parts: the Himalaya Mountains and their extensions; the flat, seemingly almost limitless river plains that include such time-honored lands as Sind, the Punjab, Oudh, and Bengal, and which collectively are known as the Indo-Gangetic plains; and the ancient rock mass which makes up the bulk of peninsular India. Besides these three divisions there are the coasts: narrow and with few good ports on the west, and on the east wider and frequently marked by marshes and lagoons. There are also the essentially Iranian, and thus outside the physical subcontinent, basins, valleys, and hills of Baluchistan, which make up a large portion of West Pakistan.

❊ Peninsular India

THE PENINSULA JUTS INTO THE INDIAN OCEAN in an approximate north-south axis: triangular in shape, the southernmost extension at Cape Comorin reaches to within less than ten degrees of latitude of the equator. Ceylon, just to the east of the Cape, is essentially part of the geological story of the peninsula. Adam's Peak, on the southwest of that island, is the first landfall for ships headed for the Bay of Bengal. It has represented "India" to thousands of voyagers for centuries even though Ceylon is a cultural entity separate from India. Yet even for Indians the peak has meaning. On the summit of the mountain is a boulder which is said to conceal a divine footprint. For Hindus the print is that of Siva, for Buddhists it is that of Gautama, for Moslems the story has it that Adam, driven from Paradise, stood penance there. Thus, though the peak is low (7,260 feet) compared with India's mountains generally, it has attained a stature unique to the eye and mind. The allusion of legend and story to such geographical features is a commonplace in the Indian tradition.

Peninsular India is ancient India in the geological sense. It is best represented by a mass of crystalline rocks that stretch from Cape Comorin north to Bihar, which outcrop near Udaipur in Rajasthan, and which form the distinctive topography of Bundelkund, the seat of that extraordinary city and rajadom of Jhansi. The ranee of Jhansi was one of the most colorful figures of the Sepoy Revolt of 1857. Her kingdom was in part the key to central India, and for a time her fierce leadership almost unseated the British Raj in that crucial area. Bundelkund marks the northern limit of peninsular India and its ancient plateau. The dense crystalline mass of the plateau is for many geologists one of the best areas on earth for research on the nature of the earth's crust. Perhaps a billion years ago these rocks were formed as a part of the continent building which distinguishes the geology of this planet. Some of these rocks were laid down originally as sediments, the depositional products of primeval seas and lakes whose dimensions have been lost eons ago; others were apparently volcanic or magmatic intrusions. All, however, have been so subject to metamorphism that their very origin is problematical and subject to scholarly dispute.

On the northwest of the peninsula proper is the Aravalli mountain chain—India's oldest mountains. Exposed to ages of erosion, these mountains still mark the landscape with their remnants. Mount Abu (5,646 feet) is the highest of the surviving mountains. It too is a sacred symbol for living man, as it is the seat of the Jains and contains their breath-taking temples of Dilwara. Udaipur of Rajasthan, one of the loveliest palace cities in the world, is situated on a mountain lake surrounded up to a height of four thousand feet by the jumbled and striking ridges of the Aravalli, at once marking both new and extremely ancient geological events.

The physical extension of the Aravalli and the Vindhya mountains, to the southeast, is contiguous with two other elevated mountain formations of great antiquity, the Satpura chain and the Western Ghats. The latter clearly mark the border of the Deccan along the western side of the peninsula as far as the mountains of India's extreme south, the famous Nilgiri Hills, seat of the primitive Toda people. The Toda, who live in an area of forested hills, were first described (1906) by the anthropologist Rivers in a classic account that revealed to the world an aspect of India more ancient than the Hindus.

With few exceptions, the most ancient crystalline rocks that make up the plateau of the Deccan have never been covered over with those primeval marine waters whose sediments so mark the formation of the great geological systems of the various periods of the Age of Reptiles and the Age of Mammals. Their stability is emphasized by their resistance and reaction to the stresses and strains inherent in the dynamic nature of the earth's crust. The plateau tends to fault in great blocks that rise or fall according to the tectonic character of the local region. In other words, the crystalline mass splits rather than bends or folds into those anticline-syncline festoons and loops which so often characterize softer strata. So massive is the Deccan resistance to horizontal stress that one theory has it that the Himalaya-Karakorum mountain system to the north bends in its characteristic way because of the stubborn stability of the old rock formations of the south. To understand this idea, one has to envision a time when the heart of Asia, what is now Tibet, Turkistan, and beyond, was flattish and covered with a great shallow sea (Tethys) with broad reaches of hilly land ringing its shores. At least seventy million years ago this vast region began not only to rise, shedding its sea waters, but to move southward like some

MAP 1   *The Indian subcontinent with certain places and areas designated.*

inexorable tide. The forefront of this ocean of land pressed against the stable plateau of India with its two sentinel land bastions, the Aravalli Mountains on the west and the Rajmahal Hills on the east. The result was a gradual crumbling of the forefront of the lighter northern mass which combined with its natural orogeny to create the mighty ranges of the Himalayas, the earth's highest and most massive. The map indicates how the Himalaya range rises in a great arc from Assam to the vicinity of the Khyber. Some authorities, as we have said, consider this curve as the expression of the resistance strength of the Deccan, which is concave at its northern center between the twin bastions of Aravalli and Raj Mahal.

❋ *The Mountain Boundaries*

IT IS A CURIOUS AND WONDERFUL THING, this festoon of the world's highest mountains that surrounds Indo-Pakistan and gives these lands their storied isolation as a continent within a continent. They divide India from the rest of Asia, and yet much of Indian tradition and history is found within their often lonely and awesome reaches. Start at Karachi on the Arabian Sea. Here is the narrow strip of land between sea and mountain which is the southernmost gate to India. A gate which witnessed the passage of Alexander west to Persia after what is probably the most ambitious military adventure in history; here Mohammad ibn Qasim led the Arab armies in the eighth century on to the conquest of Sind. Northward the Sulaiman-Kirthar Hills mark the easternmost extent of the plateau of Iran. The hills run parallel to the course of the Indus; they fringe the white plain of Kachhi, where the mean annual temperature is the highest in the world. Kachhi, however, is at the foot of the Bolan Pass, which splits the Sulaimans at the tectonic heart of that chain. At the head of the Bolan Pass is Quetta—former British military cantonment city and seat of the only artesian wells on the subcontinent. Here in 1935 over twenty thousand lives were lost in an earthquake which almost extinguished the town. Here the mountains swing north and east in concentric loops crowned by peaks bearing names, like "Throne of Solomon," that recall the story of the lost tribe of Israel. In the Bugti country, which lies in the southernmost of the mountain loops, was found the natural gas which now supplies Karachi, over four hundred miles to the south. Northward the Sulaimans form the homeland of the Pathans. The Gomel, Tochi, and Khyber passes are in Pathan country. It is important to note that this region was of stratigraphic importance as the link to Central Asia and Iran. Kipling's "the great game" was played here as Russia and Britain probed each other's wills with the pawn of the Pathan and more often his resistance: Afridi, Waziris, Mahsud, Mohmand, Afghan, Ghilzai, Peshawar, the Guides, Swat, Chitral, Mianwali, Bannu, Tank—old names, but they form the very stuff of Borderland history.

The Sulaimans are like foothills to the Hindu Kush to the north and the Karakorum farther to the east. These latter ranges are barriers between Central Asia and the Punjab plain. They are characterized by year-round snow-capped peaks, glaciers, gorges marking the course of the Indus, hidden and romantic kingdoms and principalities: Kafiristan, where wooden carvings recall an aboriginal world existent before Islam; Hunza, supposed to be a modern Shangri-la; Ladakh, where Tibetan Buddhism flourishes and which is the farthest western extension of ethnic Tibet; and Kashmir. The valley of Kashmir is well endowed by nature with mountains, streams, lakes, and forests blended together into an ecology which recalls the Altai valleys of Central Asia.

Beyond, to the east, are kingdoms that were once resplendent physical aspects of Tibet itself. Centers of Buddhism and markets for the inner Asian trade, Nepal, Sikkim, and Bhutan are both Indian and Tibetan and reflect their intermediate position while possessing unique features that give them their special characteristics. The soldierly Gurkhas, the incredible Sherpas, the primeval Lepchas, the devout Bhutanese—one is compelled to adjectives in the naming of these people just as one is forced to poetry or silence by the mountains which crown their homeland: Kanchenjunga, whose peak by agreement is untrodden by man as proper for the seat of the gods; and Everest of the Snows, the highest peak in the world. The Ganges, India's most sacred river, has its source in this region. It is said to spring from the topknot of Siva, who sits on the top of Mount Meru viewing the world.

Few and difficult are the passes that lead through the Himalaya; that is why Chinese pilgrims seeking the sanctuaries of Buddhism made their way across the Turkish deserts north of Tibet beyond the Kuan Lung Mountains to the passes across the Pamir, the Roof of the World, or through the Dzungarian Gates, and thus to Afghanistan and the Khyber. But there is one incredible break in the mountain barrier, the little known gorges of the Brahmaputra River. This river has its source near the headwaters of the Sutlej branch of the Indus system. As the Tsangpo, it flows due east, passing near Lhasa as if probing the mountain chains to the south. At last it issues to the south almost at that point where the whole mountain system bends in to form the north-south running mountain ribs of Burma and Southeast Asia and the eastern border of India. The gorge in which the river rolls from the Tibetan highlands to the Assam plain is some 18,000 feet deep, such ravines being a prominent characteristic of Himalayan rivers, including the Ganges and the Indus, that is, they are older than the mountains and have been cutting their channels deeper with each rise in elevation. The marks of old courses are to be seen across the vastness of plateau and mountain and these, with the abundant fossil records found in the rocks, tell of gentler times when physical relief was moderate and the monsoon winds swept the moisture of the Indian Ocean into the heart of now comparatively rainless Tibet.

The eastern border of the Ganges-Brahmaputra delta is marked by that group of mountains that make up the boundary between the subcontinent proper and Burma. The latter's ethnic affinities are to southeast Asia. This is emphasized by its three north-south running rivers, Chindwin, Irrawaddy, and Salween, which have inclined the Burmese to look to the Bay of Bengal as the center of tradition. Thus Burma is more akin to Ceylon and Thailand in its Hinayana Buddhism than to China or Tibet. The Indo-Burma frontier is the homeland for a variety of tribal people among whom the Nagas are perhaps most famous. Assam receives the highest rainfall in the world, over one hundred inches annually. This is the reason for the success of tea plantations and the reason why the region is a natural borderland. The mountain ranges run north-south, bracketing the rivers. Their slopes are covered with thick jungle, whose exigencies made the Burma sector of World War II the situation for one of the most difficult military campaigns in history.

This lush tropical jungle of the Indo-Burmese border, with its extraordinary monsoonal rains, is in complete contrast to the rainless aridity of the Indo-Iranian Borderlands on the opposite side of the subcontinent. Each of these regions is, however, a barrier of a kind and a zone of attraction for those who throughout time have had the adaptive capacities, either through already existing cultural heritages or by surviving the process of natural selection, to gain a productive and characteristic footing.

The mountain boundary of the subcontinent can be relatively easily traversed on its western side, much less so on its eastern, and it is almost impenetrable in its central area. The most frequent contacts of the subcontinent with Asia proper are thus to the west. Traits of Western origin have reached India overland, while in contrast, traits of Indian origin have moved eastward, generally by sea. However, when Indian traits do diffuse overland, they tend to go by the western routes, even reaching China by that circuitous course, as is demonstrated by the example of Buddhism or the calendar of the twelve beasts. The central and eastern borderland regions are noted for their peculiar ethnic character, where indigenous development syncretizes whatever is received into forms at once unique and paradoxically familiar, as, for example, Tibetan Buddhism or the iconography of Nepalese Hinduism. Isolation is also a factor in these regions and provides for the modern survival of tribal forms since extinct in areas to the south.

This emphasis upon the western Borderlands as the source of new ideas, objects, and people makes all the more important an awareness of the cultural sequences in such regions as Afghanistan, Iran, and western Central Asia. If the geographic premise is considered in its broad sense, then the cultural developments in those regions have a direct bearing upon the cultures of the adjacent Indo-Gangetic plains, a fact of vast significance to the whole of India. The Harappan civilization, the Aryans, the Kushans, and the Moguls, for example, demonstrate the fact that traits of the West diffused to India in one form or another and integrated in that plain to affect all of the subcontinent, each in its peculiar fashion. There is then a significant direction to the movement of traits to India because of the position and character of the Himalayan chain.

Where the mountains reach the Bay of Bengal or the Arabian Sea is the terminus of the orogenic divide that defines the Indo-Pakistan region as subcontinental. If the theory of the movement of the inner Asian land mass against the crystalline heart of the subcontinent is indeed correct, it is apparent that much of Asia's topography owes its origin to the interplay of the mass of the main continent with its southern fringe. A similar situation may be found in the relation of Africa to Europe. The heart of Africa, like the Deccan, is made up of ancient crystalline rocks that also fault rather than bend under stress. It may well be that the Alps are the result of a continental tidal flow brought up against the unyielding bulk of the archaic African land mass.

Africa and the subcontinent were connected by land during the Mesozoic era, or Age of Reptiles. The deposits that represent this age were laid down as the result of the erosion of mountains or other high areas like those of the Aravalli. In compensation for the uplift of these ranges it would appear that some portions of the Deccan subsided. Into the basins thus fomred flowed streams and rivers carrying their burden of erosional products. The rivers, of course, tended to follow fault-line depressions, and they thus have a linear aspect. Today these old basins and river systems are traced by the presence of sediments in which are found the fossil remains of a terrestrial and fresh-water fauna and flora. These paleontological remains are to a large extent duplicated in Central Africa and Madagascar and even resemble material from South America. Thus some authorities have envisioned a vast southern continent which eventually became divided up into its present existing segments of Africa, India, Madagascar, etc., by the subsidence or floating off of those areas now covered by the Arabian Sea and the Bay of Bengal. This "lost" continent is referred to in the literature as Gondwanaland, after the Gonds of the Narbada River region, where the formation was initially identified. There are living animal and plant forms which appear to confirm by their existence what the paleontological record indicates.

More recent studies of the Indian Ocean underline the possibility that though a land area continental in size was unlikely to have existed, it is very likely that faulted blocks were uplifted to form land bridges from time to time.[1] Gondwanaland formations are Mesozoic or perhaps early Tertiary. However the possibility that a land bridge existed until the Pleistocene between Africa and India has to be considered in view of human artifactual parallels in the Paleolithic to be discussed in a later chapter.

The over-all evidence derived from studies of the Indian Ocean and its environs in Africa, Arabia, Iran, India, Burma, and Australasia is summarized by Pepper and Everhart:

> Vertical movements occurred throughout the shield areas from time to time but were of different intensity and magnitude. In consequence, the borders of the shields contain sags which in some places are the marginal edges of basins that now lie mainly beneath the continental shelves. Coastal basins and embayments bordering the basement complex have been the sites of deposition of marine and continental sediments of widely different kinds

[1] J. F. Pepper and G. M. Everhart, *The Indian Ocean: The Geology of Its Bordering Lands and the Configuration of Its Floor*, Department of the Interior, OSGS Miscellaneous Geologic Investigations, Map 1-380, Washington, D.C., 1963, p. 29.

and amounts at times from the Cambrian on. Volcanic extrusions of different ages have been spread widely in some areas. To a large extent, tectonic movements have controlled the distribution of the continental and marine sediments. During the Paleozoic, in Africa, India, and Australia the shields were elevated, and large areas of continental sediments, varying from lacustrine to aeolian, were deposited. Near the end of the Paleozoic the shield margins were downwarped, and widespread flooding occurred. During the Mesozoic Era a thick sequence of limestone and intercalated sands and muds was deposited. Near the end of the Mesozoic, marked uplift of the continents began, and a long period of erosion followed from Tertiary time to the present. Although many uplifts and downwarps of regions have taken place within the periods in the eras, in general they have been of much smaller regional extent than the movements that marked the end of each era.

In India the end of the Mesozoic and the beginning of the Tertiary was dramatically marked by the outpourings of igneous material from fissures in the crystalline shield of the Deccan. In the Bombay region these outpourings may have reached a thickness of ten thousand feet. The flows reached as far north as Sind, where a thin layer there of less than two hundred feet is in marked contrast to the mighty lava sheets that lie one on the other in the western Deccan. Though much of this material has been eroded away, it is still a dominant land feature of the northwest of peninsular India. Study of the flows, which are principally basaltic, proves that in general they accumulated as the result of steady, rather slow outpourings rather than in an explosive manner, because of their remarkable horizontality. There are examples of tuff and ash which indicate explosive vulcanism, however, but in general these flows, which are collectively known as the Deccan trap, are almost exactly like those of the Columbia lava plateau in the northwestern United States, massive in their bulk and homogeneity, and majestic in their vastness. It is of great economic importance to India that the regur soils resulting from the erosion of the Deccan trap are among the most agriculturally productive in the subcontinent.

The close of the Mesozoic was marked by great crustal movements. It was presumably then that the upwarping of the Himalayan chain began, with a consequent downwarping of the area between the Aravalli-Vindhyan-Rajmahal hill boundary of the Deccan and the foothills of the new ranges. This effectively cut off peninsular India from inner Asia and left two great gulfs, one on the north and east, and one on the west. At first these gulfs were filled with marine waters, but by a combination of increased deposition from Himalayan rivers and a general land uplift, the seas eventually retreated, to be replaced by the Indus, Ganges, and Brahmaputra river systems familiar today. These rivers now flow on accumulations of sediment thousands of feet in thickness, and which span in time in an almost uninterrupted fashion from the Eocene period at the beginning of the Tertiary until today. Interestingly, the Eocene is marked by marine fossils which are also found high up on the slopes of Mount Everest—ample demonstration of the magnitude of the changes which so characterize the Tertiary.

The orogeny which created the Himalayas acted throughout the Tertiary and is in effect today. Many of the later Tertiary deposits were raised as foothills, and often fluvial erosion creates outcrops of underlying strata among these deposits. In the Punjab one of the more significant type series of Tertiary formations has been worked out in the so-called Salt Range. The sequence is relatively dated by paleontological evidence, in which the mammals are of greatest importance. It was here in the Siwalik strata that the extraordinarily interesting primates, Sivapithecus (Upper Miocene) and Palaeosimia (Middle Miocene), were discovered. The latter would appear to be in the line toward the orangutan, while the former suggests some relationship to the fossil primates generally grouped in the family Dryopithecidae. This family is famous for its particularly hominid-like teeth, suggesting that it bears a definite relationship to human evolution.

The Tertiary witnessed the creation of what is essentially the modern situation, modified somewhat by the geological events of the Pleistocene, to be described in the next chapter. The riverine systems are probably the best indication of the differences between the three classic divisions of geologic India-Pakistan. The rivers of the peninsula meander over Deccan trap deposits or on broad crystalline peneplains, carrying silts and gravels which are deposited along the valleys in such quantity that a comparatively small percentage of the total depositional load reaches the sea. The general direction of these rivers is east to the Bay of Bengal. This is because during the Tertiary it would appear that the whole of the peninsula was uplifted on its western side and sunk on its eastern as a result of crustal movement. The sharp walls of the Western Ghats suggest a massive faulting along the side probably matched by the subsidence of blocks now under the Arabian Sea. Of interest are the rivers Tapti and Narbada on the northwest, which flow apparently along fault lines from east to west in counterdistinction to the usual Deccan riverine situation.

In contrast to these Deccan streams are the rivers of the mountain massif of Himalaya-Karakorum. Here the rivers Indus, Brahmaputra, and Ganges and their eventual tributaries begin amid glaciers and snow fields and roar through enormous gorges, moving immense quantities of detritus to the foothills. Monsoonal rains augment the flow of these rivers so that the seasonal volume of water is immense. In the case of the Indus, for example, it is ten times that of the Colorado River and twice that of the Nile.

❊ *The Riverine Plains*

THE THIRD GREAT GEOLOGICAL DIVISION OF INDIA-PAKISTAN is that of the vast alluvial plains of the Ganges and the Indus. The Punjab of the Indus system is defined by five streams—the Indus proper and four main tributaries: the Jhelum, the Chenab, the Ravi, and the Sutlej; while the Ganges plain also includes the Gogra and Jumna systems. In effect these are wide, relatively shallow, mature rivers which move great masses of silt into increasingly more complicated meander patterns. The silt deposition raises the river bed and creates natural levees which even with human restraints often enough cause disastrous flooding. The deltas of these rivers (including that of the Brahmaputra with the Ganges) are constantly building up. In the Karachi area the Indus River deposits have widened the continental shelf to 122 miles over a distance of some 200 miles. The Ganges delta is also approximately 100 miles wide, and in few places is there a water depth of over 300 feet.

This accumulating alluvium is, of course, an agricultural resource of immense significance to the people of the subcontinent and one reason why so much of this book is devoted to the archaeology of these riverine plains.

Approximately ten thousand years ago the subcontinent would appear to have had living within its confines a population of food gatherers no greater in number probably than that of most regions of the Old World and very likely somewhat less than that of the "classic" hunting-gathering centers of Europe and the Near East. At present the same area, especially its riverine plains, is the homeland for one of the world's heaviest concentrations of population, a population that has already borne so heavily upon the land that much of its natural fecundity is exhausted. This man-created phenomenon is in contrast to the millions of years in which life of all forms has found a suitable environment in the subcontinent and left a record of successful adaptation from age to age. Even the dinosaurs or the insects with all their voracious and omnivorous capabilities have not made the impact upon the landscape that has man. In view of this fact it becomes difficult to envision an India where human population is at the minimum and the landscape still unaffected by human agency. Yet such an India did exist in a past so close to our own time by geological standards that we can still look at living survivals of that India and use these as graphic keys to that past.

Very often in considering the changes which affected the situation of past cultures or established civilizations, scholars have regarded climatic change as especially significant. Today we are more suspicious of these things and tend to qualify our ideas accordingly. The physical evidence for environmental change would seem to be twofold. The first is the intervention of human activity, which by clearing forests, tilling the soil, migrating, damming, raising sheep, goats, and cattle, diffusing foreign fauna and flora, hunting and fishing, and in the end upsetting ecologies or providing new symbiotic relationships can drastically alter the natural situation. The second factor relates to the natural changes to which all the earth's environments are subject. No environment is changeless, it is on a moving curve to something else no matter how flat that curve may be according to a time scale. The activities of man can accelerate this change. For example, it seems clear that some of the early developments of food production were in semiarid lands where the existing vegetative cover was just sufficient to retain moisture in the soil and to resist or to confine the erosional agencies of wind and water. The agricultural activities of man plus the devastation to this vegetation caused by domestic sheep and goats accelerated environmental change so that a desert appeared whose exposed surface is even today unalterably despoiled by seasonal winds and flash floods. The rather desperate efforts to avert this situation are all too evident in the archaeological record.

❋ *The Climate Factor*

THE GEOLOGICAL STORY just outlined is, of course, the proper prologue to an understanding of the Indian geographical setting, which in turn must be understood both in terms of its local natural tendencies and in terms of its relationship to man. This can only be touched on in this context, but an understanding of it in detail is a prerequisite for those who would understand the true character of any region of the Indo-Pakistan environment.[2]

The end result of this geologic history was the creation of a true subcontinent, the larger part of which is set in the midst of the warm waters of the Indian Ocean. As the mountains to the north separate the subcontinent from inner Asia proper, so the waters of the Indian Ocean tend to isolate it from other lands and continents. But this is only one aspect of the situation, for these same waters have a profound influence upon the Indian environment. In general the climate is oceanic, though areas like the Indo-Iranian Borderlands are an exception. The climate is thus warm and tropical, regional differences being largely due to elevation and amount of rainfall. The mountain bulwarks isolate the subcontinent from the cold continental winds, and this plus its geographical position close to the equator allows for a significant heating of the land. This superheating is particularly notable in April, May, and June, especially in the interior, and causes a low-pressure area to form over the subcontinent. A pressure

---

[2] See especially O. K. Spate, *India and Pakistan*, 2nd ed., Methuen, New York, 1957.

gradient is established between the high-pressure areas of the Indian Ocean and the low-pressure area of the subcontinent. The southeast trade winds, which are moisture-filled, move down this gradient across the Arabian Sea from west to east or up the Bay of Bengal from south to north and northwest. By mid-June these winds have "broken" the heat over most of the subcontinent. The monsoon, as this phenomenon is called, causes heavy rain along the Western Ghats and against the slopes of the Himalayas. Bombay, for example, receives above eighty inches of rainfall annually, most of which is monsoonal. Assam measures over one hundred inches in the same period. The parts of the Deccan behind the Western Ghats receive correspondingly less rainfall the farther to the east each lies.[3] Thus Mysore has an annual rainfall of twenty to forty inches, while Bombay and Cochin have more than eighty inches. Rajasthan, Sind, the northwest Frontier area, and a large portion of western Punjab fall outside the summer monsoon rain shadow and as a result receive less than twenty inches annually. The Thar Desert and much of central and western Baluchistan have less than ten inches annually and can thus be considered as desert regions. The Himalayan mountain slopes act as a deflector as well as a recipient of monsoon winds. They cause rain-bearing clouds to flow up the Ganges Valley into the Punjab, moving as it were along the Grand Trunk Road to the northwest "Gates" of India. This is doubly fortunate for the Gangetic plains, since it permits both a rainfall crop and the use of the rivers as a further source of moisture in the winter season. This contrasts with the lower Indus region of Sind at the southern end of the Indo-Gangetic plain, where the summer rainfall is negligible.

By September the seasonal monsoon rains are abating and by November the winter climate has taken hold. Much of this colder weather is due to cool air drawn out of the north owing to low pressures south of the equator. Thus the climate in this season is essentially continental and dry. This is the time, however, of rain and snow for high areas in Baluchistan and for the North-West Frontier area. In Quetta, for example, the bitter Khojak wind that sweeps out of the northwest often brings snow, and a similar situation occurs at Peshawar near the Khyber Pass. These moisture-bearing winds are essentially part of the cyclonic storms which originate over the Atlantic Ocean.

From March until the onset of the summer monsoon, the hot weather sets in. Though the coastal strips along the peninsula stay relatively cool because of offshore breezes, the interior regions literally bake. This was the season in British days of retreat to the hill stations, those places above the plains where because of elevation temperate climates were found. If one wants to find the now historical sites which represent in rather precise

---

[3] Spate, 1957, p. 44, records a remarkable rain distribution from the west of the Ghats eastward. "Mahabaleshwar, practically on the crest, has 261 ins., Parschgani, only 10 miles to the E., only 68; 10 miles farther on Wai has 29 ins."

fashion the British period, a visit to Simla, Ootacamund, or Murree is in order.

The extremes of heat to which the subcontinent is subjected have given rise to a series of characteristic adaptations which have tended to represent the area in Western minds even though they are often but superficial representatives of a rich and teeming cultural form. The turban, for example, is a simple head covering made from a length of cloth. Essentially it protects the head from the sun's rays. Yet it is tied in a variety of styles to represent Sikh, Pathan, Rajput, or Punjabi. Scottish-plaid turbans were created for the British-Indian army, and green turbans represent the hadji who made the pilgrimage to Mecca. The jeweled turban has symbolized the raja to the West. The sari may have been derived from the Roman toga, as some authorities suggest, but it is for Indian ladies a becoming and perfectly appropriate garb for hot weather. It usually consists of a choli piece for the upper body, a bare midriff, and wrap-around skirt made from one piece of cloth whose end can be tossed over the shoulder or head. Its versatility, lightness, and openness are particularly valuable for hot weather. The parasol may well be of Indian origin, as it is seen on sculpture of considerable antiquity. The parasol has often acted as a symbol both of royalty and even of divinity. Whatever its iconographic meaning, its popularity has doubtless been assured by its ability to cast shadows over individuals who have to move about in the bright sun. The divan, the pavilion, the portico, roof ventilators, and the lattice screen are architectural responses to subcontinental weather; the dhoti, the charpoy, the chappal sandals, and sleeping on the roof are probably also answers to the demands of this climate. These are the material responses which are part of the biology of the individual seeking a necessary balance between the external heat requirements of his body, the temperature of the air, and his comfort. But surely these are superficial aspects of greater needs and motivations which the exigencies of this kind of climate produce. It is hard to deny the attitude of mind which a sultry day produces amid the villages of rural India. It is an effort to face the day, it is better to sleep through the height of the heat, there is solace in the thought of water in the well, and coolness in the sound of Indian music. The Hindu gods and their rituals, the stories of epic action in the remote past, the use of primary colors in fabric or for wall decorations—somehow all seem right. This is, of course, not a simple matter, for the reaction of the Westerner is bound to be different. But if one contrasts with this a shopping center or a fast car in Nevada, for example, in midsummer, it seems that these American traits fight the heat and exist in spite of it. In India or Pakistan the action of man seems to be because of it. When one considers early Buddhism with its emphasis on moderation in all things or Gautama seated in the shade of the bodhi tree seeking revelation, one has to acknowledge perhaps that the climate factor has had at least some influence on the end result.

✳ *The Crops*

AUTHORITIES GENERALLY AGREE that the original vegetative cover for the subcontinent was largely arboreal. The character of these forests depends in large part on rainfall and soils. Thus the natural floral zoning is neatly prescribed. Obviously the rain forests of tropical type found in Assam and the Western Ghats and based in the alluvium of these areas are quite different from the Deccan dry, deciduous forests or those forests situated in the Deccan trap. Within an area such as the Gangetic plain there are decided differences in floral zones, between, for example, those floral communities that are found along riverbanks and those found out in the plains themselves. Elevation also plays its role in such areas as the Himalayan and Baluchistan highlands.

Because of the intensive human interference in the forest lands, the floral landscape has been drastically changed over the centuries. In places all traces of the original forest have disappeared, especially in the heavily inhabited plains areas. Even in tribal regions slash-and-burn and other clearing techniques have kept climax forests confined to forest reserves. The original regime is replaced with secondary growth; grassland mixed with acacia, tamarix, and the xerophytic euphorbia are examples of typical secondary succession in much of the Deccan plateau, the Vindhyan hills, and the marginal areas of Rajasthan, Sind, and the Punjab. Even this secondary succession is under stress in many of these areas owing to the depredation caused by goats and cattle (almost one third of the world's cattle are found in India-Pakistan) and the fuel-seeking activities of the human inhabitants. This hastens the erosion of the lands and the onset of desert conditions even though the rainfall may be more than ten inches annually. In both Sind and Rajasthan the Thar Desert has expanded its boundaries as a result of just such a situation, and many of the local land failures throughout the subcontinent have their roots in this fatal circumstance. Unquestionably Baluchistan also has been seriously affected in this way in the past, and the process continues today. The great delta regions are not subject, of course, to these problems, but even there man's interference is apparent. In Bengal, for example, the water hyacinth, introduced in late historical times, has choked the waterways and has invaded the rice fields—a handsome and determined destroyer of the old environment.

The advent of agriculture and animal domestication plus the growth of sizable populations is thus indicated as the start of a process which saw the change from an essentially closed arboreal world to one of open plains and savannahs teeming with human activity. In the complex fabric which is the story of India this factor perhaps best represents a constant. It is a phenomenon whose trace archaeology seeks; much of the material presented on these pages relates to it and can only be understood in that

Areas of wheat concentration

MAP 2   *Distribution of wheat cultivation on the Indian subcontinent.*

context. The rise and fall of civilizations, the movement of cultures and selected cultural traits, the diffusion of ideas and techniques—such phenomena are inextricably related to the fate of the physical land and its vegetation.

Without being overemphasized, this fact has always to be seriously considered if Indian history is to be understood; it is the failure truly to do so that frequently mars written histories of even the past few decades.

Two staple crops of subcontinental subsistence are wheat and rice. They are found in essentially different ecologies. Rice flourishes in moist climates, while wheat and its counterpart cereal grains, millet and barley, are most successful in temperate or even semiarid climates provided sufficient water is obtainable by one means or another. There are of course adaptive variations or ecological restrictions on this basic premise region by region, but the essential fact remains that Bengal and the Ganges Valley as far as Agra, the peninsular littoral, especially at the foot of the Western Ghats and the east coast, are the traditional centers of rice

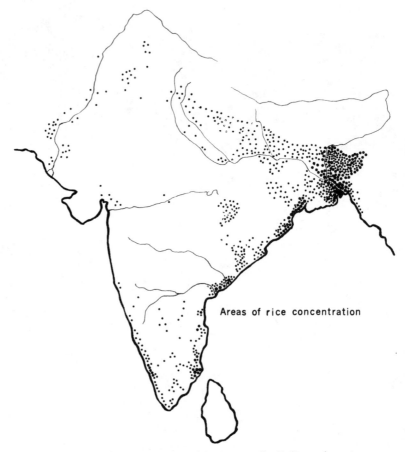

Areas of rice concentration

MAP 3   *Distribution of rice cultivation on the Indian subcontinent.*

cultivation, lying coincident largely with the heavier rain shadow, while the wheat center is the Punjab and the middle Ganges Valley. Sind, once a wheat center, is now a rice-growing area, but at the cost of the land, which the extensive irrigation necessary for rice in many places has water-logged and leached out.[4] Wheat would appear to have had a chronological priority over rice in its use as a domestic crop on the subcontinent. As will be pointed out, this has special significance.[5] The Harappan civilization, the first complex culture form to appear on the subcontinent, was based on wheat cultivation on alluvial soils found essentially in the Indus River Valley. A thousand years or so later the next great civilized development centers around Buddhism in the lower Ganges plain, and its subsistence basis is rice cultivation. At that time in Sind the old seat of the Harap-

[4] Bajra and jowar crops are now an important part of the subsistence economy and are particularly adapted to the Deccan.
[5] See p. 31.

pan civilization was minimally occupied and would not appear to achieve a civilized climax again until the advent of the Arabs at least a thousand years later. It is obvious that in these subsistence emphases our story has another prime motif in its design which would seem at least to match if not outshine the political or military motives which are so frequently alluded to in recounting subcontinental history. This is made all the more important when one considers that India is a land of villages, its population preponderantly rural. With reason one can argue that India's story is more properly that of her villages than her cities, which are often the standard point of reference in the accounts. The simple ratio of wheat and rice is a factor of enormous significance for the history of India, and it too needs to be understood here.

✳ *The Fauna*

THE FAUNAL PICTURE IS ALSO REVEALING. The subcontinent belongs zoogeographically to the Oriental region. The animals belonging to this region are those whose distribution tends to cluster in the climatic zone known as tropical Asia. This zone ranges from West Pakistan to south India and includes Southeast Asia and Indonesia up to the so-called Wallace Line, which runs just to the east of Borneo and the island of Bali. Baluchistan proper is not part of the Oriental region. However, the boundaries of the region are not sharp, as many faunal groups are found on both sides.

The closest vertebrate faunal parallels of the Oriental region are with the Ethiopian region. The Ethiopian region is in effect tropical Africa. The parallels are at the family and genus levels, but a few species are shared. This suggests that there were ties in the past (Gondwanaland or a land bridge?[6]). The arid and temperate lands to the west and north of the subcontinent belong to the Palearctic region. Transitional forms between these two faunas are numerous, and many Oriental groups (including

[6] However, Darlington's statement about fresh-water fishes is revealing: "The fish faunas of Africa and tropical Asia are very different as wholes, but share about ten primary-division families and even a few genera. These two faunas are fairly effectively separated now and they seem to have been so for a long time, except for occasional exchange of a few fishes across southwestern Asia. A few fishes, especially some cyprinids, have been exchanged by this route recently. That earlier exchanges, too, were across southwestern Asia and not across a more direct land connection is indicated by the complete absence of strictly fresh-water fishes on Madagascar. The differences between the fish faunas of Africa and Asia suggest a profound difference in the histories of the two continents. The fauna of Africa is a complex mixture of archaic and more recent fishes, the latter apparently mostly received from Asia. That of tropical Asia consists mostly of more recent fishes of groups which seem to have originated and radiated in tropical Asia. The history of Africa seems to have favored survival of old fishes; of tropical Asia, evolution of new ones." P. J. Darlington, *Zoogeography: The Geographical Distribution of Animals*, John Wiley & Sons, Inc., New York, 1957, pp. 90–91.

FIG. 1 *Fish and reptiles of the Indo-Iranian Borderlands as seen by artists living there about 2500–1700* B.C.

species) extend into temperate Asia (the tiger, many reptiles, birds). On the other hand few Palearctic groups extend into the Oriental regions, though there is some overlapping.

M. A. Smith in writing the introduction to the revised version of his volumes on amphibians and reptiles of British India divided the Indian subregion of the Oriental region into seven parts (desert area of northwest India; Kashmir and the western Himalayas; Gangetic plains; central India; the Deccan; mountains of Malabar and Ceylon; Chota Nagpur area). In the first area he included Baluchistan, the North-West Frontier Province, the Punjab, western Rajputana, and Sind. He comments: "The fauna of this area is essentially a desert one and resembles that of the desert region farther west. The majority of the genera that occur in it are not found elsewhere in India."[7]

[7] M. A. Smith, *The Fauna of British India, Reptilia and Amphibia*, Taylor and Francis, London, 1931 and 1943 eds., Vol. I, pp. 18–20.

FIG. 2   *Animals of the Indo-Iranian Borderlands as seen by artists living there about 2500–1700* B.C.

This observation gains added importance since reptiles and amphibians are less apt to be readily distributed and are slower in their adaptation to new environments than most of the higher vertebrates and probably the insects. Among the other animals native to this region the lion, elephant (now extinct), wild ass, ibex, gazelle (*subgutturosa*), black buck, and a large avian fauna are worthy of note. In effect the desert area is a transitional zone and relates closely to Iran, Western Asia, Central Asia, and ultimately to North Africa. Nonetheless, in the Indus river system there is a native Oriental fauna which is largely identical with that found in the Gangetic plains, the Deccan, and central India, the family of soft-shelled turtles Trionychidae (*chitra indica, chitra gangetica*), the gavials, the cobras, many cats, rhinoceros (now extinct in the area), mongooses, etc. The transitional nature of this border area is perhaps nowhere so well illustrated as among the vipers. Russell's viper is a well-known occupant of the riverine areas of Sind and the Punjab. Its habits would appear to incline it toward a riparian Oriental environment. In contrast is the nasty "saw-scaled viper" (*Echis carinatus*), which is apparently of Palearctic derivation and is found widely distributed in the arid belt from North Africa to Sind and beyond into the Deccan. This would appear to exemplify the extrusion of a Palearctic form into the subcontinent. The horned viper (*Pseudocerastes*), on the other hand, does not occur off the Baluchistan portion of the Iranian plateau, Cobras, however, are found in Iran and Central Asia (*naja oxiana*), and this would seem to represent an extension of Oriental fauna to the west and north.

The zoogeography of the subcontinent places considerable importance on the relation of given forms to areas outside of the region. One is concerned with derivation, with local adaptations, and with defining the characteristic features of an indigenous form. In this the field is not unlike that of archaeology.

The critical point is that the relationship of fauna to environment (ecology) is of great significance to the study of man. I have singled out Smith's description of the "desert area" of what is essentially the Indo-

FIG. 3   *Birds and plants of the Indo-Iranian Borderlands as seen by artists living there about 2500–1700 B.C.*

Iranian Borderlands and northwest India. The faunal situation there would suggest and indeed emphasize that transitional features are more important than indigenous ones in best representing the nature of life in the area. In effect this is probably true of all of India's frontiers, but less so in other frontiers than the western borderlands. The Himalayan region and

FIG. 4   *Animals of the Indus River Valley known to the citizens of India's most ancient civilization, the Harappan, 2300–1700 B.C.*

Assam are in reality transitional zones graded microscopically by climate and elevation. Similarly, when one moves east or west, north or south within the subcontinent itself, such is also the case on a much broader and less diminutive gradation. Thus Gujarat, at the same elevation as lower Sind, has much the same faunal situation, but there are differences due to rainfall and proximity to other and different ecological situations south and east.

✳ *Man and the Regional Hypothesis*

MAN BY HIS SUBSISTENCE and other activities, as alluded to above, disturbs the environment, upsets ecologies. But at the same time, unless his technological advantages permit the kind of "seven-league boots" movement exemplified by advantages such as railroads, man tends to move within ecological niches which he is familiar with and which he can exploit for his own comfort and survival. Accordingly the larger movements of food gatherers, pastoralists, and farmers has tended to be from the familiar to the familiar—to those places where his already acquired competences could be used again with small adjustment. As with animals so with man the ecological dictates are foremost in the battle for survival. This is a principle that must be fully considered in dealing with the archaeology of the subcontinent.

This consideration is, of course, liable to the danger of simplistic interpretation, for if man is a biological animal and thus keyed to an environment by an ecological relationship, he is also a social animal and his culture can adapt him to ecologies beyond his simple biological talents. He can establish symbiotic relationships with other men and with animals that are just now being ascertained in the archaeological record.[8]

The factors of geography considered, it is obvious that the subcontinent provides a variety of possibilities for the economic pursuits of man. We need to stress economics here, since the subsistence-obtaining activities of man have probably the largest role in determining the place where men live. Subsistence is, however, by no means the only reason, for factors such as defense, seclusion, worship, raw materials, and the like are other kinds of settlement motivators, and sometimes these are prime. However, archaeological evidence tends to bring out the economic situation more than any others, and this is especially true for prehistoric times. We are probably on safe ground in considering the relation of economics and geography as of maximum importance in establishing a paleoethnography.

The food gatherer will tend to settle where his game and his vegetative subsistence resources are optimum. In most ancient India he probably had the widest range of possibilities dependent upon his cultural "tastes" and the habits of the game he sought. Thus there may have been some who became adapted to rain-forest situations in Malabar and Assam, while others were situated in open-forest environments like many of the tribal people in India today. The riparian jungles and riverbanks of the plains and the Deccan, with the great variety of natural food resources found there, were certainly an attraction, while the desert areas such as the Thar and Baluchistan were the reverse as were the high Himalayas. How often the cultural variations among food-gathering groups produced barriers to exclude or include alien groups is not really known. It is clear, however, that the advent of pastoralism and agriculture saw the subcontinent increasingly divided into two basic parts: those areas where the return from agriculture in particular was optimum and thus attractive for food producers, and those where the agricultural return was less than optimum

---

[8] For example, see K. V. Flannery, "The Ecology of Early Food Production in Mesopotamia," *Science*, Vol. CXLVII (1965), pp. 1247–1256.

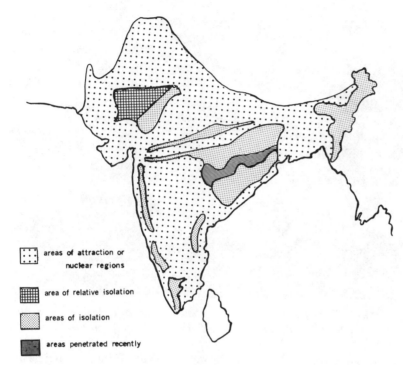

areas of attraction or
nuclear regions

area of relative isolation

areas of isolation

areas penetrated recently

MAP 4   *Areal characteristics of the Indian subcontinent* (after Subbarao).

and which were more suitable for food gathering, short-term food production, and pastoralism. The first area is marked throughout history by a
continuous settlement and often a rather dynamic process of change. The
second area tends to be more conservative, and change is less dynamic.
The historical process in which there is characteristically the rise of civilization in the first area, and with it the growth of population, the spread of
urbanization, the acceleration of foreign contacts, the rapid development
of technology, and the control of energy, sees the invasion of the second
area and its gradual compression. The late B. Subbarao, struck by these
phenomena, postulated the concept of regions of attraction, relative
isolation, and isolation. The Indo-Gangetic plains and the river basins of
the Godavari, Tapti, Kistna, Kaveri, and Narbada are examples of regions
of attraction. Areas of isolation would constitute the tribal areas of Assam,
Bihar, Orissa as well as the rainy slopes of the Western Ghats.

The areas of relative isolation would include Sind, most of Rajasthan,
the littoral along the Western Ghats, and parts of eastern Bengal and
Assam, or in other words usually those areas contiguous to areas of attraction and easy of access to those areas but possessing disadvantages both

PLATE 1 *Bhil house made entirely of thatch, branches, and mud—a type of construction of great antiquity but difficult to identify archaeologically.*

natural and historical. They were, however, invaded from time to time and can contain elements of old and new side by side.[9]

One should consider in this routes of communication which cross regions and provide reasons for their growth or demise. These routes tend to parallel the courses of rivers, as, for example, the Grand Trunk Road runs with the Ganges, and the Northwest Railroad with the Indus. Then there are the gaps and the passes that make it possible to cross mountain ranges or which ease one's way from one river system to the next. Fords, too, are obviously of importance, and their seasonal accessibility was a factor in regional interrelations. Wells, springs, oases, lakes, and streams are route regulators, and their existence has a historical reality that cannot be ignored. Routes bind regions together and permit the contact diffusion and indeed the migration of people critical to politics, if not always to regional development. Thus the accessibility, use, number, and kind of routes has great significance in the development of regional character.

The regional hypothesis may seem obvious to some, but it has to be reiterated whenever India's history or prehistory is to be considered. Subbarao himself was careful to point out the provincial aspects of

9 B. Subbarao, *The Personality of India*, 2nd ed., University of Baroda, Archaeological Series No. 3, Poona, 1958. The author summarizes the various evidences—linguistic, racial, historical, ethnic, etc.—in a brilliant study; see especially pp. 1–35. See also Spate, 1957, pp. 146ff.

regionalism or the ethnic, religious, linguistic, and other traits which can and do transcend original boundaries. But the sum of India's history would tend to support the regional idea.[10] Since this idea is predominantly based upon a geographical and economic foundation, the factors of geology, climate, fauna and flora outlined above are given prime importance.

In summation, the classical division of the subcontinent into the Himalaya-Karakorum mountain chain, the Indo-Gangetic plains, and the peninsula has a long geological history for its confirmation. This history describes the *raison d'être* of the river systems, soils, and other topographical features. Whereas the geology describes these main divisions, the climate, which is generally oceanic and is especially characterized by the monsoons, divides the subcontinent up into quite a different regional pattern with rainfall differences its basis. To this regional aspect of climate is tightly linked faunal and floral distribution, but these in turn produce another regional picture in which transitional zones are of special importance, since they bracket parts of the subcontinent with regions outside its physical boundaries. Fauna and flora are also indicative of both small- and large- scale ecological zonings which have often been radically changed by human interference. Finally, man's response to subcontinental geography is in part understood in the regional concept. This assumes that there are centripetal and centrifugal aspects to history based on regional tendencies toward productivity, mutual accessibility, and human attraction. Regional emphases vary through time, but each region's special character is continually re-emphasized by human events.

The interrelationships of the physical geography and the varied cultures of man through time are a major part of the story of human existence in the subcontinent. The archaeological evidence in the next chapters must always be considered in that light as well as in its strictly cultural historical aspect.

[10] Note Spate, 1957, p. 147, Fig. 33.

II

Earliest India

THERE IS LITTLE DOUBT that 250,000 years ago at least one form of man lived on the subcontinent. The evidence for that remote time has been accumulating ever since it was first discovered near Madras in the 1860s.[1] The artifacts that have survived to represent this most ancient India almost inevitably are familiar to the prehistorian whose special area of interest is Europe, Africa, or Western Asia. Even the regions to the east—Southeast Asia, Indonesia, and China—have a familiar prehistoric artifact representation on the subcontinent. In terms of the West, at least, there is chronological evidence that the developments which led to man's technical ability to manufacture various implements from stone were earlier there than comparable levels on the subcontinent. One cannot help but feel the strength of a diffusionist current from west to east. By no means precipitate, the wanderings that brought men and methods to the Indian subcontinent

[1] The account of the various pioneers in Indian prehistory and subsequent researches before World War II is a fascinating one, but it has been repeated on numerous occasions. The reader is referred to some of these accounts as follows: S. Piggott, *Prehistoric India*, Pelican Books, Harmondsworth, England, 1950; S. Roy, "Indian Archaeology from Jones to Marshall (1784–1902)," *Ancient India*, No. 9 (1953) pp. 4–28; A. Ghosh, "Fifty Years of the Archaeological Survey of India," *Ancient India*, No. 9 (1953), pp. 29–52; and, especially, V. D. Krishnaswami, "Progress in Prehistory," *Ancient India*, No. 9 (1953), pp. 53–79.

encompassed tens of thousands of years. Once, however, the primeval ground had been traversed and the ways and byways that led from plateau to forest to river valley to seashore or lakeside were known, it is evident that regional contacts may have accelerated. Strangely, though, where the "Early Stone Age" of India has strong extrasubcontinental parallels, the "Middle Stone Age" has increasingly few.[2] Thus the evidence so far barely suggests the presence on the subcontinent of any of the great blade-tool traditions which characterize the Upper Paleolithic of Europe and the Near East. This may change with further research, but it seems unlikely at this time. There is, however, some evidence for a developmental transition from Early to Middle to Late Stone Ages in India, at least in some areas. Here then is a strong hint of the subcontinent's role as a "refuge" area, perhaps where older traditions lived longer than elsewhere in the West and in doing so attained a characteristic quality which marks them as subcontinental. Thus though diffusion from outside the subcontinent may have been the significant factor in the origination of the Stone Ages in India, it was not perhaps as important in the development of those Stone Ages on a subcontinent where region differs from region in incredible procession from west to east and north to south. Rather the significant matter may well have been the degree of isolation or of contact that was permitted by each ecological niche to which Stone Age men were adapted. In a land as vast as the subcontinent, regional foci are more important than continental *oikoumene*. Thus there is almost a prophetic aspect to these remote ages in their demonstration of what becomes a commonplace of more recent ages.

But one is compelled to warn the ordinary reader from going farther in this chapter. For in spite of the devoted efforts of more than a handful of distinguished researchers—Indian, Pakistani, English, American—we hardly can compare the results with what prehistory has achieved elsewhere. No fossil men have been revealed, no great caves excavated, no truly early paintings or engraved bones discovered; even the animal life which so characterizes each given age is barely known. Instead we have river terraces, beds of gravel and silt, in or on which the fortunate searcher has located a number, not always large, of artifically chipped stones some of which are implements. Thanks to the arranging of these implements into typological classes and the observation of the geological associations, a relative chronological scheme is emerging and typological traditions are

---

[2] The terms Early, Middle, and Late Stone Age were arrived at by a group of prehistorians at the Conference on Asian Archaeology in New Delhi in December, 1961. They succeeded the earlier terms, Series I, II, III, IV, which were commonly used prior to this change. A caution to remember is that this terminology should be prefaced by "Indian," as it is strictly applicable to the subcontinent only. Nor is the term "paleolithic" entirely substitutable in this context.

"Nevasian" is, however, sometimes used to mean a local aspect of the Indian Middle Stone Age.

being traced on distribution maps.3 There our knowledge of prehistoric life virtually ends. Yet it is a strong start, and if on the following pages the reader is frustrated by repetitious emphasis upon this or that sequence, strata, class of tool, or if his methodology is shocked by learned speculation, it is best to remember that this work is the necessary prelude to the reconstruction by science of the prehistory which lies at the lowest part of the foundation upon which the mighty structure which is India depends.

❋ The Early Stone Age

THE PLEISTOCENE EPOCH saw initially the advent of man's immediate ancestors and then man himself. It has been customary to regard the beginnings of the Pleistocene as approximately coincident with the first glaciation of the four main glacial stages which have been determined as having occurred in the Northern Hemisphere. This would mean the beginnings of the Pleistocene would be at least seven hundred thousand years ago. However, the recent potassium-argon dating of the lowest deposits at Olduvai Gorge in Tanzania, which contain essentially Pleistocene fauna, suggests that the epoch began more than a million and a half years ago; similar dating on other continents indicates a possible duration of the Pleistocene of three to four million years. This means that the Pleistocene can now be divided into two stages: an earlier stage presumably warmer and perhaps somewhat moister than today, and a later stage characterized by the advances and retreats of continental glaciers in northern Europe and North America, as well as in the mountains in lower latitudes.

The African evidence is too new for us properly to assess its meaning to the Indian subcontinent at this time. However, it is important to note that most paleontologists and students of paleoanthropology are not particularly concerned about this temporal expansion of the Pleistocene. It simply gives more time for the evolution and emergence of the modern fauna which includes man. It also underlines how little we do know of the Pleistocene when we are able to more than double its time span even in the face of all the researches on the subject of the last hundred years.

Except for the so-called Siwalik primates the Indian prehistoric researches have produced no fossils which bear directly upon hominid evolution. This is perhaps somewhat strange in view of the discovery of fossil hominids in Africa, Palestine, Syria, Iraq, Iran, Central Asia, Java, and China; and much more so in view of the fact that ever since the 1860s men have been finding Stone Age tools in practically all the river basins in India. There is no lack of effort, however, and yearly parties of prehistorians from both the universities and the Archaeological Survey of India search the caves, rock shelters, and beaches—the likely spots for such finds. In a

3 An up-to-date summation by Gregory Possehl can be found in Appendix A.

way the lack of knowledge about the physical character of the hominids who lived in the subcontinent during the Pleistocene is not so handicapping to the research as one might think. The tool types that are found in abundance on the subcontinent are known elsewhere and often in association with one or another fossil form. It is therefore naturally assumed that there will be few surprises if fossil man is found in Indo-Pakistan; this, as any archaeologist must ruefully acknowledge, is a fatal assumption. There has, however, been a methodological flaw in approaches to subcontinental Pleistocene prehistory that is worth noting. It will be recalled from the previous chapter that the classic division of the physiography of the subcontinent is threefold: Himalayan and related mountain ranges, the Indo-Gangetic plains, and the peninsula. The mountain areas can be regarded as being strongest in their relationships to continental Asia, while the peninsula is as strongly affected by the marine world which surrounds it. The plains are affected by both peninsula and mountains—but more by the latter since that region is the source of most of the plains' rivers. In simple terms, one might expect that the discovery of stone tools in a river terrace in central India would cause investigators to look to the sea for extrapeninsula correlation; instead many studies are made noteworthy by efforts to correlate with Pleistocene cycles in the mountains, an effort fraught with great difficulties.

It is interesting in this regard that the first definitive collection of paleolithic tools was made in southeastern India in what was then called Madras Presidency. This was made by a British civil officer named Bruce Foote, whose collections were important in the establishment of prehistoric studies in India.[4] In contrast to this is the fact that the first truly comprehensive study of the Pleistocene of the subcontinent and its relation to associated artifactual evidence was performed by H. de Terra and T. T. Paterson[5] in the Kashmir and Soan River Valley region under the sponsorship of Yale and Cambridge universities in 1935. So comprehensive was this work that it has served as a model. This clear definition of Pleistocene glaciation and interglaciation with corresponding artifact association has in some ways been a trap for those working in the peninsula. Even de Terra used this study as a reference point in his brief surveys of the Narbada valley in the peninsula (with qualifications). It was natural to try to correlate the two regions of the subcontinent, but all efforts to do so have been eventually frustrated, at least in terms of the geology, since not only has there been a lack of good evidence from the intervening areas but it has also been increasingly clear that the riverine systems of the peninsula

[4] See pp. 61ff.

[5] *Studies on the Ice Age of India and Associated Human Cultures*, Carnegie Institution of Washington Publication No. 493, Washington, 1939. This study is now under severe criticism owing to reviews of the evidence by others. The work of S. Porter in Swat, carried out in 1967, is especially significant.

are not to be correlated with the Punjab river systems on any but strictly paleontological or archaeological evidence, both of which evidences have a substantial order of incompleteness at the present time.

TABLE 1. SEQUENCE OF THE PLEISTOCENE IN KASHMIR AND THE NORTHWESTERN PUNJAB

PERIOD	Upper Indus terrace in northern Kashmir	Siwalik foothills and plains in northwest Punjab, Poonch, and Jammu
Fourth glaciation	Terminal moraines 4 Glaciers in tributary valleys only T_4, loose gravel	T_4 Pink loam, silt, and gravel Reddish loam
Third interglacial stage	Erosion and uplift T_3 Degradation	T_3 Degradation (Soan industry)
Third glaciation	Terminal moraines 3, local glaciation of Indus Valley T_2, younger valley fill, boulder gravel; lake silt locally 450 feet	T_2 Potwar loessic silt, ± 350 feet (Soan industry)
Second interglacial stage	T_1 Degradation Erosion	T_1 Upper terrace gravel (Chelleo-Acheulian and Early Soan cultures)
Second glaciation	Ancient valley fill Boulder gravel Great Indus Glacier	Erosion, tilting Boulder conglomerate zone $\pm 2,000$ feet Boulder gravels in fan formation (oldest flake industry)
First interglacial stage	Erosion	Pinjor zone, $\pm 2,500$ feet Pink silt and sand Early Pleistocene fauna of Upper Siwaliks
First glaciation	Dissected trough valleys	Tatrot zone conglomerate and sand Upper Siwalik fauna

AFTER DE TERRA AND PATERSON, 1939

As is shown in Table 1, de Terra and Paterson were able to find evidence for four principal glacial and three interglacial stages in their study of Pleistocene formations in the Kashmir region. These determinations were based on detailed study along an approximate NE-SW traverse of perhaps 350 miles. The traverse ranges from more than 12,000 feet to less than 1,000 feet above sea level and extends through five physiographic regions in order: the southwestern slopes of the Himalayas; the Kashmir Valley; the Pir Panjal range, which forms the western side of the valley; the foothill country, made up in large part of folded Siwalik formations of Pliocene age; and the adjacent plain of the Punjab. In general this is a region of great instability, and there has been considerable tectonic action even in recent times so that complex folding and faulting as well as local tilting and uplift complicate the geological picture. However the Pleistocene record is in evidence on every hand. There are classic examples of glacial activity in the Himalayas: cirques, U-shaped valleys, moraines, and still existent glaciers. The Kashmir Valley is filled with Pleistocene deposits ranging from glacial outwash gravels to extensive lacustrine sediments. The Pir Panjal is characterized in the northern slopes by the tilted "Early" Pleistocene lake beds known as the Karewa, while both the foothill country and the Potwar plain have river terraces that presumably illustrate the climatic fluctuations during the ice ages.

TABLE 2. TERRACE SEQUENCE IN KASHMIR AND THE NORTHWESTERN PUNJAB

Northwestern Punjab		Kashmir
T₄ (terrace silt, sand)	Sedimentation (fluvial)	T₄ (gravel, sand)
T₃ (thin loam)	Erosion	T₃ (thin loam)
Warping		
	Sedimentation (aeolian- fluvial, lacustrine)	Third moraines
Potwar loessic silt (T₂) and gravel		T₂ (boulder gravel) Massive silt in upper Indus Valley
T₁ (gravel)	Erosion and redeposition of gravel	T₁ Upper Karewa silt
Folding		
	Sedimentation (fluvial and glacio-fluvial)	Second moraines
Boulder conglomerate (boulder gravel, ridge gravel, plains drift)	Erosion	Karewa gravel, sand
Folding		
Pinjor beds (silt, clay, sand)	Sedimentation (fluvial, lacustrine)	Lower Karewa lake beds (clay, silt)
Tatrot beds (conglomerate, sand, silt)	Sedimentation (fluvial) Erosion	Older fans (gravel, sand)
Folding		
Middle Siwalik beds		

AFTER DE TERRA AND PATERSON, 1939

Though it was the Potwar region of the plains area that produced the main evidence for prehistoric man, it was not the Potwar region alone that made possible the correlation of these remains with the stages of the Pleistocene. Rather it was the whole series of studies throughout the traverse, which include the paleontological evidence, that provided the geological framework. Its relative reliability is thus further underlined.

✳ *The Potwar Plain*

THE POTWAR PLAIN is bounded by the Pir Panjal, the Indus River, and the Jhelum. It is approximately bisected by the Soan River, which flows out of the foothill country, which here forms a front range to the Pir Panjal. On its southwestern boundary is the Salt Range, which some geologists regard as representative of peninsular India—an odd and scientifically intriguing phenomenon. The Potwar plain lies more than two thousand feet above sea level. It is traversed from southeast to northwest by the Grand Trunk Road, which crosses the Indus at Attock, at that strategic location where the Kabul River joins the Indus River. At the heart of the Potwar plain is the new capital of Pakistan, Islamabad, near Rawalpindi.

The Potwar plateau is actually a geosynclinal trough filled with Tertiary sediments some twenty-five thousand feet thick. The whole is crowned with Siwalik deposits representing the various phases of the Pliocene (Chinji—Lower Pliocene; Nagri, Dhok Rathan—Middle and Upper Pliocene) and the Lower Pleistocene in this region (Tatrot, Pinjor). It would appear that the end of the Pliocene was marked by a period of uplift and consequent erosion and this produced an unconformity between the middle Siwalik zone and the Tatrot zone. The latter represents a new cycle of sedimentation.[6]

The Tatrot sediments consist of sandstones rather coarse in composition interspersed with layers of silt or conglomerate and ranging up to almost one thousand feet in thickness. These rest on basal conglomerates. The fauna associated with these sandstones would indicate moist climatic conditions, because the crocodile, turtle, and the hippopotamus as well as the more terrestrial herbivores, the pig and the elephant,[7] are represented.

The Pinjor zone emerges apparently out of the Tatrot and is characterized by a series of pinkish silts and grayish or brownish sands. The zone varies in thickness from 500 feet to 1,500 feet outside the Potwar and from about 500 to 900 feet in the Potwar. An analysis of Pinjor silts taken from the Soan region indicates that some, at least, of these deposits possibly are aeolian loess. The fauna, though essentially the same as that of the Tatrot, is much more abundant.

De Terra interpreted this evidence as indicating in the Tatrot "a stage of quick river deposition and filling of preexisting lowlands in the Potwar

---

[6] De Terra and Paterson, 1939, pp. 253–260. See also summary in H. L. Movius, "Early Man and Pleistocene Stratigraphy in Southern and Eastern Asia," *Papers of the Peabody Museum of Archaeology and Ethnology*, Vol. XIX, No. 3 (1944), pp. 17–20.
[7] The fauna of the Tatrot zone is assigned paleontologically to the Villafranchian. However, there is some debate about the place of the Pinjor-Tatrot zones as some would have them as Pliocene (e.g., Wadia, 1957, pp. 365f.; Krishnaswami, 1947, p. 17f.).

plains," concomitant with "powerful streams and abundant rainfall";[8] Whereas the Pinjor silts suggest that "it is as if the rivers of Pinjor time had grown sluggish, meandering freely across wide flood plains. . . ."[9] To this can be added the evidence for wind-blown dust, just as occurs in the premonsoon months today. De Terra suggests a warm climate: "At best it was subtropical, like Northern Central India nowadays."[10]

The faunal evidence from the Tatrot zone in the Potwar has its equivalent in the lower Karewa lake beds on the northern slopes of the Pir Panjal. These are located in places below outwash deposits of second glacial origin.[11]

It must be remembered that the Potwar plain was not of itself glaciated but was in a periglacial situation. Then too the evidence would indicate that the foothill and Pir Panjal regions underwent uplift during the "Early" and perhaps the Middle Pleistocene. This had the effect of constantly steepening the general gradient and thus accentuating the erosional capabilities of the streams. Some care has to be exercised in interpreting the evidence for climatic conditions on the basis of the geological evidence alone. For example, loess is sometimes evidence for arid conditions when temperature extremes and short but violent periods of rainfall loosen the poorly vegetated soil cover, which is subsequently swept up by sufficiently forceful winds to carry the silt burden and deposit it as loess. Such situations occur in glacial circumstances as well as in interglacial. The Tatrot fauna is qualitatively the same as the Pinjor but quantitatively inferior, and this again can be a flaw in the argument that the Tatrot represents a different climatic situation from the Pinjor. One suggests that the accident of discovery might change the faunal picture.

Be that as it may, the consensus of a variety of older workers who have assessed all the evidence would place the Tatrot zone as representing the first glaciation of the Himalayan region and the Pinjor as the first interglacial. The Pinjor fauna marks the final climax of the Siwalik fauna that had evolved through the Pliocene. On the basis of such evidence Himalayan glaciation was apparently local, and its effects on the plains region to the south needs far more extensive study than it has hitherto received. If de Terra is correct in his views as to the role of the monsoonal winds, and we have no reason to suggest otherwise, it is clear that the essentially warm marine environment of the subcontinent modifies the local climatic situation even in the periglacial terrain of the Potwar, and much of the evidence for climatic change in the Pleistocene would here have to be considered in a

[8] De Terra and Paterson, 1939, p. 260.

[9] *Ibid.*, p. 262.

[10] *Ibid.*, p. 264.

[11] *Ibid.*, pp. 128, 129, Figs. 78, 79.

purely subcontinental light. This will certainly change some of our present views. However, the equivalence of a pluvial (rainy) stage in the peri-glacial region with a glacial stage in the Himalayan region and a corresponding interpluvial with an interglacial stage would seem justified by the evidence.

The second glacial stage was the most extensive of those recorded in the Kashmir Himalayas. It is represented by massive boulder conglomerates. The earlier Tatrot-Pinjor beds were folded and in the Potwar faulting produced a number of basins, which were covered by the conglomerates. In fact, the upper Siwalik beds in the whole region were tilted as the result of the continuing orogeny of the Himalayan area. The Pir Pinjal was further uplifted, and this plus glaciation and increased rainfall produced an erosional stage of great magnitude, thus the *raison d'être* for the great accumulation of conglomerates. The rivers emerging from the Himalayas brought down massive gravels that spread out in the valleys as fans over 1,500 feet thick. In places these gravels merge with glacial outwash trains in the Salt Range and among local ridges of the Potwar, and in the foot-hills large accumulations of gravels mark the erosional activity of local streams at this stage, while on the Potwar plateau finer gravels and sands are the equivalents of the boulder conglomerate, especially in the Soan Valley.

The fauna of the time includes such moisture-loving creatures as hippos, crocodiles, and turtles, but in addition open-forest or veld animals occur: elephants, camels, horses, buffalo, and wild cattle. This is regarded as a Middle Pleistocene fauna. Of greatest interest is the occurrence of large and apparently worked flakes of quartzite in the upper part of the Boulder Conglomerate where that formation is found as a high terrace in both the Soan and Indus valleys.

The second interglacial stage (T_1) is characterized by widespread erosion. In the Soan Valley terraces were cut initially and gravels taken from the older Boulder Conglomerates by the eroding stream action were deposited on these and later sometimes cemented. In the Potwar region and else-where gravels lie unconformably on the upper Siwalik strata. This uncon-formity marks a period of uplift and erosion in which the degradation of the Potwar region continued while the eroding streams cut their modern channels, in which were deposited the gravels. Associated with these gravels were stone tools somewhat more advanced than those associated with the Boulder Conglomerate (Early Soan, Abbevillo-Acheulian). These implements were much rolled, and in view of the fact that the researchers consider the second interglacial age of greatest length, it would appear that they were manufactured early in that interval and redeposited later among the sediments of Terrace 1. Lack of fossil evidence handicaps a reasonable conclusion as to the nature of the second interglacial environ-ment, but the Abbevillo-Acheulian-type tools are associated elsewhere

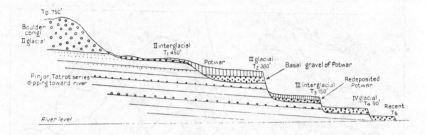

FIG. 5   *Transverse section through Indus terraces (T_D, T_1, etc.) near confluence with Soan River* (after de Terra and Paterson, 1939).

with fauna of the Middle Pleistocene, which includes elephant, hippo,
horse, and buffalo. This would comport with a somewhat temperate
open-forest ecology.

The third glacial phase is marked by two stages: (1) the creation of
aggradational terraces (T_2) by the deposition of gravels as the Potwar
rivers filled their channels; (2) the superimposition of wind-blown silts
on the gravels in considerable thickness. These silts are layered, and de
Terra suggests that this is the result of the monsoonal rains coupled with a
rather constant supply of silt gathered by periglacial winds from sediments
deposited by meltwater, the violent monsoonal rains clearing the air of its
dust and then depositing it as loess.

In the gravels were found the stone artifacts of the earlier phase (A)
of the Late Soan type. In the loess, especially its lower portions, were
found tools of Late Soan B type as well as "workshops" of early man.
Levalloisian techniques of tool manufacture (a technique of preparing
flint cores for the production of flakes) are apparent in this phase.

The monsoonal rains at one season of the year and the fine silts which
were air-borne prior to the rains suggest a climate comparable to today.
The few vertebrate representatives are the camel, bison, horse, and some
canine species indicating an open-forest terrain.

The third interglacial phase was one of extensive erosion which cut into
the previous deposits in the Potwar quite deeply. "North of Rawalpindi a
wide terrace is cut into the Potwar loess, leveling hard Murree sandstone.
The intermediate position between a low aggradational terrace (T_4) and an
upper fan or terrace (T_2) characterizes it as the same erosional stage which
is regionally documented in Kashmir, Poonch and Jammu as Terrace 3."[12]

Deposited in this terrace in the Soan Valley are loamy silts in part derived from a deposition of the Potwar loess of Terrace 2. No clear association of artifacts or fossils is found in these silts, but in view of forms found
in the next phase, it seems likely that human and animal occupancy much
like that of the previous phase continued.

[12] *Ibid.*, p. 276.

37

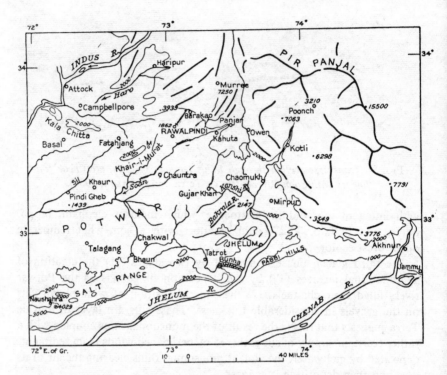

MAP 5 *Map of the region between the Jhelum and Indus rivers in the north-western Punjab* (after de Terra and Paterson).

A fourth terrace (T_4) is known in the Soan Valley and represents a fourth glacial stage. It is aggradational and consists of silts, sand, loessic loam, and gravel or largely fluvial deposits. Two sites were found containing what appears to be an evolved or very late Soan industry.

Above these fluvial deposits are layers of silt largely loessic but more often than not over one hundred feet in thickness. Within this was found "thin layers with charcoal, broken bones, and pottery."[13]

Thus the Pleistocene of the region would seem to have been most strongly characterized by (1) continued uplift of the mountains and hills with consequent tilting, faulting, and folding of the Tertiary and Pleistocene deposits; (2) strong monsoonal influences.

Further, one can add that the glaciation of the Himalayan foothills was limited to the higher altitudes, while the Potwar plateau and the Punjab plains areas were in a periglacial environment. This limitation was imposed by the fact that oceanic influences were always stronger in the subcontinental situation than in the continental. The paleontological evidence strongly suggests that at no time was an essentially cold-weather fauna present in the plains region—in effect the suggestion is that the faunal shifts were from

[13] *Ibid.*, p. 277.

38

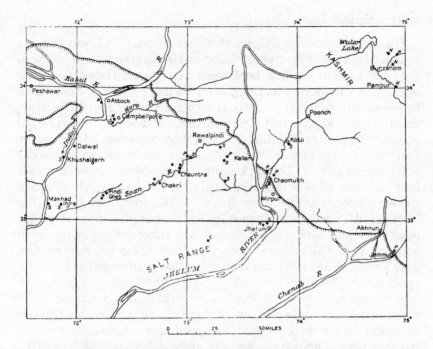

MAP 6 *Map showing distribution of prehistoric sites in the northwestern Punjab. Dentate line indicates mountain border; S, Soan industries; P, pre-Soan artifacts; N, neolithic sites (after de Terra and Paterson).*

temperate to subtropical, or in other words from the southern Palearctic Zone to the Oriental, or transition variations thereof.

The geological record as set forth by de Terra and Paterson is remarkable in the number of confirmatory relationships it has to back up the sequence. It is therefore all the more important that human artifactual remains were found in the record. These need some explanation both because they are of obvious importance to the study of early man and because they act much as a paleontological record in establishing relative sequence in India.

The occurrence of Stone Age implements in the Potwar is in the Soan and Indus valleys (Fig. 5, Map 6).

SEQUENCE OF TERRACES AND PREHISTORIC INDUSTRIES

PERIOD	Kashmir Gl. Stage	Deposit	Industry
Upper Pleistocene	4th Gl.	T$_4$	Evolved Soan
	3rd Intergl.	T$_3$ Redeposited Potwar	?
	3rd Gl.	T$_2$ Basal Gravel	Late Soan A
		Potwar Loessic Silt	Late Soan B & Acheulian
Middle Pleistocene	2nd Intergl.	T$_1$	Early Soan & Abbevillo-Acheulian
	2nd Gl.	Boulder Congl.	Pre-Soan

39

The so-called pre-Soan is represented at ten localities.[14] The artifacts were collected from the upper layer of the fan and plains gravels.[15] According to the finder's report all these implements were surface remains and their association with the Boulder Conglomerate either assumed or conjectured. In one locality (MS 163) the artifacts were mixed with "Early Acheulian" material and it appears that these were associated with the Potwar basal gravels.[16] In another case (Pl. 6) a workshop containing implements of Early Soan type was located "on limestone gravel belonging to the boulder conglomerate zone."[17] The implements are described as "big flakes made from quartzite, all in a very worn condition, with large, plain, unfaceted striking platforms at angles mostly low, varying from 100° to 125°. The bulbs are flat, but the *cores* (bulbs) are well developed, some of them very large. The upper surface is usually unflaked except for one or two small irregular scars. There is no secondary working on any but one specimen from Kallar, where small flakes of later date have been struck from the main upper surface."[18]

So amorphous a group do these tools constitute that one can as easily characterize them as by-products of the Early Soan or even Abbevillo-Acheulian industries as see them as constituting a separate entity. The fact that there is apparently one case where Acheulian and "pre-Soan" material occur together (Malakpur) and that Early Soan material is frequently found on the surface of the Boulder Conglomerate suggests this possibility. However neither Paterson nor H. L. Movius see these large flakes as in any way organic to either the Soan or Abbevillo-Acheulian industries.[19] Since the "pre-Soan" material represents the earliest evidence for human habitation of the subcontinent (second glacial stage), it is more than a little important that further field investigation be carried out.[20]

The "Early Soan" industry, in contrast to the above, is clear-cut and its association with second interglacial deposits as defined by de Terra apparently well established. The industry is made up characteristically of tools made of "thoroughly rounded water-worn pebbles and small boulders."[21] There is also a relatively small quantity of flakes. The pebble

[14] Movius, 1944, p. 25.
[15] De Terra and Paterson, 1939, p. 265.
[16] *Ibid.*, p. 282.
[17] *Ibid.*, p. 286.
[18] *Ibid.*, pp. 304–305.
[19] *Ibid.*; Movius, 1944, pp. 24–25.
[20] Professor Eldon Johnson of the University of Minnesota made a preliminary effort in 1963-1964, but his plans for full-scale investigation were apparently negated in the following year.
[21] De Terra and Paterson, 1939, p. 305.

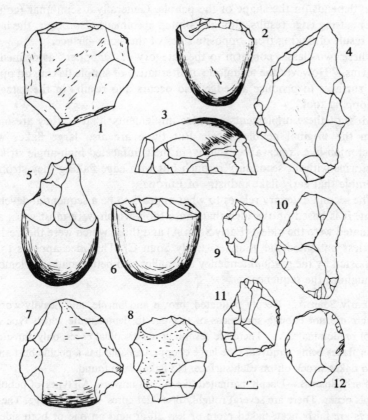

FIG. 6   *Early Soan tool types* (after de Terra and Paterson, 1939).
1—*"Pre-Soan" flake from Boulder Conglomerate at Kallar*
2, 3, 4—*Early Soan pebble tools—flat-based type*
5, 6—*Early Soan pebble tools—rounded type*
7, 8—*Early Soan discoidal cores*
9–12—*Early Soan flakes*

tools were divided into two broad categories on the basis of manufacturing technique, and state of patination and wear. The "technique" classes can be summarized as follows:

(a) *Flat-based:* a striking surface is obtained by using an irregular-shaped pebble which has a naturally or artificially obtained flat side. The flakes are knocked off toward the rounded surface of the pebble to form a working edge on the flat side or sides according to the shape of the pebble (Fig. 6). The cutting edge is usually convex. Slip-flaking often marks its use.

(b) *Rounded-pebble tools:* flakes are knocked off the original surface of the pebble, and the shape of the tool, or rather the shape of its "cutting" side, depends on the shape of the pebble. Generally a semilunar (convex side) cutting edge results, though pointed specimens also occur, the latter the result of flaking from opposite sides of the same surface.

These two classes conform to the category of "chopper" as defined by Movius.[22] However the technique or alternative of simple flaking on opposite surfaces to produce an edge also occurs and results in the category "chopping tool."

Most of these implements are core implements; that is, they are made from the original pebble nuclei. But there are also large flakes with Clactonian-like appearance; that is, in their unfaceted high-angle striking platforms without secondary retouch but with edge flaking they strongly resemble that early flake industry of Europe.

The second category relates to what appears to be a sequential development. It is based on the idea that those tools which were most worn and patinated were the oldest (Early Soan A) and those which were the freshest and less patinated the younger (Early Soan C). This idea appears to be supported by the gradual tendency to smaller and better made implements throughout the sequence.

Early Soan A.—Deeply patinated, brown and purple, and heavily worn. There are not enough specimens of this age to demonstrate which type of tool predominates. . . . There are several crude discoidal cores, only three or four flakes being removed. One large chopperlike core has a pebble butt and two flakes struck off on each surface. No flakes were found.

Early Soan B.—Deeply patinated like A, but unworn. All types of pebble tools occur. There are several roughly discoidal cores, one very large. These cores are fairly neat, flaked more or less all around on one or both sides, usually alternately. There is one large chopperlike core.

The associated flakes . . . have unfaceted platforms, the angle varying between 95° and 130°. Occasionally the platform is placed at an angle to the axis of the flake. In some specimens the bulb is more or less totally removed by an *éraillure*; in some the bulb is nearly flat, and in others it is strongly convex. There is little retouch, but in some specimens chipping resulting from utilization simulates coarse retouch and may possibly be so. The primary flaking of the upper surface is crude on the whole, often with part of the original pebble surface remaining, but in some few specimens it is much more regular. Step flaking is common. The general impression is that this industry, apart from the great number of pebble tools, has resemblances to the early Clactonian of Europe.

Early Soan C.—Less patinated, light brown; only slightly worn or not at all. All types of pebble tools occur, but type b (ii) (Fig. 6,6) is by far the most common. A probable development from this type is the disk, flaked all over

[22] Movius, 1944, pp. 10, 25–26.

one surface. A new type appears at this stage and becomes much more common in the late Soan. It is a "side chopper," roughly oval in shape, with a pebble butt and straight or convex and occasionally has some secondary working. Some of the specimens of form b (v) show no signs of utilization and may be regarded as cores alone.

Otherwise the undoubted cores are of the discoidal type with alternate lateral flaking, often with a patch of "cortex" remaining in the center of one or both surfaces. These discoidal cores resemble the Clactonian forms and also the early Levalloisian. However, another type of core appears, which is more nearly akin to other Levalloisian forms—flat, with under surface cortex and striking platforms prepared at each end by the removal of two or three small flakes.

Correspondingly, there are two kinds of flakes—those with high-angled plain platforms having the same general characteristics as early Soan B, but flatter and neater on the whole and with a greater amount of primary flaking; and those, rather fewer in number, with low-angled, simply faceted platforms. There are no definite signs of retouch but distinct signs of utilization.[23]

The Early Soan material was found in both the Soan and Indus valleys (Soan—at least four localities; Indus—at least six localities). The find spots are either on the surface of the Boulder Conglomerate or in association with the T_1 terrace or occur as heavily rolled implements obviously redeposited in the Potwar basal gravels of T_2.

As noted above, representations of the Abbevillo-Acheulian industries, which are also found in the peninsula, in Africa, Western Asia, and Europe, occur in the Potwar, especially in the Soan Valley. These take the form of bifacially flaked handaxes both of the crude, thick-butted, steeply flaked Abbevillian type and of the more refined, flatter-flaked Acheulian type of which there are various stages. The cleaver also occurs. The handaxe type which Paterson called Middle Acheulian is found (well rolled) with "pre-Soan" flakes in T_1 gravels at Locality MS 163 on the Grand Trunk Road.[24] At site P. 16, about $2\frac{1}{4}$ miles southeast of Chauntra and some 15 miles to the south of Rawalpindi, both Late Soan and Abbevillo-Acheulian implements were found. The account of the find is worth quoting verbatim:

The locality is 2 miles from the Soan River and only half that far from the dry flood plain. Its altitude is 80 feet above the Soan level, almost on the slope crest of the second ridge, which is capped by a coarse gravel. The gravel is composed of water-worn boulders and pebbles derived from Siwalik sandstones mainly, but there are also quartzite constituents such as occur in many of the ancient Soan terrace deposits. Its lower position

23 De Terra and Paterson, 1939, pp. 307–308.
24 *Ibid.*, 1939, p. 282.

in relation to the Potwar gravel is evident . . . and as this basal loess gravel is of different color and composition, we conclude that the lower gravel represents a different terrace deposit. However, no true terrace flats are preserved in the neighborhood, but this is easily understood if one takes account of the friable nature of the underlying rock and the intense dissection which it has undergone on the slope of the syncline. Adjacent to this ridge gravel and banked up against the crest of the ridge lies a pinkish sandy silt in which were found some 100 artifacts of Abbevillian and Acheulian type. The handaxes are water-worn, the Abbevillian tools more so than the Lower and Middle Acheulian tools, and they occur in greater numbers near the high terrace ledge. This may indicate that they were washed out from the ridge gravel and redeposited at a later time when the pink sandy silt was formed. The pink silt makes a slope veneer and is charged with detritus of apparently eluvial type, from which we collected a number of late Acheulian handaxes, as well as cores and flakes of the late Soan industry.

From these facts it would seem that there are two different deposits and at least two distinct types of industries. The ridge gravel can belong only to a fill stage during which the then less dissected slope was buried by ancient Soan drift. Although different in composition from the Potwar gravel, it might well represent a facies of the Potwar, for it lies nearer to the Soan tract than the higher Potwar gravels. In that event it would represent a terrace gravel of third glacial age on which the river subsequently degraded, thereby reducing its thickness greatly. This interpretation is supported by the altitude of the ridge gravel, which is intermediate between the 120-foot (third) and 20-foot (fourth) terraces of section 11, which is only a few miles upstream from this locality. Hence the gravel might be considered as of third glacial age while the adjoining sandy silt must be third interglacial, representing a thin deposit on T_3. Accordingly, the early paleolithic handaxes were embedded in a third glacial deposit and redeposited in the following interglacial stage, together with late Soan tools. Now, in view of the occurrence in place of similar early Acheulian handaxes on level 200 feet of section 5 it is probable that at Chauntra the same industry (with Abbevillian tools) originally was manufactured on a high terrace, which was subsequently denuded, and its artifacts incorporated in T_2.[25]

Thus the Acheulian material was originally made in the third glacial age and redeposited in the third interglacial stage. However, the heavily rolled Abbevillian-Acheulian implements were presumably of a stage prior to the formation of the third glacial gravels, and this would suggest the second interglacial stage in confirmation of the situation at MS 163. At Balawal, one mile farther to the south, a Late Acheulian handaxe was recovered from a cemented gravel located below Potwar sands and silts.[26] A rolled

25 *Ibid.*, pp. 289–290.
26 *Ibid.*, p. 291.

Abbevillian handaxe was found with similarly rolled Early Soan pebble implements and mixed with Late Soan implements in an "open gravel patch" in the Dhok Pathan conglomerate. The site, measuring some three thousand square feet, was the richest found by investigators in the Potwar. One hundred artifacts were collected there. De Terra believes the deposit in which this workshop was found is "redeposited Potwar of T_3 or river draft of T_4."

In summation, it would appear that the Abbevillian and Early-Middle Acheulian implements are of the second interglacial stage, the former earlier than the latter, as these are more heavily worn and patinated, and the Late Acheulian presumably of the third glacial stage and perhaps occurring in at least an early phase of the third interglacial stage. The evidence would indicate that the Abbevillo-Acheulian tradition was separate from that of the Early Soan at these stages.

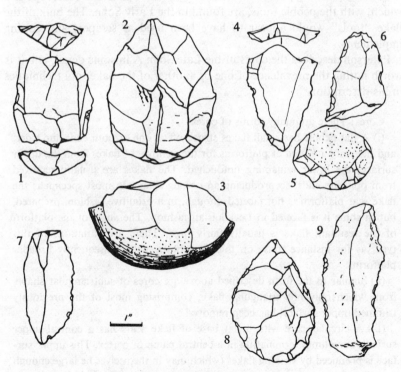

FIG. 7 *Late Soan tool types* (after de Terra and Paterson, 1939).
1–3—*Late Soan A cores*
4–6—*Late Soan A flakes*
7—*Late Soan B flakes*
8–9—*Chauntra*

✳ *Late Soan Industries and the Chauntra Site*

THE TRUE OR LATE SOAN IS BASICALLY A FLAKE-TOOL INDUSTRY which still contains the pebble tool types of the Early Soan, though these are somewhat smaller and more refined. Paterson divides the Late Soan into two industries—A, the earlier, being associated with the T_2 Potwar basal gravel; and B, being associated with the Potwar loessic silts and clays above the gravels. The industry is especially noteworthy in the full-fledged appearance of the so-called Levalloisian technique, which was suggested in prototypical form in the Early Soan. This includes the preparation of striking platforms and the production of flakes whose long axis is at a 90° angle with that platform. There is little secondary retouch of these flakes, though Paterson believes this is because of the hardness of the quartzite. A few blades also occur in Late Soan A. Abundant are the angular flakes with obtuse striking platforms which suggest the Clactonian of Europe and which, with the pebble tools, are found in the Early Soan. The bulk of the flake "tools" would appear to have been used as scrapers and cutting implements.

Paterson describes the cores of the Late Soan A in some detail, and it is worth noting the prevalence of one or another of the flake-tool techniques in his description:

Cores: There are many forms of cores.

(i) A flat pebble has small flakes struck off at one or both ends and sides, and the scars are used as platforms for the removal of flakes from the upper surface, the lower remaining untouched. The flakes are usually removed from opposite ends, so producing an oblong shape. In most specimens the flake scar platform is not faceted, though, in a primitive fashion, prepared, but in some it is faceted in Levalloisian fashion. The angle of the platform of the resultant flake is usually fairly high. There are variations of this type, as for instance those on thicker pebbles, with consequently broader platforms.

(ii) Similar to the form described above are cores of subtriangular shape, from which only one triangular flake, comprising most of the previously trimmed upper surface, has been removed.

(iii) A circular core with a flat base of flake scars has a conical upper surface, sometimes terminating in a central patch of cortex. This upper surface is produced by striking flakes (which may in themselves be large enough to utilize) from the lower surface, but their removal produces faceted platforms suitable for taking flakes off the lower surface itself. Such a process, alternately striking from the upper and lower surfaces, was continued in some specimens until the core was too small for further use.

(iv) The discoidal core is common. Flattened circular pebbles are flaked all around the periphery alternately from each surface, resulting in a roughly diamond-shaped cross section, with a more or less wavy edge. Occasionally, and especially in the larger cores, a patch of cortex may be left in the center of one or both surfaces; certain forms may thus approach type (iii). The more simple forms are Clactonian in appearance, and the flakes from them have plain high-angled striking platforms. The flaking is often very large and irregular, resulting sometimes in a more oblong core. In these irregular examples there is no secondary flaking, as there sometimes is on the regular type, to even the edge, so that the core may be used as a chopper, or maybe as a slingstone.

(v) There are a few specimens where flat pebbles have been split and the fractured surfaces alone have had flakes struck from them, producing evenly convex surfaces and so meriting the name "turtle-back type."

(vi) The chopper type of core is triangular in cross section, with a thick pebble butt and flaked on each side of the working edge. Some specimens show signs of secondary working along the edge, or else of utilization. Whether these were made purposely as side choppers or scrapers or are merely utilized cores is not certain.[27]

Late Soan B is more outstandingly a flake-tool industry than Late Soan A. The Levalloisian type of flake manufacture is also more prevalent, suggesting the techniques of the European late Levalloisian. Blade flakes are more common than in Late Soan A. This artifactual assemblage was found in rather pristine and remarkably unworn condition, suggestive of an undisturbed natural situation since they were deposited.

The Late Soan industry is the most widespread of the Potwar group. De Terra and Paterson recorded at least twenty localities.

Paterson was particularly interested in the Chauntra site (Pl. 16) because of the mixture of the Late Soan industry with the Abbevillo-Acheulian. He divides the material into three groups: (a) the Abbevillian-like handaxes, some pebble cores, and a few massive flakes, all well rolled and primitive in manufacture; (b) Early and Middle Acheulian handaxes less worn than the implements of (a); (c) fresh, unrolled implements which include cores and flakes of Late Soan type and cordate pyriforms, and pointed ovate handaxes of late Acheulian type. Paterson concludes: "It is interesting to note the parallel development in the Punjab of the Soan flake and pebble industries, alongside the Abbevillian-Acheulian complex. So far these two entirely distinct cultures have been found in contact at one site only, Chauntra, where handaxes of late Acheulian type are associated with cores and flakes of late Soan age. The specimens from this site, unfortunately, are too few for the results of this contact to be determined."[28]

[27] *Ibid.*, p. 309.
[28] *Ibid.*, p. 312.

The de Terra and Paterson study in the Kashmir-Punjab, with the previous work of de Terra and de Chardin, was truly remarkable both in the collaborative side, which brought the efforts of geologist, archaeologist, paleontologist, paleobotanist, and other scientists together, and in the substantial results, which form a solid reference standard against which to measure prehistoric evidence in the subcontinent.

❋ The Beas and Banganga Valleys

ALTHOUGH SINCE DE TERRA AND PATERSON'S WORK IN 1935 other localities outside the Soan-Potwar-Indus area have been found, the first definitive, though short-termed, field study of a comparable area was that of B. B. Lal in the Beas and Banganga valleys of the Punjab. These rivers are tributaries of the Sutlej, the easternmost of the five main rivers of the Punjab. The region is essentially Siwalik in its geology. Quartzite is as abundant as in the Potwar. It is foothill country and roughly comparable to the Pir Panjal orogenic situation.[29] Four sites were explored: Guler, Dehra, Dhaliara, Kangra.

At Guler, five terraces of the Banganga River are suggested. All of these are aggradational: T_1 565 feet, largely made up of large boulders with some silts and gravels; T_2 375 feet, silt on smaller boulders and pebbles, the latter largely redeposited from T_1; T_3 150 feet, a thin layer of silt imposed upon medium-sized boulders ($1-1\frac{1}{2}$ feet) "closely packed with pebbles." T_4 is apparently conjectural and not confirmed; T_5 30 feet, part of the modern flood plains or slightly less recent.

As a general observation Lal noted that pebble choppers predominated among the Guler tools, and this observation was extended to the other three sites. Handaxes were found, as well as discoidal cores, and flakes. The latter include "Clactonian" types and proto-Levalloisian ones also (in the Paterson sense). In all fifty-two paleoliths were recovered on the various terraces (see page 49).

At Dehra, on the Beas River, four terraces were observed. The town of Dehra stands on one that measures about 115 feet. Another terrace rises above this one to at least 200 feet. In this fourteen paleoliths were recovered from a thick gravel bed. Ten of these were choppers and four, "Clactonian" flakes.

At Dhaliara, again on the Beas River, implements were recovered from a gravel bed which because of its height may be older than that of Dehra. Four choppers were recovered and one of what Lal calls a "pebble handaxe," which is apparently a pebble struck from opposite sides to

[29] B. B. Lal, "Palaeoliths from the Beas and Banganga Valleys, Punjab," *Ancient India*, No. 12 (1956), pp. 58–92.

TABLE 3. CORRELATION OF IMPLEMENTS WITH TERRACES (*after Lal, 1956*)

TYPE	TERRACE	Terrace 3	Terraces 3 and 2 (mixed)	Terrace 2	Terrace 1	Total
TOTAL		10	18	18	6	52
Proto-Levalloisean flake, longish	F iv	..	1	1	..	2
Proto-Levalloisean flake, oval	F iii	..	..	2	..	2
Clactonian flake with retouch	F ii	1	1	2	1	5
Clactonian flake without retouch	F i	1	1	4	1	7
Non-discoidal core	E ii	1	..	1	..	2
Discoidal core	E i	..	3	..	..	3
Acheulian handaxe(?)	D ii	..	1	..	..	1
Abbevillian handaxe(?)	D i	..	1	..	..	1
'Pebble handaxe'	C	..	1	1	..	2
Bifacial 'chopping-tool' with entire periphery worked	B ii	..	..	..	1	1
Bifacial 'chopping-tool' with part of periphery worked	B i	..	1	1	..	2
Unifacial 'chopper' with lateral working-edge	A iv	..	1	..	..	1
Unifacial 'chopper' with 'fan-shaped' working-edge	A iii	2	5	2	1	10
Unifacial 'chopper' with crescentic working-edge	A ii	2	1	2	1	6
Unifacial 'chopper' with straight working-edge	A i	3	1	2	1	7

AFTER LAL, 1956

produce a pointed edge,[30] a technique more akin to chopper-chopping tool manufacture. It probably should be equated with de Terra's "beaked tool" category—a kind of awl.

Kangra is at the junction of the two rivers Banganga and Patalganga. Here a pebble handaxe was recovered from a terrace whose position was not defined.

Thus two true handaxes out of a total of seventy-two specimens were collected. There was some confusion as to the association of these hand-axes. Clearly they were subsequent to Terrace 1 and perhaps even of Terrace 2. In any case, Lal's brief survey suggests that the Abbevillo-Acheulian tradition was not very strong in the region.

❋ *The Singrauli Basin and the Rihand Valley*

IN THE BASIN OF THE SINGRAULI RIVER in the Mirzapur district of Uttar Pradesh, an important field study of paleolithic and late remains was carried out in 1959 by V. D. Krishnaswami and K. V. Soundara Rajan.[31] The district includes a small part of the Gangetic plains to the north; its central portion is characterized by foothills, the Vindhyan escarpment and the Kaimur range, which rises about five hundred feet above the level of the Ganges. The Son River forms the southern boundary of the central portion. South of the Son River three tributaries drain into the Son on a more or less north-south line (the Kon, the Dudhi, and the Rihand). The country is rugged but low in height. The country is old geologically, consisting south of the plains of gneissic rocks and other archaic groups, Gondwana and Cuddapah sediments. Important among these are the Talchir beds of the lower Gondwana series. These are assigned to Upper Carboniferous time and consist of green laminated shales and soft fine sandstones.[32] Associated with these is a bed of boulders which is regarded as of glacial origin. According to the investigators implements were found on the surface of this bed where it was exposed in the higher portions of the Singrauli basin.

However, the localities associated with the Balia Nadi, a tributary of the Rihand, are worthy of special note.

Locality I—A section exposed in the bank of the river consisting of ten feet of mottled clay within which is a bed of gravel. The clay is covered with loamy clay containing kankar on which are about eighteen inches of a light brown soil.

---

[30] *Ibid.*, Fig. 8 (15); Fig. 9 (16); Fig. 15 (3).

[31] V. D. Krishnaswami and K. V. Soundara Rajan, "The Lithic Tool-industries of the Singrauli Basin," *Ancient India*, No. 7 (1951), pp. 40–65.

[32] Wadia, D. N., *Geology of India*, Macmillan and Co., Ltd., London, 1957, pp. 180–182.

Locality II—Opposite the village of Hinauti on the southern bank of the Balia Nadi. Here the kankar is encountered in the section below a yellowish silt. At approximately five feet below the surface a three-foot pebble layer containing implements and kankar nodules occurs, below which is another three-foot layer of sand and kankar. The whole rests on the Talchir formation, which is the bedrock in the area.

Locality III, downstream from Locality II but nearby, has essentially the same setting as Locality II but is smaller. Here tools were found in the gravels as in Locality II, but these gravels rested in turn on the glacial gravels of the Talchir, the latter providing the raw material for the tool manufacturers living some 200 million years later.

The bulk of all tools found at these localities were made of quartzite. The number of implements and their type is indicated in the investigator's chart.

TYPE OF IMPLEMENT	Total	Percentage	
"Chopper-chopping" tool	17	15.5	
"Hand-adzes"	...	...	
"Proto-handaxe"	1	0.9	
Handaxes	38	34.5	} 42.7
Cleavers	9	8.2	
Cores and core scrapers	8	7.3	
Levallois flakes	8	7.2	
"Proto-Levallois" flakes	20	18.2	
Miscellaneous Clacton flakes (waste flakes excluded)	9	8.2	
TOTAL	110	100.0	

It can be seen that by far the largest percentage of the material belongs to the Abbevillo-Acheulian class. According to the account, the bulk of these are of Middle and Evolved Acheulian type. The Clactonian and proto-Levalloisian flakes form another group, while true Levalloisian flakes and flake scrapers also occur. The pebble tools they call Early Soan. However, the Paterson definition of Late Soan A associates the pebble choppers and chopping tools of the Early Soan with the Levalloisian, and on this basis one might be more inclined to consider the association here as more representative of the Late Soan A than of the Early Soan. The presence of the Evolved or Late Acheulian handaxes is not incompatible with this idea. The investigators suggest, however, that the pebble tools may be older than the handaxes, since they appear in general to be "comparatively more worn."[33]

Zeuner, observing the sections made by the researchers, was unable to assign the implementiferous gravels of these localities to any particular

[33] Krishnaswami and Soundara Rajan, 1951, p. 48.

cycle of aggradation.[34] However, in the Rihand valley there are at least two terraces resting on the Talchir bedrock. There the sequence is a gravel bed (5 feet) succeeded by a layer of reddish silt (10 feet), which in turn is succeeded by another gravel layer (2 feet) and then another of reddish silt to the surface (8 feet). In the Bichi Nala, a tributary of the Rihand, a thick aggradational phase was marked in the presence of gravels capped by over 60 feet of reddish silt. A rolled Acheulian handaxe and a Clactonian flake were washed out of this gravel layer.

The artifacts as found act like the type fossils of paleontology. There is a strong possibility that one could assign these Singrauli materials to the range of time represented by the second interglacial and the third glacial stages in the Punjab with an emphasis on the latter or even later. One is tempted to see in the erosional phase which cut into the Talchir formation its equivalent in the erosional phase that cut T_1 in the Punjab, while the aggradational terrace T_2 with its Potwar basal gravels and later silts has both a nicety of similar geological features with the aggradational terrace represented by the gravels and silts of the Singrauli basin and an equivalence in the archaeological material. We are confounded by a lack of paleontological and other necessary evidence.

Thus, at the opposite border of the plains, that which reaches to peninsular India, there is a suggestion perhaps of a correlation with the Himalayan Zone, but at this date only a suggestion. The peninsula situation is, however, now clarifying itself somewhat (see Appendix A for summary). Initially de Terra approached the peninsula by a brief field survey in the Narbada valley. His field work was an all too brief survey of some two weeks in the area between Hoshangabad and Narsinghpur.[35] His work was buttressed both by his knowledge of previous studies on the geology of the region and by field techniques sharpened by his work in the Punjab. His work became a kind of standard for prehistoric research in the peninsula as a whole but recently has come under criticism by others working in the same area.[36]

❁ *The Narbada Valley*

DE TERRA RECOGNIZED THREE SEDIMENTARY PHASES, each divided from the other by an unconformity accredited to erosional stages, and the whole situated on lateritic gravels and soils.

---

[34] *Ibid.*, p. 64.

[35] De Terra and Paterson, 1939, pp. 313ff.

[36] A. P. Khatri, "Stone Age and Pleistocene Chronology of the Narmada Valley, Central India," *Anthropos*, Vol. LVI (1961), pp. 519–530.

The uppermost of these phases is the regur, or cotton soil; the two earlier phases were labeled by him respectively from top to bottom: Upper Group and Lower Group. All of these phases were then tentatively correlated to the Punjab sequence on the basis primarily of the archaeological evidence, though Middle Pleistocene fauna were known to come from the basal gravels of the Lower Group. These gravels or cemented conglomerates produced rolled handaxes (Abbevillian) and flakes with high-angled platforms. An "Upper Acheulian" industry was evidenced by the extraction of specimens of that type from the red clay (pink silt) of the Lower Group. On Quartzite Hill (Locality 5) a deposit of "rewashed" laterite contained Abbevillian-like handaxes, one large flake with edge trimming, one chopper of Early Soan type, and two large flakes.[37] Near Narsinghpur (Locality 8) both faunal material (*Bos namadicus, Bubalus, Hexaprotodon, Elephas namadicus*) and "Late Soan"-type tools (pebble cores, a beaked tool) were recovered from gravels and sands of the Upper Group. At Locality 9, near the confluence with the Umar River, in the gravels of the Upper Group rolled Abbevillian handaxes, less rolled Acheulian handaxes and cleavers, and some Clacton-like flakes were recovered. Early Soan types were also found in the basal gravel here.

Horn cores of *Bos namadicus* and the lamellae of a molar of *Elephas namadicus* were found near the Abbevillian handaxes.

THE SEQUENCE:

INDUSTRY	Narbada	Punjab
	Cotton Soil (Regur)	T_5
	Upper Group:	
	Pink Clay	T_4
Late Soan	Sand	T_3
	Lower Group:	
Upper Acheulian	Pink Clay	T_2
E. Soan-Abbevillo-Acheulian	Conglomerate & Sand	T_1
	Laterite	

De Terra himself was very tentative about these conclusions. Khatri has objected with reason to some of his conclusions, especially to the use of the term "Soan" for pebble tools found in the Narbada valley and the concurrent suggestion that they represented an invasion of pebble-using people.[38] Khatri, after a substantial study of the same area, arrived at a somewhat different picture, one which abandons the term Soan and refers to an evolution of handaxes from a primitive phase to an advanced phase in which chopper-chopping tools were "a part and parcel of the handaxe culture, belonging to the earliest phases of its development and do not

[37] De Terra and Paterson, 1939, pp. 322–323.
[38] Khatri, 1961, p. 521.

suggest any Sohanian intrusion."[39] He also utilizes the standard of Pleistocene geology which interrelates a stage of heavy rainfall (Pluvial) with a stage approaching modern conditions, i.e., Interpluvial. The laterite, then, which he claims is nowhere as continuous as was assumed by de Terra, can be correlated with a wet phase:

PERIOD			Geological Formations	Climate	Archaeology
Holocene			Black Cotton Soil	Interpluvial	Microlithic
			Yellowish Brown Silt with Concretion	Present-day Conditions	
Pleistocene	Upper		Deposition of Cross-bedded Sand (fossils)	Current Sluggish but Water Still in Plenty	Late Acheulian and Series II
			Cemented Sandy Conglomerate (fossils)	Pluvial Water Level More Than 30′ Higher	Late Chellean to Early Acheulian
			Unconformity	Than the Present	
	Middle		Boulder Conglomerate (fossils)	Interpluvial Present-day Conditions	Earliest Phase of the Chellean Found in Both the Deposits
			Red Greasy Clay	Humidity Continued	
			Laterite (?)	Pluvial	—

Recently R. V. Joshi excavated at Adamgarh (de Terra's Locality 5) and identified an apparent Acheulian workshop there. By careful stratigraphic control he was able to provide evidence to suggest some evolvement of tool type. The assemblage as a whole, however, appears to be identified with those of the lower Narbada and Gujarat.[40]

At Maheswar, in the middle course of the Narbada valley, Sankalia was able to work out a climatic sequence based on the river deposits which actually confirms and extends Khatri's work.[41]

8 or 7	Wet Phase	Black soil
7 or 8	Temporary Flood Deposit	Kankar—sandy gravel & silt (loess resting on 4)
6	Dry Phase	Brownish silt
5	Wet Phase	Smaller trap gravel (III)
4	Dry Phase	Pink silt
3	Wet Phase	Pebbly gravel, not so well cemented as I (II)
2	Dry Phase	Pinkish silt
1	Wet Phase	Cemented pebbly gravel (I)
		Rock

[39] Ibid., p. 528.
[40] R. V. Joshi, "Acheulian Succession in Central India," Asian Perspectives, Vol. VIII, No. 1 (1966), pp. 150–163.
[41] H. D. Sankalia, Prehistory and Protohistory in India and Pakistan, University of Bombay (Bombay, 1963), pp. 52–54.

One notes the absence of laterite and also of fossil evidence at Maheswar. However, flakes with high angle and no platform and their cores appear in gravel layers I and III, as do handaxes. Gravel I has produced Abbevillian-type handaxes. Gravel III produced primarily Levallois flakes. We presume then that Sankalia's 1-2 equals de Terra's Lower Group; 3-4, his Upper Group; while 5-8 represents phases of the Upper Pleistocene to recent, the black soil of 8 or 7 equating to the regur. This sequence appears to be confirmed by Joshi in the Damoh area of Madhya Pradesh. The rivers there are close to the Narbada basin but drain to the north. Acheulian implements occur in a compact gravel lying on an eroded bedrock. Rolled Abbevillian handaxes suggest their formation prior to the formation of the gravel bed.

On the lower Narbada one of the most promising studies of all Pleistocene and human-related deposits on the subcontinent has been carried out by G. J. Wainwright.[42] This study combined both a detailed survey of the lower reaches of the river, section by section, and micromorphological examination of the soils involved. Much of the importance of this study stems from the nature of the relation of sea-level to continental glaciation. The great glacial ice sheets that covered large portions of the Northern Hemisphere during a glacial stage used a percentage of the earth's water resources. This caused a corresponding drop in sea level the world over. On the other hand, during an interglacial stage, sea level would naturally rise. These levels are often marked by extinct beaches. Such beaches have been particularly well studied in the Mediterranean area for example. Obviously the chances for world correlation of these stages are particularly good in such studies, and this kind of research is well under way in various parts of the world. The relation of the lower reaches of rivers to the rise and fall of sea level has a particularly important bearing upon studies of early man in the Pleistocene, since his artifact remains occur most frequently in riverine situations. When sea level is low, the stream gradient is increased and erosion of the river bed is the result. When sea level is high, aggradation is the result. Wainwright was able tentatively to work out the following sequence:

Phase I   *Formation of the modern soil, during which time the river attained its present level.*

Phase II   *Aggradation of sands and aeolian material. This deposit is not very thick and was almost certainly formed by seasonal monsoonal flooding.*

Phase III   *Erosion by the river to a low sea level, during which time Soil III was formed on deposits of Phase IV.*

[42] G. J. Wainwright, *The Pleistocene Deposits of the Lower Narbada River and an Early Stone Age Industry from the River Chambal*, University of Baroda, Archaeological Series No. 7, Poona, 1964.

Phase IV   *Aggradation of sands, silts, and clays in response to a rise in the
sea level.*

Phase V   *Erosion by the river to a low sea level, during which time Soil II
was formed on deposits of Phase VI.*

Phase VI   *Aggradation of sands, silts, and clays in response to a rise in the
sea level.*

Phase VII   *Erosion by the river to a low sea level, during which time Soil I was
formed on deposits of Phase VIII.*

Phase VIII   *The aggradation of the Lower Series—clays, silts, and sands (and
gravel in the upper reaches)—in response to a rise in sea level.
The Lower Paleolithic implements belong to this phase.*

Phase IX   *A phase of erosion to a low sea level represented by the uncon-
formity separating the Lower Series from the Lower Clay. It is
unknown how much of the Lower Clay was destroyed by this process.*

Phase X   *An aggradation represented by the Lower Clay, which is of unknown thickness.*

The Lower Paleolithic industries are Acheulian, apparently largely of
the evolved type. These were found at the junction of the Narbada with the
Karjan River, from the Rajpipla area of the Karjan, and from a right-
hand tributary of the Narbada, the Orsanj.[43] All of these were apparently
associated with cemented gravels or their equivalent in Phase VIII.

Wainwright also examines the sequence established by F. Zeuner for the
Sabarmati and other rivers of Gujarat whose deltas are somewhat contiguous with that of the Narbada where they debouch in the Gulf of
Cambay. Zeuner's investigation of exposed sections along the Sabarmati
indicated that there had been repeated oscillations of climate between
wetter and drier conditions.[44] Zeuner's sequence was as follows:

(P)   *Allitic weathering and formation of lateritic crusts. Climate more humid
than at the present. A hilly land surface.*

(Q)   *Mottled clay deposited in the basins of the river bed. First evidence of the
Sabarmati River being in the area where it flows today. Climate not of
the lateritic type.*

(R)   *Cemented gravel phase. The river carries coarse pebbles and deposits them
as a sheet, veiling the uneven beach and the basins filled with the mottled
clay. Climate characterized by seasonal floods; precipitation apparently
somewhat heavier than nowadays. Paleolithic man present in the area.*

(S)   *Silt phase. The river builds up its bed by shedding sands and silts.
Climate becoming drier, runoff decreasing, and the river as a result
building up its bed to form a steeper gradient. Paleolithic man continues
to be present.*

43 *Ibid.*, pp. 38–41.
44 F. E. Zeuner, *Stone Age and Pleistocene Chronology in Gujarat*, Deccan College
Monograph Series No. 6, Poona, 1950.

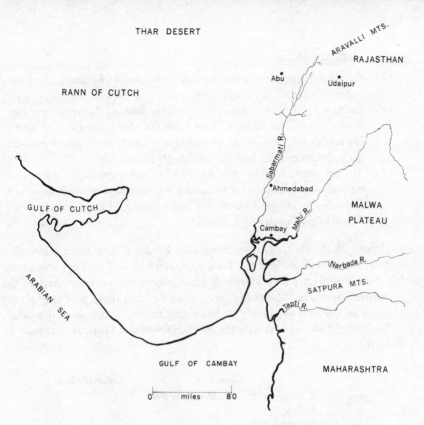

THAR DESERT

ARAVALLI MTS.

RAJASTHAN

Abu

Udaipur

RANN OF CUTCH

Sabarmati R.

GULF OF CUTCH

•Ahmedabad

MALWA
PLATEAU

Cambay

Mahi R.

ARABIAN SEA

Narbada R.

SATPURA MTS.

Tapti R.

GULF OF CAMBAY

MAHARASHTRA

0   miles   80

MAP 7   *The region of the Gulf of Cambay with the principal rivers.*

(T)   *The red soil phase. The aggradation having drowned part of the ancient land surface, the river has been able to shift its bed, presumably to a more westerly position. A red soil is formed, covering the exceedingly flat new land surface formed by the aggradation. Climate probably more humid than previously, with dry forest or scrub covering the country. The climate was, however, less humid than during the lateritic phase (P). Paleolithic man vanishes from the scene.*

(U)   *Main dry phase. Once more the river begins to aggrade, raising its bed still farther. It reappears in the area of the present river and lays down fine silts and wind-blown sand derived from the arid land surface away from the river. Gradually river action becomes less conspicuous and aeolian deposits of sand begin to dominate. The upper part of this bed appears to be purely aeolian in most places. Climate becoming drier again and culminating in an arid period.*

(V)   *After the end of the dry phase, a flat land surface was either left or (more probably) formed by subaerial denudation. Apparently a phase of somewhat damper conditions, though no soil has been found in the Sabarmati area.*

(W)   *Dune phase. More or less isolated dunes are blown over the land surface (V). Climate: a revival of drier conditions.*

57

(X) *Prepottery microlithic phase. A soil develops on the dunes. Man re-appears as the maker of microlithic tools.*

(Y) *Latest dry phase. This phase is of somewhat doubtful character, as it may be due either to a slight increase in aridity of the climate or to man's destructive influence on the natural vegetation. Pottery makers present; agricultural activities highly probable. Up to Iron Age.*

(Z) *Modern phase. Climate like that of (X), with a prolonged dry season but sufficient precipitation to maintain (under natural conditions) soil formation by chemical weathering under cover of a dry forest or scrub. Period of present-day agriculture.*

Typologically the tools associated with Phases R and S are Abbevillo-Acheulian, Middle Acheulian, Late Acheulian as well as Levallois cores, but pebble tools are also gathered, especially in the northern part of the Sabarmati drainage.[45] Sankalia feels, however, that these pebble tools are at the least difficult to classify as belonging to one tradition or the other.

Wainwright would correlate the Narbada with the Gujarat sequence as follows:

		Gujarat		Lower Narbada
	Z	*Modern (Dry with Short Wet Per.)*		
	Y	*Dry*		
	X	*Slightly Wet*		
	W	*Dry*		
	V	*Slightly Damp*		
	U	*Mostly Dry*		
	T	*Wet*		*Soil I—Phase* VII
	S	*Dry*	*aggradational*	*Lower Series—Phase* VIII
4th Gl.	R	*Wet*	*erosional*	
3rd Intergl.	Q	*Dry*	*aggradational*	
3rd Gl.	P	*Wet*	*(lateritic weathering)*	

As Zeuner and Wainwright see it, combining the knowledge of both adjacent regions, there are three wet cycles separated by two aggradational cycles. The first is marked by the lateritic weathering, which is followed by two aggradational cycles separated by a period of erosion. In the second of the aggradations, Phase VIII—(S), the paleolithic implements occur. Wainwright suggests the possibility that the lateritic weathering (P) of Gujarat is of the third glacial age. He further suggests that his Soils I, II, III, each marking low sea level, are possibly assignable to "the three maxima of the last glaciation."[46] The paleolithic industries are thus of third interglacial age, a suggestion supported by the presence of Late Acheulian and Levalloisian cores.

[45] Sankalia, 1963, p. 50.
[46] Wainwright, 1964, p. 44.

It would seem that Wainwright is leading the way to a far more convincing method of correlation, of which the lower Narbada effort is a prime example. Obviously the hope for better understanding of man in the Pleistocene of the peninsula comes from a better knowledge of the recent history of the surrounding seas.

Wainwright also had opportunity to examine paleolithic material from the river Chambal, the most important stream in Rajasthan. Here two gravel beds were revealed by Sankalia and Khatri. The lower of these contained Early Stone Age implements which Wainwright indicates are identical with those from Gujarat.[47] The material consists typically of mature and late Acheulian-type handaxes, cleavers, choppers, and Levalloisian flakes. Similar material has been found on the Chambal by Misra, Nagar, and others.[48]

The correlation of the entire Narbada River to the Wainwright sequence would seem to be an obvious step. The chart (p. 384) indicates what a tentative correlation might be. Further, if we can correlate the marine sequence on the lower Narbada with the glacial sequences of Kashmir, we might find a somewhat more promising correlation than we have had hitherto, previous efforts having been established purely on the basis of tool types and stages of wet and dry as defined for the peninsula.

✳ *Climatic Cycles and Other Peninsular Sequences*

IT IS OF CRUCIAL INTEREST that Zeuner's emphasis upon climatic fluctuation brought him to doubt whether one could, on the existing evidence, confirm the existence of cycles of pluvials and interpluvials in Gujarat. The pluvial theory is based on evidence, primarily in Africa, that the compression of the Northern Hemisphere climatic zones toward the equator during a glacial stage brought the rain-bearing wind farther south, and thus wet climates were experienced in more southerly climes when more northern areas were undergoing arctic or subarctic conditions. In the case of southern Europe and Africa, the cyclonic storms off the Atlantic would seem to have been responsible for heavier rainfall, or pluvial conditions, in the four glacial stages. In the subcontinent, which is located mostly in a tropical zone and is a part of the monsoon belt, this condition may not have existed in the same way as in regions to the west. The fact of moister conditions than at present in some areas of the subcontinent during the Pleistocene goes without saying, but the evidence for successions of dry and wet climates does not mean pluvial and interpluvial. Zeuner was careful to

---

[47] *Ibid.*, pp. 86–88.
[48] V. N. Misra and Malati Nagar, "Two Stone Age Sites on the River Chambal, Rajasthan," *Bulletin of the Deccan College Research Institute*, Vol. XXII (1961–1962), pp. 156–169.

indicate the elementary stage of our knowledge in this regard.[49] To this date essentially nothing new has been added to our knowledge of subcontinental prehistory to substantiate pluvial cycles on the scale of Africa's. It must be remembered that, in spite of repeated diastrophism in areas such as Assam and Kashmir, morphologically the subcontinent has been essentially the same since the Pliocene. Rain-bearing winds have therefore been essentially from the Indian Ocean monsoon belt and the largest precipitation generally along the Western Ghats and the Assam region. Shifts in wind direction due to low pressures over Gujarat or central India could have brought heavier rain than today to these areas. These shifts may have occurred because of higher pressures over glaciated areas in the Himalayan region. Something along these lines probably did occur, but it is hard to envision any other meteorological situation than a monsoonal one, and this in turn has been so characteristic of the subcontinent through all stages that we are hard put to find evidence for a correlative scheme by which to relate local greater rainfall with glacial stages elsewhere.[50]

The peninsula situation is of interest in the light of other sequences found there.

At Khandivli in the Bombay area, in the Konkar or coastal strip, Todd mentioned finding handaxes and Clactonian flakes associated with a lower gravel bed, but though such gravels were located later, no such artifacts were found in them. Since his section and sampling were so limited, the question is presently unresolved.[51]

However in the Godavari basin Sankalia has been able to provide something of a reliable sequence. His investigations were carried out near Nevasa, a small town on the banks of the Pravara River, a tributary of the Godavari in the traprock region of the northern Deccan.[52] The sequence, as established in sections (Fig. 8), involved a Middle Pleistocene fauna as represented by the discovery of a piece of mandible of *Bos namadicus* associated with handaxes and cleavers of Abbevillian and Early-Middle Acheulian type and a series of cores, one of which is discoid (the latter found on surface), the whole having been found in the lowermost and cemented coarse gravels (I). These larger gravels were gradually succeeded by smaller gravels and sand. Clay beds intervened between these lowest gravels and two upper gravel beds, II and III, which succeed one another.

49 Zeuner, 1950, pp. 42–43.

50 De Terra does this in H. de Terra, "The Quaternary Terrace System of Southern Asia," *Geographic Review* (Jan. 1939), pp. 109–111.

51 K. R. U. Todd, "Palaeolithic Industries of Bombay," *Journal of the Royal Anthropological Institute of Great Britain and Ireland*, Vol. LXIX (1939), pp. 257–272; S. C. Malik, *Stone Age Industries of the Bombay and Satara Districts*, University of Baroda, Archaeological Series No. 4, Poona, 1959; H. D. Sankalia, 1963, pp. 46–47.

52 H. D. Sankalia, "Animal Fossils and Palaeolithic Industries from the Pravara Basin at Nevasa, District Ahmadnagar," *Ancient India*, No. 12 (1956), pp. 35–52.

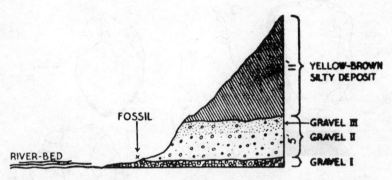

YELLOW-BROWN
SILTY DEPOSIT

FOSSIL

GRAVEL III
GRAVEL II

RIVER-BED

GRAVEL I

Fig. 8   *Nevasa: Locality I—Section along the right bank of the Pravara facing north* (after Sankalia, 1956).

In these beds occurred Indian Middle Stone Age artifacts which were thus clearly separated in the sequence from the Early Stone Age material of Gravel I.[53] Over these gravels was a thick bed of brownish sandy silt, which may be loessic. The whole was capped by a surface bed of dark soil. Thus two cycles of wet and dry periods are indicated here. The first appears to equate with the aggradational phase in which Lower Paleolithic remains are found in the Narbada basin. The fossil evidence suggests this possibility as well.

The classic area for finds of handaxe industries is of course the Andhra Pradesh and Madras region where Foote first recognized these evidences of most ancient India.

At Giddalur, in the Kurnool district of Andhra Pradesh, the basin of the Gundlakamma River, Soundara Rajan investigated a series of Stone Age sites as a member of Zeuner's Prehistoric Expedition of the University of London Institute of Archaeology (1949).[54] The sites (Giddalur I, II) are located along the Sagileru tributary of the Gundlakamma. Here was revealed a deposit of cemented gravel above a shaly bedrock which showed signs of weathering along its surface. Above the cemented gravel is a layer of fluvial silts, and this in turn is succeeded by a loose layer of pebbles. The whole section does not exceed ten feet. The author suggests that two aggradational phases are represented by the gravels. The cemented gravel layer appears to be implementiferous. This was also suggested at the nearby site of Talapalle on the river Enumaleru. The bulk of the tools of the Early Stone Age were surface finds of the Abbevillo-Acheulian type. Clactonian flakes also occur. A few pebble tools are also represented in the collection

---

[53] A fine Acheulian handaxe was, however, associated here with the Middle Stone Age materials. *Ibid.*, pp. 39–40.

[54] K. V. Soundara Rajan, "Stone Age Industries near Giddalur, District Kurnool," *Ancient India*, No. 8 (1952), pp. 64–92.

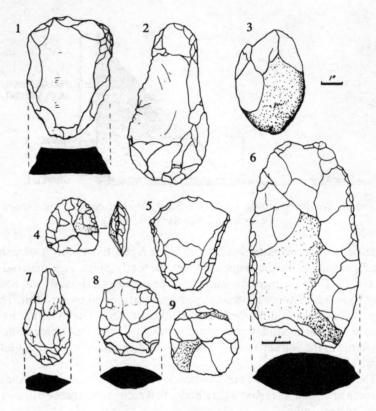

FIG. 9 *Tool types of the Early Stone Age of India.*
1—*Cleaver* (*Western Rajasthan*) (after Misra)
2—*Victoria West* (*Giddalur B*) (after Rajan)
3—*Flaked pebble* (*Orissa*) (after Mohapatra)
4—*Cleaver* (*Giddalur*) (after Rajan)
5—*Cleaver* (*Malaprabha, Khyod*) (after Sankalia)
6—*Cleaver* (*Chambal River*) (after Wainwright)
7—*Handaxe* (*Giddalur*) (after Rajan)
8—*Oviate tool* (*Giddalur*) (after Rajan)
9—*Discoid scraper* (*Nevasa*) (after Sankalia)

from Giddalur I. The tools of Giddalur II are essentially the same as those of I but somewhat smaller, and a "Levallois trend in flake-making is present."[55]

At Nagarajunakonda, on the Kistna River, Soundara Rajan found six localities (A-F) in various parts of the valley there. These localities were

[55] There is some question about the absence of Levalloisian flakes; Sankalia, 1963, p. 32 and footnote.

actually places where surface remains could be collected. The river sections involved three gravel beds (I-III) separated by silt layers, the whole covered by modern soils. At Locality C, where this section was best exposed, tantalizingly there were three rather indeterminate flakes found *in situ*: two from Gravel Bed I and the third from Gravel Bed III. The investigator's

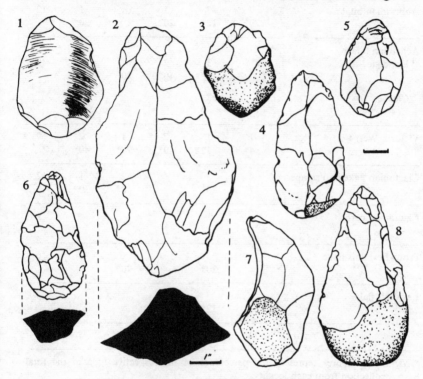

FIG. 10 *Tool types of the Early Stone Age of India.*
1—*Handaxe* (*Orissa*) (after Mohapatra)
2—*Abbevillian handaxe* (*Chambal R.*) (after Wainwright)
3—*Handaxe* (*Orissa*) (after Mohapatra)
4—*Handaxe* (*Orissa*) (after Mohapatra)
5—*Handaxe* (*Orissa*) (after Mohapatra)
6—*Handaxe* (*Rajasthan*) (after Misra)
7—*Rostrocarinalte-like handaxe* (*Nevasa*) (after Sankalia)
8—*Acheulian handaxe* (*Malaprabha, Khyad*) (after Sankalia)

surface collections were treated as distinct assemblages, and these contained Abbevillo-Acheulian handaxes, Levalloisian flakes, Clactonian flakes and blades, burins, and blade scrapers.

At the site of Karempudi, thirty-two miles from Nagarajunakonda (ESE) on the Naguleru River, Soundara Rajan found five localities containing the following material:

Type	LOCALITY					
	I	II	III	IV	V	TOTAL
Pebble tool	12 50*					12
Abbevillian biface	7 29*	3 12*	1 20*		1 20*	12
Acheulian biface Handaxe		3 12*	2 40*	1 20*	1 20*	9
Cleaver		2 8*				
Victoria West (?)	1 4*	1 4*	2 40*	1 20*	2 40*	7
Clactonian flake and scraper	4 17*	5 20*		2 40*	1 20*	12
Clactonian core		3 12*				3
Proto-Levallois flake		5 20*		1 20*		6
Levallois flake		3 12*				3
TOTAL	24	25	5	5	5	64

* *N.B.* These figures represent the percentage of the respective type in the total collection from each locality.

If we interpret this correctly, Locality I would possess only pebble tools and Abbevillian bifaces, and Clactonian flakes; Locality III possesses Acheulian and Abbevillian handaxes; Locality V is the same as III in context but also contains Clactonian flakes; Locality IV has Acheulian handaxes, Clactonian flakes and proto-Levalloisian flakes, while Locality II ranges from Abbevillian through Levalloisian but excludes pebble tools. If we were to treat these localities as sites and consider them distinct assemblages, we would have a rough sequence based on a reference standard both outside the peninsula and within. Since Soundara Rajan also arranged his surface collections from Nagarajunakonda in similar fashion, we can add them to our block of sites and assess them in a relative chronological order (see table on page 65).

RELATIVE CHRONOLOGICAL ARRANGEMENT OF KNOWN PALEOLITHIC TOOLS OF THE KAREMPUDI-NAGARAJUNAKONDA AREA (*after Soundara Rajan*)

	Karempudi					Nagarajunakonda					
	I	II	III	IV	V	A	B	C	D	E	F
No. of Tools:	24	25	5	5	5	?	?	3	?	?	?
Middle Stone Age										I	
Acheulian Levalloisian		I					I				
Acheulian Clacton flakes Proto-Levallois			I								
Abevillian and Acheulian handaxes and/or Clacton flakes	I	I		I		I					I
Pebble Tools and Abbevillian handaxes and Clacton flakes	I					?			I		I

Sankalia has very pronounced reservations about these relative chronological schemes without supporting stratigraphy and quantitative validity.[56] He is certainly justified in his criticism, for all too often such schemes when placed in print become gospel. Nevertheless, there is a value in noting relative associations from surface collections, and Soundara Rajan's efforts only point up the need to make surface collections as random in sampling for statistical purposes as they are in excavation.[57]

A number of sites are known on the coastal plain around Madras (Vadamadurai, Attirampakkam terrace, Manajanakaranai). Krishnaswami, who explored these sites, made collections from each of them as a supplement to Paterson's early work.[58]

Paterson, drawn to the Madras plain by repeated instances of finds of paleolithic vintage there, especially of handaxes, has provided a basic sequence of great importance.[59]

The Cortallaiyar River drains out of the Red Hills, to the west of Madras.

---

[56] Sankalia, 1963, pp. 36–37.

[57] The technique of surface collecting with randomness for statistical validity is frequently used in New World archaeology and should be considered as an instrument in India. J. A. Ford and G. R. Willey, "Surface Survey of the Viru Valley, Peru," *Anthropology Papers of the American Museum of Natural History*, New York, 1949, Vol. XLIII, Pt. 1., p. 38ff.

[58] V. D. Krishnaswami, "Stone Age India," *Ancient India*, No. 3 (1947), pp. 11–57; de Terra and Paterson, 1939, pp. 327–330.

[59] De Terra and Paterson, 1939, pp. 327–330.

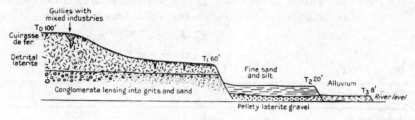

FIG. 11   *Terrace sequence near Madras—copy* (after de Terra and Paterson, 1939).

Its valley there has four definite terraces (Fig. 11), as do those of adjacent rivers. The sequence starts with the erosional plain of the basal gneiss, which is everywhere in this region. On this the depositional terrace T_D was formed. On the basic gneiss is a thick layer of boulder conglomerate, laterally lensing into grits and sands. On this and grading out of it is detrital laterite to the top of the terrace. Terrace T_1 is sixty feet above the level of the present river. This is a degradational terrace marking a period of erosion of the detrital lateritic bed of T_D. It was also a period where, in the dissected surface of the laterite, silts and sands were laid down.

The next stage saw further erosion and the creation of Terrace 2 (twenty feet) as the result of an initial laying down of pellety lateritic gravel and the later deposition of fine sands and silts. Still later further erosion and depositions produced the small alluvial terrace T_3.

According to Paterson the Middle Acheulian (Group II) tools were found in the detrital lateritic beds of T_D. At the site of Vadamadurai Tank, northwest of Madras, a great many implements were recovered, which Paterson divides into three groups.

The specimens from this site can be divided into three groups. Those of the earliest group, heavily patinated and many of them rolled, are of pre-laterite age and are found in the boulder conglomerate. The second group is of later date and has been stained red through contact with the laterite gravel laid down on top of the conglomerate. The third group, in which the specimens have no lateritic staining and little patination, belongs to a period following the removal of the gravel.

The first group can be further subdivided on grounds of patination and typology into an early and a late series. The former comprises handaxes and cores with a very deep whitish crust. The handaxes are of Abbevillian type, very crude and irregular in outline, with thick pebble butts and much cortex remaining, often on both surfaces of the tool. The flaking denotes a stone technique, producing large, deep, and very irregular flake scars. The cores are large and of a rather nondescript type, mostly oblong or circular, with rough, irregular flaking. The flakes have much cortex remaining on the upper surface, and the primary flaking, where present, is of a very primitive type. Only one or two show any signs of having been retouched. The second series in this first group, which is less heavily patinated, shows a typologic advance, especially in the cores. The handaxes are reminiscent of the earliest Acheulian and show the beginnings of a step-flaking technique, though large free flaking is still commonly used. They are slightly more regular in form, particularly one or two large pointed specimens. The cores are mostly discoidal, with fairly regular alternate flaking. The flakes, none of which shows any faceting of the platform, have less cortex and more primary flaking on the upper surface than in the previous stage, but there is still little or no definite retouch.

The second group, comprising laterized specimens, shows a definite typologic advance. The handaxes resemble the middle Acheulian and have considerably more step flaking, which is flatter and neater than before. They are much more even in outline, pear-shaped and ovate being the most common forms. The cores are mainly of discoidal type, similar to those in the preceding stage, but with more regular flaking. Most of the flakes have primary flaking covering the upper surface, but few, if any, show any definite signs of retouch, and none has a faceted platform.

The specimens in the third group have no laterite staining and but little patination. The handaxes, probably upper Acheulian in date, are of two main types, one comprising ovates with small, fairly flat step flaking, and the other including long and pointed forms with thick pebble butts and large but very neat and regular free flaking. Discoidal cores are found, also a flat type of core, oblong, oval, or square, with a platform prepared at one or both ends, for removing flakes from one surface. None of the flakes, however, shows any signs of faceting on the platform. They are mostly fairly thin, with little or no cortex on the upper surface, and a few have been retouched for use, probably, as side scrapers. Only one cleaver has been found at Vadamadurai and it belongs to this third group.

At Attirampakkam, also near Madras, a large series of Acheulian handaxes and cleavers as well as a "Levalloisian" flake-tool industry was found. These items were associated with the "basal laterite" gravel of T_2. Levallois-like flakes also occur in the loam of T_2.

Typologically, then, Early Stone Age tools conform in general to those found in the central Deccan at Giddalur and other places in the peninsula. The primary laterite of the Narbada region appears to be third glacial (see Chart p. 384). That of the Madras coastal plain is derived probably ". . . by subaerial processes from the higher laterite-forming processes from the higher laterite-forming plateaus of the hinterland."[60] Thus the detrital laterite of the coastal plain is probably post-third glacial. The boulder conglomerate grades smoothly into the overlying detrital laterite,

[60] *Ibid.*, p. 327.

suggesting a gradual change in the nature of the aggradation from a substantially fluviatile to an aeolian character, thus from wet to a drier situation. The implements typologically relate the boulder conglomerate to the Lower Group of the middle Narbada sequence. At Manajanakaranai Late Acheulian and even Middle Stone Age material was recovered from the detrital laterite beds by Cammiade.

This sequence in the Madras plain is enormously important in its revelation of an Abbevillian assemblage as an entity separate from the later Acheulian and other implement types. Its implication will be dealt with later in this chapter.

CORTALLAIYAR RIVER

			Group I
100'	T_D	BG	Abbevillian type
			Early Acheulian
		Detrital laterite	Middle Acheulian Tools Group II
60'	T_1	Erosional; sand & gravel in gullies	Late Acheulian Group III
			Flakes & cores
20'	T_2	Pellety laterite gravel	Late Acheulian handaxes & cleavers
			Levalloisian-type flakes
		Fine sand & silt (loam)	
8'	T_3	Modern alluvium	

✳ Findings at Orissa

THE PUBLICATION BY G. H. MOHAPATRA of his findings in Orissa, the most recent there, carries us definitively to the northeastern side of the peninsula.[61] The Orissan country includes a broad coastal plain which ascends into forested hilly country on the west. Five major rivers drain from the interior to the plain, where their respective deltas provide a characteristic appearance. Mohapatra spent nearly a year in the field over a total of three seasons in the districts north of the Mahanadi River examining the Pleistocene deposits in the various river valleys there. He found evidence for three wet phases separated by three dry phases. In the hill country a primary laterite was encountered above the gneissic bedrock. However, in the river valleys the lateritic layer was not exposed. Instead a mottled clay occurred over the bedrock, which in turn was covered with a cemented coarse gravel (Gravel I) (in Gravel I detrital laterite like that of the Madras coastal plain occurs unconformably above the gravels), then a thick layer of red silt, then another bed of gravel (Gravel II), and finally a variety of silts and fine gravels to the modern surface. Early Stone Age

[61] G. C. Mohapatra, *The Stone Age Cultures of Orissa*, Deccan College Dissertation Series, Poona, 1962.

materials were found in Gravel I, while Middle Stone Age tools were located in Gravel II. Mohapatra classifies his Early Stone Age collection (representing twenty-two sites) into three phases, based on technological development, as follows:

STAGE I *Block-on-block technique. Flake scars are big, deep, few, and flaked mainly from the tip region. On the whole the tools are crude.*

STAGE II *Introduction of the cylinder-hammer technique but without complete mastery. Block-on-block technique still persists in majority of the cases. Flaking is done mostly from the sides. Tools become smaller and to some extent symmetrical in form. A considerable number of miniature tools occur in this group for the first time.*

STAGE III *Complete mastery over the cylinder-hammer technique. Use of pressure flaking technique for retouching and finishing is seen on a few tools. Miniature variety of tools increases in number, showing a more varied typology with some new types of tools.*

The following are the types of tools occurring in the three stages.

STAGE I	(a) Handaxes
	(b) Irregularly flaked bifaces
	(c) Flakes
	(d) Scrapers
	(e) Irregularly flaked pebbles
STAGE II*	(a) Handaxes
	(b) Cleavers
	(c) Scrapers
	(d) Cores
	(e) Flakes
	(f) Irregularly flaked pebbles
STAGE III*	(a) Handaxes
	(b) Cleavers
	(c) Scrapers
	(d) Points
	(e) Flakes
	(f) Cores
	(g) Irregularly flaked pebbles

* Including both the large and miniature varieties.

The tool types and their percentages in the stage classes are tabled. Mohapatra calls Stage I typologically Abbevillian; Stage II, Early Acheulian; Stage III, Mid to Late Acheulian.

Absent are Levalloisian elements, as are pebble tools of the so-called Soan type, claims the author.

TOOL TYPE	Stage I	Stage II	Stage III	TOTAL
Handaxes	19	58	12	89 (47.00%)
Cleavers	—	12	3	15 (8.10%)
Scrapers	2	6	16	24 (12.97%)
Irregularly flaked bifaces	3	—	—	3 (1.62%)
Flakes	13	7	6	26 (15.13%)
Irregularly flaked pebbles	6	4	3	13 (7.00%)
Cores	—	1	4	5 (2.73%)
Points	—	—	6	6 (3.25%)
Discoids	—	—	4	4 (2.16%)
TOTAL	43	88	54	185 (99.96%)*

* This research of Mohapatra's succeeds that of Bose and Sen at Mayurbhanj.

✳ The Arrival of Early Stone Age Man

AS THE ARCHAEOLOGICAL RECORD NOW STANDS, it would appear that Early Stone Age man first arrived in the peninsula during a stage when there was more rainfall than at present. Of the three cycles of wet and dry stages now identified, at least in the more northerly portions of the peninsula, it is the wet period of the second cycle which witnessed the widespread residence of Early Stone Age man there. The fact that in some collections made in the aggradational gravels of that cycle rolled artifacts of Abbevillian or Clacton type are found as well as implements of later types fresh in appearance would suggest the possibility of an earlier advent of man in the region.

In large part the problem of the time of the advent of Early Stone Age man in the peninsula is compounded by a lack of stratigraphy in the boulder conglomerate (Gravel I). In almost all cases the implements recovered from the conglomerate or otherwise associated with it are of mixed kind, running the gamut from Abbevillian core tools and coarse massive flakes of Clacton-like appearance to refined Acheulian forms and even Levalloisian-like cores and flakes. The stratigraphic picture on the Madras plain does, however, indicate that the Abbevillian facies does exist in the peninsula. This is further suggested at Giddalur (I) and at Nagarajunakonda, as well as in Orissa.[62] Recently Sankalia has uncovered a strong hint of its presence in the middle Narbada basin and elsewhere.[63]

[62] H. K. Bose, D. Sen, G. Ray, "Geological and Cultural Evidences of the Stone Age in Mayurbhan," *Man in India*, Vol. XXXVIII, No. 1 (1958), pp. 53–54.
[63] Sankalia, 1963, pp. 238–287.

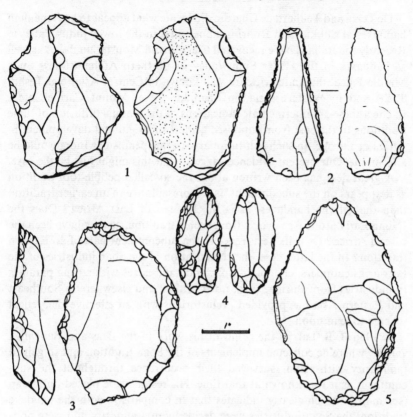

FIG. 12   *Tool types from Hazar Sum, Afghanistan* (after Puglisi).
1—*Clactonian type*
2—*Late Clactonian or Mousterina*
3—*Clactonian type*
4—*Small biface*
5—*Biface*

But the consensus, in the face of all these possibilities and sequences would tend not to put the appearance of the earliest handaxe assemblage before the beginning of the second cycle identified so far for peninsular India. On the present evidence this cannot be earlier than an early phase of the third interglacial stage (see Chart p. 384). A comparison with the situation in the Potwar indicates that the first appearance of the Abbevillo-Acheulian tradition there is during the second interglacial stage, or decidedly earlier than its appearance in peninsular India. Possibly we thus have a diffusionary scheme for the handaxe-flake tradition that perhaps presages the directional aspect of late diffusionary phenomena up to recent times.

De Terra and Teilhard de Chardin did locate what appear to be Acheulian handaxes at Sukkur and Rohri in upper Sind in the lower Indus Valley.[64] Recently the Italians have recovered Clacton and Mousterian flakes as well as handaxes in the Hazar Sum Valley of northern Afghanistan.[65] Such Middle Paleolithic industries are well known in Central Asia (e.g. Teshik Tash) and in Western Asia (in Shanidar Cave, Mount Carmel, etc.). In effect these are intermediate indications of the gradual diffusion of these traditions to the east from supposed centers of origin and development in Africa or Europe. In such a diffusionary scheme peninsular India would be a terminus. Our present evidence suggests that this might just be the case.

A great deal has been written about the so-called pebble-tool tradition as it appears on the subcontinent. Is it representative of an earlier tradition than that of the handaxes, as is the Kafuan of East Africa? Does the Indian Early Stone Age evolve from such a tradition, as may have been the case in Africa? Or is its occurrence in the subcontinent part of an Eastern tradition? In the latter case, the classification of the Soan industries of the Potwar as choppers, chopping-tools, and hand adzes with strong parallels to industries from Burma, Java, north China, and elsewhere in Southeast and Eastern Asia has provided prehistorians with an effective theoretical scheme to lean upon.[66]

In 1956 B. B. Lal, as the result of his work in the Beas and Banganga valleys, where he collected implements of the Soan tradition and so gained familiarity with them, surveyed their occurrence throughout the subcontinent as it was known at that time. His results were placed on a map (see map 8) which clearly indicates that in comparison with the handaxe tradition, the Soan industries were decidedly in a minority and were nonexistent in some localities of peninsular India. While investigators of the Early Stone Age in India have been numerous, it is not always true that they are equally able to differentiate the so-called Early Soan tradition from by-products or even incomplete implements of the Abbevillo-Acheulian tradition. Questions are continually asked in India as to the relation of any given series of artifacts to the Soan tradition.[67] Do the two traditions really occur together in peninsular India? In the Punjab these are separate until the Late Soan and are found together at one site only—Chauntra (cf. p. 43). Is there really a Soan tradition south of the Indo-Gangetic

---

[64] De Terra and Paterson, 1939, Pl. XLVIII.

[65] S. M. Puglisi, "Italian Archaeological Mission in Afghanistan. Preliminary Report on the Researches at Hazar Sum (Sainangan)," *East and West*, N.S., Vol. XIV, Nos. 1–2 (1963), pp. 3–12.

[66] This classification was the pioneer work of H. L. Movius, Jr., of Harvard University: "Early Man and Pleistocene Stratigraphy in Southern and Eastern Asia," 1944; "The Lower Palaeolithic Cultures of Southern and Eastern Asia," *Transactions of the American Philosophical Society*, Vol. XXXVIII, Pt. 4 (1949).

[67] See especially Lal's arguments in Lal, 1956, pp. 85–91.

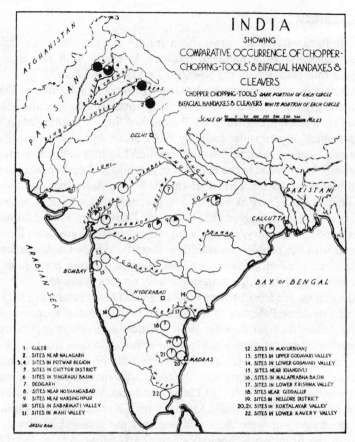

1. GULER
2. SITES NEAR NALAGARH
3,4. SITES IN POTWAR REGION
5. SITES IN CHITTOR DISTRICT
6. SITES IN SINGRAULI BASIN
7. DEOGARH
8. SITES NEAR HOSHANGABAD
9. SITES NEAR NARSINGHPUR
10. SITES IN SABARMATI VALLEY
11. SITES IN MAHI VALLEY

12. SITES IN MAYURBHANJ
13. SITES IN UPPER GODAVARI VALLEY
14. SITES IN LOWER GODAVARI VALLEY
15. SITES NEAR KHANDIVLI
16. SITES IN MALAPRABHA BASIN
17. SITES IN LOWER KRISHNA VALLEY
18. SITES NEAR GIDDALUR
19. SITES IN NELLORE DISTRICT
20,21. SITES IN KORTALAYAR VALLEY
22. SITES IN LOWER KAVERY VALLEY

JASSU RAM

MAP 8   (after Lal, February, 1956).

plains? One would tend to doubt it on the basis of both Lal's chart and
the fact that in many cases the artifacts involved are questionable as regards
any representation of another tradition but that of the handaxe-cleaver
group.[68]

Pebble-tool industries occur before the Abbevillo-Acheulian handaxes
in East Africa, and in Bed II at Olduvai Gorge the pebble tools clearly
outnumber the handaxes, which first appear in the lowest level there.
Cleavers do not appear till Bed III in this context.[69] This, according to the
excavators, is late Middle Pleistocene in time, or probably contemporary
with glacial stage three in Europe (and thus possibly in the Kashmir area).
Pebble-tool industries are known at several sites in Arabia.[70] They are also

[68] The cleaver is an axelike tool with a sharp, usually straight, cutting edge (see Fig. 9).
It is characteristically found with the handaxe industries of the subcontinent.

[69] S. Cole, *Prehistory of East Africa*, Macmillan, New York, 1963, p. 143.

[70] G. Caton-Thompson, "Some Palaeoliths from South Arabia," *Proceedings of the
Prehistoric Society for 1953*, N.S., Vol. XIX, Pt. 2 (1954), pp. 189–218.

found at Barda Balka in northeastern Iraq,[71] etc. On the other hand, a strong suggestion of a handaxe tradition is found with the chopper-chopping tool complex, in the so-called Patjitanian of Java.[72]

What, then, can we say in answer to such problems as the above? On the face of the evidence now available to us, it would appear that the pebble-tool industries as represented in the Potwar had little or nothing to do with the occupancy of peninsular India by Early Stone Age man. It is possible on the other hand, that a pebble-tool tradition like that defined by Movius for Eastern Asia existed in the Himalayan foothills and perhaps the Gangetic plains[73] prior to the arrival of the Abbevillo-Acheulian tradition in peninsular India. There is further a suggestion that a coarse flake-tool industry existed in this region even before the Early Soan. The relationships of this pre-Soan industry, though a mystery at present, are more likely to be found with the pebble-tool tradition than the Abbevillo-Acheulian, in view of their general grossness and high-angled striking platforms. But this is only hinted at by the material and by no means proved.

In the end we are frustrated by our evidence. There are no cave sites like those of France or Palestine to indicate the refinements of sequences only broadly defined in river deposits. Still less do we have any real basis for a recreation or interpretation of life so far removed in time from us. We do know Early Stone Age man tended to live near or in the river valleys, where we assume that game was abundant and that resources of wood, shell, and other necessities for his life were at hand. We lack information as to how far regions like Bengal, Assam, Nepal, Kerala, and the Tamilnad were penetrated—or were their environments too arduous or remote for men with the primitive technology of the Early Stone Age of India? Or perhaps those very regions which are now lodestones of human activity played a similar role in those remote times, which later investigation will prove. One thing is certain, and that is that there must have been an undeniable attraction for these early men in the hills and valleys of the subcontinent, for every survey produces their implements and underlines the ubiquity of their presence.

As to the men themselves we have no record at all. No fossils have yet been found to provide an answer. Yet there is a hint in the association of tool traditions with fossil man outside of India. The Soan chopper-chopping tool tradition is, for example, associated with Pithecanthropids as for

[71] R. J. Braidwood and B. Howe, *Prehistoric Investigations in Iraqi Kurdistan*, Studies in Ancient Oriental Civilization, No. 31, Oriental Institute, University of Chicago, Chicago, 1960.

[72] Movius, however, feels this is a false impression, since the technique of manufacture differs from the classic Abbevillo-Acheulian technique. Movius, 1944, p. 92.

[73] Some authorities would see a Madrassian or peninsula pebble-tool industry in counterdistinction to the Soan. Cf. K. V. Soundara Rajan, "Quaternary Pebble, Core and Flake Cultures of India," *Ancient India*, No. 17 (1961), p. 70.

example the men of Peking or Java. But pebble tools are also associated with an early modern type of man in Africa. When some fortunate researcher finally locates hominid remains in the conglomerates of the peninsula or caves of the Potwar, one or the other type of man may be revealed. It is to be hoped that whatever type he is, he might hold either a pebble tool or a handaxe in his fossil hand. It would certainly solve numerous problems!

❋ *The Middle Stone Age*

THOUGH RECOGNITION OF AN INDIAN MIDDLE STONE AGE INDUSTRY as such is relatively recent, it does appear that we are on better ground in identifying both its chronological position and its artifactual character than we are with the Early Stone Age. The industry is basically one of manufacturing flake tools from chert. Its general typological parallels are with the so-called Levalloiso-Mousterian of Western Asia, North Africa, and Europe. That is, the flakes are struck from prepared cores that are usually disc-shaped. Bridget Allchin has pointed out a second, somewhat less formal, flake-producing method characteristic of the industry, and that is the production of broad flakes or blade flakes from pebble cores that are minimally prepared. The core remaining suggests in smaller form the chopping tools of the Early Stone Age.[74] This second method of flake-tool manufacture is, according to Sankalia, much more common than the strictly Levalloisian technique.[75] This author sets forth seven classes of tool types for the industry:

(1) SCRAPERS OF VARIOUS TYPES *on* (i) *simple flakes,* (ii) *flakes with prepared platforms,* (iii) *flakes with prepared platforms and finer prepared cores, and* (iv) *simple flat nodules: hollow or concave, convex, concavo-convex; side, or square, rectangular, or crescentic flakes.*

(2) BORERS OR AWLS.

(3) POINTS (*rare*).

(4) SCRAPER-BORERS.

(5) BLADELIKE THICK FLAKES.

(6) CHOPPERS.

(7) SMALL ACHEULIAN-TYPE HANDAXES *or* BIFACES *on jasper, flint, and other fine-grained rocks.*[76]

The presence of the chopperlike cores and of the handaxes, plus the character of the second technique of flake manufacture, strongly suggests

[74] B. Allchin, "The Indian Stone Age Sequence," *Journal of the Royal Anthropological Institute of Great Britain and Ireland,* Vol. XCIII, Pt. 2 (1963), pp. 216–217.

[75] H. D. Sankalia, "Middle Stone Age Culture in India and Pakistan," *Science,* Vol. CXLVI (1964), pp. 371–372.

[76] *Ibid.,* p. 371.

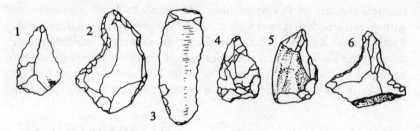

Fig. 13   *Typical stone tools of the Indian Middle Stone Age* (after Sankalia).
1—*Triangular point, Maharashtra (Bel Pandhari)*
2—*Double-edged side scraper, Maharashtra (Nevasa)*
3—*Double-edged side scraper, Maharashtra (Nevasa)*
4—*Bifacial point, Rajasthan*
5—*Borer, Maharashtra (Chandoli)*
6—*Borer-scraper, Maharashtra*

that the Middle Stone Age industries grew out of those of the Early Stone Age.[77] On the other hand, the presence of a full-fledged Levalloisian aspect suggests the influx of influences from the West. In this regard the distribution of Middle Stone Age localities is of great interest. Sankalia lists 55 site localities (see Appendix B). Of these, 8 are in the West Punjab (West Pakistan), 2 in Kashmir, 1 in the East Punjab, 5 in Rajasthan, 9 in Madhya Pradesh, 2 in Saurashtra, 12 in Maharashtra, 4 in Mysore, 1 in Andhra, 2 in Madras, and 9 in Orissa. To this list can now be added the site of Sanghao Cave near Peshawar in West Pakistan[78] and a site discovered by Dr. Sherman Minton and myself in 1959 and since revisited with Mr. Gregory Possehl and Messrs. Sharif and Mughal of the Department of Archaeology, Government of Pakistan.[79] This site is located on a gravel terrace on the right bank of the Indus River near Jherruck in southwestern Sind.

It is obvious from the above list that the Middle Stone Age is widely spread over the subcontinent. The inclusion of de Terra and Paterson's Late Soan assemblage in the Middle Stone Age by several authorities and the discovery of Sanghao Cave with its comparable typology creates a link to the West that needs much more investigation. The Allchins have brought forward evidence to suggest that the Middle Stone Age and the Late Stone Age relate in technique in the far south of the peninsula

[77] Cf. B. Allchin, "The Indian Middle Stone Age: Some New Sites in Central and Southern India, and their Implications," *Bulletin of the Institute of Archaeology*, No. 2 (1959), p. 39.

[78] A. H. Dani, "Sanghao Cave Excavation, The First Season, 1963," *Ancient Pakistan*, Vol. I (1964), pp. 1–50.

[79] To be published in American Museum of Natural History, Novitates series, by Mr. Possehl.

(Tinnevelly).[80] This would indicate the lateness of Middle Stone Age survival in the south and suggest perhaps a later arrival there and in Ceylon than elsewhere in the peninsula. On the other hand, the Late Soan of the Potwar reaches a climax in the third interglacial stage and reaches into at least the first stadia of the fourth glacial stage, a temporal situation

PLATE 2   *Flints of the Indian Middle Stone Age lying on a pebble surface of a terrace at Jherruck, southern Indus River Valley.*

which equates neatly with the spread of the Mousterian industries of the Middle Paleolithic of the West. Thus we might look for a kind of chronological inclined plane along which the Middle Stone Age diffused from west to east and from north to south.

The stratigraphic position of the industry is of interest in this regard. At Nevasa Sankalia established the stratigraphic relationship of the Early Stone Age to the Middle Stone Age, and this has been confirmed elsewhere in the peninsula.[81] Essentially it is later than the Early Stone Age, from which it is stratigraphically distinct, and it is found associated with an aggradational cycle in the peninsula which follows the aggradational

---

[80] B. Allchin, 1963, pp. 219–220; F. E. Zeuner and B. Allchin, "The Microlithic Sites of Tinnevelly District, Madras State," *Ancient India*, No. 12 (1956), pp. 8–9.

[81] Sankalia, 1964, pp. 369–371; also this book, Appendix A.

cycle with which the Early Stone Age is associated. It is thus inferred that it was during a wet phase somewhat lighter than that of the Early Stone Age that the Middle Stone Age of the peninsula began. The later part of the Middle Stone Age saw the onset of drier climatic condition.[82] It seems that Middle Pleistocene fauna is possibly associated in the Middle Stone Age localities, but much more remains to be collected before the true nature of the association is established.[83]

❋ Sanghao Cave

THE CAVE SITE OF SANGHAO is located in the hill country in Buner and close to the border of the district of Mardan. It is located near an old route which gave access to the Shahkot Pass. The cave is set in a bed of cemented boulder conglomerate. Dani, the excavator, has compiled a composite section for the region which helps to place the Sanghao material into the late geological and climatic picture, with the warning that this section is tentative!

UNIT	Correlation	Climate
1. Recent alluvium	Recent	Warm, dry
2. Kalpani Lake beds	Late or post-glacial	Warm, moist
3. Younger loess, in places red-stained at base	Last glaciation	Cool, dry
4. Cemented gravel and breccia	Last interglacial	Cool, moist
5. Older loess, in places fine clay	Penultimate glaciation	Cool, dry
6. Laterite zone	Penultimate interglacial	Warm, moist

The cave is known locally as Parkho-darro Cave (Sanghao is a nearby village which lends its name to an area in which there are numerous caves, Parkho-darro being one of them). The main cave measures 80 feet long by 35 feet deep by 14 feet high. The floor was divided up into three parts by rock falls. The first season of excavation was in the nature of an exploration to find the depth of the deposit and its character. Dani reports a total depth of 15 feet from the top to the bedrock. The deposit is layered into twelve different strata, each separated from the next by an ash and charcoal line. The talus in front of the main deposit also was layered and was equated accordingly. These layers represent five main periods:

PERIOD I (at the bottom)—Inside phases (12)–(10); outside layer (6A).

A variety of scrapers, blade-flake, tanged and triangular point, gravers or burins, made predominantly of quartz.

[82] An excellent account of the present state of these climatic studies is given in Sankalia, 1964, pp. 373–374.

[83] *Elephas antiquus, Bos namadicus* are both definitely found in association. *Ibid.*, p. 374. Survival of earlier fauna in these regions has always to be considered.

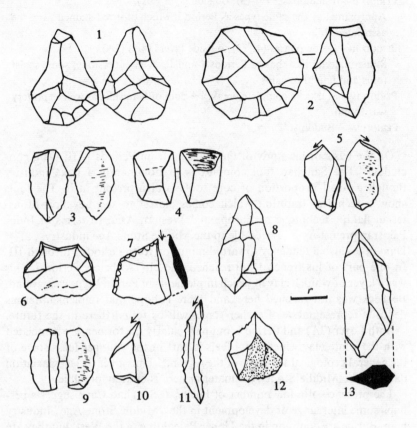

FIG. 14 *Tool types from Sanghao Cave* (after Dani).
1—*Small handaxe—Trench B, Layer 3*
2—*Discoidal core scraper—Trench B, Layer 11*
3—*Leaf-shaped scraper—Period I*
4—*End-scraper (red-stained)—Period I*
5—*Scraper-cum-point—Period I*
6—*Borer, notched on both sides—Period I*
7—*Burin or graver—Period I*
8—*Triangular point—Period II*
9—*Blade flake side-scraper—Period III*
10—*Graver or burin (red-stained)—Period III*
11—*Chert blade point—Period III*
12—*Triangular point—Period III*
13—*Pointed ends side-scraper—Period III*

PERIOD II—Inside phases (9)–(5); outside layer (5A).

Approximately the same types as Period I. Much of it red-stained from the associated soil.

PERIOD III—Inside phases (4), (3); outside layers (4A) (3A).

Stone material like that of Periods I and II. A hammerstone, some schist tools and faunal remains.

PERIOD IV—Marks "a complete break." A coin of Kanishka as well as pottery was found.

PERIOD V—"Buddhist."

On the basis of his study of the material from Periods I–III, Dani concludes: "The Sanghao tool complex is predominantly a flake industry though a small proportion of core tools is also present in it. The tools show a technical tradition which comes closest to the Levallois-Mousterian flaking technique of Europe and Western Asia. In terms of Indo-Pakistan prehistory it is referable to the Middle Stone Age industry. . . ."[84] Dani notes also a tendency toward diminution from Periods I through III. In one part of his trench Dani reached a level (7A) below Period I. This was a layer of whitish clay in which implements of Period I type were found. Bedrock was not reached here, and there is hope that implementiferous deposits representative of earlier stages will be found there in the future.

Both Layer (7A) and Period I, but particularly the former, are associated with the white clay which Dani feels is part of the younger loess stage of the general geological sequence of the region.[85] Thus an early last glaciation date for the Middle Stone Age material here is entirely possible.

The presence of a fair number of burins at Sanghao Cave suggests perhaps some later stage of development in the "Middle Stone Age" industry here. Burins are common in the Upper Paleolithic of the West, but they are uncommon in both the peninsula and in the Late Soan of the Potwar. A flaked core with platform intact from Period I also suggests that the blade-manufacturing techniques of the Upper Paleolithic of regions farther to the west were not unknown at Sanghao. It may well be that the Periods II and III at Sanghao are perhaps a bit later than we can presently estimate, in view of this kind of evidence.

❋ Middle Stone Age Man

AT TESHIK TASH in Soviet Central Asia a Mousterian industry is associated with remains of Neanderthal man. Mousterian-like implements are also found in Northern Afghanistan.[86] Several Mousterian-like flakes and

---

[84] Dani, 1964, p. 17.

[85] *Ibid.* , p. 14.

[86] Puglisi, 1963, Figs. 7–8; also unpublished collection made by L. Dupree now in the American Museum of Natural History, New York.

cores were recovered by geologists of the Geological Survey of Pakistan in 1951 associated with an extinct beach in the Mashkel basin of Baluchistan. (Accounts of these finds were unfortunately not published.) This evidence, faint as it is, does demonstrate some extension of Middle Paleolithic industries toward the subcontinent. On the other hand, at Kara Kamar in northern Afghanistan, Carlton Coon found a blade-tool industry of Upper Paleolithic vintage and of a type unknown (so far) on the subcontinent.[87]

The net result of the research on the Indian Middle Stone Age so far has been to establish its relative position as regards the Early and Late Stone Ages and to set forth substantial but nonetheless woefully incomplete evidence as to its position in the Pleistocene period. It is clear also that the men of the Middle Stone Age found the subcontinent entirely suitable for their hunting and gathering pursuits, for they spread from the Himalayas to the extreme south and from Sind and the Punjab to Orissa and probably to Bengal.[88] The change from using quartzite or traprock as raw material for implements in the Early Stone Age to using the silicas, like chert and flint, in the Middle Stone Age of the peninsula is worthy of note.[89] It suggests, then, that not only were these early men motivated in their roaming by the availability of game or plant foods but the raw material for their tools was also a strong reason for local settlement or familial migration. The fact also stands out that river valleys were prominent in their settlement seeking. Many of the localities are high on promontories overlooking river valleys. Here sources of stone were available. But equally we can ponder the very good possibilities that the riparian forests or those of the hills round about were Stone Age man's habitat. For if stone was a material of utility, so were wood, fiber, and gourds. It is the stone alone that survives, and this is certainly so small a proportion of all materials used in that remote time that we can indeed wonder how truly valid these pathetic remains are to evidence that life. However, the surface of the research has hardly been scratched, and the continuance of increasingly intensive field work and laboratory study in both Pakistan and India assures that much more evidence will be gathered and that the men of the Stone Age of the subcontinent will emerge a little more clearly out of the past.

[87] Carlton S. Coon, *The Seven Caves*, Knopf, New York, 1957; also C. Coon and E. K. Ralph, "Radio-carbon Dates for Kara Kamar, Afghanistan," *Science*, Vol. CXXII (1955), pp. 921–922.

[88] The distribution of sites so far located is similar to that of the Early Stone Age in that it excludes Assam, Kerala, and Bengal. However, oral reports of Stone Age implements found in both West Bengal and East Pakistan suggest that our distribution will continually enlarge as the research moves forward.

[89] Sankalia, 1964, p. 374.

III

The Prelude to Settled Life

T HE CLOSE OF THE ICE AGE IN THE NORTHERN HEMISPHERE saw decided changes in local environments as the climatic zones shifted with the retreat northward of the glaciers and the consequent rise in sea level everywhere. In Europe regions once tundra now became the seat of coniferous forests, which in turn became increasingly deciduous as arctic climates moved north of the southern Baltic Sea.

In Western Asia, which had been largely unglaciated, such large scale change apparently did not occur. However, there is evidence accumulating to show that periods of wet and dry climate alternated during the period after 12,000 B.C. The whole series of cycles would appear to have moved gradually from at least a relatively moist stage to the modern situation of relative aridity. As late as 3000 or 2500 B.C., these cyclic shifts do not appear to have been abrupt or of great scale. When one considers how little moisture is needed to make previously desert soils flower on the one side and how readily man can change his environment on the other, evidences for climatic change have to be weighed carefully by researchers. The research for Western Asia is only in its infancy in this regard.

In the period between 10,000 and 8000 B.C. there was all over Europe and Western Asia a wide variety of cultural adaptations. The Upper

Paleolithic of Europe, just previous to this time, had been a remarkable climax of cultural achievement by *Homo sapiens*. In such places as the Dordogne of France, the foothills of the Pyrenees, the hills and valleys of Central Europe, the evidence suggests that man was evolving from the simple band level of social organization to one of more complexity. This probably was motivated in part by the need for collective efforts of large scale not only in the economic pursuits of hunting and gathering but in ceremonial activity, the latter permitting a more formal interaction with the animistic qualities of nature than ever before. Totemism and sympathetic magic, belief in an afterlife, shamanism, chieftainship are suggested by the evidence available. These traits were apparently acquired during the Upper Paleolithic. With the end of that age it appears that both old and new populations, whatever their derivation, rather than moving about in the fashion of older ages were more restrictive. Some indeed were so adapted to a dependence upon certain kinds of animals and plants that they moved with the fauna and flora as in the past. But largely as environments changed and populations grew, men increasingly exploited that ecology which was at hand and which was paradoxically familiar in spite of change. Unquestionably experiments were made with the natural environment as far as the ingenuity of man and the elasticity of his particular cultural form permitted. Thus, after 10,000 B.C., we are bewildered by the archaeologist's use of a great number of names all designating particular cultural forms or situations but each an entity of itself. Hamburgian, Zarzian, Sebilian, Magosian, Azilian, Tardenoisian, Maglemosian, Capsian, etc., are all designations of intensive food-gathering and -collecting cultures operating within reasonably restricted areas. This is in contrast to the earlier Stone Age terms such as Abbevillian, Acheulian, Mousterian, Gravettian, etc., which have a far broader and less regional meaning.

Thus, characteristically, these post-Pleistocene hunting and gathering cultures tend to regionalization. The focus of this tendency seems to have been a propensity for a specific kind of game or foodstuff, though naturally this is only at the center of a total use of the available resources. Thus in the northern temperate zone of Europe we have shellfish gatherers, stag hunters, reindeer hunters, and fishermen. Coon, in identifying levels of the period at Belt Cave near the Caspian shore of northern Iran, was compelled to use such terms as vole eaters and seal hunters. These emphases are, of course, reactions in part to environmental changes, but the implication is that wherever cultures of the period were situated, they were exploiting that particular environment to the utmost of their technological abilities. There is evidence that a wide variety of plant life was exploited for the derivation of whatever of their qualities could be used. The food use of hazelnuts at Star Carr in Yorkshire and wild cereals at Mount Carmel in Palestine are good examples of this activity.

Such variety in the daily habit of men is perhaps symptomatic of cultural differences. A territoriality is apparent. Bounds are set to spheres of activity which tend to confine people to their established realms. This, along with the characteristic adaptation to a particular environmental setting, places a limit as to what can be obtained from areas outside of these realms. It is not until later, when interdependence characterizes the situation of contiguous or even distant societies, that trade and other interregional contact is important and some of the cultural lines become correspondingly blurred.

✳ *The Technology*

AN INTENSIVE EXPLOITATION OF THE LANDSCAPE within a variety of ecological and assumed cultural bounds, then, is the hallmark of the period and of the cultures that are characteristic of this late version of a hunting and gathering life that men had been living since the Lower Paleolithic. The technology is relatively complex. The full-fledged use, respectively, of the bow and arrow, the harpoon, the lance, fishhooks, nets, and the sickle is typical. The most characteristic implement is the composite tool. This is made by hafting small stone blades or flakes to a bone or stick handle. This required the creating of small flints (blades or flakes) with sharp cutting edges and a prepared surface or edge for hafting. The term "microlithic" is used to express this diminution. Points, burins, and arrowheads are also diminutive, probably in direct response to the manufacturing technique fashionable at the time rather than to the lack of big game, which some experts have suggested.

The composite tool was in these remote times an innovation of enormous significance. In a way it can compare in importance to such other innovations in human history as cementmaking and smelting, for it provided men with a versatility in their tool repertoire never before attained. To realize what is meant here requires that one considers the fact that all men at whatever period in time have the same biological potential for using materials and sources of energy. Men of Altamira twenty thousand years ago had the same potential for using atomic energy as a high-school boy has today. Both possess identically the necessary intelligence and the physical dexterity. Two major differences stand out, however: the understanding of the world around him which the high-school boy receives from accumulated knowledge, and the tool repertoire which enables him eventually to turn that knowledge to use. In other terms, the relationship of Stone Age man to modern man is like that of the scientist to the engineer in that the former develops the theory through scientific (empirical) method while the latter instruments it through technology. So many times in history the scientific discovery remained nonutilitarian, since the instrumentation was not available to exploit that discovery. The case of Hero's steam engine of the first century A.D. is a fine example of this relationship, but there are a multitude of other examples in history.

It is therefore not improbable that some men who were confined to the technological abilities of an earlier Stone Age knew the advantages of this or that resource but were unable to exploit it except in a clumsy and inefficient way. Stones like chalcedony, for example, shatter like glass when struck, and it was not till the technique of pressure flaking ensued that chalcedony was effectively used. Yet undeniably early Stone Age men were familiar with the sharpness of an edge made from chalcedony. The denseness and weight of some of the igneous rocks certainly had their attraction for food collectors of the Paleolithic, but it was not until the innovation of grinding that these could be really used. Nor was there in the handaxe, the cleaver, and the scraper the potential for such innovations. These implements were complete in themselves and, though providing a limited range of usage, nonetheless were excellent for their intended purpose; however in their manufacture the toolmaker learned the potential of stone for other tools. Eventually this experience led to innovation and another step was evolved.

The advent of the blade tool in the Upper Paleolithic of the West opened new horizons. The blade is sharp-edged; when backed by flattening one edge, the blade becomes an effective knife. A variety of other possibilities are found in the simple blade. A transverse blow at one end produces a burin or engraver point at one end; two opposite nicks provide a point if on one end, or a single or double notch for hafting if on the body. Scrapers and gouges of various kinds also are readily obtained from the blade; so are chisels and saw teeth. All through the Upper Paleolithic one can see the improvement and amplification of blade tools. With such tools wood and bone could be carved, shaved, engraved, and punched as never before.

The so-called Mesolithic of Europe, which succeeds the Upper Paleolithic there, and indeed largely evolves from it, saw a further amplification of blade-tool usage by the reduction of its size, thus adding another spectrum of activity to what was already possible. This was the full development of the technique of cutting or slashing by hafting many small blades together. One tended to cut a variety of materials less by weight and force of arm and more by sicklelike swings of arm and implement, or by back-and-forth sawing motions along a chosen line.

The period is characterized, then, by a variety of implements of which the composite tool is the most representative. So successful indeed was the technological level that it has apparently lasted even to recent times; in the Narbada River valley, for example, tribal peoples were still making microliths as late as the eighteenth century A.D. At that time they apparently seized upon sources of European bottle glass as raw material for their microliths,[1] microliths which, if it were not for the material from which they are made, are in every other way identical with those of the Stone Age!

The stone implements of the period were of course also a means to create other and perhaps more complex implements from wood, shell, leather, etc., and all these together created the capability for the manufacture of such things as canoes, special traps, free-standing pole or rafter-and-beam structures, wooden pails and pots, tubes, sledges, and for the carving of such things as totemic or other iconographic devices or symbols. With man possessing such technological capability, the exploitation of the landscape became extraordinarily possible. With the right tools, deep rivers could be crossed, shelter provided where one wished, animals corralled, supplies in bulk moved from place to place, containers made for whatever needed containment. Whatever the game, a device could be created to obtain its meat, fin, or bone. Basketry, matmaking, nets, even musical instruments (leather and wood drums, for example) are other physical exemplifications of this stage of technological development.

❈ *The Mesolithic*

THIS TECHNOLOGICAL LEVEL is the culmination of the innovations and inventions of the Upper Paleolithic of the West. A straight line of development can now be drawn from the Lower Paleolithic to the Mesolithic. Not all the evolutionary steps are clearly defined, but the results are apparent enough to demonstrate a gradual acceleration of technological achievement until the climax is reached in the Mesolithic. In turn one can understand why the diffusion of the technology of the Mesolithic provided for the potential of food production. But it should be emphasized that it was the technological capability for food production only that was diffused. It was as if a coping saw and a plane should be given to a child or an amateur. His use of these implements would be only for those things immediately obvious, or in other words for what was familiar. He would be unable to develop the wider use of these tools as known to a craftsman. In other words, he would not be able to fulfill the full potential of his tools without the need to do so or the knowledge of how to do it. Nevertheless, paradoxically, the fact that he possesses the tools provides him with the technological capability.

The evidence would seem to be reasonably conclusive that in Europe and Western Asia the culmination of the Mesolithic was reached. It seems, then, that aspects of the mesolithic technology diffused to Central

[1] A. P. Khatri, "Rock Paintings of Adamgarh (Central India) and Their Age," *Anthropos*, Vol. LIX (1964), pp. 764, 766–768.

and Southern Asia. Each environment in the path of the diffusionary movement presented its natural and indigenous cultural problems, which were solved partially by specific technological adaptations. These were, of course, matched by accompanying ecological and social adjustments about which we have little information indeed. Thus the people of Belt Cave manufactured the weapons for seal or vole catching, while the Natufians of Mount Carmel used the technology for cutting wild cereals and hunting gazelle.

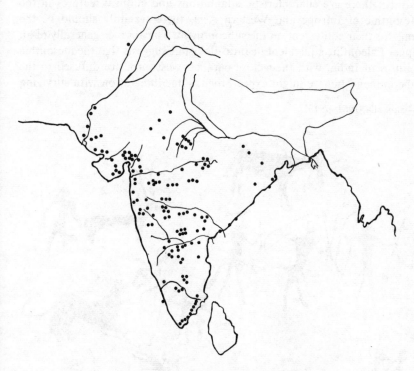

MAP 9   *Distribution of "mesolithic" sites.*

To say that the mesolithic technology spread like wildfire is certainly near the truth as compared to the far slower diffusion of the premesolithic Stone Age. Thus, by 4000 B.C., it is entirely possible that a full-fledged mesolithic-type culture flourished near the very tip of India in the Tinnevelly region of Tamilnad. If indeed Europe was the point of origin of the mesolithic achievement, then in something like six thousand years it had spread over halfway across the Old World. This may be a symptom of the utility of the technology and its almost universal applicability.

Distribution maps of "Mesolithic" cultures in Indo-Pakistan show that they were established almost everywhere in the peninsula, in Gujarat, and in Sind. In the peninsula they were located apparently in savannah or park-land country. In speaking of the Chota Nagpur Plateau, Sankalia observes: "Everywhere the site was situated on the old river terraces and plateaus and away from the present river valleys."[2] In other words, the adaptive capability of the cultures in India was such as to enable them to adjust to a variety of ecologies in the uplands. This observation has of course to be qualified by temporal considerations, but it is nonetheless significant.

But if there are characteristic adaptations and cultural features in the Mesolithic of Europe and Western Asia, there certainly should be the same for their equivalent on the subcontinent. The absence generally of an Upper Paleolithic equivalent in Indo-Pakistan suggests that the mesolithic cultures of India, with their close parallels westward, are diffused to the subcontinent, but we might expect, then, some integration with surviving

[2] Sankalia, 1963, p. 131.

FIG. 15 *Rock drawings and paintings of possible mesolithic derivation.*
  1—*Mahadeo Hills* (after Gordon)
  2—*Kupgallu, Bellary* (after Gordon)
  3—*Mahadeo Hills* (after Gordon)
  4—*Mahadeo Hills* (after Gordon)
  5—*Mahadeo Hills* (after Gordon)

traits of the Indian Middle Stone Age.[3] Because such appears to be the case in a few instances, there appears to be a tendency among some scholars to regard the Mesolithic as an indigenous development out of the Indian Middle Age. While this is probably true of some objects, it does not on the face of it seem to be the true situation. It goes beyond coincidence that identical forms are found in Iran, for example, in somewhat earlier and certainly contemporary context. Throughout the entire range of subcontinental prehistory and history one has to keep three principal characteristics of change and development in mind: (1) what is directly or implicitly parallel with adjacent regions outside; (2) what is peculiarly Indian because of indigenous development; (3) what is regional and expressive of local emphasis rather than the entire subcontinent. The case of these mesolithic assemblages of India serves to point up the need there is to keep these characteristics in mind.

But before describing more particularly the applicability of these points, we should survey some of the key sites.

❊ *Key Sites*

B. B. LAL EXCAVATED THE SITE OF BIRBHANPUR IN 1957. The site is located in the highest of two terraces above the river Damodar in the Burdwan district of West Bengal. There are other such sites in the neighborhood. Two trenches were sunk into the terrace. The first (Trench BBP-1) involved a lowermost layer of decayed whitish sandstone, above which was a layer of mottled silty sand. In turn a layer of lateritic gravel with stone fragments (hardpan?) was uncovered on an implementiferous level of earth mixed with coarse granules mostly of quartz and hematite. This layer, which lay below a surface soil of light brown sandy earth, contained a microlithic assemblage. The second trench (BBP-2) had much the same section. The lowermost layer was of mottled silty sand like phase (4) of BBP-1. On the pock-marked surface of this silt was the implementiferous layer composed of reddish silty sand with lateritic pebbles. A thin granual sand layer, also with lateritic pebbles, was above this, and the whole was covered with the light-brown sandy earth of the first trench.

In addition to digging these trenches Lal found clusters of microliths nearby in places where erosion had washed away the layers above the

---

[3] At Khandivli near Bombay, Commander Todd revealed what he has called "a blade and burin" assemblage between the Middle Stone Age levels and the mesolithic which might be called an Upper Paleolithic (Todd, 1939). But since Todd's time this assemblage has not been confirmed elsewhere in India. Rather, those who study the problem see a transition from the Middle Stone Age industries to the microlithic material. Thus, for example, Malik, who reworked Todd's sites, makes the "blade and burin" industry part of the Middle Stone Age (Malik, 1959, pp. 43ff.).

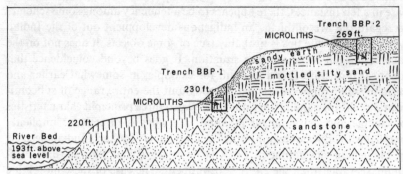

FIG. 16 *Damodar terraces near Birbhanpur* (after Lal). *Microliths were found in the mottled sandy silt levels at localities BBP-1 and BBP-2.*

implementiferous layer. These clusters were from ten to thirty yards from one another, the whole representative of a sizable Mesolithic settlement.

The collections made by Lal indicate an absence of pottery but a large body of lithic material. Somewhere over four hundred finished tools were recovered, but in this only one specimen each of a trapeze and a triangle (?) were found. Lal interprets this to mean that the industry here is essentially nongeometric, as these shapes are characteristic of so-called "geometric" microlithic cultures in the West (see Fig. 17). The tools were made out of a variety of materials, with quartz by far the most common. The tool types include lunates, points, borers, burins, and scrapers, and of course a variety of cores, fluted and otherwise, as well as blades. The bulk of the tools are an inch or less in size. An off-find was a stone (6 inches by 4 inches by 2 inches) in association with the microliths that because of its having a pitted depression on one side suggested to the excavator that it might be an anvil. Another interesting discovery in Trench BBP-2 was of some ten pits, or holes, of different sizes and depths; similar holes were found in one of the clusters. No particular orientation (possibly circular) was determinable, but one cannot avoid the possibility that these are "post holes." The anvil was found within the area encompassed by these "post holes."

Soil sampling of the site was carried out, and in a remarkably perceptive study Dr. B. B. Lal, an archaeological chemist with the same name as the excavator, sets forth data upon which to build some view as to the climatic conditions at the time of settlement. Using this study, the excavator concludes: ". . . the deposits immediately preceding the microlithic deposit . . . were formed under hot and humid conditions, which he [Lal, the chemist] is inclined to assign to the last pluvial phase of the Pleistocene, and . . . with the setting in of milder and drier climatic conditions, Mesolithic man appeared on the scene. The microlithic deposit was finally sealed by a

$2\frac{1}{2}$ to 3 ft. thick deposit of sandy earth, which, as the analysis has shown, was laid down under semi-arid conditions and has undergone weathering in the course of time. On this basis, the microlithic industry may be placed vaguely somewhere early in the Holocene."[4] Birbhanpur is thus a good candidate for a truly early date for the microlithic industries.

[4] B. B. Lal, "Birbhanpur, A Microlithic Site in the Damodar Valley, West Bengal," *Ancient India*, No. 14 (1958), pp. 4–48.

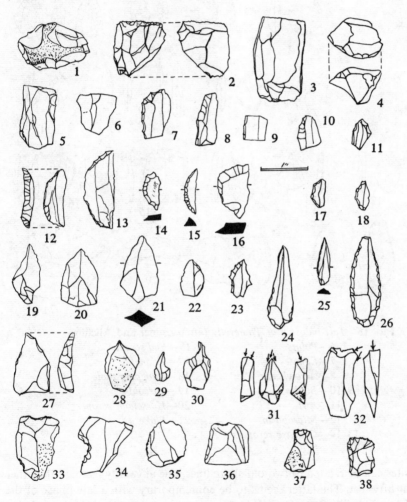

FIG. 17 *Tool types from Birbhanpur* (after Lal).

1–4—Cores	19–27—Points
5–11—Flakes	28–30—Borers
12–16—Lunates	31–32—Burins
17–18—Trapeze	33–38—Scrapers

Far to the south, in the coastal Tamilnad, Frederick Zeuner and Bridget Allchin found a series of sites among the sand dunes of the Tinnevelly district. These dunes (*teris*) are essentially fossilized and are associated with old shore lines. The present coast is one of bars and lagoons, the latter slowly being filled. Dune building continues today. The

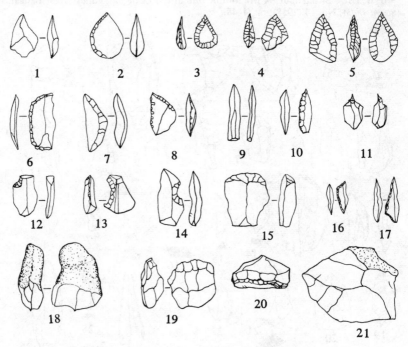

FIG. 18   *Teri industry of Tinnevelly* (after Zeuner and Allchin).

1–5—*Points*	15—*End scraper*
6–7—*Lunates*	16–17—*Triangles*
8—*Arrowhead*	18—*Chopping tool*
9–10—*Blades*	19—*Discoid*
11—*Awl*	20—*Horsehoof scraper*
12—*Microburin*	21—*Flake*
13–14—*Concave scrapers*	

sites can be related to two old shore lines, one at twenty feet and the other at fifty feet. The latter seems to be contemporary with a late phase of the Indian Middle Stone Age. It is the twenty-foot shore line which produced the classic *teri* sites of microlithic industries. The investigators have worked out a stratigraphic section in a study of the possible geological correlations. Essentially a bleached soil level (A) of recent or just subrecent times overlies a red-cemented sand level (B). This can be interpreted as representing initially the foundation of a lagoon and sand-dune situation, after which a phase of weathering occurred during which the sea level dropped to about its present level and the modern lagoon and dune situation ensued. The microlithic tools of several of the sites are heavily stained red, indicating that they were deposited before the weathering period, and perhaps even before the first *teri* formation. This stratigraphic picture is of great importance, since the local sea-level correlation has, as on the lower Narbada, an extra-Indian potential. Zeuner and Allchin tentatively have suggested that the sea level of the twenty-foot shore line might be the postglacial eustatic maximum, which took place around 4000 B.C.[5]

The industry of the *teri* uses chert and quartz for the manufacture of microlithic forms from blades and flakes (see Fig. 18). Some of these forms are geometric. An important and unique type is the bifacially pressure-flaked point. These points and the technique of manufacture are apparently unique in India. They do occur in Ceylon, however, and in fact the Tinnevelly *teri* industry is common enough on that island, where it occurs in caves and also on coastal sites.[6]

Bridget Allchin sees in these coastal and Ceylonese industries, after a close study of them, a transition from the Middle Stone Age industries. The process, as she sees it, is one of gradual change: "All these examples give the impression that the change from one group of techniques to another was effected without a sudden break; by the acquisition of new techniques and dropping older ones bit by bit, rather than by a sweeping change."[7]

In Gujarat Sankalia was able systematically to examine the microlithic industry sites found there in a program of field work in the 1940s in which he was assisted by F. Zeuner.[8]

Over eighty sites are known in Gujarat, and these are regarded as a mere sample of what was once an immense settlement of the region. The locale of the sites is the open, sandy, and gently rolling alluvial plain of northern and central Gujarat. Through the region meander, or have meandered, a number of small rivers and streams. At times of high water, inundation lagoons occur here and there in the hollows between the hill undulations. The hills and the riverbanks were the locations of the settlements of Microlithic-tool-using peoples.

[5] The site description is based on Zeuner and Allchin, 1956, pp. 4–20.

[6] B. Allchin, "The Late Stone Age of Ceylon," *Journal of the Royal Anthropological Institute of Great Britain and Ireland*, Vol. LXXXVIII (1958), pp. 179–201.

[7] Allchin, 1963, pp. 210–234.

[8] H. D. Sankalia, "Investigations in the Prehistoric Archaeology of Gujarat," Baroda, 1946. See also Sankalia, 1963, pp. 143–194; Sankalia, *Excavations at Langhnaj, 1944–63*, Pt. I—Archaeology; Part II—The Fauna (with Juliet Clutton-Brock); Part III—The Human Remains (with S. Ehrhart and K. A. R. Kennedy): Deccan College Building Centenary and Silver Jubilee Series No. 27, Poona, 1965; B. Subbarao, 1958, pp. 69–75.

The most important of the investigated sites is the composite site, or group of sites, known as Langhnaj. With F. Zeuner's soil analysis as a guide, a stratigraphic picture was drawn up.

SECTION

Layers 1, 1a, 2, 2a Dark brown sand	Sand 1'–3'	Per. III. Modern pottery, iron, and microliths
Layer 3—Upper half	Sand 3'–4'	Per. II. Old pottery, microliths, Mace-head or ring stone
Layer 3—Lower half	Buried soil	Period I. Pure microlithic culture with most of the human skeletons and animal remains, like rhinoceros
Layer 4—Upper half	4'–5'	
Layer 4—Lower half and below	Kankar and sands	

AFTER SANKALIA, 1963, p. 145

The implication of the site locations close to inundation lakes is that the climate was wetter than today. This conforms in Zeuner's climate sequence to phase (X), or essentially subrecent time.[9]

At the site of Rangpur on the river Bhadar, considerably to the south of Langhnaj but also on the alluvial plain of central Gujarat, Rao found a "Microlithic" industry of "Langhnaj type" in a gravel lense formed by previous floods of the Bhadar River of the northern and western sides of the site. The level is clearly separated by a layer of silt from the Harappan level, which represents the next cultural assemblage in the sequence there.[10] The excavator assigns a tentative date to this material of 3000 B.C.

The industry of these Gujarat sites consists of the usual blade and flake tools made generally of chert and agate (see Fig. 19). The presence of trapezes and triangles would assign the assemblage to the geometric class. A ground-stone "digging-stick weight," however, is associated with the industry in Period II, and hematite rubbingstones are also found in that period. A long bone with side teeth may be a harpoon and is found at Langhnaj.

Remarkable were the human remains found at Langhnaj, some apparently buried in a flexed position (E-W and W-E) in the midst of or close to the settlements. Study of the remains by Karve and Kurulkar, and later by others, revealed a tallish, slender people, longheaded and somewhat prognathous.[11] A strong possibility exists that some of these people were killed by blows to the head.

[9] Zeuner, 1950; however Zeuner has given up the idea of a wetter phase in his last publication, 1963, p. 15. See also F. E. Zeuner, "Microlithic Culture of Langhnaj, Gujarat," *Man*, Vol. III (1952), pp. 129–131.

[10] S. R. Rao, "Excavations at Rangpur and Other Explorations in Gujarat," *Ancient India*, Nos. 18–19 (1962 and 1963), pp. 5–207.

[11] H. D. Sankalia and I. Karve, *Preliminary Report on the Third Gujarat Prehistoric Expedition*, Deccan College, Poona, 1955; Sankalia, 1963, p. 146; Sankalia, 1965.

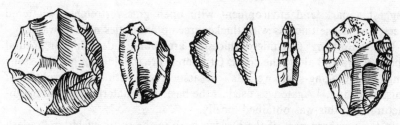

FIG. 19 *Microlith types of Langhnaj* (after Sankalia).

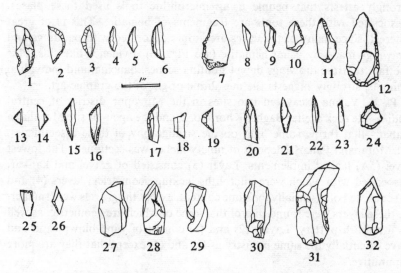

FIG. 20 *Microlith types from Salsette Island* (after Todd).

1–6 —*Lunates*	24—*Awl*
7–12—*Blunted backs*	25–26—*Rhomboids*
13–16—*Triangles*	27–29—*Burins*
17–19—*Trapezoids*	30–32—*Flakes*
20–23—*Drills*	

Dentalium beads, presumably from the Gulf of Cambay, were also found. However, of exceeding interest were the remains of wolf.[12] Domesticated dogs are known from the Natufian of Palestine, wolves are tameable and this one may represent an effort in that direction in response to the tendencies of the time. The rhinoceros is evidenced by a shoulder blade artificially pitted which may have been used as an anvil in making microliths. The buffalo, antelope, swamp deer, black buck, hog deer, the nilgai, mongoose, fish, and the tortoise appear in the faunal record, and there is evidence that these were all killed for food. This faunal picture would

[12] Sankalia, 1965, Pt. I, p. 7.

suggest a park-land environment with open grassy stretches, scattered trees, and dense thickets with thicker tree communities next to water.

In the Bombay area microlithic sites are found on the higher ground above rivers and along the coast. Of interest are the finds of ground-stone rings or "digging-stick weights" in association with the microliths of Salsette Island.[13] Agate was used as the basic raw material for tool manufacture, and this was obtained locally.

In the northern part of the Deccan both in the south of Uttar Pradesh and in Madhya Pradesh rock shelters and caves are common. The evidence strongly attests that people using microlithic tools used these places. Associated with these tools are fragments of hematite. This is of great interest, since many of the caves are amply decorated with paintings and drawings made by using hematite (see Fig. 15). Evidence like this, plus the fact that the drawings depict hunting scenes, dancing, and individual animals, strongly suggests the mesolithic origin of the graphic art.[14]

R. K. Varma excavated two sites in the Mirzapur district of central India—the rock shelter Baghai Khor No. 1, and the open-air site Morahana Pahar—that throw some light on the stratigraphy of these assemblages. At Morahana Pahar a deposit of ninety inches was sectioned. The lowest level (5A) lacked implements. Layer (5) consisted of gravel and kankar, associated with which were microliths lacking geometrics; layers (4) and (3) consisted of essentially the same content, except the gravels were smaller. In these layers were found microliths, some of which are geometric, as well as a reddish pottery. Layers (2) and (1) consist of wind-blown sand and have essentially the same industry as (3) and (4) except that they are more diminutive.

Similarly at Baghai Khor an implementiferous deposit of fifty-five centimeters was excavated.

The Baghai Khor rock-shelter had a deposit of 55 centimeters comprising four distinct layers. Layer 4 yielded non-geometric microliths but no pottery. The tool types comprise blunted-back-blades, lunates, awls, and burinate tools. Layer 3 yielded, besides non-geometric microliths, a few small sherds which can be divided into three groups. The first group consists of hand-made pottery of coarse grayish section. It is ill-fired and ochre-washed. The second

[13] K. R. U. Todd, "The Microlithic Industries of Bombay," *Ancient India*, No. 6 (1950), pp. 4–16.
[14] Bridget Allchin feels the evidence makes the drawings of microlithic origin. B. Allchin, 1963, pp. 222–223. On the other hand, B. K. Thapar has doubts as to this possibility. See B. K. Thapar, "Mesolithic Phase in the Prehistory of India," *Indian Prehistory: 1964*, V. N. Misra and M. S. Mate, eds., Deccan College Postgraduate and Research Institute, Poona, 1965, p. 71. R. K. Varma implies that at least some of these rock paintings from Mirzapur district are contemporary with the microlithic users. See R. K. Varma, comment to V. N. Misra, "Mesolithic Phase in the Prehistory of India," pp. 75–76.

group of pottery has a thin section and ochrish red slip. The third group also has a thin section but it is better fired and well-made. It has a reddish slip. Layer 2 yielded microliths of both non-geometric and geometric types associated with pottery similar to that found in Layer 3.

An extended human burial in articulated condition was found buried under Layer 2. The burial pit was cut into Layers 3 and 4. The bed-rock over which the skeleton lay directly was dressed in order to provide a raised platform for head and feet and a comparative depression for the body. Due to later pits, part of the skull and face was damaged. The orientation was west-east. The whole skeleton was found covered with thin stone chips.

Also in the Mirzapur district around the Kaimur a group of rock shelters and open-air sites known as Lekhahia were excavated under the direction of G. R. Sharma. These produced the same sequence as that revealed by R. K. Varma at Morahana Pahar and Baghai Khor.

PHASE I—Nongeometric prepottery microliths, heavily patinated.
PHASE II—Geometric tools without pottery.
PHASE III—Geometric tools with pottery.
PHASE IV—Geometric and diminutive tools with pottery.[15]

In Lekhahia Rock Shelter I, besides rock paintings some seventeen burials were revealed. Each of these was on its back in an extended position and so closely associated were microlithic tools that it may well be that these tools should be considered as grave goods. All but two of these skeletons were oriented west-east, with head to the west. It would appear that the bulk of the burials were of the middle phases of the rock-shelter occupation.

Other rock shelters and cave sites containing both paintings and a level of geometric microliths are well known, especially in the Mahadeo Hills.[16]

In Mysore, in the more southerly regions of the Deccan, "microlithic" sites are widely found on the surface. In one area, known as Jalahalli, in a valley, Todd located some of these microliths in a reddish soil below the black soil of the surface. This again points up the fact that some of the microlithic industries are found in a stratigraphic context that strongly suggests some antiquity. In contrast the term "microlithic" has also been applied to the stone tools found at the very late site of Brahmagiri (see page 326), which confuses the issue a little.[17] This is because while we

---

[15] After V. N. Misra, "Mesolithic Phase in the Prehistory of India," *Indian Prehistory: 1964*, pp. 76–79.

[16] See D. H. Gordon, "The Stone Age Industries of the Holocene in India and Pakistan," *Ancient India*, No. 6 (1950), pp. 64–90.

[17] R. E. M. Wheeler, "Brahmagiri and Chandravalli 1947: Megalithic and other Cultures in Mysore State," *Ancient India*, No. 4 (1947–1948), pp. 250–252. See also M. Seshadri, "The Stone Using Cultures of Prehistoric and Protohistoric Mysore," London, 1956.

tend to consider microlithic cultures as having typological relationships, we tend to fail to understand that they may lack organic or cultural ties. The typology, then, becomes almost meaningless.

❋ The Development of Microlithic Industries

WHEN WE CONSIDER THE CHRONOLOGICAL POSITION of these "microlithic" industries, it becomes clear that the time range is considerable. For example, the use of bottle glass as a source of material for "microlithic" manufacture (see p. 85) in central India brings the tradition at least to the eighteenth century A.D. In the other direction, the Tinnevelly evidence, the location of the "microlithic" deposit at Rangpur, and the early occurrence of microliths at Langhnaj indicate that dates prior to 3000 B.C. are entirely possible. In a microlithic industry found some four feet in the upper alluvium in the Balia Nadi of the Singrauli basin, Krishnaswami saw an echo of a "degenerate Upper Palaeolithic blade tradition."[18] Lal's Birbhanpur material is also suggestive of an early dating. Again, at Tinnevelly, Allchin's suggestion of ties to the Indian Middle Stone Age establishes a continuum of considerable time depth in which one would be hard put to determine exactly when one tradition can be clearly separated from the other. Malik also makes this suggestion for the Bombay area.

Allchin makes a good case for the division of these industries on the basis of materials used, the quartz-users being predominantly southern and possibly eastern central India (e.g. Birbhanpur).[19]

Lal goes a step further and suggests that the quartz industries are generally nongeometric.[20] This would certainly appear to be the case for almost the whole of eastern India as far as the Tamilnad.

The problems of determining the place, character, and distribution of these industries are difficult in themselves, but the matter is further complicated by a tendency to call any small stone artifact "microlithic" and thus by implication to relate it to the particular tradition which seems to lie chronologically after the Indian Middle Stone Age and before the advent of food production. Because the term "microlithic" is used in Europe in connection with the Mesolithic, this implication cannot help but be apparent in the Indian context.

The Asian conference in New Delhi in 1961 decided to call these microlithic industries the Indian Late Stone Age. The implication is, of course, that they are representative of the last major phase of hunting-gathering before the advent of agriculture. At Bellary, for example, Subbarao un-

[18] Krishnaswami, 1953, p. 65.
[19] Allchin, 1963, pp. 220–221.
[20] Lal, 1958, p. 38.

covered a "microlithic" level below that of the "Neolithic" there.[21] If the evidence continues to accumulate to prove developmental ties to the Indian Middle Stone Age, the natural evolution of food-gathering life to this its latest phase will be proven and the indigenous background for the phase sketched in. In this context, the diffusionist theory outlined at the beginning of this chapter will be capable of misinterpretation.

Yet we are brought face to face with the almost certain fact that a process of diffusion brought essentially microlithic types to the subcontinent. The backed blade, the trapeze, the triangle, and the arrowhead cannot be considered as anything else but representative of the compound tool and the bow and arrow. These rather complex traits are also symptoms of fundamental ways of life in which sizable communities developed, as the concentration of sites at both Langhnaj and Birbhanpur suggests. It is very possible that a tribal society is indicated. On the other hand, the wide distribution of the microlithic industries and their frequent association with caves and rock shelters modest in size suggests roving bands probably made up possibly of no more than segmented familial groups. Perhaps both social groups were common. Certainly, if some of the rock drawings are indeed of Indian Late Stone Age origin, societies of reasonable complexity are indicated.

In effect, then, the Indian Late Stone Age has a very specific meaning even as a classification device. It means that period dominated by a hunting-gathering food-collecting way of life which, if present distribution maps are reasonably indicative, was prospering all the way from the Indus River Valley across the Deccan to the Tamilnad. In this it was far more widespread than either of the two earlier ages. The people were regionalized in this period in that there are coastal, riverine, plateau, and even semiarid or desert aspects. More than likely the more tropical areas were also included in their realm. These people possessed the bow and arrow and made microlithic tools, almost all of which are duplicated in cultures known in the West. It is a point of interest in this regard that the Baradostian of Shanidar Cave in northeastern Iraq contains within its various phases elements of both the earlier Mousterian and the later microlithic. The implication is, of course, that these stages of development everywhere include factors of indigenous character as well as integration with new elements brought in from outside.[22]

The straight-line duplication of types of the Indian Late Stone Age in the Zarzian of Iraq and the mesolithic levels of Belt Cave is also striking and convincing. Undeniably a way of life did move to the subcontinent in a period after 9000 B.C. and before 4000 B.C. But when that cultural form diffused to the regions of the subcontinent, where it was to be established,

[21] B. Subbarao, *Stone Age Culture of Bellary*, Deccan College Dissertation Series No. 7, Poona, 1948.
[22] Cf. Braidwood and Howe, 1960, p. 154.

it is increasingly obvious that it encountered the surviving representatives of the Indian Middle Stone Age.

✳ *Mesolithic Culture of the Subcontinent*

THOUGH OUR KNOWLEDGE OF THESE CULTURES STILL REMAINS POOR, the existing evidence hints tantalizingly at their character. If we consider their earliest manifestation as that which is found at Period I in Langhnaj and in Lal's site at Birbhanpur, we might expect pole houses or lean-tos as the shelters for large communities of people who gathered their principal sustenance by hunting animals of the rivers and lakes of the region. At Salsette Island near Bombay as well as in Gujarat there is a strong suggestion that closeness to lakes and marshes was important to the food-gathering abilities of the time. This, too, has a strong second in the dune dwellers of Tinnevelly. One suspects that swamp reeds, reptiles and amphibians, fish and the marsh birds were all grist for their economic mills. Inland in the high terraces of rivers and amid the hills and plains of the plateau, rock shelters and caves were important as shelters but seemingly more for smaller groups than for the coastal or lagoon dwellers. Some of these sites in the inland areas are factory sites where resources of stone were available and yet not too distant from established hunting grounds.

The graves of Langhnaj hint of a belief in an afterlife where the daily-life articles of the living were necessary to a proper existence. Strange, however, is the fact that many of the burials show marks of a violent death. Were they victims of battle, or were they sacrifices to the animistic forces recognized by hunting-gathering people almost universally? The suggestion of grave goods is, however, a clue to a belief in magic and to the recognition that the spirit of the dead person had need of magic's help in the after-world.

The remarkable faunal remains found at Langhnaj prove the intimacy with which these men lived with the animals they hunted. It is unnecessary to remark that they knew the habits of their prey. We can ponder one thing, however, and that is whether their good knowledge of animals and their constant pursuit of this resource led to such things as pet keeping, corralling, or providing fodder just to see how close animals as individuals or as groups would come to men. In other words, was the interaction of man and beasts, and indeed plants and man, of sufficient intensity that the potential of domestication was present? The buffalo and the wolf were there, and such animals are potentially domesticable. The doughnut-shaped stones from Langhnaj (Period II) and Salsette Island could be maceheads, but they could as well be digging-stick weights. The digging-stick allows for the effective planting of cereal grains in moist riverine mud.

It is significant that Sankalia can speak of the microlithic sites of northern Gujarat and tell of "hundreds of sites." Every issue of *Indian Archaeology*, the annual report of the Archaeological Survey of India, reports on literally dozens of sites found in Rajasthan, Malwa, Bundel-kund, and areas to the south. This would substantiate the idea of comparatively large populations interacting and yet regionalizing at the same time. Such interaction increases the chances for innovation as communities transmit, diffuse, reject, improve, and motivate new ideas. It is perhaps an act of independent invention that "pressure flaking" should develop in Ceylon and the Tamilnad far from possible contacts with extra-Indian regions where the technique was well known and yet the wide-flung distribution of the technique may be expressive of the selective interactions of the time.

One can remark, as I have above, on the tendency to call later industries "microlithic" that are certainly far from being "mesolithic" in the sense which I have underlined. Yet this tendency is perhaps a recognition of the continuity of the "mesolithic" tradition which apparently made such an impact on the development of the cultures of the subcontinent. R. J. Braidwood, in his presidential address at the centennial celebration of the Archaeological Survey of India in New Delhi in 1961, perhaps in response to too great a tendency on the part of scholars to look to Western Asia for the origin of all food production, remarked that one thing that should be looked for on the subcontinent was what these Indian Late Stone Age people were doing. Were they experimenting with local potentially domes-ticable plants and animals, as had the first food producers situated on the hilly flanks of the Fertile Crescent? Indeed, did they have successes? In the light of later evidence for the early development on the subcontinent of the domestic chicken, humped cow, water buffalo, rice, and perhaps other cereals, these questions must be pondered.

The Indian Late Stone Age means, then, full-fledged hunting and gathering in the sense of the Mesolithic of Western Asia and Europe. It also means a manipulation of the local environment which could have led to food production. It is true that we need to know a great deal more, but there are clues to important events in the human story in India at this stage—and clues eventually lead to graphic truths.

IV

The Beginning of Settled Life

Τ HE EXEMPLARY, FAR-REACHING, AND CONTINUING archaeological researches in Western Asia and Egypt of the last several decades have provided an outline of the steps ancient man took in his evolution from intensive food collection to full-fledged food production.[1] The record is remarkable in its relative completeness, even though there are numerous gaps and limited factual evidences. It would appear that out of the intensive use of the different environments in which man found himself during just postglacial time, as outlined in the last chapter, there arose the intentional manipulation of the life cycles of certain plants and animals to provide stable resources of foodstuffs and other material—in other words, food production by means of agriculture and animal domestication. In particular, the cereals wheat (especially emmer, or *Triticum dicoccum*) and barley (*Hordeum*), the leguminous plants (lentils, peas, vetch and vetchling), the goat (*Capra hircus*), and the sheep (*Ovis orientalis*) were selected out by man and by processes still being studied became the economic basis for the first village life.

[1] Among the most important of these researches are those of Braidwood, Childe, Reed, Helbaeck, Soleki, Perrot, Kenyon, and Mellaart (see Bibliography).

102

❋ *The Primary-Village and Subsequent Phases*

THE MOUNTING NUMBER OF SITES for a primary-village phase being discovered in Western Asia, especially in the highland areas of Iraq, western Iran, Syria, and Turkey, indicates that these regions were the centers for this major development in the human story. The primary-village phase began there somewhere in the time period after 8000 B.C. and before 6500 B.C. In all cases a partial dependence upon food gathering is still retained whether the village community is small, like Jarmo in Iraq, or large, like Catal Hüyük in Turkey or Jericho in Palestine.[2]

Primary-village dwellers knew how to make pottery, weave mats, make plaster, cut stone; they indulged in painting and modeling and had rather complex cults centered around animal representations, sacrifice, and ablution. Buildings were often set aside for these purposes.

Two phenomena characterize the next phase: a gradual evolution into developed village life, and a gradual diffusion of food production of Western Asian form to the west and south, but earlier apparently to the east. For the first there is evidence for larger communities living on the borderlands between the highlands where primary-village farming had its origin and on the great alluvial plains where later civilizations were to develop. These communities by 4000 B.C. had domesticated cattle (*Bos*) and pigs (*Sus scrofa*), flax (which they cultivated), and pomegranates, dates, pistachios, almonds, and other fruits. They were using native copper, had boats, and were involved in a moderate trade for obsidian, shells, and probably leather, coloring matter, and perhaps certain semiprecious stones and other exotica. Village communities of as many as 250 to 500 or more individuals were common enough, and with less dependence upon hunting as a secondary economic resource than in the primary farming phase. We can recognize, therefore, the growth of a full-fledged sedentary society less self-contained than the earlier primary villages. This means, simply, that an increasing number of specialists became necessary to handle effectively the administration of a society whose families lived together the year round and whose collective effort in the cultivation of crops and the herding of food animals provided a total production which exceeded the individual subsistence requirement for that year—in other

---

[2] The problem of the status of Tell-es-Sultan (Jericho), a low-lying site of considerable scale in the Jordan valley next to a spring, has not yet been satisfactorily resolved. Was it a community whose economic basis was essentially an as yet unevidenced agriculture? Or was it a peculiarly successful food-gathering society whose successes permitted the development of true village life equal to that of the food producers? The point is that the intensive use of the environment so characteristic of the Mesolithic need not have evolved to food production. It could also result in a fuller and more efficient use of non-domesticated food resources, which if they are present in sufficient and recurring quantity, can produce a stable economy out of which village life could evolve.

words, a society with a surplus which could be used for the acquisition by barter, or rather exchange, of things not found locally or, more important, which could be used to pay for the services of someone whose yearly duties did not require work in the field. We note in this period the manufacture of fine pottery beautifully painted with motifs in geometric or naturalistic styles in both black and polychrome. This is the production of professional potters. It is symptomatic of the use of surplus foodstuffs to pay for the services of a professional. How much this applied to weaving, stonecutting, wood carving, shellwork, brickmaking—which crafts were common enough at the time—we are uncertain, but we can be reasonably secure in feeling that the appearance of these crafts in full array is a measure of the consequent success of agriculture and domestication. Beyond this we are hard put to create the society of these villages. Many of them stored their crops in silos in or amid their houses; frequently the dead, especially children or women, were interred in the floor of the house, and the burial with ornaments, red-ocher staining of the bones, the presence of daily-life objects, and the flexed position of many of the bodies suggests a belief in an afterlife. Monumental building, in the form of walls, towers, and "temple" structures, also occurs. All these things suggest a social organization of some complexity: a village chief and/or a council of elders, as well as priests or shamans, and craftsmen were probably normal to such communities. The most important aspect of this level of development is the rapidity with which it changes. In Mesopotamia, where the record from the last phase of food collecting to the rise of civilization is most complete, we are carried in a few thousand years from simple societies hovering between the cave life of their ancestors and the timid beginnings of village life to the full-fledged and aggressive urbanization of the Sumerians. Change is the hallmark of that record. What is relatively complete in Mesopotamia is less so elsewhere in Western Asia, but almost anywhere where a portion of the story emerges we are witness not only to rapid indigenous development but to the increasing interdependence of one region with the next.

The diffusion of food production and village life especially to the east is the second aspect of the time from 8000 B.C. onward. The archaeological record is nowhere so complete as in Western Asia proper; nevertheless, we have strategic places where the movement is reasonably clear. Before we examine some of the sites, we must reiterate that a mesolithic society, as defined previously, contains the potential for food production, provided it is in contact with what is potentially domesticable. The argument for diffusion has validity only when it pertains to what on the present evidence was naturally characteristic of the environment of Western Asia prior to domestication, such as the wild forms of wheat, barley, goats, sheep, and cattle, which have been shown to be as a whole a constellation of domesticates native to that region, and when such forms are found in other regions at later dates than those of Western Asia in associational contacts that indicate they moved as a complex. In other words, wild wheat may be native to Afghanistan, for example; thus a mesolithic society could have domesticated it there independent of the West, but when a cultivated wheat is found in an early site in Afghanistan associated with domesticated barley and goats (both not native to Afghanistan) it is probable, but by no means certain, that the whole complex was diffused from Western Asia, where all are found in domesticated form presumably at an earlier date.

✳ *The Iranian Plateau*

THE IRANIAN PLATEAU is the block of land that intervenes between the Fertile Crescent countries and the subcontinent. The plateau is essentially a great Tertiary basin with broad mountain chains thrust up at its rim and isolating the interior from the surrounding regions such as Central Asia and the great river valleys of the Indus (east) and the Tigris-Euphrates (west). The interior of the plateau is made up of subbasins, and deserts with interior drainage. On the east the basins are squeezed between the Koh-i-Baba mountain ranges of central Afghanistan and the coast ranges of Makran on the Arabian Sea. The Koh-i-Baba merge with the Hindu Kush and the Pamir-Karakorum-Himalaya chain on the east, while, to the north of central Iran, the Elburz Mountains intervene between the Great Salt Desert and the Caspian Sea, merging with the Caucasus on the north-west. The Zagros Mountains are a southern offshoot joining the Caucasus to the coastal range of the Persian Gulf and the Arabian Sea. Only on the northeast, where the hills are lower and phase down into the spacious plains and deserts of Central Asia, is the plateau rim less well defined by geography.

Too far to the west to be affected directly by the rains of the monsoon and too far to the east to be affected strongly by the Atlantic and Mediterranean, the plateau is largely an arid desert. The high mountains, however, receive rainfall, and the resulting water supply drains toward the interior and provides moisture for a broad belt of vegetation between mountains and desert.

It is obvious that since there has been no great climatic change on the plateau since Pleistocene times, this geographical situation prescribes what men can do and what they can't do quite neatly.[3] Early agriculturists obviously tended to grow their crops in the belt between mountains and desert, within which there are of course varied ecologies, which in turn could be adapted to according to the elasticity of one's food-production

[3] One of the most important studies on the question of geography and climatic change in Iran is that of H. Bobek, 1953/1954, whose studies indicate the parallels of the ancient and modern climates and their differences. See H. Bobek, "Klima und Landschaft Irans in vor- und frühgeschichtlicher Zeit," *Geographischer Jahresbericht aus Österreich*, Vol. XXV (1953/1954), pp. 1–42.

techniques. Later, with the development of such characteristic water-procuring mechanisms as the khanat and the water wheel, and the development of strains of hardy plants which needed less moisture for their growth, more marginal areas could be utilized. Essentially, however, agriculture flourishes in two great wings with the great central deserts between. The northern wing is broad in its extension eastward from the Zagros region, narrow where the desert is close to the Elburz in the region of Tehran, and rather stringy and dentiform east of that region as it merges into the arid regions of Central Asia and as it creeps up river valleys like that of the

MAP 10   *Regions of the Indo-Iranian Borderlands and parts of the Iranian plateau.*

Murghab and the Oxus and the Hari Rud in western and northern Afghanistan. To the south, the lower wing is broad-based in the Zagros and increasingly narrow from the Shiraz region, or Fars, to the coastal ranges, after which it is interrupted by arid stretches in the great east-west-running valleys that cross south of the Great Desert to Baluchistan. Here there are oases and sometimes well-watered deltas, like that of Seistan in the delta basin of the Helmand. Here, too, in the southern foothills and alluvial plains of the Koh-i-Baba ranges there are rich patches of fertile soil and water at such localities as Girishk and Kandahar.

Of the two wings, the northern is naturally more amply endowed for food production and has the continuity. It is a natural path running from the Zagros to the Altai and the Dzungarian Gates, the natural entry to China. Indeed, a string of early farming-village sites has been traced from the Zagros to the Vale of Ferghana (Tepe Asiab, Tepe Sarab, Ali Kosh, Tepe Guran, Solduz, Tepe Sialk, Chashma Ali, Tepe Hissar, Anau, Djeitun, Chopran Tepe, Namazga, Geoksyur, Kara Tepe, Chust). While the interconnections between such sites are not altogether clear in every case, sufficient evidence has been gathered to show that village life based on a closely comparable technology existed there before 3500 B.C. As early as 1942 Donald McCown was able to show what stylistic ties, principally in motifs of pottery painting, existed between such disparate sites as Tepe Sialk on the western end of the Great Salt Desert and Anau in Turkmenistan.[4] There also is a chronological differential to indicate a movement from west to east of food production and its village life. The nature of this kind of evidence can best be ascertained by a view of the contents of a few of the key sites.[5]

✳ *Key Sites: Sialk*

TEPE SIALK is located close to a spring in an oasis situation. There are two mounds on the site. At the base of the north mound (Sialk I) were found the habitations and artifacts of villagers who who combined farming, fishing, and hunting to provide their sustenance. Sheep, goats, and cattle are attested, as well as pottery, rib-bone sickles, maces, hoes, the sling, carved figurines, native copper, awls or pins, and cosmetics. Their huts were pisé-walled and modest in size. Burials within or among the houses are of bodies flexed and with bones stained with red ocher.[6]

The last levels of the north mound and the lower levels of the south mound (Sialk III 1-7) follow in order of sequence and attest the elaboration of village life. Mud-brick houses, increasing use of native copper, crowned

[4] D. E. McCown, *The Comparative Stratigraphy of Early Iran*, Studies in Ancient Oriental Civilization, No. 23, Oriental Institute, University of Chicago, Chicago, 1942.

[5] This discussion does not include sites of western Iran, especially from Khuzistan and the Lake Urmia region, since their relationships have been briefly sketched in the general outline above and their affinities initially are largely to the west as a part of the "hilly flanks" zone. The reader can find much of this material in R. J. Braidwood, *Prehistoric Man*, Chicago Natural History Museum Popular Series, Anthropology, No. 37, Chicago, 1957; Braidwood, 1960, pp. 130–152; R. H. Dyson, Jr., "Archaeology and the Domestication of Animals in the Old World," *American Anthropologist*, Vol. LV (1953), pp. 661–673; Dyson, "Problems in the Relative Chronology of Iran, 6000–2000 B.C.," *Chronologies in Old World Archaeology*, R. Ehrich, ed., University of Chicago Press, Chicago, 1965, pp. 215–256; R. H. Dyson, Jr. and T. C. Young, "The Solduz Valley, Iran: Pisdeli Tepe," *Antiquity*, Vol. XXIV (1960), pp. 19–28; T. C. Young and P. E. L. Smith, "Research in the Prehistory of Central Iran," *Science*, Vol. CLIII (1966), pp. 386–391; Frank Hole and Kent V. Flannery, "The Prehistory of Southwestern Iran," *Proceedings of the Prehistoric Society for 1967*, Vol. XXXIII, pp. 147–206.

[6] Excavated by R. Ghirshman, *Fouilles de Sialk, près Kashan, 1933, 1934, 1937*, Musée du Louvre, Département des Antiquités Orientales Série Archéologique, T. IV-V, Paris, 1938–1939.

in the later levels (Sialk III 4-7) by a full-fledged metallurgy including casting, plus stamp seals and a fine and elaborate painted pottery that in the later levels is wheel-made—these represent the increasing sophistication of the village culture. A matter of great interest is the gradual change of pattern in the painting of pottery from a strict horizontality in which geometric and natural motifs were rather precisely and rhythmically depicted to an eventual breakup, found in the latest levels (Sialk III 7), in the painting of scenes (see Fig. 37).

✳ *Djeitun*

THE LATEST PHASES OF THE SIALK VILLAGE SEQUENCE (Sialk III) are closely paralleled in northeastern Iran at Tepe Hissar and in southern Turkmenistan at Anau and Namazga Tepe, demonstrating an identity of cultural form and indeed actual contact between western Iran and the northeast.

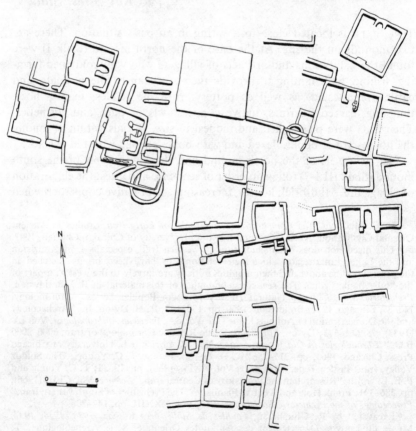

FIG. 21 *Settlement plan, Djeitun* (after Masson).

The Russian material, however, is of great interest in that it provides a clearer picture of early village life than any of the Iranian sites excavated so far and it also has two sites (Djeitun and Chopran Tepe) of farming villages that are demonstrably earlier than those of Sialk. They thus demonstrate a very early phase of essentially Western food production at the borders of Central Asia.[7] The site of Djeitun lies on a finger of higher land overlooking a marshy area just south of the Kara Kum desert and in a region which receives some drainage from the hills of the Kopet Dagh. Essentially the site represents one period dating to at least the sixth millennium B.C. The settlement was large, something over 150 by 100 meters. The portion excavated revealed simple squarish huts up to five meters in diameter built up of pisé walls. The buildings interconnect, giving a sense that a housing unit consisted of several of these houses. Circular structures, a platform, and small compartmented units suggest that work and storage buildings were part of each presumably familial complex. Possibly storage pits were located within some of the houses, as were fine built-up hearths of pisé. The artifact assemblage is particularly full, consisting of a fine range of objects largely in stone, clay, and bone. The stone industry consists of a series of microlithic tools including triangles, crescents, trapezes, backed blades, arrow points, drills, and scrapers of various kinds. Coupled with this industry are fine long blades whose edges have been nibbled purposely or by use, as well as transversely broken and secondarily flaked burins or engravers—artifacts suggestive of a food-producing culture. Ground-stone quadrangular axes, disks, rubbers, and metates complete a marvelous mixture of implements of the hunt and of domestication. Bone objects include needles, points, and tubular beads, some of which are notched or engraved. Clay articles include some enigmatic pointed or flattish objects that look like parts of some kind of game, and a fine group of animal figurines depicting probably goats and sheep (?). The pottery corpus includes open bowls, jars with flaring rim, and cups—one of which is pedestaled. Many of these vessels are painted with simple geometric designs or just rows of wavy lines. Shell ornaments are also found in the habitations.

Djeitun represents a graphic example of the eastward diffusion of the food-production techniques known earlier in Western Asia. Its locale close to the slopes of the Kopet Dagh indicates that these early food producers were clinging to the familiar ecological situation that was found in the foothill country all the way to the Zagros. Essentially this situation included a perennial source of water, a soil resource capable of supporting an annual cereal crop, and resources of game nearby. Goats and sheep also require grass and leafy trees, so it is possible that the forest cover of

[7] V. M. Masson, *Trudii Yushno-Turkmenistanskoi Archaeologicheskoi Komploksnoi Ekspeditsii*, Akademiya Nauk Turkmenskio SSR, Ashabad, 1960, Vol. X, esp. pp. 37–109.

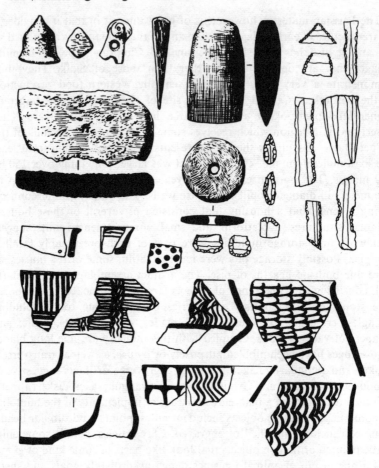

FIG. 22   *Material culture of Djeitun* (after Masson).

the slopes of the Dagh, as well as in the lower watered areas, were a logical part of the desired environment. However, Djeitun's proximity to the Kara Kum desert is like that of Sialk to the Dasht-i-Kavir and it may well be that resources there were equally desirable. However, beyond the Kara Kum are the riverine lands and the steppes of Central Asia. Djeitun represents, then, a people on the verge of entering another world where the herding of food animals and the horse will for thousands of years outdo agriculture in importance and by so doing affect the course of history in a peculiarly dynamic way. One wonders if these primitive farmers still clinging to the techniques that made the mesolithic phase of Western Asia the most successful of all the stages of food gathering but who were already herding flocks of goats and sheep (?) were laying the foundation for that Central Asian way of life.

There is a slight gap in the sequence after Djeitun, but it is apparent that the development that led to the stages represented at the lowest levels at Anau, Kara Tepe, and the sites of Namazga and Geoksyur, the next in the sequence, involved a gradual shedding of the food-gathering aspect of daily life, an improvement in agricultural practices, and an increased contact with regions to the southwest. Essentially, then, the later stages of this

FIG. 23   *Material culture of Namazga (II)* (after Masson).

Turkmenistan sequence are familiar, since they are parallel to that previously outlined for Sialk though having their own stylistic character. The distribution shows a large number of sites scattered along the base and amid the foothills of the mountains. Most of these demonstrate continuity of occupation at least into the third millennium B.C.

✳ *Northern and Western Afghanistan*

DJEITUN, EARLY AS IT IS, is not apparently the only representative of this stage of food production in the region. In the Hindu Kush mountains, to the south of Mazar-i-Sharif, capital city of northern Afghanistan, Louis Dupree developed excavation in a rock shelter known locally as Ghar-i-Mar (Snake Cave). This is located on a high terrace of the Balkh River near the town of Aq Kupruk. A narrow trench was sunk to a depth of approximately ten meters, where a yellowish red clay was encountered, apparently sterile, before the season was ended. Some three meters of levels containing historical material were first encountered. Below this occurred a gap, and then there were levels which were essentially prehistoric and defined by layers of gravel. The excavator further divides these layers on the basis of their artifactual content into Neolithic (Gravels I) and Mesolithic (Gravels II). The latter has an industry which has a lower phase: "blade cores, microblade cores, end scrapers, burin combination tools, blades, bladelets, burins, points, shouldered points, and keeled scrapers. . . ." Hearths and animal bones attest to true habitation. The upper layers of Gravels II, which date around 6600 B.C. (8650±100), contain much animal bone and an industry of "long thin blades including sickle blades, burins, and end scrapers or blades." A one-meter gap of sterile sand exists until the lower level of Gravel I. Within this latter level a nonceramic neolithic industry was encountered: "sickle blades, side scrapers or blades, point burins, backed blades, and cores" along with a polished bone point. A pocket of sheep or goat dung was associated with this level. A radio-carbon date for the level places it around 5200 B.C. (7220±100).

The upper layers of the Neolithic of Ghar-i-Mar are dated around 5000 B.C. (7030±110). These contain a flint industry: ". . . sickle blades, perforators, end scrapers, and blades. One possible angle burin (graver) was found, as well as several worked bone fragments." Two types of pottery were recovered: "a crude, soft, limestone tempered ware with simple rounded rims and flat bases, and a better fired ware with distinctive zig-zag incisions," the latter resembling pottery of a type found in Russian Turkistan as early as 5000 B.C. Sherd impressions of a fiber or basketry were also recovered here.

The excavator sees the northern slopes of the Hindu Kush as part of an ecological situation similar to that found in Western Asia. "I suspect that the wheat-barley complex developed in a general longitudinal (34° to 40° N.) zone at an altitude of 500 m. to 1500 m. above sea level. The idea of agriculture would have easily and quickly spread across the foothills in any direction in this zone. . . ."[8]

The Dupree material has its parallels at Djeitun and in the Caspian region at Belt and Hotu caves, and one can expect that more such early material will be found in this zone as research continues. Northern Afghanistan is essentially part of the Oxus River basin, with the drainage of tributaries from south to north and that of the great river itself to the west and northwest. The narrow plain which merges into the foothills of the Hindu Kush on the south was known in ancient times as Bactria. It is marked in its fertile stretches with hundreds of mounds running in grand and sporadic array from Shibarghan into the mountains east of Khanabad, where an old trade road begins the ascent into the Pamirs. The tentative archaeological work that has been done on this region, with its emphasis

[8] L. B. Dupree, "Prehistoric Archaeological Surveys and Excavations in Afghanistan: 1959–60 and 1961–63," *Science*, Vol. CXLVI (1964), pp. 638–640.

TABLE 4
GHAR-I-MAR CAVE,
NORTHERN AFGHANISTAN
(after Dupree 1964)

Av. Thickness (cm,)		Stratigraphy	Field Numbers
	10	Recent Nomadic	
	60	Early Islamic: *ca.* 10–13th centuries A.D.	
KUSHAN	150	Brick Levels: Nomad Levels * Hv 426	*Listed by name*
	25	Red-Brown Earth Below Nomad Level * Hv 427	1000
? SCYTHIAN	25	Dark Grayish Brown Earth	1001
		———————— 1st mil. B.C.	
	30	Red Earth Above Gravels I	1002
		Cultural Gap	
? NEOLITHIC — GRAVELS 1	70	Upper Layers Gravels I * Hv 429	1003, 1004, 1008 1009, 1010, 1011, 1012 1013, 1014, 2000
	50	Large Pockets of Mollusks: Gravels I Hv 428	1005, 1015, 1016
	50	Powdery (Decayed) Gravels I	1006, 1017, 1018, 1019
	70	Red-Brown Gravels I	1007, 1020, 1021 1022, 1023, 2001
	100	**Sterile Gray-Sands-I**	1024, 2002
? MESOLITHIC — GRAVELS 2	60	Upper Layers: Gravels 2: * Hv 425	1025, 2003
	30	Lower Layers: Gravels 2	1026
	250	**Sterile Gray Sands-2**	1027
GRAVELS 3	40	Gravels 3: Only Small Pit Dug: No Cultural Material Yet	1028, 2004
	? ?	Yellowish Red Clay: Small Pit ? ? ? ? ?	?

on finding sites of a given period only, has left the area largely an archaeological blank. The result is that the developmental sequences now known for
late prehistoric man in Turkmenistan and Iran have no parallel in northern
Afghanistan. Dupree's work and a handful of painted potsherds gathered
here and there in the plain are, however, symptomatic of what may well be
one of the most fruitful areas for the study of prehistoric times.

The fact that these early sites are always found near resources of perennial water suggests that systems of well irrigation and water storage were
not known. Climatically the wet season in the Oxus and Turkmenistan
region is in winter, when cold rains, some quite violent, come from the
north and west. Summers are quite hot and rainfall scarce, so water for
crops comes generally from the rivers and streams that flow from the
mountains toward the Oxus. However, many of these sink into the Bactrian
plain and water can only be obtained by means of wells. These early prehistoric villagers were thus confined to the inner fertile valleys and spurs
of fertile land among the foothills where water was obtainable from perennial streams the year round, but especially in summer when the crops were
growing. This settlement pattern apparently prevented the use of the plain
proper until later times when systems of irrigation made settlement there
possible. The fact that the Oxus River is a sensitive international border for
much of its length makes exploration close to that stream difficult, but it
is entirely possible that early settlements will be found close to the flood
plain of that perennial stream of central Asia.

Donald McCown, in his classic study of the sites of the later prehistoric
assemblages of Iran, divided them, primarily on the basis of the stratigraphic position and ceramic typology, into "cultures." Those for northern
Iran were the Chashma Ali culture (Sialk II, Anau IA, and Chashma Ali
IA, upper and the Hissar culture (Hissar I-IIA, Sialk III); his Sialk culture
is essentially Sialk I and possibly the lowest phase of the little-known site
of Chashma Ali (IA, lower).[9]

Almost all of our newer evidence on early village life in northern Iran
is earlier than McCown's Sialk culture, and little except the important addition of the Russian work in Turkmenistan has been done to amplify
effectively McCown's research in these late periods. It is clear, however,
that not only was food production well established in the north but up to
the third millennium B.C. villages had multiplied and begun to settle
marginal lands both south and north. The northern and eastern expansion
into Central Asia, best exemplified at the site of Chust, was to have a
strong influence on the beginnings of early China.[10] This needs to be
referred to in connection with the site of Burzahom in Kashmir, but this
aspect had little to do with the spread of wheat and barley food production to the subcontinent.

[9] McCown, 1942.
[10] See Appendix C.

It is the southern diffusion from the northern wing that has a particular importance to the prehistory of the subcontinent. As early as 1943 Stuart Piggott, an English archaeologist of note, pointed out the parallels between northeastern Iran and northern Baluchistan,[11] and he elaborated on this in a later study.[12] V. M. Masson confirms Piggott's thesis and extends it to include Turkmenistan.[13] The stylistic ties can be elaborated quite neatly (see Figs. 34, 35, 36, 37).[14]

Such is this evidence that we can be reasonably secure in postulating a diffusionary movement from the northeast to the northern Baluchistan region in the period after 3500 B.C. We are confounded, however, in tracing the details of this movement, for intermediate evidence is of the faintest kind. Charles Wilkinson, one of the excavators of the Islamic site of Nishapur for the Metropolitan Museum of Art in 1936, found an early prehistoric site nearby, but time did not permit excavation.[15] In western Afghanistan, Dupree and Fischer surveyed the Shaharak valley, to the east of Herat, and found no definite prehistoric remains.[16] In the summer of 1965 I was able, in the company of Mr. Gregory Possehl and my wife, to survey briefly some thirty miles along the left bank of the Hari Rud from Herat eastward, as well as a shorter distance on the right bank. A brief visit to mounds along the road from the Iranian border to Herat was also made. Neither of these all too brief efforts resulted in the discovery of a trace of prehistoric occupation in the vicinity of the river. A part of the reason for this is the fact that the talus bluffs are sharp, rising as much as thirty feet in places, and thus effectively divide the flood plain from the rest of the valley, which is generally arid except where irrigation water is raised onto the bluffs. The modern villages are situated on the bluffs overlooking the valley and may well rest on prehistoric foundations, however.

The Hari Rud, which drains out of the mountains of central Afghanistan westward, is the only source of perennial water in the vast region to the south of the mountains of Khurasan and along the western fringe of the central Afghan ranges. Much of this territory is desert country broken here and there by an oasis or in close to the mountains by a patch of fertile soil watered by a local stream or spring upon whose vagaries a small

---

[11] S. Piggott, "Dating the Hissar Sequence; The Indian Evidence," *Antiquity*, Vol. XVII, No. 68 (1943), pp. 169–182.

[12] Piggott, 1950.

[13] Masson, 1960, especially pp. 30–31.

[14] The terms Early, Middle, Late Hissar, as used here, mean as follows: Early Hissar: Hissar IA-IB (in part), Sialk III 1–3 (4). Middle Hissar: Hissar IC(B), Sialk III(3) 4–5 (6). Late Hissar: Hissar IC-IIA, Sialk III 6–7, 7b.

[15] C. K. Wilkinson, "The Iranian Expedition 1936," *Bulletin of the Metropolitan Museum of Art*, Vol. XXXII (1937).

[16] Dupree, 1964, p. 638.

PLATE 3   *The cave site of Ghar-i-Mar, northern Afghanistan.* (Courtesy of
Louis Dupree.)

population depends. Nowadays a modern highway, along which a vehicle
can speed for hours at no slower a rate of speed than sixty miles per hour,
traverses this country which in not too distant times required a long and
difficult journey if one wished to cross it. The modern highway skirts to
the north of the town of Farah, which marks the point where the mountains end and the Registan deserts of southern Afghanistan begin. The
plain around Farah is watered by the Farah Rud and is well cultivated.
There are a number of sites there, one of which, Tepe Barangtud, is
certainly prehistoric.[17] Its pottery, which is of the black on buff prehistoric
painted type, indicates affinities with areas farther south, in Seistan;
Farah, in fact, is the northern gateway to this great delta region of the
south. Seistan is the delta for the river Helmand—one of the famous
streams of antiquity, whose source is near Kabul, capital of Afghanistan.
This river flows out of the mountains near Girishk, another major stopping
point on the route that connects Farah with Kandahar, Afghanistan's
second city. The Helmand River splits the Registan desert of southern
Afghanistan in two and flows south until turned by the high ground along
the present border with Pakistan, then flows due west until it enters the
Seistan plain, into which it flows from the south, spreading out into a broad
shallow *hamun*, or lake.

---

[17] This site was first visited by Miss Beatrice de Cardi in 1948, and by me in 1951.
It has never been excavated.

PLATE 4 *The wind-swept desolation of the Dasht-i-Zirreh of Seistan. The seated figure is gazing toward the remains of a prehistoric cemetery.*

 ❋ *Seistan*

SEISTAN OCCUPIES THE LOWEST ELEVATION of the great Tertiary basin of southern Afghanistan. The perennial water of the Helmand makes Seistan an oasis in the midst of deserts. The climate is subject to extremes, especially in summer, when temperatures above 120° F. are common enough. The hot summers are mitigated somewhat by the so-called "wind of 120 days," which blows from May to September out of the northwest. High-velocity winds are frequent in this period, and these velocities are matched in winter. The British boundary surveyors there shortly after 1900 recorded winter blasts up to 120 miles per hour.[18] It is winter too when what little rainfall there is descends.

In spite of the climate, Seistan has excellent assets in perennial water and alluvial soil. The wind, in fact, also has its beneficial side, since it drives off insects and its steady blowing out of the northwest makes possible the orientation of roof ventilators through which the wind is funneled to screens of soaked reeds or branches, resulting in decided coolness in the rooms beneath. It also is used for windmills.

[18] G. P. Tate, *The Frontiers of Baluchistan*, London, 1909. See also Tate, *Seistan, Memoir on the History, Topography, Ruins and People* (2 vols.), Government of India, Calcutta, 1910–1912.

Seistan was a critical station on the route from Kerman, in southeastern Iran, in medieval times. From Seistan caravans could journey up the Helmand valley or at least stay in its proximity in the long journey across the Dasht-i-Margo to Kandahar. Such was the route taken in reverse by Krakocrates, one of Alexander's generals, on the return from India. Routes connecting northeast Iran to Kandahar, however, tended either to cross the mountains from some point on the Hari Rud or by staying close to the southern foothills to avoid the longer route via Seistan and the Helmand River valley. It is thus no coincidence that throughout history Seistan has had closer ties to Kerman and the Makran coast, and to the Persian Gulf, than to other parts of Iran.

However, the place has always had an air of mystery about it, and it shows mightily in the sacred, legendary, and historical accounts of Iran. Rustam, the great folk hero of the *Shah Namah*, is said to have been born there, while Zoroaster, founder of Persia's great faith, found refuge in Seistan in the sixth century B.C. with Vishtaspa, father of the Achaemenid king, Darius the Great. Many are the stories connected with the Kuh-i-Khwaja, an extinct volcanic neck which, buttelike, sticks up out of the flat delta and is the seat of numerous temple ruins. In many ways Seistan is the last great center of strictly Iranian tradition on the road to India.

British surveyors and travelers from about 1860 on had noted that Seistan was strewn with ancient remains. It was Sir Aurel Stein, however, who discovered that the area to the south of the great *hamun* was the locale of numerous sites of prehistoric time. He collected from several of these, and his material established the fact that the prehistoric culture represented was essentially of southern Iranian type.[19] In the winter of 1950-1951 we managed to set up a base camp near Chahar Burjak in the extreme south of the Afghan portion of Seistan. From here we could cross the Helmand River at a point where the river turned north to empty into the *hamun*.[20] From prehistoric times into the Islamic period a considerable volume of water used to flow out of the Helmand due west into what is now called the Southern Delta, where Stein found the prehistoric remains on the Iranian side. This old branch of the Helmand River has a discernible dried-up course known as the Rud-i-Biyaban. Along the banks of this extinct stream one can see the remains of a thousand years of occupation made all the more dramatic by vestiges of irrigation channels and reservoir systems of considerable complexity.

The prehistoric sites are frequently marked by black-topped mesa or buttelike outcrops of alluvium. It would seem that one of the main attrac-

19 Sir M. A. Stein, *Innermost Asia. Detailed report of explorations in central Asia, Kan-Su, and eastern Iran*, Oxford University Press, London, 1928.
20 Walter A. Fairservis, Jr., "Archaeological Studies in the Seistan Basin of Southwestern Afghanistan and Eastern Iran," *Anthropological Papers of the American Museum of Natural History*, Vol. XLVIII, Pt. 1 (1961), pp. 1–128.

tions of this part of Seistan was its resources in copper, for the black topping of the outcrops is principally the slag resulting from copper smelting. Inevitably the slag is mixed with the potsherds, bone, and other habitation debris of the prehistoric occupation. In other prehistoric sites a checkerboardlike appearance has resulted from the accumulation of habitation debris in the rooms of the village. With the wind erosion of the mud-brick walls of the houses, the debris within sank in place, marking the interiors which the walls once surrounded. Broken pottery, like the slag, frequently has acted to preserve the surface beneath from erosion, so that as the surrounding soil was swept away by the fierce and constant winds, the sherd- or slag-capped areas rose out of the landscape like towers. Indeed, shortly after the time of Christ the then rulers of Seistan used these prehistoric "towers" as the foundation for a limes, or protective line, across the Southern Delta. Wonderful is the work of the wind in such situations, for when we stumbled onto a prehistoric cemetery in a veritable maze of buttes, we discovered that some of the graves were above our heads! The wind had not only cut the surrounding earth away but had undercut some of the remains, so that we were able to remove the funerary appurtenances of men of prehistoric times who had been buried here by plucking the objects down from above our heads!

In such circumstances the archaeologist has little to excavate; the wind has done it all! But it has also obscured whatever stratigraphy was present.

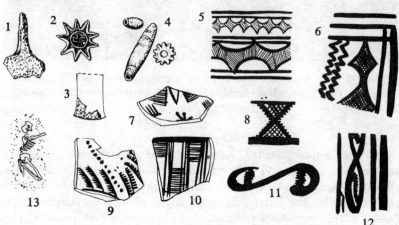

FIG. 24 *Material culture of prehistoric Seistan.*
1—*Dagger or spear blade (bronze)*
2—*Metal seal*
3—*Axe blade (bronze)*
4—*Stone beads*
5–12—*Typical designs on pottery*
13—*Flexed burial*

However, analysis of our findings along with those of Sir Aurel Stein indicates that generally one major phase of prehistoric occupation is represented (see Fig. 24). This was a phase of developed farming which flourished here probably around 3000 B.C. From all we can establish, these people probably lived in mud-brick squarish houses in settlements varying from a few families to probably as many as six hundred to a thousand souls. They were extensive users of copper, which they made into pins, needles, axes, knives, beads, bangles, and possibly figurines. This

PLATE 5 *The wind-excavated grave of a prehistoric villager in southern Seistan. The knife blade is roughly opposite the vertebrae, the blade pointing toward the flexed legs.*

copper was mined, smelted, hammered, and possibly cast. They were fine carvers of stone and were particularly fond of vessels made out of alabaster, though they did carve steatite or more darkish stone into comparable vessels. The latter they often engraved with geometric designs. Beads of lapis, carnelian, and agate were apparently very popular. They wove mats and probably cloth (of an unknown fiber) and made baskets. As potters they made a variety of shapes with a buffish clay on which they frequently painted geometric and occasionally natural motifs in black. Very common and quite extraordinary in its delicacy was a light gray pottery which too was often decorated with black painted designs. Stamp seals may well have been used, but only one problematical one has been found.

Leaf-shaped arrow points and delicate needlelike blades of flint indicate a fine technique of chipped-stone tool manufacture even though copper and polished or ground stone seem to have taken much of the place that chipped stone held in earlier cultures elsewhere.

The dead were buried in a flexed position in cists made of mud brick. Funerary furniture was placed with the corpse and included pottery, jewelry, and such objects of daily life as tools and weapons.

Sheep, goats, and cattle are indicated but not confirmed, owing to the fragmentary nature of the remains. Some large stone grinding slabs suggest that agriculture was practiced. Indeed, the well-watered Southern Delta must have provided a good crop. This, with the copper and other natural resources, must have provided a good basis for the simple economy of these prehistoric men.

Yet one is puzzled by the fact that the evidence is nearly everywhere of one kind. It is as if prehistoric man reached here in one movement, flourished for a time, and then for unknown reasons left. Of course, the vagaries of a delta may be the answer. The Helmand River alluvium may well cover earlier and later periods of prehistoric time—perhaps newer investigations will reveal what Stein's work and our earlier researches could not. The Italians are presently working at Rudbar nearby (App. H).

One thing is clear, however, and that is that the cultural representation we do have evidence for is southern in its affinities. It directly relates to the Makran and to such desert basins of southeastern Iran as that of Bampur (see Fig. 25). In other words, an arm of the southern "wing" of prehistoric Iranian farming culture had reached Seistan late in the fourth millennium B.C., demonstrating how much slower these southern regions were in the diffusion eastward than the north, on the present evidence. This leads to a suspicion that geographical factors were playing a particular role in providing the Toynbeean challenge to which farming cultures here were late to respond. For it is clear that between Fars, where earlier food-producing cultures have been found in some abundance, and such regions as Seistan lie only pockets where water and soil combine to make year round settlement possible. Thus we are brought to the question as to whether the diffusion of wheat and barley farming from the west toward the east in these southerly regions was a kind of oasis-hopping or whether a developed technology and an understanding of hydrology made possible a control of resources between these oases. Was it the reservoir or the khanat or the water wheel that made possible human occupancy of regions where there was no perennial water? Or perhaps a social organization which provided for storage of foodstuffs for specialists and farmers alike in months of drought? Seistan suggests an answer to these questions. It suggests that perennial water was still a necessary concomitant of settlement. Prehistoric man around 3500 B.C. in these regions still lacked the means to make the desert flower.

✳ *The Kandahar Area—Mundigak*

THIS WOULD SEEM TO HAVE CONFIRMATION of a kind in the next major fertile region to the east, and indeed the last within the inner Iranian physiographic zone proper. Kandahar City is located at the foot of the Koh-i-Baba ranges where the Argandab River and its tributaries, like the Tarnak, debouch from the mountains. The Argandab eventually joins the Helmand River near Kala Bist and Lashkari Bazaar, Mahmud of Ghazni's old winter capital. Mahmud controlled the passes from Kandahar eastward and so was able to cross into the subcontinent at will. His will took the form of numerous devastating conquests, which underlined how very much the people of the subcontinent were vulnerable to the northwest frontier, a frontier which on the Afghan side centers in its southern aspect on Kandahar.

In the same season as the exploration of Seistan, our party was able to survey the fertile plain to the south and east of Kandahar City proper.[21] This plain is a kind of rough right triangle lying on its side. The southerly boundary is the Tarnak River, which runs close to the dune bluffs of the Registan. To the north the mountains and then the Argandab River incline to the west till joined at the apex of the triangle by the Tarnak River. Eastward the land is generally barren. In this area there are numerous sites, two of which are most certainly prehistoric: Deh Morasi Ghundai and Said Kala.[22] Four cuts were made in Deh Morasi Ghundai, two of which reached virgin soil. The evidence indicates that the site represents a single phase of developed village farming. The artifacts recovered include both black on buff and gray pottery, some of which is typologically like that of Seistan. Spindle whorls suggest weaving, and abundant fragments of copper attest to that industry. Alabaster vessels and compartmented stone seals found here are familiar in comparable-period sites in Baluchistan as well as in those of northeastern Iran. Dupree, who made one of the cuts (Cut 4) in the site, recovered a piece of native iron which obviously had been flaked as if of stone. He also recovered two stone hoes along with evidence for barley cultivation.[23]

Most interesting perhaps was the find of a peculiar pedestal-based goggle-eyed figurine of a female found associated with a brick structure

---

[21] Walter A. Fairservis, Jr., "Preliminary Report on the Prehistoric Archaeology of the Afghan-Baluchi Areas," *American Museum Novitates*, No. 1587 (1952), American Museum of Natural History, New York.

[22] See Appendix D for list of sites in the Kandahar area.

[23] L. B. Dupree, "Deh Morasi Ghundai: A Chalcolithic Site in South-Central Afghanistan," *Anthropological Papers of the American Museum of Natural History*, Vol. L, Pt. 2 (1963), pp. 59–135.

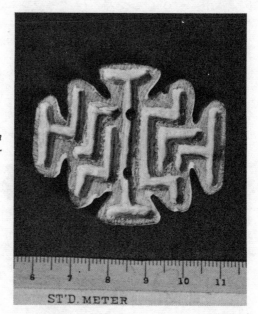

ST'D. METER

some forty-five by twenty-eight centimeters in size. The forehead of the figurine is incised and smeared with red paint (Fig. 38). Near it were some pottery, goat horns, a seal, a piece of hollow copper tubing, and an alabaster cup. Cut 4 was made at a high point at the east end of the mound, and this so-called "shrine" appears to have been enclosed in a building or compound of mud-brick walls. The evidence from Cuts 1 through 3 indicates that this building was in the midst of a habitation area made up of smallish mud-brick buildings. Thus it was either a kind of household shrine or a public building within the village. The latter seems more likely in view of the evidence elsewhere (see p. 145).

Said Kala Ghundai was also briefly examined by the sinking of two *sondages.* One of these went down somewhat over six meters before water rushing into the sides of the cut made further excavation impossible. The material from the upper levels of the site was essentially the same as that from Deh Morasi Ghundai (B), but with a suggestion of a slightly earlier phase (A). Below these levels, without a perceptible break, were levels containing an assemblage of crude handmade and basket-marked pottery with here and there some fine wheel-made potsherds to indicate that the people of those days were at least familiar with the products of the more advanced technique.

One came away from the Tarnak-Argandab sites with a sense that they represented a localization of strong traditions of developed village farming.

To the north of Kandahar City is a valley above the valley of the Argandab River called the Kishk-i-Nakhod, where the French Archaeological

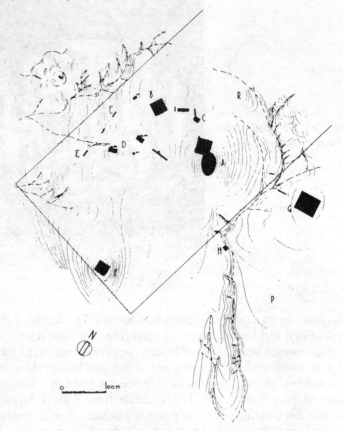

MAP 11 *Plan of the site of Mundigak. The dark areas mark the points of excavation* (after Casal).

Mission in Afghanistan discovered the prominent prehistoric site of Mundigak in April, 1951.[24]

The critical locale is the largest point (150 meters at the base) (Tepe A) of an extensive deposition which spreads out apparently contiguously. It is (or was) conical in shape, rising some twenty meters above the plain. This plain is situated on the route along which caravans historically have moved to and from Herat and where the seasonal nomads move between the highlands and the lowlands.

The excavations provided evidence for seven main periods, of which the first four are of importance here.

Period I (the earliest) consists of five subperiods. The two earliest of these were probably representative of a seminomadic people who lived in

[24] Some ten seasons of excavation have produced a definite stratigraphy for this region.

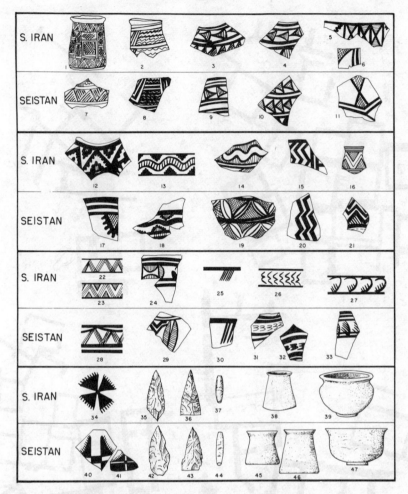

FIG. 25 *Comparison of certain artifact styles found in southeastern Iran (Bampur area) with those found in Seistan. (The southeast Iranian material is principally of the Khurab stage—see Appendix H.)*

tents or temporary pole houses of some kind. These were succeeded in subperiod 3 by people who built semipermanent pisé houses. In phases 4 and 5 the remains of small houses made of crude brick, sometimes on pisé and stone foundations, were uncovered. Those of phase 5 indicate that larger, more extensive structures than those of phase 4 (3 meters by 1.75 meters) were made. Some of these were rectangular and divided into two rooms. Hearths occur in the centers of the main rooms, and in the midst of the houses occasional ovens or kilns were located. Some of these were

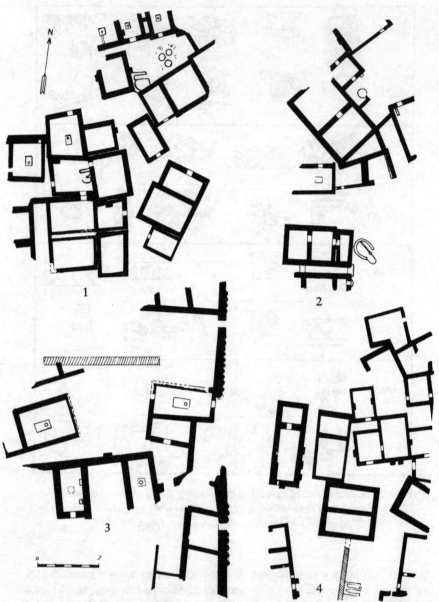

FIG. 26 *Characteristic house plans for Periods I (2), II (4) III (1) and IV (3) at Mundigak. The colonnaded facade of the large structure of Period IV is shown in plan (3) (after Casal).*

apparently for pottery manufacture. Actually the excavator's period division here can be criticized, since there is a sharp division between his subphases 3 and 4 not only in architecture but in artificial content. The characteristic pottery of subphases 2 and 3 is a painted ware, black on red; in the nearby Quetta valley at Kile Gul Mohammad there is a similar black-on-red ware. This ware is wheel-made and has its closest typological affinities to McCown's Chashma Ali culture in northern Iran (see Fig. 34), a fact of immense significance. The succeeding phases 4 and 5, however, not only contain examples of the Kile Gul Mohammad ware but add the jars and cups and design repertoire, including black and red polychrome painting, familiar in Quetta as the Kechi Beg wares, and which in turn have their equivalents in the early Hissar culture of northeastern Iran (Fig. 35).

Figurines of cattle begin to appear in phase 3 and those of humans in 4, but both copper and alabaster were apparently used from at least phase 2 on. Interestingly enough, handmade pottery occurs in all phases but in a decided minority. The excavator rightfully comments that this whole period seems to reflect the arrival of a culture already full-blown. As he would see it: "Il paraît plus probable que les premiers occupants de Mundigak venaient d'ailleurs et qu'après avoir pendant un certain temps utilisé le site comme une halte, ces nomades s'y fixèrent. Mais ils amenaient avec eux des éléments d'une civilisation déjà évolvée."[25]

Period II is divided from Period I by a thick layer of soil mixed with habitation debris and ash. This may well mark a period of destruction of the old village, or it may simply mean the cleaning of one section for new construction. Period II in its earlier phases (1 and 2) continues the same kind of architecture as in Period I. There is, however, a feeling of denser occupation, since there are more houses within the same space. The characteristic house seems to have been rectangular, as before, but divided into a small room (*ca.* 2 by 4.5 meters) and a larger room (*ca.* 4-5 by 6 meters), which were connected by an interior door, in a typical case (Fig. 26). Interesting was the finding of a well amid the houses, sunk deeply into the virgin soil but passing through the layers of earlier habitation. The curb of the well was of brick, and its sides within the habitation layers were of pisé. The last phase of Period II (3a and 3b) witnessed the construction of houses seemingly without doors to the outside, though they are essentially the same in plan as the earlier houses. One speculates as to whether this meant that the walls were supports for a wooden superstructure or an upper living story, or whether, since floors of beaten earth with hearths are present, access to the interior was obtained by ladder, as occurs elsewhere in the ancient world. The pottery of the period is surprisingly crude compared with that of Period I, and though some of the familiar types of that period occur, the wares are dominantly handmade. Sling

[25] J. M. Casal, *Fouilles de Mundigak, Mémoires de la Délégation Archéologique Française en Afghanistan*, Librairie C. Klincksieck, T. XVII, Paris, 1961.

stones, stone arrow points, and a crude stone button seal were found in these levels. Spindle whorls (cone-shaped) and bone points are also common. The whole period, however, has few innovations or additions and seems to represent a kind of leveling off. Perhaps the outside interests that caused the diffusion of new patterns and techniques were weak in this period.

Period III, on the other hand, witnessed a kind of florescence. Not only are the ceramics found in Period II continued but there is a gradual reduction in the number of handmade wares, so that by phase 6 the percentage of these within the total of all wares is only 15 per cent. The period is marked, however, by the exuberant painted pottery which both by form and by design belongs to a family of wares found from northeast Iran to north central Baluchistan. This style is the marker of the Middle Hissar culture in the northeast (Fig. 36), and it is practically potsherd for potsherd

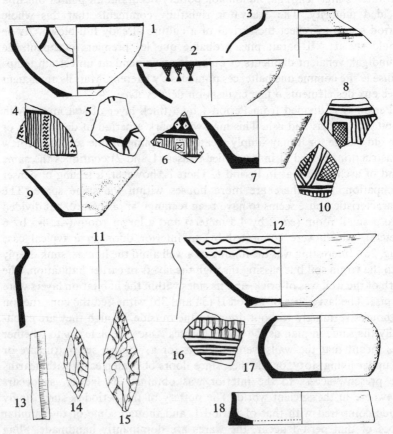

FIG. 27 *Characteristic artifacts of Periods I (1–10) and II (11–18) at Mundigak (after Casal).*

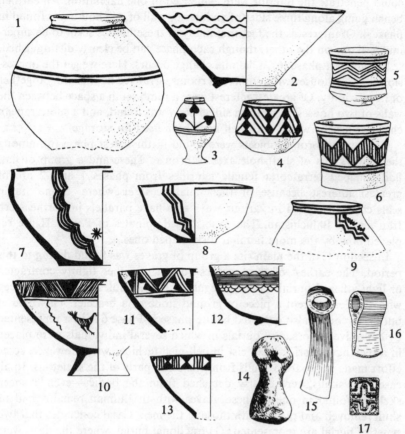

FIG. 28 *Characteristic artifacts of Period III at Mundigak* (after Casal).
1–14—*Pottery and clay objects*
15–16—*Bronze axes*
17—*Clay seal*

identical with that of the so-called Quetta ware first made known by Stuart Piggott.[26] The structures of phases 1 through 5 are not unlike those of the previous periods, but with greater emphasis upon what appear to be small blocks of rooms (up to five), each giving access to the outside but with few inner connections. Wells within the dwelling area appear to continue. There is some evidence for wooden rafters though the method of using them is not quite clear. One house, however, contained a central pillar, suggesting a support for a long span. Small windows set so the sun's rays

[26] S. Piggott,"A New Prehistoric Ceramic from Baluchistan," *Ancient India*, No. 3 (1947), pp. 131–142. See also Figure 28.

could penetrate the interior were evidenced in one habitation. An earthen bench going along three sides of an interior wall of one house was found in phase 4. Of interest is the fact that many of these houses seem to be superimposed one on the other, though each phase can be clearly distinguished.

In the latest phase (6), a definite change occurs. Here we get the impression of large houses with numerous rooms, arranged haphazardly together or in proximity. Of greatest interest were a tomb set in a space between the walls of two houses, in which a single body was found, and a subterranean chamber nearby which may well have been used for storage.

Copper and bronze objects were found in this latest phase (6), among them two kinds of shaft-hole axes of bronze. These and a group of flat, fiddle-shaped terra-cotta female figurines from phases 1 and 2 are of greatest interest because of their analogues, elsewhere. Stone stamp seals compartmented in various ways also have parallels in northeastern Iran and in Baluchistan. The cone-shaped spindles of Period II are replaced now by the more familiar disk-shaped ones.

In section C of the main site a group of graves was found dating to this period. The earliest of these graves consist of either tightly contracted or lightly flexed burials laid in irregularly shaped holes. Little was placed with the dead except a piece of ground stone or a bracelet. This type of burial, of course also occurred before phase 6. Phase 6 is best represented by collective, or ossuary, burials in which several individuals were placed in a rectangular brick-lined cist in pell-mell fashion, with, however, some effort made to separate skulls from the other parts of the skeletons. In all cases the skulls were clearly detached from the bodies—even a sheep skeleton found in one of these graves with the human remains had its skull removed and placed with those of the men. Casal concludes that two types of burial are represented: (1) fractional burial, where the dead were defleshed elsewhere; (2) burial of partially dissected corpses or of parts of corpses. As with the single graves, little grave furniture was found.

Period IV witnessed the vast expansion of what had been in the previous period a substantial village. The whole of the site was now occupied. So vast is the occupation apparently that the excavator speaks of an urban period. However, there is no break between periods III and IV, and pottery, seals, figurines are similar, with certain critical differences to be mentioned in context.

Characteristic of the period in all its three phases was the construction of monumental buildings on high points of the site (Tepes A,B,G). In addition, a great enclosure wall was built, apparently both to connect these high points and to enclose the main and highest mound (Tepe A). These high points connected by the wall are referred to by Casal as "bastions." They are essentially units of small compartments connecting with one another and apparently once inhabited. The main wall was made up of an inner and outer wall with a passage between (ca. 2 meters). The outer wall was about 1.20 meters thick and reinforced on the exterior by rectangular buttresses of brick. The inner wall was thinner, 1 to .75 meters. The wall foundations were dry stone set in a mud or clay mortar to a height of about 1 meter. On this the main brick structure was constructed. There are traces of steps, indicating that access to the unknown height of the wall was readily obtained.

The "bastions" were placed at angles of the main wall, and their exterior faces were buttressed in a similar fashion. The main wall was traced for almost three hundred meters. The north and south walls were not followed but appear to be intended eventually to enclose the main mound. In the other direction, apparently a second wall was extended to the west to provide an enclosure for that inhabited area, but its extent was not traced.

Almost due east of the main mound, some two hundred meters away, a small hillock rises on which an unusual structure was found. It appears to

Fig. 29 *Characteristic artifacts of Period IV at Mundigak (after Casal).*
1–14, 16—Pottery and figurines of clay
15—Bronze pin

have been a building devoted to ceremonial activity. It was surrounded by a compartmented wall faced with pointed or toothlike buttresses or decorative elements. Within, and separated from the wall by a passage, as well as being slightly elevated above it, was a building made up of square or rectangular rooms varying in size from a few meters to six or seven meters in length. Hearths and traces of brick flooring occur here and there within these rooms. The most interesting of these chambers was one in the western part of the building. In its southeast corner stood a square block of masonry. Against its two exposed faces were benches or tables. The whole of the block and these objects were plastered or painted white. A third bench or table, also plastered in the same color, was located on the east wall nearby. At approximately the center of the room was a large rectangular hearth somewhat elevated and painted red on its sides. On its western side, another bench was placed a bit lower than the hearth.

In a kind of court to the west of the chamber, and on which the chamber opened, another hearth was found, somewhat oval in shape and considerably elevated. Both this part of the court and the floor of the little chamber were ash covered, suggesting an extensive use of the hearths. Starting close to the wall of the hearth chamber and following the slope of the court to where a sump was located at the foot of the enclosure wall was a drain made up of fitted pottery units.

The most important building, or at least the most prominent, is the so-called palace which was situated on the highest part of the site (Mound or Tepe A). Because of erosion the plan of the building in its entirety was somewhat obscured, but enough remains to evidence a truly monumental structure. This building went through at least three renovations. Essentially, however, it consisted of a striking brick half "colonnade." Against a brick wall, half cylinders of bricks were set and topped by a brick frieze of step design. The whole was set on a brick foundation fronting on a paved court (?). It was plastered or painted white. This portico was pierced in several places, giving access to a series of rooms and small courts, some of which contained hearths. In the third and last of the major renovations of this building, long rectangular structures (E-W) were set in the northern court in front of the colonnade and the fine façade ruined. These later structures contain traces of drains, niches, and stairs leading to a vanished superstructure. Their formality suggests a public building. However, Casal indicates the possibility that the structure was defensive, based on the presence of arrow points, sling pellets, and signs of conflagration.

Behind the old colonnade a massive platform some five meters thick was built, and behind this another wall was constructed. Access through the old colonnade was still obtainable by entering a small chamber in the west, which in turn gave access to a stairway onto the platform. On the south side of the platform a colonnade emulating the first one was apparently constructed, but little of it remained. A doorway through this

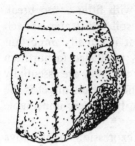

FIG. 30   *Stone head of Period IV (3) at Mundigak* (after Casal).

colonnade, however, gave access to a series of small apparently doorless chambers on the south. An enigmatic depression, a drain probably, was found on the eastern end of the main platform.

The two phases of Period IV which follow were difficult to trace archaeologically. It does appear that the "palace" and building on Mound G (Tepe G) were deserted. Perhaps the population was decreasing or changes were occurring to make the large settlement of the first phase less practicable. In any case there is no question but that the larger part of the inhabitants remained.

In general the artifacts of the later phases of Period IV show some changes in style. There is a tendency in the painting of pottery toward the use of naturalistic design, both floral and animal, and toward a breakdown of the strict geometry of the earlier phases. The familiar "Zhob mother goddess" found at Deh Morasi Ghundai appears in Period IV (1-2) (Fig. 29: 10, 14), but the type is replaced in the last phase by a far less finished form. However, it was in this latter phase that a fine white calcite head of a man was recovered. The head is distinguished by a hairband dropped in the back that is familiar in style to one known from Mohenjo-daro (Fig. 30). Stone stamp seals are abundant throughout the period. Another artifact of importance, because of its analogy in northeast Iran, is a spiral-headed pin of bronze. Bronze or copper objects, such as mirrors, lance heads, hooks, and pins, are evidenced for the period.

Alabaster vessels are attested. But of great interest, because they are widely found, especially in the south (see p. 125), are stone vessels carved with geometric designs familiar in the painted pottery. Other objects of importance to stylistic correlations elsewhere are clay model houses also painted with the pottery designs. These are especially familiar in the Quetta Valley.

Period V shows some continuity with the last phase of Period IV, but new elements are introduced that lead to other problems of protohistoric time which will be described later (see p. 359).

The sequence at Mundigak, while reflecting outside influences, also stresses continuity. One period follows another with little or no break between, suggesting that the same resources of soil and water as well perhaps as trade were durable throughout. What is equally important is the fact that the Mundigak sequence is closely paralleled in northern Baluchistan—so much so, in fact, that one can say that they are essentially of one and the same tradition. More distant but nonetheless direct is the relationship to northeastern Iran, to which region there were undeniable continuing connections.

The Mundigak sequence is remarkable in its expression of primitive beginnings in Period I (1-3), after which we witness a gradual physical expansion of settlement, an increase in population, and an increasing sophistication of cultural form, climaxed in Period IV by a development which suggests the presence of temples, palaces, and other large public structures requiring large collective effort, a corps of specialists, and hierarchical leadership. This result is so contrary to the usual line of development among these early farming communities of the Iranian plateau that it is obvious that different factors are at work in this area. If we dismiss the idea that the evidence shows an indigenous evolution unique to the Kandahar region, which idea is indeed unsupportable, it becomes obvious that other influences were involved, influences derived from sources other than those of Iran. The proximity of the subcontinent points the way.

❋ Baluchistan—The Quetta Valley

EAST OF KANDAHAR the central Afghan ranges join with the Sulaiman Mountains in upland country where cultivation is confined to watered valleys or small grassy slopes and plateaus. Large areas are barren and settlement relatively sparse until one enters the Sulaimans, which lead to the plains of the Punjab and the valleys of Baluchistan. The country is, then, the transition zone from the Iranian plateau proper to the subcontinent; there is a descent from the upland country to the plains. Historically the one who controlled the line Kandahar-Ghazni-Kabul dominated the passes to India. This fact caused many a heated conference in high circles of nineteenth-century London and St. Petersburg. Sufficient for our purposes to note that at this end of the Iranian plateau geography sets one's face firmly toward the subcontinent. Though archaeological exploration of this region (Kandahar-Ghazni-Kabul-Peshawar-Fort Sandeman-Kandahar) is by no means complete, sufficient work has been done to indicate that only in the southern portion (Kandahar-Fort Sandeman and vicinity) did late prehistoric man settle his villages in any density. The largely rocky and soil-poor valleys inhabited today by the Pathans were

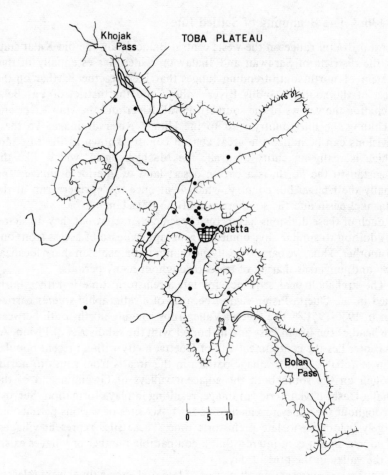

MAP 12 *Map of the Quetta Valley showing site distribution.*

not of great attraction, nor indeed could they be developed for adequate food production by the means then at hand.[27]

The picture is entirely different, however, from Fort Sandeman south and west, in that region known today as eastern Baluchistan. Here the valleys are broad, though largely barren, and sources of water vary from abundant (Zhob, Hab, Porali, Anambar rivers; artesian wells; springs) to very poor.

Baluchistan can be divided naturally into four broad regions: the northeast, running from the Gomel River valley in a great loop south and west to include the Zhob, Pishin, and Anambar river systems of the districts of Zhob and Loralai and the well-watered Quetta Valley; the flat plain of Kachhi, lying in the cul-de-sac between the Bugti hills in the east and the

[27] Dr. A. H. Dani reports orally that his recent explorations (1967) in the Waziristan region discovered a few sites of late prehistoric vintage.

central Brahui range on the west; central Baluchistan, the old Kalat state of the districts of Sarawan and Jhalawan, which lies essentially in that system of north-south-trending ranges that includes the Kirthar on the west of the southern Indus River Valley; and the district of Las Bela, including the valleys of the southern Porali River and the Hab River and including the hill country west to the Hingol River drainage. To these divisions can be added the great coastal country known as the Makran, which is really an entity of itself; the Mashkel basin, which, like the Registan to the north, is a barren desert land of interior drainage; and finally the Chagai hill country, which is at once the northern rim of the Mashkel basin and the southern rim of the Registan.

Each of these divisions has its own specific character, but they do share, in addition to similar environments, geographical ease of access from one to another. Thus, we paradoxically encounter in Baluchistan sharp localization and universal sharing of traits throughout many periods.

The archaeological sequence for late prehistoric time is rather fairly fixed in the Quetta-Pishin region because of stratigraphic studies carried out in 1950-1951.[28] The Quetta Valley runs roughly north-south between the head of the Bolan Pass and its border with the subdistrict of Pishin. At its center lies the cantonment city of Quetta, a city with a present population of 250,000. The drainage pattern in the area is from south to north, though on the south both the adjacent valleys of Gwandin and of the Bhalla Dasht have interior drainage, resulting in playa formation. Surveys throughout the valley revealed some thirty-six sites of various periods but largely belonging to late prehistoric time. These sites represent villages, of course, and it is of interest that a comparable number of villages exists in the valley in the present day.

Four sites, representing all phases of late prehistoric time, were selected as important for excavation, and the results of these excavations then provided a standard by which to place the remainder of the sites in the valley and in adjacent regions in their relative chronological position. It should be emphasized that the prime aim of this work was to provide just such a standard. There were neither funds nor time to extend the excavations so as to determine fully the available evidence for the way of life of each period involved. This is the obvious next step and one which we have wanted to take for these many years, but we have been thwarted by a plethora of difficulties.

Of the excavated sites, Kile Gul Mohammad (Q-24), located just north of Quetta City, proved to be of greatest importance, since it provided evidence for the earliest occupation by food producers of Baluchistan so

---

[28] Walter A. Fairservis, Jr., "Excavations in the Quetta Valley, West Pakistan," *Anthropological Papers of the American Museum of Natural History*, Vol. XLV, Pt. 2 (1956), pp. 169–402.

far known. In a cut which reached a depth of 11.14 meters it was discovered that the lowest 5 meters was representative of a people who, when they first occupied the site, built their huts of pisé and probably wattle and daub. They had herds of goats, sheep, and cattle, and the presence of one or two sickle blades suggests that they cultivated a cereal crop. They also had ground-stone tools as well as those of chipped flint. In the earliest phases (KGM I) these people do not seem to have used pottery, but later they did employ a crude handmade, sometimes basket-marked, ware (KGM II) which they occasionally painted with simple wavy lines. In these later phases mud brick was commonly used for the houses, though pisé was also common. Points and spatulalike implements of bone also occur in these levels, the latter only in the later phases.

Kile Gul Mohammad is located in the plains near the Zarghun Mountains, out of which flows the Hannah River. The evidence indicates that this river became braided in its course across the plain and that these early people settled, therefore, near one of its branches. Other sites of this early phase were located within a few miles of Kile Gul Mohammad (Q.17, 25, 29, 34), and all but one of these (Q-17) were in the proximity of a water course. The exception was located on the tip of a gravel talus overlooking the riverine plain. It is of interest that these sites are concentrated in or about the most fertile and best-watered part of the valley. In Pishin, to the north, however, a site (P-6) of the same period was located on a knoll which rose on a gravel bluff or terrace of a perennial running stream, the country close about being unsuited for agriculture.[29]

This early phase is widely represented in northern Baluchistan. Surface remains indicate its presence in the mound of Periano Ghundai near Fort Sandeman on the northeast and in the heart of the great mound of Dabar Kot far to the southeast in the district of Loralai. Here, too, it has been found at the site of Rana Ghundai (Ia) and in the little mound of Sur Jungal (I) (see pp. 149f.). Recently Miss Beatrice de Cardi has identified it in the northern part of southern Kalat at the site of Anjira (Anjira I), and its latest phases are represented probably in the very earliest levels of Casal's Mundigak Period I. This distribution suggests a northern concentration

---

[29] Nothing quite comparable to the lowest levels at Kile Gul Mohammad (KGM I) has yet been found elsewhere in Baluchistan. The cut at these levels was no more than a meter square, and we can wonder as to whether a true sampling of the level was obtained. For this reason I have placed both KGM I and KGM II in the same phase and treated them as one here. Questions have been raised as to whether one should call KGM I preceramic or aceramic or perhaps ignore it as a kind of bad dream. The fact is that KGM I has at least a dozen phases of occupation (or habitation) represented in it and that there is a slow and gradual appearance of pottery in KGM II, suggesting a slow acceptance of the trait. What is significant is the fact that both KGM I and KGM II are essentially the same cultural assemblage, and as R. J. Braidwood indicated at Jarmo, whether or not pottery was present at one time or another can be overplayed to the detriment of the essential point—the presence of a characteristic way of life.

of early food producers, and this may well be true. In any case it is closest to the routes of diffusion from northern Iran. Radio-carbon dates obtained from samples taken from the upper phase of Kile Gul Mohammad I gave dates around 3300 B.C. (5300 ± 200), so it is entirely possible that the first settlements of this type in the region may go back to as early as 4000 B.C.

Kile Gul Mohammad III witnesses the full appearance of the open-bowl black-on-red-decorated and wheel-made pottery that occurs in Mundigak Period I, phases 2 through 5. This is known locally as Kile Gul Mohammad black on red ware. It was first identified at this site but has been described for Mundigak. In all particulars this level equates with that of Mundigak (Period I[3-4]). The evidence demonstrates larger population and more permanent settlement than hitherto. In the Quetta Valley, sixteen sites have been identified as belonging to this period. Whereas the bulk of these are found in the area where Quetta City now stands, in the most fruitful part of the valley, a few (Q-6, Q-9) are located close to the walls of side valleys in areas that are essentially marginal, that is, where water sources such as streams and springs are uncertain.

Without a break these settlements of the Quetta Valley continue, growing larger in size and increasing to eighteen in number. A new pottery type, called locally Kechi Beg ware but well exemplified in Mundigak (Period I5), arrives full-blown at this time. This ware is truly a climax in the ceramic history of the region. It is a thin, beautifully made ware usually of a buff color and fired quite hard. It takes the usual form of deep, open vases, bowls, and jars. Typically, bands of black interspersed with delicately painted sigmas, hachures, willow leaves, dots and dashes, panels, and even occasionally an animal are used for decoration. So delicate is the painting

PLATE 7   *The Quetta Valley from the site of Damb Sadaat.*

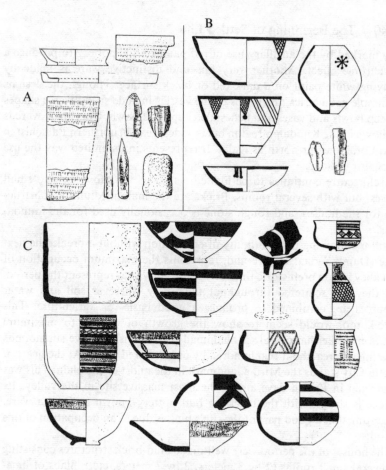

FIG. 31 *Characteristic artifact styles of prehistoric periods identified in the Quetta Valley.*
A—Kile Gul Mohammad I & II
B—Kile Gul Mohammad III
C—Damb Sadaat I

that one gets the impression the potter used a brush made of one or two hairs or fibers. In the Quetta sequence the later levels of this phase are found at both the upper part of Kile Gul Mohammad (IV) and the lowermost level of the mound of Damb Sadaat, or Mian Ghundai[30] as well as at the type site near the village of Kechi Beg. This later phase here is particu-

---

[30] Naming a site is one of the headaches of archaeology in Pakistan. Typically a site is named after the local or nearest village. In turn, many of these villages are named after the headman who is in authority at the time. Upon his demise the name is changed to that of his successor. Woe to the visitor who wants to find Abdullah Damb (mound of Abdullah) when Omar is now headman! In the case of Damb Sadaat, Stuart Piggott, who first described it, referred to it as Mian Ghundai, using its Pushtu reference. The local villagers, being Brahui, called it Damb Sadaat. We have chosen in our surveys to use such names only when tradition has proved their longevity. We tend to use a number system in combination with local names.

larly marked by the ancillary use of red paint on the pottery to produce a polychrome effect. Another very fine and distinctive ware is made by applying white paint on a dark red or black surface. Though the designs are simple geometrics, the forms of the vessels include such diverse shapes as deep bowls and vases and pedestaled cups and bowls. This black ware is unknown in the Kandahar region but is widespread in northern Baluchistan from Loralai as far north as Kalat. It represents in its limited way the use of local traditions.

Architecture continues to be limited, as far as we know here, to small houses, but with several rooms. Bricks are the main medium of construction for the houses, and rough stone is occasionally used for the foundations.

Still maintaining the continuity of occupation without a break, the next stage (Damb Sadaat II), we find, represents the maximum occupation of the valley in late prehistoric time. At least twenty sites represent the period, and they are scattered throughout the valley wherever soil and water resources are combined to produce a good basis for agriculture. This period, too, would seem to show the growth of villages to maximum size. Some, like that of Faiz Mohammad (Q-9), consist of five submounds covering an area about two hundred by one hundred yards. At the heart of Quetta City stands the Miri, a landmark in the midst of the plain. This was an arsenal in British days and is the most massive site in the valley. Its surface is strewn with the black on buff pottery known as Quetta ware, suggesting that a good part of the site's bulk is due to an occupation of this period.

The houses of the period were well-made mud-brick structures consisting of several small rooms (2 by 3 meters, 2 by 7 meters, etc.). Slabs of limestone were used in wall foundations frequently. In some of these houses both fire pits and ovens were located. These "ovens" resemble the "bread" ovens of modern Pakistan which are used for making *khnan* or *chappatti*. They consist of a pit made from a bottomless pottery vessel surrounded by brick. It would appear that charcoal was burned either within the vessel or, in one case, around it, the bread being made by flattening the flour paste against the inner side of the vessel. In some houses large jars attest to inside storage facilities.

Fire pits were made of brick, lined and outlined to provide a confined area. Some of these pits were a meter and a half in length and are found in rooms only two meters in width—an impossible situation suggesting possibly that the roofs of such places were left open. However, in one instance of such a fire-pit chamber, a stone door socket was found *in situ* at its entrance. In view of the extreme cold of the Quetta Valley in winter, one might speculate upon the possibility that some kind of superstructure or conduit was over this chamber conducting heat to occupants above or in the proximity.

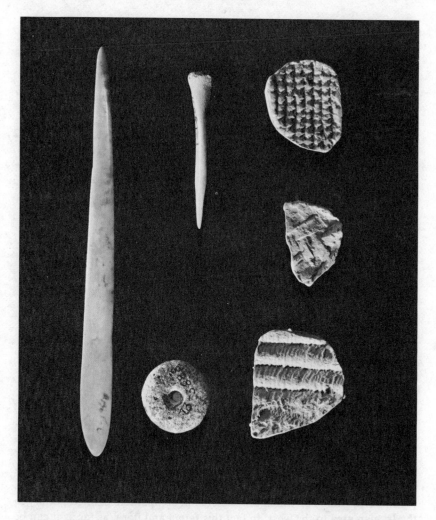

PLATE 8 *Indications of weaving from the site of Damb Sadaat (II), Quetta Valley. The clay impressions on the right were made from impressed pottery; the evidence from top to bottom: bast-fiber cloth, reed matting, basketry. In the center are a bone needle and a stone spindle whorl; on the left, a rib-bone thread separator or perhaps a spatula.* (Courtesy Lee Boltin.)

The artifacts of the period are familiar from Period III at Mundigak. Generally, compartmented stamp seals, animal figurines, chipped- and ground-stone objects (including alabaster vessels, palettes, or metates, clay or stone balls, copper, and, of course, the pottery have their analogues in the Kandahar site, as they do at Rana Ghundai, Sur Jangal, and Dabar Kot in Loralai, and at Periano Ghundai near Fort Sandeman in the Zhob district to the east. Though the Quetta ware is outstanding, the appearance

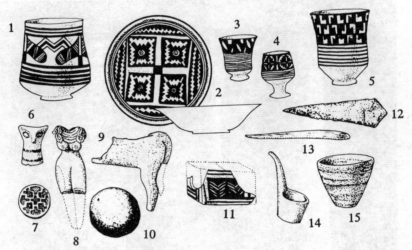

FIG. 32 *Characteristic artifacts at Damb Sadaat II, Quetta Valley.*

1–5—*Pottery*	12—*Bronze knife or dagger blade*
6, 8, 9—*Figurines (clay)*	13—*Bone spatula*
7—*Stamp seal*	14—*Clay ladle*
10—*Clay ball or rattle*	15—*Alabaster vessel*
11—*Model clay house*	

of a magnificent gray ware is worth noting. This we have called Faiz Mohammad gray ware (Fig. 33:2). It consists of deep, open bowls and shallow plates painted on their interior with a series of concentric lines capped at the rim by a single line of loops. The lines surmount the lower portion of the bowl and plate, which is painted with a variety of geometric or naturalistic motifs. Among the latter are fish, birds, snakes, and pipal leaves—none of which are depicted in comparable painted pottery in the Iranian area to the west; in fact this fauna and flora, as far as it can be identified, is common to the subcontinent.

Two other groups of objects make their fullest appearance in this phase. The first is that of figurines of human females and of cattle. The former group consists largely of delicately modeled terra-cotta pieces an inch or somewhat more in size. The figures are full-breasted and distinguished by the depiction of heavy necklaces and strands of hair reaching to the top of the breasts and made by the appliqué method (see Fig. 32:8). The legs are bent forward at the knee and are footless and end in a rather grotesque tapering fashion. No heads have yet been found for this form. Cattle figurines, though more common in the next phase, occur in this one. They possess prominent dewlaps and are painted with black stripes.

The second group of objects is that of the potters' marks. These first occur as early as the first phase of the Kechi Beg ware appearance here, but by this period they are very common. They consist of marks made on

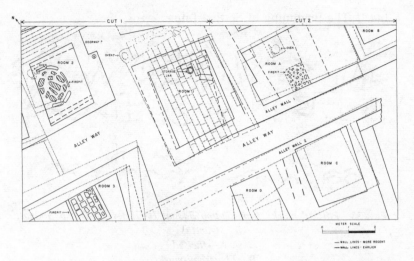

FIG. 33   *Plan of the settlement found in Damb Sadaat II levels, Damb Sadaat, Quetta.*

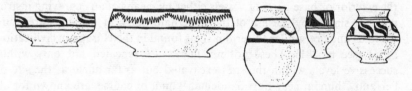

FIG. 34   *Pottery of Damb Sadaat III, Quetta Valley.*

PLATE 9   *Clay stamp seal from the Quetta Valley (DS II) of late prehistoric date.*

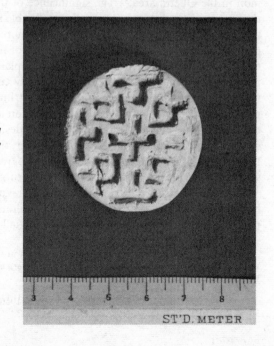

FIG. 35   *Potters' marks from Damb Sadaat II-III levels, Damb Sadaat,*
Quetta.
A—Incised
B—Fingernail-marked

the exterior or base parts of vessels either by means of an engraving instrument or simply by the use of the fingernail. Some of the signs are quite
complex and are similar to certain signs found in the Harappan civilization
script (see p. 281). These potters' marks are repeated not only within
successive levels within the sites excavated but as far afield as the site of
Periano Ghundai near Fort Sandeman[31] and, of course, are known for all
phases of Period IV at Mundigak,[32] though it appears they are most common in the Quetta area.[33] The significance of these potters' marks is that
they represent a system of mutually intelligible symbols commonly accepted through time and space. They are a step more advanced than the pottery
painting described as being an integral part of these developed village cultures in their appearance across the Iranian plateau. In the case of pottery
painting there may well have been originally certain iconographic meanings assigned to the symbols employed, but in this region, at least, such
meanings are by now improbable. So common are these painted vessels in
the habitation sites and so numerous the designs that one suspects the
symbols used are merely decorative. However, the potters' marks are hardly decorative. They suggest concepts such as trade-mark, personal possession, place or person of manufacture, or even good luck!

The final prehistoric period in the Quetta Valley (Damb Sadaat III) is
best represented by the construction of buildings located on the highest
part of a site. The one structure which is partially known was discovered in

---

[31] W. A. Fairservis, Jr., "Archaeological Surveys in the Zhob and Loralai Districts,
West Pakistan," *Anthropological Papers of the American Museum of Natural History,*
Vol. XLVII, Pt. 2 (1959), p. 354, Fig. 59.
[32] Casal, 1961, Figs. 87, 93, 105.
[33] They also occur in northern Kalat. Fairservis, 1956, Pl. 31: pp, qq, at Nushki, Pl.
30:Z.

the uppermost levels of the site of Damb Sadaat.[34] It would appear that, as at Mundigak, the lower habitation layers were leveled somewhat to provide a seat for the building. The building appears to have been essentially a brick platform at least thirty feet wide on one side. In its midst were drains made out of rough limestone blocks. Though the superstructure has not survived, it appears that there were several rooms there, some of which had low beams like those of the "palace" of Mundigak (see p.132). Indications are that a stone bench stood at one time against the southern wall of the platform. There is evidence that spur walls, some almost three meters thick, led from the platform to lower portions of the mound. A dramatic feature connected apparently with the formation of the building was discovered, namely, that its main wall rested upon a small stone-built hollow in which was found a human skull minus its lower jaw. Apparently this indicates some formal consecration of the building.

In the vicinity of this structure some eight female figurines were found, among which were those of the so-called "Zhob mother goddess" type (mentioned earlier) known from Mundigak and Deh Morasi Ghundai (Fig. 38:1). In addition, in Damb Sadaat III levels were uncovered fragments of cattle figurines painted with stripes, even including the horns. A design of unusual interest because of its resemblance to the "yoni," a symbol of the female organs used in Hinduism, is the tear pattern painted on the forehead of some of these animals.

Model houses, clay rattles, stamp seals, copper, alabaster cups, and a repertoire of pottery vessels which, though it includes much of the earlier Quetta-ware types of form and design, tends to simplification are common to the period. This period is the last major prehistoric phase in the valley. It does represent, however, a falling off of the number of villages to ten, though it appears that it also represents larger occupation of fewer places, as if the population were more centralized, as is suggested at Mundigak Period IV, its contemporary. After this period there was a rapid depopulation or at least a decrease in the occupation of the valley, which does not return to a size comparable to its prehistoric levels until Islamic times.

The developments in this final period of prehistoric times in the Quetta Valley have striking parallels in the Kandahar region. The process which is outlined in both areas begins with what appears to be the impermanent establishment of a simple herding-farming life which, after successive stages of more permanent and increasingly elaborate and sophisticated evolvement, is climaxed by a stage where identical emphases upon relatively large populations settled around monumental and presumably public buildings are manifest. It is in these later stages that we are confronted with new elements in the culture unfamiliar in Iran. Among these are the

[34] See L. Alcock, "Appendix i, The Pottery, Site Q8, Cut 1," in Fairservis, 1956, pp. 212ff.

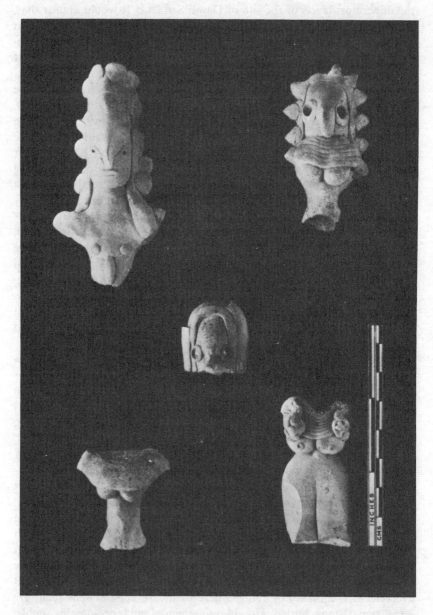

PLATE 10   *Female figurines from northern Baluchistan The type seen in the upper right-hand, center, and lower left-hand positions is commonly known as the "Zhob mother goddess." She is found at sites near Kandahar, Fort Sandeman, Loralai, and in the Damb Sadaat III levels at Quetta. The upper left figure was found on the surface at Damb Sadaat. The lower right lady is from Damb Sadaat (II), Quetta Valley.*

fauna and flora depicted, the peculiar and characteristic figurines, the potters' marks, and certainly the buildings with their drains. They are suggestive of other traditions and perhaps of other peoples.[35]

❋ *Zhob and Loralai*

IN THE DISTRICTS OF LORALAI AND ZHOB, to the east of the Quetta Valley, the story, insofar as our evidence is concerned, is essentially the same as in Quetta. In the Fort Sandeman area, near the junction of the Zhob River with the Gomel, two sites of prehistoric time are well known: Periano Ghundai and Moghul Ghundai.[36] At the former site no deep digging has ever occurred. The place is located close to the banks of a local tributary of the Zhob in the middle of the valley, and the surface remains uncovered indicate that occupation of the site was as early at least as the middle phases of Period I at Mundigak and the third main horizon at Kile Gul Moham-mad (KGM III), owing to the presence of the wares such as KGM black on red and a variety of handmade ware. There is also evidence that the sub-sequent periods are also represented. It is the latest levels, which Sir Aurel Stein probed with some trenches in 1927 and which we were fortu-nate enough to survey in 1950, that produce more definitive evidence. These late levels divide into an earlier phase, which we call the Zhob cult phase, and a later but related phase, the Incinerary Pot phase. The In-cinerary Pot phase is characterized by the burial of individuals in vessels after disarticulation and some cremation. These burials were in the floors of houses. These houses, about which little is known, were made of mud brick resting on stone foundations.

The Zhob cult phase, the earlier, is characterized by the presence of the same goggle-eyed, hooded female figurines known in Damb Sadaat III and in Period IV of Mundigak (Fig. 36:1,4). Leaf-shaped stone arrow

---

[35] A basic difference exists among archaeologists somewhat as the result of training and academic emphases. The historically oriented scholar tends to interpret archaeo-logical evidence in terms of the arrival of new people, in terms of events, and in terms of direct contacts between areas; the anthropologically oriented scholar interprets in terms of the culture process, that is, the always unstatic nature of human culture, which is in-evitably inwardly evolving without necessarily receiving an external stimulus but which, upon receiving that stimulus, tends to trait readjustment or integration without com-pletely losing its entity. Complete change, according to this view, takes place only when the traditional cultural bounds no longer can encompass the adjustments which have occurred, that is, when one can no longer identify the culture by its once established trait configuration. This anthropological orientation characteristically colors the interpreta-tion of New World archaeologists as against that of the Old World ones—which sharpens the controversies.

[36] See (Sir M.) A. Stein, *An Archaeological Tour in Waziristan and Northern Baluchistan*, Memoirs of the Archaeological Survey of India, No. 37, Government of India, New Delhi, 1929, pp. 33–49.

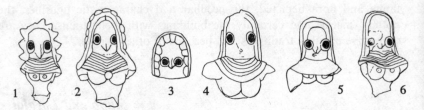

FIG. 36 *The so-called "Zhob mother goddess," which is found widely in the Afghan-northern Baluch areas. It is a remarkable example of the common cultural expression of the prehistoric times in these regions.*

1—*Quetta, Damb Sadaat III*
2—*Kandahar, Deh Morasi Ghundai IIa*
3—*Loralai, Sur Jangal III (?)*
4—*Kandahar, Mundigak IV (1)*
5—*Zhob, Periano Ghundai (Zhob cult phase)*
6—*Loralai, Dabar Kot (Stein's Cut E)*

points and one of bronze and more magnificent bull figurines of terra cotta are also characteristic of this period. A fine black on red pottery also occurs, some of which suggests the famous Harappan pottery. The presence of this pottery plus such objects as graters, string-marked vessels, and lunate-incised bowls typical of the Harappan civilization suggests the Zhob cult's contemporaneity with at least one phase of that urban culture.

At Moghul Ghundai, a site located close to the valley wall to the south of Periano Ghundai, essentially the same picture emerges, including the presence of the Zhob mother goddess and bull figurines amid the ruins of what once had been a structure made of boulders obviously of some size.[37]

To the south of the Zhob valley is the district of Loralai, in the basin of the Anambar River, which eventually as the Nari River debouches onto the plain of Kachhi near Sibi at the foot of the Bolan Pass. Here are three well-known sites—Rana Ghundai, Sur Jangal, and Dabar Kot—but there are numerous others of both prehistoric and historic times located here.[38]

Dabar Kot is certainly the largest site of its kind in Baluchistan. It stands some 113 feet above the Thal River plain, and cultural debris is scattered over that plain in many directions for hundreds of yards. Not

[37] On our initial visit to the site we assumed this stone was part of a sangar, or small fort, of comparatively modern times. Subsequent visits have convinced us that the stone rubble was part of a prehistoric building of a late phase of the site's history. The association of the Zhob goddess plus certain pottery types seems to confirm this. Cf. Fairservis, 1959, pp. 359–360.

[38] The Buddhist period is particularly well represented while the Islamic period is but poorly so. It appears that a significant population rise did not occur until the British took over the area in the latter part of the nineteenth century.

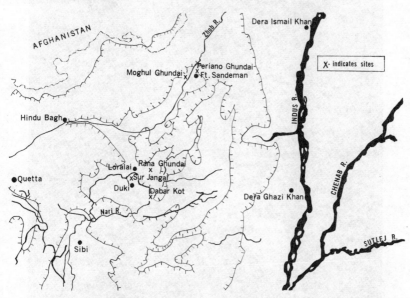

MAP 13 *Location of certain sites in the districts of Zhob and Loralai, Baluchistan.*

all of this great mass is prehistoric. There is ample evidence for an extensive Buddhist structure as well as other, probably later, occupations there, but the ceramic evidence indicates that probably every prehistoric period (which can be represented ceramically) that is found in Quetta is found in this site. More than likely the very early phases of Kile Gul Mohammad are also there. We know nothing of these occupations except by comparative inference, however. But high on the site Aurel Stein made a test excavation[39] which revealed the presence of a mud-brick building equipped with drains, which were partially made by using fired brick. Associated with this building was the familiar Zhob mother goddess (Fig. 36:6) as well as a compartmented seal, some clay bangles, and a potsherd of Harappan type. This association suggests that the same situation existed here as at Periano Ghundai—the contemporaneity of the Harappan civilization with the latest prehistoric phases of Baluchistan and southern Afghanistan. In fact, at Dabar Kot and at nearby Duki mound (L-6) an extensive Harappan occupation did occur, probably at the time of the latest phase of the Zhob cult period.

In the midst of the narrow Baghnao Valley of the Thal River, some ten miles northwest of Duki mound and about a thousand feet higher in elevation, is the little site of Sur Jungal. It was first examined by Stein in 1927 and later revisited and "tested" by *sondage* in 1950 by an American

[39] Cut E, Stein, 1929, pp. 59–60.

PLATE 11   *Bull's head found in the "Zhob cult" levels at the site of Periano Ghundai, near Fort Sandeman, Zhob district, Baluchistan* (Courtesy Lee Boltin.)

Museum of Natural History team.[40] These investigations indicate that the site represents three major phases of prehistoric village life. The first equates to the third phase at Kile Gul Mohammad (III), and the last to a late phase of the occupation at Damb Sadaat (II-III). Not only are the ceramic analogues precise but in addition there are familiar objects such as model houses and the Zhob mother goddess to confirm this correlation. The limited excavation attests the presence of small houses of mud brick for all periods. The northern part of the mound is the highest (*ca.* sixteen feet), and in this area rather large walls were encountered at levels of Sur Jangal II-III affinity, indicating that a substantial structure of some kind was located there.[41] The interest of the site lies in its suggestion of a major

[40] A. Stein, 1929; Fairservis, 1959, pp. 293–300.
[41] Cf. Fairservis, 1959, Fig. 8.

economic shift. In all the sites of Baluchistan and Afghanistan which we excavated, the faunal remains inevitably showed that sheep and/or goats were more numerous than cattle, though cattle were common enough. At Sur Jangal, however, cattle remains by far outnumbered those of sheep and goats. The Sur Jangal potters, working in the Iranian tradition of ware painting, created some wonderful vessels, on some of which are depicted lines of both humped and humpless cattle. All of these have widespread horns, which occur among some varieties of domestic cattle even today.

Though both Duki mound and Dabar Kot are near enough to Sur Jungal, there is no evidence for Harappan influences there. In this regard it is noteworthy that the plain on which the former sites are located is less than 3700 feet above sea level. The area is ecologically transitional between the uplands of Baluchistan and the Indus River Valley. Here the olive, the date, and the dwarf palm are found, since the region possesses a warm and seasonally not too extreme climate. Notable is the fact that the region receives some summer rain as a result of the diversion of some monsoonal winds westward from the Punjab.

Sur Jangal, a thousand feet higher, is located in a typical upland valley of Baluchistan. Here a scrubby desert vegetation attests to a succession growth as the result of the removal of the original forest cover by man and his beasts. Presumably the villages of Sur Jangal, like those of modern villages at the foot of the valley, drew their water from the Thal River in wet seasons and from the relatively high water table in dry. Cattle, unlike sheep and goats, need a more luxuriant vegetative resource for their sustenance, however, and one can therefore speculate that the villagers of Sur Jangal may have moved their herds back and forth to seasonal pastures. The plains to the south must have had obvious summer advantages.

The village of Sur Jangal was occupied continuously for probably somewhere short of one thousand years. In this period of time it remained small in population, in contrast to the situation elsewhere in the same period. The emphasis upon cattle, which is in this region a southern trait even though the culture involved is essentially northern, suggests that adaptations to local ecologies were occurring as shifts toward the Indus River Valley went on in the movement eastward.

The site of Rana Ghundai is less than twenty miles from Sur Jangal, but it is five hundred feet higher in elevation. It is located a few miles east of Loralai town, the district headquarters. The area is known as the Bori tract, and its climatic situation is the reverse of that of the Thal plain. Here winter rains, like those of the Quetta Valley, are from the west, and the months of November through February are significantly harsh. In other words, Rana Ghundai is located in a typical upland plateau environment. The plain about has a number of sites upon it representing a wide range of settlements from prehistoric to Islamic times. Rana Ghundai has attained an importance in archaeological literature probably beyond its actual

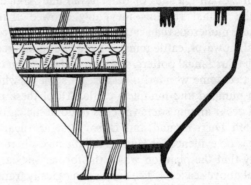

FIG. 37 *Bull vase from the site of Rana Ghundai, Loralai* (after Ross).

value. For many years it provided the only reasonably reliable stratigraphic picture in Baluchistan. This was due to the careful observations of a British officer stationed in Loralai. Brigadier Ross and his wife noted that the local populace were digging away the mound to use the earth, which is rich in organic residues, as fertilizer for their fields. The sheered walls of the site provided a section from which pottery and other habitation debris could be removed in sequential order. Ross published his work and Stuart Piggott refined it so that the outlines of a picture emerged.[42] As a part of our study of the prehistory of the Borderlands, a visit was paid to Rana Ghundai in 1950 to check Ross's section.[43] Those investigations provided ample evidence that the Rana Ghundai sequence except in its earliest phase (Ia) is directly parallel to that of Sur Jangal. The earliest known phase at Rana Ghundai (virgin soil was never reached) appears to be like that of the second major phase at Kile Gul Mohammad, in which handmade wares and chipped-stone tools are associated with small brick-made huts. At Rana Ghundai there are also later periods (IV-V), of little concern to the present context.

The site is situated in the midst of a flat alluvial plain of some fertility. Here presumably cereal crops were cultivated in the summer months. Ross recovered some sheep, goat, and cattle bones, and these animals are depicted in the famous painted pottery (usually black on red) along with the black buck of the uplands (Fig. 38). Of interest is the fact that rarely among these animals are depicted the humped cattle known to have been used by the inhabitants of the more southerly sites.

In the three major sites of Dabar Kot, Sur Jangal, and Rana Ghundai there are thus differences of environment and consequent economic ad-

[42] E. J. Ross, "A Chalcolithic Site in Northern Baluchistan," *Journal of Near Eastern Studies*, Vol. V, No. 4 (1946), pp. 291–315; S. Piggott, 1950.
[43] Fairservis, 1959, pp. 300–308.

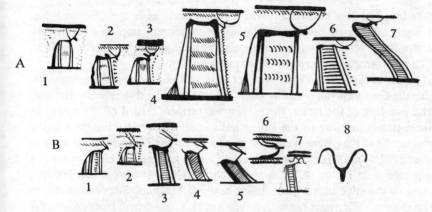

FIG. 38 *Animals as painted on prehistoric ceramics of northern Baluchistan.*

A—*Cattle*
1—*Rana Ghundai, Level D*
2—*Sur Jangal II*
3—*Sur Jangal I*
4—*Sur Jangal II*
5—*Rana Ghundai, Level D*
6—*Sur Jangal III (?)*
7—*Sur Jangal III (?)*

B—*Goats, ibexes, sheep*
1—*Rana Ghundai, Level D*
2—*Rana Ghundai II*
3—*Rana Ghundai III (?)*
4—*Sur Jangal III*
5—*Sur Jangal III (?)*
6—*Rana Ghundai III (?)*
7—*Rana Ghundai, Level E*
8—*Sur Jangal III (perhaps a bull)*

justments. But in the material culture known to us the analogues outweigh the differences. It is obvious that at one span of time the three sites possessed the same cultural form. From all appearances this meant village life with habitation in small mud-brick houses of one or several rooms and the local manufacture of a variety of pottery, stone tools (both ground and chipped), bone tools, and probably objects of copper, if not bronze. Designs in the painted pottery were mutually familiar, as was the Zhob mother goddess in the last major prehistoric phase.[44] Toward the end of that phase, Sur Jangal was abandoned and Rana Ghundai virtually so, it appears. However, at Dabar Kot the Harappan civilization appears full-blown, apparently both as a contemporary influence in the last prehistoric phase there and as a successor. Though only thirty miles from the Bori tract, where were situated village sites like that of Rana Ghundai, the Harappan culture did not move into that region; apparently environmental factors were as significant in this restriction as cultural ones (see pp. 1–2). In this sense the relationship of these sites illustrates the fact that the upland cultures were early moving into southerly regions where the environment

---

[44] None of these "goddesses" have been found at Rana Ghundai, however—more probably the accident of nondiscovery, in view of the investigations there. This is especially valid since the upper levels at the site have virtually disappeared.

was less and less like that of the uplands and, as is the case with Sur Jangal, making necessary adjustments in economic emphasis to do this. Later the reverse seems to have been happening—the southerly cultures, like the Harappan, were moving into the uplands.

South of the Quetta Valley proper in cul-de-sacs among the mountains, like the Gwandin valley and Isplenji, places which tend to interior drainage and ponding of the water, the prehistoric farmers settled on the shores of these ponds or close to the valley walls in spurs overlooking their fertile shores. That they were successful is proven by the representation at such sites of almost all phases found in the Quetta sequence. This story can be repeated west of the valley as well as at Panjpai, Mastung, and Nushki, close to the edge of the great desert basin of Mashkel. Sites essentially of the Quetta Valley time range and type are also found with frequency as far south as Kalat City. Nowhere in these areas are we confronted with the concentration of village sites which is obtained in the Quetta Valley, however. Basically a spring, a high water table, or, as in Isplenji, a possibly perennial lake is the reason why settlement was possible.

❋ *Central Baluchistan—The Surab Region*

CENTRAL BALUCHISTAN IS BOUNDED ON THE EAST by the Kirthar Ranges, which front on the Indus Valley, and on the west by the rim of the Mashkel basin. It is a mountainous country, with the ranges trending north-south. The region is thus roughly a series of corridor valleys running between the desert to the west and the front ranges of the Indus to the east. To the south the westerly corridors swing west with the mountains to parallel the Makran coast. The northernmost corridor is the Rakhshan valley, while the southern is the Kej valley. Both of these are natural avenues west to southeastern Iran. In the southernmost district, that of Jhalawan, the valleys are relatively narrow and tend to be pinched in at either end, as the road leads through gorges. Several important streams, such as the Hingol, the Hab, and the Porali, have their headwaters here and eventually drain out along the Arabian Sea coast. Others, however, turn eastward and break through the Kirthar ranges to enter the Indus Valley proper. The most important of these is the Mula River, which does, of course, provide a passage to the Indus plains for the traveler leaving Kalat.

It is clear, then, that in addition to the broad passage which connects Kalat with Quetta on the north there are good routes of ready communication in every direction in the region. Prehistoric sites occur all along these routes and the side valleys off them. In areas such as Kolwa, at the head of the Kej valley, and in the valleys south of Surab there are concentrations of these sites, such concentrations being coincident with the availability of good soil and water.

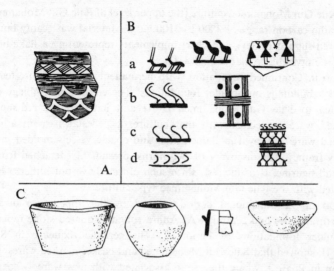

FIG. 39   *Typical pottery types of central Baluchistan* (after de Cardi).
A—*Zari ware*
B—*Togau wares* (*the lettered motifs demonstrate typological develop-ment in Period III, Anjira*)
C—*Anjira wares*

The region has been explored from time to time by archaeologists since 1900, the work of Hargreaves, Stein, and de Cardi being particularly significant,[45] especially that of the latter. Stein managed to survey the region and record the locations of a great many sites. He carried out some excavations, but these had limited value. Miss de Cardi has managed to establish a stratigraphic sequence both by observing the exposed section as Ross did at Rana Ghundai and by carrying on limited but strategically placed excavations. She worked at two sites in the Surab region, Anjira and Siah damb, and was successful in establishing five periods with typological ties elsewhere as follows:

PERIOD I. A neolithic occupation derived probably from the Sialk culture of Iran. At Anjira a seminomadic settlement could be related to Period II

[45] H. Hargreaves, *Excavations in Baluchistan 1925, Sampur Mound, Mastung and Sohr Damb, Nal*, Memoirs of the Archaeological Survey of India, No. 35, Government of India, New Delhi, 1929; Sir M. A. Stein, *An Archaeological Tour in Gedrosia*, Memoirs of the Archaeological Survey of India, No. 43, Government of India, New Delhi, 1931; B. de Cardi, "A New Prehistoric Ware from Baluchistan," *Iraq*, Vol. XIII, No. 2 (1951), pp. 63–75; B. de Cardi, "New Wares and Fresh Problems from Baluchistan," *Antiquity*, Vol. XXXIII (1959), pp. 15–24; B. de Cardi, "British Expedition to Kalat, 1948 and 1957," *Pakistan Archaeology*, Vol. I (1964), pp. 20–29; B. de Cardi, "Excavations and Reconnaissance in Kalat, West Pakistan," *Pakistan Archaeology*, Vol. II, No. 2 (1965), pp. 86–182; J. M. Casal, "Nindowari," *Pakistan Archaeology*, Vol. III, No. 1 (1967).

of the Kile Gul Mohammed culture (the upper level of Kile Gul Mohammad had a radio-carbon range of 3500 to 3100 B.C.). Material was scanty but included red-slipped pottery and chert implements representing a flake-blade industry comparable to that of Sialk I–III.

PERIOD II. Continued occupation, with permanent settlement attested by mud-brick buildings on boulder foundations. The cultural assemblage corresponded to Kile Gul Mohammed II–III and included the red-slipped burnished ware associated with that culture, a pedestal base in a gray burnished ware unknown in Baluchistan, and coarse vessels molded inside basketry frames. The discovery of two horns, presumably detached from a small bull figurine, is of interest, since such objects have not hitherto been associated with the Kile Gul Mohammed type culture.

PERIOD III. A transitional period marked by the appearance of new architectural styles and ceramics. At Anjira roughly squared stone replaced the boulder foundations of Period II. The ceramic sequence in Siah, Trench II, showed that Kile Gul Mohammed and basket-marked wares were common in Phase i, where they were associated with new wares—Togau[46] and a bichrome ware of Amri-Kechi Beg type. The earlier wares had virtually ceased by Phase ii. This phase marked the building of a massive "podium" at Siah, later destroyed and replaced in Phase iii by domestic buildings with which were associated Zari ware[47] and fine cream-slipped pottery decorated with geometric patterns. For the most part though, some animal designs and a little true polychrome serve to identify the ware as a local variant of the Nal culture (see p. 158 f.). Three stages in the devolution of the Togau frieze could be demonstrated stratigraphically through Phases i–iii, beginning with Stage B. From the occurrence of Amri-Kechi Beg wares, the beginning of this period is best related to the end of Kile Gul Mohammed IV and to Damb Sadaat I.

PERIOD IV. A period which coincided in part with the Quetta-culture occupation of Damb Sadaat II. At Anjira it was marked by expansion and rebuilding, with well-squared masonry replacing the rougher stonework of the previous period. Fine Nal wares were predominantly cream slipped and were decorated with polychrome or bichrome designs of great variety, in

46 The term Togau refers to a black on red painted ware usually having the form of an open bowl with a painted frieze just below the interior lip. The motifs vary, but characteristically they are animals such as goats, ibexes, or birds. Miss de Cardi has been able to demonstrate stages of stylization of these animals which are useful in determining sequential phases wherever the ware occurs. The type is associated with the Kechi Beg ware of KGM IV in the Quetta Valley, but it is so similar in color, shape, and design to the KGM black on red ware that at the very least we feel there is a generic relationship. De Cardi suspects this as well. De Cardi, 1965, pp. 128–134.

47 Zari ware is a ceramic group defined by de Cardi: "Zari ware is a hand wheel-made reddish buff ware with large grits. It is slipped about equally commonly in black or red, the slip being thick. . . . The most usual form is a globular jar of medium size." This painting of the vessel is frequently in white with black outline. The ware is strongly suggestive of the dark slip and white on dark slip type of Period IV at KGM and of Kechi Beg.

PLATE 12 *Reddish bowl of Chashma Ali type suggesting a generic relation-ship of design motif to Togau ware; northern Iran.* (Courtesy of the Metro-politan Museum of Art.)

zoomorphic, naturalistic, and geometric styles. A cordoned color-coated ware (Anjira ware) was used for heavier domestic vessels together with a granulated ware. . . .

PERIOD V. While erosion had removed the stratigraphical evidence, the presence in superficial layers of Periano wet- and reserved-slip wares and designs of Rana Ghundai IIIC style points to contact with, if not the arrival of, a people whose advent in northern Baluchistan can be assigned to about the beginning of the second millennium B.C. Their culture can be recognized in the final perod at Damb Sadaat, and at Mundigak, Afghanistan, in Period IV (2-3).[48]

This remarkable accomplishment of Miss de Cardi's, even though, as must be in these days of limited time, budget, and reluctant government permission, it is primarily a ceramic sequence, does provide a reasonably solid stratigraphic picture. As she has pointed up, there are specific ties to the Quetta sequence. As in northern Baluchistan, a continuity of occupation from seminomadic beginnings up to a time of elaboration and expansion of permanent settlement can be demonstrated. It does appear that the final stage here was not as monumental as in the northern areas, and we do not have a full demonstration on these sites of the "Zhob cult" aspect, as is

[48] De Cardi, 1965, pp. 93–94.

seen, for example, in Damb Sadaat III. Possibly the economic basis for it was unobtained in this rugged land even though the cultural form was apparently known in Miss de Cardi's Period V. The elaboration of Period IV suggests that a settlement climax was achieved at that time and that then there was some falling off of population.

✳ *The Nal Settlements*

THIS PERIOD IV IS OF CONSIDERABLE INTEREST, since it reflects the influences of the so-called Nal culture, which was first clearly described by the excavations of Hargreaves at Sohr Damb near the village of Nal in central Jhalawan.[49] This is a mound site of some scale (1,016 feet by 600 feet by 40 feet at the highest point). It is situated in the midst of modern cultivation, the water for this being obtained by irrigation.

The Nal cultural remains were located beneath a habitation level that rose to the top of the site and which belonged apparently to phases of the so-called Kulli culture of southern Baluchistan (see p. 215). In his principal digging Hargreaves excavated two converging trenches (A and E) on either side of an old excavation made by Colonel Jacobs of the Hazara Pioneers in 1908. He cleared the intervening area (Area A). He uncovered a series of some fourteen rooms which were outlined by stone walls that apparently had provided the foundations for mud-brick houses. The houses give the impression of being well laid out and less haphazard in plan than those, say, of Mundigak at a comparable time. In this they compare to those known in the Quetta Valley and at Kechi Beg and Damb Sadaat. Hargreaves was unable to identify any doors in these walls, but hearths were found in the rooms. The stratigraphic picture and the proveniences of artifacts are unclear from the report, so it is difficult to assess the correct affinities of objects found. However, it is apparent that these people used copper for the manufacture of bar celts, chisels, lance heads, and other tools and weapons. They had a variety of ground-stone objects, including grinding stones, celts, and containers. They made beads in various forms out of agate, and perhaps out of lapis lazuli. Most striking of all is the pottery, which includes the Kechi Beg white on black open bowls but most distinctively the Nal-type wares. These include wheel-made canisters, bowls with inward-turned rims, and flat-sided bowls—all with ring bases. It is the decoration which makes this ware the most distinctive in Baluchistan, a land which in prehistoric times must have had more than its share of master potters. The Nal ceramic style is basically the repetition of a motif or pattern by multiplying its outline, often in concentric fashion. Red, blue, or yellow pigment is often applied to the spaces between outlines or to fill out a motif. The designs include a range of

[49] Hargreaves, 1929.

FIG. 40 *Characteristic artifacts and styles of the Nal culture of Baluchistan.*

geometric motifs, many of which occur in northern Baluchistan. Animals and plants also occur. In the case of these motifs, techniques of hachuring and rather precise geometric drawing were used. Of great correlative interest is the use of designs drawn in the hairline brush technique associated with the Kechi Beg wares in the Quetta Valley and elsewhere.

So many burials were found in the excavations that the place is often referred to as the necropolis or the cemetery. These burials as a whole do not seem to be associated with the habitations excavated. The exceptions are an adult and two children who were found individually in little brick caches. The adult was partially flexed and lying on its left side. No funerary furniture was found with it, however. The greatest number of remains were fractional burials. Some of the body parts were found in vessels of the Nal type. An example of this situation suffices to represent the whole:

Group B in A-6.—In clearing the floor of A-6 a collection of thirty-two vessels was discovered. . . . Part of a long bone was lying over one vase, many were scattered among the pots and two long bones were lying together. The whole group of bones and vessels lay in an area 9′ 9″ by 3′ 3″. No skull was found with these but eight days later when removing the earth at the north-west corner of A-6 the skull of an adult was found all alone. This may have been part of Group B but it was fully three feet distant from the nearest vessels. Even with this skull nothing like a complete skeleton was recovered, no pelvic bones, no shoulder blades, no vertebrae. On examination it was found that eighteen of the thirty-two vessels contained earth only. One was quite empty, having been covered by another vessel. The remaining vessels all contained bones or bone fragments mixed with earth. Two phalanges were in

PLATE 13 *Nal pottery associated with the early Kulli livels of southern Baluchistan. These examples from the Edith Shahr site, Complex A, and from Niai Buthi I, Las Bela.*

one vessel, parts of two small ribs in a second, three metatarsal or metacarpal bones in a third and so on. It is not clear whether these bones were originally placed in the vessels or later found their way into them, but the latter seems the more likely in this particular case as bones were more frequently near the top of the pots. This may be considered as typical of a form of fractional or incomplete burial of which some twenty-six examples were discovered.

Lt.-Col. Sewell and Dr. Guha report that these human remains were of four persons, namely, two adults, a youth of about eighteen years, and an infant of about one year. Bones of a bird and a small mammal were also recovered with this group.[50]

These fractional "burials" were apparently all later than the habitation, since they were mostly separated from the floor of that level by distances of anywhere from two inches to four feet.

The evidence indicates that Nal-type settlements were dominant in

[50] Hargreaves, 1929, pp. 21–22.

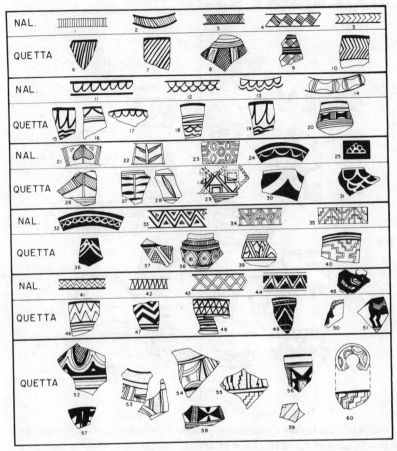

FIG. 41 *Comparative typology of the Nal pottery with equivalents in the Quetta Valley. The Quetta material is largely of Damb Sadaat II levels in the Quetta Valley.*

central Baluchistan south of Kalat in the period represented by Damb Sadaat I and II in the Quetta Valley (especially the latter) and by de Cardi's Period IV in the Surab area.[51] There is an obvious parallel in burial customs between the fractional burials at Nal (Sohr Damb) and those of Period III at Mundigak, and, in fact, painted pottery in the Nal style was found at that site in Period III.[52]

Several surveys of the Surab region demonstrate that the Anjira-Siah-Damb sequence is represented widely. Surface remains indicate the presence of such definitive pottery types as Togau, Kile Gul Mohammad, Nal,

[51] De Cardi, 1965, pp. 93–94.
[52] Casal, 1961, Figs. 52–45, Figs. 60–135.

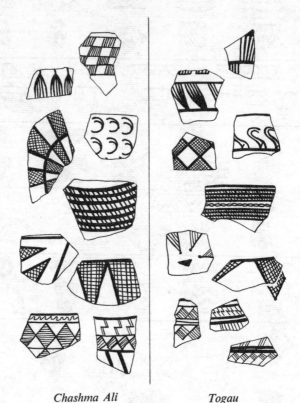

Chashma Ali   Togau

FIG. 42   *Typological similarities of painted pottery designs found in northern Iran (Chashma Ali culture) and in Baluchistan (Togau). There is perhaps a thousand-year lag from north to south.*

Zari, Anjira, and related wares. Miss de Cardi plans to publish her surface survey collection, which includes some fourteen or more sites in this region. Stein, Field, members of the Pakistan department of archaeology, and we have, however, visited the area. The evidence indicates a rather sparse occupation of the valley from Rodinjo south to the Khuzdar region (some fourteen prehistoric sites in a linear distance of perhaps eighty miles). This figure will change, of course, with later intensive surveys, but this is perhaps an indication of the relatively sparse population of the region as compared to that of the Quetta Valley at a comparable time (see Appendix F).

South of Nal and the Khuzdar area are numerous sites located with some density in such regions as Kolwa, at the head of the Kej valley, leading to the Makran, the Wadh, Drakalo, and Ornach valleys, and northern Las Bela. These sites have several things in common (see Map

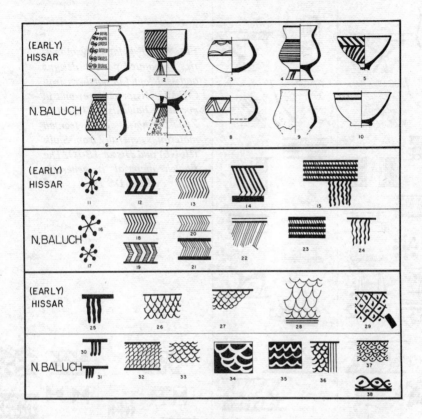

Fig. 43 *Typological similarities of painted pottery designs found in north-ern Iran (Early Hissar culture) and in northern Baluchistan (Quetta-Zhob-Loralai). The Iranian material is generally from Sialk III (1) and Hissar IA. The Baluch material is generally from KGM III to DS II.*

16). First, there is little evidence for the early occupation of the type represented in the Quetta Valley and at Anjira for Period I there (KGM I-II, Period I Anjira Siah-Damb). There is, however, evidence for the next period, that represented by the Kechi Beg type settlement (or Kechi Beg-Togau), and for the Nal settlements. Most prominent, however, is the culture known as Kulli, from a site discovered in Kolwa by Sir Aurel Stein which represents a peculiar and significant cultural elaboration that can only be understood in another context.

The diffusionary line which runs from western Iran to the northeast, through Afghanistan and into the heart of Baluchistan, is, as is suggested in the foregoing, rather explicit. (Figs. 42, 43, 44, 45.) Chronologically

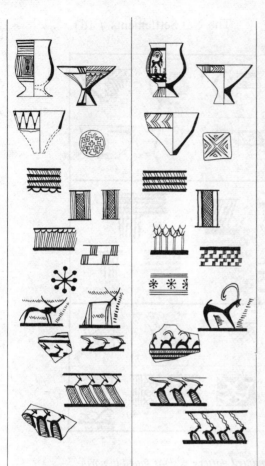

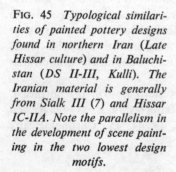

FIG. 44 *Typological similarities of painted pottery designs and seal found in northern Iran (Middle Hissar culture) and in northern Baluchistan (Quetta-Zhob-Loralai). The Iranian material is generally from Sialk III(4–6) and Hissar IB-IC. The Baluch material is generally from DS II.*

FIG. 45 *Typological similarities of painted pottery designs found in northern Iran (Late Hissar culture) and in Baluchistan (DS II-III, Kulli). The Iranian material is generally from Sialk III (7) and Hissar IC-IIA. Note the parallelism in the development of scene painting in the two lowest design motifs.*

the evidence indicates that the Nal settlements probably date to a period around 2500 to 2000 B.C. (see Appendix F). They are typologically analogous to the northern cultural assemblages and as such may be said to represent the southernmost extent of those assemblages as well as the last manifestation of them as a part of a purely Iranian ethos. However, there are stylistic elements in the Nal that suggest that other traditions were exerting their influence, a subject of the next chapter.

The Prelude to Civilization

T HE ADVENT OF FOOD PRODUCTION in the northern and central portions of Baluchistan began the process which was to lead to the development of civilization in the Indus River Valley. But before this happened, an important prelude was necessary. This involved the spread of settled life into southern Baluchistan and, at the same time, its diffusion into the Indus River Valley proper. In both areas the environment required adaptations which profoundly affected the character of the cultural forms or styles. Similarly, social and cultural changes are hinted by the evidence which effectively preluded the civilization that was to come.

The archaeological evidence, still frustratingly weak, is nonetheless sufficient enough at present to outline the shifts from an essentially Western Asian developed village life to one which we can term "Indian." What follows is an account of what this evidence is and how it might be interpreted. (Absolute dates for these chapters can be found in Appendix E.)

✳ The Diwana Site

IT IS SINGULARLY IRONIC that the Hab River, one of the finest in Baluchistan, flows through some of its most unproductive country. Only three or four village settlements of reasonable size exist north of the modern dam site at Band Murad, while to the south the settlement at Hab Chauki is a mere checkpoint on an east-west road and the remainder of the occupation in that area is represented by a few huts on the plain and a fishing village or two by the sea! Yet the Hab is a perennial stream, and in its upper waters, patches of lush vegetation and deep pools recall the riparian splendors of the Indus. As if to confirm this, crocodiles still float about in these waters, in complete contrast to the arid valley and barren mountains all about!

In 1960 an American Museum of Natural History survey reached a point on the Hab nearly one hundred miles north of Karachi. The local village is called Diwana and marks a place where there is a main pass across the Kirthar ranges into Sind. A traveler can, in less than forty miles, reach Tando Rahim Khan at the northwestern edge of Lake Manchhar and can thus be essentially in the Indus River basin.

Just north of Diwana a series of small stone-covered low mounds, many of which exhibit traces of wall lines, was encountered. This complex of mounds covers an area about 150 yards long (N-S) by 125 yards in width. Here the valley is about 6 miles across; the Hab River itself lies about 2 miles west of the site, which is in turn located on the talus or possibly a terrace close to the western foothills of the Kirthar range. Between the site and the river there is a belt of scrub growth on a silt soil which, given moisture, is very cultivable. In fact, several small modern villages appear close to the river and use that portion of the land immediately at hand to which they can raise water. The site, however, is far from the river. This initially seemed unusual, except that, as it turned out, its situation was perfectly viable.

On the north of the site a nullah (arroyo) leads from the silt plain eastward to a gap in the front hills next to the site—a distance of about 300 yards. Here the hills rise above 500 feet, and in the vicinity of the gap, which is perhaps 150 feet across, they narrow considerably into two opposing tonguelike spurs. Beyond these spurs there is a large ellipse-shaped basin formed by the spurs of the front hills and the main mountain on the east, the latter rising over 1500 feet. This is a natural catch basin, and the ancient farmers took advantage of it by constructing a 25-foot-high dam of sandstone blocks across the gap. The dam was probably at one time about 75 feet long but is now broken on its northern end. In its lowest level the dam is at least 25 feet thick and was certainly built to withstand considerable pressure.

This natural reservoir and the subsequent dam were apparently the *raison d'être* for the existence of the site. The slope of the valley to the river would have expedited control of the waters caught behind the dam as they were released into irrigation canals at the head of the slope. Unfortunately, no aerial photograph is available of the place, but traces of the irrigation system may well appear when one is taken.

The highest part of the site itself is a mound on the northeast corner near the nullah. The material of the structure in the mound is stone, cut like the blocks of the dam, and this excellently reveals a plan of a building. The building was a flat platform with a low ascending ramp and step arrangement on the southern side at least. Traces of two circular depressions (*ca.* seven feet in diameter) occur in the midst of the platform.

Smaller and perhaps less formal dwellings can be traced in the rubble on the west of the site.

Ceramics were found in abundance. The most typical is a fine ware painted black on a buff or reddish surface. The designs are painted with considerable finesse, delicate hairline fringes on the basic design motif being characteristic. A fine gray painted ware is closely related to this pottery in its design repertoire. Open bowls with painting along the interior rim area were popular vessel forms.

These ceramics appear to be a local variation on the Nal, and they are known, as one might expect, from sites in the Lake Manchhar region and points south in the hill country, which is known locally as the Kohistan.[1] In these contexts they appear before the arrival of the Harappan civilization.

It would appear that the period of occupancy of this Hab River site (listed as Hab-1) was one where every effort was being made to utilize the resources of the valley. The dam is a response to an arid climate where rainfall is sparse and water precious. The prehistoric farmers were certainly superior to the modern inhabitants of the Hab valley in their efforts to handle this environmental situation, for they were not defeated by the high banks of the Hab River. Rather they caught the runoff before it descended out of reach so that the whole of the silt plain was made available for their cultivation, whereas today the local villagers are barely able to gain subsistence from patches of soil by painstaking water raising or the use of primitive diverting devices on the river.

Archaeological exploration of the broad and reputedly very fertile valley of the Saruna branch of the Hab River, which takes off just above this site, is virtually nil. However, there are excellent descriptions of great dams, or gabarbands, there at Pir Munaghara and Ahmad Band.[2] Sites are also reported. Since there are several excellent routes connecting Sind with Jhalawan that pass through the Saruna valley, it is more than likely

---

[1] N. G. Majumdar, *Explorations in Sind*, Memoirs of the Archaeological Survey of India, No. 48, Government of India, New Delhi, 1934, Pls. XXVIII, XXIX.

[2] Hughes-Buller, "Gabarbands in Baluchistan," *Annual Report of the Archaeological Survey of India*, Director General of Archaeology, ed., Government of India, Calcutta, 1903–1904.

that this fact plus the fertile soil made the Saruna valley an important part of the Nal settlement.[3]

❊ *Kohtras Buthi*

THE RELATIONSHIP OF THE NAL SETTLEMENTS TO DAM BUILDING is best shown by the remarkable site of Kohtras Buthi, which is situated near the head of the Baran Nai valley. This valley is roughly parallel to that of the Hab River. However, this stream is much less voluminous. Kohtras Buthi is about forty miles to the southwest of the Hab River site. It lies in a strategic position near the junction of routes into Taung, where a large prehistoric site of unknown affinity is reported,[4] and the so-called Landi Road to Lake Manchhar.

The site is near the bank of the Baran River. It is essentially located on a hilltop which rises some ninety-five feet above the river plain. The steep slopes of the hill on the east, west, and north effectively preclude easy access to the top. On the gentle slope to the south a series of two walls made of boulders set in dry-stone fashion impedes the way. The inner wall was apparently buttressed by a series of at least four bastions. Through this wall an entrance was made that led into the habitation area, which was reached across an open "courtyard." Majumdar, the discoverer, writes:[5]

Amongst the ruins we could trace the outlines of countless rooms, both large and small (stone-built), grouping themselves into blocks separated from one another by alleys. The greater part of the area covered by ruins is divided into two sections by a long ridge which runs north to south, and along the two sides of the ridge houses were erected one after the other. Coming near the courtyard, the height of the hill diminishes from 95 feet to 64 feet. A little to the north of it some excavations were conducted, in the course of which a number of rooms forming a small house and an alley running by its side were fully exposed. The alley proceeded from the courtyard, and a passage branching off from it gave access to the interior of the house. There were further discovered a small flight of steps at the southwestern corner, and near the entrance a bath measuring 5½ feet by 3 feet.

[3] An important book which notes these areas adjacent to Sind is by H. T. Lambrick: *Sind: A General Introduction*, History of Sind, Vol. I, Sindhi Adabi Board, Hyderabad, Pakistan, 1964. See especially pp. 50–69.

[4] Lambrick, 1964, pp. 59–60.

[5] Majumdar, 1934, p. 133.

PLATE 14 *The Baran Nai near Kohtras Buthi, southwestern Sind.*

To the west of the site, on the Taung fork, gaps in the hills are filled with massive stone walls much as at the Diwana site on the Hab. One that was nearby was measured by Majumdar and found to be about 400 feet by 30 to 35 feet (at top) and over 20 feet in height. At the foot of Kohtras Buthi two stone walls cross the gaps between the site and adjacent hills.

The ceramic evidence relates the site to the Nal tradition.[6]

This kind of evidence strongly indicates that under the direction of skilled engineers the population was able to construct effective systems of water control which enabled them to utilize the local soil resources to their maximum. Even in distant Kharan, in the western part of Kalat on the rim of the Mahkel basin, Stein found dams which made possible a Nal settlement. At Toji, in northeastern Kharan, low stone dams measuring about 4 to 5 feet high and 8 feet thick and some 100 yards or more in length were placed across nullahs that ran close to the site. These would appear to have been intended for a kach system where the alluvial soil would settle behind the dams.[7]

In Kolwa, Stein also recovered evidence for the relationship of a gabar-band or dam system to a Nal settlement. Near Kallag mound two low dams were found lying across the drainage slope in successive order. These would appear to have been intended to prevent the runoff from collecting

[6] The term "Amri" has been used to describe an assemblage which was first identified by Majumdar at the site of Amri in the Indus Valley, where it occurs in pre-Harappan context. This term has been, in consequence, widely used wherever its analogues are found in Baluchistan. However, in order to show its association, we have come up with such terms as Amri-Nal, Amri-Quetta, etc. This is symptomatic of a too general use of the term to include many typological series. The Amri material appears to derive from Baluchistan out of the Nal-Kechi Beg-Quetta tradition, and the term should only be used in the Indus Valley, where its definition by the recent excavation of Casal has some local precision. Where the term is used here, it relates generally to the Casal material.

[7] Sir M. A. Stein, 1931, Pl. 1.

into a deep nullah and so being lost. Instead the dams could divert water to the fields lying below the slope.[8]

A similar situation also occurs at Ughar Damb in the Mashkai River drainage of Jhalawan.[9]

❋ *Nal Settlements and Water-Control Systems*

THIS WIDE DISTRIBUTION OF NAL SITES and their water-control systems in the southern reaches of Baluchistan represents a triumph over the exigencies of the region. The use of stone both as boulders and in cut blocks gave these farmers a fine advantage in salvaging the soil and water resulting from the short but violent rainstorms usual to these regions. The degree to which earthen embankments and wood supports were used is, of course, unknown, but we can assume with some assurance that every resource was utilized in these irrigation systems.

It can be noted that basically two systems were employed both separately and in conjunction with each other: the kach system, by which alluvial soil was accumulated behind the "steps" of low dams laid across the slope drainage, and the reservoir dam. The latter is of two types: a dam like that of the Hab River Diwana site, where waters were presumably accumulated in a catch basin and released slowly to the fields, and a diversionary system, where the dams were placed as weirs to divert the waters into canals leading to the cultivation. We can assume that weirs of various kinds were also used in the rivers wherever practicable.

The gabarband system had its beginnings in Baluchistan at least as early as the period of the Nal settlements. It is still practical today. Basically southern Baluchistan produces one crop of grain a year. This is primarily a *khushkaba*, or rain crop. The slope of southern Baluchistan generally is from north to south except on its eastern fringe, where local streams (Mula, Kolachi) flow into Sind through gaps in the Kirthar range. The principal rivers flow south, however, and pass through valleys where settlements are heaviest. Thus the Hingol begins in the Surab region and passes through Gidar, Gresha, Nal, and Jhau before crossing through the coastal ranges to the sea; the Mashkai, with the Nundara, drains the region of Jebri and Gajar and joins the Hingol in Kolwa; the Porali begins in the Wadh area just south of Khuzdar and Nal and flows through the hill country to the plain of Las Bela. The Hab, of course, is the principal north-south-running stream in the hill country east of Las Bela proper. These river systems with their local tributaries were the seat of early settlements of Nal type. With the exception of the Welpat tract of Las

---

[8] *Ibid.*, pp. 113–114.

[9] *Ibid.*, pp. 146ff. There is also a suggestion of dams located near Sraduk, a site of Nal affinity near Panjgur in Makran. *Ibid.*, p. 45.

Bela, Saruna, and possibly the Gidar tract, soil resources are very limited. Cultivation is best nearest to the riverbanks. However, in most of the small valleys and in parts of the large, alluvial soil is present for considerable stretches above the immediate vicinity of the rivers. These stretches can be cultivated as khushkaba fields after rains, provided there is enough rain. For the wheat and barley farmers of prehistoric times the restraining dams they were able to build across the gaps in the surrounding hills or across the courses of small intermittent streams provided a water resource in addition to the seasonal rain itself. In consequence, water could be strategically placed and more effectively used over a longer period of time than was possible by simple khushkaba dependence. High evaporation plus some leakage probably did not allow for storage of water in reservoirs over periods of more than a few months, or indeed in some cases for a few weeks, but obviously for whatever period it was, the water supply was that much the greater. Almost all the major valleys and many smaller ones, like those of Drakalo, Wadh, and the Ornach, exhibit traces of stone dams on the slopes or in the gaps of the surrounding hills, attesting the fullest possible use of the alluvial soil in those valleys. Correlatively, extensive occupation of these valleys is proven by the number of sites of the period (see Appendix F).

The wide distribution of the Nal-type settlements includes for the first time the low-lying alluvial plains of the southern Indus River Valley, or western Sind, and the district of Las Bela. De Cardi has noted Nal pottery well down toward the Mula Pass in the Mula River valley at Jahan.[10] At the large site of Judeirjo-daro near Jacobabad in southern Kachi, Raikes found ceramic material suggesting pre-Harappan occupation there that included a canister of Nal type as well as a number of sherds with painted designs familiar to the Baluchistan culture.[11] De Cardi also found similar material at Pathiani Kot at the foot of the Mula Pass.[12]

❊ Other Nal Settlements—Lohri, Damb Buthi, Tharro Hill

To THE SOUTH OF THIS REGION, Majumdar's work around the Gaj River Pass into Sind produced ample evidence for Nal settlements there both in the valley approaches at sites around Rohel-jo-kund and in the plain at Rajo-dero.[13] (Majumdar was killed by bandits on the last expedition—a martyr to his science).

[10] B. de Cardi, 1964, pp. 20–29.

[11] Raike's collection is stored in the Pakistan Department of Archaeology laboratories in Karachi.

[12] De Cardi, 1964, Pl. III: 8, 9 (?).

[13] K. Deva and D. E. McCown, "Further Exploration in Sind: 1938." Ancient India, No. 5 (1949), pp. 12–30.

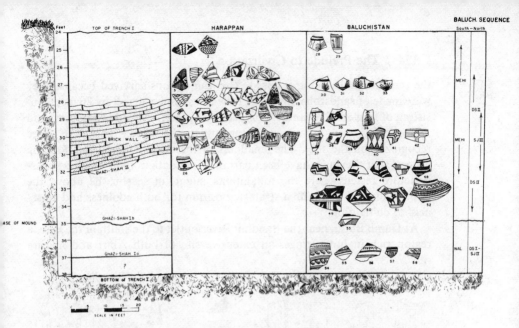

Fig. 46   *The sequence at the site of Ghazi Shah comparing Harappan type pottery with that of Baluchistan type. The material of Ghazi Shah Ia is called Amri A; Ghazi Shah Ib is called Amri B elsewhere.*

It is around Lake Manchhar, at the foot of the Phusi Pass and close to routes from the Kohistan previously described, that a truly major settlement of the Amri type (see page 170 note) was located by Majumdar.[14] Lake Manchhar is a shallow body of water connected to the Indus system by the western Nara and by an outlet to the east, the Aral (see p. 230). It is also the catch basin for the mountain torrents that flow from the Kirthar in the west and the Lakhi hill tracts on the south. The lake is subject to seasonal expansions and contractions as the result of these sources.

Majumdar's survey revealed an Amri settlement close to rivers and streams near their point of debouchment onto the flood plain of the western Nara-Lake Manchhar system.[15] Some sites were close to hot springs (Ghazi Shah, Damb Buthi). These sites are representative of small villages (a few hundred feet in diameter) where inhabitants built house walls of mud brick often set on boulder foundations. Often these villages were located on spurs or hillocks above what had once been the cultivated area (Damb Buthi; Naig, Chauro), but the majority are found in the low area at the foot of the hills or spurs (Ghazi Shah, Gorandi, Pandi Wahi). Several sites, in fact, were located directly on the Nara-Lake Manchhar plain. The site of Lohri, for example, which is situated to the north of the lake, is inundated annually and for a large part of the year is just above water level. Here Majumdar found a kind of checkerboard plan caused by

14 Majumdar, 1934.
15 See Map 16.

the remnant walls being exposed. The foundations survived because they were made of sandstone blocks. A little house some 30 feet by 26 feet, consisting of four small chambers (6½ feet by 4½ feet), two side chambers, and a "veranda," was excavated (belonging to the middle period of three recognized on the site). The smallness of the chambers and the flooding suggest that they may have been part of a foundation upon which a superstructure rested where the inhabitants might, in season, be above the flood while still retaining a strategic position for both coolness and closeness to cultivation.

At Damb Buthi, near the Bandhni River outlet to the south of the lake, a region rich in hot springs, an extensive site of both Amri and mature

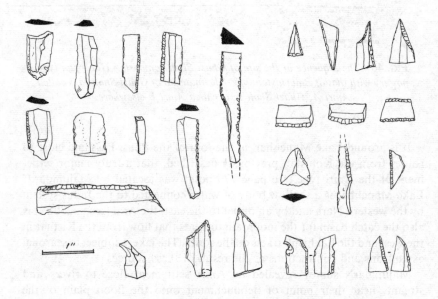

FIG. 47   *The flint industry at Tharro Hill.*

Harappan type was located. The two cultures were, however, separated on the hill which was the locality of the habitation. Here Majumdar excavated a number of doorless small rooms, in some of which he encountered fractional burials of the type uncovered by Hargreaves at Nal. A good deal of artifactual debris was associated with the human remains, including a variety of pottery, flint flakes and cores, terra-cotta and shell bangles, and a stone bead. Interestingly, a mussel-shell container was uncovered still holding a quantity of red ocher. The site would appear to have been a necropolis of some kind.

One of the largest of these sites was located upriver from Damb Buthi near Bandhni village. Here two mounds, one of which is some 400 by 230 yards in size and about 29 feet in height, were discovered. Majumdar was also able to trace prehistoric remains of the period right across the valley. In turn, his trek up the Bandhni revealed how heavily that valley had once been occupied by these prehistoric people, for right up to the watershed, sites of the culture were located (Bandhni, Chauro, Dhal), and indeed beyond to the Baran Nai basin and along its course to the vicinity of Thana Bulla Khan, some seventy-odd miles from Karachi, the line of occupation could be followed (Pokhran Landi, Khajur, Arabjo Thana, Ahmad Shah, Othmanjo Buthi) (Map 16).

The most southerly of the Amri sites is that of Tharro Hill, located close to the Indus delta some eleven miles west of Tatta, the old capital of Sind. This is a natural hill which rises some thirty feet above the alluvium. It is one of several in the area, on some of which flint flakes and cores and other "workshop" debris have been recovered. At Tharro Hill the Amri settlement is marked by the line of a stone wall intended to enclose a small settlement within which signs of habitation are numerous. The hill is littered with the remains of shellfish and this food resource may well have been the reason for the attraction of the place when the Indus River deltaic meander brought waters nearer to the site or, as is equally likely, the sea coast was nearer and tidal streams flowed close by. The flint industry found at Tharro Hill is not completely of Amri affinity (Fig. 47). The characteristic form found is a short trapezoidal blade apparently intended to be hafted. Small points, backed blades, and polyhedral cores are also common, and long blades of a type known to be associated with the Nal and Harappan cultures also occur. But the strong possibility does exist, however, that a late microlithic-type industry is represented, perhaps indicative of an occupation earlier than the Amri. An identical industry minus the long blades is known from a collection made on the Lyari River near Karachi[16] and from one made on the former golf course at Karachi.

❋ *Amri*

THE MOST FAMOUS OF THE SITES of the period found by Majumdar is that of Amri. The site is located south of the Lakhi Hills, which jut eastward into the Indus Valley just below Lake Manchhar. It is therefore less than twenty miles as the crow flies from the Bandhni River sites, to which access can be obtained over the Lakhi Hills by various footpaths. A part of the site is, in fact, situated on a gravel terrace close to the Indus River.

16 D. H. Gordon, *The Prehistoric Background of Indian Culture*, Mandhuri Dhirajlal, Bombay, 1958.

The site as a whole is at a low elevation and subject to flooding from the river. It is therefore located at the margin of cultivated alluvium, the river being some 1500 meters away to the east. Majumdar was able to evidence the fact that the Amri levels there were pre-Harappan by some limited excavations on the site. This conclusion was confirmed later at the sites of Ghazi Shah, Pandi Wahi, and Lohri in the Lake Manchhar region.

In 1959 J. M. Casal, the excavator of Mundigak, began a three-year campaign at Amri in an effort to expand Majumdar's work.[17] Casal excavated at two mounds (A and B) on the site, which stretches perhaps a distance of four hundred by three hundred meters. The Amri levels may, however, be considerably less than this in area, since both Harappan and Muslim remains are found above them. Casal, in fact, found that the earliest Amri occupation had been confined to Mound A.

Casal carried his excavations farther than Majumdar and reached virgin soil in both mounds. He was able to distinguish four phases in the purely Amri levels (Period I):

Period IA (the earliest) produced no structural remains, but a trench on the western border of the settlement was perhaps a canal. Handmade pottery amounts to over 80 per cent of all recovered, but the typical Amri wheel-made pottery, some of it painted in black and red, also occurs. (The Togau C type of pottery also was found, giving a neat typological tie to Miss de Cardi's Period III in central Baluchistan.) Some copper, shell, or terra-cotta bangles, sling stones (?), and flint blades of the "long" type were found also.

Period IB produced two levels of structures made from mud brick. One room had walls which rested on a three-foot-deep foundation trench filled with gravel. The plan shows small contiguous and rather regular houses made up of several chambers, the largest being some three by six meters in size. Large pottery vessels, for some unknown reason, perhaps storage, occur in the floors or yards of some of the houses. The pottery changes little from Period IA but includes now a dish-on-stand type, a familiar shape in the later Harappan civilization.

Period IC demonstrates the maximum Amri-period expansion at the site and is represented by three to four phases of building. Two entirely different kinds of habitations occur. The first are long (over six meters by three to four meters), rectangular, apparently flat-roofed, houses with mud floors, sometimes raised. A door at ground level gave access to the interior. Within the house the "storage" jars of IB type were common. In one case wooden posts were found in the walls, probably as supports for a light roof.

The second type of construction resembles Majumdar's findings at Lohri of little compartmented houses. These cell-like structures of mud

17 J. M. Casal, *Fouilles d'Amri*, Publication de la Commission Des Fouilles Archéologiques Fouilles du Pakistan, Librarie C. Klincksieck, Paris, 1964.

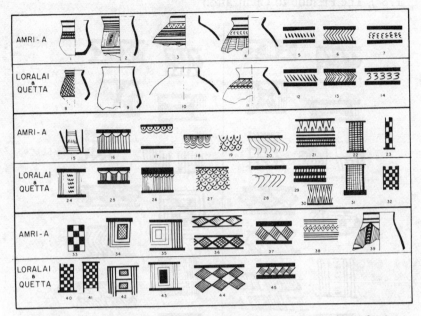

FIG. 48 *Comparative typology of painted pottery motifs in the early Amrian levels in the Indus Valley and those in the Quetta-Loralai areas in northern Baluchistan. The Baluchistan material is generally of Damb Sadaat I-Sur Jangal II affiliation.*

brick did not contain signs of habitation. They are obviously too small for that (some measure only a meter or two square). Obviously these structures were erected to support a superstructure. Significantly, there is considerable space between some of the house units, and here, as against the outside of these buildings, the hearths and other marks of daily life were found. One can envision the populace sleeping much of the year on their roofs—a common enough custom in torrid Sind today. Pottery tradition continues to sustain the Amri types, but now wheel-made forms amount to nearly half of all those found.

Period ID essentially continues IC but with considerable replacement of the older buildings. A new building of the compartmented or cellular type was constructed. Two of the compartments were connected by a door. Casal found parts of the same vase in all the little rooms and with justice assumes that the inhabitants lived on the roof (of wood) and that when it collapsed, probably through fire, the vase was scattered about. The pottery is essentially the same as that of Period IC but is a bit more florid and depictive—animals were common themes and provide a delightful, almost comic, touch (for example, the turtles in Figure 1).

It is interesting that all through this period potters' marks occur, most of which are simple engravings on the exteriors of the vessels.

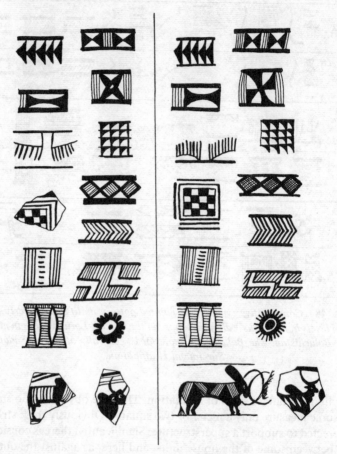

FIG. 49 *Comparative typology of painted pottery motifs in the late Amrian (B) levels B in the Indus Valley (left) and those in the Quetta-Loralai areas in northern Baluchistan. The Baluchistan material is generally of Damb Sadaat II affiliation.*

Period II is marked by the leveling of the structures of Period ID and the construction of buildings apparently identical to those of the earlier period. In phase B (the later) a large mud-brick platform with postholes was constructed on the west of Mound A, but its use is unknown. An increasing number of Harappan ceramics in this period is found, indicating that culture's growing influence.

Period III is the Harappan period at the site. The initial Harappan occupation would appear to be of the mature type (IIIA). It is followed by a transitional phase (IIIB), leading to a late phase (IIIC) like that at Mohenjo-daro (see p. 302), and at last by a Jhukar level (subperiod IIID) (see p. 353).

A study of faunal remains at the site indicates that cattle (*Bos taurus*) predominated in Period I, but sheep, goat, and the donkey also were present. Gazelle was hunted (or herded?) in the period. In the Harappan period (III), while cattle still predominate by far, the number and variety of wild animals hunted is large. These include the gazelle, deer, rhino, bear, boar, gavial, land tortoise, and turtle. Some of these are shown on the painted vessels (Figs. 1, 2, 3). The presence of the "domesticated" donkey in Period I is of importance, since as a beast of burden the donkey plays a significant role in the movement of produce throughout Western Asia in the third millennium B.C.

No good evidence for the character of the agriculture was obtained, but both the size and the elaboration of the buildings and the settlement itself plus the amount of habitation debris and duration of occupancy point inevitably to a successful adaptation of agriculture to the Indus Valley environment. (Of note in this regard was Majumdar's discovery at the sites of Dhal and Rohel jo-Kund of stone rings, which would qualify as digging-stick weights. None were found, however, at Amri.)

❊ *Kot Diji*

IN UPPER SIND ON THE EAST BANK OF THE INDUS RIVER, about fifteen miles south of Khairpur and some thirty odd miles from Mohenjo-daro, is the small site of Kot Diji.[18] The place is close to the walls of a medieval fortress and like Amri is on the margin of the cultivated plain. The fort itself is situated on a rocky hillock on whose talus, or perhaps its lower reaches, the prehistoric site rests. The place was excavated intensively for over a month by the Department of Archaeology, Government of Pakistan, under the direction of F. A. Khan. It had previously been visited by Ghurye in 1935, and collections made then reside in the Prince of Wales Museum in Bombay. Khan's work, short as it was, is definitive for the site. Excavations took place in the high portion of the site (Area A) and in a lower area to the east (Area B). The whole site area is relatively small, being only about six hundred feet by four hundred feet. Khan revealed that the upper levels of Area A phases 1 to 3 were Harappan and that the lower levels (phases 4 to 16) to bedrock belonged to an assemblage he calls Kot Dijian (3A is transitional). The Kot Dijian, while having its local aspects, is, however, a variant on the Nal-Amri cultural type, whose traces are described above. The often exuberant painted designs familiar in the Baluchistan and western Sind situation are rare here, but in general the equivalences are more than casual (Figs. 50, 51). There are also analogues to material from the Quetta sequence, including the potters' marks.

[18] F. A. Khan, "Excavations at Kot Diji," *Pakistan Archaeology*, No. 2 (1965), pp. 11–86.

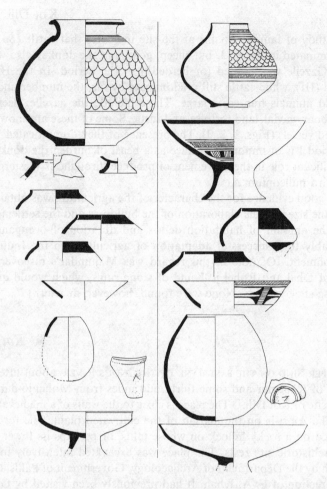

FIG. 50   *Comparative typology of pottery of pre-Harappan Kot Diji (left)*
and of pre-Harappan Amri (Amri B type).

The Kot Diji levels contained the mud-brick walls, often with stone foundations, of houses where, in some contrast to Amri, Lohri, and other sites of western Sind, the inhabitants lived at the ground level. Some of these walls are massive, measuring up to five feet in thickness. Mud-brick floors, large *in situ* vessels, and fireplaces, often brick-lined, were common to these houses. In one case (phase 7) a stone-lined drain was let into the lower layers. The excavator revealed large brick-lined ovens which he calls "community ovens" and which are a common feature of the Kot Dijian levels. In addition, a kiln complete with funnel was unearthed.

The Kot Dijian levels on the high part of the site (Area A) were surrounded by a thick, high wall. The base of the wall rested on bedrock. Its lower portion consisted of undressed limestone blocks for a distance of

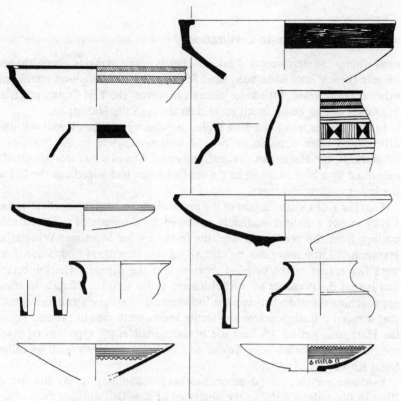

FIG. 51 *Comparative typology of pottery of pre-Harappan Kot Diji (left) and of pre-Harappan Amri (Amri B type).*

10 feet on which a mud-brick extension was raised for at least another 12 to 14 feet. A mud-brick revetment rested against the outer face while at the corners at least "bastions" were constructed, one of which was cleared to reveal its width to be 20 feet and its length some $31\frac{1}{2}$ feet. Large buildings not sufficiently cleared to ascertain their plan were noted within the walled area. Apparently this wall enclosed the entire settlement in its early stages, but later some of the inhabitants lived outside the walls in what Khan calls the "Lower City." This lower area was subject to flooding, perhaps from a nearby stream, for large limestone blocks were found in phase 4, apparently used to dam or divert floodwaters. Within the walls, however, the habitations were pressed right against the inner face.

Generally speaking, the Kot Dijian remains were singularly poor in artifacts. Bone and shell objects (some of unknown use), spindle whorls, clay discs, stone balls, a terra-cotta figurine of a bull (head), and a fragmentary bronze bangle were recovered from them. The flint-stone industry includes leaf-shaped arrowheads, sickle blades, knives, and polyhedral cores. Grinding stones also occur. Interesting because they are found in the Kot Dijian levels here but are common to the later Harappan culture are such things as terra-cotta "cakes," beads, clay bangles, cone-shaped objects (which may have been used for spindles), and dish-on-stand and other ceramic vessel forms. In general, however, the Kot Dijian material impresses one as being much more delicate than the Harappan.

In the last stages of the Kot Dijian occupancy, the large wall fell into disuse, and after a phase or two of final occupation by the "original" inhabitants, the Harappan occupation began. The two cultures are clearly separated by a burned layer, as if a conflagration had wiped out the last of the lower occupation there.

That the Kot Dijian variant of the pre-Harappan occupancy of the Indus Valley is not a unique matter is indicated by the finds of a comparable pottery from the predefense deposits found by Sir Mortimer Wheeler at Harappa.[19] Little more can be said about this important find, since there were few traces of the original dwellings in the deposit. The important fact is that the presence of this settlement so far into the Punjab, in effect approaching the doab between the Indus and the Ganges, strongly suggests that a rapid diffusion across the fertile Indus plain was in process *before* the Harappan period. (A new site of the "predefense" type was reported recently. It is located near Taxila and includes a cemetery. It is called Sarai Khola (see App. K).

Evidence for this phenomenon has been accumulating. At the site of Bhut in Bhawalpur state, to the northeast of Kot Diji, surface finds of the Kot Dijian ceramics have been made. The site is located close to the channel of the river Ghaggar, an intermittent monsoonal stream often equated with the ancient Sarasvati, a river of legendary tradition. The water of this stream now dies out in Rajasthan and does not now reach to its Hakra branch in Bhawalpur but surely did so in ancient times.[20] In the same region A. Ghosh, late Director-General of Archaeology in India, surveyed the Rajsthan sites in Bikaner in 1950 and found a great many sites, a percentage of which are Harappan, but at least seven are of the Kot Dijian type or at least have that type represented among them: Dulmani(?); Chak 11, Chak 21, Chak 75; Kalibangan; Mathula(?); Metasar 2; Nohar; Sothi A(?), Sothi D(?).[21] Of these sites Kalibangan has been the subject of much field research over the past several years under the direction of Shri B. B. Lal and Shri B. K. Thapar. This site consists of two mounds on the left bank of the Ghaggar River. The larger mound is on the east, the smaller

[19] Sir M. Wheeler, "Harappa 1946: The Defences and Cemetery R 37," *Ancient India*, No. 3 (1947), especially pp. 90–95, Pls. XL–XLII.

[20] For a balanced discussion of the nature and history of this, see Spate, (1957), pp. 485–488.

[21] I am enormously grateful to both Shri A. Ghosh and Shri B. B. Lal for the opportunity given me on several occasions to study the fine collections in the Indian Archaeological Survey's ceramic storage area at Safdarjang, New Delhi.

Fig. 52 *Pre-Harappan painted pottery motifs from the site of Kalibangan (after Lal and Thapar).*

to the west; together they cover a quarter of a square kilometer. The excavations have revealed that the main occupation is of the mature Harappan type (see p. 306), but in the lower levels of this Period (II) the Harappan material is mixed with non-Harappan material.

As at Kot Diji, this settlement was enclosed by walls, in this case solely of mud brick. Two structural phases are recognized: the earlier when the wall was somewhat less than two meters in width (1.90 meters average) and a later when the wall was widened between 3.70 and 4.10 meters. The space enclosed was about 250 meters in the north-south line and apparently only about 180 meters east to west. The "English bond" method of brick construction was used and the wall mud-plastered at various points (brick size, 30 × 20 × 10 cm.). The pottery is characterized by painted wares largely of the black on red (surface) variety. Occasional use of white as another adjunct color occurs. The designs are largely geometric, though faunal and floral elements occur. It has strong suggestions of stylistic ties to Kot Dijian wares (Fig. 52). The other objects found, such as the flint work, copper, terra cotta and shell bangles, stone mills, etc., also recall Kot Diji. Copper axes found at Kalibangan have not been found so far at Kot Diji.

The excavations indicate that between the end of the pre-Harappan settlements and the arrival of the Harappans there may have been a short phase during which the site was abandoned, perhaps because of earthquake. The mixing of the two traditions already mentioned suggests that the old inhabitants had contact with the new arrivals (see App. K).

This mixture also occurs at Amri (Period II) and at Kot Diji (3A) as a kind of transitional period. In the lower levels of the western mound pure pre-Harappan levels are found at Kalibangan (Period I).[22]

[22] See *Indian Archaeology, A Review*, 1960–61 edition, Report of the Archaeological Survey of India, New Delhi, pp. 31–32; Government of India, 1961, 31–32; also B. B. Lal, "A New Indus Valley Provincial Capital Discovered: Excavation at Kalibangan in Northern Rajasthan," *Illustrated London News*, March 24, 1962, pp. 454–457. Cultural Form, July 1967 pp. 78–88; Ministry of Education, Government of India.

The accumulating evidence, then, indicates that not only was a descent into the Indus River plain made by prehistoric farmers but their activities carried them far from their original home in Baluchistan. This argues for the success of an adaptation to the western Indian environment. While we do not know the true nature of the agriculture which made settlement possible, the closeness to rivers and streams in each case points to the flood plain as the obviously cultivable area. Inundation canals to carry rising floodwaters as far as possible into the old alluvium are likely; but since no certainty could have been attached to the degree of annual flooding, this extension by man of the flood plain would seem to have been primarily aimed at obtaining a surplus when possible. The basic subsistence must have required a more modest and dependable cultivated area; thus the proximity to the rivers.

It is unfortunate that we have virtually no evidence as to the kind of crops cultivated. However, in the Harappan period, wheat and barley are attested and were presumably the staples of that civilization (see p. 18). We can therefore assume a similar wheat and barley dependence in pre-Harappan times. What is unclear, however, is the difference in variety of these crops between that originally grown on the Iranian plateau and that now grown in the riverine plains of the Indus Valley. After all, upper Sind is known as the hot center of the world, while the monsoonal Punjab and the arid climate of northern Rajasthan present environmental problems which would seemingly require some adaptive changes in the crops grown.

Similarly, while cattle, sheep, and goats are evidenced for these settlements, we cannot be certain these are the same as those of the highlands. Indeed, sheep do not do well in these lowlands, and both goats and cattle can develop all kinds of hoof difficulties if kept purely on a moist alluvial soil. Pasturage would be required on high or at least well-drained ground part of the year. It is probably no accident that both in Baluchistan and in Sind the humped bull makes his appearance in these or the later Harappan settlements. Are indeed humped cattle the mark of a necessary adaptation accomplished by these men in crossing an indigenous wild *Bos* with the domestic cattle of the plateau?

In any case the existence of these settlements attests their economic success. The social adaptations, however, have probably a more significant meaning in view of the civilization that arose soon afterward on the identical ground. To gain some idea of what is indicated the second area of pertinence we should consider is Las Bela. Las Bela has been so little known that a more detailed description of the region is in order here. At the same time, this gives the reader an idea of what problems are encountered in an initial field survey.

✳ *Las Bela—The Geography*

THE FIRST ARCHAEOLOGICAL EXPLORATION OF LAS BELA was carried out by Sir Aurel Stein as late as 1942, and a brief report on the trip was published by him in 1943.[23] Unfortunately, Stein died before he could complete the final report on the archaeology of the district, and his manuscript was never published. Donald McCown apparently saw some of the material because he postulated an early red ware he called Niain ware, after that found by Stein at the site of Niai Buthi near Las Bela. This ware McCown regarded as being similar to the Togau ware of de Cardi.[24]

The only other source of information on material of archaeological interest is the *Baluchistan Gazetteer*.[25] This is based on information furnished by British officers and officials who traveled there from 1833 on. These travelers located various remains and recorded local legends about them. Strangely, though the district is readily accessible from Karachi, there has been little interest in the place.

There remains, however, the return march of Alexander from Patala (Hyderabad) through Gedrosia to the area around Kerman. In this march Alexander's troops apparently crossed the Hab River (Arabius), which is the present boundary of the southeastern portion of the district, and then, turning north, reached the town of Bela (Rambacia); after a battle there with a people called the Oreitai, they moved due west through the Jhau.[26] This march, with its account of hard battles in the district, would seem to indicate that there was a sizable population there and that it was comparatively well organized, an indication which in no way is contradicted by the soil and water resources presently known.

The Las Bela district is the smallest in area of the former Baluchistan states (Makran, Kharan, Kalat, Chagai)—7,043 square miles; and it has the densest population—11 persons per square mile. Over 70 per cent of its people are involved in agriculture.

The population distribution is significant. Las Bela proper is a wedge-

[23] Sir M. A. Stein, "On Alexander's Route into Gedrosia: an Archaeological Tour in Las Bela," *Geographical Journal*, Vol. CII, Nos. 5–6 (1943), pp. 193–227.

[24] D. E. McCown, "The Relative Stratigraphy and Chronology of Iran," *Relative Chronologies in Old World Archaeology*, R. Ehrich, ed., University of Chicago Press, Chicago, 1954, pp. 56–68; see also p. 62.

[25] *Baluchistan District Gazetteer*: Las Bela, 1907.

[26] Stein makes a good case for this route, which is now apparently generally accepted by classicists. See Stein, 1943.

shaped piece of alluvium fanning out from border mountains on the north to its shores on the Arabian Sea around Sonmiani Bay. Appended to this area, primarily by political events, is a long arid coastal strip running west to the borders of Makran. Within this strip only the shrine at Hinglaj and the small port of Ormara are worth noting. Neither of these evidence remains of any considerable antiquity.[27] On the east there is a series of parallel valleys set in a group of mountain ranges varying in height from an average of 4,500 feet on the north to less than 1,000 feet on the south. The only valley of any importance is made so by the perennial Hab River, which runs about 240 miles from the northern Hab Ranges to the sea. On the south the Hab forms the boundary between Las Bela district and the federal district of Karachi.

The most fertile area (Welpat) of the district is watered perennially by the flow of the Porali River. This important stream rises in southern Jhalawan in the mountain area just south of the line formed by the two towns of Khuzdar and Nal. The Porali drainage is thus an important link in the route to both Makran and Kalat. Further south, Porali tributaries provide access to the east, and there are several caravan routes branching to the upper Hab valley or to the Mhri valley and thus to western Sind.

About twenty-five miles north of Bela town the Porali River valley begins to widen. Until then it has been confined between high mountain walls, with only patches of cultivation possible here and there along its shores. About ten miles farther south these patches become almost contiguous along the western bank. The surrounding hills are of poorly cemented boulder conglomerate, and the actual channel is a stone-strewn bed with the water flowing in several meandering streams. The silt bluffs on the west bank are of considerable height, and the local populace is kept busy annually reinforcing branch and thorn-bush weirs that channel the water at key points onto the silt plain. This plain opens out about eleven miles north of Bela, where it is less than three hundred feet above sea level. Here the Porali becomes braided and meanders southward between its high silt and gravel banks until it vanishes into the alluvium in the vicinity of Jakhra some forty miles south of Bela. In seasons of high water the Porali was said to reach the brackish swamp areas just north of Sonmiani, but presently a dam system at Jakhra prevents this.

The alluvial plain around Bela, from the mountains south, is called locally Welpat. The cultivable area is in shape like an elongated oval, with a taper at both ends. The talus fans on the east of the valley form one boundary, and the high, arid silt bluffs on the west of the main Porali channel form a boundary there (see Pl. 18). In general, the area west of the Porali is uncultivable, even though additional water is frequently available via the Kud River, which joins the Porali just south of Bela.

[27] Stein, 1943, p. 202ff.

The cultivable area tapers out of the main Porali valley about twelve miles north of Bela; it grows to its greatest maximum just a few miles north of Bela town and is already tapering inward by the time it reaches the town itself. South of Bela, the cultivation forms a long, narrow, often broken, strip between the Porali on the west and the talus fans on the east. This strip broadens somewhat at Uthal, some forty miles southeast of Bela, after which it ends rather abruptly, cultivation farther south being sporadic.

Except for this cultivated strip, the bulk of Las Bela proper is a flat, desiccated alluvial plain broken here and there by the channels of inter-mittent streams from the mountains, or by an isolated field or two supplied by wells. About 60 per cent of all villages in the district are found in the Welpat-Uthal strip, and two thirds of these are in Welpat, where Bela town, the district capital, is also located. One hundred and two villages are located in less than 280 square miles.[28]

The climate of Las Bela is characteristic of western Baluchistan as a whole. Rainfall is less than ten inches annually, and it usually occurs in the winter months. The district itself is outside the summer monsoon rain shadow. Temperatures are high in summer and moderate in winter. The climatic situation emphasizes the great importance of the Porali River as a dependable source of moisture the year round.

Of significance is the fact that though Las Bela is a part of Baluchistan, its basic population is non-Baluchi. Census reports indicate:

Baluchi	ca.	9,000
Brahui		7,000
Jatt		5,000
Lassi		38,000

The Baluchi-Brahui element has been the dominant ruling group. The historical affinities of this group are to Kalat and Makran and eventually to Iran. The Jatts, too, belong elsewhere, their main center being in the Kachhi and Sibi districts. However, the Lassi appear to be indigenous to Las Bela. Their language is closely related to that of Sind, and most of their cultural affinities appear to be Sindi rather than Baluchi. The name Las Bela is Sindi and means "forest of the Lassi." The great emphasis of the Lassi is upon farming rather than upon the warlike nomadism of the Baluchi of the past, and in this they emulate the Sindi. In this regard it is said that some Lassi consider themselves as of Arabian descent, as fre-quently occurs among several groups in Sind.

There is a decided Negroid strain among the Lassi, probably deriving from the period when the Arabs, dominant in both Makran and the East African areas, were maintaining a slave trade and probably using certain African groups in their military forces. It is of interest that beehive-

[28] Figures based on census of Pakistan, 1951.

shaped houses occur in Las Bela, and these, along with such objects as the Somali shield and spear, would indicate a strong influence from the Arabian Sea-East African center. It is quite possible that such influences go back earlier than the Arab period.

Holdich has called Las Bela a "true gateway."[29] It is less than seventy miles to Bela town from the Kolwa area on the Mashkel River, or less than two days' journey on good camels via the Jhau Pass. This route touches upon the Nal River almost halfway along, and this provides a continuing source of water. The Mashkel River valley is the natural route into Makran and points west. It is less than 100 miles to the Indus River via the routes previously outlined (*ca.* 125 miles to Mohenjo-daro as the crow flies). South of Bela town there is the natural route taken by Alexander along the eastern side of the alluvial plain. This, in turn, reaches the Hab River area near its mouth, whence it goes southeast past Karachi and the Malir oasis to the Indus River and beyond. This open area on the south, with its access to the Arabian Sea coast, may have made ports such as Sonmiani of great importance in the past, though Patala, Daibul, and Karachi are historically more famous, since they centered on the Indus River routes.

The Arab invasion of Sind under Mohammed ibn Qasim in A.D. 711-712 began in Makran, and we can presume that it crossed into Las Bela via the Jhau Pass because, as tradition has it, General Haroun, one of Qasim's officers, was killed near Bela and his supposed tomb is still regarded with respect by the local populace. The traditions indicate that the Arabs then invaded Sind, attacking Daibul on the coast and then, significantly, Sehwan near Lake Manchhar on the Indus. Both these cities were readily accessible from Bela. Thus it would seem from the historical accounts of Alexander and later the Arabs that Las Bela had an important role as a gateway to India.

A final geographical feature should be noted. The abundant water and rich fertility of the Welpat tract in particular is a matter of some wonder for those who have wandered over Baluchistan. Most valleys in Baluchistan are cultivated on a narrow margin of survival. Water resources are tapped by the *karez*, or well, systems, and it would also appear that in the past surface water was diverted by damming the channels of normally dry streams. Soil resources too are very limited, and villages are widely scattered. The concentration of villages in Welpat is therefore unusual in Baluchistan. Even more unusual, perhaps, are the great numbers of fine old trees, including date palms, which give the district its name, "forest of the Lassi." Excellent crops of wheat, millet, mustard, castor beans, bananas, dates, and truck products are harvested each year, and one of the satisfying aspects of the place is the well-fed condition of cattle, horses, sheep, and goats. The natural advantages of the area around Bela are such that it is

---

[29] T. H. Holdich, *The Gates of India*, London, 1910.

greatly superior to most of western Baluchistan. These advantages plus its accessibility must have made the region highly attractive from very early times.

✳ *Niai Buthi*

SIR AUREL STEIN SURVEYED THE ORMARA AREA and included both the western portions of Las Bela proper and the gorge country of the Hingol River up to and including the Jhau Pass. Stein records a few sites on this initial portion of his survey and regards them all as late or medieval

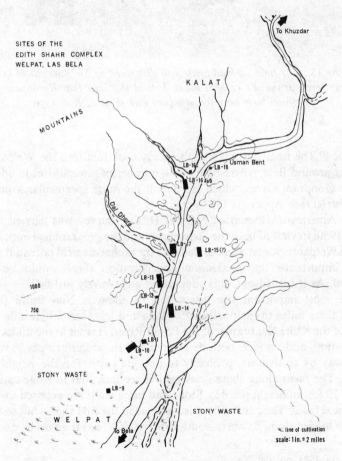

MAP 14 *Sites of the Edith Shahr Complex, Welpat, Las Bela.*

PLATE 15 *Las Bela—a mud-brick wall excavated by Sir Aurel Stein in the upper levels at the site of Niai Buthi. It is at this level that Harappan-type artifacts have been found mixed with those of Kulli type.*

Islamic.[30] The final stage of Stein's survey took him into the Welpat sub-district around Bela, where he noted a number of mound sites in addition to the Gondrani Caves, which are one of the more spectacular aspects of the district (see Appendix G).

An American Museum of Natural History survey was carried out in 1959-1960. In view of both the Stein report and the geographical importance of the Welpat region, it was decided that the archaeological potential was of such importance that maximum concentration there would be most fruitful. As it turned out, this conclusion was entirely justified.

The most important site discovered by Stein is Niai Buthi (LB-6), about three miles to the northeast of Bela and less than a half mile to the west of the Kulri Nai branch of the Porali River. It is set in the midst of the cultivation, and, in fact, both its eastern and its western slopes have been cut away by cultivators, probably to provide earth for the neighboring lands. The faces along these sides exhibit sections that in some cases run up to 20 feet in height (Pl. 15). Stone and brick walls are exposed throughout these faces. The cutting has also elongated the side somewhat so that it is now longer along its north-south axis (*ca.* 400 feet) than on its east-west

[30] Stein, 1943, pp. 198–208.

axis (*ca.* 300 feet). The mound rises somewhat above 40 feet and has a broad saddle shape at its top.

Stein made two cuts into the site above the thirty-foot contour on the southern portion of the western slope. The walls of these excavations have partly collapsed, but enough remains to indicate that he did not go much deeper than two meters in trenches not more than three to four meters in width.

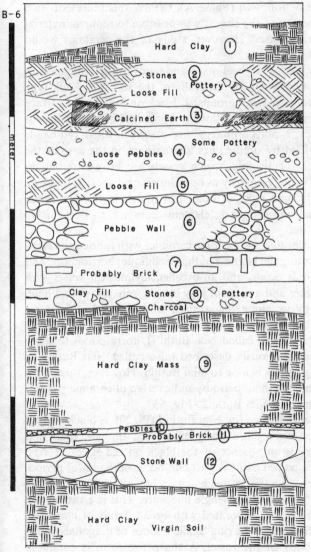

B-6

meter

Hard Clay ①

Stones ②
Pottery
Loose Fill

Calcined Earth ③

Some Pottery
Loose Pebbles ④

Loose Fill ⑤

Pebble Wall ⑥

Probably Brick ⑦

Clay Fill Stones ⑧ Pottery
Charcoal

Hard Clay Mass ⑨

Pebbles ⑩
Probably Brick ⑪

Stone Wall ⑫

Hard Clay Virgin Soil

FIG. 53 *Section from the western face of the site of Niai Buthi, Las Bela. Two main periods in a habitation of Kulli type are shown: Niai Buthi I: 3-12; Niai Buthi II: 1-2.*

Taking advantage of the exposed wall on the western side, we removed pottery *in situ* down to virgin soil, a vertical distance of something over 5 meters (5.40 meters). In addition, surface collections were gathered from all over the site.

One observation of some importance was that red-fired brick occurred only on the top of the mound. A brick wall was exposed in Stein's cut (southwest) along the east wall (Phase B). At the base of this (Pl. 15) was a thin charcoal line, below which was a hard clay mass within which a few mud-brick lines could be followed (Phase A). Clearly this represents two phases in a late occupation of the site. It was possible to remove material *in situ* from both these phases. However, study of the ceramics would indicate no important differences.

The pottery in both phases is wheel-made and tends toward thickness in construction. The painted wares are generally of the so-called Kulli type and can be divided into three main groups: 1, black on buff slip or surface (decoration on the sherds *in situ* is confined to horizontal lines, in a broad-line drawing technique); 2, polychrome painted vessels in which red bands and black designs divided by simple lines alternate or, in the case of the latter, act as a border. These polychrome vessels are brown or buff in background color and occur primarily as open bowls or dishes; 3, black on red slip designs that include pipal or other leaf motifs in the Harappan style, as well as animal and geometric elements common to Baluchistan (see Pls. 21, 22).

In addition to the decorated wares, some ceramics with fabric-impressed rims were found, indicating the lateness of that technique; herringbone and comb-loop incised sherds occur, and an excellent cylindrical vessel with holes through it. A grater and a piece of clay bangle were also found here.

The section made by us along the western wall revealed at least six phases of building. Preliminary studies of the *in situ* material indicate that the uppermost phase, now called Niai Buthi II, corresponds to those phases of the Stein cut previously described (also called Niai Buthi II). The five lower building phases belong to Niai Buthi I. However, there is no clear break between the two main periods, and overlap of ceramic styles is apparent in the last phase of Niai Buthi I (Fig. 53).

The characteristic ceramic type for Niai Buthi I (Pl. 20) is black on buff slip or surface painted ware more finely made, i.e., thinner, than that of Niai Buthi II.There is an absence of the black on red styles of Niai Buthi II. Though black on red painted wares do occur in the lower period, their design repertoire is like that of the black on buff slip type. A characteristic type is given the name Buthi single-line ware. This is a rather thin ware of finely levigated paste, decorated with broad bands of chocolate brown or black running around the rim. Shallow loops or diagonals sometimes run along the body of the vessel. A sharp rim form is common. Buthi black on buff slip is also a fine ware, with deep straight-sided or

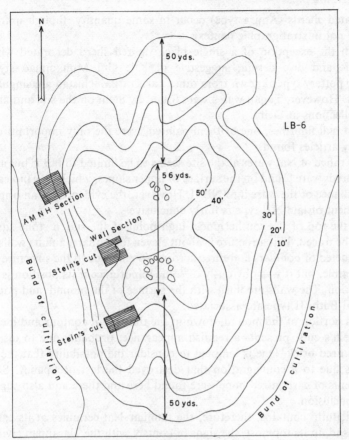

MAP 15   *Excavated areas at the site of Niai Buthi, Las Bela.*

tapering jars and open bowls characteristic. Designs are cleanly painted, even though broad brush strokes were used. Animals, floral patterns, and a limited number of geometrics make up the design repertoire.

Several sherds of Nal-type ware were recovered in Niai Buthi I and on the surface of the site (Plate 13). Of considerable interest for its tantalizing suggestions of a generic relationship to wares found in both Kalat and Quetta are examples of white paint on black slip pottery found on the surface (Zari or Kechi Beg white on dark).

Indus Valley affinities are clearly expressed in the surface recovery of examples of graters, incised fruit stands, and string-marked pottery, the latter frequently possessing a red slip (Plate 19). This material is confined to the upper portion of the site, where it was found *in situ*, and thus is of Niai Buthi II association.

Of interest is a single example of incised stone ware. Raised-ridge-decorated sherds (Anjira type) occur in some quantity, though unfortunately not in stratigraphic context.

With the exception of a single black on red sherd decorated with a triangle and disc design, suggestive of Kile Gul Mohammad style,[31] earlier pottery types known from other parts of Baluchistan are singularly absent. However, Togau wares were found by Stein on the site and are in the collections at Delhi.

Two bull figurines, one of them painted, were the only important non-pottery articles found.

The range of Nal wares at the site seems to be limited to NB I, but a few Nal sherds were found on the surface of upper slopes, which may indicate a continuance of the ware into NB II. However, the evidence for an original settlement of late Nal type is fairly conclusive.

On the top of the southernmost high point of the site, a stone square could be traced. This structure is about eleven feet square, and its walls are constructed of boulders laid three across. No entrance to the structure was perceptible, but it was obviously of some importance if its position is any indication. The walls are flush with the surface of the mound, and pottery of Niai Buthi II type are associated.

This portion of the mound, down to the thirty-foot contour and including Stein's cuts, presents a reddish appearance, probably due to disintegrated fired brick. One is tempted to consider the possibility that the red here is due to a conflagration that destroyed the last occupancy. Some fragments of carbonized bone were found here and there and also suggest this conclusion.

Niai Buthi contains, therefore, the familiar Nal ceramics at its earlier levels and, in its topmost, the signs of contact with the Harappan civilization. Between and amid are the pottery types which were first identified by Stein at the site of Kulli, the largest in Kolwa. The earlier phases of the Kulli (Niai Buthi I) are related to the ceramic corpus familiar in the last phases of pre-Harappan occupation of such sites in the Indus area as Ghazi Shah Ib (Fig. 46), Amri (periods ID-IIA), and in Baluchistan in the upper layers (areas D, F, and upper layers of A) of the mound of Sohr Damb, Nal. This sequence to this point is parallel to that of the northern sites, and indeed the identical picture emerges in the study of sites in Kolwa, Jhau, Drakalo, Wadh, and the Ornach (Appendix F). It is the later levels of Kulli affinity that produce unfamiliar elements: incised stone vases, incised fruit stands, graters, and a heavy, exuberantly painted pottery in which scene or friezes of not particularly orderly or geometric style are depicted (Pl. 21).

[31] Fairservis, 1956, Design 9.

✳ *The Edith Shahr Complex*

THE GREATEST SURPRISE WAS OBTAINED in moving to the northern extremity of Welpat. The discoveries there throw considerable light on these late phases as well as the earlier (Map 14).

Near the village of Usman Bent, at the border of Jhalawan and Las Bela, the Porali River crosses the one-thousand-foot contour line and in so doing debouches from the gorge country into a continuously broader valley. The river itself meanders over a bed that in places extends over a half mile. The eastern bank consists primarily of arid plains of boulder conglomerate, while the western follows suit except here and there where silt banks support patches of local cultivation. These silt alluvial deposits become broader as the river proceeds southward. They are confined between the talus fans of the hills and the river bed until, approximately eight miles south of Usman Bent, the hills drop away and the river flows out onto the plain of Welpat.

The archaeological resources of this eight-mile stretch of valley are such as to make it one of the very most important areas in the Indo-Iranian Borderlands. Within the area there are at least five hundred structures of one kind or another clustered into groups or strung out along the valley. Almost all of these structures are of stone construction and are therefore remarkably preserved. Many have walls standing above four feet, and the ground plan for a great number of buildings is readily traced. In most cases it seems apparent that the stone construction was to support walls of brick or wood that have long since disappeared, but there are not a few structures complete in themselves.

The discovery of this archaeological treasure was carried out piecemeal, and initially we were not aware of the continuity of the sites. Description of them can be accordingly set forth in the same way. The whole complex is named after the first site discovered, Edith Shahr (LB-1).

Preliminary examination of the material indicates that there are at least two major periods represented: Complex A, the earlier; and Complex B, the later.

COMPLEX A: Sites of this complex are of Kulli cultural affinity or, in Las Bela, generally contemporaneous with Niai Buthi II. In addition, there are decided traces of earlier occupation (Niai Buthi I).

LB-1 (Edith Shahr type site): This extensive site is located near the southern tip of the 750-foot spur on the right bank of the Porali River. A portion of the southern edge of the site extends under cultivated fields and is separated from those fields by an irrigation canal. The main site is actually located on a gently sloping spur of the hill. The entire area covered by remains measures at least two thousand square yards (Pl. 16).

PLATE 16 *Las Bela—the southernmost site of the Edith Shahr Complex. On the right begins the main cultivated area of Welpat; the Porali River can be seen flowing down the center of the valley. The site lies at the foot of the slope. The jumbled mass marks the large structures which readily identify the site. Note the remarkable preservation of the structures in the middle ground.* (*Complex B*)

LB-1—Main mounds: The largest portion of the site is taken up by four principal mounds (height about thirty-five feet to about twenty feet at the lowest) and smaller surrounding masses obviously related in some way to the higher ones. Boulders were used as the principal building material, and, as a result, the aspect of these mounds is of enormous heaps of stone, shapeless in outline. Close inspection of the mounds indicates that their height is very likely not because of superimposed levels of cultural debris but because they represent large structures. The ceramic evidence would seem to confirm this conclusion, since it appears to represent one period only.

In spite of the collapse of the walls, generally enough remains to indicate that this part of the site contained an elaborate complex of interrelated buildings. The northernmost high mound rises about 30 feet. At the ground level on the southern side there are traces of a massive stone wall running about east-west; 20 feet in from this wall and about 7 feet higher there is another stone wall running parallel to the first one. Approximately 20 feet farther in and about 8 feet higher the top of the mound begins its rise as a kind of rectangular platform, running north-south, from which large spurs branch off at right angles descending gradually east and west. The top of this mound, as with the other higher mounds, has a considerable quantity of fired brick—obviously the remnants of the topmost structure.

It would appear that this structure was built ziggurat-fashion, i.e., in receding and rising stages. On the top of the highest stage was set a narrow, probably F-shaped, structure. Though not as apparent as in this mound, the other high mounds do have traceable wall lines suggesting the same structural pattern.

The 30-foot mound, just west of the mound described above, not only exhibits the same method of construction but at its northernmost part has an ascending spur, probably about 15 feet in width. The spur itself is divided into compartments which suggest storage pits or perhaps small

PLATE 17 *Las Bela—a boulder wall of Complex A affiliation at the site of Edith Shahr. Some of these walls have been preserved to a height of six or more feet.*

tanks. The platform appears to have been about 30 feet long running about north-south and about 24 feet wide. There are a great many indications that a substantial fired-brick structure was constructed here. Curious is the fact that at the south end of the platform the area recedes to a kind of backbone of stone about 5 feet wide, on either side of which are the remnants of a sharp slope downward. After a distance of about 30 feet, a line of stones no wider than 3 feet across indicates a kind of drain, after which there is trace of a rectangular stone structure about 10 feet wide, beyond which three walls run at right angles to the ground.

All about this rather elaborate platform there are ample indications of spurs having run off at right angles. In one case there is the trace of an alleyway dividing the large platform from a smaller and somewhat lower one on the east.

One is tempted to envision these spurs as sloping ramps or stairways leading to the various platforms. It is difficult to understand what else they might have been used for, as the method of construction would not seem to have required buttresses.

Among the smaller mounds and rather amorphous heaps of stone that occur along the south and west access of this part of the site, there are tantalizing traces of walls that give promise of revealing building plans with a minimum of excavation. One particularly interesting series of buildings on the southwest reveals a number of streets and alleyways, indicating a complex of structures. One of these has a stone-paved floor in the midst of which appears a round hollow like a well or drain. There is the trace of a similar "well" in the next building.

Just east of the largest mound, in an area taken over by the local Moslems as a graveyard, there is a very large stone building. Rectangular in shape, it measures about 215 feet in length by about 45 feet in width. Its walls are 5 feet thick and are made of large boulders, some of which, 3 feet long, are laid in parallel rows between which smaller stones are placed. Traces of numerous entrances, some with stairs, along its long side indicate that the building must have been used for some activity involving numbers of people.

Another structure of some interest is a stone circle located near one of the high mounds on the northern part of the site. This circle is about 25 feet across and has an entrance of sorts on its northwestern side. The walls are from 3 to 4 feet thick.

LB-1—Settlements: The most provocative structures on the site are separate from the main mounds and are located on the northwest, though traces of similar buildings extend for several hundred yards to the south of that point. A cluster of over forty buildings, whose foundations stand on the average over two feet high, and some five feet, is an extraordinary survival from the past. The boulder construction of the walls is such that

PLATE 18   *Las Bela—one of the Complex A sites of the Edith Shahr Complex. The aerial photograph shows how the site is situated high on a bluff on the left bank of the Porali River. Note the apparently formal layout of the main and monumental part of the site. A wall can be seen running eastward from the site, then turning north to form a huge compound.*

they seem little disturbed and give us a wonderful opportunity to envision with little effort a settlement of the second millennium B.C.

The buildings are set slightly higher than the main part of the site because they are nearer to the hillside. They are generally rectangular in shape, with the long axis varying a few degrees off the north-south line. Streets or lanes run between the structures, and these passageways vary from 3 to about 15 feet. Some of the structures are gathered about large open areas, forming a kind of courtyard which may be as wide as 40 feet.

The buildings are of varying size, but an average measurement of 75 by 21 feet was obtained for the simple rectangular structures. Clearly traceable are interior walls dividing the structures widthwise. Stones set out here and there opposite wall breaks formed entrance steps. Walls are usually around 2 feet in thickness. The interiors of all these structures are filled with hard earth and pebbles, and generally surprisingly few traces of habitation. One wonders if this original floor level was flush with the top of the stone foundations, as the steps outside might indicate.

Two rather elaborate structures in this complex of buildings are worthy of mention. The first is rectangular in plan, with an open end facing south. From the open end there appear to be traces of a slope upward, the ruins of either stairs or, very likely, a ramp. The other structure I have called the "Great Building." It consists of a group of elevated, narrow buildings gathered around a "court." Ramps and steps lead into this inner area from all sides. At the southern end two squarish piles of boulders may be the remnants of towers or outlying monuments of some kind.

Common are parallel rectangular buildings with no more than a six- or seven-foot-wide alley between, and this higher than the surrounding area, as if the two structures were meant to be joined.

LB-1—Other observations: A modern irrigation channel running along the southern side of the main site exposes numerous large boulder walls, and the area is strewn with sherds (NB II type), figurines, and particles of bone.

Exposed on the southern face of the irrigation channel are two large vessels. They are approximately three and a half feet high and are sheared in half by the irrigation. In the bottom of one, pieces of slag were recovered, but no other indications of firing were found, so the use of these large vessels is still uncertain.

Also exposed in this same face is a cist burial of which only the leg bones remain. The burial "chamber" is two feet wide and covered over with flat thick stones. The side appears to be hard clay, perhaps brick. The position of the bones indicates an extended burial.

Another burial was found in the midst of the cultivated area just south of the irrigation channel. This is a simple extended burial with the skeleton laid out on a north-south axis (head north) and on its side, facing west. The cranium had been exposed and was almost totally eroded, but enough remained of the skull and neck bones to indicate that this head had been sharply bent forward. That fact and the surrounding accumulation of prehistoric sherds (though not directly associated) may indicate that the burial is not Islamic, as its general position may imply, but perhaps of the period of the main site.

Nal wares were recovered on the site, particularly along the eastern side of the mound area next to the modern footpath. Here there are a number of stone foundations exposed, indicating rather small dwellings. Niai Buthi I wares also occur in the site, and it would appear, then, that an earlier occupation than the main one must have existed.

Again, one cannot help but note the reddish aspect of the tops of the main mounds. As at Niai Buthi, this is caused by the exposure of fired-brick debris, but again one is tempted to consider a major conflagration as one aspect of the final occupation of the site.

LB-14: About two and a half miles to the northeast of LB-1, on the eastern side of the Porali River bed, the bluffs rise abruptly to something over one hundred feet, gradually tapering down for the next half mile south. Inland about four hundred yards a low ridge runs parallel to the high ground of the bluffs. Between the two parallel rises, the ground slopes down to a flat, shallow valley which broadens out to the south. This valley was apparently of some importance in antiquity even though the land is arid and uncultivable (Pl. 18).

At the southern end of the high river bluff the area is strewn with boulders in exactly the fashion of LB-1. As at the latter site, walls are readily traced, though, unfortunately, little can be discerned as to the form of the buildings. Near the top of the highest mound a marked depression indicates a drain or storage pit set in the midst of a paved floor (hole is about four feet across). The general position of those walls that are traceable indicates a series of buildings built to conform with the side slope.[32]

Branching off to the east from these mounds, the remnants of a wall cross the small valley to the parallel ridge, turn north along the ridge for about four hundred yards, and then turn again, running west across the valley to ascend the river bluff. The wall then returns to the mounds, thus enclosing an area at least 1600 yards square.

In the midst of this enclosure, somewhat to the southern end of the valley, a large rectangular structure (axis north-south) is worthy of note. This is constructed of large boulders and includes a tier of white stones. The building is over one hundred feet long, and its walls are six feet thick. It is divided into three equal compartments, with entrances to each on the east.

South of the wall, along the valley, traces of a number of structures are found. Among these are small rectangular buildings similar to those of LB-1 and a fine stone circle, like the one at the latter site, with its entrance on the east-southeast.

Finally, on the highest bluff overlooking the valley, but north of the turn in the wall, there is a square structure with remnants of a wall connecting it with the main wall previously described; another wall runs east, then north, from this square. The structure may well be a watchtower foundation on account of its very prominent position.

Ceramics on this site so far recovered are entirely of Niai Buthi II type. Fruit stand, bull figurines, and graters of conventional type also occur (Plate 19).

LB-13: Approximately a halfmile, somewhat north of west, across the Porali River, the large site of LB-13 is perceptible from LB-14. This

32 Of large-stone construction; one stone probably weighing half a ton.

site is in the gravel bluff about thirty-five feet above the bed of the Porali. Here the ground is flat, and at one level it broadens out as one goes north. Numerous north-south-running ravines divide the site somewhat along its western edge. Here rising ground, terrace fashion, provides a setting for rectangular structures of Complex B, as well as two stone circles of that complex (see p. 362). The mass of ruined buildings extends about seven hundred yards to the north.

The Complex A structures appear to be limited to the south and east positions of the site. Here are the familiar large heaps of boulders within which are traces of walls. Around the two principal mounds numerous incomplete wall lines indicate a variety of rectangular and square buildings. One mound has several wall lines, suggesting a squat pyramidal form with a flat top, but too little can so far be traced to confirm this impression.

Some Nal ware was recovered here, as well as Niai Buthi I and II wares, and a number of plain wares, suggesting perhaps a longer Niai Buthi I occupation than at the other sites.

LB-17: Located about three quarters of a mile north of LB-13, this large site is very similar in its layout; that is, it consists of a series of mounds in the south and east, whereas to the north and west are numerous structures of what appear to be Complex B. The site is on the terrace between the western ridges and the Porali River bed. Its length, north-south, is about a quarter mile in all by no more than about two hundred yards at its widest.

The site was observed from a helicopter and photographed. Unfortunately, there was no opportunity to visit the place, and there is consequently no ceramic evidence to confirm the impression that the large stone-covered mounds high on a dominating part of the site are of Complex A. But in view of the evidence at the other sites, this is certainly not unlikely.

LB-16: A little over one mile north of LB-17, on the same side of the river and situated, as are the other sites, between the river bed and the western ridges, the site of LB-16 stretches about a half mile north-south and about three hundred yards east-west, though some presumably Complex B buildings are perceptible about a half mile to the northwest.

The site is the largest in terms of number of structures so far found, but most of these belong to Complex B. However, on the eastern edge of the site, overlooking the river, is a large mound of boulders, within which the usual wall lines can be traced. Here a well-like hollow appears on the southern side of the mound. The mound itself is quite compact, but it rises only about fifteen feet, again giving the impression of a squat, flat-topped building. All about are the usual tantalizing traces of structures belonging to the same period.

Pottery is of Niai Buthi II type, though a few sherds of Nal ware were also found.

The Complex A, or Kulli-type, settlement is found outside Las Bela in Wadh, Ornach, and Drakalo, to the north, and in Kolwa, to the west. The

PLATE 19   *Objects of the late Kulli culture found in Complex A, site of Edith Shahr, Las Bela.   Upper left—Basket-marked pottery, which persists from earliest times here.   Middle left—Small stone mortar.   Lower left— Part of a terra-cotta "cake," a type commonly found at Harappan sites. Upper right—Painted bull figurine.   Middle right—Two clay bangle fragments and a piece of the body of a clay cart.   Lower right—Fragment of a clay "grater."*

PLATE 20 *Pottery usually associated with early Kulli levels in southern Baluchistan. These examples are from the Edith Shahr site, Complex A, Las Bela.*

use of stone for monumental structures characterizes these remains. Typically there is a central mound and around it traces of a massive enclosure wall. Access to the central mound or platform, as in Las Bela, is by a ramp or stairway. Drains let into the central mound and/or in associated structures are indicated.[33]

[33] J. M. Casal has recently opened excavations in the site of Nindowari in the Ornach. No final word as to his results there has been forthcoming as yet, but preliminary reports appear to confirm the above; see addended bibliography.

A tendency to centralized settlement and a diminution in number of villages in a limited area such as the Ornach is evidenced by sites throughout the region.

❋ *Mehi and Kulli*

THE SITE OF MEHI, located some forty miles to the southwest of Nal, casts some further light on the nature of the Kulli culture. The site is roughly circular and very large (300 by 330 yards by 50 feet at its highest part). Stein explored the western slopes and the highest part of the site (also in the west) with trenches. Trench I was carried for 75 feet up the slope of the mound, from the 10-foot contour to a kind of flat terrace somewhat south of the high mound. On the surface of this terrace, Stein found numerous fragments of both bull and human female clay figurines. On the terrace itself Stein expanded his trench laterally in two directions (trenches II and III). Their depth appears not to have exceeded 4 feet at the maximum. He encountered no structural remains in this excavation.

The area explored by Stein turned out to be a cemetery in which cremated remains were sometimes buried in vessels or sometimes in the ground. Intimately associated with these burials were copper tools, beads, and terra-cotta figurines representing women, bulls, and birds. Stein was unable to determine whether the material surrounding these burials was contemporaneous with them or had intruded as the result of the burials of the cemetery builders. His text offers little to solve this problem.

Trench IV was dug up the slope of the highest part of the mound. The excavation was carried to a depth of six feet. Some rough stone-wall foundations were encountered in the highest portion of the mound. Stein describes a roughly painted black on buff jar (see Pl. 21) which has a design consisting of a kind of "bug-faced" bull standing between spiky trees and over sketchily drawn ibexes. This typically Kulli design and its execution he regards as contrasting with the finer black on red slip wares of trenches II and III and, therefore, as later. However, figurines were also found in Trench IV, and similarly decorated sherds were found in the lower trenches.

It is of comparative interest that the incinerary urns illustrated by Stein are of the plainer variety. Some were directly comparable in form and decoration to those found in the Incinerary Pot phase at Periano Ghundai (see p. 147). The female figurines of Mehi are clearly analogous to those of the Zhob cult. The goggle eyes, necklaces, shoulder form, pedestal bases, hanging hair, and hoods (when they occur) obviously represent the same basic composition (Fig. 54). The bull figurines are generally somewhat cruder than those of the Zhob cult, but have parallels in Damb Sadaat III in the Quetta sequence (see Fig. 54:21, 22). Parallels to the bird figurines are also found in the Quetta Valley (see Fig. 54:23, 24).

PLATE 21 *Pottery usually associated with late Kulli levels in southern Baluchistan. These examples found by Stein at Mehi.* (Courtesy of the Archaeological Survey of India.)

PLATE 22 *Pottery associated with the late Kulli phase of southern Baluchistan. The middle upper and lower motifs are known in the Mature Harappan of Sind. From the site of Mehi.* (Courtesy of the Archaeological Survey of India.)

Decorated sherds excavated in trenches I through III display interesting similarities of design to those of the Quetta Valley. The spiked trees in the bottoms of open bowls (see Fig. 54), the horizontal triangle and diamond motif, and the alternate verticals are examples of these design parallels.

The figurines are found in Damb Sadaat III context, while the designs are generally in Damb Sadaat II in the Quetta sequence. We might thus hypothesize that the cremation vessels and the associated figurines belong to a later phase of the Kulli culture (Niai Buthi II) which was dug into an earlier occupation phase (Niai Buthi I). The earlier phase is characterized by the more geometric designs and finer wares, including Nal types, the later by the florid designs of animals and the Zhob-like vessels previously described. A hint of this possibility is given by Stein in that none of the funerary vessels described is decorated in the earlier style.

Kulli, the largest mound in Kolwa, very probably represents the principal prehistoric settlement there, at least for one period. It measures 400 by 300 yards and is about 30 feet high at its highest point. The surface collection illustrated by Stein is dominated by the exuberant black on red slip decorated pottery familiar in the cremation phase at Mehi. Included are female figurines and painted terra-cotta bulls, exactly as recovered at

Mehi and as found at Niai Buthi II levels in Las Bela. Not infrequent are black on red slip sherds with dark red bands used as an auxiliary decorative feature.

Stein initially cleared some little rooms of a stone-walled structure (I) located on the top of the southeastern portion of the mound. His excavations included trenching along the outside edges of the walls and clearing within them. The building may have been part of a temple or palace complex, as no doors were observed. This might indicate that the little rooms were probably used for grain storage and intended to be entered from above. Steps leading upward were found in one of the chambers, suggesting that there had been an upper story in the structure. Within these rooms terra-cotta bull figurines, fragments of copper, lapis lazuli beads, bone and glass(?) bangles, a grater, and grinding implements were found. The pottery included storage vessels decorated with raised wavy bands and black on red slip canister jars decorated with buglike animals identical to those of the latest phase at Mehi. Sherds of this latter type were common both inside and outside the structure.

Additional excavations were carried out in the eastern slope of the site by trenching upward from the twenty-foot contour into the thirty-foot plateau (Trench V). Terra-cotta bulls and female figurines were very common in this trench. These differed in no wise from those of Mehi and Complex A-late-phase in Las Bela. The pottery type was also identical to that found in the structure at the top of the mound. However, some fine unpainted gray-ware bowls were found which are of interest as possible links to the Bampur area.

Nothing in Stein's material suggests an earlier level equivalent to that of Nal, but the geometric motifs on the sherds (even though these are dressed up with ancillary red bands) may be derived from an earlier phase equivalent to that at Mehi. However, evidence for this assumption is also lacking. It may well be that the entire site was of the late Kulli period and that its mass was accumulated from the destruction (traces of fire everywhere present in the structures) of an elaborate and extensive building complex of which Structure I formed a part.

❋ *Village Settlement of Southern Baluchistan*

EVEN WITH THE LIMITATIONS of the restricted and incomplete field work that must for a time qualify any conclusions, what we do have is evidence enough to prove that the prologue to civilization or indeed civilization itself was present in the period around and after 2500 B.C. in these regions. In the previous chapter a description was attempted to show that to the north, in the Kandahar area, Fort Sandeman, Loralai, Duki, and the Quetta Valley, a continuity of occupation of these regions is amply demonstrated by the archaeology. From semipermanent village camps, the record shows a more and more permanent settlement with expanding population in terms of larger and more numerous village sites, followed in a final phase by a diminution in number of villages but a centralization in the remainder. These late villages are characterized by dominating monumental structures formal in aspect. This history is repeated in the southern regions

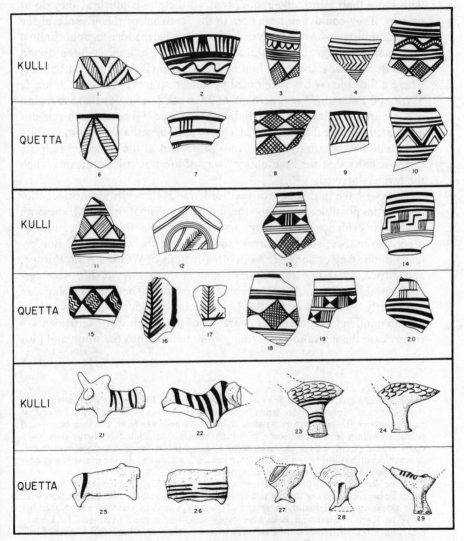

FIG. 54 *Comparative typology of pottery designs and other artifacts of Early Kulli levels and those of the Quetta Valley sequence. The Quetta material is of Damb Sadaat II-III affiliation.*

except that there is no evidence for the first phase; it would seem that southern Baluchistan was initially occupied by farmers of the type familiar to the second period at Mundigak and Sur Jangal, and to the third at Kile Gul Mohammad—those who were already fully dependent on agriculture and limited pastoralism and who constructed permanent villages close to their cultivation. It may be that more definitive field work will reveal succinctly the traces of the always far-reaching pastoral nomads who, with more than a little likelihood, roamed these hills much as they do at present. They could well have been in the forefront of the advance of the agriculturalists, who themselves had a partial dependence upon animal husbandry. Though a microlithic "settlement" has never been found in the Borderlands, there is a hint at Tharro Hill (Fig. 47) and at Sukkur, where a flint quarry has been noted by numerous individuals, including de Terra and Paterson,[34] and perhaps at Jherruck (see p. 76) that the region was occupied during the Late Indian Stone Age.[35] The shellfish remains associated with the flint industry at Tharro Hill suggest a familiar mesolithic situation. The proximity of the Amri settlement at the same site suggests the possibility that the "mesolithic" way of life was still flourishing when the farmers arrived.

Thus we have in this part of the Borderlands three distinct socioeconomic entities possible: hunting-gathering, pastoralism, farming. Of these we have clear evidence for farming, and partial or possible evidence for the other two in these southern areas, and indeed in the whole of the Borderlands in one way or another. As in other regions of Western Asia, Europe, and Africa, symbiotic relationships among these ways of life were certainly established as early as they came into contact. These relationships are not clearly evidenced in the Borderlands, but obviously they have to be kept in mind in interpreting the character of these prehistoric settlements.[36] In any case the migration of farming communities into the south and into

[34] De Terra and Paterson, 1939.

[35] These old quarries are at Sukkur, still being used. In 1961 during the renovation of the facilities at Mohenjo-daro, stone from Sukkur was used as a foundation for tourist pathways over the site. It was possible to pick out artifacts from the then uncovered paths, including flint tools, some of which certainly antedated Mohenjo-daro to a considerable extent, as, for example, some Indian Middle Stone Age cores and flakes. A magnificent neolithic axe a foot or more in length was found during our visit and now can be seen in the Government collections in Karachi!

[36] The *Baluchistan District Gazetteer* for Jhalawan (1907), for example, in describing nomadic life there, says of the nomads (p. 64): "In spring and summer they wander with their flocks in the highlands in search of pasturage and in October and November move to Kachhi, Sind and Bela where they supplement their livelihood by labour, and return to their homes in March"; (p. 142): "Permanent villages and owners of irrigated land who are not flockowners arrange for their supply of milk during the spring and summer by hiring sheep and goats which are in milk from some flockowner with whom they are acquainted. They are generally kept by the hirer until their milk becomes dry."

the Indus River Valley probably was not a movement into an uninhabited region, no matter how sparse the indigenous population.

In another way, too, the development in the south differs from that in the north. The southern regions are generally more arid, and rainfall is of a more torrential kind. Permanent settlement in the south was initially, then, subject to greater seasonal stress than in the north, where rainfall was more constant. Early settlements in the south were generally strung out along the valleys; in the north they are more concentrated. There is a strong suggestion that, site for site, those of southern Baluchistan from the Khuzdar-Nal area south are larger than those of the north in comparable periods, bespeaking a concentration of population wherever good sources of soil and water were found. An important aspect of this, however, must be noted. At Bandhni, Majumdar's survey of the site indicated that though the site consisted of two low mounds, one covering an area of

MAP 16   *Prehistoric sites in the region of southwestern Sind.*

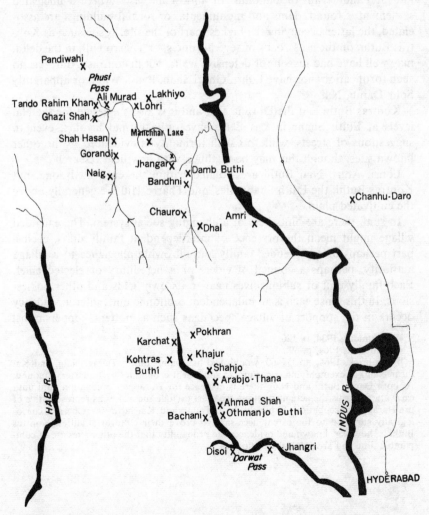

about 400 yards by 230 yards and the other somewhat less, excavations in one area showed that the habitation there rested on the bedrock.[37] Lambrick, former superintendent of census in Sind and a keen observer of archaeological evidence, who visited Pandi Wahi in 1942, remarks: "Within a quarter of a mile, in various directions, are the remains of single houses and groups of houses, much denuded and covered with pottery fragments and flint flakes."[38]

At sites such as Ghazi Shah, Amri, Tharro Hill, and Lohri, the settlements are much more concentrated. At Amri and Lohri the house types differ in that the dwelling places appear to have been raised above the ground with storage beneath. There is no denying, however, the concentration of population that existed behind the walls of such sites as Kohtras Buthi and in such places as Kot Diji.[39]

We thus have two kinds of village settlements: nucleated, like Kohtras Buthi, the Diwana site, Sohr Damb; and extended, as, for example, we find at Pandi Wahi or Bandhni. In almost all cases where a nucleated settlement is found, dams and monumental or formal buildings are associated, the latter occupying the highest part of the site. A site such as Kohtras Buthi, on the crossroads of several routes, or Tharro Hill, in the delta, may well have had reason for defensive walls, but in contrast Amri has no such fortification, nor have Lohri, Ghazi Shah, Pandi Wahi, or apparently Sohr Damb, Nal.

Kohtras Buthi and the Diwana site, and it is also suggested for the Nal levels at Edith Shahr in Las Bela, have quite formal layouts, even to suggestions of streets, while no such formality is evidenced in the other known sites, though this may be qualified with new field research.

Lohri, Amri, Niai Buthi are situated within the cultivated zone, but Kohtras Buthi, the Edith Shahr sites, and Tharro Hill are generally above the cultivated plain.

In sum, there are hints here of a changing social system. The extended village might mean the presence of interdependent family units, each a part perhaps of an extended family and all owing allegiance to a village authority, perhaps a council of elders or a hereditary or elected chief. Each family unit or subunit lives near to its own fields and other possessions. In this sense each is an independent economic unit; interdependency occurs in the support of village specialists such as potters, coppersmiths,

---

[37] Majumdar, 1934, p. 120.

[38] Lambrick, 1964, p. 59.

[39] Lambrick, 1964, pp. 59–60, would also list Damb Buthi, Taung, Naig, and Kai (near Naig) as exemplifying concentrated settlement around a "headquarters" mound. At both Damb Buthi and Naig there is evidence for Harappan occupation, and until excavation reveals the actual situation, we must exclude these sites as representative of pre-Harappan occupation. Similarly, both Taung and Kai have never been archaeologically surveyed to the extent necessary to prove their cultural affinities. Kohtras Buthi is, however, known and evidences the probability that the other sites are of comparable time and are culturally analogous.

stonecutters and in the communal interest in bringing in the harvest, celebrating the religious festivals, carrying on the interfamilial relationships, observing the regulation of personal or communal property, and acting in common under a chief in time of danger or need. We can assume that the essential cohesive factors here were language, common recognition of symbols, mutual dependence on identical resources of soil and water, shared traits of custom in the *rites de passage* of birth, marriage, and death, possibly village endogamy, and that range of religious and mythic beliefs common to agriculturalists in which fertility or the lack of it have a magico-religious basis.

The burial customs in which children or perhaps occasionally women are buried among the houses strengthens our feeling that strong familial village life linked the living and even the dead. In contrast, however, are the later fractional burials where the dead were apparently exposed until the soft parts were gone and the bones then tossed into a mass grave willy-nilly. Yet even these graves were apparently situated close to the habitations and the wants of the dead in afterlife anticipated with some funerary furniture. At Sohr Damb, Nal, the ossuary-type burial apparently succeeds that of single interment among the houses, and a similar situation occurs in Period III at Mundigak (see p. 130). The former is an ancient custom of neolithic man, the latter almost an antithesis, requiring other beliefs and other cultural forms.

The nucleated settlement, with its great stone drains, massive enclosure walls, and formal structures as well as its concentrated populations, is unquestionably the result of organization beyond that demonstrated for the ordinary village.[40] Lambrick is so impressed by these settlements that he calls them "townships." Whether they are this or not, problems of urban life were undeniably at hand. To make these populations act collectively for the construction and maintenance of dams or walls may not have been so difficult as sustaining civil order, with so many individuals rubbing shoulders. In this regard the character of the nucleated-settlement population might be guessed at. Kohtras Buthi and the Nal Edith Shahr settlements are located in areas where the available cultivable soil is less than that available in the case, for example, of the Lake Manchhar sites or Amri. A consequence of this is, of course, the hydraulic engineering enterprises of Kohtras Buthi. However, the Hab River site near Diwana, with all its formality, is situated at the edge of a considerable fertile plain (pp. 166f.). It does not seem too speculative to assume that we have here evidence for motivations other than agriculture and its direct needs. The massive enclosure walls are evidence for an authoritative system; the formal ramped buildings of the Diwana site attest to ceremony requiring the special offices of priest or clerk or both; the stone dams require water regulation for the collective good. In other words, we are led by our evi-

[40] Comparative statistics on size and population estimate are found in Appendix L.

TABLE 5. LATE PREHISTORIC SITES OF SOUTHERN BALUCHISTAN

STAGES	LAS BELA	WADH	DRAKALO	ORNACH	NAL
later stages	L-10	W-1 W-3 W-5 W-9 W-12			
V	L-4 L-5 L-7 L-13 L-12	W-10 W-6 W-7 W-12 W-9 W-8 W-11	D-1	O-1 O-2 O-6 O-7 O-10	N-2 N-5
IV	L-2 L-3 L-6 L-1	W-2 W-3 W-4	D-4	O-5 O-4	N-3
III	L-9 L-11	W-6 W-5 W-9	D-2 D-3	O-8 O-2 O-3 O-9	N-4 N-5 N-1 N-2
II					
I					

Regional representation of late prehistoric sites of southern Baluchistan arranged according to stages represented generally by surface collections. Later stages are incomplete. Regions are arranged from south (left) to north (right). Note the apparent abandonment of sites between Stages IV and V.

dence to the idea of the beginnings of a class structured society. Robert Redfield, an American anthropologist who was among the pioneer students of the character of civilization divided primitive man from civilized man primarily on the basis of the motivation for social interactions. Primitive man acts according to a *moral* order where his activities are carried out without fail because each individual is an integral part of the whole which is the common good, and that whole, his culture, provides the rules for his actions through tradition; in the urban situation, the moral order is no longer the principal force in governing the actions of civilized man; the complexities of daily life with all their shifting values require the super-imposition of common standards observed by all and stated in terms of law backed by authority. In this sense, moral order is the governing element in village life, and the technic order of law that of the cities. Thus the transition from village life to urban sees the onset and acceptance of the technic order, while the moral order's role in the society changes. The interactions between and among classes can be moral, but in the regulation of urban activities, authority has to be imposed across the classes, and there is a certain amount of coercion necessary. Class systems are interdependent systems, with each class requiring something in terms of capital, leadership, energy from the other. It is of greatest interest, then, that we have in these pre-Harappan cultures contrasting settlements and a strong sense of social change. A change perhaps from a moral order toward a technic one.

Copper, bronze, cut stone, agate, steatite, flint, shell, bone, wood, reed, pigments are not all local in each case. Trade was certainly a part of the scene, as the situation of some of the sites indicates. It is no miracle in this regard that archaeologists are able quite readily to recognize these settlements over such great distances on the basis of ceramics. These ceramics were probably not carried by traders but were largely made locally in terms of a shared tradition, a tradition which certainly did not confine itself to ceramics.

The Kulli "culture" is the south Baluchistan end product of these developments. It is contemporary with Period IV at Mundigak and with Damb Sadaat II–III in the Quetta Valley, and is thus pre-Harappan in its early phases and in its latest phases contemporary with the mature Harappan civilization of the Indus River Valley. Here we have clear signs that the centralized nucleated village, and indeed town life, was achieved. The Las Bela situation is strikingly illustrative in this regard. The bulk of the nucleated Complex A sites, with their significant monumental and formal structures, are located in the most unproductive part of the Welpat area. The ordinary village sites are, however, located in the midst of the rich cultivated plain to the south.[41] The Edith Shahr sites are large and evidence sizable popula-

---

[41] Niai Buthi, previously described, and Buband, a site of late Kulli type discovered by Stein in 1941, are the two now known.

tions clustered around monumental buildings whose function was most probably ceremonial. Obviously the presence of these sites close to but not within the most productive part of Las Bela speaks for a symbiotic relationship with the villages. In its simplest sense this might mean food for ceremony, or vice versa. How much control was held by the inhabitants of the formal sites over the villages of the cultivated plain is, of course, uncertain, but the fact that both seemed to flourish is indicative of a continually successful relationship, whatever it was.

❋ Indianization

THE EVIDENCE, THEN, points to a flourishing world in pre-Harappan times in which trade, groups of specialists, structured societies, symbiotic relationships (pastoral-village, village-"town"), and small rather interdependent communities had their place. It was a world where another process was under way in addition to the trend toward nuclearization. This is what one might call "Indianization."

It is clear that up to and partly including the period of the Nal culture, the prime motivations for change, that is, for the use of new styles and innovations, had come from northern Iran. In the next chapter some of the evidence for influences from southern Iran will be described. But an examination of the developments of the Nal-early Kulli and the Quetta-Amri-Mundigak III, etc., stages shows clearly that non-Iranian changes were under way. The most apparent symptom of this is in the always graphic pottery painting and other decoration. Here, sometimes using the same design styles as found in Iran, the potters present a whole repertoire of non-Iranian motifs, among them the pipal leaf, the humped bull, the hooded snake, the black buck, the gavial, and the soft-shelled tortoise. The ramped platforms, with their drains and evidences of human sacrifice (see p. 145), are non-Iranian, as are the hooded goggle-eyed female figurines with heavy necklaces, the unusual potters' marks; the astonishing number of clay bangles which characterizes some of the sites and the increasingly heavy emphasis upon cattle as a food, ceremonial, and perhaps draught animal are not found in the Iranian plateau on the same scale. The clustering of village communities around a central mound or "citadel" and the construction of houses with living quarters on a second story are apparently unique to this region. Other traits can be listed, but enough has been mentioned to indicate that not only were these settlers utilizing the local environment for their style motivations but they were changing to another way of life uniquely their own and yet paradoxically part of another world, the world of the subcontinent, whose true borders they or their relatives had crossed when they left the hills of Baluchistan and entered the Indus River plain.

VI

✻✻✻✻

The Origin of
the Harappan Civilization

C IVILIZATION IS THE MOST COMPLEX CULTURAL LEVEL reached by man. Its symptom is the city. The city is in turn the result of the centralization of a variety of interdependent activities under an effective administration. The variety and number of activities and the nature of their administration may differ from city to city, but what is held in common is a subsistence basis sufficient to provide for the daily needs of the population required for those activities and their regulation. The character of the city, then, depends on its subsistence basis, the character of its administration, and the spectrum of activities interrelating in the same locale. Obviously there is a great range of possibilities for differences among cities even in the same civilization. In ancient Sumeria, for example, there were many cities, each having its own characteristic patron deity, traditional history, and *raison d'être*: Nippur was a holy city; Babylon, at least in its later phases, a trading mart; while Ur, Umma, and Lagash were situated in the midst of cultivation and by the canals that made that cultivation possible.

To a certain extent a quantitative measure has to be applied, for example, in order to differentiate a large village from a small city. Villages of late prehistoric times were, in many parts of Asia and Europe, like the self-contained colonial villages of New England with their numerous home industries rather than like the simple farming communities of parts of Mexico or Southeast Asia with which one tends to equate those of ancient times. The metal smith, potter, weaver, brickmaker, priest, carpenter, leather worker, stonecutter, trader, herdsman, are typically evidenced in the archaeological remains of some of these villages in one way or another. In any class-structured society, such as that implied for the Nal-Kulli development, some of these professionals form separate groups with status equivalents dependent upon kin or capital. They have a symbiotic relationship within the society, and their services are recompensed in terms of either other services or raw materials. However, the economics of a situation may shift to a supply-and-demand basis. In times of famine the demand for the services of the brickmaker, carpenter, mason, and other members of the building professions may decrease, while in times of plenty members of these professions may be in such demand that a competitive situation emerges in which the specialist is wooed by offers of more than the going rate. In such situations the bonds of tradition established by long precedent are strained to the utmost. The more interdependent such groupings within the society become and the more specializations there are, the less and less potent are traditional values (this is not confined to the economic area alone, as pointed up in Chapter V and as we shall see); hence the need for regulation of the society by a mutually acceptable governing body which can act with authority. Such bodies are characteristic of civilization. It is important to note, however, that traditional practices have evolved in many village societies to provide for a great many exigencies, and thus the need for outside authority has often not arisen. Nonetheless, certain societies witness the failure of traditional practices and replace them with administrative bodies. By so doing, they take a step toward civilization. In this sense the city and the village differ most fundamentally in terms of the number of professions, social interactions, and services necessarily administered by a central authority.

However, groups of villages formed in the same locale, as, for example, in the Ornach or Wadh valleys, almost certainly collectively acted for the construction of dams or for defense. Intervillage links are demonstrated by the identity of artifacts from site to site. These can also be taken to mean that social and politico-economic relations were strong. Village exogamy was common, so that familial ties probably ran like a spider's web linking the whole of a settled area. Common sanction of fields and pastures, common attitudes toward strangers and toward the nomadic people whose annual visits had to be handled to mutual satisfaction, common access to water, common reaction to earthquake and storm, to disease and to surplus tightened intervillage bonds. The universally found motifs such as the bull figurine and the goggle-eyed mother goddess and the motifs found in the painted pottery further emphasize a mutual tradition. The widespread potters' marks described previously and the common use of stamp seals of compartmented form also emphasize the homogeneity of traits of these cultures. House types, village layouts, and burial customs strongly hint of the widespread sameness of social form.

In contrast to the "closed" system, which label one might apply to the local village system as outlined above, is the "open" system of civilization which has resulted from the breakdown of aspects of that "closed" system.

A civilized society is similar to a pair of scales that requires constant adjustment because different weights are placed in one pan or the other. To remain intact, civilizations have to stay in balance, but the complexity and constant development of civilized institutions continually throw them out of balance. Unlike village cultures, which are in balance and thus "closed," civilizations are out of balance and thus "open." In one sense, civilizations are a patchwork of expediencies resulting from the efforts to readjust. The longevity of a civilization depends upon its keeping its later expediencies from obliterating the original premise of the civilization.

It is that premise that must be understood in order to find the reason for a civilization. Rather than look to outside sources, one might reasonably ask what had happened to the institutions at the village level to cause the move to civilization. What had happened to the "closed" system to start the move to civilization?

Civilization is rooted in human sentiments, and its origins, wherever they occur, are difficult to follow, whatever the sources at hand. Yet hints are found in our own time. The United States was, in 1776, a collection of states each of which had its own traditions and interests, whatever was held in common. These states banded together against the British, won a victory, and became a nation. The nation was possible because the leadership was able to emphasize collective interest over individual interest. The years that followed, mixed as they were with the stresses and strains produced by the Industrial Revolution, saw a rural America turned into an urban world of a complexity that requires computers to sort it out. The ingredients that produced the world power that is the modern United States were by no means all economic. Religion, art, science, politics, military and historical accident, etc., have all played their role. Similarly, the rise to civilization anywhere in the world is as complex a matter.

❋ *Harappan Civilization, Egypt, and Sumer*

THE HARAPPAN CIVILIZATION, which arose in the lower Indus River Valley somewhere after 2300 B.C.,[1] is India's first and in the chronology of world civilization the third, behind Sumer and pharaonic Egypt. The civilizations of Egypt and Sumer arose probably a thousand years earlier. From

[1] See Appendix E.

the foregoing, it can be said that these civilizations came into being because of the need to centralize human activities under an authoritative regime as the result of the failure of traditional means to handle effectively the increasing complexity of human relationships, in whatever category or group of categories. The civilizations are all riverine; that is, they are all intimately connected to river systems which provide the environment for their main subsistence base—the cultivation of cereal grains. Each is spread out along its respective river valley for hundreds of miles. With each there are large and small centers of population, but intercommunication was relatively easy. Systems of writing, weights and measures, iconography and standards of cutting stone, of brick size, vessel form, seal usage, and the like are widespread, and in each case their associative distribution tends to mark the bounds of each given civilization or its sphere of influence.

In Sumer there is a multiplicity of urban centers situated at strategic positions in a network of irrigation canals. In both Egypt (Old Kingdom) and Harappan India there are a few urban centers and a great many villages, and large-scale canal building was not a typical activity in the same way as in Sumer. Trade was important in Sumer and less so in Old Kingdom Egypt; in the Harappan civilization it was perhaps even less so than in Egypt. Whereas Sumer is marked by intense intercity rivalry and was subject to invasions from outside her borders, both Egypt and the Harappan civilization remained in comparative isolation. In Egypt's case, however, fierce wars between district states, ending in the superiority of one, mark her historical beginnings. Such does not seem to be the case for the Harappan civilization.

Whereas Sumerian civilization is speculative, pessimistic in its world view, inventive and dynamic generally, both Old Kingdom Egypt and Harappan India are striking in terms of their conservative-seeming cultural form. The hieroglyphic writing of the Egyptians and the undeciphered seal writing of the Harappans, for example, are in clear contrast to the ever more efficient and pragmatic cuneiform of Sumer. The rapidity with which art styles change in Sumeria is almost opposite to the stability of those styles in Egypt and in the Indus River Valley civilization.

There are numerous other comparisons one might bring out, but in discussions purporting to relate the origin of the Harappan civilization to the Sumerians, these contrasts have to be underlined. In effect, one civilization was not transported to another environment. Whatever the influences that moved from west to east, and some certainly did, they affected an already determined situation.

This is, of course, a simplification of what is a complex process, but it does underline the need there is to look within the villages of the Borderlands for causes rather than to stride with seven-league boots from Tigris to Indus.

In the previous chapters evidence has been presented to show that, at least in the Nal-Amri period and its northern equivalents, prehistoric villagers had moved into the Punjab, to Rajasthan, and into Sind. Similarly, a descent was made into the low-lying alluvial areas of Las Bela. In all cases where enough material has been unearthed, we are confronted with evidence for a successful adaptation to the new environment. Villages are well seated by sources of soil and water, and the inhabitants have lost nothing as compared with their equivalents in the uplands. As indicated in the first chapter, the Borderlands are a transitional zoogeographic sub-zone, and man finds much that is familiar among the fauna and flora whether in highlands or lowlands. Nevertheless, there are style changes that show at the very least a drifting away from the original cultural form, that with which the descent to the plains was made. In eastern Sind, Bikaner, and perhaps the Punjab, we have the style which we might call the Kot Dijian, after that type site;[2] in western Sind the Amri style; while south central Baluchistan and Las Bela, that of the Nal and early Kulli cultures. In Kachhi and northeastern Sind there is increasing evidence for a local style which is in part derived from northern and central Baluchistan. This we might call the Early Harappan. By this we mean the Harappan artifact form and decoration, not the civilization (note App. K).[3]

The sites of the Early Harappan locus have not yet been excavated, and their size is obscured by the presence of both pre-Harappan and Mature Harappan occupations. Both the type sites of Gandava (Pathiani Kot) and Judeirjo-daro are very large (the latter measures 600 yards north-south and 500 yards east-west by some 25 to 35 feet in height). There is a suggestion of an early Harappan horizon at Mohenjo-daro. As does the Amri, it represents a successful settlement on the Indus River Plain.

Thus, about 2300 B.C., the early Kulli-Nal, the Amri, the Kot Dijian, and the Harappan "cultures," all of which were generally similar, were all well established in riverine environments with vast resources of soil and water available, the technical means to exploit these resources already developed, and the whole empirical tradition of food production derived from Iranian ancestry making possible knowledgeable approaches to the problems of

[2] The term "style" as used in these contexts pertains to the characteristic form of the culture that the assemblage of artifacts gathered by the archaeologist defines.

[3] The characteristic artifact features of the Early Harappan phase include the following: (1) unpainted clay bangles often squarish in cross-section; (2) characteristic Harappan figurines; (3) unpainted clay balls (rattles?); (4) plain pottery thicker in construction than Kot Dijian or Amrian, often with comb-incising; (5) globular vessels; (6) miniature vessels, unpainted; (7) Harappan painted motifs but drawn more crisply and finer than in the later Mature phase; (8) Harappan-style dishes with a distinct break between the broad rim and the bowl of vessels; (9) pedestal vessels or dish-on-stand with rims painted black, often with black circle painted decoration on interior; (10) frequent occurrence of Nal, Kot Dijian, and Amrian motifs in pottery painting; (11) toy carts, made with solid bodies.

Fig. 55 *Comparative typology of painted pottery designs of Bakun A, southwestern Iran, and Bampur-Makran, southeastern Iran. The Bampur-Makran material (right) is generally of the Khurab stage (see Appendix H).*

the new environment. Significantly, centralization was a process almost universally found in the Borderlands, from Kandahar to Las Bela, but it was a process that was to accelerate for the Harappan culture as it was for the Kulli, reaching urban proportions. An elaboration was to occur with this "urbanization" on a scale sufficient to place the Harappan civilization in the ranks with Sumer and Old Kingdom Egypt. Why did this happen?

✳ The Raison d'Être—*The Outside-Influence Factor*

THE ANSWER IS PROBABLY AT LEAST THREEFOLD if not more. First of all, there is the outside-influence factor to consider. R. H. Dyson, Jr., a leading American figure in Iranian archaeology today, in a recent paper summarizing the relative chronology of Iran from 6000 to 2000 B.C. in relation to the Mesopotamian sequence, the archaeological standard in Western Asia, divides Iranian prehistory into eight horizons based on stylistic and cultural criteria:*

Horizon	Probable Distribution	Date
1. Soft-ware Horizon	Luristan-Caspian Shore-Fars	6200–5500 B.C.
2. Jarmo-Related Horizon	Kermanshah-NW Khuzistan	ca. 6100–5900 B.C.
3. Hassuna-Related Horizon	Central Zagros to Central Iran (Sialk I$_{1-3}$)	5900–5100 B.C.
4. Halaf-Related Horizon	Central Iran (Sialk I$_{4-5}$) via Kermanshah	4800–3900 B.C.
5. Ubaid-Related Horizon	SW Khuzistan (Susa A)-Luristan-Kermanshah-NW Iran	
	Central Iran (Sialk II)-Caspian Shore-NE Iran; Fars (Tall-i-Gap I)	
	A later phase to Sialk III$_7$-Hissar IIA, etc.	
	A later phase in Fars Tall-i-Gap II-Tall-i-Bakun A III to southwest (?)	5000–2700 B.C.
6. Uruk-Jamdat Nasr-Related Horizon	SW Khuzistan-Kermanshah (Sialk IV) Fars?	3500–3000 B.C.
7. Early Dynastic-Related Horizon	SW Khuzistan (Susa D)-Luristan Kermanshah-NW Iran	
	Fars-Bampur-Khurab-Seistan-Kulli	2800–2000+ B.C.
8. Northern Gray-ware Horizon	NW & NE Iran W & S	2600 B.C.

* After DYSON, 1965, pp. 217–220.

It can be seen from this chart that two major movements across Iran affected the Borderlands. The first is outlined in Chapter IV and fits into Dyson's Ubaid-Related Horizon, though possibly elements from previous horizons, such as that described for Sialk I (p. 107) and Djeitun, may have preceded it. This is essentially a northern diffusion, and its effect in the Borderlands has been described (Chapter IV). Dyson's Early Dynastic-Related Horizon, however, is the second major movement eastward, and he as well as others sees its eastern terminus in the Kulli culture of southern Baluchistan. In effect, the inference one can make on this basis is that some traits of Early Dynastic Sumeria diffused to Baluchistan. Since Early Dynastic Sumer is Sumerian civilization at its height, this movement eastward has to be recognized as an important factor in the rise to civilization of the Indus River Valley cultures. Too little is known about this movement, however. Stein's excavations in the Bampur-Khurab and Makran areas (see Appendix H) produced the bare bones of a sequence there.[4] It is clear that the Bakun A culture has a direct relation to that of

4 However, note C. C. Lamberg-Karlovsky's recent work at Tepe Yahya (in App. H).

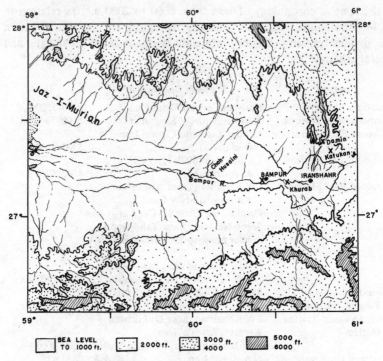

MAP 17   *The Bampur region of southeastern Iran.*

Bampur and Makran (see Figs. 55, 56). In turn, Seistan is a northerly off-shoot of the same cultural horizon (Fig. 25). Recent work at the site of Tal-i-Iblis in the Mashiz Valley in southeast Iran indicates that occupancy of the Kerman mountain area in southeast Iran was at least as early as 4000 B.C.[5] In a sequence of six levels it is in the later (Tal-i-Iblis 4-5) that evidence for Mesopotamian contact or direct influence occurs, in the form of beveled-rim bowls. The next period was lost on the site by modern destruction of the mound, but it appears to have been the period of greatest prosperity and population in prehistoric times there. (Stein estimated Tal-i-Iblis to measure some 1200 meters by 800 meters.)

The Kerman ranges in their NW-SE trend are a natural highway between the barren coast and the Great Salt Desert, since their higher altitudes provide for year-round sources of water. Tal-i-Iblis is one point along this route. However, the descent to lower altitudes at Bampur, Seistan,

---

[5] J. R. Caldwell, "Tal-i-Iblis—The Kerman Range and the Beginnings of Smelting," *Illinois State Museum Preliminary Reports*, No. 7, Springfield, 1966. See also "Investigations at Tal-i-Iblis," *Illinois State Museum Preliminary Reports*, No. 9, J. R. Caldwell, ed., Springfield, 1967.

and the Makran on the roads to the eastern part of the Borderlands prevented the concentrations of population apparently common enough in the Kerman mountains.

The Makran is essentially a series of parallel east-west-running valleys largely desert but relieved here and there by sources of water either as springs or as part of the Kej or Rakshan river systems. Coastal Makran consists of low ranges and a broad alluvial plain across which wind the often dry river courses that drain those ranges or the valleys beyond. Rivers like the Dasht act as natural avenues connecting the interior valleys with the coast. Near their mouths are important seacoast towns, while the oases of the interior are the seats of small farming communities. The prehistoric sites of Bampur and Makran are small in size, in keeping with the poverty of natural resources. Shahi Tump, for example, near Turbat, in the Kej valley is only about eighty-five yards square. This is an interesting site in that it typifies the cultural affinities of the whole region. Though it

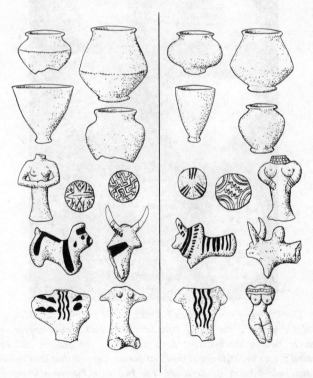

FIG. 56 *Comparative typology of pottery and other artifacts of Bakun A, southwestern Iran, and Bampur-Makran, southeastern Iran. The Bampur-Makran material (right) is largely of the Khurab phase, with some Kulli. The female figure with extended legs is of Damb Sadaat II affiliation.*

FIG. 57 *Funerary pottery from Shahi Tump.*

PLATE 23 *Pottery from the site of Shahi Tump, near Turbat, Makran. The examples evidence a variety of influences. The bulk would appear to have decorative ties to southeastern Iran. However, the graters and the five decorated pieces in the lower right-hand corner suggest that they are derived from the Indo-Iranian Borderlands. The two with the meandering painted lines belong to a type known in Baluchistan as Faiz Mohammad gray ware, while the hook-pattern fragment on the right is of the Togau type. All in this plate belong to the precemetery phase of the site.* (Courtesy of the Archaeological Survey of India.)

was poorly excavated by Sir Aurel Stein, enough is known to reveal something of its sequence. Basically there are three phases, the two earlier representing an occupation of the Khurab type common to eastern Iran (Appendix H). A cemetery was cut into a late phase of the Khurab. The burials were flexed (E-W), and each was surrounded by several pottery vessels, some containing the ashes of animal bones or food offerings. Beads indicate that necklaces encircled the necks of the dead. Copper implements, including a shaft-hole axe and a spearhead, were also found associated, as was a copper seal. The pottery consisted largely of open bowls and cups painted in black on buff or gray with geometric designs familiar to the Bakun-Kerman area (Fig. 57). A terra-cotta bull, a piece of a toy cart, a fragment of a grater, and a steatite carved vessel all seemed to be associated with the cemetery. These objects are probably of Kulli origin.

The Kulli also shows up in the coastal settlement of Sutkagen-dor on the Dasht River (see p. 266), but this material is of both Iranian and early Kulli type. Here incinerary pot burials recall the Incinerary Pot phase in the Fort Sandeman region (p. 147) and the incinerary burials at Mehi (p. 205).

The intimacy with which typically Iranian artifacts mingle with those of Kulli type in Makran makes the problem of differentiation difficult. So confused has the picture become that some researchers have even claimed that a Kulli element is present in Oman and the Bahrein Islands of the Persian Gulf! This is primarily because those traits which we are claiming for Kulli are probably of western origin and are indeed largely part of that diffusionary movement outlined by Dyson. The charts (Figs. 55, 56) are of great interest in this regard. Here not only do we have precision in comparing pottery forms and designs, but in the figurines remarkable resemblances are found. In particular the pedestal-based examples (Fig. 56) are of importance, as with the Zhob mother goddesses, which are also of the pedestal type, for if such figurines are the representation of a religious cult, then one might expect that certain architectural forms and rituals might also have diffused with them. Similarly, stone vases found in the Indus Valley, Mehi, Shahi Tump, Bampur, Khuzistan, and Early Dynastic Sumeria are indicative of the directness of the diffusionary line.[6]

There is no evidence for the large-scale water-control systems of Nal-Kulli type in the Kerman, Fars, Bampur, or Makran areas, nor any good evidence for potters' marks or writing of Harappan type. Metallurgy, as shown in Seistan, Bampur, and at Shahi Tump, is excellent, and there are good parallels in spear points, knives, axes, and the like to what is known of these tools at Kulli, Nal, and the Harappan sites.

[6] F. A. Durrani, "Stone Vases as Evidence of Connection Between Mesopotamia and the Indus Valley," *Ancient Pakistan*, Vol. I (1964), pp. 51–96.

The evidence is therefore strong that this late but important diffusionary movement overland from southern Mesopotamia and Khuzistan again played a part in the development of the style of the late, if not the early, phase of the Kulli culture and undeniably the Harappan civilization (see pp. 296f.). This is the first factor.

❋ The Second Factor—The Subcontinental Setting

A SECOND FACTOR in any answer to the riddle of the origin of the Harappan civilization returns to the subcontinental setting. The Indus River is one of the mighty streams of the world. It has twice the flow of the Nile River and ten times that of the Colorado. It is the recipient of waters from both the mountains of eastern Afghanistan and the Himalayas, and in its course it is joined by all the principal western Punjab rivers. So great is its alluvial soil burden that it creates enormous levees and raises its bed in the southern Punjab and in Sind. Disastrous floods result when these natural levees are broken, and man has for millennia battled to withstand them. The meander pattern in Sind is that typical of the late maturity of a river, and there has been a tendency for shifts to the west.[7]

At Kashmor above Sukkur, the river is some sixty to eighty feet above the plain to the west. In pre-Arab and early Arab days, the river seasonally flooded this plain as far as the modern town of Jacobabad. The floodwaters then flowed south into what is known as the Sind Corridor and into the western Nara. The Nara is a stream that flows close to the foothills of the Kirthar ranges; its water sources are the streams of those ranges and the floods of the Indus. Eventually these waters empty into Lake Manchhar, which, rising to a certain level, pours its flood through the Aral Channel on the southeast bank into the Indus; but when the Indus is higher, the reverse occurs.

On the east the Thar Desert and a series of rocky outcrops in the area around Khairpur and Kot Diji contain the alluvial belt there. There is a channel, about which little is known, which was at one time part of the Hakra-Ghaggar river system but which also received some flood from the Indus River proper. This is the eastern Nara, whose outlet is south in the Nawabshah area, and much of whose development has occurred in recent years owing to a canal system in the Nara Channel fed by the Lloyd Barrage at Sukkur—a triumph of British engineering.

The gradient of the Indus River from Sukkur south to the sea is about nine inches per mile. The flatness of this gradient is, of course, underlined by the ease with which the country is flooded. A rise of fifteen feet in the

[7] Maneck B. Pithawalla, *A Physical and Economic Geography of Sind*, Sindhi Adabi Board, Karachi, 1959.

PLATE 24 *A view westward across the "Great Bath" on the main mound at Mohenjo-daro. Note the great flatness of the Indus plain, an indication of past riverine action.*

inundation season can flood areas ten miles or more across. In periods before protective bunds were raised, the difference of a foot or two in flood level could spell the difference between safety or disaster for communities located many miles from the river itself.

The vastness of the Indus floods in Sind, even in an average year, is reflected in Lake Manchhar and the smaller *dhands*, or inundation lakes. In the inundation season the river water flows into the Aral Channel, normally an outlet for the lake, and enters the lake to expand its border considerably. It is this, plus the water received from the north (see Map 18), which provides the Manchhar area with its abundant resources of alluvial soil.

The basic crop of Sind has been wheat until recent times. Wheat is a rabi, or winter, crop and is sown in the fields after the inundation in November-December; it is reaped just before a new flood in April. Since the land gradient is low, the water table is high, and the moisture retention of the soil is good even in the dry air of Sind, the construction of an extensive irrigation system beginning in medieval Islamic times at least has caused a gradual rise in the water table, which reached a paradoxical climax with the British construction of the Lloyd Barrage at Sukkur in 1932. More acreage was brought under cultivation because of the new irrigation, but much land has been lost because the drainage was unable to offset the final rise of water table, which leached out the soil and left the *kalar* soil, saline and uncultivable.[8] To this situation wet rice cultivation, a

[8] S. Piggott, whose book *Prehistoric India* is a classic of its kind, considered these leached fields a part of the Harappan scene, but this is not tenable on the present evidence. For example, see Lambrick, 1964, pp. 72ff.

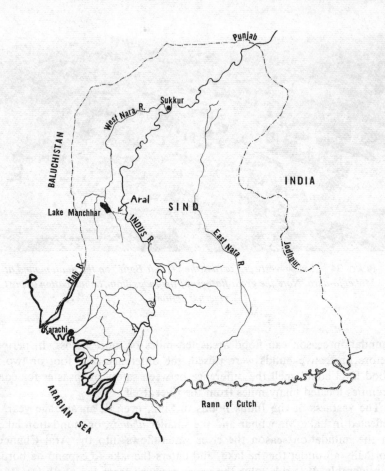

MAP 18 *The former province of Sind, showing principal drainage systems.*

kharif, or summer, crop, has certainly contributed—so much so, in fact, that the Government of Pakistan has now forbidden rice growing in some areas.

The parallel of Sind to Egypt is obvious in that both regions have depended upon the annual deposit of alluvial soil in the fields to provide for new cultivation. As for the distribution of Harappan sites in Sind proper (exclusive of the hill sites), they are found close to the active flood plain of the river or to the *dhands* which depend on the summer floods. There is no question that the flooded areas of the valley were of critical importance to that ancient civilization. Presumably, its people may have sought to extend the floods by means of inundation canals, but basically the active flood plain of the river was sufficient. Even today over one million acres of Sind land belong to the active flood plain. The soil of these flood plains is the *kacho*, a light loam which is the most productive of the local soils.

Unlike the Nile, however, the Indus River is far less confined to its principal bed. Its soil load is at least twice that of the Nile and its deposi-

PLATE 25   *The dry bed of the eastern Nara near the Rann of Cutch, West
Pakistan.*

tional rate somewhat higher. Accordingly, it tends to build up its bed until
the river is actually above the surrounding plain similar to the Tigris
and Euphrates rivers in southern Mesopotamia. The river, overflowing
and breaking through its banks, finds new channels in the lower lands,
where it repeats the process. This plus the meander pattern, which in terms
of total river length is constant but which changes as one or another meander is cut off, causes in time river floods across the valley in opposite
directions, with a correspondingly wide distribution of alluvial soil. This
soil remains fertile, provided it is watered sufficiently and not leached out
by ponding or made hard and uncultivable through drying out.

The natural forest cover in Sind was at one time a tropical type of jungle
in the watered areas, but an increasingly xerophytic and sparse growth
occurred closer to the barren areas of Thar and Kohistan. The evidence for
this situation is found in modern Sind, where forest preserves flourish as
soon as man and his animals are forbidden their depredations (see Appendix I). This area was in prehistoric times the homeland of a great variety of
game of both Palearctic and Malaysian affinity, in keeping with the region's
transitional nature (Figs. 1–4). The elephant, buffalo, antelope, black buck,
rhinoceros, tiger, lion, leopard, cobra, python, water snake, gavial,
tortoise, turtle, rabbit, shrew, and monkey are all evidenced in the artifacts
of the prehistoric inhabitants.

The food producers who settled in the Indus River Valley were thus in
possession of an environment whose resources were enormous, comparable in every way to those of Egypt and Mesopotamia. Whereas the Indus
delta region was not as important as that of the Nile or the Twin Rivers

231

because of a peculiar relationship of monsoonal seas to the river flow, which may have confined the delta, the river to the north was a natural highway to the Punjab, probably the richest farm land on the subcontinent.[9] It can be said that for prehistoric farming the Indus River Valley offered an almost limitless advantage in terms of soil and water. It must be remembered that all our evidence derived from southern Afghanistan, Baluchistan, and Iran confirms the fact that these farmers were superbly capable of using the alluvial soil of the valley for magnificent crops of wheat and barley. As their settlements in the arid highlands indicate, they were very successful in the exploitation of limited sources of soil and water. To Sind they brought the same capabilities, but now their soil and water advantages were infinitely improved. We do not have statistics for estimating the number of man-hours it took to produce one bushel of wheat in Baluchistan as against the same amount in Sind, but we can be certain that the Sind version had a decided superiority.

Thus the Indus River Valley, "Young Egypt," as it was called in early British days, was capable of supporting the urban life which is civilized life by dint of its subsistence advantages, a second factor in the development of the Indus civilization.

✳ *The Third Factor—Social Readiness*

A THIRD HAS BEEN TOUCHED UPON PREVIOUSLY. In its broadest sense it can be summarized as social readiness for civilization. In effect, the transition from the "closed" system of the early villages to the "open" system of the developed-village phase as known in the Borderlands was the preparation for civilization. The appearance of a structured society provided one essential for the next step, the ultimate centralization under an authoritative control of some kind. Specialization set requirements for trade and a value system; agricultural dependence and large populations motivated institutionalized religion; intervillage and regional rivalries were prerequisites for the coming to power of authoritative leaders, as were large-scale engineering works. Class division, whether on the basis of wealth or profession, required interclass relationships that must have been continually changing as the technology advanced, as the external contacts increased, as the seasons fluctuated with their apexes of abundance and depths of hunger; indeed certain familial values were themselves challenged when wealth became a class status symbol.

A very significant phenomenon in this category is the shift of the highland villages to the Indus River plains. That this was the result of a desire for land and water is a reasonable conclusion. The highlands could not be as dependable from year to year as the great river valley. Undeniably the

[9] The problem of the Indus River delta is discussed in Lambrick, 1964, pp. 20ff.

success of food production in the high areas of the Borderlands produced its own problems of population growth and the need for expanded resources. Important was the problem of fractionalization of the land. When the father dies, his sons inherit his possessions. However, with land limited, the constant division of it through several generations diminishes its size for each inheritor. To avoid this, some sons move away to set up their own homes, still respecting their kinship ties to the home village. Thus another mechanism for movement to other regions is built into the social organization and its economic aspect. In the later prehistoric villages, class units such as that of the coppersmiths, with their intervillage relationships, may not have accompanied the individual villages in their shifts to the plains. The dependency of the villages on the coppersmiths would be no less, and something therefore had to be done to tempt or to coerce this class into the move. It is this lack of unanimity in action that again and again raises the specter of demand. Once an interdependence has been created, it is difficult to live without it. If our example of the coppersmiths has validity, at least by way of illustration, we can envision a shift to the plains as moving these specialists farther from their traditional resources of raw material. Thus they must have set up mechanisms, via trade, annual pilgrimage, proxy, or otherwise, by which their sources could be continued. Such problems multiplied even further if the raw material had to be transported from afar, for then its costs would necessarily have been higher. Should there be middlemen, costs would have to include their labors. Whether such things were explicitly stated in terms of value equivalents or rates of exchange, or by institutionalized controls which required the services of each individual, is, of course, unknown to us. We must be content with the knowledge that such problems existed.

As suggested previously, symbiotic relationships with pastoralists are a commonplace of the Borderlands. At Sur Jangal we have a strong hint that some villages were specializing in cattle husbandry. We also have abundant evidence for the extensive herding of sheep and goats in all parts of the Borderlands. Apparently besides yielding hair and wool and milk, these animals were slaughtered regularly at the yearling stage. Certainly in places like the Bugti country, the northern plain of Kachhi, and much of Jhalawan, herding was more dependable than agriculture. Though goats and sheep appear in the Harappan civilization, it was cattle that were the dominant form of livestock. In such emphases we have strong hints of cultural differences, and it is not too difficult to envision equitable relationships established between sedentary agriculturalist and nomadic pastoralist, or between highland herder and plains farmer. Each community would thus be at the hub of a complex network of interrelationships between specialists, traders, herders, and farmers—all of which would be seriously affected should that community be forced or desire for any reason to move away.

Among the institutions for which we have a fair amount of evidence is that of religion. The formal buildings of the late phases of prehistoric occupation of the Borderlands (Mundigak IV, Damb Sadaat III, Kulli, etc.) are at least in part for ceremonial purposes, in which ablution, sacrifice, fire, fertility both human and cattle, as well as the construction of a "temple" building in the midst of and dominating the habitations, were involved. These late phases of the high Borderlands are in large part contemporary with the Harappan civilization, so they may well have been derived from the Indus Valley; but their wide acceptance gives a strong suggestion that it was not simply an imposition of a foreign faith but rather the formalization of what was already accepted widely. In this formality a priesthood class becomes tangible—specialists to administer the ceremonies, which surely were of some elaboration if the architecture is in any way an indication. Again, the support of a priesthood and the ceremonies they preside over requires economic resources and a common acceptance of the meaning of the ceremonies.

The fact that the ceremonial structures dominate when they appear (with the possible exception of the colonnaded building at Mundigak) may mean that the priesthood shared authority with secular chiefs, or indeed dominated a class pyramid (or sandwich). In this regard we have little indication of war weapons in these communities. The spearheads are light, the arrow points and sling balls seem more for the chase than for fighting. Even the so-called fortress wall or citadel at Kot Diji is not a very convincing defensive work, cluttered as it is with habitations, and it certainly is not in a very dominating position in comparison with the hill fortress of later times just to the east. Secular chiefs for war on the scale of Early Dynastic Sumer are not hinted at in this region. Rather, the whole region seems to have been quite peaceful. Conflict with tribal hunters or occasionally recalcitrant nomads likely occurred, but we have little hint of it. Priestly control of authority in such situations is more probable than not.

Thus this social aspect of the origin of civilization in the Indus Valley can be summarized as follows:

The evidence indicates that the valleys of the high borderlands were by the beginning of the third millennium B.C. the seat of numerous small Iranian farming villages. The cultivators and the pastoralists exploited what resources there were very extensively with the aid of traditional technology and farming knowledge. This exploitation led to a surplus which made possible both a population increase and the support of a growing number of local specialists in trades such as metallurgy and stone-cutting. At the same time, changes in the local ecologies due to this exploitation imperiled the ability of local villagers using traditional methods to provide a secure and augmenting subsistence foundation to support the growing populations.[10] This provided a reason for developing nontradi-

[10] In villages where land inheritance is a significant factor in the preservation of the

tional methods, among which systems of water and soil control were prominent. Whether some of these systems were independently created or were the result of diffusion from the west is unclear. It does appear, however, that intervalley and thus interregional contacts were strong and therefore the spectrum of diffusionary possibilities was wide.

The social organization of the traditional village would appear to have been based on some system of uni-local residence such as is common enough among historical peoples of the region, since there is little change in even an individual house from phase to phase in any one period and both children and women are buried in the floors. In villages where presumably a single family lived, the eldest adult, probably male, would have been the source of authority sanctioned through custom. In villages consisting of several families, some council or clan group made up of the traditional authorities of each family would have guided affairs. This might include the appointment of a leader in times of crisis. Or village rule might have been left in the hands of a hereditary chief or headman whose position was sanctioned by kinship.

The fact that these highland valleys always contain several or more villages, depending on their resources, and that these villages are homogeneous in the assemblage of traits which represent them suggests that not only in the style of such things as pottery, tools, house type, and religion were they related but that the social organization provided for firm kin-intervillage relationships most probably because of local village exogamy resulting perhaps from limitations on land inheritance. In such cases degrees of distinction according to land holdings and (or) mythic or actual prowess of ancestors or contemporaries may have set certain families apart.

Also to be considered is the economic role of village smiths, potters, weavers, and other specialists and their relation to the land. Where a familial sharing of land existed the resulting wealth was presumably shared. The whole resources of the family could be used to develop the economic base. Indeed, to a high degree, division of labor within the family, by which for example wives wove or made utilitarian non-wheelmade pottery while the males tilled the soil, made the family highly independent. Interdependence, however, existed certainly in the support of smiths and in the economic relationships to pastoralists, for example, whose production of hides, hair, and raw materials were significant in the village economy. We can presume that some trade in such items as shell and colorful stones also created some interdependences.

family lineage and prestige, the fractionalization of the land (if, for example, there were a number of eligible heirs) would make it unworkable after a generation or two. In such cases non-heirs tend to move away or to maintain familial prestige in other ways. Intra- and interfamilial rivalries over land could have been a factor in augmenting the duress which the exploitation of a limited amount of land can bring. A pool of non-productive but kin-related workers could develop from such reasons.

The shift to an economy that demanded the organized labor of people from several villages to construct dams and public buildings and to support an increasing number of specialists which came about as the result of economic need (already outlined above) intensified the traditional village social organization. What seems to have taken place was the literal acknowledgement of interdependences by the formalization of classes based on family prestige, wealth, or occupation already implicit in the village and indeed in the total settlement of each valley. Thus, once innovation was accepted, the mechanism to make it work was already available. Leadership in dam building, for example, could be obtained by recognition by the familial authority of the individual or individuals capable of doing the job. Failure or success, efficiency or lack of it, were the selective factors which made certain individuals more desirable than others. Local beliefs, knowledge of which had been implemented through learned tradition, now required change to meet new circumstances. As social interrelationships changed the need for direction in such areas as myth and ritual and the formalization of iconographies and pantheons produced the priest specialist and his "college" of theocratic consultants. The precarious relationship of the individual to his "luck," so characteristic of primitive belief, was no longer sufficient when the whole population was dependent on the universals of the natural world for success in farming.

A need for insurance in ritual and assurance in dogma motivated the formalization of religion to serve the whole society, not simply the individual. This in turn had a physical aspect in the creation of "temples" and the attendant class of religious specialists.

Whether the architectural form of these "temples" was a borrowing or not from the west is not as important as the fact that the local faith was not imposed from outside but grew out of local belief. Nothing in our evidence suggests otherwise.

Characteristically, the focus of individuals into nonfarming occupations results increasingly in a sharper distinction and categorization of society. These occupational groups tend to be created on the same familial basis as that of the farmer. The property basis is changed but the father-to-son pattern of learned behavior remains the same. Thus the adults teach the children not only the requisite social behavior but the skills of their particular occupations as well.

Group distinctions, however, can motivate the creation of classes where traditionally more recognition of total value to society is given to one group than to another. Characteristically, wealth becomes a significant factor. With an increase in number and kind of specialization a redistributive system necessary to provide for all the nonproductive people (those not involved in subsistence activities) must be formalized and in turn the redistributors may create their own hierarchical subsystems. The accumulation of wealth becomes a marker of class because it represents the very real power of one class or another to manipulate the economic system. Thus not only are classes given position in a hierarchy that is structured on the basis of their worth to the society but also according to their economic power. In such circumstances classes tend to become endogamous, and though by custom they give recognition to the village organization as a whole, they actually relate by kinship only to a part of it. Their true relationships to the village settlement are largely in terms of their role in the interdependence of services and production.

As with the two kinds of villages described earlier, the villages which generally lack hierarchies are derived from an ancient and traditional way of life; the villages whose remains suggested a structured society are the result of the changes necessary to adapt new economic and social conditions. However, both can and do occur in proximity to one another: the structured settlement situated in a more dominant location relative to dams, routes, and other strategic advantages, or, in Harappan context, in the midst of the fields, and the simple village close to the cultivation and sources of water. In a valley such as Welpat or the Ornach where both kinds of villages occur, we can assume that the authority prevalent in the structured village is dominant over the whole valley. In fact, the homogeneity of artifacts between villages suggests that the exchange of goods and services was a constant in their relationships. Each hierarchical village then is a prominent hub in a network of villages, a network which ensures that what affects one community affects them all. This qualitative and functional role of the hierarchical village enables us to label it a "town." By this term we mean also its transitional character between village and city.

But the varied micro-environments of the Borderlands are motivators for equally varied economic dependences, as mentioned earlier. The village network not only includes the settlements of cultivators on the local alluvial plain but extends to semicultivators, semipastoralists, and pastoralists whose stable situation in one or another ecological niche requires varied degrees of dependence on those in another niche. The whole then not only tightly interrelates in any one region but also, owing to practices of transhumance, common culture, trade, etc., there are relationships on an interregional basis which strain the standards of local social systems to encompass them. Whereas the old simple village life (for example, early Nal) was reasonably self-sufficient, the new, more complex situation has to relate not only to the local sphere of activity but also to a far-flung extralocal cluster of custom, belief, and technique. In the competition between local or "little" social systems and interregional or "great" social systems, it is the latter that eventually dominates. We find abundant expressions of this phenomenon everywhere, varied locally only by style differences such as in number of bracelets and necklaces on figurines.

But the needs and events that motivated change indigenously in the

Borderlands also led to a high degree of experimentation. The modification of traditional ways of doing things and the shifts in social organization which made such things as familial custom less important than regional custom also made the traditional adherence to ancestral locales less dogmatic. The pragmatic aspects of water control, soil engineering, commerce, and the accumulation of wealth made the search for good land and other resources as important as the cyclic and repeated exploitation of local resources. The shift of highland villagers into the Indus River Valley was motivated by precisely the same factors as was the technological and social innovation that made possible continued and successful settlement in the highlands. Population pressure or a few bad crop years could have been the trigger for dynamic shifts to the great valley. In this regard the problems which had to be solved before extensive settlement in the valley was possible could be solved in the atmosphere of innovation and experimentation characteristic of the time.

The move into the Indus River Valley did not take place as a migratory movement during which the highlands were abandoned; it would appear, rather, that the network described above was extended by degrees with consequent shifts of population according to the successful settlement of region after region. As a consequence the links between regions were not broken until that time long after the dawn of civilization on the Indus River when both highlands and lowlands were almost deserted. This meant that the diffusionary channels described by Dyson were generally effectively open and the innovations of the West could play their role in stimulating style and technological development in the Borderlands.

The urbanization process so necessary to the definition of a civilization would appear to have come about as the inevitable result of the direction already taken by the villagers of the Borderlands. What was lacking in the highlands was the space and the natural resources to stimulate the process. In the Indus Valley both were at hand. With little technological innovation but with an already largely established hierarchical system the organization necessary to handle the problems of settled life in the valley was created. Large populations, increasing number of specialists, surpluses of subsistence crops, storage (since a one-crop-a-year harvest was typical), and the maintainance of religious, social, legal, and political forms mutually recognized by the population—these were the kinds of problems which needed solutions as settlement was established.

The walled towns of the highlands had their equivalents in the cities and towns of the lowlands. But, as will be seen in the next chapters, such cities were only a small part of the settlement of the lowlands and indeed were not typical of the settlement as a whole, for the greater number of sites are villages of a type long familiar in the Borderlands. Thus in the network of settlements which characterized the time only certain nodes were selected out as urban centers. Their character is the subject of the next chapter.

Though we lack evidence we vitally need, what we do have is an awareness that the process which created the civilization on the Indus was logically the result of processes already underway in the Borderlands.

These speculations on the social side of pre-Harappan and Early Harappan villages are not without some foundation, as the reader may have gathered, but we cannot, of course, truly determine just what the situation was. There is just enough evidence, however, to indicate that these early societies had the social capability and the incentive for civilization.

The diffusion of new traits from Mesopotamia, the richness of the great valley, and the technological and social readiness of the existent cultures are the ingredients for the genesis of the Harappan civilization. There is, however, significantly another factor—India herself.

As will be shown in the next pages, the civilization that arose in the Indus River Valley, whatever its antecedents in Iran or elsewhere, is nonetheless uniquely subcontinental. It has a particular character that clearly differentiates it from other civilizations of the ancient world, and in this particularity one can trace the roots of some of later Indian civilization. The Harappan civilization is a unified civilization made cohesive by a common theme, an ethos universally understood. The Early Harappan stage must have seen this theme, this motive, created, and its creation eventually gave the Harappan culture dominance over all its neighbors. In one form or another it was to last perhaps a thousand years, and may well have endured to the time of the Buddha as an important aspect of ancient Indian life. The real riddle of the Harappan civilization's origin is the *raison d'être* for its Indianness. A hint of an answer can be obtained by an examination of the civilization itself, the subject of the next chapter.

VII

The Harappan Civilization

As FAR AS ARCHAEOLOGICAL INVESTIGATION HAS GONE, all the evidence would indicate that the heartland of the Harappan civilization was the Indus River, especially its lower reaches below Sukkur, or what is known as the land of Sind. As Egypt is known as the gift of the Nile, so Sind is the gift of the Indus River. In fact, the very name "Sind" is a corruption of the term "Sindlur," the local name for the Indus River. Her "gift" is a broad, flat plain of some twenty thousand square miles, through and over which the river meanders to the sea.

The previous chapter provides some details of the local geography, but in the context of the Harappan civilization certain points need to be emphasized, or re-emphasized, as the case may be.

❋ The Geography

(1) The Indus River is in its mature stage in Sind and southern Punjab. This means that characteristically the river meanders over the plain. Its silt deposition is very great, and in consequence of this the river builds natural levees which are broken in times of high flooding. There are recorded changes

of the Indus River channels in history.[1] The effect of such changes on established cities there is to cause their abandonment or to motivate drastic action by man to save them.[2]

(2) The climate of Sind is arid, and only in lower Sind are summer monsoonal rains at all influential, and these only occasionally.

(3) The six summer months, April through September, have earned Sind, especially upper Sind, the reputation of being the hottest place on earth. The breathless fierceness of a Sind summer has colored the writings of many an author.

(4) The watered alluvium, especially in the Indus River flood plains, is highly productive, and given opportunity, natural vegetation grows there quite luxuriantly.

(5) The Indus River, Lake Manchhar, the *dhands*, and the Eastern and Western Naras are excellent sources of food fish.

(6) The celebrated salt-covered tracts in the vicinity of traditionally productive zones like Larkana are primarily the result of recent irrigation practices and cannot be said to be typical of ancient times, even though natural leaching does occur, especially in the Indus River delta.[3]

These geographic factors are essential to an understanding of what caused the particular florescence of a village society into a full-fledged civilization of a particular character. They also must be a part of any theory as to the decline of that civilization.

❊ *Mohenjo-daro*

IT IS PERHAPS UNFORTUNATE for interpretations of the Harappan civilization that that civilization is best known through excavations at its cities. After the initial discoveries of Harappa and Mohenjo-daro, some thirty campaigns were carried out at those massive sites; one was carried out at the smaller but nonetheless comparable site of Chanhu-daro, and more recently at Lothal in Gujarat. Since at this writing upwards of 150 sites of the Harappan civilization are known and of these only about five or six can be said to represent cities or towns (Mohenjo-daro, Harappa, Chanhu-daro, Pathiani Kot, Judeirjo-daro, and Lothal—the first two being the largest), the rest representing villages, it is clear that we can not over-

[1] Lambrick, 1964, pp. 191ff.

[2] Among the cities of Sind whose importance waned with river changes, according to fact or tradition, are: Patala (?), Brahmanabad-Mansura, Alor, Bhamphore. Some cities and towns have disappeared because of floods, as, for example, did Muradabad.

[3] *Indus River Basin Studies*, Division of Engineering and Applied Physics, Harvard University, Harvard Water Resources Group, Contract No. 14-08-0001-8305, 1964, pp. 2–3.

MAP 19 *Plan of the site of Mohenjo-daro.*

emphasize the urban at the expense of the rural—which is in effect what our evidence tends to do.

Of all the Harappan sites, however, Mohenjo-daro is by far the most impressive. It covers an area of some 240 acres, of which something less than one third has been excavated. This site is located in the Larkana district of upper Sind several miles to the east of the railroad station of Dokri. It is close to the right bank of the modern Indus River channel and were it not for protective bunds would probably have disappeared in large part in the last several decades. As it is, flooding occurs in the summer months right up to the bunds, and the local village of Hasan Wuhan to the northeast can only be reached by boat.

The site of Mohenjo-daro falls readily into two parts: a high artificial mound rising to about forty feet on the west; and a low, undulating, and much broader area on the east.[4]

North and east of this low area are scattered remains, suggesting that the site extended considerably beyond the apparent bounds of the visible

[4] The excavated areas on the site are named after the principal archaeologists who worked them. Thus HR is Hargreaves; DK is Dikshit; VS is Vats.

PLATE 26   *Mohenjo-daro from the southeast, looking toward the main mound or citadel, which is crowned by a Buddhist stupa.*

site. In fact, the Pakistan Archaeological Department officers who are resident there often show visitors walls just below the surface of waters on the east. This is in contrast to the situation on the west of the high mound, where recent excavation in connection with improvements to the area produced only river sand. This suggests that there is a possibility that Mohenjo-daro was once in an island situation, vested by some branch of the Indus. More than likely, however, this sand is indicative of ancient flooding. To the north of the site there are remnants of brick embankments of some size which may be ancient bunds intended to divert the riverine floodwaters from the main site. On the south there are also remnants of walls and other remains. Among them are what appears to be a brick-lined pit of a size approaching a rectangular reservoir perhaps forty by sixty yards in extent, though the dimensions are not clear owing to the lack of excavation. In view of the great brick-lined depression at Lothal (p. 270, Pl. 42), these pits at Mohenjo-daro deserve the attention of future investigations.

Striking is the broad sandy area which lies between the west and east units of the main site (Map 19). There appears little doubt that this area, low-lying as it is, was subject to flooding in ancient times. One wonders what arrangements were made to bridge the two major mounds in that situation. Even more intriguing is the possibility that this area was made into a deliberate pool, of which the revetments in the west mound and the newly discovered ones on the HR side of the east mound were the artificial bounds.[5] Another puzzling feature is the narrow low-lying valley which runs east-west between the excavated areas VS and HR, the so-called East Street (Map 19). A modern pathway leads along this stretch, connecting the depression between the two major units of the site and the pro-

[5] G. F. Dales, "The Decline of the Harappans," *Scientific American*, Vol. CCXIV, No. 5 (1966), pp. 92–100.

PLATE 27 *Cultural stratum of Harappan times between two strata of riverine silt, proof of the temporary status of settlements close to the Indus flood plain. Picture was taken at a point midway between the river and Mohenjo-daro.*

tective bund on the east. Without the bund, of course, the paths would run unimpeded to the Indus River. In the winter of 1959-1960, directly after some local rain, I was shown this area by some officers of the Archaeological Department of Pakistan. On both sides one could observe very clearly masses of mud brick surmounted, or in some cases matched, by walls of fired brick. Here and there the brick bulwarks would recede or advance, to conform apparently with the structures which fronted on the valley.

I made a later visit in company with the late Professor Frederick Zeuner, and observations strongly suggested to us both that one might have reason to suspect the presence of a canal or artificial channel. Such water systems are certainly within the bounds of probability, especially in view of the accessibility of the river and the use of boats attested for this civilization. However, until excavations are carried out with such problems in mind, we must be tantalized by these possibilities without admitting them as facts.

It is the western mound that above all catches the visitor's eye (Pl. 26). Dominated by a ruined stupa of the Kushan period dating to the second century A.D., it can be seen for several miles around. Clearly, in Harappan times the landscape was indeed dominated by the structures there. Sir Mortimer Wheeler has carried out the most recent and most effective excavation in this part of the site, and his conclusions are in large part definitive.[6] Wheeler has defined three major building periods there without having reached virgin soil on account of the modern high water table, even though an effort in 1950 reached twenty-six feet below the surface of the modern flood plain. (In 1964–65 G. Dales reached virgin soil at thirty-nine feet below the modern plain.) The central feature of the mound is a massive mud-brick platform protected, at least on its western flank, by an embankment some forty-three feet in width which in later times had to be continually reinforced. Below the platform, which belongs to the most productive period of building on the site and which for various reasons can be known as of the mature period of the Harappan civilization (Period II) (see p. 306), are remnants of walls of buildings of an earlier phase (Period I) probably of the mature period.[7]

The builders of the great platform also provided for enclosure walls interposed between rectangular bastions and broken now and again by gates. This system of bastions, enclosure walls, and gates is poorly known, since it is presently revealed only at the southeastern corner of the site and by a fired-brick tower and a small gate (postern) on the west.

The west mound has a depression running east-west which serves to divide the northern and higher area from the southern, or lower, area. The latter is poorly known, even though some excavation was carried on there in the past. What is revealed is a rather bewildering and rather meaningless series of walls, pillars, wells, drains, and the like which obviously indicate structures of some formal importance. Of these there is one known to the excavators as the Assembly Hall. Badly preserved, it is

---

[6] Sir M. Wheeler, *The Indus Civilization, History of India* supplementary volume, 2nd ed., Cambridge University Press, 1962. This is the classic study of the Harappan civilization, and the reader is strongly advised to supplement this chapter by reading this excellent account.

[7] The late period is one of deterioration (see p. 306).

nonetheless one of the most striking monuments at Mohenjo-daro. It consisted of a broad pillared hall opening principally to the north, i.e., toward the highest part of the site. Twenty rectangular pillars approximately five feet by three feet in size supported the roof. The pillars were arranged in rows of four with five pillars to each row. In the aisles so formed were carefully laid strips of brick pavement bordered by bricks laid on edge.[8]

Behind the pillared hall are the remnants of a fine paved room some twenty-two feet in length from north to south that is linked by its paving to the main hall. Unfortunately, the eastern portion of these structures has been destroyed, but it would appear that behind the main hall and its annex on the south was a walled court with a well. To the northeast and apparently contiguous with the Assembly Hall complex was a series of small chambers belonging to a large structure. One of these chambers contained a dark stone apparently placed in its situation with deliberate purpose. Since this stone is of size (2' by 1' 7" by 1' 2½") and its top is flat and polished, it is difficult to ignore it. It merely accentuates the problems of interpreting these remains.[9] This building complex, located as it is in such a prominent position, must have played a significant role in the life of the city. Yet nothing found in association even hints as to its role. One cannot help but speculate, however, that it was constructed in response to a formality urged by religion or government. Was it indeed a place of assembly or perhaps a place of audience? Wheeler rightfully refers to the Achaemenid pillared hall of audience, the apadana, in this context, and such a comparison is certainly called to mind.[10] Marshall thought the spaces left between paving strips in the aisles of the main hall might have supported benches. An interesting feature occurs before the northern entrance of the hall. Three circles of brick were found, measuring some three feet across and three feet high, which almost certainly protected the vulnerable trunks of trees whose shade would have been welcome whatever the purpose of those who visited before the main building. Thus, present speculations are directed to more or less the same conjecture.

It is the group of buildings to the west of the stupa on the highest part of the mound that command the visitor's attention. Of these, the Great Bath is the most striking. The structure consists of an outer series of small rooms (except on the west side) and an inner colonnade or recessed

---

[8] Marshall's report, the original account of the site, would place at least some of these pavements in a slightly later period, but their position argues for their contemporaneity. Sir J. Marshall, ed., *Mohenjo-daro and the Indus Civilization*, Vol. I, Arthur Probsthain, London, 1931, p. 161.

[9] Marshall suggests it was possibly used by a leather cutter or sandal maker (1931, p. 167); this hardly comports with the elaborate buildings with which the stone is associated.

[10] Sir M. Wheeler, *Early India and Pakistan*, Ancient Peoples and Places Series, Glyn Daniel, gen. ed., Frederick A. Praeger, New York, 1959.

PLATE 28   *The Great Bath of Mohenjo-daro, showing the surrounding colonnade and the bathing stairs.*

pillars running around the pool proper. The latter is rectangular, and access to the waters was obtained by flights of steps set into the middle of the opposing short sides. The pool measures about 39 feet by 23 feet and is approximately 8 feet deep. The stairs into the pool terminate on platforms which are a little over a foot from the bottom of the pool; they are 3 feet in width and extend right across from one side to the other. The pool was made waterproof by lining it with bitumen along the outer edge of the containing walls and binding this layer with a thin wall of brick backed by a rammed clay filling. There is evidence that the steps were covered by wooden treads slotted into the sides of the stairs and fixed with bitumen.

The bottom of the pool is composed of bricks laid on end, their long axes running north-south. In the southwest corner a drainage hole penetrates through the western wall of the pool, eventually reaching a fine corbeled channel made of fired brick some 2 feet in width and high enough to walk along. This channel curves to the north and then after some 35 feet tends to the west, probably eventually emptying through some outlet set in the mud platform described previously. Mackay noted that a narrow chamber through which the pool drain passed to the corbeled channel was once covered by a flat-timbered roof, as evidenced by the slots for receiving squared beam ends found on either wall. Of great interest is a deliberately made manhole about 2 by $3\frac{1}{2}$ feet which gave access into both the chamber and the corbeled passage. Obviously this was used to permit the cleaning of the drainage system. The floor of the pool slopes toward the drain hole, and the latter was probably closed by a plug of some kind. Water for the pool was obtained from a brick-lined well located in one of the chambers on the eastern side of the structure.

The outer walls of the Great Bath building measure from six to something over seven feet in thickness. Some four entrances penetrated this massive enclosure. Of these those on the south (two) and east (one) are the most important. The former gave access to a long narrow chamber nicely paved and having a drain at its eastern end. Two small chambers of unknown usage occur at either of the long ends of this vestibule; access to the fenestrated aisle leading around the pool was obtained through a door set toward the eastern end of the north wall.

The small chambers along the eastern side of the structure may have been dressing or service rooms of some kind. The well room has already been mentioned. This had a separate entrance from the street and may have served a double function, being both for the users of the pool and for the individuals who were carrying out their sundry tasks in the immediate vicinity.

Chamber 19 of the excavator's plan is the northernmost of the small rooms and is of interest in that it contained a bathroom with a drain emptying out to a main sewer line, which ran along the street; it also contained a stairway which led to an upper story of the bath. The fact of an upper story appears to be confirmed by the presence of two water (?) chutes set into the wall which drained into brick boxes immediately adjacent to the building.

At least four chambers were found in the northern third of the structure at one period, but these were subdivided, and in fact the northernmost units were filled in and that part of the building raised in a later development.

Just north of the Great Bath is a group of buildings whose use is unknown. However, the one immediately adjacent to the Bath consists of two rows of bathrooms set on either side of a narrow line which contains a main-line drain that carried water to the south and probably eventually turned west. The descent was about 1 foot in 68. The individual bathroom measured about $9\frac{1}{2}$ by $5\frac{1}{2}$ feet. The paved floors in each gently sloped toward the doorways, where tunnels carried the water into the main drain. Privacy was apparently a consideration, for doorways are arranged so that one could not see into the opposite room while standing in a doorway of the opposite wall. The doorways, too, do not open to the middle of the room but to one side. Each room also contains a flight of stairs. This makes one suspect that the drain lane was actually a service corridor where servants moved back and forth carrying water to the bathrooms from a well found in the chamber just to the north and where the drainage system could be curated. The users of the rooms lived, or at least carried on their principal activities, on a floor above, descending with all due modesty to perform their respective ablutions in perhaps assigned bathrooms below.

Beyond this building, whose closeness to the Great Bath suggests related functions, one comes to a veritable rabbit warren of structures badly preserved but having some rooms within which paved floors and drains indicate the same concern for water for one reason or another as do the more southerly buildings. It is notable that at this point one is at the highest part of the whole site. The difficulty of raising water to these heights has to be considered in speculating over the function of these buildings.

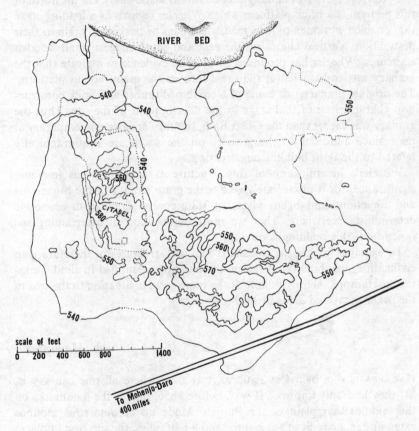

MAP 20 *Plan of the site of Harappa.*

Across the street to the east of the Great Bath is a big rectangular building that for some inexplicable reason is called the "college" by the savants who interpret these things. It is a jumble of walls, drains, stairways, and a fine open court. Obviously it is an important part of the complex of buildings on the platform around, but "What is it?"

To the west of the Great Bath, thanks to the painstaking work of Sir Mortimer Wheeler, we appear to be on firmer ground.[11] On the southeast are the remnants of a fine stairway some twenty-two feet wide which led from the plain to the top of the platform. This put the individual adjacent to a structure which Wheeler has called the Granary. In ancient times this was distinguished by a superstructure of timbers set on some twenty-seven square or rectangular brickwork units. The passages between these units "ensured the circulation of air beneath the main body of the granary overhead." The whole formed a massive podium of formidable size (150 feet by 75 feet initially, but additions made later). On the north of this podium is a brick platform which Wheeler regards as a loading stage that enabled workmen to haul readily the bags or baskets of grain to their destination. Vertical chases on the east and south suggest small wooden staircases. Wheeler has produced substantial evidence to indicate that the granary was constructed at the same time as the main mound platform. The original granary was made of a combined timber and brick construction characteristic of that stage in the development of the site. Thus the granary was earlier than the Great Bath, but they are also contemporary in part, since additions to the granary on the south are stratigraphically related to the Bath building construction.

Wheeler's identification of this structure as a granary has immense significance, for it immediately recalls the grain storage of the Sumerians and Egyptians and opens vistas of state control familiar to economic determinists everwhere. That we must use caution in ascertaining the function of this building is obvious.

To examine further the so-called "citadel" structures of the Harappan civilization, we should first review the buildings identified in similar context at Harappa, before looking at the more secular situation to the east in the other excavated areas at Mohenjo-daro.

✳ *Harappa*

HARAPPA IS ONE OF THOSE FRUSTRATING SITES where all one can say is, "If they had only known." It was, before 1856, one of the landmarks on the middle Ravi plain of the Punjab. Made up of numerous mounds extending in a circuit of some three and a half miles, the site rose in places up to sixty feet. Early reports noted its immensity. General Alexander Cunningham, who initiated much of the development of the Archaeological Survey of India, even describes buildings found there without realizing their true antiquity.[12] From 1856 to 1919 a systematic destruction of

[11] *Ibid.*, 962.
[12] Sir Alexander Cunningham, Archaeological Survey of India reports, Vol. V, 1872–73.

Harappa was carried on thanks to the inevitable stupidity of so-called "practical" men whose shortsightedness plagues us now more than ever. The Lahore-Multan link of the Indian Railroad required a firm footing to pass over the muddy and oft-flooded plains of that area, and the presence of that great mass of ancient fired bricks was too good to be true. It was a natural quarry and remained so until an enlightened government finally put an all too tardy stop to that usage. The major excavation report that resulted after some twelve seasons of excavations produces plan after plan showing fragments of the walls and pavements which once were part of fine structures but which now, like a broken weather vane, point nowhere.[13]

The plan of the site (Map 20) shows that at one time the river flowed close by and that it has since shifted some six miles to the north, in keeping with its maturity. Thus, as with Mohenjo-daro, proximity to the river was clearly a necessity in picking the settlement location. Similar to the Sind site, this one contains a high mound which marks the western portion of the place, and there is a lower and much larger complex of remains to the south and to the east.

In characteristic fashion Sir Mortimer Wheeler chose Harappa as critical for renewed excavation in formulating the plans for his directorship of the Archaeological Survey. Equally characteristically, he chose the high mound as his area of concentration. A disgruntled colleague once remarked that in planning to excavate the French look for likely places to find temples, the Germans seek palaces, the British head for citadels, and the Americans inevitably find kitchens! The ethnocentrism becomes glaring when they all discover the same buildings!

Wheeler's exemplary excavations indicated that on the original site villages of Baluch affinity had once existed (see p. 182). Successive floodings occurred before the Harappans, in a mature stage of their civilization, arrived. The Harappans constructed a tapering wall 45 feet wide at its base that was protected by a mud and brick band and a fired-brick revetment. These walls made a rough parallelogram about 460 yards by 214 yards, the long axis extending from north to south. Within this, as at Mohenjo-daro, a great mud-brick platform was raised, in places up to 25 feet in height. On this were constructed fired-brick buildings whose various vicissitudes went through at least six phases. These buildings have, for identification purposes at least, practically vanished, but a drain and a well remain to suggest the same obsession with water as at Mohenjo-daro. Vats, the original excavator, also found forty large vessels set in a line next to a building. He called them postcremation urns because scraps of carbonized bone were found within them, but little more can be said, for we need proof that these scraps were of human bone before we can ponder the parallel with modern Indian custom.

[13] M. S. Vats, *Excavations at Harappa*, Government of India, New Delhi, 1940.

Wheeler's work on the enclosure walls indicated that the main entrance was on the north but that on the western side a bastion overlooked a series of ramps and terraces which led through gates till a final rise by means of a ramp or stairs to the platform. Other bastions were identified along the walls and suggest an effective system of defenses. Wheeler indicates three phases in the construction of these "defenses." The last included an enlargement of the northwest corner system and the blocking of the above-mentioned gateway, as if the occupants were under external stress and needed to improve or reinforce their defenses.[14]

To the north of this walled mound and between it and the old river bed were found a series of remains of much importance. The first of these to note are Wheeler's granaries. These are closest to the river bed, and in fact Wheeler feels that a revetment found on the southern end, plus the lack of space to the east and west sides of the structure, indicates that the granaries faced toward the river and thus could be supplied by river transport. The granaries proper were set on a pounded-earth platform about 4 feet high. The granaries appear to have been a bit more elaborate than their equivalent at Mohenjo-daro. A central aisle ran between two large units composed of six granaries each. These measured 50 feet by 20 feet respectively and in form consisted of three narrow parallel brick units and two outer walls. These provided the foundation for wooden floors apparently, and the spaces between each unit were in effect the air passages to provide necessary circulation. Stairways in the central circle and ramps along the sides gave access to the storage areas, which, according to the original excavator's report, had doorways both at one end and on the two long sides. Wheeler points out that the total floor space available (ca. 9000 square feet) is quite close to that available at the Great Granary at Mohenjo-daro.

About one hundred yards to the south of the granaries are a series of brick circles arranged in lines. These measure ten to eleven feet in diameter. Vats had identified seventeen of these and Wheeler another of them.[15] The circles typically have a hole in the center and concentric rings of edge-on-bricks. Wheeler's careful work resulted in the identification of straw or brick in association with his platforms. Vats had already found cleaned wheat and husked barley in the central hole of another.[16] Wheeler, reasoning by analogy with similar customs elsewhere, feels that the Harappans used wooden pestles to pound grain in the "mortar" of the central hole.[17]

Another industry is indicated by the presence of sixteen furnaces nearby

14 Sir M. Wheeler, 1962b, p. 22.
15 Vats, 1940; R. E. M. Wheeler, 1947–1948.
16 Wheeler, 1947; Vats, 1940.
17 Wheeler, 1947; Wheeler, 1962, p. 23.

that apparently used cow dung as fuel; metallurgy is indicated but not confirmed.[18]

A remarkable group of buildings is found just north of the walled platform. These are essentially a series of well-planned houses probably once surrounded by a compound wall. At least fourteen houses are indicated, running in two east-west lines of seven houses each. A narrow lane divided one row from the others, the northern row opening on the lane and the back of the southern row of dwellings. Each house was rectangular and measured approximately 55 by 24 feet. One entered at one short end through an oblique passageway into a long room, or more probably a court, some 23 by 20½ feet in size, beyond which was a small room. Brick paving apparently was much used in these houses, as with most structures of the Harappan civilization. The houses, though in lines, were separated, and no sharing of a common house wall is indicated. Wheeler sees these structures as the result of "a piece of government planning" and as indicative of "ranges of barrack-like quarters within a walled compound."[19] These, together with the granaries and the "serried lines of platforms for pounding grain," plus of course the walled "citadel," suggest social and political elements of significance to an understanding of the Harappan civilization.[20]

The structures so far described relate in large part to the high mounds, or as Wheeler calls them, the "citadels," of Harappa and Mohenjo-daro. They present a formal aspect. Though such formality can be found in other areas of these sites, there is nonetheless a feeling that the more varied daily life of the times took place in each away from the "citadel." This is confirmed by the abundant habitation debris found by the excavators and in part by the bewildering labyrinth of lanes, doors, drains, and walls which, in spite of the formality of over-all plan, characterized the low-lying remains east of the high mounds. It is to Mohenjo-daro, with its extensively excavated and better preserved remains, that we must look to obtain a view of the more informal situation. To a lesser extent what is depicted there is confirmed at the more recently excavated sites of Lothal, Chanhu-daro, and Kalibangan (see pp. 261–273).

❋ *Settlement of Mohenjo-daro*

THE PLAN AT MOHENJO-DARO was that of a grid. The broad main street ran north-south, while narrower lanes ran east-west, often terminating in smaller north-south streets whose termini were often blocked by house walls, though lanes led the wayfarer at right angles away to east and west.

[18] Vats, 1940, I, 470; Wheeler, 1962b, p. 23. These are, however, probably of later date than the granaries.
[19] Wheeler, 1962b, pp. 23, 24.
[20] *Ibid.*, pp. 24–26.

PLATE 29   *A view of "Main Street" in the DK area at Mohenjo-daro.*

There were at least six of these blocks, rectangular in shape and consistent in size (*ca.* 800 feet by 1200 feet). This would indicate modular planning of an advanced type not unlike that of Tell el Amarna. An examination of the plan for the HR area is revealing in that it shows that the characteristic house unit was large and consisted of a number of rooms surrounded by a thick outer wall fronting on the streets and lanes. This outer wall measures as much as five feet, and even within the houses thick walls (three feet or more), buttresses, and thick platforms were common. The outer walls also have an outside batter of 2° to 6° from the vertical. Almost every house had a stairway or stairway leading up; water pipes, and chutes within the walls used for disposing of matter from above are frequently found; windows on the streets and lanes are infrequent; many of the rooms are so small as to bar their use for living purposes. This kind of evidence makes it certain that the families resident at Mohenjo-daro lived in upper stories, made most probably of wood supplemented by reed matting, or light screens of mud brick. This is apparently confirmed at Kot Diji, where reed mat-marked impressions were found in the Harappan levels.[21] This upper-story living underlines the response to the climate that man must make to flourish in Sind.

There is certainly some correlation between the heat factor and the efforts made to bring water to the houses. One of the striking features of the site is the fine brick wells (inside diameter two to three feet) which

[21] Khan, 1965, Pl. Vb; see p. 18.

stand now above many of the ruined buildings. Many of these wells were private and often had outlets within rooms of the houses. One such room, for example, was about two feet higher than an adjacent room, and in it was found a paved floor, curbed by brick, for bathing that stood before two very excellent privies. These were set against the wall, through which outlets led to a drain in the lane outside.[22] Frequently pottery piping was used to carry water to the main drains. This piping was both vertical, for the conveyance of waste from an upper story, and horizontal. Bathrooms are common enough at Mohenjo-daro, the bathing floor properly sloping to its drain, as in the bathrooms of the "citadel" mound. Cesspits as well as drains were used for the disposal of waste.

Lattice work in stone as well as probably in other materials covered openings in the thick walls and gave light without glare. Interesting are the corbeled brick arches used for wall niches, drains, and in a few cases as

[22] Marshall, 1931, Vol. I, p. 207.

PLATE 30   *Reconstruction of plan of House VIII at Mohenjo-daro* (after Marshall, 1931).

SCALE

PLATE 31 *Reconstruction of plan of House XIII at Mohenjo-daro* (after Marshall, 1931).

passageways. The thickness of the walls is certainly a protection against heat, and one can consider some of the wall openings as possibly secured with wet cloth or matting, thus cooling the interior. Windows as a rule are absent, however, as remarked above, and only doorways (3 feet 4 inches in width) break the monotony of the exterior walls.

The habitations of Mohenjo-daro give one the impression of being the homes of a well-to-do class with plenty of servants available to cook and otherwise carry out the daily chores. A few kilns or furnaces are recorded among the houses, and in one case a series of brick-lined pits were found, suggesting to the excavator that they were used for dyeing. But few signs of other than home activities have been found at Mohenjo-daro.

Basically the Harappan house was a series of rooms arranged around a court within which household activities such as breadmaking and presumably washing were carried out. Presumably these rooms were for storage, cooking, ablutions, etc. Access to an upper story was by an interior stair-

PLATE 32 *Well in the lower city, Mohenjo-daro.*

way. Some of these houses may have had two courts and a corresponding augmentation of service rooms.

Though the bulk of the buildings to the east of the "citadel" at Mohenjo-daro appear to have been residences, there are a few whose function seems to have been public. One of these is strongly suggestive of the ceremonial structures described for the late prehistoric phases of the highland areas of the Borderlands. Wheeler describes it as follows:[23]

> ... the so-called House A1, bounded on the north by "South Lane" and on the west by "Deadman Lane." The significance of the plan is not brought out by the published record, which amalgamates walls of very different periods and is in several respects incomplete. The numerous additions apart, the nucleus of the plan is a high oblong structure, 52 ×40 ft. with walls over 4 ft. thick and a partial infilling of mud brick. It was approached from the

[23] Wheeler, 1962b, pp. 40–41.

south by two symmetrically disposed stairs parallel with the frontage, access to which was provided in turn by a monumental double gateway between two irregular blocks of buildings. In the inner sector or court of this gateway is a ring of brickwork, 4 ft. in internal diameter, of a kind which has been conjectured to represent protective enclosures round (sacred?) trees. Just inside the adjacent room to the east of the gateway was found a bearded human head, 6.9 ins. high, carved in white limestone from the neighbouring Baluch hills. The upper lip is shaven, as in other Harappan (and Sumerian) heads; the hair is bunched in a bun at the back and bound across the forehead with a narrow fillet. The ear is a formless oval with a small central hole; the eyes are designed for inlay of shell or faïence. Nor was this the only sculpture found in or about the site. "On the top of the wall above the western flight of steps" lay a headless seated figure of alabaster. Three days

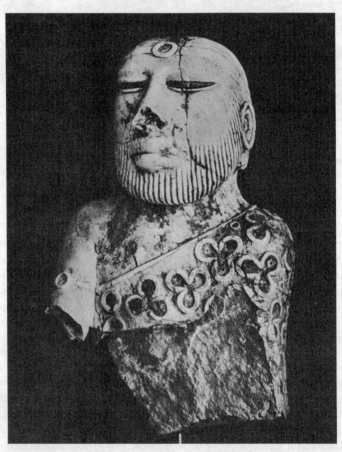

PLATE 33 *Harappan "priest," steatite, from Mohenjo-daro* (after Marshall, 1931).

later a part of a head of the same figure was found 45 ft. to the north, in "South Lane," and the next day the remaining part of the head was recovered in the courtyard of an adjacent house. "As the three pieces so widely separated were all found in the superficial debris, it seems likely that they were scattered after the site had been destroyed and abandoned, though the image appears to date from a very early period." Be that as it may, the figure is of extraordinary interest. It is 16½ ins. high, and represents a seated or squatting man with his hands resting on his knees, one a little higher than the other; the head is bearded and wears a fillet passing over the receding forehead and hanging down in two strands at the back; the eyes have lost their inlay. Details are worn away, but there is a hint of clothing, at least over the lower part of the body.

In determining the use of the building we thus have at present the following

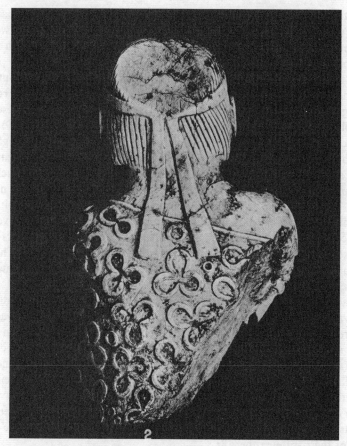

PLATE 34   *Rear view of Plate 33. Compare with head from Mundigak,*
Fig. 30 (after Marshall, 1931).

data: it is massively built but of relatively small size; it is approached in monumental fashion by two symmetrical stairways, a provision quite out of scale with any domestic or industrial purpose; the stairways are themselves reached though an impressive double entrance at the lower level, and within the entrance is a small circular enclosure apparently designed for the protection of a tree or other object—possibly even of the statue whereof the head was found only a few feet away; and finally, amongst the rare sculptures of Mohenjo-daro, a second was broken in the same vicinity, and its major part was found actually on the site of the present building. The combination of circumstances, though not determinate, inclines towards the identification of the structure as a temple, and it can at least be said that there, more amply than anywhere else at present in Mohenjo-daro, the conditions for such identification are supplied. The re-excavation and adequate record of this site are particularly desirable.

In the same HR area a series of ten rooms arranged in two equal parallel rows (N-S) divided by a narrow passage is of some interest. A well is located at one end of the passage. Each house unit is divided into a front and back room, the former having a doorway to the street and a paved floor for bathing with drain and associated pit or pottery sump outside. To the south and directly associated with this complex are two rooms facing to the west, one of which contains a well. To the east of these is a complex of four small chambers, one of which contains a bathing floor.

The principal units of this complex measure some seventeen to eighteen feet by ten feet and are thus capable of being used as living quarters. They are located across a narrow street from a massive building which has a counterpart in scale in an incompletely excavated structure to the northwest. The former, at least, appears not to have been a typical habitation and may well qualify as a public or formal building which was served by the occupants who had their quarters across the street. There appears to be a close parallel here to the unit houses found at Harappa (p. 253). There is also a rough parallel to the formalized bathrooms with their living quarters above to the north of the Great Bath (p. 248).

Mackay, one of the excavators, continued work carried on by a previous excavator, Dikshit, on the western side of the DK area. Here was uncovered a large courtyard paved with mud brick and surrounded on three sides at least by a series of rooms. Some of these rooms were paved, and there are at least two wells located at the southern end of the structure. Mackay saw in the location of the building close to the edge of the city, its abundant water, and its large open courtyard the possibility that it was a khan or caravanserai where travelers arriving at the city might tether their beasts in the court and ascend to an upper story for the night or the duration of their sojourn there.[24]

[24] E. J. H. Mackay, 1938, pp. 118–119.

PLATE 35   *Grinding (?) pits in a courtyard of the lower city, or habitation area, of Mohenjo-daro.*

Evidence for industrial activities other than those described for the "citadel" is singularly sparse at Mohenjo-daro. However, on the main mound (Mound II) at Chanhu-daro, a large site on the eastern side of the valley about eighty miles south of Mohenjo-daro, considerable evidence for the presence of artisans was found.[25] A large rectangular building entered at one side from the street contained a series of brick-made crisscrossed flues on which was placed a single layer of bricks on which were compartments. MacKay found a large number of small steatite beads finished and unfinished amidst the ruins of this structure and suggested that it was possibly used as a factory for glazing them. In a courtyard next to the building as well as within the building itself a good many copper, shell, bone, and steatite (seals) objects were found, some also incomplete. In Lothal in Gujarat the presence of the coppersmith, the bead maker, and others was attested by finds among the buildings (see p. 267f.).

The grid pattern with its modularity, the street drains, cesspits, pipes, the generally rectangular small rooms on the ground, the brick-lined bathing floors, the presence of wells in and among the buildings, the stairways, etc., are found in the habitation areas so far as they are now known at Harappa, Chanhu-daro, Lothal, and Kalibangan. In other words, the

[25] E. J. H. Mackay, *Chanhu-daro Excavations 1935–36*, American Oriental Society, Vol. XX, Museum of Fine Arts, Boston, 1943.

PLATE 36 *Main drain in a street at Mohenjo-daro.*

evidence is overwhelming for town planning of a singularly advanced kind. It bespeaks of such professions as the pipe maker and layer, the sanitation engineer, the well maker, the architect, the brick mason, and the carpenter, the last of these to cut and lay the big beams which almost certainly had to be stretched across the lower chamber walls to uphold the superstructure. The Harappan use of fired brick, which was not unknown in Mesopotamia, was nonetheless carried to sophisticated lengths. A gypsum mortar was commonly used to bind the brick tiers, but it is rather odd that so few footings have been found. Dependence for foundation support was apparently the virgin soil, pounded earth, or the remains of previous walls. The absence of stone resources in these areas, of course, limited what could be accomplished.

The effect on the modern-day observer of moving between these seemingly endless walls of brick is one of monotony, and so impressed Stuart Piggott that he summarized the Harappan civilization in a classic comment: "The secrecy of those blank brick walls, the unadorned architecture of even the citadel buildings, the monotonous regularity of the streets, the

PLATE 37   *An alleyway in the lower city of Mohenjo-daro.*

stifling weight of dead tradition all combine to make the Harappan civilization one of the least attractive phases of ancient Oriental history."[26]

There is ample evidence that plastering of walls with a mud plaster was common practice. Whether this was decorated in any way we do not know. But certainly a good deal of the monotony of the city's streets was relieved by the wooden superstructures, which may well have reflected in painted, carved, cloth- and mat-covered surfaces the color, exuberance, and humor which is found in the artifacts of the Harappans.

❋ *Villages of the Harappan Civilization*

IN THE FACE OF WHAT WE KNOW about the cities of the Harappan civilization, we have almost nothing to mark down for the villages. At Kot Diji F. A. Khan found that the Harappan levels were marked by "a well-regulated town-plan with lanes . . . ." The modular plan evident in the

[26] Piggott, 1950, p. 201.

cities was found here as well as at Chanhu-daro. The houses were doorless, and thus roof life is postulated. Khan found what appears to be a "bath-tub," consisting of a pottery container with an incised intersecting-circle decoration on its interior. However, no drains were revealed in the houses, but ovens, storage vessels, and hearths were uncovered. Here limestone foundations massive and deep-set were common to the Harappan levels.

The prime interest in the excavation at Amri being stratigraphic and the Harappan occupation so limited, little is added to our knowledge of village life from that site. An almost similar situation occurs generally with the Lake Manchhar sites and those of Majumdar's trek up the Bandhni Nai to the Baran Nai and the Karachi area. At Naig near a hot spring, Harappan remains were scattered along the entire slope of a hill one hundred feet high. The houses of the Harappan occupation were at least possessed of stone foundations, which is all the surveyor could ascertain in the time permitted there. Somewhat better is the evidence from Ali Murad, where hasty excavations revealed a massive stone wall apparently encircling the occupation area. House walls were immediately adjacent to the main wall. This wall was recessed at intervals, and at one point there was a deliberate

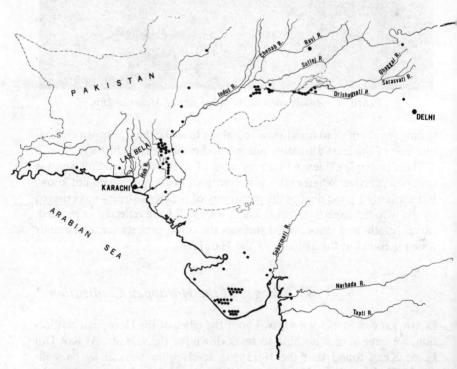

MAP 21 *Distribution of sites of the Indus civilization* (after Wheeler and others).

PLATE 38 *The almost completely eroded Harappan site of Amiliano on the Malir River near Karachi. It is a good example of a nucleated mature Harappan village.*

gap, as if a gate had once existed there. Near this was a ruined stone-lined well.

At Damb Buthi, as at Naig, the Harappan remains covered the entire slope of a high hill. This site is also located near a spring. Of great interest is the fact that whereas at Amri sites such as Ghazi Shah, Pandi Wahi, and Kot Diji the Harappan remains are mixed with and are superimposed upon earlier levels, at Damb Buthi the earlier material is found unassociated at another part of the site. At Dhal Harappan remains were again found scattered over a hillside. At the front of this particular hill, however, was a "rampart" wall of some substance.

In these small Harappan sites there seems to be some tendency to enclose the upper or higher areas, much as occurs in the "citadel" at Harappa and Mohenjo-daro. Even in the remote vastness of the Makran coast, George Dales, of the University Museum of the University of Pennsylvania, found a similar situation at the westernmost Harappan sites of Sutkagan-dor and Sotka-koh. These sites are located in strategic positions athwart trade routes leading to the Kej River valley and the Arabian Sea coast. Sutkagan-dor was first examined but briefly by Sir Aurel Stein in 1927; Sotka-koh, however, was discovered in the Dales survey of 1960.[27]

27 G. F. Dales, "A Search for Ancient Seaports," *Expedition*, Vol. IV, No. 2 (1962), pp. 2–10.

Sotka-koh is located about nine miles north of the coastal town of Pasni; it is situated on a rock outcrop on the eastern side of the Shadi Kaur Valley in an alluvial plain. A stone wall runs for over 1600 feet along the eastern edge of the site, and on higher ground were located the stone foundations of the buildings presumably enclosed by the wall.

Sutkagan-dor divides into two parts: a "citadel" located on the sandstone outcrop jutting above the alluvial plain of the Dasht River, and a "lower town." The "citadel" area was enclosed by a massive wall of semi-dressed stones; in one place the base of this wall is twenty-four feet thick. There are also traces of bastions here and there. The enclosed area is rectangular, with the long axis north-south, and is almost "large enough to hold four football fields." The main entrance to the "citadel" was presumably on the southwest, where traces of massive towers enclose a passageway some five and a half feet in width. Within the enclosure traces of regularly arranged structures of some three major building phases were disclosed. The "lower town" is apparently of Kulli affiliation and recalls the situation at Damb Buthi.

In the Malir River area just east of Karachi are three Harappan village sites (Map 21): Nel Bazaar (or Allahdino) is a large mound close to the river on its west bank; Amiliano is a flat gravel-covered area to the north of Nel Bazaar bisected by the Thano Bulla Khan-Karachi road and close to the Malir; Hasan site (SI-6) is located about twenty-one miles northeast of Karachi and in an alluvial stretch of a branch of the Malir, the Malir itself being about four and a half miles farther to the east. The three sites are small, none over 100 yards in any direction. All are located in the midst of or at the fringe of a modern cultivated area. The Hasan site is actually located on a gravel bluff that rises some 6 to 12 feet above the alluvium which lies to the north and east. The highest point of the site is approximately 18 feet above the plain. Examination of that point revealed a rough stone structure with a hole at its highest point. The remainder of the site is marked by traces of stone walls.

The Malir River area, like much of the Kohistan country between Karachi and the Indus Valley, is cultivated by a kach system (see p. 171). It is therefore of no small interest that both Amiliano and the Hasan site are located in the vicinity of modern kach dams. The inhabitants of the latter site may even have built a ruined stone dam which is located some fifty yards to the west. This dam originally had an opening in its southwest corner, the lowest point in the kach system, where even today considerable moisture accumulates. The modern kach dams are of earth, but they utilize the stone dams wherever possible. The fact that the site is so intimately connected with an area whose cultivation depends on a kach system seems to be fairly conclusive evidence that the system was in vogue in Harappan times.

The high part of the Hasan site has a more ruinous counterpart at

Amiliano, and these strongly suggest that a traditional village plan provided for the construction of a formal and presumably public building on the highest part of the site, about which the village habitations were clustered.[28]

Another kind of rural site is Naru Waro Dharo, located about six miles north of Kot Diji. The area is a sandy stretch of high ground some twenty-five feet above the plain. Though Harappan artifacts were scattered all over the sand, excavation of only a few inches revealed virgin soil. There was no indication of structures of any kind. The excavator surmises, then, that the place was a temporary camp, the housing consisting of single thatched-roof huts.[29] One possible reason for the site's existence may have been the need to bring cattle to high ground in the flood season to avoid the hoof diseases prevalent in moist soils.[30]

❋ *Harappan Sites in Gujarat and Elsewhere*

THE SITE OF LOTHAL, while not in the Indus River Valley proper, is nonetheless a Mature Harappan site contemporary with an equivalent phase at Mohenjo-daro. It is located in Gujarat near the head of the Gulf of Cambay. This region is extraordinarily flat, and the numerous villages stand like islands in a calm sea of green cultivation or brown earth, according to the season. The site is just above sea level, and there is evidence that the Sabarmati River or one of its branches flowed close to the site, at one time to the west and in a second stage to the east. S. R. Rao, the excavator, also carried out a survey of Kathiawar, Kutch, and southern Gujarat. He or his colleagues were able to find some eighty-five sites of Mature or Late Harappan affinity, the majority of which were located close to the coast and presumably represented a coastwise migration from the southern Indus Valley. Lothal, however, is taken by Rao to represent a seaport, much as is the town of Cambay, famous in medieval times for its trade across the Arabian Sea.

At its height (Phase II) Lothal was apparently a walled town, rectangular in shape, approximately 1000 by 750 feet in size, the long axis of the town being north-south. Three quarters of the town was apparently devoted to habitations and factories. In the latter category a substantial bead factory for the production of carnelian, agate, opal, crystal, and other stone beads

---

[28] It may be that in Amiliano, as at Harappa and Mohenjo-daro, the formal buildings, whether constructed on natural outcrops or artificial platforms, were traditionally located on the west of the site. This is the situation also at the Hasan site.

[29] *Pakistan Archaeology*, No. 1, 1964, p. 43.

[30] This was suggested by F. A. Khan in conversation some years ago. His written report on the site, however, suggests that it might have been a temporary refuge area.

PLATE 39   *The low-lying mound of Lothal on the flat plain of Gujarat.*

has been found, while a coppersmith's house was also evidenced on the
north of the enclosure. The habitation area reflects the usual Harappan
block plan with its familiar streets, lanes, and drains. The author describes a bazaar and refers to what must have been very comfortable living
quarters:[31]

> Houses were constructed in straight rows on mud-brick platforms on one
> or either side of the street. When rebuilt in later phases, the alignment
> remained more or less the same. Lanes joining the main street at right angles
> ran parallel to one another. The north-south street flanked by shops of two
> or three rooms each in the Lower Town was the main bazaar . . . where
> shell-workers, coppersmiths, goldsmiths and bone workers lived. Their
> equipment consisting of anvils and ovens, crucibles and muffles, drills and
> chisels, have been recovered from the workshops and their neighbourhood.
> Houses were fairly large and comfortable and their walls ran in cardinal
> directions. Most of them had a long but narrow verandah in the front, a
> central hall, and two or three small rooms. They stood about a meter above
> the road level, and a rectangular projection from the plinth provided the
> necessary approach. Every house had a bath and a kitchen, the former being
> built of kiln-burnt bricks. The sullage water was drained off through a
> private drain into a soakage jar embedded in the street close to the plinth
> wall . . . and at times enclosed by bricks. The narrow passages between
> the houses provided an approach to the rear side of the house from the main

[31] S. R. Rao, 1962, p. 21.

PLATE 40   *Buildings on the "citadel" at Lothal.*

PLATE 41   *Drains running off the "citadel" at Lothal.*

street. The built-up area of a house of average size with three rooms and a verandah was 59 sq. meters. Larger houses measured 13.4 × 6 meters. The largest house in the Lower Town had six rooms and a hall measuring with an overall area of 176 sq. meters. The walls were .9 to 1.4 meters thick and plastered with mud and lime. A high percentage of lime was used for plastering floors of drains and baths. The house floors were paved with mud bricks and, in very rare cases, made up of terracotta balls and pellets.

The southeast corner of the site is known as the "acropolis." Here a mud-brick platform some twelve feet in height was raised to support two blocks of buildings, access to the top of the platform being obtained by means of a ramp which led from a gate set approximately in the middle of the south wall of the main enclosure. Rain water and sewage were removed from the acropolis by two large drains sloping north and south to cess-pools. In addition, each house of the acropolis had its own bath with corresponding local drain. On one part of this raised area were twelve small blocks with channels or divisions between that were set on a mud-brick platform (measuring 45.5 by 42.5 meters). These resemble the so-called granary at Mohenjo-daro. Indeed, husks of rice were found in the mud plaster of the structure. Rao found some seventy-five terra-cotta sealings there and has the opinion that it was more than likely a warehouse.

The most remarkable structure at Lothal is the so-called dock (Pls. 42, 43). This is a rectangular depression of some size, 219 by 37 meters, en-

PLATE 42   *The great dock at Lothal. The sluice is in the foreground. The main site is off to the left.*

PLATE 43   *The great dock at Lothal; the entrance for ships is presumed to be on the immediate right.*

closed on all sides by fired-brick walls and connected to the acropolis by a great platform (240 by 23 meters) which Rao calls "the wharf." Supposedly, ships entering via tidal channels from the Gulf of Cambay were at high tide floated over a gap in the southeastern corner. Brick walls found in 1961 outside the dock and alongside the channels are regarded by modern engineers as means of reducing erosion brought by the fluctuation of the tides.

A spillway in the south wall of the dock was equipped apparently with wooden sluice doors set in grooves. Thus, the water level in the dock enclosure could be maintained no matter what the tidal level without. Rao has argued that this structure proves Lothal was a seaport, as against its being a conventional Indian tank. His points are worthy of notice:

(1) Fired bricks are not required for a tank. Mud brick or mounded earth is sufficient.

(2) There is no ramp or stairway to reach the always fluctuating water level. The sides are vertical.

(3) There is definite indication of a loading platform.

(4) The silt in the basin is saline, and shells associated with it are marine.

(5) Saline water would have been useless for drinking or irrigation.

(6) Post holes in the enclosure walls suggest tie posts for ships.

(7) Anchor stones have been found in the basin itself.

However, these arguments have been convincingly refuted by Leon Leshnik (*American Anthropologist*, Vol. 70, No. 5, October, 1968, pp. 911–922).

PLATE 44 *Kalibangan—view of an excavated thoroughfare. The figures in the foreground are walking on the earliest street level.* (Courtesy of the Archaeological Survey of India, Government of India.)

At Kalibangan by the Ghaggar River (see p. 182) the Harappan "town" occupation (KLB-2) was similar to that of the other sites: a fortified citadel and settlement based on a grid plan with "oblong blocks of houses, sub-divided by lanes and thoroughfares." A main thoroughfare over seven meters in width ran through the middle of the site. The houses were the usual rooms around a courtyard. Drains, a well, stairway, etc., are all familiar features. Interesting, however, were oval or rectangular "fireplaces." In the center of each of these was a cylindrical or rectangular brick block, around which the fire was built. The terra-cotta "cakes" were apparently used in this "ritual."[32]

At the mound of KLB-I (the higher) on the site mud-brick platforms were built over the pre-Harappan levels; on these were apparently formal buildings, one of which had an elaborate drainage system and a room in which were aligned several rectangular fireplaces. On the southern side of the mound a massive wall complex was uncovered, indicating that this "citadel" was walled.

In sum, the sites of the Harappan civilization demonstrates a variety of *raisons d'être*. In almost every case these are fairly explicit: agriculture, trade (?), and sources of water. Agriculture, of course, was the predominant

[32] *Indian Archaeology, A Review*, 1962–63 edition, p. 30.

PLATE 45 *Kalibangan—salient on the southern face of the fortification wall of the citadel.* (Courtesy of Archaeological Survey of India, Government of India.)

occupation, and in practically all cases the sites are located close to soil and water resources. In this and in the pre-Harappan site situations the overwhelming coincidence of modern village and ancient site, almost side by side or at least in close proximity, bespeaks a common dependence upon the same resources of soil and water—a fact of some importance to the interpretation of the ancient situation.

There is a formality about the Harappan sites—village, city, or town—which argues for a "formal" and authoritative mother tradition rather than an authoritative and coercive administration. In other words, the old tradition of "this is the way we have always done things" typical of village life was still a paramount factor in the daily activity. From what we know about Harappan village sites, there is characteristically an "acropolis" as well as a habitation area, if only on a very much smaller scale than in the urban sites. The "acropolis" in the village would seem to be simply a public building set above the habitation areas. This structure, too small to be inhabited, must have been used to perpetuate something shared across the Harappan world. It is difficult to conceive of this as having been anything else but a religion.

❋ The Artifacts

OF ALL THE ARTIFACT GROUPS OF THE HARAPPAN CIVILIZATION the seals provide the most graphic picture of that culture's life, and yet the seals frustrate because it is upon them that the Harappans cut their writing, a writing so far untranslated and thus mysterious.

1

2

3

4

5

6

7

The bulk of the seals are of steatite carved intaglio, though a few copper examples have been recovered. These are usually square or rectangular with a perforated boss at the back, for carrying or stamping purposes. At Harappa tiny seals of the same shape are common; also a number of round seals are found (a few cylinder seals also occur). Characteristically an animal is depicted standing before a rather enigmatic object which is very probably an emblem or standard of some ritual significance. Above the animal's back is the writing, pictographic in aspect and numbering anywhere from two or three to eight or so separate characters. The animal most often depicted is a bull-like creature with horns thrust forward (1). However, the water buffalo (2), a short-horned buffalo (3), a fine humped bull (4), the Indian rhinoceros (5), the elephant (6), the tiger (7), and the gavial (8), as well as mythological or imaginary creatures (9, 10, 11), also occur. In addition simply rectangular or square seals with a single inscription are not uncommon. Seals with single symbols, such as the swastika (12), the endless knot (13), the multiple cross (14), or the grid (15), occur. Rectangular or squarish examples cut with what seem to be scenes are of considerable interest, since they permit tantalizing glimpses into the lost world of India's first civilization.

One is struck by the number of scenes in which attitudes or acts of adoration or sacrifice occur. One of the finest examples of this phenomenon was found in the VS area at Mohenjo-daro (16). Here we see a central figure in what appears to be a dancing or perhaps a mudraic position on a platform. Below and on either side two men kneel, facing him, while behind both are great cobras poised like canopies above their suppliant forms. An extraordinary central figure of similar type was found in the so-called "lower city" at Mohenjo-daro (17). This shows what appears to be a deity wearing a buffalo-horn headdress, numerous bangles, bracelets, and a V-shaped collar or necklace. His face is furrowed or painted, and he is in the same attitude as the figure in the previous seal. On either side however, are wild animals—a rhino and a buffalo on the right, an elephant and a tiger to the left. A hyena figure appears just above the tiger, while below the platform (or throne) a goat (?) looks up. This figure also occurs by itself. An unusual example seems to show the same individual looking upward (18).

Of considerable interest because of their similarity to the Gilgamesh motif of Mesopotamia are the seals showing a powerful man holding two hapless tigers by the throat (19). In the same category is the scene of a horned and tailed individual who apparently has leaped from a tree on the back of a tethered (?) tiger (20, 21). This suggests individuals wearing masks.

A tree spirit or deity seems to have had an important place in the ancient iconography. In one seal from Mohenjo-daro we are witness to the offering (sacrifice) of a goat by a kneeling man to a figure who stands in the midst of a bush or tree (22). A quiet row of individuals, some of whom may be women wearing peculiar head-dresses, watches the scene. A similar scene with a ram or painted bull (?) occurs (23). Here the audience has long pigtails. In another example a tiger turns his head to gaze at a figure with a horned or feathered headdress who is also crouched in a tree (24). A scene of a ram before the same horned figure in his tree suggests sacrifice (25). Greatly impressive are the scenes showing two powerful figures uprooting trees

16

17

18

19

20

21

22

while a braceleted individual stands between them (26).

A rectangular sealing from Harappa suggests that human sacrifice was practiced. A seated woman, her hair rather disheveled, raises her arms in apparent resignation, while before her an armed man stands as if preparing to strike (27a).

Other possible nonhuman or superhuman types are a figure who is part tiger and (27) part man but who wears a ram headdress and a hunter who, with bow and arrow and horned (28) headdress, suggests something out of the Upper Paleolithic or Mesolithic of Europe rather than something from an early civilization. Hunting, indeed, seems to have had an important place, for we have an example of a hunt in which the hunters have shot an antelope or deer (29). The beast has been hit twice, and a third hunter is aiming his arrow for the *coup de grâce*. Another example apparently depicts the stabbing of a buffalo by a courageous fellow who steps on one lowered horn while thrusting his spear home (30). In another case the position of the buffalo's head and the flying spear suggest that the hunter has missed and is in danger of being gored (31). The tiger appears in a sealing from Harappa, apparently being drummed up or serenaded by a man who carries in horizontal fashion a cylindrical drum (32).

One of the most intriguing of all the scenes depicted among the seals and sealings is that which shows individuals apparently bull-leaping in the Cretan fashion, that is, somersaulting from the horns of the animal into the air—both forward and back (33a). The figures are carved in a modeled linear fashion that is atypical—a style that occurs on only a few other seals (33b). The fact that segmented beads are usual to Crete as well as that a few signs in the writing system suggest Linear A writing might prove a Cretan connection, a not unexpected phenomenon in view of the fact that Cretan sea-faring dominated the eastern Mediterranean from perhaps 1900 to 1450 B.C., dates which overlap those of the Harappan civilization.

Animal spirits or representatives of godlike powers are suggested in some seals (34, 35), where a scorpion or insect of some kind is the central unit with tiger, elephant, buffalo, and rhino (?) arranged right and left as in the great scene described previously.

Processions of animals are known, but more intriguing is the procession which depicts individuals carrying what appear to be standards (36). The central bearer carries a bull, while behind him is the cuplike emblem often seen before the bulls; before is a capped or turbaned bearer with a tassel or flag on a pole. A standardlike motif is seen (37), where two unicornlike bull heads twist about on a pole which is apparently the trunk of a stylized pipal tree.

Dancing figures (38) recall the famous bronze girl sculpture found by Marshall (39), suggesting that dancing was very much a part of the life of the times.

Only one scene aside from the hunting ones, however, seems to depict a daily occupation (40a). This shows some women busy gathering something near the foot of a bird-filled tree. The trays and other objects with them suggest that they might be winnowing. However, for all the emphasis which must have been placed upon agriculture and animal husbandry, there is surprisingly little of it found in these seal scenes. Rao has found an example of what may be a seed drill at Lothal (40b), and there is an example or two of a man holding what seems to be a basket before a tree (41). The depiction of cattle is seemingly to emphasize the power and strength of the bull rather than the more useful products and service which are derived from cattle. Nowhere is a donkey shown, but goats and presumably sheep are occasionally illustrated.

One fortunate find was made in the upper levels at Mohenjo-daro by MacKay. This is a splendid seal depiction of a river-going ship (42). Clearly seen are its high prow, its central cabin, and its double steering oar. It looks to be keelless and of shallow draft, like those ships of predynastic

23

24

25

26

27

27a

28

30

31

32

33 a

33 b

34

35

Egypt. Before the cabin are poles apparently to hold standards, and in this too there is an echo of prehistoric Egypt. At Lothal terra-cotta ship models were recovered, and Rao has ascertained three types of boats from these. These include flat-bottomed bargelike craft; the type represented in the Mohenjo-daro seal but with keel; and the best example at Lothal, which has a sharp keel, pointed bow, and a blunt stern. There is a hole in the stern, suggesting that it once held a mast. Rao also found pottery on which may be depicted a multioared boat.[33]

The vast bulk of the seals depict a combination of a single animal with the "standard" before him and the writing above. Of interest is the fact that the single-horned bull, the most common subject apparently, is painted on the neck, horns, and shoulders, a phenomenon found in the figurines of the Quetta Valley (Fig. 32) and indeed in modern India. On a series of small copper tablets found at Mohenjo-daro the seal animals are curiously depicted, some bearing symbols drawn on their bodies which resemble vital organs (43, 44, 45)—a form of hunting magic used widely among primitive people. Of interest in these tablets are the rabbit (46), a two-headed llamalike creature (47), and a horned hunter (48).

It is the writing that has aroused the great interest of many in the Harappan civilization. Writing is the use of symbols for sounds, ideas, or objects, and the symbols are mutually recognized by the society. Of all the criteria for defining civilization it is perhaps most important, for it represents a level of sophistication in which a culture can convey complex concepts by means of symbols through time and space with explicitness. The vital statistics of the script can be stated all too briefly: approximately 400 signs are known; the inscriptions are short and formal even in the case of graffiti; the writing is from

[33] S. R. Rao, "Shipping and Maritime Trade of the Indus People," *Expedition*, Vol. VII, No. 3 (1965), pp. 30–37.

right to left, but where there is a second line, it is from left to right. However, there are some additional notes one might make to fill out the picture (see also Appendix J):

36

37

(1) Authorities in general agree that the writing is syllabic. The estimated number of signs is more than 350 and probably less than 425. This puts it in a class with Egyptian, i.e., more than Linear B and less than cuneiform (Sumerian). It seems not to be ideographic, though undoubtedly some ideographs are used.

(2) It seems clear by inspection that a large number of signs are determinatives or serve as such on occasion. For example, the symbol for fish is like a fish. In other cases it appears to be definitely syllabic, especially in its appearance without marks for number, as in the middle of an inscription.

38

It is obvious that we can identify many symbols by reference to those seals in which scenes of daily or ritual life are depicted. Animals, humans, plants are discernible, and by reference both to the scenes and to the artifacts some utensils can be identified as well.

(3) As probable syllables, it appears that all those symbols which are apparently identical with or very likely evolved from pottery marks known in the Quetta Valley are good candidates (Fig. 58).

(4) Noteworthy are certain signs which are partitioned in various ways. The oval or diamond symbol appears in at least four principal forms that may be related: (1) empty or with a dot; (2) with a V-shaped division mark at the top; (3) with four V-shaped or other-shaped divisions, giving a compartmented appearance; (4) with spokes, giving a wheel-like appearance. This group often has several strokes next to the signs. We have to consider these signs as a family obviously. Possibly they refer to time (day signs or sun signs) or seasons.

Frequent are the same signs with other marks inside, such as a plant form. Sometimes these ovals overlap or link in a characteristic fashion.

39

40 a

40 b

41

42

43

44

45

By reference to numbers now known these may refer to given quantities if the seals involve specific amounts, as some of them seem to do.

Of interest is the halving of signs; the pipal leaf stands alone intact and as a half. This may indicate lengthening and shortening of a given vowel, or perhaps vowels and half vowels.

(5) Attention will have to be paid by future decipherers to the number system. It is important to try to ascertain what strokes most probably represent numbers and which are separations or even diacritical marks, as Langdon and Gadd, who originally studied the script, have guessed.[34]

(6) The animals depicted on the seals may have reference to what is meant in the inscriptions. The association of signs with the animals and the repetition of combinations need analysis.

(7) There may be pairings of combinations.

The lack of long inscriptions and of cursive writing suggests strongly that the writing had limited use. Of course there is always the chance that much writing was done on perishable materials such as the palm leaf or tree bark; however, we have really very little hint as to that possibility. The fact that the bulk of the writing occurs on seals suggests that it is simply a seal writing, an extension of the intent of the seal. In general we have two categories of seals: seals used as amulets, and those used as representations of the individual, his family, clan, or whatever group or institution he belongs to. There is of course a mystique about a seal; it acts in the absence of the owner as if he were present. Thus, a sealed package stamped with the owner's name is not opened by those for whom it is not intended. The fact that sealings have been found widely in the Harappan world emphasizes their

---

[34] Again, the basket (?) symbol which occurs so frequently at the beginning or end of an inscription may be the marker of quantity, indicating that the vertical strokes are to be regarded as numbers. The association of the basket (?) symbol with these strokes needs analysis.

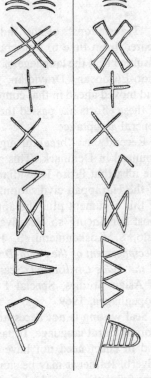

role as signatures, probably of individuals (note Appendix J, p. 419).

Students of the writing note that rarely is a combination of signs repeated, which also tends to underline the probability that the writings are the names of individuals. There are, however, a large number of seals on which multiple strokes occur, suggesting numbers. Frequently these occur with signs, suggesting that quantity is meant, or in other cases the juxtaposition of animal or plant signs with numbers may mean so many fish, men, etc. Rarely are more than twelve strokes used, and it may well be that some of the signs used, represent numbers above twelve. So-called diacritical marks by a sign may have vowel connotation, but they could also mean that the object depicted is meant rather than its sound, or vice versa. Thus we puzzle over the material and are frustrated by its secrets.

46

47

48

49

50

51

"Translations" of the Indus script have appeared from time to time, but all of these have assumed that the language of the Harappans was Indo-European, Dravidian, or something else and moved ahead in that context. However, none of these efforts has passed the tests necessary for general acceptance.

Recently a "breakthrough" has been announced in Denmark. This appears to rest on the idea that Proto-Dravidian was the language of the Harappan civilization. The presentation of this argument plus the approach used is the most convincing so far advanced. See A. Parpalo, S. Koskenniemi, S. Parpalo, P. Aalto, *Decipherment of the Proto-Dravidian Inscriptions of the Indus Civilization*, Scandinavian Institute of Asian Studies, Special Publication No. 1, Copenhagen, 1969.

Seal writing is not necessarily writing derived from the oral language. It has its own meanings and in effect need not have verb, adjective, or adverb. Rather it may be simply a kind of label specifying the individual or his god, house, or belongings, much as a heraldic device uses iconographic elements limited in number in countless ways to name the individual or an institution. Except for the numbers, which suggest bookkeeping and thus more mundane motivations, one cannot help but feel that the Harappan script is of this character. It appears to be a script a full step above the potters' marks of pre-Harappan times but below the complexity of early hieroglyphic Egyptian or Sumerian, which was already ideographic. The script has little preamble except possibly in the potters, marks. Throughout its known history it shows little or no change and disappears with the Harappans and their seals. Though it is writing in one sense, it does not appear to have been much more meaningful to the Indus people than the repeated motifs that appear on their pottery. However, tomorrow's shoveling may reveal a room full of tablets and change this so limited interpretation.

There are numerous figurines of terra cotta some of which are coated with faïence, found on Harappan sites. Common among these are those of females (49–54). The figurines are crudely modeled; ornaments, headdresses, eyes, belts, etc., are often in appliqué. They indicate that the turban or at least a cloth wrap-around head covering was common enough, that women may have worn "topless" wrap-around clothing (55), and that elaborate hairdos with the hair spread in a fan shape above the head (56) were in vogue. Ornaments of many kinds, bangles, necklaces, and earrings being particularly prominent, are depicted not only on the figurines but are themselves found in great numbers on the sites. Clay bangles often occur in such abundance that in any random sample of finds they are among the most common. Shell, bone, iron, agate, turquoise, carnelian, some rather poor lapis lazuli, and steatite were conventional materials used for the manufacture of beads. Segmented beads known elsewhere as characteristically of Cretan or Aegean manufacture may well be Mediterranean in derivation, while beads ornamented with the trefoil pattern found in Akkadian Mesopotamia suggest contact with that area.

Marshall was particularly fortunate in his recovery of gold jewelry, which included necklaces with barrel-form beads and disk spacers (57), finger rings, hairbands, ring- and cone-shaped earrings. Collars of round beads arranged in rows between spacers as well as long cylindrical or tubular stone beads with gold spacers are especially handsome. Disk beads with central tubes occur and are known from Sumeria. The Harappan female in full regalia must have been very striking indeed.

Two extraordinary statuettes were found at Harappa. The first is of gray stone and is of a young woman dancing. She is headless, and parts of her legs have been broken off. Her left leg is thrust forward and to the side as if she were about to twirl. The other statuette is of a

52

53

54

55

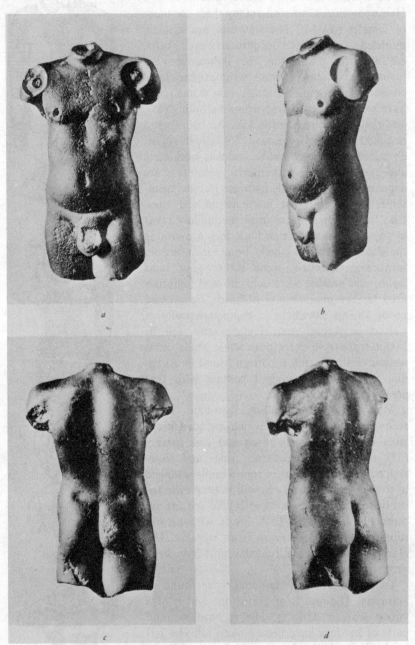

PLATE 46 *Figure of man in red stone found at Harappa* (after Marshall, 1931).

male (Pl. 46), also headless, and his arms and
legs are missing as well. This is modeled in red
sandstone and is so sensitively executed that
were it not from the site one would have thought
it of Gandhara or Gupta origin.

Males are not as well represented as females in
the figurine category. One or two naked fellows,
a rather odd seated gentleman with either his
tongue sticking out or a pronounced chin
beard (58), and an individual with cap and a scarf
or necklace (59) like those individuals represented
in the procession (36), are representative. The
most real representation is that of the "priest."
This is made of steatite and is in its present broken
state about seven inches tall (Pl. 33); a mature
male who is bearded and wears a head ornament
which drapes over his skull in the same fashion
as the hairband of the head found at Mundigak
(Fig. 30). A trefoil-decorated robe drapes over
his left shoulder. The interiors of the trefoils
are filled with red pigment. A similar head but
less complete shows that the hair was tied in a
bun. There is also a seated figure which looks
particularly Sumerian (61). In some contrast to
this Sumerian flavor is the limestone figure of a
ram resting on a plinth (62). It is bearded, and
its frontality resembles nothing so much as an
Egyptian statue of a ram.

The bulk of the figurines are of animals, and
these are delightful indeed. My wife, who has been
drawing them during field work, divides them into two categories: serious work and conventional
work (Fig. 59, 60). The latter category pertains
to the larger group of figures which almost
caricature the animal by emphasizing such features as the ear of the rabbit, the horn of the
rhino, and the plumpness of the pig. In this
category also are crude representations of animals
made with the same pinched and appliqué
technique of many of the human figures. This
category includes animals with wheels, toy
carts which are practically identical to those used
today in Sind, and figures with movable heads
and limbs. Little faïence squirrels and mon-

56

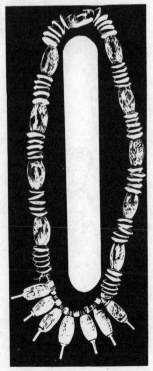

57

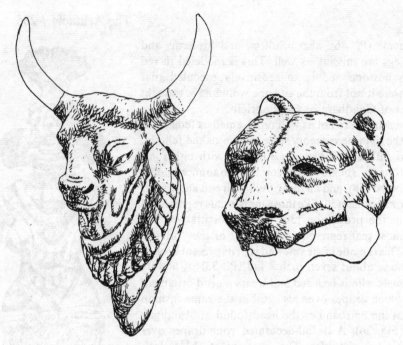

FIG. 59 *Terra-cotta animal figurines, Mohenjo-daro. Examples of "serious" work.*

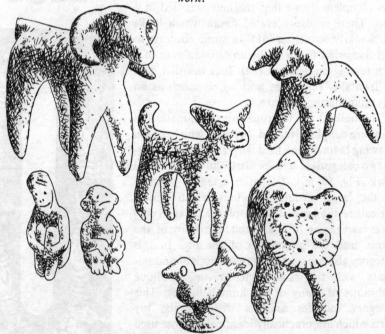

FIG. 60 *Terra-cotta animal figurines, Mohenjo-daro. Examples of "amusing" or conventional work.*

keys are among the delights of this art. In effect
we can regard these as toys precious to the life
of Harappan children. One who doubts this probably has never lived with children, for even a
modern home's habitation debris where there
are children includes parts of toys! Serious work
can also be regarded in part as a class of toys.
Here the modeling is done with high skill and
great attention to detail. The result is a beautiful
little sculpture which certainly should rank high
in the history of animal art (Fig. 59).

The pottery corpus is a varied one and demonstrates that ceramics had great popularity and a
wide variety of uses (Figs. 61, 62). Dish-on-
stand vessels (fruit stands) with narrow tapering
bases, beakers, pointed-base jars, handled cups,
jar stands, perforated cylindrical vessels, and
cricket cages (?) are noteworthy in addition to
the variety of vases, pans, and plates conventional to these early cultures. The painted pottery is characteristically black on a red background, and its motifs are equally divided
between geometric and naturalistic, with trees,
birds, fish, and animals in the latter category
rather exuberantly displayed. In general the
pottery is florid, heavy, and well made. It is in
great contrast to the delicate vessels of pre-
Harappan cultures, and the emphasis on scenes
in the painting as well as the identical conventions of drawing demonstrates that the Harappan
painted wares are the final phase of the old
Borderland and Iranian painted pottery tradition, much as the late Kulli is in southern
Baluchistan, with which it is contemporary
(Fig. 63).

Games and toys other than dolls seem to have
been widely used in Harappan times. We have
such things as the ball and spiral-mountain
toy, pottery rattles, throw-sticks in bone or
ivory, dice, miniature vases, and possibly the
enigmatic terra-cotta "cakes," which may have
been counters. The latter are triangular-shaped
objects which often bear signs of having been
close to fire. One theory would have these used

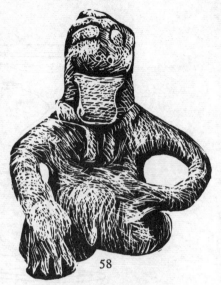

58

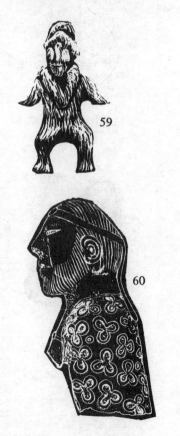

59

60

FIG. 61   *Harappan pottery from Mohenjo-daro.*

61

as supports for cooking vessels. However, they are also found commonly enough in drains and thus may have been used for toilet purposes.

Numerous objects relating to a variety of pursuits have been found in Harappan sites, and the list can be extended almost limitlessly: stone spindle whorls; ivory, bone, and metal needles; clay buttons; chipped- and ground-stone quadrangular axes; mortars and pestles; grinding stones; "digging-stick" whorls; flint blades; bone combs; rubbing or beater stones; clay spoons; clay and stone model houses; maceheads; clay sling missiles; bronze, copper, and silver vessels; copper hooks; bangles; arrow points; ivory, bone, faïence, and shell inlays for furniture or other wooden objects.

Copper and bronze tools and weapons, both full-size and miniature, were manufactured.

FIG. 62 *Harappan painted vessel from Chanhu-daro* (after MacKay).

The weapons were apparently not very formidable: a leaf-shaped flat-sided lance or spear (an example of a ribbed lance head was found by MacKay in the upper levels at Mohenjo-daro), axe heads, the previously mentioned barbed arrow points, and daggers are the known metal weapons. This is seemingly evidence for the lack of standing armies, though there is apparently a change to heavier, more effective types in the upper levels at Mohenjo-daro. Cleavers, chisels, points, gouges, mirrors, and razors were also made in metal. The quadrangular axes were certainly capable of cutting the local trees and from their comparative commonness appear to have been widely used. A shaft-hole bronze axe head (63) found in the upper levels at Mohenjo-daro is atypical. Such axes are

62

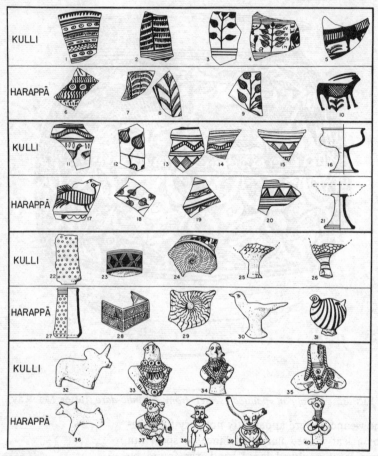

FIG. 63 *Comparative typology of pottery designs and certain artifacts of the Kulli culture of Baluchistan and those of Harappan civilization.*

known from such sites as Hissar (III) in northeastern Iran and are presumably derived from Central Asia or the Caucasus. Interesting is the fact that some of the flat axes are inscribed with the signs of the Harappan script.

A bronze covered cart and animal-headed pins from Harappa show that some of the metal work was used for toys and decoration. The animal pins depict goats apparently and suggest a resemblance to similar pins known from western Iran.

Weights are well known at Harappan sites. These consist of blocks, large and small, made from a variety of stones. The smaller ones were used in scales, a few of which have been found. These weights are both binary (lower) and decimal (higher). Reifler has traced equivalents in both Mesopotamia and China, indicating an almost universal recognition of at least some of the values (unpublished ms. by Erwin Reifler).

Linear measurement was apparently well standardized. MacKay by good fortune found a piece of shell marked in regular fashion and quite clearly intended as a rule (64). Nine divisions remain, and from circular markings at two places five units apart it would appear that a decimal system was in vogue. Each division is approximately 0.264 inches wide, or a five-unit total of 1.32 inches. Thus a foot in the decimal system would be 13.2 inches, which fits into a widespread system of the ancient world. Similarly Vats and Wheeler provide evidence that the "cubit" was also used.[35] Thus both the smaller and larger units of measurement were used in building and presumably to lay out fields. And in terms of the researches on the meaning of the Harappan script, one wonders which of the symbols that appear with the number marks mean cubit, foot, or other measurement units.

The assemblage of artifacts gathered from sites of the Harappan civilization is formidable. The exploitation of resources of stone, metal, clay, wood, ivory, bone, leather, shell, etc., is full-bodied. The systems of measurement, of writing, of technology, of building underline the complexity of the culture which produced them. The discovery of fragments of cotton found clinging to a metal tool at Mohenjo-daro adds another dimension to the civilization. Cotton does not become common in the Mediterranean world until sometime after 700 B.C. Presumably the Harappans, who lacked linen, arrived at the domestication of cotton as a response to a need which animal hair and hide and plant fiber did

[35] Sir M. Wheeler, 1962b, p. 67.

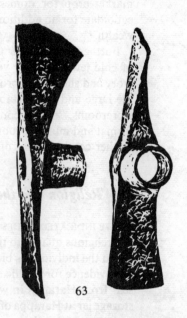

63

64

not fulfill. Cotton might have been a luxury and perhaps thus become a market crop for domestic consumption. In any case cotton is a good candidate for an additional prop to a class system based increasingly upon wealth.

Further evidence for the wealth of the time is furnished by the presence of gold jewelry, silver vessels, and such exotics as stone-cut lattice work, ivory and shell inlay, bronze mirrors and razors, faïence toys, and of course the large and comfortable houses complete with baths, drains, stairways, storerooms, service courts, etc. The splendor of the Great Bath and the formal and multiple-room buildings in the "citadel" at Mohenjo-daro are further confirmations of accumulated wealth.

✳ *Religion and the Movement of the Harappan Civilization*

AS WE INDICATED IN DESCRIBING the seals as well as the architecture there is a religious quality to the Harappan civilization that is difficult to ignore. From the individual's birth to his death one can detect its traces. Initially the evidence for phallic emblems, the depiction of pregnancy, the unusual seal from Harappa in which a birth of a plant(?) is depicted, a find in a storage jar at Harappa of a lingam, the prevalence of representations of bulls and human females, and the apparent sacrifice of animals or indeed of humans to a deity intimately connected with vegetation (p. 275) strongly suggest cults related to regeneration, cults of fertility. At maturity the formal processions, the ablutions of the Great Bath, the priesthood suggested by the sculptures and the "citadel" structures, the use of masks and horned headdresses, the iconographic elements such as the man-tiger and bull or goat figures, the tree deity, the "Gilgamesh" motif, the painted or decorated animals on the seals, the enthroned figures before which individuals kneel, etc., relate to a complexity of myths, animism, ceremonial preparation, and formal rites to a variety of powers.

At death it seems that, in the earlier phases at least, burial within the houses in the old neolithic manner occasionally occurred. Hargreaves found a burial in a house in HR-A at Mohenjo-daro in which the individual has been laid on his left side with his head resting on his left hand, facing east. At Harappa, Cemetery R 37 contained some fifty-seven burials, one of which had been encased in a wooden coffin, while another had been placed in a mud-brick cist. Generally the burials were extended north-south and included funerary furniture such as personal ornaments plus a good deal of pottery, some of which may have contained food. Fractional burial on the order of that indicated at Mundigak (Period III, see p. 130) may have been practiced in the late phases at Harappa. At Lothal a cemetery also of a late phase was located by Rao just outside the main occupation area on the northwest. The graves were extended north-south as at Harappa and also included some funerary furniture. In these instances double burials were found, in one case the sex of both being male. Again the funerary furniture and the formality of these burials suggest a belief in an afterlife for which some preparation was necessary.

Yet what we have seems halfhearted, as if these were burial conventions without vital beliefs, something like the situation in the later periods of pharaonic Egypt. Rao has suggested that fire worship was practiced at Lothal, and he ascribes the singular absence of the artifacts mentioned above that point to religion.[36] He is, of course, describing the situation at a site remote from the Indus Valley and largely later in time than the Harappan of that valley. However, Lothal is so close to the classic Harappan pattern of town planning and artifact content that it has to be considered as a definite part of the tradition.

This raises a problem of interpretation. The Harappan civilization may have begun in the region of upper Sind, Kachhi, and perhaps the Bugti hills, but it moves rather rapidly north, south, and east. There is ample proof of this rapid movement at such sites as Kot Diji, Kalibangan, Harappa, Pandi Wahi, Ghazi Shah, and Amri where Mature Harappan occupation is literally superimposed upon and often mixed with the earlier non-Harappan occupants. Further, the Harappan occupation at these sites (except Harappa) is short-lived, and only in the large sites, such as Chanhu-daro and Mohenjo-daro, do we have extensive late phases showing a durable but deteriorating occupancy. Sind is apparently gradually abandoned, and the new foci are in the Punjab, northern Rajasthan, and Saurashtra. At one period, perhaps around 1900 B.C., one might have roamed from Kathiawar to the Punjab via the Indus and found the familiar settlements of the Harappans all thriving contemporaneously; but this was a rapidly changing situation.

Nevertheless, the pottery, bangles, fruit stands, seals, terra-cotta "cakes," weights and measures, town planning, drains, graters, bath tubs, etc., were duplicated so precisely wherever Harappan settlement occurred that as Wheeler has stated, ". . . the Indus civilization can . . . claim a larger area than any other of the known pre-classical civilizations."[37] However, he also speculates: "Behind so vast a uniformity must lie an administration and economic discipline however exercised, of an impressive kind."[38]

It is extraordinarily difficult to understand this conformity, but we can at least conclude from the rapidity of movement (less than five hundred years) that there was very little in opposition in the areas moved to; thus change was not so likely to have been induced from contact with indi-

[36] Rao, 1962, p. 29.
[37] Sir M. Wheeler, 1962b, p. 3.
[38] Ibid.

FIG. 64 *Artist's view of interior of Harappan house in the Mature period.*

genous cultures. The fact of rapid movement is of itself apt to provide for the preservation of traditions, since there would have been little time for great change;[39] moreover, the direct diffusion of Harappan traits in such an unchanged fashion indicates that the Harappans were themselves the carriers, for otherwise integration of the Harappan tradition with local style traditions would have occurred. In this sense the Harappans would appear to have been greatly superior, technologically and organizationally at least, to the cultures they came in contact with, probably of food collectors and herders. This may have been like the conquest of the

[39] Some minor change can be observed, however, in such things as pottery types, painted designs, seal writing; details of this have not yet been published by the excavators of Harappan sites.

Indians in the New World by Western Europeans. However, while this may have been true for the Punjab, Saurashtra, and points south and east, it was not so in Baluchistan and southern Afghanistan. Here the late phases of developed-village farming culture were undeniably influenced by and in contact with the Harappan civilization, as evidence trade objects, style shifts, and the parallel formality of those phases. The Kulli of southern Baluchistan has so much in its assemblages of Harappan types, even including the plethora of bangles, "cakes," pottery forms and decoration, figurines, etc., that it has on occasion been misconstrued as Harappan. The platforms and drains and also some artifacts of the last phase of pre-historic occupancy in the Quetta Valley (DS III) and of Period IV at Mundigak as well as similar artifactual suggestions in the Zhob-Loralai regions evidence a common acceptance of some of the trait styles of the Harappan civilization without showing an entire loss of the local traditions. If we regard the traditions of the Harappan civilization as the "Great Tradition," much as we regard Sanskritic Hinduism in modern India, then these Borderland cultures are in reality folk or "little-community" variants on the main theme.[40] The main theme has to be more than a simple socioeconomic concept of class and wealth, since that is subject to many variables; rather, one has to consider a religious theme, evidenced, as has been outlined, both for the cultures of the Borderlands and for the Harappan civilization. Religious ideas are readily adapted to local concepts—witness Tibetan Buddhism or popular Hinduism; when religion falls into conjunction with and in fact helps to accelerate shifts in social and economic emphasis, it receives ready acceptance. That such shifts were under way has been the subject of two previous chapters.

Thus, movement by the Harappan civilization into the western part of the subcontinent proper was rapid, dynamic, and direct. That civilization's ramifications which will be described in the next chapter were, however, much wider than the geographic space it occupied. To the west, however, in the high Borderlands, the Harappan expansion, while direct along the main lines of communication (Makran coast, Bolan Pass, Duki), was largely in the nature of the diffusion of certain traditions and styles developed in the Indus Valley and integrated with existing local cultures which, paradoxically, were ancestral to the civilization. The diffusionary lines were within an established network (see pp. 237–238). The result was a vast *oikoumene* which was now Indian in character and doomed, in the Borderlands at least, to be short-lived.

[40] This use of the terms "Great" and "Little" tradition is based on R. Redfield, *The Primitive World and its Transformations* (Cornell University Press, Ithaca, 1953) and McKim Marriott, "Little Communities in an Indigenous Civilization," *Village India*, M. Marriott, ed. (University of Chicago Press, Chicago, 1955), and others. (See also p. 237.)

VIII

The Decline of the Harappan Civilization

AMONG THE SEALS OF MOHENJO-DARO are a few cylinders some of which are carved in a fashion foreign to the Harappan civilization. There are also in Harappan context the so-called "Persian Gulf seals," small, round, buttonlike objects usually with animal designs which have been found on Bahrein and Failaka in the Persian Gulf. One is noted at Lothal, and there is a scattering of circular seals found in the Indus Valley sites. In the riverine situation some thirty seals of Harappan type are known in Mesopotamian context.[1] Of these only eleven have any definite stratigraphic association; seven of them are probably of the Akkadian period, and four are of later periods. Peculiarly, many of the so-called Indian seals found in Mesopotamia are round or buttonlike rather than square, the conventional shape for the Harappan seal. However, when this evidence is added to the fact that there are a number of other objects which either by direct trade or by stimulus diffusion were derived from the West (stone boxes, dice, measures [?], faïence, wheeled vehicles, etched and segmented beads, trefoil patterns, "Gilgamesh" motif, shaft-hole axes, knob-decorated

[1] C. J. Gadd, "Seals of Ancient Indian Style Found at Ur," *Proceedings of the British Academy*, Vol. XVII (1932), pp. 191–210; see also B. Buchanan, "A Dated 'Persian Gulf' Seal and its Implications," *Studies in Honor of Benno Landsberger*, (1965), pp. 204–209. (An excellent recent discussion of the real problem.)

pottery, gold disk beads, spiral-headed pins, the ram sculpture [style], etc.), it is clear that the Harappan civilization, remote as it was from the great centers of the antique West, and emerging at its fringes, still in a very real sense was a part of that West. In other words, as the ancient world became more international, a characteristic of the later phases of earliest

PLATE 47 *Fish caught in the Indus River near Mohenjo-daro. Such fish are depicted in the vase painting of ancient times and were certainly an important part of the diet.*

civilization, the Indian region began to play its part. Some scholars see in the Sumerian account of trade with an eastern land known as Dilmun or Tilmun a reference to the Indus Valley civilization. There is nothing, however, in our present evidence to indicate that this trade was more than a hit or miss affair. Contact by land and possibly by coastal sea roads there surely was, but it would seem to have been rather the result of movement by many carriers intermediate in the Iranian region than the deliberate and direct efforts of Sumerian or Harappan traders or their agents. However, the seals indicate that the Mesopotamians at least were aware of the Indian area. This awareness occurs in a period probably after 2000 B.C. when the Sumerians were in decline and the period of Isin-Larsa was marking the last phases of their dominance. It was the heyday apparently of the merchants of Ur and Lagash, since their trade to the east is well recorded.

It is entirely possible that had the early Mesopotamian civilization continued to flourish, direct contact with western India would have become almost as routine as it became later. The improving of sailing techniques, the use of the domesticated horse, donkey, and possibly camel,[2] as well as the lure of precious stones, and possibly of cotton cloth, dyes, ivory, and spices ensured this happening. However, throughout Western Asia a decline set in partially due to overexploitation of natural resources, partially to ineffective administration, partially to foreign invasion, but all in all largely to a loss of the tradition and styles that acted as a unifying matrix. People still lived in the old cities, but their entity as Sumerians became increasingly meaningless. This is, of course, a complex matter and beyond the scope of this writing, but it is sufficient to note that the recognition of the Indian market was only just taking place when the great change occurred.

It is necessary to note this phenomenon because the "trade" between India and Mesopotamia seems to have been somewhat one-sided. This imbalance raises questions as to the Indian polity, for had Indian traders been determined to exploit the Mesopotamian market to meet the demand for luxury items, one can be certain this would have occurred well into the Old Babylonian period of Hammurabi, an event for which we have no clear evidence. In fact, the evidence we do have is that after 1900 B.C. the Harappan civilization declined in Sind and the southern Punjab, and its centers shifted to Gujarat and the Doab. But these new areas were generally peopled by villagers whose endeavors outside Lothal and a few minor "port" sites were largely rural.

We have in the previous chapter discussed some of the characteristics of the Harappan civilization and in so doing underlined the conservative, generally uniform quality of its cultural style. It is of value to review some of these facts and to list some of the conclusions one might reach in analyzing this evidence.

---

[2] A camel scapula was found at Mohenjo-daro (Marshall, 1931, I, 28), and a camel is represented on a copper from Khurab (see Appendix SE Iran).

✳ *The Harappan Cultural Style*

(1) We have no direct evidence for kings or rulers, secular or sacred, except the possibility that the "citadels" at such sites as Harappa and Mohenjo-daro are indeed the seats for such authorities; we have, however, in the town planning evidence for strong central control.

(2) We can assume that a class system was characteristic of Harappan society. This is based on evidence for specialists of various kinds, for possible centralized authority, for elaborations of houses and material possessions reflective of wealth.

(3) The conformity of Harappan artifacts everywhere when sites of the civilization are identified indicates that conventions of building, art style, technology, and religion were strongly observed.

(4) The evidence indicates rapid diffusion of Mature Harappan culture in all directions.

(5) The Harappan writing was generally limited to seals and was therefore intended to be used as a means of elaborating the seal's role as an identifier and as a statement of personal property. The writing was possibly used in accounts, but aside from the "messages" of the seals and the pottery or metal marks, there is no indication it was ever used as a means of more complex communication.

(6) Technology in brickmaking, in gold, silver, bronze, and copper work, in cut stone, and in other comparable and generally utilitarian industries was of considerable sophistication.

(7) The basis of the economy was agriculture and cattle husbandry. In general Harappan sites are located close to sources of water, and in the case of the large rivers and the dhands, next to the active flood plain.

(8) In the Harappan sites of southern Sind generally as well as in Baluchistan (Dabar Kot, Sotka-koh, Sutkagen-dor) the Harappan occupation arrives suddenly and is short-lived. This is not so at large sites such as Mohenjo-daro, Chanhu-daro, and Harappa, where one may speak of a "Late" Harappan.

(9) The sum total of Harappan sites of the mature stage is over one hundred. Of these perhaps four or five sites would qualify as cities.

(10) There is nothing to indicate the relationship of these cities to the villages except that they share the same artifacts as a whole.

The impression one gains from a study of the Harappan civilization is that it is a civilization still emerging out of an essentially village ethos. It is paradoxically a civilization more villagelike than citylike in the Western sense. It is like Sumerian "civilization" in the latest phase of the Ubaid period, just before the vast changes noted which were to come in the Uruk period that followed. It is more advanced technologically than the Ubaid cultures were because of both indigenous development and outside influence, and this tends to veil the fact that for all its sophistication, the Harappan civilization lacked the dynamism that led to the innovation which was historical Sumeria.

In part the Sumerian accomplishment came about because there had been long settlement in the Sumerian land, compared with which settlement in the Indus River Valley was quite short. The rapid movement of the Harappans into Saurashtra, Rajasthan, and the Punjab was because they already possessed the necessary techniques and skills to exploit the agricultural resources of those lands; these were largely pre-Harappan in origin but now amplified and perfected probably by influences from the west. In contrast to the Sumerians the Harappans evidence little indication of an evolutionary development toward the florescence which is the Early Dynastic climax. We are struck by the full-blown quality of Harappan civilization—pragmatic, utilitarian, changing dynamically only in its trait of widespread settlement. If a village can be understood to be extended over a thousand miles, then the Harappan "civilization" is such a village.

However, there are still the great cities of Mohenjo-daro and Harappa, and these surely are as urban as any city ought to be. If our faint evidence is correct, the Harappan villages and towns are really only the "cities" in miniature, and conversely, the cities appear to be elaborations of the village in plan and in activity, except that there is no question that the cities, with their blocks of well-to-do homes, were centers of wealth and, from the variety of materials and industries found there, approaching an economic system where the laws of supply and demand were about to bring developmental changes. The centralization represented is of formidable kind, and if our population estimate of some 40,000 souls living together at Mohenjo-daro has any validity,[3] an administration of authority and strength must have been established to keep matters in hand. But this administration was apparently not sustained in its authority by despotic power; there are no indications of military garrisons, written edicts—in effect, of coercion. The population was essentially attuned to a behavioral pattern which, like the relation of father to son, clearly set down the actions of each member of the populace. It was again the moral world of the village expanded to an urban setting.

One cannot but be impressed with the urban order, the modular planning, the uniformity of the great Harappan sites. There is little indication of the twisted and chaotic lanes of the traditional Eastern city with its confusion of byways and thoroughfares. Rather it is as if each segment of the population knew precisely that there was only one way to live together

[3] Walter A. Fairservis, Jr., "The Origin, Character, and Decline of an Early Civilization," *American Museum Novitates*, No. 2302 (1967); also this book p. 305.

—by conformity to a time-honored plan given its validity by one's fore-fathers.

It is here that the Harappan religion probably had its strongest hold. The seal references to a tree deity, to tiger "gods," to supermen, etc., seem to refer to an animistic world more common to hunters than to agriculturists. There is almost a humor in the distortions of beasts' heads into pinwheels, and in the false elephant trunk placed on the head of a bull (pp. 274–291). The seal material seems remote from the formality of the great "public" situations of the "citadels." It suggests that while a primitive animism was a theme in the ritual life, it was not the main theme.

The best candidates for "temples" are those structures which are raised high on platforms in which drains, baths, and fire pits of one kind or another are found. Ceremonial ablution, ritual purification, fire sacrifice, possibly ritual drinking, and the priestly offering of animals and humans are all suggested by the evidence. A supreme deity or deities for whom these rites were necessary emerges from this kind of evidence. Yet we have little suggestion as to whom or to what such rites were devoted. After some twenty field campaigns we have barely a clue as to the Harappan pantheon: no images, icons, texts, or proof of a temple.

There is, however, the evidence that each Harappan site was an emulation generally of the next one. Everyone had his place in the settlement. Here, then, is a society whose traditions were so strong as to support without apparent question the almost exact repetition of the familiar both in everyday activities as well as in the creation of new settlements. This is not an act of law or despotic authority, for indeed both law and despotism are notoriously subject to arbitrary or expedient change. It is rather the expression of a society to which the traditions lend their moral basis, their mystique, which sets forth the dharma in such a fashion that change is a disharmony and counter to the nature of the society.[4]

Thus the class structure seemingly had its roots in religion, had the sanction of the world beyond one's ken, much as is found in the villages. Here, then, India stands forth. The relationship among the classes, among individuals was governed by dharma. Surely one's well-being in a world where each had his place depended on fulfilling the purpose for which one was given that place originally. The process of Indianization mentioned previously would then have had its fulfillment in this ultimate character of the Harappan civilization. Familial ties were strong, the dead lived elsewhere, but in view of the grave goods placed with them it is clear that the living owed the dead a service, perhaps extending to the particular dharma for which one was responsible. Thus living and dead related to an ultimate cycle linking past to future.

---

[4] In contrast, we have abundant evidence that the preceding periods were times of considerable and constant change (see Chapters IV–VI). This final phase with its seemingly antichange quality may be deceptive, since it is short-lived comparatively.

As indicated previously the movement from highlands to lowlands was apparently not precipitate as a whole. The ties between villages were kin-related initially but time and distance weakened such links so that what remained was the legend of ancestral derivation from elsewhere along with the economic and "great tradition" interdependence. The network that linked village to village, town, and city was widespread and no unit existed in isolation. The network at the height of the Harappan civilization included communities of the highlands of variant cultural styles such as that of the Kulli. It also included the settlements of Gujarat and the Punjab. Each community had its local orientation, its "little" style, while at the same time participating in the "great" style or tradition in which it had an established role.

That these speculations may seem farfetched is admitted, but they do offer a reason why there is so much uniformity among Harappan sites, both village and town or city, and are probably nearer the truth than is the assumption that despotism, religion, or otherwise was solely responsible for the civilization's character.

✳ *The Deterioration of Harappan Civilization*

IN THIS LARGER SENSE THEN the answer to the question as to why the Harappan civilization fell is that it didn't fall! It simply stood at the beginning of the mainstream of Indian culture and faded into that current, having brought to it acts of faith, class morality, aspects of technology, and perhaps a cosmology which heralded the eventual supreme achievement that was medieval India.

However, there are literal facts that caused both movement and change, which can be interpreted as decline and fall. At Amri, Jhukar, and Chanhu-daro in Sind there is evidence for a rather miserable culture known as the Jhukar which succeeds the Mature Harappan (Appendix F). Casal at Amri regards the Jhukar as simply a phase of the Late Harappan. It contains many Harappan-type artifacts but lacks the typical seals, though it has some "button seals" of possible Iranian type. It has a polychrome pottery, however, which is in part motivated by Harappan painted design but which also suggests other influences. A similar-type ware occurs in the Fort Sandeman region and at Dabar Kot and Rana Ghundai in Loralai, suggesting that the Sind type might have been derived from the hill country.[5] In any case, there is no significant break between Jhukar and Harappan levels at the excavated sites of Amri and Chanhu-daro.

At Mohenjo-daro the Mature occupation deteriorates in the Late Harappan to the destruction or covering over of the fine buildings of the earlier period with hundreds of miserable huts; refuse and brickbats

[5] Fairservis, 1959, p. 316 and *passim*.

FIG. 65   *Cemetery H urn, black on red designs.*

choked the streets and the grand avenues; the "citadel" itself was surmounted by poor habitations much as were ancient Rome, modern Boston, London, and New York. Here was certainly a breakdown of dharma. In fact, the discovery of a number of skeletons of men, women, and children who apparently met violent death in the dark lanes of this final phase of the city's life underlines civil disorder and even outside raiding.[6]

At Harappa a post-Harappan cemetery known as Cemetery H that consists of two strata has been uncovered. The lower stratum (II) contains extended burials oriented generally with heads to the east or northeast. The funerary furniture consists of red wares painted rather exuberantly with designs of animals, birds, plants, and humans in black. The vessels are often dishlike, but pedestal feet occur commonly. The later level (I) consists of urn burials in which young children were buried whole but adults were fractionalized and skull and long bones only placed in the urns. There are also red wares elaborately painted with black designs. As Wheeler has pointed out, the lack of Harappan material in Cemetery H suggests a gap between the cultures, a fact somewhat supported by his excavations in 1946.[7]

In general these later phases only suggest that the Harappan civilization,

6 G. Dales, however, disputes this meaning of these skeletons. Dales, 1962b.
7 Sir M. Wheeler, 1959.

in Sind at least, deteriorated because of some inner weakness. The question of the cause of the decline has some resolution in a study of the economic basis of the Harappan civilization. Essentially the situation at Mohenjo-daro must stand for the whole of those communities located on the alluvial plain under the same stresses but on a lesser scale.

The crops identified or assumed to have been cultivated by the Harappan civilization include: wheat, barley, peas, figs, mangos, pomegranates, melons, dates, bananas (?), and sesamum. This is exclusive of cotton and other possible truck garden produce, which are known to have been culti-vated. These are generally winter crops in modern Sind. We also are aware of the herding of cattle and to a lesser extent of goats and/or sheep. Based on a comparison with house size relative to number of persons in a house-hold in modern rural Sind, population estimates can be obtained for the ancient situation, since we know something about the habitation area. In turn, a caloric intake per individual of 2500 per day can be used as a conservative estimate as to the ancient nutritional intake. On this basis a series of vital statistics can be obtained for Mohenjo-daro (Table 6). The fact that the active flood plain was apparently cultivated (as in Egypt) plus the indication that only a rabi, or winter, crop was sown stresses the need there must have been for a well-planned system of storage, another reason for a centralized administration.[8] Because flooding refertilized the soil, it cannot have been regarded as a seasonal disaster; but its extent, as in Egypt, could mean the difference between a lean and a pros-perous year. The need to live near the flood plain made hazardous the situation of the living area. Thus, the large walls of structures, the abundant use of fired brick, the platforms are probably partially the result of attempts to maintain the city proper in the midst of floods. There is abundant evi-dence for flooding on the site (see Plate 27). There are at least nine building periods at Mohenjo-daro, apparently repairs after flooding.

As the population grew and the cultivated area was extended, the city became more and more vulnerable to the vagaries of the river. Each flood season had within itself the potential for rich harvests or for famine. In addition, cattle forage and wood for fuel and building were daily required and caused a constant draw upon the primary forest and grass cover. The local environment was therefore undergoing change because of man's efforts.[9] We do not know whether this caused more devastating floods, soil leaching, and crop loss, but since the subsistence basis for the city was so subject to fluctuation, any shift would affect the economy.

[8] An attempt to describe the economics of the Harappan civilization is contained in Fairservis, 1967.

[9] The argument as to climatic change having been a factor seems now to have been largely resolved in favor of the belief that the ancient climate was essentially the same as it is today. Cf. R. L. Raikes and R. H. Dyson, Jr., "The Prehistoric Climate of Balu-chistan and the Indus Valley," *American Anthropologist*, Vol. LXIII (1961), pp. 265–281.

TABLE 6
ESTIMATED VITAL STATISTICS FOR MOHENJO-DARO, INDUS FLOOD PLAIN (*After Fairservis, 1967*)

Acres, Sq. Ft.	No. of Houses	GENERAL Individuals Per Acre	Acres Cultivated	Wheat Acreage	Fodder in Acres	Annual Fodder Requirements, Tons
5,500,000	3164	1.86	25,812	22,715	3097.5	41,535

CATTLE

No. of Cattle	No. of Work Bullocks	No. of Milk Cows	No. of Cattle Young and Aged
8754.8	3226.5	2610	2918.3

FODDER, IN TONS

Annual Fodder (Wheat/straw, 1/1)	Fodder Cultivation, 12% of Total Acreage	Cultivated Fodder	Grazing for Forage
8130.1	619.5	8749.6	32,785.8

POPULATION

	Males	Females	Total
Total	21,792 52.5%	19,458 47.5%	41,250

Males, Ages 0–9	Females, Ages 0–9	Males, 60+	Females, 60+	Productive Population Males	Females	Total
7527 35%	7122 36.6%	14.6 6.5%	1070 5.5%	12,849	11,266	24,115

DAILY DIETARY REQUIREMENTS PER INDIVIDUAL, IN CALORIES (TOP) AND GRAMS (BOTTOM)

Diet	Cereal	Vegetables	Fruit	Oil and/or Seeds	Sugar	Fish and Meat	Dairy Products	Other
2500	1600	50	50	100	100	200	125	375
933.4+	477.6	14.8	76.9	14.6	33.3	160	156.2	—

The decline of Mohenjo-daro and other large sites was very likely in part due to the inability of the agriculturists to produce enough to support growing populations. The *sailaba*, or flood-plain, agriculture alone, even with inundation canals, while enormously productive, was too uncertain after a certain production level was reached.

Harappan villages located in different environments would seem to have had the reverse problem from that of the cities. Many of the village sites were located in areas where soil resources were limited, as in the Bandhai Nai and Malir regions. Here were no refertilizing river floods, and thus the kach system was used to conserve and renew the soils. This is an indication that the Harappan farmers lacked full knowledge as to soil fertilization and were unable to contend with fertility loss except by making efforts to bring new soil. The shift in the villages would then seem to have been an effort to seek new cultivable fields.

✳ *The Phases of Harappan Civilization*

THE PATTERN AS IT EMERGES shows three main phases in the history of the Harappan civilization with numerous subphases. The *Early Harappan*, as outlined in Chapter V (p. 221), is still largely hypothetical, since a site of that phase has not been excavated. The *Mature Harappan*, as exemplified at Mohenjo-daro, is the fullest expression of the Harappan civilization. The *Late Harappan* marks the deterioration of the civilization, as previously described, and the advent of foreign traits (Jhukar, etc.) presumably derived from the highland portions of the Borderlands or, in the case of Saurashtra, from the Deccan or the other semisettled non-Harappan regions.

Phases of the Mature Harappan are found in southern Sind, in the Punjab (Harappa, Multan), in Bhawalpur, in northern Rajasthan, and in Saurashtra. They also occur in such Baluchistan sites as Dabar Kot, Duki, (Loralai), and in Sutkagan dor, Sotka Koh, and Bala Kot (see Appendix F) on the Arabian Sea coast. Where there is an earlier pre-Harappan occupation, the Harappan occupation seems to have been imposed rather suddenly. There is some mixing for a short period, and then the Harappan is dominant.

At Rangpur in Gujarat the Harappan settlement (Period IIA) is clearly separated by a layer of silt from the earlier Period I (see p. 94). This settlement was contemporaneous with Lothal (A) and seemingly marks a late phase of the Mature Harappan. It is followed by directly derived but changing phases of the Late Harappan (IIB or IIC) in which there is a falling off in the execution of pottery painting and of architecture. There is something of a revival in the last phase of this period (IIC), but as the excavator comments: "The conspicuous absence of the perforated jar, goblet, beaker, jar with micaceous red slip and terracotta triangular 'cake' is the culmination of a process of gradual replacement of certain old forms by the newly-evolved ones. It may also indicate a change in food-habits and social customs."[10] This latter part of Period II can be called Late Harappan in the same sense as used in Sind.

Period III at Rangpur is the period of large villages marked by a fine lustrous red ware which the excavator feels has evolved from Harappan ceramics. Rao concludes:

From the foregoing details it becomes abundantly clear that the Lustrous Red Ware culture was not an intrusion from elsewhere but a local development of the Harappa culture itself with such modifications as were necessitated by the new circumstances and isolation forced on it. Gujarat was the epicentre of the Lustrous Red Ware culture, and as such it would be unreasonable to think that this culture was an intrusion from elsewhere. A new type or a new painted motif might have been borrowed, but the culture as a whole was basically Harappan.[11]

Since the excavator estimates that his Period III at Rangpur dates to about 1000-800 B.C., it is clear that the Harappan civilization has a long life in Gujarat, certainly longer than enywhere in Sind.

Of great interest is the faunal list made up for Rangpur on the basis of a study of the remains found in the various phases. For Period IIA, the Mature Harappan, there are Indian humped cattle (*Bos indicus*), which the zoologist identifies with modern Indian cattle, the domestic buffalo (*Bos bubalus*), goats (*Capra hircus*), sheep (*Ovis vignei*), and the domestic pig (*Sus Scrofa cristatus*).[12] Plant-life remains were also studied.[13]

The occurrence of rice husk (*Oryza sp.*) in Period IIA and of pearl millet, or bajra, in Period III is of particular importance, since it indicates at the minimum a direct contact of man with these potentially domesticable plants—whether he had domesticated them or not is unknown.

At Lothal the earliest Harappan there is of the Mature type (Lothal A); Lothal B, on the other hand, is much like Rangpur in the late phases of Period II, with which it was probably contemporary.[14]

---

[10] Rao, 1962–1963, p. 23.

[11] *Ibid.*, p. 25.

[12] Bhola Nath, "Animal Remains from Rangpur," in Rao, 1962–1963, pp. 153–160.

[13] S. S. Ghosh and K. R. Lal, "Plant Remains from Lothal," in Rao, 1962–1963, pp. 161–177.

[14] Radio-carbon dates for Lothal:

LOTHAL A			
IIIB	2005 ± 115 B.C.	TF-27	
IIIB	1995 ± 125 B.C.	TF-26	
IIIB (end)	2010 ± 115 B.C.	TF-22	
IVA	1900 ± 115 B.C.	TF-29	
LOTHAL B			
VA	1865 ± 110 B.C.	TF-23	
VA	1810 ± 140 B.C.	TF-19	

TABLE 7

PHASE RANGE OF CERTAIN SITES OF THE HARAPPAN CIVILIZATION

EARLY	MATURE	LATE	
	_____		SUTKAGEN DOR
	Mixed Levels	Jhukar	
Amrian Levels	_____	_____	AMRI
_____			
		Jhukar	
		_____	CHANHU-DARO
	Mixed Amrian Levels?		
Levels	_____		GHAZI SHAH
		Jhukar	
		_____ _____	JHUKAR
Suggested Early Harappan Occupation	Pre-Platform Platform	Very Late Occupation	
_ _ _ _ _		_ _ _ _ _	MOHENJO-DARO
Kot Dijian Levels	Mixed Levels		
_____	_____		KOT DIJI
Possible Early Harappan			
_ _ _ _ _	_ _ _	_ _ _	JUDEIRJO-DARO
Basic Baluch. Village Occupation before Harappan Settlement	Harappan	?	
_____	_____	_____	DABAR KOT

PHASE RANGE OF CERTAIN SITES OF THE HARRAPAN CIVILIZATION

EARLY	MATURE	LATE	
Pre-Defense		Cemetery H	HARAPPA
	Mixed Levels		KALIBANGAN
		PG Ware	RUPAR
		PG Ware	ALAMGIRPUR
	Very Late Evolved Harappan	Lustrous Red Ware	RANGPUR
	Very Late Evolved Harappan	Lustrous Red Ware	LOTHAL

There are a great many Harappan sites, or sites of Harappan affinity, in Gujarat. Rao has tabled these on the basis of the Rangpur sequence. Thus, for Period IIA there are 5 sites; IIB—60; IIC—63; III—16. Here, then, we see a mushrooming of settlements of the Late Harappan phase degenerating, reviving, and finally surviving in new form.[15]

As far south as the Narbada (Mehgam, Telod) and the Tapti (Bhagatrav), Harappan sites have been located. The Narbada sites are near the sea and are of Late Harappan type (Rangpur IIB), while surprisingly Bhagatrav is of the Mature type (Rangpur IIA). Its proximity to river and sea suggests that, as at Lothal, it is a small seaport. Thus from the Tapti gate to the Deccan to Sutkagen-dor, which lies on a route between the sea

[15] In Kutch the site of Desalpur, an apparent seaport contemporary with Lothal A, extends the line of Harappan sites between Sind and Gujarat and suggests that sea connections were sustained. Cf. Rao, 1962–1963, p. 188. Recently G. Possehl has added several dozen more sites in Gujarat (unpublished dissertation).

and the interior of Makran, there is a line of possible seaports establishing for a short time an arm of the sea road between disparate parts of the coastal subcontinent. It would not be surprising to find occasional Harappan objects as far south as Kerala or Ceylon in view of this distribution.

At the other extreme, some seventeen miles west of Meerut and twenty-eight miles northeast of Delhi in the Ganges Valley, is the site of Alamgirpur, the locale of a small Harappan settlement, the earliest of a series of four occupations, each clearly separated with a gap between. What little is known of the Harappan occupation suggests that it represents a Late Harappan phase. At Rupar on the Sutlej in East Punjab two Harappan phases were found, below an occupation of the so-called Painted Gray Ware culture. The earlier phase is of the latest Mature Harappan, the later of Late Harappan type with new forms appearing in the ceramic corpus.

In the West Punjab the last phases of Harappa appear to belong to a Mature period, unless Cemetery H is representative of a very late revival of sorts—an unlikely hypothesis. Finally, at Kalibangan in northern Rajasthan the earliest Harappan occupation is of the Mature type, and there is apparently representation of Late Harappan as well.[16]

✳ The Abandonment of Harappan Sites

THE HARAPPAN CIVILIZATION can thus be said to have "faded away" rather than to have been extinguished completely. The abandonment of such sites as Mohenjo-daro, Harappa, Lothal, etc., was certainly due to a variety of causes, of which a few have been described. Flooding of these places because of their vulnerability close to meandering rivers was apparently a factor. One can tolerate just so much, and then, provided the promise of a better situation is there, one will move on. Recently R. Raikes, a hydrologist, has set forth a theory that tectonic action in which sea-level rise was involved caused a further decrease in the Sind gradient and that as a result the Indus River waters were for a long time ponded, thus making such sites as Mohenjo-daro subject to destroying floods— hence their abandonment.[17]

Sir Mortimer Wheeler, the one who commands the greatest knowledge of

---

[16] Radio-carbon dates for Kalibangan are:

Late level of Harappan	2095 ± 115 B.C.	TF-25
Late level of Harappan	2045 ± 75 B.C.	P-481

A single sample of charred grains from the Late Harappan at Mohenjo-daro has produced a date (TF-75) 1760 ± 115 B.C. B. B. Lal "A Picture Emerges—an assessment of the Carbon-14 datings of the proto-historic cultures of the Indo-Pakistan subcontinent," *Ancient India*, Nos. 18–19 (1962, 1963), pp. 213–214.

[17] R. L. Raikes, "The Mohenjo-daro Floods," *Antiquity*, Vol. XXXIX (1965), pp. 196–203.

subcontinental archaeology, had held to a theory that the forts referred to in the Rig-Veda, that earliest and most descriptive of the Vedic Aryan narratives, were those of the Harappans. The Aryan invasion of India, which is generally thought to have begun about the middle of the second millenium B.C., was apparently resisted by the inhabitants of the Indus Valley and the Doab. Who but the Harappans possessed the fortifications stormed by Indra and his followers? The great walls of the "citadel" at Harappa could exemplify a need for defense. Thus, if the Harappans still survived behind those walls by mid-millennium and if the Aryan invasion was of the dynamic kind recorded in the Rig-Veda, then there is every reason to believe that Wheeler's theory has some basis. In any case it substantially locks the beginnings of traditional Indian history with the archaeological picture of the Harappan civilization.[18]

Obviously, however, there is no single cause for the decline of the Harappan civilization. Its wide and generally conformist distribution from Alamgirpur to Bhagatrav suggests rapid movement and identical motivations. In one sense the Harappans merely accelerated the diffusionary process that brought food production across Iran to the Borderlands. This movement was substantially caused by the same drive for good soil, water, and forage for cattle, sheep, and goats.

A distribution map of the spread of the Harappan civilization placed over the map of the conventional regions for cereal growing shows that the Harappans flourished essentially in the wheat-growing regions of Sind, Punjab, and Gujarat. Just below Delhi, on the northeast and south of the Tapti River, begins the significant change to the great rice-growing centers. This suggests that the Harappan farmers pushed to the limits of a known environment, beyond which they could not go, since their subsistence, wheat cultivation, could not effectively function. Is it coincidence that in the Mature and Late Harappan levels of Rangpur and Lothal rice husks have been found? Native rice is found in Gujarat and the Punjab, and the Harappan farmers were familiar with it, though they may not have grown it. But perhaps it was experimented with until at last a successful development permitted the change from wheat to rice and the door was opened to the lower Ganges Valley and to south India. This would have been indeed a factor that caused the final disappearance of the Harappan style. It is probably no sudden accomplishment that the rise of prosperous kingdoms in the Oudh, Bengal, and Bihar regions occurred after 1000 B.C. The rice subsistence foundation had possibly been established by descendants of the Harappan civilization. This is a speculation, of course, but what little evidence we have points to the Harappans as the first experimenters with that crop which was to open the rest of the subcontinent to food production.

[18] See Sir M. Wheeler, *The Indus Civilization*, 3rd ed., Cambridge University Press, Cambridge, 1968, pp. 129–134, for his latest views.

IX

"Uncivilized" India

IN CONTRAST TO THE ABUNDANT EVIDENCE we have for the late prehistoric cultures and their evolution in the Borderlands and immediately adjacent regions, there is almost nothing known of the rest of the subcontinent in a comparable time range. The evidence we do have is in part described in a previous chapter (III). From this we gather that most of the subcontinent was inhabited by mesolithiclike food gatherers. But there are tantalizing traces of other ways of life. Meager as these traces are, they hint of significant regionalized developments that prelude the shape of historical India.

✳ *Burzahom*

DE TERRA AND PATERSON, in their survey of the Srinagar district in the Kashmir Valley, happened on a site called locally Burzahom. This place was marked by a group of large stones arranged in a rough semicircle. Limited excavation at the place produced a coarse pottery and some polished stone axes. At the time nothing was known about the significance of this material. However, sometime later Lauristan Ward of the Peabody Museum of Harvard University studied this material and recognized that

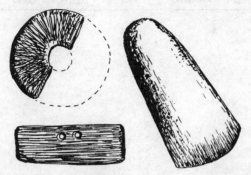

FIG. 66 *Stone disk, rectangular knife, polished stone axe from the early levels at Burzahom.*

its affinities were to Central and Northern Asia. Indeed, it could very easily be misconstrued by the unknowing as from a site of neolithic China.[1] In 1960-1961 the Archaeological Survey of India began a thorough excavation of the site. Four phases of occupation have been described.[2] The latest phase belongs to a period dating to 3rd-4th century A.D. Earlier than this is the phase (II) of the large stones (megaliths?). With these were associated a unique wheel-made red ware, some poor examples of black burnished ware of the next earliest phase, and a few polished stone axes and bone tools. Some of the burials of the types found in next phase (II) occurred here as well. This phase contained mud and mud-brick houses. Some of these houses apparently were built on mud platforms. Postholes, partitions, and storage pits suggest the character of the structures. There were also polished stone axes and gouges tapered and ovoid or quadrangular in cross section and polished bone tools, including harpoons, awls, and arrowheads. The pottery was of black burnished type and included, in addition to the conventional forms of basins and vases, a funnel-shaped vessel. Some of this pottery was decorated by incision. A charred pit contained animal bones, those of deer being most abundant.

Burials in this place were in oval or circular pits in the midst of the houses. Four of the human burials were in the crouching position, though some were secondary burials. Red ocher stain on the bones was found in each case. "Pet" animals were sometimes buried with their human masters or mistresses. However, animal burials also occurred. One burial was of five wild (?) dogs and the antler of a deer. For the rest, complete and incomplete burials of dog, ibex, and wolf were encountered.

The earliest phase at the site (I) was formed by "pit dwellers." Their pit

[1] L. Ward, "The Relative Chronology of China Through the Han Period," *Relative Chronologies in Old World Archaeology*, R. W. Ehrich, ed., University of Chicago Press, Chicago, 1954, p. 134.

[2] *Indian Archaeology, A Review*, 1953–54 and 1961–62 editions.

TABLE 8. COMPARATIVE CHRONOLOGY OF GENERALLY POST-HARAPPAN SITES OF INDIA-PAKISTAN

Date	Ahar	Gilund	Navdatoli	Nevasa	Daimabad	Jorwe	Nasik	Hastinapura
600								
400								
200								
0	C							
	Rang Mahal							NBP WARE
200	IIB						NBP	
								?
400	A NBP & Iron							
600								Painted Grey Ware
800		IIIC		Jorwe Ware	III Jorwe Ware	Jorwe Ware	Jorwe Ware Microliths	
			Jorwe Ware					
1000		IIIB		?	II Malwa Ware			Yellow Ochre Ware
			Malwa Ware					
1200		Navdatoli						
		Cream Slipped Ware in Upper Levels		IIIA Black and Red with White Paint	I Ties to Brahma-giri IB			?
1400	I Painted Black & Red or Cream Ware							
1600			Painted Black & Red or Cream Ware					

Sonpur	Cemetery H	Taxila	Charsada	Gandhara Grave Complex	Moghal Ghundai Cairns	Mundigak	Ghul Ware	Londo Complex B
		Sirkap						
	Rang Mahal Like ?				Kushan craftsmanship with Hellenistic influence			
								TYPE III
BP Ware		Bhir Mound						
npur ck and d Ware	OR		Wall					
								TYPE II
				Ceramic tie to lowest levels at Charsada			?	
npur ck and d Ware			?					
	Very evolved Harappan ?							
								TYPE I
						VII		
			?					

structures were circular or oval and some 1½ to 2½ meters in depth, with the mouth of the pit quite narrow. Ash was found in the bottom of some of these structures. Two pits were connected by an underground corridor in one example. Others had inclines, and one had a step down. Postholes and evidence for reed matting suggest the character of the roofs. Polished stone axes, other stone objects, including ground-stone rings (digging-stick weights or maceheads) and rectangular knives pierced with holes, and bone tools like those of Phase III were also found in this occupation. Gray ware was the dominant pottery, though some burnished red ware also occurred. The former included pedestal-based bowls and jars with flaring rims. The bulk of the gray ware was mat impressed or cord-marked and handmade.

That Phases I through III were not unique in Kashmir has been confirmed by the discovery of nine other sites in the valley of the Jhelum River in the Anantorag district (Begagund, Gotkral, Hariparigom, Jayaderi-Uadar, Olchibag, Pampur, Panzgom, Sombur, Thajiwor).

In general there appears to be a continuity from Phases I to III, as if III were the last manifestation. Radio-carbon dates for Phase I have been obtained (TF-13 1850±130; TF-15 1540±110 B.C.).

There is little doubt that we have here a southern aspect of the late prehistoric cultures of Central and Northern Asia (Fig. 66, Plates 48,

PLATE 48 *Burzahom—dwelling pit of the early phase of the neolithic occupation.* (Copyright—Archaeological Survey of India, Government of India.)

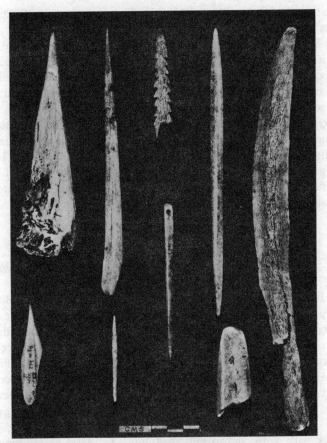

PLATE 49   *Burzahom—bone tools from the neolithic strata.* (Copyright—
Archaeological Survey of India, Government of India.)

49). Textured pottery, rectangular knives, bone harpoons, pit houses,
polished stone celts of ovoid or quadrangular type, and stone rings all
have direct analogies in such places as southern Siberia (Minusinsk,
Transbaikalia), Mongolia, Manchuria, and northern China. Dog eating,
flexed burial, pole houses are also found in Eastern and Northern Asia. The
deer bones would evidence food gathering, but the stone rings and possibly
the celts suggest that some agriculture was practiced.

Burzahom represents a movement out of Central Asia toward and into
the subcontinent of a more limited kind than that out of Western Asia
previously described. However, one of the surprises of the archaeological
investigation of the old North-West Frontier Province and the Punjab is
the absence of late prehistoric sites. It may well be that future investigation
of these regions will reveal a deeper penetration of the Burzahom cultural

form into the alluvial plains from its highland home. In any case Burzahom represents the southernmost expression of a widespread North Asian complex. It represents a movement that may well have started with the Mesolithic of Europe and which survived in the fertile valleys of Kashmir and perhaps Nepal, Tibet,[3] Hunza, Baltistan, and Ladakh. It is so clearly inner Asian that one finds difficulty in including it as a part of subcontinental archaeology except for the fact that it is in the river system of the subcontinent. It is also a less important but nonetheless definitive manifestation of one of the cultural streams which were through time directed toward India. In this one is reminded of the historical travels of the Chinese monks Fa Hsien and Hsuen Tsang, who were later to travel out of inner Asia to India via High Asia. These travels were somewhat anticipated by the prehistoric cultures of the type found in Kashmir (see App. K).

✳ Eastern India

EASTERN INDIA, or the regions of Assam, parts of Bihar, Orissa, and Bengal, is in proximity to southern China, Burma, and southeast Asia. The frontiers of these areas are, as has been pointed out elsewhere, mountainous, jungled, and generally difficult. Thus, influences back and forth were slow and gradual, and it was not until sea trade was established across the Bay of Bengal and through the Straits of Malacca that contacts accelerated. Southeast Asia, in its late prehistoric phases, appears to have been occupied largely by food gatherers who possessed crude pottery (impressed or cord-marked), ground- and chipped-stone implements (celts, gouges, etc.), bone tools, bark cloth, and various shell, bone, and terra-cotta ornaments and tools. Apparently there were highland hunting peoples living in rock shelters, and coastal or riverine peoples much of whose subsistence came from shellfish and who probably lived in reed or pole shelters. However, a limited agriculture was also practiced.[4] The dates of these late prehistoric occupations, which probably went through at least three major stages, are from perhaps 3000 B.C. to the time of Christ or shortly thereafter.[5]

Eastern India can be broken into two main geographic zones: the river basins, and the hills and plateaus. Dani regards the river basins as essen-

---

[3] Megaliths have been reported from Tibet; cf. J. N. Roerich, "The Animal style among the Nomad Tibes of Northern Tibet," *Seminarium Kondakovianum* (1930), pp. 33–35.

[4] Southeast Asian archaeology as a whole is woefully lacking in definite, detailed, and long-range excavations of key sites. Much needs to be done before each part of the region takes a full place in prehistoric accounts.

[5] The best recent summary of this area and its relation to eastern India is by A. H. Dani, *Prehistory and Protohistory of Eastern India*, Firma D. L. Mukhopadhyaya, Calcutta, 1960.

tially zones of attraction, while the hills and plateaus are in effect refuge areas. The extremely limited archaeological study of the late prehistoric cultures of eastern India provides little other than a substantial number of stone tools gathered generally from the surface of the ground. These fall into certain classes (see Map 23). Of these classes faceted axes, shouldered axes, and rounded-butt adzes and axes are the most important. Hammerstones, chisels, perforated stones, etc., are also collected, but it is the axes or axe types which are typologically of greatest importance. Generally these are made from hard stones such as flint and basalt; however, the material used seems to have depended on what was available locally.

Dani divides the axes into two main groups: Group I consists of tools manufactured by three different techniques used either singly or in combination: chipping, pecking, grinding. Aside from chisels, hammerstones, wedges, wedge-shaped axes, and perforated stones, rounded-butt axes of two main classes belong with this group of stone tools. Class I consists of axe blades with median cutting edge formed by bifacial grinding; Class II, axe hammers with broad end flat or blunted.

The rounded- or pointed-butt axe has some variety of form in India, but it is widely distributed from Assam well down into the peninsula. Wheeler found them at Brahmagiri in northern Mysore in the lowest (and earliest) of three different periods of occupation. Here they occurred with crude pottery, "microliths," and some "scraps" of bronze and copper. Wheeler, on the basis of the thick deposition (eight to nine feet) which represents this phase, considers a date of perhaps 700 B.C. as a reasonable estimate of its chronological place.[6] At Sanganakallu some thirty miles away, Subbarao also found similar axes. At both this site and Brahmagiri the succeeding occupation is megalithic, and there is evidence for overlap, suggesting that a more advanced iron-using people (the megalith builders) was not only contemporaneous with but overcame in some way the more primitive axe-using indigenous population.

Axes of this type are also found as far north as Burzahom in Kashmir. They are singularly absent in the Indo-Iranian Borderlands and are rare in Southeast Asia. They are very common in southern and northern China, however, where they occur both as axes and as adzes. The adze type is rare in India however.[7] Dani feels that they are essentially indigenous to India but qualifies his view in consideration of the Chinese evidence.

With Group II, however, we are on better ground as far as evidence of external sources is concerned. Group II in Dani's classification includes faceted tools, shouldered tools, splayed axes, the "bar chisel, and thin-sectioned broad axes." The last-named of these is well known in Assam and was found in the Santal Parganas.

---

6 Sir M. Wheeler, 1959, p. 85.
7 Cf. Dani, 1960, p. 93.

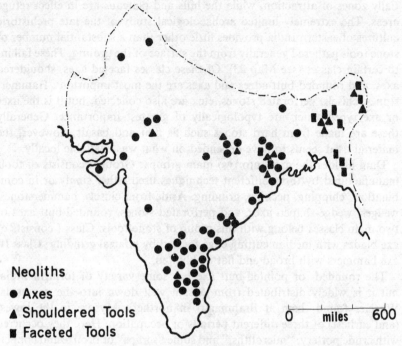

Neoliths
- **Axes**
- ▲ **Shouldered Tools**
- ■ **Faceted Tools**

MAP 22 *Distribution of certain tool types on the Indian subcontinent*
(after Dani).

The faceted tool with unifacially bevelled cutting edge is an excellent cutting tool, tending to be small in size. The tool in general is found in Ranchi and Mayurbhanj. It occurs in both triangular and rectangular forms, the latter having a wide distribution in India, including Bihar, Orissa, Assam, and even Darjeeling.

Relatives of the faceted tool are the shouldered axes or hoes, which appear to have been made in the same way—perhaps by a sawing technique.[8] These shouldered tools range throughout eastern India as far south as the Godavari River. They cluster in Orissa and Assam on distribution maps. They even are found inside the fortifications of such sites as Kausambi in the Ganges Valley and Rajgir in Patna. Neither the "bar celt" nor the splayed axe occurs in enough collections to warrant any conclusions about either one.

Faceted tools and shouldered axes are widely distributed throughout Southeast Asia and even occur north of the Yangtze and in Japan. Their eastern derivation, therefore, seems fairly confirmed.

[8] Dani, 1960, p. 225.

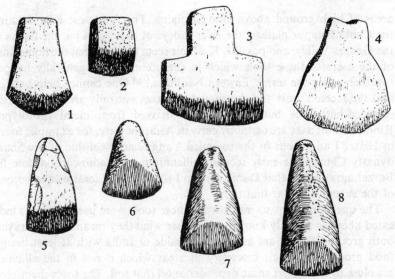

FIG. 67   *Stone tool types of eastern India* (mostly after Dani).
1—*Faceted tool, Assam*
2—*Faceted tool, Assam*
3—*Shouldered axe, Assam*
4—*Splayed axe, Assam*
5—*Rounded- or pointed-butt axe, Assam*
6—*Rounded- or pointed-butt axe, Assam*
7—*Rounded- or pointed-butt axe, Brahmagiri*
8—*Rounded- or pointed-butt axe, Brahmagiri*

Since these implements are largely known from surface collections, their date and relative chronology are somewhat hazy. Wheeler's estimate from the work at Brahmagiri indicates the survival of the use of this type of tool probably at least to the time of Christ. At Tamluk, in the Midnapur district of West Bengal, a faceted tool was found in the earliest level which in turn was succeeded by a Sunga occupation; thus it belongs to a period before the second century B.C. Recently, at Daojali-Hading in the United District of Mikir and in the North Cachar Hills in Assam shouldered axes, faceted tools, and apparently pointed-butt axes were found in association with a crude grayish pottery marked with cord and basket impressions. Grinding stones were also found in some abundance.[9] Unfortunately for those who consider the absence of metal a sign of great age, an iron bar celt resembling the faceted tool was found on the surface of the site. The site itself lies on a hillock between two nullahs.

Dani has noted that in general these ground-stone tools are found in

[9] *Indian Archaeology, A Review*, 1953–54 and 1961–62 edition.

areas of high ground above alluvial plains. The Assamese hills, Sikkim, the Chota Nagpur plateau, the river valleys of eastern India, the flanks of the Ganges Valley, and possibly Kashmir seem to have been the homelands of the users of these tools which in the literature are generally lumped together under the term "Eastern Neolithic."[10] One cannot help but feel that the faceted tools and the shouldered axes not only are later than the rounded-butt axes but may well be derived from metal prototypes. Rounded-butt axes are certainly early in Asia; they are, for example, found in Hissar I and occur in the so-called Yang Shao Neolithic of pre-Shang dynasty China. The early second millennium B.C. radio-carbon date for Burzahom suggests that Dani's Group I tools were at least on the borders of the subcontinent at that time.

The question is not so much when these tools were used, which as indicated above is roughly known, but rather what they mean. It appears that both groups of tools are associated outside of India with at least limited food production. Their discovery in areas which if not in the alluvium are close to it suggests some dependence on that soil. The tools themselves include adzes and possibly the hoe as well as the axe. The recent Assamese finds show that grinding stones were part of the tool repertoire. The typological ties to Southeast Asia and to south China further suggest that the character of food production in those regions was identical with that in India wherever in the subcontinent the tools appear. The faceted and shouldered tools are probably post-1500 B.C. in Southeast Asia, and much of the settled life of that region did not develop until well after 1000 B.C. with the advent of rice production. Are these tools, then, the representatives of the beginnings of rice cultivation in the regions where shortly that cultivation would form the basis for the development of another Indian civilization? Such places as Tamluk, Kausambi, Rajgir, and Sisulpargarh, in whose confines these tools were found, would one day be the metropolitan centers of considerable and prospering states. Do we have in these faceted sawn and ground tools an eastern counterpart of the earlier advent of food production, described in previous chapters? We have no direct answers to these questions.

Yet each year of field work indicates that these tools mark no casual settlements but rather permanent, well set up and adapted communities of people who found in the particular environment of eastern India and probably the flanking slopes of the Ganges Valley the necessary and perhaps ideal setting for their subsistence activities. Faint as our evidence now is, it nonetheless indicates that an influence of considerable scale was

---

[10] The discussions that have blossomed forth as to the derivation of this phase are beyond the scope of this book. However, it is worth noting that there are opposing views as to the origin of some of the axe types. Some see Western Asia as the source, others an indigenous development; however, all are generally agreed that the shouldered axe or hoe is from the East.

diffusing from the East. Whether this means Eastern methods and objects of food production is unknown, but we have in this amorphous cultural assemblage of Eastern India a strong candidate for this kind of diffusion at any rate.

✳ *The Central Deccan*

A REMARKABLE SERIES of archaeological studies in the southern portion of the central Deccan in the upper courses of the Krishna, Bhima, and Tungabhadra rivers has been carried out, particularly by F. R. Allchin and his associates, in recent years. The region consists of basement rocks and presents a peneplain landscape broken only by granitic domes and rock hills consisting of great boulder piles. It is a semiarid area with an annual rainfall of somewhat less than twenty-five inches.

Sites representing numerous historic periods are scattered over the region, but it was Allchin's work principally that established the presence of an occupation of neolithic type. Two sites in particular can claim our attention: Piklihal and Utnur.[11]

Over thirty sites of the region have been identified as consisting of layers of ash often separated by earth strata. Allchin excavated one of these sites, Utnur (see Map 23). The excavation indicates that the ashmounds represent a single complex of pastoral peoples who kept cattle. The ashmounds were in reality stockades within which the cattle were penned. At apparently regular intervals the accumulated cattle dung was fired *in situ*. Thus motivations for this were of several kinds, suggests Allchin:

First the dung was allowed to accumulate because there was at that time no practical use for which it was required. Then the time came when dilapidation of the stockades made it desirable to rebuild. The complete burning of the pen, stockades, accumulated dung and all, would be an excellent preparation for remaking it upon a clean, drained base. The start of the seasonal migration would be the obviously ideal time for such a burning as there would be several months during which the fire could exhaust itself and the site cool. But the starting points of the seasonal migrations, in whichever direction, would also be those points of the year at which important religious celebrations took place, and if—as we may now confidently assert—our Neolithic pastoralists were not cut off from the main streams of cattle keeping tradition wherever they manifest themselves in Eurasia, then the presence of cattle bonfires and Needfires at such times would be not only in order, but even

---

11 F. R. Allchin, *Piklihal Excavations*, Andhra Pradesh Government Archaeological Series, No. 1, Hyberabad, 1960. See also F. R. Allchin, *Utnur Excavations*, Andhra Pradesh series, No. 5, Hyderabad, 1961; and his *Neolithic Cattle-Keepers of South India —A Study of the Deccan Ashmounds*, Cambridge University Press, Cambridge, 1963.

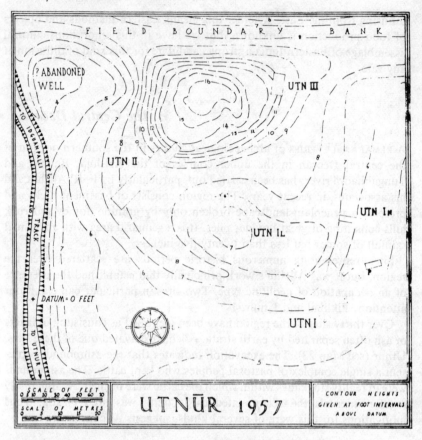

MAP 23   *Plan of Utnur ashmound* (after Allchin).

demanded. Thus the favourable material basis provides a justification for folk religious practice of this kind. In view of the continuity which we have repeatedly found between the culture of the Neolithic pastoralists of the Deccan and modern groups in India, it may also be not unreasonable to infer that the modern Pongal, Holi and Divali ceremonies contain, along with other traits deriving from other streams of culture history, traits deriving directly from their culture.[12]

A radio-carbon date of 2160 B.C. ± 150 years has been obtained for an early phase (IB) at Utnur. Allchin found evidence for five major burnings and other smaller ones. Initially the site was occupied by cattle users who created a *dongo*, or thorn hedge, to pen their beasts (Period IA). These people possessed pottery, stone tools, and probably built their huts of branches and brush. The next phase (IC) saw the creation of a post stock-

[12] F. R. Allchin, 1961, p. 75.

ade possibly consisting of two concentric rings. Later periods (II-IV) saw in general elaborations or simplifications of post-stockade construction. In the last phase, however, an ash wall was combined with a thorn fence.

Allchin relates the Utnur cattle complex to the so-called Deccan or South Indian Neolithic. This cultural grouping is most clearly defined at the site of Piklihal. At that site lower and upper phases have been determined lying immediately under deposits of the Iron Age. Apparently the earliest settlers built terraces on and about the small hills on which their habitations were placed, even to the point of using the natural rock shelters. As Allchin sees it, the boulder terraces were made for a variety of purposes: as retaining walls for habitations; for cattle penning; for cultivation. In the latter case the general aridity of the region probably required the conservation of cultivable soil, much as motivated the kach system in southwestern Sind. However, the terraces are small, and Allchin suggests that some form of millet was grown. Hunting was probably an effective supplement to the diet, as evidenced by the finds of rock "bruisings" and paintings associated with the site that depict buffalo, gazelle, and deer. However, sheep, goats, and cattle were herded and may, in the latter case, as suggested at Utnur, have been the principal subsistence resource.

Burials of the Neolithic phase in the Deccan were in the extended position with grave furniture consisting of daily-life utensils and probably some food offerings. Burial was in close proximity to the habitation area. Ground- and chipped-stone implements include splayed axes, chisels, rubbing stones, mortars, and balls (rubber, sling pellets?), etc. The blade-tool industry suggests some ties to the Indian Late Stone Age industries in that lunates and backed blades are found. Apparently these people hafted the simple blades with little or no secondary preparation. In general, however, the stone industry is rather nondescript.

The pottery (Allchin labels these A wares) was made either by the hammer-and-anvil technique or by the slow wheel. There is a great variety of colors: ocher yellow, black, gray, buff, brick red, brown, etc., mostly the result of firing. Burnishing of the vessels' surfaces occurs in about 50 per cent of cases. A large variety of forms occurs (Fig. 68). The most interesting among these are legged stands, perforated pots, carinated bowls, and hollow-footed bowls and cups. Various treatments of the vessel surface for decorative or utilitarian purposes were carried out. These include incising, rusticating, and painting, the latter in black-brown over a brown- or sienna-colored surface. The designs painted are single geometrics or parallel lines.

The pottery includes a channel spout, lug and other handles, lipped bowls, and other features which suggest strongly to Allchin similar types found at Shah Tepe in northeastern Iran.[13] Of interest, too, is the fact that

13 F. R. Allchin, 1960, pp. 61–62.

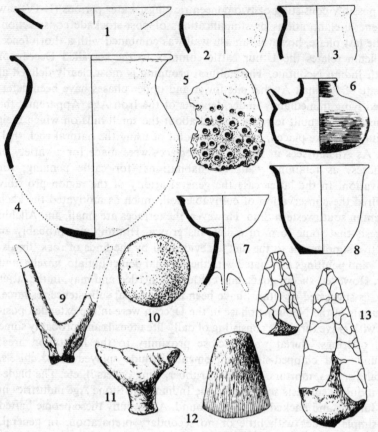

FIG. 68   *Artifacts of the Deccan Neolithic (mainly from Piklihal) (after Allchin).*

1–8—*Pottery*   10—*Clay ball*
9, 11—*Clay figurines*   12–14—*Stone axes*

some of the neolithic wares (A4 and A5) are common to both the Upper Neolithic and Iron Age levels at Piklihal.[14]

A small group of terra-cotta figurines was recovered from the neolithic levels. These include humped bulls, modeled birds, and a male (?) human torso.

At the site of Brahmagiri, also in Mysore State, as is Piklihal, but some ninety miles to the south, Wheeler recovered evidence for a culture of

[14] Allchin classifies the pottery at the site into four general categories: A Ware—neolithic; B Ware—red, black, and red-and-black pottery, which represents typical wares of the Iron Age, early historic and medieval type; C Ware—imported wares of the early historic period; D Ware—modern wares whose traditions can be traced back.

comparable type to that of Piklihal which he calls the Brahmagiri Stone Axe culture.[15] As at Piklihal there is an overlap with the succeeding culture, which at Brahmagiri is megalithic and can be dated not earlier than the third century B.C.[16] The characteristic features of this assemblage at Brahmagiri include coarse gray wares (IA-IB) and painted and incised wares (IA) like those of Piklihal. The blade-tool industry is also like that of Piklihal, but the abundance of pointed- or rounded-butt axes is in some contrast to the much more limited representation at the northern site. As in the Upper Neolithic at Piklihal, an example or two of copper or bronze is associated.

Burials include the familiar extended type and those of infants who were buried in large urns set amid the habitations. No house plans were revealed, but postholes indicate the kind of construction used.

At Tekkalakota in the Bellary District two phases of occupancy were noted. These were primarily distinguished by ceramics. However, it is the burials that give a strong suggestion of change. The earlier phase at the site had fractional burials but the later contained extended burials in a number of interconnected vessels. A black and red ware peculiar to these multiple-vessel burials was recovered.[17] Children were buried in urns.

At Sanganakallu, about forty miles to the north of Brahmagiri and not far from Tekkalakota a similar occupation was found. As at Brahmagiri there is an overlap with a succeeding megalithic horizon. An earlier level clearly separated from the neolithic levels seems to be of Late Indian Stone Age vintage.[18]

The evidence from these two sites and from Hallur in nearby Dharwar district shows that proximity to rivers and hills was important in the selection of living sites. The rocky hills and the river banks were important settlement areas. Here the people built circular houses made of poles and mud-plastered bamboo screening. These houses were some five meters in width and the grass roof (conical?) was supported by central pillars. The house foundations were of stone rubble overlaid by a layer of packed earth which was plastered. Clay or stone hearths are found in these houses.

In addition to cattle and sheep (?) pastoralism, a limited agriculture was apparently practiced. Species of grain (*Dolichos biflorus*) and millet

[15] R. E. M. Wheeler, "Brahmagiri and Chandravalli 1947: Megalithic and other Cultures in Mysore State," *Ancient India*, 1947–1948, pp. 199ff. The occupation was eight to nine feet in depth.

[16] Sir M. Wheeler, 1959, p. 163. Wheeler defines two phases of the Stone Axe culture at Brahmagiri (IA—earlier, IB), IA being somewhat more elaborate than IB.

[17] M. S. Nagaraja Rao and K. C. Malhotra, "The Stone Age Hill Dwellers of Tekkalakota," Poona, 1965.

[18] M. S. Nagaraja Rao, "New Evidence for Neolithic life in India: Excavations in the Southern Deccan," *Archaeology*, Vol. 20, No. 1 (1967), pp. 28–35; also, Subbarao, 1948.

(*Eleusine coracona*) were grown and these plants are adapted to a semi-arid climate such as is found in the southern and central Deccan.

Fishing, hunting, herding, and cultivation are all attested to at these sites and these are expressive of extensive use of the environment. Fecundity may have been worshipped in a formal fashion since there are depictions of bulls in figurine, pictographic, and painted forms. In this regard the burial of children in globular urns (like a pregnant female in shape), often within the houses, and in an embryonic position, has suggested to the archaeologists that there might have been a belief in reincarnation, the globular urn symbolically representing the womb into which the child is making his spiritual reentry.

At Maski, just east of Piklihal, B. K. Thapar of the Archaeological Survey of India also found a similar assemblage (Period I) below megalithic levels (Period II). Faunal analysis was made at Maski and the other sites and revealed the presence of fresh-water mussels, rats, squirrels, buffalo, goats, and sheep. The remains of sheep and short-horned humpless cattle were most abundant, however. Ground-stone axes like those of Brahmagiri were very scarce, a few only being found on the surface. The blade-tool industry was much in evidence, as was the pottery. Beads of amethyst, chalcedony, coral, shell, paste "glass," carnelian, and agate were also common.[19]

COMPARATIVE STRATIGRAPHY OF SOME DECCAN NEOLITHIC SITES

Utnur	Piklihal	Maski	Sanganakallu	Brahmagiri
	U. Neol. IB	I	IB	IB
IV				
III	L. Neol. (IA)		IA	IA
II				
I				

In sum, this southern culture in its apparent home area has a time range of late third millennium B.C. to at least the fourth century B.C. Initially it appears that essentially pastoral peoples took advantage of the hills of the region perhaps for protection and certainly for the rock shelters found there. The importance of Allchin's work at Utnur cannot be overemphasized, for if the radio-carbon date stands up, we have evidence for another pre-Harappan cultural form. Allchin would relate the pastoral peoples of this period eventually to northeastern Iran. However, the situation at Sur Jangal in the Loralai district of Baluchistan (see p. 151) suggests that one trend in the gradual change which saw the shift toward the Indus River Valley was the increasing emphasis on cattle raising. The Harappan civiliza-

[19] B. K. Thapar, "Maski, 1954: A chalcolithic site of the southern Deccan," *Ancient India*, No. 13 (1957), pp. 12–13.

tion itself is to a considerable extent cattle dependent. Thus the pastoralism of this southern region may have resulted from a Borderland genesis.

Herding people, with their wide range of subsistence seeking, are apt to be in the advance guard of settled life. Such may well be the case in peninsular India. Accordingly, one can envision a pastoral people moving southeast out of Sind into parts of Rajasthan and Gujarat, finding open grassland in these places and eventually drifting south on the Deccan plateau, leaving a few traces of their passing.[20] In the Raichur-Bellary region of the Karnatak the wanderings may have ended. Here was grassland and shelter, but beyond to the east and west were the more jungled hills of the Ghats and the tropical or marshy shores of the seas—environments not conducive to animal husbandry. It is not too difficult to imagine that the microlithic element in this blade-tool industry was adopted from hunting-gathering peoples who we know were living in these regions for a considerable length of time (Chapter III).

The Utnur people are an expression of a pastoralism in which the temporary camp is a characteristic of the traditional wanderings. Typically, movement is restricted to traditional routes. It would seem from the flimsy and conformist quality of the settlements as they are presently known that the whole community owned the herd and there were no class distinctions. The fact that there are many ashmounds in the region suggests that these pastoral people were indeed members of tribes made up of scattered but integral units consisting probably of extended families. (Utnur is only two hundred feet on a side—see Map 24.) The fact that the mounds reflect identical traditions such as dung burning, stone tool manufacture, pottery types, and stockade building indicates that these units were in contact. Perhaps the sodalities here were clans or chieftainships. It is of interest that an infant's burial was found in the proximity of the supposed habitation area. Here is a hint of the idea that the newborn dead were not truly dead but perhaps, as among the Andaman Islanders, merely waiting for a new body to inhabit; therefore the familial units of the tribe did not isolate the mortal remains of the deceased for fear of separating the spirit of the dead from its true family. In such customs the familial unity through time is expressed. As Allchin has pointed out in connection with certain Indian traditions, once started these customs have a way of surviving.

The Lower Neolithic saw the fullest development of pastoralism but within restricted and traditional territories. It also saw the increasing development of agriculture as a supplement to the main diet. Allchin has pointed up the tendency at Utnur toward better stockades, and we can consider the evidence of terracing at sites such as Piklihal (in both its Lower and Upper Neolithic phases) as indicative of a trend toward more permanent settlement. If Allchin is correct in his speculation that some form of

[20] A channel spout was found at Kot Diji by Ghurye in 1935 (see Pl. 50).

PLATE 50 *Spouts belonging to gray vessels found by G. S. Ghurye at the site of Kot Diji in northern Sind in 1935. They resemble types found widely in northern Iran.* (Courtesy of the Prince of Wales Museum of Western India, Bombay.)

millet was cultivated, we again have an adaptive factor within India, rising probably from the knowledge of cereal growing brought from the Borderlands.

It is in these more permanent settlements also that one can trace the old Borderlands traditions not only in pottery but in such customs as the making of bull figurines and the burial of the dead, complete with funerary furniture, in the vicinity of the houses (see p. 121, for example).

The long life of this cultural tradition—some two thousand years if our estimates are correct—suggests that a degree of isolation was present and that the life of these people was beautifully attuned to the demands of the environment. Yet it is significant that there is a strong suggestion that the practice of periodic wholesale burning of the stockade corrals became increasingly less common. This, plus a shift toward ash or earth stockade walls topped by thorn hedges and away from wooden-post stockades, indicates perhaps that wood had become scarce. Cattle dung became, as it is today, a valuable source of fuel and is used in Indian village life from the foothills of the Himalayas to Cape Comorin.

✳ The Overall Pattern

UP TO THIS POINT such cultural entities as that of Burzahom, the eastern Indian ground- and chipped-stone industries, and the pastoralists of the southern Deccan can be said to be either culturally independent of or possibly earlier than the Harappan civilization. Each is reflective of an adaptation to a particular part of the subcontinental environment. Incomplete as our evidence is, we still have enough to prove that already the heterogeneity which is so characteristic of historical India was developing region by region.

These cultures are barely visible to us, since they are represented by limited excavations and surveys. However, in sum, they are part of the same pattern, the shift of food producers to areas where their methods were able to exploit local environments to the limits of the available technology. There was little elaboration possible for these small communities, and we are probably entirely correct in considering their social level as no higher than the simple tribal horizon. Kashmir, the southern Deccan, Assam, and the hills of Bihar, Orissa, and Bengal were on the fringe of regions where major developments in the evolution of village life and civilization were about to or already had taken place. Thus in isolation they lasted for considerable lengths of time with little change, and it is quite possible that even today the traditions and indeed aspects of this way of life have survived to color the subcontinental scene.[21]

APPROXIMATE DIMENSIONS OF ASHMOUND SITES
IN VARIOUS DISTRICTS OF MYSORE AND ANDHRA PRADESH
(*after Allchin, 1963*)

BELLARY DISTRICT

Kupgal[1]—*ca.* 180′ × 180′ × 8′–15′

Kupgal[2]—*ca.* 150′ × 150′ × 10′

Sanganakallu— ?

Halakundi[1]—*ca.* 180′ × 180′ × ?

Halakundi[2]—*ca.* 90′ × 90′ × ?

Gadiganur[1] } "Small ashmounds, neither of any
Gadiganur[2] } great height" p. 50

Sanaraspur—75′ × 55′ × 5′–6′

Lingadahalli—*ca.* 762′ in circumference

Kanchagara Bellagallu—210′ × 120′

Kurikuppa   ?

Suguru—"A small flat mound"—p. 51

Kakhalla   ?

Gudikallu—"A large cinder mound"—p. 51

Nimbapur—135′ × 54′ × 10′–14′

Kudatini (Budigunta)—150′ × 100′ × 25′–30′

---

[21] The Bhils, for example, still eat dog. Dog eating is found in both Northern and Eastern Asia. Note also Allchin's feeling as quoted on pp. 323–324.

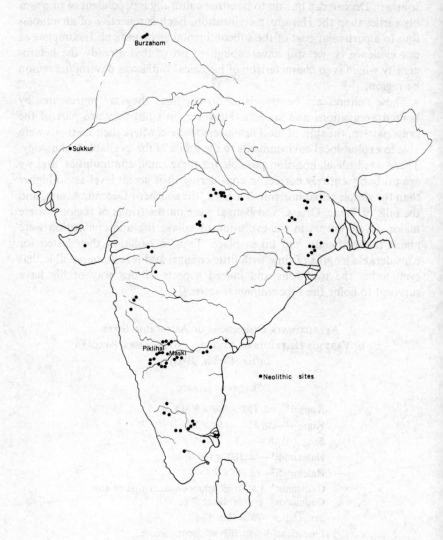

MAP 24 *Sites of "neolithic" type.*

RAICHUR DISTRICT

Hire Benakal   ?
Chikka Benakal   ?
Sirupur—50′ × 30′ × 1′
Piklihal (ashmound)   ?
Lingsugur   ?
Yergunti   ?
Kurkundi   ?
Wandalli—200′ × 150′ × 22′
Gaudur—325′ × 250′ × 10′
Manvi   ?
Sirwar   ?
Budinni   ?

MAHBUBNAGAR DISTRICT

Utnur—*ca.* 200′ × 200′ × 3′–10′
Machanpalli[1]—100′ × 50′ × 5′
Machanpalli[2]—100′ × 50′ × 5′
Talmari-Kutukuru track—280′ × 250′ × 20′

GULBARGA DISTRICT

Benkanhalli—46′ × 16′ × 7′
Thanmandi Thanda—100′ × 100′ × 15′
Hanamsagar-Kodekap path—150′ × 150′ × 15′
Mallur—20′ × 20′ × 5′
Ranjan Kullur   ?
Kupi   ?

X

The Fringes of Civilization and the Spread of Village Life to South India

THE ADVENT OF THE HARAPPAN CIVILIZATION in both the Ganges Valley and up to the flanks of the Malwa plateau and the Deccan proper had an immense effect. This effect was in some contrast to such developments as the so-called Deccan Neolithic described in the previous chapter. The Harappan civilization was after all the bearer of sophisticated technological advances in metallurgy, architecture, agriculture, animal husbandry, transport, and the like. At the same time the degree to which any of these advances were accepted or diffused would of course depend on a number of factors, including their utility to the receivers and that intangible, their social acceptability. The cultures which were either contemporaneous with or later than the Harappan civilization east and south of its settlements were themselves derived from pre-Harappan cultures or originated in a strange compact of Harappan, indigenous, and late Iranian traits. The researches of the past two decades have given us evidence as to the existence of these cultures, but little has been done on the processes which created them. They are remarkable in their demonstration of hybrid backgrounds and enduring traditions.

✳Ahar, Gilund—The Banas Culture

IN SOUTHEAST RAJASTHAN near the beautiful Rajput city of Udaipur is the site of Ahar, where a characteristic culture of the region was first identified.[1] This is a mountainous area from which on the east flow the rivers Banas and Chambal. It is an important region in the history of Rajasthan but one of comparative isolation.

Two periods are defined at the site. The earlier (I) is divided into three phases and represents the prehistoric occupation. It is dated by the radio-carbon method as ranging from approximately 1800 B.C. to 1200 B.C.[2] Period II is also divided into three phases and contains northern black polished ware (IA) and red ware of Rang Mahal type (IB, C). These are of early historical time.

The characteristic house of Period I was made of mud brick set in a foundation of stone. In the mud of the walls nodules of quartz were mixed as a strengthening factor. The houses were sizable, thirty feet by fifteen feet in one case.

Agriculture is evidenced by the presence of manos and metates and husks of an as yet unidentified cereal. Deer were killed for food, and there is little evidence for domesticated animals. Stone tools are completely absent, and the suggestion has been made that copper was the tool-making medium. Indeed not only are a variety of copper objects (flat axes, bangles, rings) found but there are good sources of local copper, one reason for the historical attraction of the area. Incised decorated terra-cotta whorls or beads are among the clay objects found.

The pottery has variety, and the workmanship is quite sophisticated.

The early Aharians manufactured a variety of pottery fabrics and forms for the manifold household uses. . . . In this the so-called painted black-and-red ware played only one of the roles; while its delicately painted dishes and bowls, some on stands, and small water vessels (lotas) served as "table" ware for eating and drinking, bright red-slipped vessels, some exquisitely decorated on the neck and shoulder, with cut, incised and appliqué ornaments, provided various sizes of storage vessels. But this was not all. There were at least two or three parallel series in black, blotchy grey, tan and coarse red ware. Almost all these were ornamented in one way or another up to the shoulder or the belly, leaving the lower portion coarse. In fact this part of the vessels was intentionally 'rusticated' or made coarse by the application of sand, because probably the vessels were kept buried in the ground or because they were meant for rough use as cooking. Often these vessels are thinner from belly downward, and so their top-heavy, beautifully decorated upper portion alone have survived, leaving us numerous fragments of the former.

[1] R. C. Agrawal, *Indian Archaeology, A Review*, 1954–55, pp. 14–15.
[2] Four dates from Agrawal, 1966 (see Appendix E).

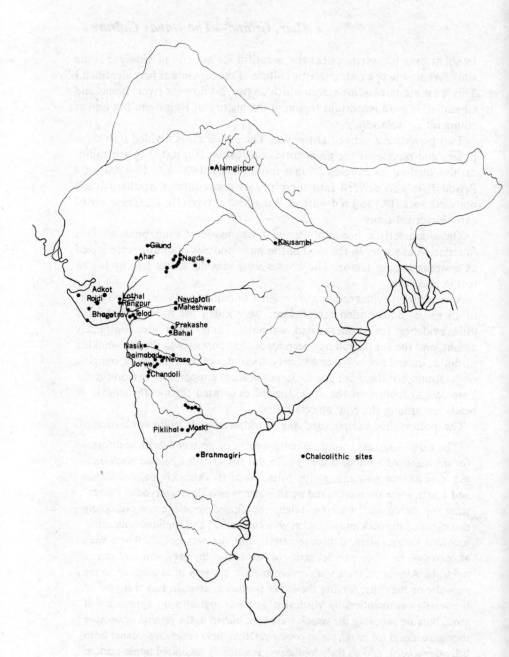

MAP 25 *Location of certain sites of "chalcolithic" type.*

Two or three other wares completed the pottery ensemble of the Aharians. The first is a stoneware-like fabric made of compact, extremely well levigated clay and well fired, so that the sherds give a metallic sound when struck. Lightly slipped in tan, orange, chocolate or similar hues, it has fine burnished, at times even polished surfaces. So far, only fragments of dishes or plates with slightly inturned rim and cut or grooved below the rim and plates with stepped outgoing rim and stems of dishes-on-stand have been found from the lower levels. It is possible that all these form part of a vessel such as dish-on-stand, or of a dish which rested on an exquisitely made stand. Whatever it is, this pottery is quite distinctive and might have had an exotic or foreign origin. Such certainly is true in the case of a thin buff ware and cream-slipped painted in crimson blackish red. Some 30 sherds of both these, probably belonging to two vessels occur, again in the lower levels. It was formerly believed that the white-slipped ware figures only in the top layer of the Chalcolithic, but this view has now to be given up. Secondly, the buff ware recalls similar ware from Amri in Sind and Nal in Baluchistan and farther afield in Iran, rather than that of Navdatoli (which might be imitation). The Ahar buff ware is indeed an import.[3]

Sankalia's suggestion that a pre-Harappan element exists among the pottery types again emphasizes the probability that much of western India was occupied by food-producing cultures before the advent of the Harappan civilization.

At Gilund, some forty-five miles to the northeast of Udaipur, another food-producing culture of the same type as at Ahar has been identified recently.[4] Here two mounds located side by side were investigated. The eastern mound turned out to be of historical time, but the western was only occupied during the prehistoric period. Four structural phases of this period were defined by the excavators. The earliest was of a rather amorphous structural complex in which long walls of some two and a half to three feet in thickness ran north-south in parallel lines. These were joined on the south by east-west walls which in turn were the starters for more parallel north-south walls. The space between the parallel walls was filled in with sand, and some of the wall surfaces were plastered. This structure is so monumental and formal in aspect that it undoubtedly represents something other than a mere habitation.

The next subphase produced a mud-brick house, while the third included five circular or oblong pits some three to four feet in diameter. These were brick with white clay worked with sand. The purpose is unknown, but storage is suggested.

Probably to these middle subphases can be assigned a structural complex which consists of:

3 Sankalia, 1962, p. 189.
4 *Indian Archaeology, A Review*, 1959–60, pp. 41–46 (excavations headed by B. B. Lal).

A main wall, running west–east and then turning north-northeast, with a cross-wall on the inner side and a parallel wall, following the alignment of the main wall, on the exterior. Made of kiln-burnt bricks (14 × 6 × 5″) over a stone-cobble foundation and having a width of 1 ft. 10 in., the main wall (including) the return was traced, without reaching the end on either side, to a length of 36 ft. It had a hard reddish plaster, about an inch in thickness, consisting of sand and clay mixed with 15 per cent of lime. The cross-well on the interior, measuring only 1 ft. 2 in. in width, was traced to a length of 7 ft. 6 in. The outer wall running parallel to the main wall at a distance of 4 ft. 6 in., was marked by two openings, one of which, measuring 3 ft. in width, provided entry into the complex in the form of a downward earthen ramp consolidated with rubble-pitching. The outer opening was not fully excavated, but it seemed to follow the general pattern of the former. At three places along the main wall, near the junction of the main wall and the cross-wall and near the inner face of the outer wall close to the first referred-to entrance were noticed charred remains of wooden posts.[5]

The last subphase evidenced less well contructed buildings, the walls being made up of "large Kankar-nodules and mud, mud-faced externally with stone rubble, mud and burnt brick-bats, and mud-bricks." Evidence provided by the impressions of split bamboo and reeds in chunks of rammed earth indicated an earthen roof over or mixed with a bamboo and reed understructure.

The stone industry was limited and of the blade-tool type and included microliths. Fragments of copper were recovered, but there was apparently an absence of ground-stone axes or adzes. However, manos and metates of ground stone as well as sling pellets (?) are evidenced. Beads in agate, chalcedony, steatite, and terra cotta were found. Terra-cotta animal figurines include bulls and a series of what the excavator calls "gamesmen" —chessmenlike figures with animal heads.

The pottery included the black and red painted ware known at Ahar but found throughout Gilund. However, there are burnished gray and red wares, plain and painted black wares. A small number of black on cream painted potsherds along with the black on red pottery were found in the upper levels. This is especially interesting, since the cream painted wares are found to the south in the Deccan at Navdatoli in the lower levels there (Periods I and II—see p. 340), while the black on red ware is also known at that site in the lowermost level of Period III. Dish-on-stand forms in the red and black-on-red ware suggest Harappan contacts or influences. Cut spout vessels of the plain red ware, strap-handled vases in the gray ware, and high-necked jars suggest Iranian types of the general gray ware family known in the late third millennium B.C. to the mid-first millennium B.C. Finally, a fine polychrome ware (black, red, and white on red) was found only in the lower levels.

[5] *Indian Archaeology, A Review*, 1959–60, p. 43.

Gilund and Ahar represent well-established village communities lying just outside the sphere of direct influence of the Harappan civilization. The presence of microliths, the hint of pre-Harappan origins for some of the pottery, the large houses built according to a local style, the apparent emphasis upon copper as a major tool-making material, the peculiar and characteristic pottery types are demonstrative of influences as far-flung as the central Deccan and northeastern Iran or Seistan.[6] All add up to a localized situation of sufficient cultural stability to stand on its own in spite of the integration with the Harappan styles of cultures lying to the south, west, and north. There is a suggestion here that the large houses with their sizable hearths were the homes of extended or multiple families.[7] This is in contrast to the Harappan civilization with its habitations apparently constructed in order to house various classes or specialists. Though the radio-carbon dating and the comparative stratigraphy indicate that these villages were in existence at a period when the Harappan civilization was waning, there appears to be little doubt that not only are these cultures not derived from the Harappans but they are representative of non-Harappan cultures peculiar to the subcontinent. Their derivation, like that of the pastoralists of the Karnatak, was most probably ultimately the food-producing cultures of prehistoric Iran. However, it is obvious that just as the pastoral cultures of the Deccan differ from these village cultures of southern Rajasthan, so today do the traditional forms of the same regions differ in the modern situation. The amazing thing about the phenomenon is not that there is a common origin behind these cultures but that their expression of regional variation, of differing tradition, is already apparent in the second millennium B.C. The Harappan civilization diffused to the fringe of other cultural traditions, and it is no wonder that at such sites as Lothal, Rangpur, and in the Banas culture sites, we are witness to the integration of influences from the subcontinent with the classic Harappan.[8] Traces of the pottery of these Rajput cultures can be followed across Malwa to Bihar and perhaps to Bengal, where it appears in Burdwan at the site of Rajar Dhipi.[9] At Nagda on the Chambal River sizable structures, one of which indicates possible fortification, were found on the lowest levels there (Period I).[10] The pottery associated with this occupation

---

[6] A gray ware of a type common to northeastern Iran at Hissar II–III is found at the site of Nad-i-Ali near Chakansur in Afghan Seistan; see Fairservis, 1961.

[7] Cf. Sankalia, 1963, p. 190.

[8] Agrawal, 1966, however, sees strong Harappan elements at Gilund and includes among them the terra-cotta bulls, burnt brick structures, gamesmen, and possibly the inverted firing of pottery. We must await further study and publication of the material. These cultures are known now as the Banas culture, with Ahar and Gilund as the type sites.

[9] Sankalia, 1963, Fig. 74 C.

[10] *Indian Archaeology, A Review*, 1955–56, pp. 11–19.

was most characteristically a handsome black on red or cream painted ware, the motifs of which ranged through an astonishing variety of subjects from geometrics to animals and plants—all executed with a fine and imaginative skill. The style recalls the exuberance and indeed some of the painted motifs and vessel forms of pre-Harappan Kalibangan, to which it may be ultimately related (see Fig. 52). This ware is known generally as Malwa ware.[11] A blade-tool industry at Nagda includes special serrated or saw-toothed blades probably used as sickles and microliths.

✳ Maheshwar, Navdatoli, and the Malwa Cultural Complex

IT IS TO THE SOUTH on the middle course of the Narbada in Madhya Pradesh that the best archaeological demonstration of the character of these settlements has been obtained. The sites of Maheshwar and Navdatoli consist of two mound complexes located opposite one another at a ford used immemorially as a link between north and south. Of the two sites Maheshwar, on the north bank, evidences little of the late prehistoric occupation, being principally an area first fully settled shortly before the time of Christ and until the present being a place of much historical inhabitation.[12] Navdatoli, on the other hand, was the seat of a large prehistoric settlement.

This site is actually made up of four mounds no more than ten feet in height. The earliest settlement was upon the black soil common to the region (see p. 54). Sankalia, the excavator, suggests that this may mean the clearance of the jungle, which almost certainly caused the blackness of the soil, the result of the weathering of the original alluvium.[13] This initial occupation, which starts around 2000 B.C., was of a village which at one phase or another probably contained some fifty to seventy-five houses, or about two hundred inhabitants, as the excavator suggests. The houses were round, square, or rectangular and were of post and screen construction. As at Ahar, the houses were spacious, one being 40 feet by 20 feet, though smaller huts, probably storehouses, were found amid the larger. In a later phase (II) the main houses were smaller, 10 feet by 8 feet, suggesting a

---

[11] Sankalia (1963, p. 197) has noted similiarities also at Sothi.
[12] The sequence there is as follows:
     PERIOD I—Microlithic—gap
          II—Central Indian Chalcolithic
          III—Northern Black Polished Ware—Iron Age
          IV—Early Medieval—dating ca. first to fifth century A.D.
[13] Sankalia, 1963, pp. 197–198. This description is based in part on H. D. Sankalia, B. Subbarao, and S. B. Deo's *Excavations at Maheshwar and Navdatoli 1952–53*, Poona-Baroda, 1958.

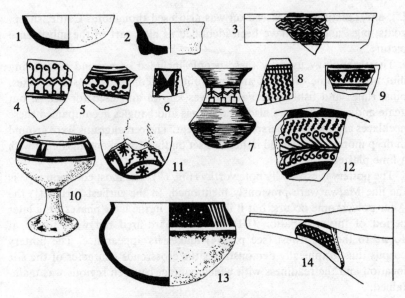

FIG. 69 *Pottery of Period III at Navdatoli (after Sankalia).*
1—*Coarse ware*
2—*Coarse ware*
3—*Carinated bowl with chocolate slip, black paint*
4—*Painted red ware or Malwa black on red*
5—*Painted red ware or Malwa black on red*
6—*Painted red ware or Malwa black on red*
7—*White-slipped ware*
8—*Painted red ware*
9—*Painted red ware*
10—*Painted red ware goblet*
11—*Painted red ware globlet (?) fragment*
12—*Painted red ware or Malwa black on red*
13—*Painted black and red ware*
14—*Channel-spouted painted red ware*

social shift probably from a single extended-family house to the smaller nuclear-family abodes. However, all the houses in all phases are close to each other. Occasionally between rows an open space, perhaps for bazaar purposes, was found.

These people were farmers, initially growing two kinds of wheat as a staple (*Triticum vulgare compactum* and *Triticum sp.*). In the second major phase (II) rice appears as another, though apparently limited, staple. Throughout the entire occupation legumes of all kinds were eaten. Five have been identified: lentil (*Lems culinaris Medikus*), black gram (*Phaseolus mungo*), green gram (*Phaseolus radiatus L.*), green peas (*Lathyrus sativus*

L.), and *Lathyrus sp.* Linseed oil was also used thoughout. Cattle, sheep, goats, pigs, and deer have been identified as also part of the subsistence picture.

The technology used by these people included compound tools using flint blades, some of which are "microlithic"; copper was used for axes, pins, rings, and fishhooks. Faïence was known and used for beads, but agate and carnelian were also used. Rings and bangles accompanied these necklaces as objects of personal adornment. The cereal grains were ground in deep mortars and baked in hearths set on the ground and plastered with a lime plaster.

The pottery is especially noteworthy (Fig. 69). The most common type is the fine Malwa ware previously mentioned. In the earliest period (I) the Ahar polychrome occurs, but it is not found in the later phases. In a later period of this occupation (III) the thin, hard-fired red ware found at Jorwe to the southwest (see p. 344) makes its appearance. The pottery corpus thus graphically demonstrates the crossroads character of the site location and the readiness with which contact between regions was maintained.

More provocative perhaps are white-slipped wares of Periods I and II which in some of their forms resemble vessels from Iran. This is true also of a teapot bowl form of the third period in the Malwa type which has a channel spout. A study of these wares of the third period at Navdatoli shows analogies to a ware called Londo in Baluchistan which can be dated probably to post-1000 B.C.[14] Carinated bowls of various kinds, the spiral or inverted hook design, incised and appliqué wares are notable parallels in this regard (Fig. 69).

Navdatoli, therefore, is certainly in the same cultural continuum as Ahar, Nagda, Gilund, and other sites of the north or, in other terms, what is called "the Malwa Chalcolithic." But in its latest period (III) it is clear that its position on a major trade route is bringing in new influences, presumably along the old Gujarat-Sind routes. Indeed, around 700 B.C. it would appear that traits of the Iron Age borne perhaps by newcomers from the Gangetic region via the Ujjain route ended the story of the old settlement, which by then was over a thousand years old.

✳ *Areas to the South*

ASPECTS OF THIS MALWA CULTURAL COMPLEX, at least as it is known at Navdatoli, are far-reaching in areas to the south. At Nevasa, on the Pravara River tributary of the Godavari River and close to the Western Ghats, a single phase of prehistoric occupation was found. (The depth of

14 B. de Cardi, (1951), pp. 63–75.

the deposit was about five feet.[15]) The evidence was for houses similar to those of Navdatoli. Most interesting and very common were child burials. The infant's body was placed in two urns placed mouth to mouth and apparently set into the floor of the houses. The very few adult burials recovered were also in the house floors. They were fully extended and had funerary furniture in the form of pottery and jewelry. Often these burials were somewhat fractionalized, and one adult skull was stored in a funerary urn. Child burials also contained funerary goods, including necklaces, bangles, and small vessels.

Examination of a few of these child burials revealed the possible presence of millet and a suggestion that both cattle dung and oil were used in the funerary rites.

Even more important, a string of copper beads in one burial demonstrated that silk was spun from cocoons on a cotton nep. Thus both fabrics are attested.[16]

The pottery is generally the Jorwe ware noted in Period III at Navdatoli. The copper and stone industries were also similar to those of the Navdatoli site.

At Daimabad, also on the Pravara, a sequence of importance for its comparison meaning has been determined:

The Chalcolithic deposits are naturally thick and divisible into three sub-periods. In Period I is discernible a meeting of the Brahmagiri I and Navdatoli I cultures, if the observations regarding the pink-slip painted pot are correct. The latter recalls similar slipped pottery from Prakash and Navdatoli. Other pottery is mainly handmade, decorated with incised and appliqué decorations. Lithic blades, terra cotta and other beads and an extended adult skeleton buried right in the house make up the remaining features of this phase or period. Period II is marked by increase in black-on-red pottery of Malwa type (one having a channel-spout) and designs, as well as in stone blade tools, terra cottas of a dog and a bull and a burial in a specially dug pit. In Period III Jorwe-Nevasa becomes supreme. It is also noted for the occurrence of two terra cotta human figures, a stone mace-head or ring-stone and remains of houses—circular or rectangular in plan. The floors of the houses were rammed with clay mixed with husk and plastered with lime. Burial in houses continued, but remarkable is the position of a skeleton surrounded by 14 post-holes indicating a canopy and 'lying-in-state before a burial.'[17]

15 *Indian Archaeology, A Review*, 1959–60, pp. 26–28; 1960–61, pp. 19–20. The site is called Ladmod locally.

16 Flax is also evidenced at a comparable time. Sankalia, 1963, p. 221; See also Deo and Ansari, 1965, pp. 195–201.

17 Sankalia, 1963, p. 203.

The lowest level at Nasik contains a blade-tool industry with microliths associated with Jorwe ware. This level, as is true at so many sites in the Deccan, lies below an occupation of the Iron Age represented by "Northern Black Polished Ware." At Jorwe a similar combination of blade-tool industry with microliths associated with the black-on-red Jorwe ware was found. The site, a series of mounds, was found to represent but one period. However, here six celts of "low grade bronze" were also recovered.

The site of Chandoli lies on the banks of the Ghod tributary of the Bhima River some thirty-odd miles northeast of Poona, and is south of Jorwe, Daimabad, and Nevasa. It represents a small village settlement much as do the more northerly sites of the Malwa complex. To this complex there are numerous ceramic, technological, and stylistic ties. However, of considerable interest are gray wares of the Central Deccan Neolithic as well as ground stone axes, and urn burials such as those of Tekkalakota. In effect we have in Chandoli a reflection of the integrative process which brought about the blend of the more advanced sedentary culture of the north with that of the south.[18]

To the north, at Bahal in the Girna Valley, as well as at Eran on the Bina, this culture type also is represented. It thus appears in its distribution to reach from Brahmagiri in Mysore-Karnatak to well along the Chambal River system in Malwa. In large part it is located in the hill country in the upper or middle reaches of valleys and near or upon major north-south trade routes, which of course accounts for the similarity of objects found. Surveys are revealing scores of sites now within this broad distribution. It marks as nothing else does the full-fledged advent of food production on the subcontinent proper. Within the time range of some twelve hundred or more years during which this culture was dominant, the Indian life in these areas became increasingly one of village oriented society and less and less the band or tribal social form speculated for Utnur. In the period not only were the villagers slowly changing their techniques of farming and building because of outside influence (diffusion of millet, bronze, cotton) but they were innovative in their own pragmatic way—so much so in fact that we may well credit them with the development of silk weaving, rice growing, and the techniques involved in using some of the legumes.

In spite of these advances, the fact that these cultures were relatively unchanged when Buddhism was already flourishing in the Ganges Valley demonstrates perhaps an innate conservatism that in future centuries was to characterize much of southern India. Paradoxically, then, as village life gained a surer foothold in the south because of innovation, it also spread a stability and love of tradition which contrasts with the north, where change was more rapid and tradition less meaningful.

18 See Deo and Ansari, 1965, for site description.

XI

The Vedic "Night"

THE STORY HAS BEEN REPEATED FOR MILLENNIA, sung in temples, chanted in halls, told by word and actions of how a warrior people came out of the vastness of inner Asia through the passes of the northwest to fall upon the fortified cities of India and to conquer: riding horse-drawn chariots, driving herds of cattle, sheep, and goats, worshipping cosmic deities like Indra of the thunder and Agni of the fire, sacrificing, quarreling, gambling, drinking, singing, dancing—the Rig-Veda account of the Aryan tribes is one of the oldest epics in the world. It is part of an oral tradition which lies at the heart of Hinduism. The Aryans were a pastoral people moving along routes already ages old, a people already affected by the sedentary world with which they were in contact even before arriving in India. They were organized into a rough class system headed by warrior chiefs whose rank was retained partially by accumulated wealth counted by herds and partially by prowess in battle. They spoke an Indo-European language and both by speech and cosmology were one with that group of pastoral nomads who inhabited the heart of the Eurasian continent in the early second millennium B.C. and whose later migrations so profoundly affected the ancient world.

After their conquest of the Punjab plain and the middle Ganges Valley, tradition has it that the settling-in process by which Aryan and non-Aryan people were integrated included the development and the change of the Aryan religious forms to more universal significance. The Brahmanas explained the meaning and form of Vedic ritual, while the Upanishads philosophized and speculated upon them. It would seem that these later treatises were aimed at reinforcing the Vedic beliefs and rituals, which time and new environments were changing, and also at converting non-Aryan and presumably indigenous people.

The Mahabharata records a split between these kingdoms of the Aryans and an internecine strife that was climaxed in an epic battle in the central Ganges Valley in which the gods and men of many lands fought to the death. Afterward the victors seem to have settled in, with the broad reaches of the peninsula and the lower Ganges Valley yet before them. The Ramayana, in turn, tells of the kidnapping of Rama's wife Sita by Ravanna, a demonic king of Lanka (Ceylon), and her eventual rescue by Rama, aided by his ally Hanuman, the monkey king.

These two epics illustrate the spread of an essentially Indian tradition to south and east. As with the previous diffusion of traits from the west—handaxes, microliths, pastoralism, agriculture, bronze, etc.—the initiating ethos was now Indianized, that is, while still related generically to its origin, given peculiar character and suitability by its Indian environment. Thus this *literary* evidence confirms in its way the archaeological evidence which we have viewed in previous chapters.

✳ Archaeological Evidence for the Aryans: The Copper Hoards?

WHEREAS THE LITERARY TRADITION describes the Aryans in great detail so that their culture, their chronicles, their movement stand out vividly, the archaeological evidence for them is scant. For a time people deliberately sought for traces of the Aryans among the sites of the north and indeed unearthed several reasonable candidates for Aryan occupation. Sir Mortimer Wheeler and Stuart Piggott both hypothesized that the walled cities attacked by the Aryan invaders were the walled cities of the Harappans,[1] a conclusion that has still not been entirely negated, for there seems to be little question that the long duration of such cities as Harappa and Mohenjo-daro placed them in a chronological position which would have made their late phases contemporary with the traditional date (1500 B.C.) for the beginning of the Aryan invasion. Robert von Heine-Geldern, an Austrian anthropologist of great perception, saw in the finds of single or hoards of bronze and copper tools the mark of the Vedic Aryan. Since some of the tool types (trunnion celt, a sword from Fort Munro, socketed

[1] Piggott, 1950, pp. 262–263 (note especially the excellent Chapter VII on the Aryans); R. E. M. Wheeler, 1947, p. 82.

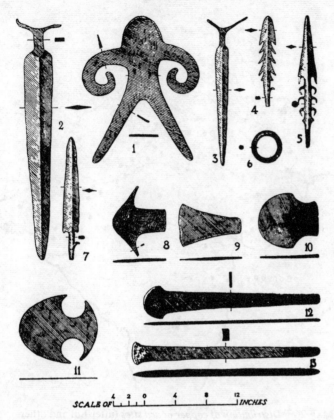

FIG. 70   *Characteristic artifacts from copper hoard sites* (after Gordon, 1958).

axes, adze-axes, etc.) have almost exact analogues in the Caucasus, south Russia, and Iran, the line of at least a trade from inner Asia to northern India could be drawn with some historical precision.[2] However, B. B. Lal has shown that the Fort Munro sword, the socketed axe, etc. (Fig. 70), with their West Asiatic analogues, form a group not found in the Gangetic basin and should not be confused with the copper hoards, which are. Further, the West Asian group is made of bronze, while the other group is solely of copper.[3] Thus the flat axes, shouldered celts, antennae sword, anthropomorphic figures, harpoons, and bar celts belong more character- istically to an Indian assemblage than any other. The shouldered celt of copper, in fact, resembles that of stone, and thus it is possible that an

[2] R. von Heine-Geldern, "Das Dravidaproblem," *Sonderabdruck aus dem Anzeiger der phil.-hist. Klasse der Österreichischen Akademie der Wissenschaften,* So. 9 (1964), Jahrgang.; also R. von Heine-Geldern, "Archaeological Traces of the Vedic Aryans," *Journal Indian Society of Oriental Art,* Vol. IV (1936), pp. 87–113.

[3] B. B. Lal, "Further Copper Hoards from the Gangetic Basin and a Review of the Problem," *Ancient India,* No. 7 (1951), pp. 20–39.

MAP 26 *Distribution of copper hoard sites* (after Lal and others).

eastern Indian locale is specified. As remarked in the previous chapter copper flat axes, antennae swords or daggers, and rings are found in more southerly areas (Jorwe [Chandoli], Navdatoli I, Rangpur II, Khurd [Rajasthan]). These are perhaps also demonstrative of an indigenous development. The critical point is that axes, swords, rings, and the like are basically the same the world over. Craftsmen motivated by local traditions and styles may vary both the form and the decoration and still retain the function. In fact, as we come up in time, local variation becomes increasingly apparent.

A tantalizing clue as to the possible stratigraphic placement of the copper hoards is provided by the fact that at two sites, Busauli and Rajpur Parsu in Uttar Pradesh, objects of the copper hoards have been found apparently as surface remains. At both these sites an ill-fired, thick, ocher-washed pottery was found but unassociated with the copper, though the implication of such an association is strong. This pottery is found in the earliest occupational levels (I) at Atranjikhera in the Etah district of

Uttar Pradesh and at the storied site of Hastinapura, which is situated some sixty miles to the northeast of Delhi (the place is referred to in the Mahabharata and other texts as the seat of the Kaurava kings).

Little more can be said about the copper hoards and their association except that all in all the evidence, slight as it is, suggests that they are, in type at least, unfamiliar in the West and that in fact they probably are part of an indigenous development perhaps derived ultimately from a technological advance diffused from the West but then more definitely Indianized. The bar celts, the harpoons, and the anthropomorphic figures are certainly unique to the subcontinent. The association at Navdatoli, Chandoli,[4] and Rangpur suggests, moreover, that there is a distinct possibility that these copper hoards may have been derived at least generically, from cultures contemporary with at least one phase of the Mature Harappan. In effect, then, the copper hoards would seem to have nothing to do with the Aryans (see App. K).

❋ Painted Gray Ware

A BETTER CASE CAN BE MADE for the makers of a pottery called the Painted Gray Ware. This is a fine wheel-made pottery, gray in color, thin in section, and painted with black or red geometric designs (Fig. 71). At Hastinapura Lal found this ware was a characteristic of his Period II. The remains of this period at the site include evidence for rice, wattle-and-daub huts, glass bangles, animal figurines (humped bull), copper arrowheads and other small objects, iron slag (in the later phases of the period), weights of jasper and chert, bone needles, and the bones of cattle, pigs, sheep, and horses. The settlement would seem to have been small and impermanent if we consider this evidence. Further, the presence of iron and of the horse in the middle Ganges Valley is especially interesting, since with little doubt their situation at Hastinapura is at least sixth century B.C. Period II is clearly separated from Period III by a flood level during which the place was abandoned. Period III is marked by the mud-brick houses of a substantial settlement. The characteristic pottery of the period is the famous Northern Black Polished Ware, which is also found far south in the Deccan (see p. 344).

Another suggestion of the affiliation of the Painted Gray Ware with the early Vedic accounts has been made by a remarkably perceptive series of investigations carried out by B. B. Lal. Since over thirty sites are mentioned in the Mahabharata or belonged to the stories by tradition, Lal systematically visited each one. His investigations were necessarily limited by time and other duties, but they nonetheless revealed that almost all the sites

---

[4] *Indian Archaeology, A Review*, 1953–54 and 1961–62 editions. This site, located on the bank of the Cod River in the Poona district of Maharashtra, produced a fine "tanged" handled dagger associated with Malwa ware.

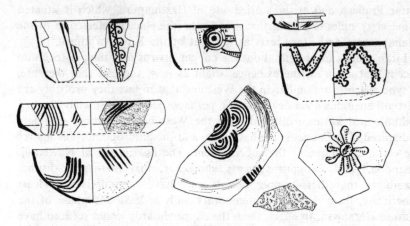

Fig. 71 *Painted Gray Ware from Hastinapura, Period II* (after Lal).

had in common the Painted Gray Ware in their lower levels.[5] These could be added to sites such as Ahichchhatra in the Bareilly district of Uttar Pradesh, where the ware was first found. Since Lal's original work, investigators have added to the list of sites, which now range as far east as Vaisali in Bihar in the Ganges Valley and south to Ujjain in central India. Significantly, the ware is found underlying such great urban centers as Kausambi near Allahabad, the embattled center of Panipat, and Mathura. The main area of occupation was apparently the eastern Punjab and the central Ganges Valley, with perhaps sections of northern Rajasthan. At Rupar, near the Harappan site of Kotla Nihang, the Painted Gray Ware occupation was found overlying at least two phases of the Harappan. The earlier of the two phases is of late Mature type, while the later is clearly Late Harappan. After this later phase the site was deserted for a period of unknown duration, at the end of which the Painted Gray Ware occupation began. In turn, this period was succeeded, as is common in the Gangetic region, by an occupation characterized by the Northern Black Polished Ware. No structures were found in the Painted Gray Ware levels, apparently a phenomenon of these levels everywhere. This again suggests the impermanence of the settlements. The stratigraphic relationship to the Harappan period is also confirmed at Alamgirpur near Delhi, the most easterly Harappan site presently known.[6] Here iron objects were found throughout the Painted Gray Ware occupation (II).[7] These objects

[5] B. B. Lal, "Excavations at Hastinapura and other Explorations in the Upper Ganga and Sutlej Basins 1950–52," *Ancient India*, Nos. 10–11 (1954–1955), pp. 5–152, especially pp. 138ff.

[6] On Rupar, see *Indian Archaeology, A Review*, 1953–54, pp. 6–7; for Alamgirpur, *Indian Archaeology, A Review*, 1958–59, pp. 50–55.

[7] The excavators thought the phase of this period represented at Alamgirpur was late.

include "a spear-head, barbed arrowhead, and nails or pins." Rice was also recovered as well as some terra-cotta toy animals (bull, ram), complete with wheels! The houses were undefinable, apparently because of their original construction by the wattle-and-daub method.

In all this, what evidence we do have suggests the arrival of not only a new cultural form to the Gangetic region, but perhaps a new people, since there appears to be very little indeed to connect this cultural assemblage with either the Harappan or the Malwa or earlier cultures.

At Sonpur, in the Gaya district of Bihar, excavations under the direction of Dr. B. S. Verma and Shri L. A. Narain of the Jayaswal Research Institute of Patna revealed three periods of occupation. The earliest (I) was subdivided into two phases, A and B. IA revealed a settlement in which crude red and black wares of uncertain affiliation occurred. The houses of the occupation were untraceable, and it is suggested that they may have been of wood. Subperiod IB had a fine wheel-made pottery typified by black, and black and red ware. Postcremation pit burials were apparently located among the houses, though the character of these, as in the previous subperiod, was undefinable. Most significant perhaps was the discovery of a large quantity of charred rice in a broken storage jar. The succeeding period (II) on the site is characterized by the appearance of the Northern Black Polished Ware and also by the continuance of the red and black ware of the previous period, indicating that the early period was not too remote in time from Period I.[8] The Sonpur excavations are important on two counts: first, they demonstrate that rice cultivation was a part of the subsistence base, undoubtedly its most essential part in the absence of wheat and barley, in those areas of the Gangetic Valley where it later flourished and where it forms the basis of the great urban development of which Buddhism was a part; second, there is the very real possibility that the relative primitiveness of the earliest culture revealed at Sonpur is indicative of impermanence of settlement possibly due the rapid movement of rice farming across the Gangetic plain—perhaps a kind of slash-and-burn technique was used. At Kausambi, Sharma found the walls of a palace whose earliest phase was constructed prior to the appearance of the Northern Black Polished Ware. These walls were "of random rubble, huge undressed stones being set in lime-mortar."[9] Associated with these walls were pottery types analogous to Navdatoli Phase III, Rangpur IIC and III, etc. "Some of the sherds bore paintings in black characteristic of the Central Indian Chalcolithic culture complex."

Such evidence as this, and it certainly will accumulate as the current pace of archaeological research in India continues, suggests that the Jumna-Gangetic region was originally settled—at least in one part, the southern—

---

[8] *Indian Archaeology, A Review*, 1960–61, pp. 4–5.
[9] *Ibid.*, 1962–63, pp. 32–33.

by food producers whose origins derived from the line of the pre-Harappan (Kalibangan, etc.) and Malwa (or Central Indian Chalcolithic) cultures, and that it was settled in its western and northern parts by the Harappans. Increasingly the Malwa cultural strain shifted eastward to the lower Gangetic Valley, probably because of successes in rice cultivation and possibly jowar that made their region attractive. Here they came in contact with primitive food gatherers and food-producers (of Southeast Asian kind), peoples still using microlithic tools or the eastern ground-stone axes, as indicated in the earlier levels at such sites of Uttar Pradesh as Rajghat and Prahaladpur and in West Bengal at Pandu-Rajar-Dhibi. The arrival of central Indian food-producing methods seems to have revolutionized the lower Gangetic region, for not only were there many small settlements scattered across the plain, cutting away the jungle, but in places such as Kausambi the roots of an urban center were seated, perhaps as a response to a need to trade for raw and manufactured materials. These centers were late in appearing and are in some contrast to the impermanent village communities whose pioneering efforts cleared the land for rice cultivation and whose first traces archaeology is just now recognizing.

In the Doab, however, the Harappan decline, as remarked previously (p. 311), may well have been due to too close an adherence to a traditional method of cultivation which became insupportable. The disappearance of Harappan settlements seems to have left the region relatively unoccupied for a time. What settlements are found there are represented by the ocher marked pottery and seem both primitive and widely scattered. The contemporary centers of activity were in the Deccan and more than likely in the lower Ganges Valley (see App. K).

The arrival of whatever people are represented by the Painted Gray Ware settlements caused a rather sudden rise in population and a widespread acknowledgment of the same cultural form. Temporary houses, iron tools and weapons, cattle, horses, wheeled toys, dice, glass are attested, as is the fact that the settlements cluster in the locale of the stories of the Mahabharata and the tradition of the Puranas. The evidence suggests a sudden arrival, considerable movement about, and a rather abrupt demise.

Are we then examining the evidence for an essentially pastoral people possessing a limited agriculture who are in a second stage of movement that brought them initially from inner Asia to the western Borderlands and the Punjab? Are these Painted Gray Ware assemblages related in some way to the Vedic account?

❋ Post-Harappan Remains—The Punjab, Sind, the Northwest Frontier

THE ANSWER MIGHT BE SOUGHT among the post-Harappan remains of the Punjab, Sind, the northwest frontier area, and Baluchistan. These remains fall into two general categories: those, such as the Jhukar of Sind and

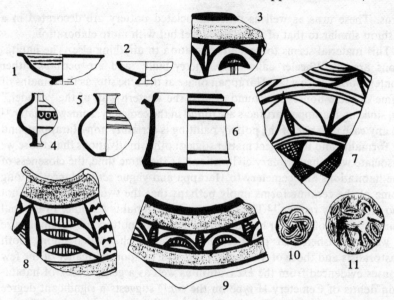

FIG. 72 *Pottery (1–9) and seals (10–11) characteristic of the Jhukar "culture" of the Indus River Valley.*

Cemetery H at Harappa in the Punjab, which seem to have a generic relationship of some kind with the previous Harappan civilization; and those which represent new influences or new cultural forms.

For the first category little can be said. Casal feels that the Jhukar as he revealed it at Amri (see p. 302) is simply a late manifestation of the Harappan there rather than a new cultural successor, which idea has been expounded previous to Casal's work. Indeed an examination of the Jhukar material, scant as it is, would seem to confirm Casal's idea.[10]

Cemetery H lies to the south of the "citadel" at Harappa. Here in two distinct levels a large number of burials were found. The lower level (II) contained slightly flexed burials, some of which may have been fractional. The funerary furniture consisted of a fine variety of black on red pottery; characteristic forms in this ceramic corpus are pedestal-footed vessels and dish lids. The latter are particularly striking, since they are handsomely painted with motifs that include human beings, plants, birds, bulls, fish, all rather stiff and formal (Fig. 65). Level I, the later, contains urn burials of infants and fractional burials of adults, the latter also in part placed in

[10] Besides Casal's Amri report an examination of the Jhukar material from Chanhudaro (MacKay, 1943, esp. Pls. XL to XLVIII) shows little that would not be regarded as of Harappan derivation. The Jhukar does not contain the characteristic Harappan seals and the Jhukar pins with curled heads, the socketed axe (Pl. LXXII) are non-Harappan, but such traits seem to be obviously the result of later influence and usages rather than of a significant cultural change.

urns. These urns as well as other associated pottery are decorated in a fashion similar to that of the earlier level but with more elaboration.

This material seems to bear little relation to anything else. The habitations are, as Wheeler calls them, "jerry-built" and are perhaps either contemporary with a late Harappan phase at the type site, as the remains of some of these houses are found against the western wall of the "citadel," or, since no Harappan artifacts are found in the cemetery, somewhat later.[11] In any case the style of the pottery painting is certainly non-Harappan, and its formality and the subject matter suggest other motivations than those we associate with that primary civilization. At the same time, the closeness of the habitations and cemetery to Harappa and vague resemblances among some of the ceramic forms imply perhaps that the two cultures were not too temporally remote.[12] The Cemetery H material is a riddle. Fractional burial, the use of urns for burials, and perhaps the pottery motifs emphasize a well-established cult practice, a practice which occurs among both pastoralists and those of a sedentary life. The temporary quality of the few houses evidenced from the excavation as well as a general lack of habitation debris of Cemetery H type on the site[13] suggests a significant degree of impermanence. Therefore, it is not impossible that the people of Cemetery H are representative of new settlers perhaps from beyond the Khyber. For the moment, the case must rest with that possibility.[14]

In the Punjab one naturally turns to the northwest frontier when seeking evidence for the routes taken by invaders, a part of the second category of investigation. Generally speaking, the sites so far excavated in this broad region evidence little that is clearly pre-sixth century B.C.[15] Recently

11 Cf. Sir M. Wheeler, 1962b, p. 56.

12 A Swedish expedition under the direction of Hanna Ryth has excavated the site of Rang Mahal in Bikaner, Rajasthan, not far from Kalibangan. The ware, a black on red painted ware, found at that site has a wide distribution in western India. It can be dated to about the time of Christ. It bears a resemblance to Harappan pottery and may well represent the survival of that tradition, which by the way may still survive in modern wares. Some scholars see also some typological ties to the Cemetery H ceramics, a fact that, if proven, might help in relating the material. Cemetery H ceramics are known from Bahawalpur (Ratha Theri, Lurewala). Trihni ware, a black on red painted pottery found in the Lake Manchhar area, is also apparently of that or the Rang Mahal tradition.

13 Perhaps due to the original destruction of the place for a railroad bed in the nineteenth century.

14 There is also the consideration of the Incinerary Pot phase at Fort Sandeman (p. 147).

15 The earliest levels at Bhir Mound at Taxila are perhaps sixth to fifth century B.C. Sir J. Marshall, A Guide to Taxila, Department of Archaeology in Pakistan, Cambridge University Press, Cambridge, 1960, p. 4.

Wheeler's excavation at Charsadda near Peshawar may have reached levels no more than a century or two earlier than Alexander's invasion in the fourth century B.C. Sir M. Wheeler, 1962a.

excavations carried out by the Italians in Swat[16] have produced remains which suggest to the excavators "that the material of Swat has points of contact with Iranian production, and especially with that of Northeastern Iran; it seems to us particularly close to the ceramic production of the locality of Tepe Hissar IIB." Since that level of the Iranian site can be dated at least as early as the first quarter of the second millennium B.C., it is obvious that the Swat sites have a great importance to the problem of the post-Harappan occupation of the Gandharan plain. The sites are cemeteries found at these localities: Buthara II, Katelai I, Loebanr I. All these share the same characteristics.

The burial tombs consist of two small chambers, one above the other. The upper chamber (*ca.* 2 to 2½ meters square by 2 meters deep) was generally empty. The lower chamber, separated from the upper by stone slabs, was smaller and contained the human remains with accompanying funerary furniture. The burials were either inhumation, in which case the corpse was placed on its side (N-S) in a flexed position, or cremation, probably after fractionalizing. At Katelai not only was a portion of the cemetery there devoted to child burial but in the midst of the necropolis two complete skeletons of horses were recovered.

The pottery generally is either red or gray, wheel-made and burnished or polished, and consists of a number of forms (Fig. 73), pedestal goblets, some hourglass-shaped, and a floral-like vessel being particularly striking.

[16] C. S. Antonini, "Preliminary Notes on the Excavation of the Necropolises found in Western Pakistan," *East and West*, Vol. XIV, Nos. 1–2, (1963), pp. 13–25.

FIG. 73   *Clay objects from the necropolises of Swat* (after Antonini, 1963).

Decoration consists of simply incising, but occasionally holes are made that suggest a human face. A jar cover has a handle shaped like a horse. Flattish figurines, usually of human females, with incised, punctate, and appliqué features were also found. Metal objects consisted of bronze or copper pins with flat or pyramidal heads, a harpoon, knives, and other blades, one of which is leaf-shaped with three central grooves and has a circular disk as a base. Gold circular earrings, silver or iron leaves, and two iron (?) spearheads complete the list of metal objects found. Beads of carnelian, chalcedony, and glass, spindle whorls, a stone macehead, a group of bone discs, and a pierced pendant (a bracelet) were among the other objects recovered with the human remains.

Ahmad Hasan Dani of the University of Peshawar has recently extended the range of these grave "people" first identified in Swat. He has found evidence for them in Dir (Balambat, Timargarha, Ziarat), in Bajaur (Inayat Qila) and in Mardan (Panjpir, Jamalgarhi). He has also found evidence of them in the Indus River valley to the east of Swat (Gorband). He has termed this complex the "Gandhara Grave Culture." Based on both typology and a limited stratigraphy he has divided the material into three periods, the latest of which is earlier than the Achaemenid Persian occupancy (or conquest) of the Gandhara Plain (late sixth century B.C.). On the basis of the grave types the three periods are defined:

PERIOD I—Complete burial with copper
PERIOD II—Cremation and burial with copper
PERIOD III—Fractional and multiple burial with copper and iron

The people of these periods apparently placed their settlements on the alluvium and near to the foothills of the river valleys. Dani suggests that the hills provided pasturage for their cattle. They also had the horse. They practiced some agriculture, and circular and rectangular storage rooms have been found. In general, the grave furniture is similar to that found in Swat though there are distinct period differences, especially in ceramics. The whole is dominated by gray and red wares: In this Dani sees the Italian material as fitting to his Periods II and III. Stacul who analyzed the Swat finds also divided that material into three periods and made his latest period contemporary with Wheeler's lowest levels at Charsada (sixth to fourth centuries B.C.).[17]

Jettmar has produced evidence that Dani's Period III may well be of seventh to sixth century B.C. date. This is based on a comparison of a three-holed cheek piece of iron found by Dani with similar ones found in Soviet Central Asia.[18] A recent radio-carbon date for Dani's Period I

[17] Stacul, "Preliminary Report on the Pre-Buddhist Necropolis in Swat," *East and West*, Vol. XVI (1966), pp. 37–79.
[18] K. Jettmar, "An Iron Cheek-piece of a Snaffle Found at Timargarha," *Ancient Pakistan*, Vol. III (1967), pp. 203–209.

(3380±60 years, Heidelberg) places that period in the late second millennium.[19]

Thus continuity of occupation is attested for an agricultural people who had the horse and cattle and who lived in and about the Gandhara plain for almost a thousand years. Their connections to Central Asia and Iran are definite, though of what character we still do not know.

There is a vague resemblance in the pottery to that of the Jhangar assemblage of Sind. Jhangar is post-Harappan at Chanhu-daro.[20] What is known of it is scant. The Jhangar occupation was apparently of short duration, the buildings of the time being no more than huts of reeds. The pottery which represents it is black or gray in color and is often incised. A linked group of three vessels or a triform vessel has a counterpart in a painted red ware found at Shahi Tump in Makran. The triad vessel from Swat may also be a distant relative of this ceramic habit.

We may also remark a possible link between the urn burial custom of Swat and Cemetery H at Harappa. A corrugated stem of a pedestal vessel is found in the Painted Gray Ware level at Hastinapura,[21] and the use of terra-cotta disks at both sites, perhaps the mutual presence of copper pins, and certain bead forms suggest a course for future investigation.

The Gandhara Grave Culture is a good candidate for a representative of the "Aryans." Horses, horse furniture, contacts with Inner Asia, suggestion of high capability in metallurgy, etc., plus the chronology, and indeed the direction given in the ancient literary accounts, make such candidacy viable. However, it is a candidacy only since the archaeological work in this important region is only just now coming into its own in Dani's capable hands.

The literary evidence, as B. B. Lal among others has shown, is there. The Rig-Veda, the earliest account, tells of the coming of new people to the northwest; the Mahabharata stories record the movement to the middle Ganges Valley; the Ramayana is the final episode, which sees Bengal, Orissa, and Ceylon within the geographic bounds of the Vedic tradition however it is defined. Broadly reviewed, this literary trail is a good one.

Yet the Aryan invasion is a literary account. It was probably not an invasion of hordes of Central Asian nomads who in great and overwhelming waves swept from the steppes to the Doab. It is more likely that Indo-European-speaking pastoral tribes of a variety of traditions and probably of a diversity of ethnic backgrounds gradually infiltrated the fertile plain from Peshawar to the Punjab. This pattern of movement is more character-

---

[19] A detailed account of Dani's work on the Gandhara Grave Complex can be found in *Ancient Pakistan*, Vol. III (1967), pp. 1–407.

[20] MacKay, 1943, Pls. XXXIX–XL.

[21] Lal, 1954–1955, p. 50, Pl. XXX.

istic of pastoral peoples than the great migrations historians are prone to dramatize. As pastoralists they may have established traditional seasonal routes but at least initially were unlikely to settle in large permanent sedentary settlements. Thus their traces archaeologically are less likely to be in terms of habitation and more likely to be necropoli or even isolated monuments. In the thickly settled Punjab of today traces of old campgrounds probably have long since disappeared, and it is only the more permanent settlements of a later stage which will be found.

The traditional story of the Aryan migration into India comports, however, with the record of such movements elsewhere in Asia during the second millennium B.C.—especially in its latter half. Other regions of the Borderlands present some evidence bearing upon this protohistoric period of relative unrest.

The region south of the Khyber Pass is hilly, relatively barren, and crossed by routes that follow the courses of rivers flowing generally east-west. Some of these rivers, such as the Kurram and the Gomel, are mentioned in the Rig-Veda, and their valleys were apparently under the control of some of the early Vedic groups.[22] The Gomel is a particularly important route, connecting southern Afghanistan, Ghazni, and the Zhob River valley of northern Baluchistan with the Indus plain and the southern Punjab. The country today is the homeland of the Pathans, some of whom, like the Wazirs and Mahsud, were particularly aggressive in the days of the British Raj. The region is rather poorly explored archaeologically. Sir Aurel Stein found a number of sites in his surveys there in 1927, especially in the vicinity of the towns of Tank and Bannu. These, however, are principally of Buddhist affiliation. Both stamped and mold-made or impressed wares as well as those ceramic types known in Rajasthan at Rang Mahal were found, but nothing to suggest earlier occupation.

At Moghul Ghundai, near Fort Sandeman and south of the Gomel, a series of low stone cairns was found on the hillside above the prehistoric site (see p. 148) by Sir Aurel Stein.[23] Many of these cairns contained fragments of human bones, possibly cremated, plus coarse whitish pottery and some iron objects. This last group includes corroded knives, spearheads, leaf-shaped arrowheads and in one case a triangular barbed arrowhead, along with a silver bangle and a little bronze "cosmetic" jar. A surface find of some small bells, jade and carnelian beads, was made by a local villager apparently amid the cairns. A bronze ring cut intaglio suggested to the excavator Kushan or Gupta workmanship, while an appliqué-decorated vessel was reminiscent of the "Hellenistic." In the Quetta Valley a cairn site was found south of Quetta cantonment. In it were located a variety of iron and bronze arrowheads, some of which are identical with those of

[22] Stein, 1929, pp. 46–47.
[23] *Ibid.*, pp. 46–49.

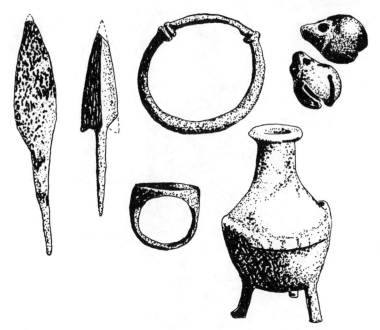

FIG. 74   *Metal objects from the cairns at Moghul Ghundai (Zhob).*

Moghul Ghundai.[24] The presence of the so-called "Ring Ware" in association with the cairn would date the material to a period certainly later than the birth of Christ (see Table 8). Stein's suggestion of Kushan or Gupta derivation for the cairns of Moghul Ghundai seems, therefore, to be near the truth. A number of scholars have referred to the finds at Moghul Ghundai as possibly having something to do with the Aryan movement into the subcontinent.[25] It would seem that the candidacy of the site is slight in view of the above. Comparable material, by the way, does not appear at Mundigak until Period VII.[26]

At Mundigak Period V, which succeeds the climactic period of the prehistoric occupation (see p. 133), shows in its ceramics and some of the building that the older traditions were still known, but Casal, the excavator, finds in the new ceramics which characterize the period analogues to ceramics identified in Ferghana in Central Asia—especially Chust—and would therefore suggest the coming of a new people from that region. The principal structure unearthed was a massive public building of unknown function. It was approached by a long ramp which presumably

[24] Fairservis, 1956, Pl. 52, also p. 350.
[25] Sir M. Wheeler, 1962b, p. 99.
[26] Casal, 1961, Fig. 140: 26–28.

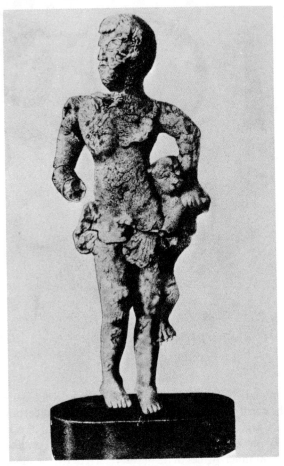

PLATE 51   *Bronze statue of Hercules found in the Quetta Miri in the nineteenth century. A rare photograph. The piece has since disappeared.*

led to an inner court or building mounted on a platform. The impression
one has is of a sedentary culture but with new traditions motivated by
trade and some human movement; there is nothing, however, in the known
remains to truly define its character.

Period VI marks a gradual abandonment of the Kandahar site. Interestingly, carinated bowls and vessels with steep sides known in Period V
continue. These types have a wide distribution in areas to the south. Iron
also appears in this period.

Period VII was marked by a fine granary (?) on top of Mound A and a
general revival of settled life at Mundigak. Casal would date this period to
the first half of the first millennium B.C. If this is so, the preceding periods

mark the time range in which the Vedic period began. There is little at Kandahar to indicate the changes which may have occurred. Perhaps it was too out of the way, too localized. In the period of the Achaemenid Persian kings the Kandahar region was known as Arachosia and was part of the empire in name only, since recalcitrant tribes of the surrounding mountains made travel through there difficult. In fact, the Great Trunk Road led north of the Koh-i-Baba and then turned south along routes commonly used today to connect northern Afghanistan with Kabul and Peshawar. Kandahar in those days had minimum importance. Perhaps the Mundigak sequence demonstrates this. Certainly surveys in the region as far south as the borders of the Registan district have produced nothing which shows flourishing occupation here after the major prehistoric occupation until Partho-Sassanian times.[27]

The survey of the region of Quetta-Pishin shows a definite falling off of village sites after the climax marked by Damb Sadaat III. We can conclude that the valley was still inhabited but like Mundigak increasingly less so. Again there is no clear evidence for the arrival of new people. An odd, thick painted pottery, first found by us on the site of Kile Gul Mohammad, turned out to have wide geographic distribution, ranging as far as the central Hari Rud valley in western Afghanistan, to the site of Kaudani near Fort Sandeman, and down into Loralai (Moghul Kala). It is both hand- and wheel-made and often decorated with bands or zones of appliqué strips, some incised or painted. The forms seem to have been principally deep or shallow open bowls. The ceramic, named "Ghul ware" in its most primitive form (Type I), bears a resemblance in shape, manufacture, and decoration to a ware found by Beatrice de Cardi on sites throughout Jhalawan and Sarawan. This is the so-called "Lando" ware.[28] Lando ware is thick, often handmade, and painted with black or reddish on brown surface. Its forms include carinated deep bowls. Its painted design repertoire includes hanging spirals, birds, and stylized horses' heads as well as floral motifs or simple geometrics. De Cardi saw analogues in this ware with that of Cemetery B at Tepe Sialk and originally put it around 1100 B.C.[29] Most interesting is the fact that Lando ware is associated on its sites with a thick appliqué-decorated pottery, particularly in Jhalawan. This ware is

[27] See Appendix D, p. 393. Louis Dupree's excavations at the cave site of Shamshir Ghar show a definite rise in the habitation of the region during Partho-Sassanian times. Kandahar was, of course, important in Islamic times. L. B. Dupree, "Shamshir Ghar: historic cave site in Kandahar Province Afghanistan," *Anthropological Papers of the American Museum of Natural History*, Vol. XLVI, Pt. 2 (1958), pp. 137–312.

[28] De Cardi, 1951. Recently Mr. Raikes (1963) has described a ware he found at Pirak near Sibi in Kachhi. He feels it is extremely early on the basis of broad parallels with wares found in Western Asia. After examining "Pirak ware" in Karachi, I feel it is simply a variation of the Ghul-Lando-Complex B wares to which it has several significant parallels: handles, designs, and construction.

[29] She has since revised this estimate to post-800 B.C. (1964, p. 25).

Fig. 75   *Lando ware* (mostly after de Cardi).

found as the characteristic ceramic in Las Bela for what is called the Complex B assemblages found in that district's northern reaches (Pl. 52).

❋ *Complex B*

Complex B is one of the most remarkable archaeological remains in Baluchistan. It is worth detailing here the nature of the remains (Pls. 52–55). The complex was found in close proximity to the remains of Complex A (see pp. 195–205). The sites of the complex are as follows:

LB-2: On the slope of the hill on the western side of LB-1 there is a large stone circle made up of several tiers of large boulders that form walls four and a half feet thick and enclose a space thirty-two feet wide. The walls stand about three feet high and are broken at the eastern side by an entranceway. Associated with this circle is a heavy, tempered, thick ware decorated with appliqué bands, loops, and verticals which, in turn, are incised, pinched, or punctated (Pl. 52). A fine plainware with flaring rim on globular vessels was found, as well as a few sherds of a red-slipped ware, thin and well made with traces of black painted bands. A few fragments of prehistoric pottery were also picked up within the circle.

The ceramic tradition is completely different from that of Complex A, but the fact that stone circles almost exactly like that of LB-2 are found within the Complex A structures (see p. 198) poses a problem unsolved on the basis of present evidence.

Close to LB-2 are a few rectangular structures which on the evidence of LB-10 may belong to the period of LB-2, even though no ceramics were recovered there.

PLATE 52 *Pottery associated with Complex B sites of southern Baluchistan. These examples from Las Bela.*

LB-10: The terminal slopes of the western hills along the Porali valley that are immediately adjacent to the cultivated area dramatically overlook the entire Welpat plain.[30] Here, beginning at a point almost immediately overlooking the site of LB-1 and thereafter extending over four thousand feet down the spur to the south and west, is the extraordinary complex of structures known as LB-10.

On the highest part of the hill above LB-1 there are several small heaps of stone, as if there had been small square structures here—perhaps watch stations. Several hundred feet to the southwest, on the backbone of the spur, the remains of a long wall run for about 2600 feet to the squarish

[30] For a description of Las Bela, see pp. 185ff.

building that is the beginning of the major building complex. The traces of the wall foundations indicate that it was about $2\frac{1}{2}$ to 3 feet wide. Here and there larger piles of stone indicate that there were towers, or at least higher points, along the wall. At one place in the wall, almost two thirds of the way along, two of these heaps seem to be on either side of an opening, as if a gate or entranceway had been there.

The first structure along the wall line is a squat rectangle (30 by 50 feet) with walls about 4 feet thick and an entrance in its western side. This building, though slightly askew, is the dominant structure of a group of low-lying buildings. The main wall forms the southern edge of this complex, while its northern edge is limited by a group of rectangular structures. Of interest is the group of oblong stone cists along one side of a building; on the surface of one were found odd fragments of as yet unidentified bone but initially it appears human. Just south of this group are traces of an "avenue" of white stones extending to the west.

The main wall curves to the north, acting as the boundary on that side for a large complex of structures. It disappears amid a group of rectangular buildings that extend for a considerable distance to the north, but just west of the northernmost structure faint traces of a wall appear. This suggests a gradual return to the southwest, thus enclosing the entire site— but centuries of erosion have obscured the evidence for this.

The more than one hundred structures between the wall and the cultivation are of considerable variety. Most numerous are rectangular buildings whose orientation is generally east-west, though there is no strict adherence to this. Some buildings, in fact, line up considerably south of west (Pl. 53). Generally, the buildings average 15 to 25 feet in width, but the lengths vary considerably. Lengths range from 25 to 125 feet, with the 50- to 80-foot range most common. However, one enormous building stretches 245 feet. In places only the outline of these structures still remains, more or less flush with the ground; in other cases there is simply a series of rises to mark the location of destroyed buildings. However, in the majority of cases the walls rise several feet in the air, in some cases 5 feet and in others only 1 foot. Many of the structures are compartmented, and three-room structures are not uncommon.

There is a tendency for these rectangular buildings to be gathered into clusters. Occasionally a building will have a kind of "wart" at the side of one end, presenting a kind of modified L-shape in plan. Sometimes T-shaped structures are formed this way, and occasionally a narrow stubby extension appears at the end of a building.

Square buildings occur, though in the great minority. These are generally small (24 by 24 feet), have no particular orientation, and in most cases have no indication of an entrance, which is generally true of the rectangular structures as well. In one building, however, there is the trace of an entrance ramp.

PLATE 53 *Las Bela—Complex B structure of Edith Shahr Complex at the edge of the Welpat cultivation. Some of the circles are, however, corrals made of stones to hold the animals that belong to the houses by the cultivation. A Complex B mound site is indicated by the arrow.*

A large compartmented structure similar to the one in LB-14 (Complex A) also occurs in LB-10. This is approximately 40 feet wide by 75 feet long. The walls are 7 feet thick, and there are traces of entrances on the long southwestern side. A 9-foot-thick wall divides the building into large rooms.

Among the more provocative structures are the stone circles. Two of these are similar to that of LB-2. One measures about 42 feet in diameter, has 6-foot-thick walls and an entrance to the northwest. The other is about 55 feet in diameter, its walls about the same thickness as those of the first, and its entrance almost due west. In both a tier of white stones was used as a feature of the wall building.

The circles in the second group were obviously intended to be mere outlines. Of the nine traceable ones, three are made up of a double line of stones imbedded upright in the ground, probably no more than 1 foot deep, and protruding 4 to 12 inches out. These are carefully chosen white boulders set 1 to 1½ feet apart in regular order. Two of these circles measure about 45 feet across, and at the center there is a large stone surrounded by a pile of smaller white stones (Pl. 54) as if there had been a support platform for the larger stone which had collapsed. In the other case only the smaller stones are found. One of these large stones is white, the other of ordinary rock color. No entranceways are discernible.

The remaining circles are small, usually no more than 20 feet across, and are outlined by a single line of stones—though there may be exceptions to this, since most of these circles have suffered from time. Characteristically, these small circles are set very close to the corner of a rectangular building,

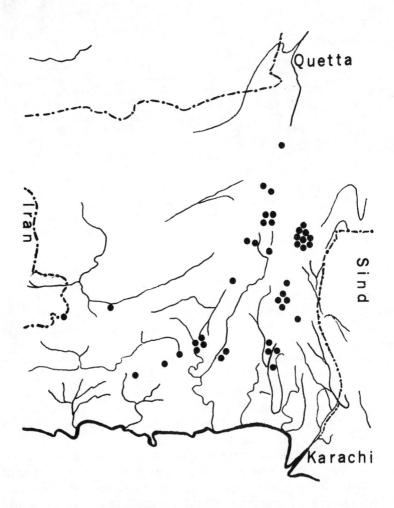

MAP 27 *Distribution of sites of Complex B and Lando type in Baluchistan*
(after de Cardi and others).

PLATE 54 *Las Bela—a white stone circle of Complex B, Edith Shahr Complex LB-10.*

PLATE 55 *Las Bela—a section of double-rowed stone circle of Complex B, Edith Shahr Complex. Each stone is fixed in place.*

in some cases as close as 6 feet. There is no consistency about the corner of the building chosen.

"Avenues" of white stones occur clearly in three instances, and there are traces of a possible fourth. All of these are on a general east-west axis, though there is a 10° variance. The best preserved "avenue" is 520 feet long and is about 10 feet wide at its outside dimension, though it has an inner avenue formed by another line of stones about 2 feet apart on either side. This avenue terminates at either end in small piles of stones undistinguished in form. A smaller avenue, approximately 9 by 140 feet, ends in an ellipse at its western end.

Finally, attention should be brought to the outlines of small huts or houses on the southwestern point of the site. These are interesting primarily because they appear to be less formal than the foregoing.

Sherds are not abundant on the site, but the principal pottery is the coarse, thick ware, some with appliqué decoration, already encountered at LB-2. In addition to coarse round handles, lugs also occur in this type. There is also a dark-slipped ware, apparently representing small-mouthed jars. A few sherds of prehistoric painted wares, an incised fruit stand (with concentric line dividers between "comma" incisions, which is atypical of the Harappan type) (Pl. 52), and a fragment of a bull figurine were also found, as well as a flat bronze arrowhead.

LB-9: Located about two miles to the southwest of LB-10, in the midst of the cultivation, LB-9 is a circular earthen mound rising about 15 feet. Its interior is hollow, descending to perhaps slightly less than 10 feet above the level of the plain. Within this hollow the diameter is about 140 feet. Quantities of stone strew the slopes of the site, indicating that some stone construction was involved. No entrance area could be traced.[31]

Pottery here is of the same type as at LB-10.

LB-13: Groups of rectangular structures generally oriented north-south occur frequently on the north and west of this site, some on the flat plain on which the Complex A structures are located and a few to the west on the higher bluffs. Notable are the traces of a white-stone "avenue." A large square structure, 45 by 42 feet, with entrance on the east, may perhaps be Moslem, though there is no mihrab area on the west, which is common to comparable Moslem stone squares. Far out on the northwest of the site are two isolated stone circles of the LB-2 type. The two circles are in a north-south line, about 140 yards apart. Both are about 42 feet in diameter, and one has an entrance on the southeast; the other appears to be the same, but this is not certain because of its ruined condition. The walls of these circles are some 5 feet in height, and they are very impressive.

[31] LB-9 is also on one of the main routes of the area.

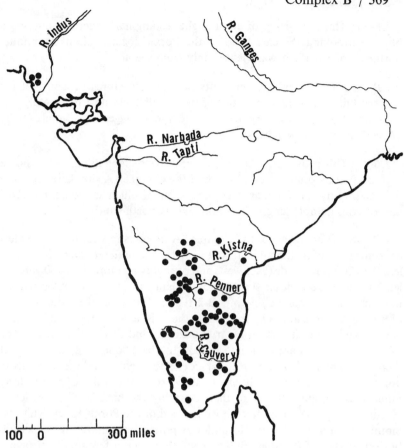

MAP 28 *Distribution of "megalithic porthole" cists.*

Traceable on the surface of the site, close to the main groupings of rectangular structures, are rather extensive layouts of regular rows of houses, both square and rectangular.

LB-14: A scattered group of rectangular buildings and at least one stone circle outlined like those of the second group of LB-10 are located in the broad area to the south of the Complex A structures. However, our initial examination was cursory and produced only ceramics of Complex A, but this may not hold up when future work is possible.

LB-15: This is a group of about eight rectangular structures high on a bluff overlooking the east bend of the Porali, located about four miles northeast of LB-13. It was viewed only from the air.

LB-11, LB-12: Here are remnants of small structures on spurs of the western hills along the right bank of the Porali opposite LB-13. Only one structure (LB-11) has some good wall-line traces, suggesting a square (12 by 12 feet), perhaps a watchtower.

LB-17: This provocative site has at least five rectangular structures on a high bluff at its southern end. North of the Complex A site there are more than twenty-five rectangular structures, some of which are compartmented and of considerable length. The long axis is north-south.

LB-16: The area west of the Complex A mounds represents the greatest concentration of rectangular structures so far encountered. Here, in an area less than 200 yards wide (east-west) and probably no more than 400 yards in length, there are at least sixty buildings laid out in erratic but generally parallel rows. A stone circle of LB-2 type is found on the eastern fringe of this concentration. On the north there is a wide tree-filled nullah, beyond which another series of structures is found on the high land. Some of these structures are even laid out on the backbone of a ridge so that there is an abrupt drop-off on either side. The orientation here varies from north-south to almost exactly east-west. On the east of this last area a stony mound rises about 20 feet so that, counting the high bluff on which it stands, its top is some 60 feet above the bed of the Porali River. This last mound did not produce the Complex A pottery in quantity, as expected, but rather that of Complex B. There are, however, a few sherds of black-on-red slip painted pottery, suggesting an earlier occupation.

LB-18: Flight over the area north of LB-16 revealed here and there on both sides of the river a few of the rectangular structures associated with Complex B, as well as some square and circular stone buildings, most of the latter probably being of Moslem origin, however. There was no indication of any extensive occupation such as we had found elsewhere, and after we reached a distance of about six miles north of LB-16, the canyon terrain appeared and even the meager cultivation of this part of the Porali valley virtually disappeared.

LB-8: Approximately three miles east-southeast of Bela town and therefore outside the immediate Welpat area, the site of LB-8 has to be considered in the range of Complex B. This site is a cluster, as it were, of about twenty-five rectangular buildings on the talus fan of the eastern hills set back about 300 yards from the edge of the cultivation. The buildings are oriented somewhat east of south.

Several buildings have indications of entrances on the long sides, which is somewhat atypical of Complex B structures. The ceramic evidence is very scanty, but what there is indicates Complex B associations.

LB-7: In the area of the Khamkho Nal Pass, approximately ten miles to the southeast of Bela, there are a number of stone structures high on the arid gravel terraces at least two and a half miles east of the cultivated area. These structures consist of single boulder-outlined circles, and stone squares with entrances on the east. It would appear that these are of Moslem origin, but there may be several of Complex B affiliation. Ceramic evidence is practically nonexistent, and there is no means of clarifying this problem as yet.

✳ *Complex B—Summation*

ONE OBTAINS THE IMPRESSION OF A FORMAL, ORGANIZED SOCIETY with a considerable emphasis upon ceremony in the character and placement of these monuments. Whether this is a correct view or not remains for future research to decide. Nevertheless, it is necessary at this point of our studies to underline certain features.

(1) Generally speaking, there is surprisingly little pottery or other artifactual material to be found among the ruins when compared to other sites in Baluchistan.

(2) The homogeneity of the buildings from site to site indicates an acceptance of certain traditional ideas and a functional agreement.

(3) The position of the sites on the arid talus fans, terraces, and bluffs above the cultivated areas, and dominating them as it were, parallels a similar placement pattern in Complex A and would in the same way tend to emphasize formal planning.

(4) The elaborate stone circles, avenues, and the parallel rows of rectangular buildings are at variance with what is known about traditional building forms in village Baluchistan.

These four points are self-explanatory and need little further comment. We might mention, though, as regards the first point, that more often than not, not a scrap of pottery could be found on or about a building. Accordingly, it does not seem likely that these were habitation sites, though the odd rows of squarish houses on some of the sites may well have been temporary homes for those who carried on the functions whatever they were.

Again, as with Complex A, the ceremonial aspect takes priority in our speculations. It seems hard to regard the stone avenues as anything else but ceremonial structures. They lead nowhere, and their orientation is generally consistent. The second group of stone circles may have been the ground plan for, say, a domed house, yurtlike in appearance, and accordingly one would expect to find some entrance arrangement, but the circles are unbroken.

The long wall of LB-10 is so thin that it does not seem possible that it rose to any great height, and, in addition, its placement would hardly make it a feasible place to defend.

If one were to follow along on this train of thought, it would appear that the Complex B sites are necropolises (dearth of cultural debris, nonhabitation aspect of the rectangular structures—perhaps multiple burials *à la* chamber of tombs, placement above the cultivation, great number) or ceremonial centers (avenues, stone circles, unusual structures like the large compartmented squares, dominating position in the valley, etc.) or perhaps, least likely of all, official residences of a ruling class (formalized structures, enclosure walls, elaborate building arrangements such as the clustering of buildings or the arrangement near a main wall, position above the plain).

That the plain was cultivated extensively during this period would seem obvious from the elaborate nature of the buildings and their number. We have, of course, some proof of the occupancy of the plains in site LB-9, though this too appears to be a formal structure and probably not a village mound.

The critical chronological relationship between complexes A and B has to be considered, particularly if we regard Complex B as representative of a new cultural tradition if not actual invasion. The fact that Harappan elements are part of Complex A gives the problem a critical importance, bearing as it does upon the so-called "collapse" of the Indus Valley civilization (see p. 296).

Admitting the poverty of our evidence as it presently stands, we might suggest that there is no great temporal gap between the two complexes. We have to consider the following in this regard:

(1) The close juxtaposition, if not the superposition, of the remains (Pl. 16).

(2) The apparent sharing of structural forms, such as the stone circles and probably the rectangular buildings.

(3) The apparent survival of Complex A traits at sites where no Complex A occupations occur.

(4) The concentration upon the same localities for building.

One is tempted to consider the possibility that the reddish appearance of the tops of the mounds of LB-1 and LB-6 is the result of conflagration brought on by invaders who obviously were the possessors of Complex B traits. In view of the above, this classic view of events would not seem to be tenable. In contrast, we have to consider the possibility that Complex B is an outgrowth of Complex A. This, too, would appear to be untenable in view of the ceramic evidence, the real absence of many critical Complex A traits, and the peculiar structural forms of Complex B. One might expect transitional elements, which are at present almost absent from the record. An incised fruit stand (Pl. 52), with its unusual treatment suggests such a transition, as does the similarity of certain structures mentioned above. The possibility of red-slip wares surviving as a part of Complex B might also be considered. But all these factors are inconclusive.

There is another consideration at hand, and that is the outside source for Complex B traits. This too is inadequate. The coarse appliqué ware is unreported from the surrounding areas of Sind, Kalat, and Makran, though this does not mean that it is absent there. Field[32] records a stone circle in Makran, but his description does not include ceramic evidence.

We did not find similar wares in Seistan, nor can we find reports from eastern Iran (south or north) with accounts of this type. In Turkmenistan, Masson reports an appliqué ware with simple ring handles (Yaz Tepe I) which might be a candidate for comparisons with Complex B coarse ware.[33] But this is, of course, too far afield for any valid conclusion. In the Quetta Valley we made some attempt to fix the few sherds of appliqué ware found there into a general chronological scheme.[34] But there is no real comparison possible of those wares to the ones of Las Bela except to note that both use a similar decorative technique. The Quetta study does, however, confirm in a general way the protohistoric position of appliqué pottery.

There seems little doubt that there is a close relationship of Lando ware to Complex B even though it is not found in Las Bela. In turn, the Ghul wares of the north suggest a strong generic relationship. Are we, then, in possession of evidence for a major shift from the Iranian plateau toward the subcontinent?

A traveler moving along the old road to Hyderabad from Karachi via Thano Bulla Khan would see from time to time stone boxes made of four or more upright slabs near his road. In fact a sign reading "Hyderabad," complete with arrow, is painted on the side of one of them near the Malir River (Pl. 56). These boxes constitute other evidence for the shadowy period after the Harappan civilization. They are usually found in clusters though occasionally single ones are encountered. They measure on the average three by five feet. In a few cases one of the upright slabs is pierced with a sizable hole. A covering slab is also frequently found, though in all the boxes I have encountered this has fallen or been removed.

---

[32] H. Field, "An Anthropological Reconnaissance in West Pakistan, 1955," *Papers of the Peabody Museum of Archaeology and Ethnology*, Vol. LII (1959).

[33] V. M. Masson, "Ancient Agricultural Cultures of Margiana," *Materiali i Issledovaniya po Archaeologii USSR*, No. 73 (1959), Pls. 22–23, 26–28. Yaz Tepe I is dated just post-1000 B.C., p. 93.

[34] Fairservis, 1956.

PLATE 56   *Southern Sind—stone cists near Karachi on the road to Thamo Bulla Khan.*

Though no excavation has yet been made on these remains, some have been so eroded that some idea of their contents can be obtained (Pl. 57). They appear to have held cremated human remains. Odd fragments of pottery found among the fragments of calcined bone indicate that the burials had some funerary furniture. The pottery is reddish and has a sharp break at the shoulder, but too little has been found to identify the forms clearly.

At some of these sites in the region stone circles are also found. Generally, all these remains are situated on ridges or dominating slopes. So numerous are they that it is very likely that systematic exploration will extend their range as far as Hyderabad or even Lake Manchhar. They are found at present as far north as Hinidan in the Hab River valley.

Though stone cairns are known as far west in Makran as Jiwanri, these seem late and at present unrelated to anything else. However, the Karachi "megaliths," if so we can call them,[35] suggest a relation to the famous megalithic remains found especially in southeastern India.[36] Here urn burial, porthole slabs, stone circles, and the like are characteristic of these remains.[37] The late date for these Indian megaliths, now generally accepted,

[35] Wheeler has noted previous reports on these remains R. E. M. Wheeler, "Five Thousand Years of Pakistan," *Royal India and Pakistan Society* (1950), pp. 34–36.

[36] Slab graves were found by Dani in his investigations of the Gandhara Grave Complex. These were burials but the use of slabs here may be related to the similar use in the Karachi area. Both graves contained cremated remains. (Dani, 1967.)

[37] The "megalithic" remains are of at least post-fourth century B.C. date and constitute other problems beyond the scope of this book. Excellent summaries of the megaliths of south India can be found as follows: V. D. Krishnaswami, "Megalithic Types of South India," *Ancient India*, No. 5 (1949), pp. 35–45; K. R. Srinivasan and N. R. Banerjee, "Survey of South Indian Megaliths," *Ancient India*, No. 9 (1953), pp. 103–115; N. R. Banerjee, "The Megalithic Problem of Chingleput in the Light of Recent Exploration," *Ancient India*, No. 12 (1956), pp. 21–34; L. von Fürer-Haimendorf, "The Problem of Megalithic Cultures in Middle India," *Man in India*, Vol. XXV (1945), pp. 73–86; Sir M. Wheeler, 1959, pp. 150–169.

PLATE 57   *Calcined human bone lying in the remains of a stone cist, Dam-lotti area, near Karachi.*

PLATE 58 *Las Bela—a view of some of the caves of Gondrani. For an idea of the scale note the man in the middle foreground.* (Courtesy D. Powell.)

suggests that they were derived, much as other traits in the past, from the northwest, the Karachi region being one of the obvious bridges between east and west. It is of interest that so far as archaeological research now goes, the earliest remains in Kerala in southwestern India are of megalithic type. As such, the region seems to have been the last to be settled by food-producing man, while Sind was the first on the geographic subcontinent.

One might inquire whether a connection exists between Complex B of Baluchistan and the megalithic remains of the Karachi area. At present they are far apart in aspect. Perhaps the Karachi settlements were more modest developments out of the splendors of the Complex B type. We simply do not know. Yet phases of movement are more likely than one or two giant steps. As the literary accounts record the settlement of vast areas of India region by region, whether dealing with the Aryans or the Arabs, so the archaeologist must make a similar assumption. It is probably no coincidence that there are suggestions of Lando ware genesis among some pottery decorations and forms in the third period at Navdatoli or that urn burial was used at Swat and Cemetery H, or that portholes are found in the stone boxes of Karachi and the Madras region, etc. Fürer-Haimendorf has suggested that the distribution of megaliths in southern India was approximately that of the modern distribution of Dravidian speakers. The fact that Brahui is an isolated Dravidian language still existent in Baluchistan suggests a point of origin. Under this thesis Dravidian peoples were pushed south into the Peninsula. Was it the Aryans who caused this migration? The question cannot be answered on the present evidence. But the presence of comparable megaliths in the Borderlands gives some support to this idea. Fürer-Haimendorf also uses modern ethnological data to support his argument. Though there have been a considerable number of archaeologists who oppose his view, the fact is that his idea has considerable substance and there is little as yet to show that it is untenable.[38] The problem that archaeology faces in tracing the validity of such relationships depends on an understanding of the processes that move men to go or to stay, as the case may be.[39]

❀ *The Movement to the Subcontinent*

WITH THE DECLINE OF THE SETTLEMENTS of prehistoric man in the Borderlands, it may well be that a few centuries elapsed before the next major inhabitation took place, a few centuries during which nature was able to recover from the blows occasioned by overexploitation of the scant resources of soil and natural vegetation. The shift of presumably pastoral people to the Borderlands from the west may have been brought about by the attractions of a revived land where grass and water were once again available. Once they were there, the old process began again which moved men down to the Indus plains and beyond to adapt to new conditions and to change old traditions, yet still keep an identifying trace of them. That is probably why archaeologists, in speaking of the relationships of such entities as Swat, Cemetery H, Jhangar, Lando, Complex B, Megaliths, Painted Gray Ware, and the like, are tantalized by hints in the material, of ties east and west and yet are hard pressed to define them. Nonetheless, what evidence we do have demonstrates that from the Khyber to the Arabian Sea old ways were dead or dying and for many centuries new peoples and cultures crossed the terrain to become absorbed in the mainstream of India and to contribute their bit to its heterogeneous quality. Many peoples and cultures must have come; some we have evidence for in the texts, in the layers of excavated sites, or on the surface of old mounds. The literature has probably exaggerated the Aryans to the exclusion of others who also found India. Perhaps it does not, for at the moment our archaeological instruments are almost mute, or indeed perhaps we have already found the answer and know it not.

[38] Christoph von Fürer-Haimendorf, "New Aspect of the Davidian Problem" in *Indo-Asian Culture*, vol. II, No. 3, 1954, pp. 238 ff.

[39] A book by N. R. Banerjee (*The Iron Age in India*, Delhi, 1965) has arrived too late for its deserved reference in this text. Banerjee relates the Aryans to the Indian Iron Age, which became full-fledged after 1000 B.C. Dani's work in the northwest was not available to him at the time he wrote his book.

Epilogue

❀ Urbanization, Buddhism, and Process

TO MANY THE GREAT ACCOMPLISHMENT OF INDIA in the centuries before Christ was Buddhism. During the sixth century B.C. the Buddha was born, the princely son of a warrior chief of the Sakya. There seems to be some dispute among scholars as to just who and what the Sakya were. One would have them as clans ruled by "popular assemblies."[1] Another calls them a hill tribe.[2] More traditionally, Sakya is a kingdom ruled by King Suddhodana and his queen, Maya. The distinction is of some importance, for a kingdom implies a society with classes: nobility, priesthood, merchants, army, peasantry. A tribe can be merely a series of households united by pantribal bonds that include clans. Clans recognize kin ties to a totemic or other ancestor. Clans act as economic and social units and, as mentioned above, may be administered by assemblies from time to time. The distinctions are rather explicit for each of these units, and the confusion in their usage reflects the relatively poor evidence we have as to the Buddha's life.

[1] C. Collier Davies, *An Historical Atlas of the Indian Peninsula*, Oxford University Press, Oxford, 1953, p. 2.
[2] W. T. de Baryed, ed., *Introduction to Oriental Civilization, Sources of Indian Tradition*, Columbia University Press, New York, 1958, p. 93.

TABLE 9. THE MOVEMENT OF URBANIZATION FROM WEST TO EAST IN NORTHERN INDIA

	2500–1500 B.C.	1500–1000 B.C.	1000–500 B.C.	500–1 B.C.
Bengal				Mainamati
				Mahasthan
				Tamluk
Orissa				Jaugada
				Sisulpalgarh
Bihar				Pataliputra
Central Ganges Valley		Hastinapura	Kausambi	Mathura
		Ahichchhatra	Jhusi	
Punjab & NW Frontier	Harappa			Charsada
				Bhir Mound, Taxila
Sind	Mohenjo-daro			

Two facts are increasingly clear however. The first is outlined in the chart (Table 9). Here archaeologically demonstrable urbanization has reached the middle Ganges Valley and is extending eastward by 500 B.C., if not earlier. Throughout the traditional story of Buddha's life not only do we encounter descriptions of capital cities like Kapilavastu, Rajagriha, Vaisali, and Benares, but we also discover aspects of urbanization in the material culture so far as it is mentioned: at Kapilavastu we find the young Siddhartha placed in a palace complete with harem, he has a stable of horses with grooms, there is a school at which he studies, he meditates in an enclosed garden, robes and objects of great richness and variety are part of his daily life.

The second fact is Buddhism itself. For basically early Buddhism seems to be both a protest against and a direction out of a complex way of life in which ambition, social inequality, civil strife, hunger, disease, temptation, superstition, riches, poverty, and the like are prevalent. The young man discovers these things and seeks a way out. The answer achieved in the great enlightenment under the bodhi tree near the town of Gaya is essentially an urban response: "Suffering comes from desire; eliminate desire and there is no suffering." How? In effect, return to a moral order: "right conduct, right thoughts."

Buddhism is a reaction to an order outside the seasonal harmonies of rural life. Farming societies, part of the closed-village system and closely keyed to the seasonal stresses and leisures which characterize the year's cycle, know laws which need not be stated in so many terms. The requirements that nature makes if the crops are to be sown, cultivated, and harvested continually point to the immutable fact that one's labor is the essential ingredient for good crops when the soil is rich and water abundant. No farmer need be told of the dharma of birth, life, and death. It is always before him. Nor need he seek in asceticism the fundamental truths of a mortal universe.

The Buddha is not addressing a rural audience but the urban classes who, divorced from the farmer's world, are suffering because, as with all urban men, they do not comprehend the timelessness of the natural world. They are divorced by civilization from the exigencies of the natural environment. They have the leisure to suffer their own particular hells, those which have arisen out of the search for wealth, power, love.

After the great battle of nations at Kuruksetra described in the Mahabharata, the Queen Mother of the Kauravas, viewing her slain sons, cries out in agony, "Why? Why?" It is for this particular pain that the Buddha seeks an antidote. How can man escape the suffering which is his as a mortal caught in complexities of his own creation? It is not among men that the Buddha finds his answer, even though he tries to do so. It is alone under a tree, sustained only by the milk brought in a bowl by a village girl. In a sense it is a return to nature—a nature which urban life has sublimated.

In turn it is the kings, queens, princes, merchants, who become the Buddhists, while in the villages Krishna, Rama, Ganesha, Lakshmi, Kali, Parvati, Siva, and Vishnu, and a pantheon of local spirits and deities grow out of roots that may be as old at least as the Harappan. In the end Buddhism, in spite of all the kinds of changes, adjustments, and integrations typical of urban culture, vanishes from the subcontinent, leaving the ancient Hindu beliefs of the stable rural world dominant.

Buddhism is, according to this interpretation, a sure sign that urbanized life had reached the lower Ganges basin. In its early monuments there is a strong suggestion that that early civilization which created Buddhism was a hybrid of many traditions. The stupa may be derived from the Central Asian burial mounds perhaps brought to India by the Aryans; the chaitya, or cave temple, harks to an earlier day when microlith-using hunters sought caves for seasonal shelter or ritual; the great pillars of Asoka are strongly suggestive of Achaemenid Persia. The civilization is based upon a subsistence crop, rice, which by Buddha's time may have had hardly a thousand years of cultivation history. Buddha himself is a Sakya. His people are comparative foreigners. Their ancestors are part of that "Vedic night" just described. One of the most poignant parts of the story of the Buddha is his farewell to his horse; more than a pet, it was a comrade, a friend—a relationship found among Cossacks, Kazaks, and Mongols, and a Central Asian trait old indeed by the time of the Buddha's ancestors.

To the student of Indian archaeology the names are familiar: Central Asia, Iran. Combined with local tradition, they are the ingredients which make up the genesis of Indian civilization. The story of prehistoric India, which stretches back to a time so remote that it conforms to a Hindu Kalpa of untold generations reaching to a primordial world, nonetheless repeats again and again the pattern which was not to change until the East India Company ships moved up the Hooghly.

But if the Buddha represents the fulfillment of a pattern already ancient, he is also symbolic of a uniqueness which is subcontinental, which is India. Whatever the diversity of her genesis, India is more than the sum of her parts, and this marvelous truth must always haunt those who would interpret her most ancient story.

Appendixes

APPENDIX A:

Comments on the Chronology of Stone Age India

By GREGORY POSSEHL

EVER SINCE THE FIRST RECOGNITION of a true Stone Age in peninsular India by R. Bruce Foote in 1863, the chronology of the various tool assemblages has been imperfectly known. In the early part of the 1930s de Terra and Paterson, working under the auspices of Yale and Cambridge universities, made some contribution to placing many of the finds from northwestern India into a relative chronology. They made an intensive study of the river terraces and moraines of the Soan Valley in modern Pakistan. From this study they concluded that there were four major periods of glacial activity in Kashmir.[1] Into this scheme they were able to place many surface finds of paleolithic material. De Terra and Paterson's work has remained a standard of comparison since that date for most Pleistocene studies, even in peninsular India.

Since 1939 much good work has been done on the Indian Paleolithic. Most of the evidence has come from peninsular sites, distantly removed from the Kashmir mountain area. Thus, there is some validity in attempting to relate these sites to one another before direct correlations are made to glacial activity in the more northern latitudes. The chart, "Comparative Stratigraphy of Stone Age Sequences in India" (p. 384), shows that there is considerable geological homogeneity for those formations in peninsular India which have been shown to contain Early and Middle Stone Age materials. One of these formations can tentatively be related to relative levels of sea level. Thus it may be possible to fit most of the formations into a world-wide glacial sequence based on these sea levels.

[1] H. de Terra and T. T. Paterson, *Studies on the Ice Age of India and Associated Human Cultures*, Carnegie Institution of Washington, Publication No. 493, Washington, 1939, pp. 220–225.

TABLE 10. COMPARATIVE STRATIGRAPHY OF STONE AGE SEQUENCES IN INDIA

	Gujarat	Narmada (after Wainwright)	Narmada (after Paterson)	Narmada (after Khatri)	Maheshwar	Chambal
		Sea Level				
	Z Brown Topsoil — Modern	I — Modern				
	Y Dry (Probably Sand) — Dry	II Aggradation due to Seasonal Rain — Rise			7-8	
	X Soil — Wetter; Microliths	III Soil III — Low		Yellow-Brown Silt; Microliths	6 Brown — Dry	
	W Dune &s Sand — Dry	IV Aggradation as in VI — Rise			5 Gravel III — Wet; Late Soan-like Levalloisian Technique	
	V Subaerial denudation — Wetter	V Soil II — Low		?		
GRAVELS III					4 Pink Silt — Dry	
	U Aeolian Sand — Main Dry Phase	VI Aggradation Silts and Sands — Rise	Pink to Yellow Clay; Tools like Late Soan Early Paleolithic Flakes & Cores			
SILTS & SAND II					3 Gravel II — Wet	
	T Red Soil — Drier Upper Acheulian Proto-Levalloisian Evolution of Tools in R	VII Soil I — Low	Sands or Gravels Conglomerate (Cross-bedded at Times); Low	Cross-bedded sands; Late Acheulian Middle Stone Age		
GRAVEL II					2 Pink Silts — Dry	
	S Silts	Gravel; VIII Sand — Acheulian Handaxes; Rise	Red Clay; Upper Acheulian Handaxes	Sandy Conglomerate; Late Chellian to Early Acheulian		
SILTS & SANDS I			unconformity			
	R Cemented Gravels — Wet Handaxes Pebble tools Levalloisian-like flakes	Silt	Cemented Conglomerate; Abbevillian Handaxes Acheulian Handaxes Pebble Tools	Boulder Conglomerate	1 Cemented Gravel — Wet; Handaxes "Clactonian" Flakes	Gravels Handaxes Pebble Tools Proto-Levalloisian
GRAVEL I		IX Erosion of clay — Low				
	Q Mottled Clay? — Low	X Clay	(Not Reported) ? ; Low	Red Clay; Abbevillian Handaxes?		
CLAY						
	P Laterite — Wet		Laterite	Laterite		
LATERITE						

Increase in aridity

Graves noted by Sankalia and Khatri with Middle Stone Age Tools

			Modern Situation	
			Glacial Retreat	
			III	
		Seasonal Flood Silts	Inter.	
	Gravel III 2 Flakes	Microliths	4th GL	
Gravel III		Late Middle Stone Age		
Middle Stone Age		Fine Sandy Gravel		
	Silt		II	
		Red or Yellow Silt	Inter.	
		Dark Brown Clay		
	Gravel II	Fine Gravels or Sand	I	
Gravel II (clay)		Middle Stone Age		
Middle Stone Age		Early Middle Stone Age		
		Fine Gravel		
	Loose Pebbles			
	Pellety Laterite Gravel	Gravels		
	Late Acheulian Levalloisian Technique			
	Middle Stone Age Tools			
Small Gravel and Sands	Fluvial Silts	Silts and/or clays		
Levalloisian Flakes	Sands	Sandy Clay with		
	Levalloisian Silt	Late Acheulian Flake Tools		
	Silt	Reddish Silts		
	Cemented Gravels			
	Handaxes "Levalloisian-like" flakes			
	Flake of Early type	Gravels I	Early Stone Age	
Cemented Gravels	Cemented Gravels	Gravel I	3rd IGL	
Handaxes		Handaxes Choppers Cleavers Levalloisian-like Flakes		
	Detrital Laterite	Many types of handaxe Pebble tools Choppers		
	Middle Acheulian	Cemented Coarse Gravels Secondary Laterite		
		Mottled Clay		
		Clays (Drier)		
		Laterite	3rd GL	
		Laterite (Wet)		
		Talchir		

The chart shows a correlation of some of the best-stratified paleolithic localities in the subcontinent. In the compilation of material for the chart, an attempt was made to keep each of the authors' own terminology wherever possible. Many of the terms used—for example, color designations and particle sizes—are highly subjective determinations, and we felt unwilling to accept the burden of attempting to change them. Thus, where discrepancies seem to occur, it is left to the reader to interpret them. However, even with this subjective limitation, considerable agreement can be seen between the various sites recorded on the chart.

A reasonable examination of the chart will reveal that there are seven major geological strata represented. The first sign of paleolithic man comes in stratum 3 or Gravel I. Below this gravel conglomerate there are two other formations: first, there is a clay often mottled blue, brown, or reddish; below the clay is a laterite, of highly variable thickness. These two formations are always archaeologically sterile, with the one possible exception of Khatri's Narbada sequence.[2] Each of the sites where the laterite and/or the clay is not recorded has Gravel I resting on bedrock.

The first archaeological formation is, then, Gravel I. Typologically speaking, the artifacts from this deposit are highly variable. They range from assemblages containing Abbevillian handaxes and Clactonianlike flakes on the Narbada, through pebble tools, cleavers, and Acheulian handaxes, up to signs of the beginnings of the Levalloisian technique on the Chambal, Sabarmati, and other rivers. Whereas some localities have produced artifacts of only one type or another, and some authors have suggested that there were two or three different cultural units in India at this time, the over-all picture is one of great mixing of stone-working techniques.[3] Thus, it would seem that paleolithic man entered India at the time when the Levalloisian technique, in its broadest form, was just becoming known.

The widespread nature of these gravels and their well-developed state would lead one to conclude that men first came in a relatively wet period. More will be said of this formation in this connection later; however, the next phase, Silts and Sands I, appears to be relatively less wet than the gravels.

The first silts and sands are found as universally as the gravels. Often they are stained or weathered red to pink. Archaeologically this deposit is not as productive as the first gravel; however, several sites have tools assignable to the stratum. The evidence, drawn chiefly from the rivers Sabarmati and Godavari and from Madras state, indicates that there is a line of development out of the older tradition underlying it. There are fewer of the very ancient types (i.e., cleavers, pebble tools, and Abbevillian handaxes) and a refinement of the prepared-core and faceted-platform techniques. In other words, there are the beginnings of something like a Middle Paleolithic.

A second gravel or soil weathering phase is stratified over the first silts and sands. This marks a break with the past, since handaxes are quite rare now. When they do occur, they are small, well made, and in association with a developed Middle Stone Age assemblage. The nature of the geological deposit is slightly

[2] A. P. Khatri, "Stone Age and Pleistocene Chronology of the Narmada Valley, Central India," *Anthropos*, Vol. LVI (1961), pp. 519–530.
[3] B. B. Lal, "Palaeoliths from the Beas and Banganga Valleys, Punjab," *Ancient India*, No. 12 (1956), pp. 85–90.

variable from site to site; however, it marks a definite change in all cases from the stratum preceding it. In general the rivers show a rejuvenation in their competence, probably due to greater rainfall. In some areas a soil horizon is developed, for example, at the mouth of the Narbada[4] and in Gujarat.[5]

Following Gravel II is another silt and/or sand stratum. Judging from the evidence in Gujarat, this is a marked dry phase. Archaeologically the phase is almost barren. The sites which do contain tools—Nevasa and localities on the river Dahisar, near Bombay—indicate that this is a time of the developed Middle Stone Age. Some of the sites and river valleys do not contain strata comparable to this level; therefore the validity of our sample drops a little.

The last widespread formation associated with tools in the subcontinent is Gravel III. Lack of a great deal of evidence limits our interpretation; however, the Middle Stone Age is well represented in the deposit. In fact, it is better documented than in the preceding phase. The assemblages of artifacts contain all of the characteristic Middle Stone Age tools. These range from small, very refined handaxes to borers, points, scrapers of many kinds, and thick bladelike flakes.[6] In those sites where a gravel was not accumulated a soil horizon developed. This is consistent with the climatological inference from the river deposits.

For the period following Gravel III there is too little evidence for general statements to be made. There seem to be very few sites to fill in the period, however crucial it might be. During the time in question there is undoubtedly a continued development of the Middle Stone Age. This is, in India, followed by a Late Stone Age characterized by microlithic blade tools. A true blade and burin industry is singularly lacking in the subcontinent in spite of some early hopes.[7] Moreover, the exact point and nature of the articulation between the Middle Stone Age and the Late Stone Age has yet to be uncovered. This is a priority task in the archaeology of India and Pakistan.

There is one site which may provide the evidence needed to fill the gap. Sanghao Cave is located in northern Pakistan not very far north of the city of Peshawar. There has been one season's work done on the site. Unfortunately only a preliminary report is available now;[8] however, when the excavations are complete, more should be known. The cave contains three periods of Middle Stone Age material. These are rather homogeneous throughout; however, there is a tendency for the tools to become smaller as they proceed upward in time. The Levalloisian technique is well attested, with some tendency toward "Mousterian"-type pointed flakes. Most interesting are the blade flakes. These occur in some quantity throughout the deposit. Thus, this site may have great importance, and if some reliable geological and faunal data can be derived from the excavations, it will surely provide a base line for comparisons to all other sites in the subcontinent.

It will be noted that no attempt has been made to include paleontological data in the scheme thus far. This was done purposely, for the following reason:

[4] G. J. Wainwright, *The Pleistocene Deposits of the Lower Narbada River and an Early Stone Age Industry from the River Chambal*, University of Barodar, Archaeological Series No. 7, Poona, 1964, p. 8.
[5] F. E. Zeuner, *Stone Age and Pleistocene Chronology in Gujarat*, Deccan College Monograph Series No. 6, Poona, 1950, pp. 9–10.
[6] H. D. Sankalia, "Middle Stone Age Culture in India and Pakistan," *Science*, Vol. CXLVI (1964), p. 371.
[7] K. R. U. Todd, "Palaeolithic Industries of Bombay," *Journal of the Royal Anthropological Institute of Great Britain and Ireland*, Vol. LXIX (1939), pp. 257–272.
[8] A. H. Dani, "Sanghao Cave Excavation, The First Season, 1963," *Ancient Pakistan*, Vol. I (1964), pp. 1–50.

The Pleistocene fauna of India is very insecurely known. Not only are the finds limited, but they have never been successfully related to finds outside of the subcontinent in any systematic and controlled sense. Thus, whereas it is true that generally the genera and species (i.e., *Bos namadicus*, *Equus*, and *Elephas sp.*) referred to by the various investigators are Middle or Early Pleistocene in date outside of the subcontinent, this fact has never been established inside India. Therefore, we have no independent means of verifying that they are indeed chronological markers there. It may be a distinct possibility that these creatures lived on into the Upper Pleistocene here, as they apparently did in many parts of Africa. The two areas are quite comparable in many climatological and ecological aspects; furthermore, these genera and species which are so important as type fossils for the Pleistocene are quite undependable as environmental markers. They are wide-ranging animals who can survive in comparatively rigorous environments and will persist through time long after many other smaller creatures with similar adaptations have vanished. Much more important for paleoecological studies are the small mammals and reptiles with restricted ranges and highly sensitive ecological positions. Apparently little or no time has been directed toward their study in India, and yet they would seem to be the key to a solution of the problems at hand.

At the right of the chart (p. 385) there is a tentative indication of a glacial stage for each of the deposits. The process for arriving at this correlation was the following: Zeuner's work in Gujarat was used as the standard for the whole chart. This was done since he seemed to have developed a sequence which was sensitive to morphological changes and which had chronological depth; therefore, it could be directly related to all of the other sites in a relatively simple way. More importantly, it could be directly tied to Wainwright's work at the mouth of the Narbada, and from there to the various sea levels associated with the periods of glaciation.

The Red Soil Phase (T) of Zeuner is the equivalent of Soil I of the Lower Narbada, Soils II and III of the latter have not been recorded elsewhere. Silt Phase (S) is equivalent to the Lower Series on the Lower Narbada, and the cemented gravels underlying these silts and clays can be correlated and regarded as being of the same age.

The age of these three soils representing three phases of low sea-level is therefore clearly of crucial importance.

If one is prepared, on the basis of the evidence so far accumulated, to assign them to the three maxima of the last Glaciation, then it is clear that the implement-bearing gravels are of Last Interglacial age. This interpretation also implies that the period of lateritic weathering is assignable to the Penultimate Glaciation—a conclusion in accordance with the pedological data.[9]

Thus, according to the geological and archaeological data, it would appear that all of the sites contain representative sections of Gravel I.

Then all of the implements are of last interglacial age or later. The proposal that the gravels were a product of a wet period and therefore could be correlated

[9] Wainwright, 1964, pp. 43–44.

to a period of glacial activity[10] is thus dismissed. Rather, they are probably a product of local interglacial river activity, and are not as significant a marker as was presumed. Instead, they would seem to be correlated to a period of low sea level, and this is much more secure an indicator of major glacial activity than rainfall.

Gravels II and III are, then, the first two stadia of the last glaciation. Soil III in Wainwright's sequence has no over-all equivalence in this chart, but it would continue the sequence. Thus, the Indian Middle Stone Age is wholly contained within the last glacial period and is not of interglacial date.

The foregoing has attempted to show that the entrance of man into the subcontinent as it has been documented so far was comparatively late, being in the third interglacial or Upper Pleistocene. All of these and subsequent remains are found in geological formations which can be correlated with one another and tentatively to a series of low sea levels, and from there to glacial maxima and minima outside of the subcontinent.

[10] G. C. Mohapatra, *The Stone Age Cultures of Orissa*, Deccan College Dissertation Series, Poona, 1962; H. D. Sankalia, *Prehistory and Protohistory in India and Pakistan*, University of Bombay, Bombay, 1963.

A P P E N D I X   B:

Middle Stone Age Sites in India

After H. D. SANKALIA*

River	No.	Site	District	Location
Indus	1	Campbellpur	Attock	W. Pakistan
Indus	2	Khushalgarh	Kohat	W. Pakistan
Indus	3	Makhad	Kohat	W. Pakistan
Indus	4	Injra	Kohat	W. Pakistan
Soan	1	Rawalpindi	Rawalpindi	W. Pakistan
Soan	2	Malakpur	Rawalpindi	W. Pakistan
Soan	3	Chauntra	Attock	W. Pakistan
Soan	4	Chakri	Attock	W. Pakistan
Poonch	1	Kotli		
Jhelum	1	Rohtas	Jhelum	Kashmir
Sutlej	1	Ror	Kangra	E. Punjab
Sukri	1	Dhaneri	Pali	Rajasthan

* *Science*, Vol. CXLVI (1964), p. 367.

River	No.	Site	District	Location
Guhiya	2	Danasani	Pali	Rajasthan
Luni	3	Luni	Jodhpur	Rajasthan
Shivna	1	Mandasor	Mandasor	Madhya Pradesh
Shivna	2	Nahargarh	Mandasor	Madhya Pradesh
Wagan	1	Hajiakheri	Chitorgarh	Rajasthan
Kadamali	2	Nimbahera	Chitorgarh	Rajasthan
Betwa	1	Gonchi	Jhansi	Uttar Pradesh
Dhasan	1	Sihora	Jhansi	Uttar Pradesh
Kopra	1	Khojakheri	Damoh	Madhya Pradesh
Son	1	Gara	Sidhi	Madhya Pradesh
Son	2	Umaria	Shahdol	Madhya Pradesh
Narbada	1	Devakachar	Narsinghpur	Madhya Pradesh
Narbada	2	Barman Ghat	Narsinghpur	Madhya Pradesh
Narbada	3	Saguna Ghat	Narsinghpur	Madhya Pradesh
Narbada	4	Maheswar	Nimad	Madhya Pradesh
Bhadar	1	Rojdi	Madhya	Saurashtra
Bhadar	2	Jetpur		
Tapti	1	Manjrod	W. Khandesh	Maharashtra
Tapti	2	Udhamgarh	W. Khandesh	Maharashtra
Godavari	1	Nandur Madhmeshwar	Nasik	Maharashtra
Godavari	2	Belpandhari	Ahmadnagar	Maharashtra
Godavari	3	Kalegaon	Ahmadnagar	Maharashtra
Pravara	1	Nevasa	Ahmadnagar	Maharashtra
Wuna	1	Nagpur	Nagpur	Maharashtra
Wardha	1	Patala	Wardha	Maharashtra
Bhima	1	Koregaon	Poona	Maharashtra
Mula-Mutha	1	Poona	Poona	Maharashtra
Kandivli-nala	1	Kandivli	Thana	Maharashtra
Kistna	1	Salvadgi	Bijapur	Mysore
Ghatprabha	1	Bagalkot	Bijapur	Mysore
Malaprabha	1	Taminhal	Bijapur	Mysore
Tungabhadra	1	Nittur	Bellary	Mysore

Ralla Kalava	1	Renigunta	Chittoor	Andhra
Arani	1	Vadamadurai	Chingleput	Madras
Korttalaiyar (Cortallaiyar)	1	Attirampakkam	Chingleput	Madras
Brahmani	1	Jhirpani	Sundergarh	Orissa
Brahmani	2	Kurhadi	Sundergarh	Orissa
Brahmani	3	Tumkelaghat	Sundergarh	Orissa
Brahmani	4	Harichandanpur	Dhenkanal	Orissa
Brahmani	5	Bhalitundi	Dhenkanal	Orissa
Baitarani	1	Jagannathpur	Sundergarh	Orissa
Baitarani	2	Ramla	Keonjhar	Orissa
Khadkei	1	Bijatala	Mayurbhanj	Orissa
Khadkei	2	Kandalia	Mayurbhanj	Orissa

APPENDIX C:

Notes on the Origin of Chinese Civilization and the Eastward Diffusion in Central Asia

THE YIN-SHANG DYNASTY (*ca.* 1700 to 1000 B.C.) ostensibly marks the emergence of civilization on the north China plains. As such it is the latest of the so-called primary civilizations (in this sense—those which lie at the base of the great traditional civilizations) to manifest itself in Asia. Though the pace of archaeological exploration of China has accelerated under Communist Chinese rule, there is surprisingly little new evidence to help clarify the origin of the Yin-Shang. However, several points are brought out by the evidence at hand:

(1) The Yin-Shang is later chronologically than the Mesopotamian (3100 B.C.) and Indian (2300 B.C.) civilizations. In fact, the Mesopotamian civilization is already part of a far-ranging *oikoumene* which touches on the Balkans, Egypt, Central Asia, and India by the time of the Yin-Shang. The recent findings in Greece (Nea Nikomedia) and Central Asia (Djeitun) evidence the widespread existence of food production and concomitant settled life by the seventh millennium B.C. This is followed in these and adjacent regions by accelerating and widespread development of sophisticated and innovative techniques in such specializations as weaving, brickmaking, animal and plant domestication, and metallurgy. For Central Asia at least, the evidence indicates the spread of these traits to Ferghana and the Altai probably by 3000 B.C.

(2) Pre-Shang settlements have been known in north China and Kansu since the 1920s. The more recent field work on the mainland has amplified this

material enormously. The evidence proves that the North China Plain was thoroughly settled by food producers prior to the emergence of the Yin-Shang civilization. Dr. Kwang-chih Chang of Yale University, in describing one of the stages of this settlement, the so-called Lungshanoid, points out that a number of traits foreshadowed the subsequent birth of civilization in the Huangho Valley.[1] He lists these as: (a) the permanent settlement, the large area of the farming villages, and the advancement of agriculture; (b) the specialization of industries, which had been considerably developed as shown by the appearance of wheel-made pottery in some of the areas; (c) the village fortifications, indicating the need for defense and hence the frequency of warfare between settlements; (d) the oracle bone, the prone burial, and the concentration of jade objects in certain places within the village, which material may imply an intensification of the differentiation of individual status; (e) the regional variation of style and the possible importance of the residential group at the community-aggregate level, which foreshadowed, if it did not indicate, the formation of urban networks and the beginning of regional states. One of these local states eventually succeeded in expansion and conquest and is subsequently known as the Yin-Shang.[2]

In other words, the setting for civilization was already prepared. In this the parallel with the situation in the Indus River Valley is quite close (p. 221). Examination of this pre-Shang material, however, indicates its hybrid origin. There are elements reflective of an indigenous development, but these seem to be in part the adaptation of already established techniques to local patterns. These indigenous elements include sericulture, jade carving, certain pottery forms, certain decorative motifs, the cultivation of hemp, kaoliang, and possibly rice, and the creation of characteristic tools and weapons such as the halberd, axe, and hoe. There are also North and Central Asian traits which are found widely from Burzahom (p. 312) to the Transbaikal and into the Caspian-Aral Sea regions. These traits include semisubterranean houses, cord-marked pottery, harpoons, the semilunar knife and hunting equipment such as the bow and arrow, probably stamped earth or pisé structures, tattooing or face painting, and dog and wild-ass usage. We might also expect certain shamanistic rituals and beliefs, as well as tailored clothing. Of eventual Western origin are the cultivation of wheat and millet; the raising of domestic cattle, sheep, goats, and pigs; flexed burial with accompanying funerary furniture; pottery making, especially painted pottery and several decorative motifs; lime plastering; and some agricultural implements, including the sickle and perhaps the spade.

The agglomeration of these traits into that characteristically Chinese sedentary complex which becomes the basis for the rise of Chinese civilization is, of course, a matter of great complexity. There is a hint that North and Central Asian hunting-gathering peoples were initially on the scene. The late Lauristan Ward of Harvard University suggested this possibility, with the addition of some sedentary pursuits.[3] Kwang-chih Chang sees cord-marked pottery as one of the very first cultural elements that appeared during the initial emergence of the neolithic stage in north China.[4] One can imagine such a cultural horizon as

---

[1] Kwang-chih Chang, *Archaeology of Ancient China*, Yale University Press, New Haven and London, 1963, p. 136.
[2] *Ibid.*, pp. 136–137.
[3] L. Ward, "The Relative Chronology of China Through the Han Period," *Relative Chronologies in Old World Archaeology*, R. W. Ehrich, ed., University of Chicago Press, Chicago, 1954, p. 130.
[4] 1963, p. 56.

providing the setting into which moved traits of Western origin whose diffusion was in response to the same stimuli as were found in Western Asia in the millennium after 6000 B.C. The uneven integration that occurred, whether rapid or slow, created those indigenous and characteristic styles which we associate with the Chinese tradition. Some authorities, either by implication or by direct comment, would deny the broad diffusionary movements that brought settled life to north China from the West. However, the facts that we have ample evidence for diffusion of the traits of sedentary life across Iran to the Altai and that some of these traits as a complex are associated with the appearance of Chinese sedentary cultures in what is apparently a fitting chronological context are difficult to overlook. China appears to be in somewhat the same relationship to this diffusionary phenomenon as is India. As Ward stated, "It seems quite clear that China was never separated from the rest of Asia by an iron curtain and that the development of Chinese culture was stimulated from period to period by the acceptance of traits, many of them fundamental, which had their origin in Western Asia."[5]

(3) The Yin-Shang civilization has its characteristic styles mostly derived from its indigenous and earlier cultural setting, as outlined above. Among these styles can be included the form of writing, the special forms of bronze vessels and their iconography, certain vessel shapes, and the domestication of the water buffalo. But there is also ample evidence that the developments in Western Asia and adjacent Central Asia strongly affected the Yin-Shang cultural manifestation. This evidence includes the appearance of the spoked-wheel chariot, the domestic horse, certain bronze implements, libation sacrifices, mass human sacrifices in connection with ritual or royal burials of a characteristic kind, and probably hierarchical government, the idea of writing, and some techniques in metallurgy.

[5] Ward, 1954, p. 140.

A P P E N D I X   D :   *Sites of the Kandahar Area*

Site	Location	Period*
Khr-1	On road following N bank of Arghandab River, 4 miles NE of junction with Kandahar-Farah Road	D–B
Khr-2	On road to N of Arghandab River, *ca.* 10 miles from junction with Kandahar-Farah Road	D–C
Khr-3	300 yards to S of village of Panjwai	D–B
Khr-4	4 miles E of Panjwai	D–B
Khr-5	4 miles E of Panjwai, 1 mile S of road	G_1–G_1

* For an explanation of the code used in this column, see p. 398.

Khr-6	6 miles E of Panjwai, 1¼ miles to S of road	D–C
Khr-7	6½ miles E of Panjwai, 1 mile S of road, at village of Salawa	D–C
Khr-8	7 miles E of Panjwai; ¾ mile S of road, 1 mile NE of Khr-7	D–C
Khr-9	7½ miles E of Panjwai, 1 mile S of road	D–C
Khr-10	1¼ miles S of road, 1 mile from Khr-9 (E)	H₂–G₂
Mundigak		I–G₃, F–E
Day Gulamon		D–C
Monsor Castle		D–C
Mound in Tamak Area	MKA Bench Mark No. 368	C–B
Arghandab-I		C
Kajakai Fort		B
Old City Kandahar		C–B
Kish Kin Hut Fort		D–C
Shamshir Ghar Cave (Dupree 1958)		E–C
Lashkari Bazaar		C
Nad-i-Ali Fort		B

A P P E N D I X   E: *Selected Radio-Carbon Dates for South Asia*

The list of radio-carbon dates for South Asia is constantly being augmented and for various reasons revised. The group shown here is based on a variety of sources, especially those obtained from the Tata Institute of Fundamental Research, Bombay (TF), and the University of Pennsylvania (P). The dates are based on the half-life of radio-carbon 5568 ±30 years Before Present. Subtraction of 1950 years gives the B.C. date.

Site	Laboratory Number	Affinity	Date
Ahar, Rajasthan	TF-31	Chalcolithic	3130 ±105
Ahar, Rajasthan	TF-32	Chalcolithic	3400 ±105
Ahar, Rajasthan	TF-34	Chalcolithic	3570 ±135
Ahar, Rajasthan	TF-37	Chalcolithic	3165 ±110
Ahar, Rajasthan	V-54	Chalcolithic	3835 ±95
Ahar, Rajasthan	V-55	Chalcolithic	3825 ±120
Ahar, Rajasthan	V-56	Chalcolithic	3715 ±95
Ahar, Rajasthan	V-57	Chalcolithic	3975 ±95
Ahar, Rajasthan	V-58	Chalcolithic	3890 ±100
Atranjikhera	TF-191	II Painted gray ware	2890 ±105
Atranjikhera	TF-289	IB Black & red ware	2550 ±105
Atranjikhera	TF-291	II Painted gray ware	2415 ±100
Burzahom, Kashmir	TF-10	Neolithic	2580 ±100
Burzahom, Kashmir	TF-13	Neolithic	3690 ±125
Burzahom, Kashmir	TF-15	Neolithic	3390 ±105
Burzahom, Kashmir	TF-14	Neolithic	3860 ±340
Burzahom, Kashmir	TF-123	Neolithic	4055 ±110
Burzahom, Kashmir	TF-127	Neolithic	3935 ±110
Burzahom, Kashmir	TF-128	Neolithic	4205 ±115

Site	Laboratory Number	Affinity	Date
Burzahom, Kashmir	TF-129	Neolithic	3670 ±90
Butkara	R-194	Grave	2425 ±40
Chandoli	TF-42	Chalcolithic	3035 ±115
Chandoli	TF-43	Chalcolithic	2905 ±100
Chandoli	P-472	Chalcolithic	3157 ±68
Chandoli	P-473	Chalcolithic	3184 ±68
Chandoli	P-474	Chalcolithic	3099 ±185
Damb Sadaat, Baluchistan	P-522	Period II	4378 ±196
Damb Sadaat, Baluchistan	L-180B	Period I	4348 ±350
Damb Sadaat, Baluchistan	L-180C	Period II	4375 ±412
Damb Sadaat, Baluchistan	L-180E	Period II	4357 ±361
Damb Sadaat, Baluchistan	P-523	Period II	4029 ±74
Damb Sadaat, Baluchistan	UW-59	Period I	4330 ±70
Damb Sadaat, Baluchistan	UW-60	Period III	4030 ±160
Eran	P-525	Period II	3193 ±69
Eran	P-526	Chalcolithic	3136 ±68
Eran	P-527	Chalcolithic	2515 ±58
Eran	P-528	Chalcolithic	2878 ±65
Eran	P-529	Chalcolithic	3869 ±72
Eran	TF-324	Period IIA	3130 ±105
Eran	TF-326	Period IIA	2905 ±105
Eran	TF-327	Period I	3280 ±100
Eran	TF-329	Period I	3300 ±105
Eran	TF-330	Period I	3220 ±100
Eran	TF-337	Period I	3355 ±90
Ghar-i-Mar (Snake Cave), Afghanistan	Hv-425	"Mesolithic"	ca. 6700 B.C.
Ghar-i-Mar (Snake Cave), Afghanistan	Hv-428	Ceramic Neolithic	ca. 5270 B.C.
Ghar-i-Mar (Snake Cave), Afghanistan	Hv-429	Ceramic Neolithic	ca. 5080 B.C.
Hallur	TF-570	Early Iron Age, layer 4	2970 ±105
Hallur	TF-573	Early Iron Age, layer 5	2820 ±100
Hallur	TF-575	Chalcolithic, layer 7	2895 ±100
Hallur	TF-580	Neolithic, layer 14	3560 ±105
Hastinapura, Uttar Pradesh	TF-80, 82	Period III	1940 ±110
Hastinapura, Uttar Pradesh	TF-81	Period III	2015 ±95
Hastinapura, Uttar Pradesh	TF-83	Period II	2220 ±110
Hastinapura, Uttar Pradesh	TF-85	Period II	2385 ±125
Hastinapura, Uttar Pradesh	TF-88	Period III	2225 ±110
Hastinapura, Uttar Pradesh	TF-90	Period II	2270 ±110
Hastinapura, Uttar Pradesh	TF-91	Period II	2450 ±120
Hastinapura, Uttar Pradesh	TF-112	Period II	2260 ±95
Kalibangan, Rajasthan	P-481	Harappan	3879 ±72
Kalibangan, Rajasthan	TF-25	Harappan	3930 ±110
Kalibangan, Rajasthan	TF-138	Harappan	3075 ±100
Kalibangan, Rajasthan	TF-139	Harappan	3775 ±100
Kalibangan, Rajasthan	TF-141	Harappan	3705 ±110
Kalibangan, Rajasthan	TF-142	Harappan	3635 ±100
Kalibangan, Rajasthan	TF-143	Harappan	3510 ±110
Kalibangan, Rajasthan	TF-145	Harappan	3895 ±100
Kalibangan, Rajasthan	TF-147	Harappan	3865 ±100
Kalibangan, Rajasthan	TF-149	Harappan	3675 ±140
Kalibangan, Rajasthan	TF-150	Harappan	3740 ±100

Site	Laboratory Number	Affinity	Date
Kalibangan, Rajasthan	TF-151	Harappan	3800 ± 100
Kalibangan, Rajasthan	TF-152	Harappan	3615 ± 85
Kalibangan, Rajasthan	TF-153	Harappan	3910 ± 110
Kalibangan, Rajasthan	TF-154	Pre-Harappan period	3665 ± 110
Kalibangan, Rajasthan	TF-155	Pre-Harappan period	4195 ± 115
Kalibangan, Rajasthan	TF-156	Pre-Harappan period	3740 ± 105
Kalibangan, Rajasthan	TF-157	Pre-Harappan period	4120 ± 100
Kalibangan, Rajasthan	TF-160	Harappan	4060 ± 100
Kalibangan, Rajasthan	TF-161	Pre-Harappan period	3930 ± 100
Kalibangan, Rajasthan	TF-162	Pre-Harappan period	3940 ± 100
Kalibangan, Rajasthan	TF-163	Harappan	3910 ± 100
Kalibangan, Rajasthan	TF-165	Pre-Harappan period	3800 ± 100
Kalibangan, Rajasthan	TF-240	Pre-Harappan period	3610 ± 110
Kalibangan, Rajasthan	TF-241	Pre-Harappan period	4090 ± 90
Kalibangan, Rajasthan	TF-244	Harappan	3250 ± 90
Kausambi	TF-221	Period III (NBP)	2385 ± 100
Kausambi	TF-225	Period III (NBP)	2285 ± 105
Kayatha	TF-396	Chalcolithic III	3575 ± 105
Kayatha	TF-397	Chalcolithic III	3350 ± 100
Kayatha	TF-398	Chalcolithic III	3520 ± 100
Kayatha	TF-399	Chalcolithic II	3525 ± 100
Kayatha	TF-400	Chalcolithic II	3800 ± 105
Kayatha	TF-402	Chalcolithic III	3240 ± 100
Kayatha	TF-680	Chalcolithic I	3850 ± 95
Kili Ghul Mohammed, Baluchistan	UW-61	Period I	5260 ± 80
Kili Ghul Mohammed, Baluchistan	L-180A	Period I	5497 ± 500
Kili Ghul Mohammed, Baluchistan	P-524	Period I	5474 ± 83
Kot Diji, Lower Indus Valley	P-179	Level 5, Late KD	4161 ± 151
Kot Diji, Lower Indus Valley	P-180	Level 5, Late KD	4083 ± 137
Kot Diji, Lower Indus Valley	P-195	Level 4, Late KD	3925 ± 134
Kot Diji, Lower Indus Valley	P-196	Level 14, Early KD	4412 ± 141
Lekhania	TF-417	Burial in rock shelter	3560 ± 105
Lothal, Gujarat	TF-19	Harappan	3650 ± 135
Lothal, Gujarat	TF-22	Harappan	3845 ± 110
Lothal, Gujarat	TF-23	Harappan	3705 ± 105
Lothal, Gujarat	TF-26	Harappan	3830 ± 120
Lothal, Gujarat	TF-27	Harappan	3840 ± 110
Lothal, Gujarat	TF-29	Harappan	3740 ± 110
Lothal, Gujarat	TF-133	Harappan, Period IIA	3740 ± 110
Lothal, Gujarat	TF-135	Harappan, Period IIA	3405 ± 125
Lothal, Gujarat	TF-136	Harappan, Period IA	3915 ± 130
Mahisadal, West Bengal	TF-389	II, Early Iron Age	2565 ± 105
Mahisadal, West Bengal	TF-390	I, Chalcolithic	2725 ± 100
Mahisadal, West Bengal	TF-391	I, Chalcolithic	3235 ± 105
Mahisadal, West Bengal	TF-392	I, Chalcolithic	2950 ± 105
Mohenjo-daro, W. Pakistan	TF-75	Late Harappan	3600 ± 110
Mohenjo-daro, W. Pakistan	P-1176	Mature Harappan	3801 ± 59
Mohenjo-daro, W. Pakistan	P-1177	Mature Harappan	3895 ± 64
Mohenjo-daro, W. Pakistan	P-1178A	Mature Harappan	3802 ± 59
Mohenjo-daro, W. Pakistan	P-1179	Mature Harappan	3913 ± 64
Mohenjo-daro, W. Pakistan	P-1180	Mature Harappan	3828 ± 61
Mohenjo-daro, W. Pakistan	P-1182A	Mature Harappan	3702 ± 63
Mundigak	GSY-50	Period I, 5	3945 ± 150
Mundigak	GSY-51	Period III, 1	2995 ± 1110
Mundigak	GSY-52	Period II, 1	3480 ± 115
Mundigak	GSY-53	Period III, 5	4185 ± 150

Site	Laboratory Number	Affinity	Date
Navdatoli	TF-59	Chalcolithic	3380 ± 105
Navdatoli	P-200	Chalcolithic, phase IIIA	3457 ± 127
Navdatoli	P-201	Chalcolithic, phase IIIA	3492 ± 128
Navdatoli	P-202	Chalcolithic, phase IIIB	3503 ± 128
Navdatoli	P-204	Chalcolithic, phase IIIC	3449 ± 127
Navdatoli	P-205	Chalcolithic phase IIID	3294 ± 125
Navdatoli	P-475	Chalcolithic phase IIIA	3455 ± 70
Navdatoli	P-476	Chalcolithic phase IIIB	4125 ± 69
Nevasa, Maharashtra	TF-40	Chalcolithic	3110 ± 110
Nevasa, Maharashtra	F-40	Chalcolithic, Jorwe	3110 ± 110
Nevasa, Maharashtra	P-181	Chalcolithic, Jorwe	3106 ± 122
Niai Buthi (Las Bela), Baluchistan	P-478	Niai Buthi II	3740 ± 64
Noh	UCLA-703A	Painted gray ware series	2480 ± 250
Noh	UCLA-703B	Painted gray ware series	2690 ± 220
Paiyampalli	TF-349	Neolithic	3340 ± 100
Pandu Rajar Dhibi	—	Period II (Chalcolithic)	1012 ± 120
Rupar	TF-209	Period III, NBP	2365 ± 100
Sanganakallu	TF-354	Neolithic	3440 ± 105
Sanganakallu	TF-359	Neolithic	3400 ± 100
Sonegaon	TF-379	Chalcolithic, Jorwe	3150 ± 90
Sonegaon	TF-380	Chalcolithic, Jorwe	3230 ± 105
Sonpur	TF-376	Pre-NBP period	2510 ± 105
T. Narsipur	TF-412	Neolithic	3645 ± 105
T. Narsipur	TF-413	Neolithic	3345 ± 105
Tekkalakota	TF-236	Neolithic, period I	3395 ± 105
Tekkalakota	TF-237	Neolithic, period I	3465 ± 105
Tekkalakota	TF-262	Neolithic, period II	3460 ± 135
Tekkalakota	TF-266	Neolithic, period I	3625 ± 100
Tekkalakota	TF-277	Ash pit (Iron Age)	2220 ± 105
Utnur	TF-167	Neolithic, period IIA	3890 ± 110
Utnur	TF-168	Neolithic, period IIIA	3875 ± 110
Utnur	BM-54	Neolithic, period IB	4120 ± 150

Additional Dates, 1968–74

(The following carbon dates are given on the 5568 half-life with reading on the 5730 half-life in parentheses.)[1]

Site	Laboratory Number	Date	
Sarai Nahr Rai	TF-1104	10,050 ± 110	(10,345 ± 110)
Bagor	TF-786	6,245 ± 200	(6,430 ± 200)
	TF-1007	4,585 ± 105	(4,715 ± 105)
	TF-1009	5,620 ± 125	(5,785 ± 130)
	TF-1005 and 1006	3,945 ± 90	(4,060 ± 90)
Adamgarh	TF-120	7,240 ± 125	(7,450 ± 130)

[1] *South Asian Archaeology*, p. 10.

(The following C14 dates based on half-life = 5730 yrs. in years B.C.)[2]

Hallur	TF-580	1710 ± 105
(Dharwar, Mysore)	TF-576	1425 ± 110
	TF-585	1195 ± 100
	TF-570	1105 ± 105
	TF-575	1030 ± 105
	TF-573	955 ± 100
Paiyampalli	TF-349	1485 ± 100
(North Arcot, Madras)		
Palvoy	TF-701	1965 ± 105
(Anantpur, Andhra Pradesh)	TF-354	1590 ± 110
Sangankallu	TF-355	1585 ± 105
(Bellary, Mysore)	TF-359	1550 ± 105
Tekkalakota,	TF-266	1780 ± 105
(Bellary, Mysore)	TF-237	1615 ± 105
	TF-262	1610 ± 140
	TF-239	1540 ± 105
Terdal	TF-684	1935 ± 100
(Bijapur, Mysore)	TF-683	1770 ± 120
T. Narsipur	TF-412	1805 ± 110
(Mysore, Mysore)	TF-413	1495 ± 110
Utnur	BM-54	2295 ± 155
(Mahboobnagar,	TF-167	2050 ± 115
Andhra Pradesh)	TF-168	2040 ± 115

[2] *Radiocarbon and Indian Archaeology*, p. 78.

(The following C14 dates, B.C. are based on half-life = 5730 years.)[3]

Inamgaon	TF-1086	1535 ± 150
	TF-1085	1440 ± 105
	TF-1087	1405 ± 105
Nevasa	TF-40	1250 ± 110
	P-181	1250 ± 125
Songaon	TF-379	1290 ± 95
	TF-383	1330 ± 100
	TF-382	1340 ± 100
	TF-380	1375 ± 110
	TF-384	1565 ± 110
Chandoli	TF-43	1040 ± 105
	TF-42	1170 ± 120
	P-474	1240 ± 110
	P-472	1300 ± 70
	P-473	1330 ± 70

[3] *Radiocarbon and Indian Archaeology*, p. 140.

APPENDIX F: *Sites of the Indo-Iranian Borderlands and the Indus River Valley*

THE FOLLOWING TABLES are substantially a record of the bulk of archaeological sites known in West Pakistan. There are gaps in the record caused by oversight or lack of knowledge that can be filled out as time goes along. The number in the leftmost column is a registry number used by our expedition in the field. The period range is largely an approximation based on what evidence there is at this time. It refers to the table below.

By counting the number of times sites represent given periods some idea can be obtained as to the scale of population and the areas of settlement in time. Noteworthy is the evidence that the prehistoric and Harappan periods mark the heaviest settlement of the Borderlands, apparently not to be matched again until Islamic and Modern times.

A—1800 to present
B—1300 to 1800
C—500 to 1300
D—300 to 500
E—800 B.C. to 300 A.D.
   E_1—800 to 350 B.C.
   E_2—350 B.C. to 100 A.D.
   E_3—100 to 300 A.D.

F—1400 to 800 B.C.
G_3—1900 to 1400 B.C.
G_2—2300 to 1900 B.C.
G_1—2500 to 2300 B.C.
H_2—2800 to 2500 B.C.
H_1—3000 to 2800 B.C.
I—3500 to 3000 B.C.
J—4000+ to 3500 B.C.

The abbreviations refer to Stein, Dales, Fairservis, Field, Raikes, de Cardi, Dupree, and others; the numbers are the reference dates or, in case the material is unpublished, the year of the field work.

No.	Site	Source	Location	Period Range
Zhob (Baluchistan)				
1	Periano Ghundai (Z-2)	St 29	Near Fort Sandeman	I–G_3
		Fa 59		
2	Kaudani (Z-4)	St 29	Near Fort Sandeman	G_3, E, D
		Fa 59		
3	Mata Kaudani	St 29	Near Fort Sandeman	G_3, E
4	Moghul Ghundai (Z-3)	St 29	Near Fort Sandeman	G_3, E
		Fa 59		
5	Urusko Zhara	St 29	Near Fort Sandeman	G_3
6	Tor Sharghalai	St 29	Sandiyar	E
7	Tor Sharghalai II	St 29	Sandiyar	E
8	Tor Sharghalai III	St 29	Sandiyar	E
9	Sang	St 29	Fort Sandeman	D
10	Kabulzai	St 29	Near Hindu Bagh	E
11	Z-1	Fa 59	27 miles from Fort Sandeman	?
12	Moghuli Khankai	St 29	Hindu Bagh	B
13	Murgha Fakirzai	St 29	Hindu Bagh	B
14	Karezgai	St 29	Hindu Bagh	G, D
15	Murgha Mehtarzai	St 29	Hindu Bagh	G, B
Loralai (Baluchistan)				
1	Spina Ghundai	St 29	Loralai	D
2	Zara Ghundai	St 29	Wahar	?

No.	Site	Source	Location	Period Range
Loralai (Baluchistan) (*continued*)				
3	Firoz Khan Ghundai	St 29	Wahar	D(?)
4	Chaperkai Hill	St 29	Wahar	E
5	Sre Sharghalai	St 29	Duki	D
6	Nimkai Ghundai	St 29	Duki	D
7	Ghalawa Ghundai	St 29	Duki	E(?)
8	Sawal Kala	St 29	Duki	E, C, B
9	L-1 (Kowas)	St 29 Fa 59	Kowas village on Quetta-Ziarat Road, 10 miles west of Ziarat	H₁–G₁
10	L-2	Fa 59	Ziarat Road, 4 miles west of Sinjawi	I–G₁
11	L-3	Fa 59 St 29	3 miles east of Sinjawi	I–G₁
12	L-4 (Sur Jangal)	Fa 59 St 29	Midway between Duki and Sinjawi	I–G₁–G₁
13	L-5	Fa 59	Near Shahr Jahangir village, Loralai	F–D
14	L-6	Fa 59	3 miles northeast of Duki	I–G₁
15	L-7 (Bala Spina)	Fa 59 St 29	Near Sinjawi	?
16	L-8 (Tor Dherai)	Fa 59 St 29	*ca.* 7 miles southeast of Duki	D
17	L-9 (Dabar Kot)	Fa 59 St 29 Noet 1898*	*ca.* 10 miles southeast of Duki	I–G₁, F–D
18	L-11	Fa 59	4 miles west of Sinjawi	?
19	L-12 (Rana Ghundai)	Fa 59 St 29 Noet 98 Ross 46	7 miles east of Loralai	J–G, F–D
20	L-13 (Moghul Kala)	Fa 59 St 29	*ca.* 15 miles northeast of Loralai	I–G₁, F, E, D, C
Quetta-Pishin (Baluchistan)				
1	Riasa Ghundai	St 29	Pishin City area	C, D
2	Kuchnai Ghundai	St 29	Pishin City area	G
3	Spina Ghundai	St 29	Pishin City area	G–B₁
4	Sra Kala	St 29	Pishin City area	D–C
5	Babari Ghundai (P-4)	St 29 Fa 56	Saranan village	D
6	Akhpara Ghundai	St 29	Pishin City area	F(?)
7	Ishan Khan Kila (P-84)	St 29	Pishin City area	D–C
8	Mata Ghundai	St 29	Pishin City area	G(?)
9	Majo Mill	St 29	Surkhab Valley	G, B
10	Kranai Hill	St 29	Surkhab Valley	G₁–G₁
11	Pir Alizai	St 29	Gulistan	G₁
12	Safid or Spina Ghundai (P-1)	St 29 Fa 56	Pishin, near Habibzai village	D–B
13	Kasiano Dozakh (Q-34)	St 29 Fa 56	Quetta Valley	K–G₁, F
14	Tirkha Ghundai	St 29	Quetta Valley	C–B
15	Baleli (Q-29)	St 29 Fa 56	Quetta Valley	J

* F. Noetling, "Reise nach Baluchistan," *Zeitschrift für Ethnologie und Verhandlungen,* Berliner Gesellschaft für Anthropologie, etc. Vol. 30 (1898), pp. 250 ff.

No.	Site	Source	Location	Period Range

Quetta-Pishin (Baluchistan) (*continued*)

No.	Site	Source	Location	Period Range
16	P-2	Fa 56	1½ miles north of P-1	D–B
17	P-3	Fa 56 St 29	Near Pir Alizai village, Quetta-Chaman Road	G₃, A
18	P-5 (Kila Bhutasi)	Fa 56	1 mile west of Pishin	B
19	P-6 (Lal Ghundai)	Fa 56	15 miles from Khanozoi on Pishin-Khanozoi Road	J
20	P-7	Fa 56	½ mile south of P-6	B–A
21	P-8	Fa 56	Sahib Khan village near Bostan	H–G₂
22	Q-1	Fa 56	Gwandin Valley	A
23	Q-2	Fa 56	Gwandin Valley	A
24	Q-3	Fa 56	Gwandin Valley	A
25	Q-4	Fa 56	Gwandin Valley	A
26	Q-33	Fa 56	Gwandin Valley	H₁–G₂
27	Q-5	Fa 56	Bhalla Dasht area	A
28	Q-6	Fa 56	Bhalla Dasht area	H₁–G₂
29	Q-7	Fa 56	Near Nishpa Tunnel	A(?)
30	Q-8 (Damb Sadaat or Mian Ghundai)	Fa 56 Piggott 47	Near Mian Ghundi levy post	H₂–G₂
31	Q-9	Fa 56	Zarakhu Valley	H₁–G₂
32	Q-10	Fa 56	3 miles south of Sariab levy post	D
33	Q-36	Fa 56	Near Hasani village, west of Mile Post 14 on Quetta- Sibi Road	H₁–G₂, F
34	Q-11	Fa 56	Sariab levy post vicinity	B(?)
35	Q-12	Fa 56	Sariab levy post vicinity	B(?)
36	Q-13	Fa 56	Sariab levy post vicinity	G₂
37	Q-14	Fa 56	Sariab levy post vicinity	H₂
38	Q-15	Fa 56	Sariab levy post vicinity	H₂–G₂
39	Q-16	Fa 56	Sariab levy post vicinity	G₁–G, F
40	Q-17	Fa 56	Sariab levy post vicinity	I–H₁, G₂
41	Q-18	Fa 56	Sariab levy post vicinity	H₁–G₂, D(?), C–B
42	Q-19	Fa 56	Quetta Miri	H₁–G₂, F–A
43	Q-20	Fa 56	North of Mile Post 5 on Samungli Road	G₂–G₂
44	Q-21	Fa 56	Near Khaizi village on Samungli Road	A(?)
45	Q-22	Fa 56	Near Sheik Manda village	F–E
46	Q-23	Fa 56	Southwestern outskirts of Quetta City	H₁–G₁
47	Q-24 (Kili Gul Mohammad)	Fa 56	Near Kili Gul Mohammad village	J–G₂, F–E
48	Q-25	Fa 56	1 mile east of Chashma village	I–G₂, F–E
49	Q-26	Fa 56	½ mile southeast of Chashma village	H₂–G₂
50	Q-27	Fa 56	100 yards southeast of Q-26	A(?)
51	Q-28	Fa 56	½ mile south of Chashma village	H₂–G₁
52	Q-30	Fa 56	Near Mile Post 8 on Quetta-Pishin Road	H₁, F–E, C, B, A
53	Q-31 (Dhozakh Khansian)	Fa 56	Baleli vicinity	D(?), C–A

No.	Site	Source	Location	Period Range

Quetta-Pishin (Baluchistan) (*continued*)

No.	Site	Source	Location	Period Range
54	Q-32	Fa 56	1 mile southeast of Chashma village	H_1–G_1, E, C–A
55	Q-35	Fa 56	Aghbarg Valley	H_1–G_2
56	Q-37	Fa 56	Near Panjpai levy post, Sarawan, Kalat	G_1–G_2
57	Khairabad	PA 65*	30° 42′ N, 67° 4′ E Bershor Valley	D–C
58	Dab Khanzai	PA 65	30° 43′ N, 67° 5′ E Bershor Valley	?
59	P-10 (Manzakai)	Fa 65 (unpublished)	Near village of Manzakai, south of Pishin City	H_2–G_2

Sibi District (Baluch-Kachhi)

No.	Site	Source	Location	Period Range
1	Judeirjo-daro (Discovered by R. L. Raikes)	PA 64	18 miles northwest of Jacobabad	G_1–G_3
2	Pirak (Discovered by R. L. Raikes)	PA 64	*ca.* 7 miles south of Sibi	F–D
3	Luni	PA 64	8 miles northeast of Sibi	D
4	Dranjan Site	PA 64	36 miles west of Sibi in Bolan Pass	D
5	Rindi Mound	PA 64	4 miles west of Dadar in mouth of Bolan Pass	D–B
6	Kotra	DeC 51, 59–64	Gandava	G_3–F
7	Pathiani Kot I	DeC 51, 59–64	Gandava	G_2–G_3, F(?)
8	Pathiani Kot II	DeC 51, 59–64	Gandava	F
9	Pathiani Kot III	DeC 51, 59–64	Gandava	F
10	Fatehpur	DeC 51, 59–64	Gandava	?

Sarawan (Kalat Division-Baluchistan)

No.	Site	Source	Location	Period Range
1	Salukhan	St 31	Kalat to Mastung	G_1–G_2
2	Saiyid Maurez	St 31	Kalat to Mastung	I–H_2
3	Sampur Damb	St 31	Kalat to Mastung	D–C
4	Spet Bulandi	St 31	Kalat to Mastung	D–C
5	Bundakhi Damb	St 31	Kalat to Mastung	H
6	Malghori Damb	St 31	Kalat to Mastung	I
7	Khwaja Zabor	St 31	Kalat to Mastung	H(?), F–E
8	Khad-i-kohing	St 31	Kalat to Mastung	F–E, B
9	Kullu Kalat I	St 31	Kalat to Mastung	F–E, B
10	Kullu Kalat II	St 31	Kalat to Mastung	?
11	Kafir Kot	DeC 51, 59–64	Panjpai	G_1–G_3
12	Tor Wenai (Tor Ghundai)	DeC 51, 59–64	Panjpai	G_1–G_3
13	Mobi Damb	DeC 51, 59–64	Pringabad	H_2–G, B
14	Kulloi	DeC 51, 59–64	Brinchinnau	G_1–G_3
15	Shahr Sardar	DeC 51, 59–64	Brinchinnau	H_2–G_3
16	Kardagap	DeC 51, 59–64		?
17	Zahrazai	DeC 51, 59–64	Mungachar	G
18	Kullu Kalat	DeC 51, 59–64	Mungachar	I, F–E
19	Togau	DeC 51, 59–64	Chhappar	I–G_2
20	Damb Zerga	DeC 51, 59–64	Ziarat	H
21	Malki	DeC 51, 59–64	Kalat	I–H, E–F, D
22	Khwaja Zubeir	FAK†	22 miles from Kalat City	I–G_1

* PA stands for Pakistan Department of Archaeology.
† FAK stands for Fazlur A. Khan, Director of Archaeology for Pakistan.

No.	Site	Source	Location	Period Range

Sarawan (Kalat Division-Baluchistan) (*continued*)

No.	Site	Source	Location	Period Range
23	Damb Goram	FAK	22 miles from Kalat on Surab Road	H_2–G_2
24	Kaptun Bra	FAK	20 miles southeast of Kalat City	H_1–G, D
25	Damb Kulu	FAK	12 miles west of Kalat City	H–G
26	Mandai	FAK	Kalat	H_1–G_2
27	Isplinji I & II (Discovered by R. L. Raikes)	PA	Isplinji village in Isplinji Valley	I–G_2
28	Sardar Khel Damb	PA	Near Sardar Khel village	H_1–G_2
29	K-1	Fa 56	1 mile south of customs barrier, Lak Pass	H_2–G_2
30	K-2	Fa 56 Har 29	4.5 miles northwest of Mastung	F, D–C

Chagai-Bolan Pass (Baluchistan)

No.	Site	Source	Location	Period Range
1	Ch-1	Fa 56	Nushki Mound, Nushki	H_2–G_1, F, D–C
2	B-1	Fa 56	1 mile south of Bibi Nani levy post, Bolan Pass	G_1–G_3, F, D–C
3	B-2	Fa 56	*ca.* 5 miles north of Kirta, Bolan Pass	H_2–G_2

Jhalawan (Kalat Division-Baluchistan)

No.	Site	Source	Location	Period Range
1	Surkh Damb	St 31 Fie 59	Surab	D–C
2	Neghar	St 31 Fie 59	Surab	F–E, B
3	Thok Valley I	St 31	Entrance to valley	I–H_1
4	Kuki Damb	St 31 DeC 64	At entrance to valley	I–H_1
5	Benn Chah	St 31 Fie 55	Surab	I–H
6	Ghalaihk	St 31	Kolwa (Jhalawan)	J(?)
7	Ziarati Damb	St 31	Kolwa (Jhalawan)	B–A
8	Thale Damb	St 31	Kolwa (Jhalawan)	H_2–G_2
9	Marastan Enclosure	St 31	Kolwa (Jhalawan)	G_2
10	Pak	St 31	Kolwa (Jhalawan)	H_2–G_2
11	Gate Dap	St 31	Kolwa (Jhalawan)	H_2, B
12	Segak	St 31	Kolwa (Jhalawan)	H_2–G_2
13	Rodkan	St 31	Kolwa (Jhalawan)	H_2–G_2, C–B
14	Old Balor	St 31	Kolwa (Jhalawan)	H–G_2
15	Ashal	St 31	Kolwa (Jhalawan)	H_2–G_1
16	Madak Kalat	St 31	Kolwa (Jhalawan)	H_2–G_1, B
17	Sahar Kalat	St 31	Kolwa (Jhalawan)	?
18	Hor Kalat	St 31	Kolwa (Jhalawan)	H_2–G_1
19	Jaran	St 31	Kolwa (Jhalawan)	H_2–G_2
20	Zik	St 31	Kolwa (Jhalawan)	H_2–G_2
21	Chambor	St 31	Kolwa (Jhalawan)	?
22	Malar (gabarbands)	St 31	Kolwa (Jhalawan)	?
23	Kallag	St 31	Kolwa (Jhalawan)	H_2–G_2(?)
24	Cheri Malar (Kamar-band)	St 31	Kolwa (Jhalawan)	H_2–G(?)
25	Chahi Damb	St 31	Kolwa (Jhalawan)	H_1–G

No.	Site	Source	Location	Period Range
Jhalawan (Kalat Division—Baluchistan) (*continued*)				
26	Singi Kalat	St 31	Kolwa (Jhalawan)	G_2
27	Gushanak	St 31	Kolwa (Jhalawan)	H_2-G_1, E–F
28	Kulli	St 31	Kolwa (Jhalawan)	H_2-G_2
29	Bazdad Kalat	St 31	Kolwa (Jhalawan)	H_2-G_2
30	Awaran	St 31	Kolwa (Jhalawan)	H_1-G_1, E–F, B
31	Kambar Damb	St 31	Kolwa (Jhalawan)	F–E
32	Firoz Khan Damb	St 31	Kolwa (Jhalawan)	F–E
33	Sohran Damb	St 31	Kolwa (Jhalawan)	C–B
34	Kambaro Damb (Bedi)	St 31	Kolwa (Jhalawan)	F–E
35	Gat Barat (gabarbands)	St 31	Awaran to Jhau	?
36	Tikri Damb	St 31	Awaran to Jhau	H_2-G_2
37	Karam Shah Damb	St 31	Awaran to Jhau	C–B
38	Siah Damb (Nundara)	St 31	Awaran to Jhau	H_1-G_2
39	Spet Damb I	St 31	Awaran to Jhau	F–E
40	Spet Damb II	St 31	Awaran to Jhau	F–E, B
41	Siah Damb (Jhau)	St 31	Awaran to Jhau	G_1-G_2
42	Adasta Damb	St 31	Awaran to Jhau	G_2-G_3
43	Dedari Enclosure	St 31	Southern Mashkai Valley	?
44	Mungal Chauki (gabarbands)	St 31	Southern Mashkai Valley	?
45	Sohr Damb (tank)	St 31	Southern Mashkai Valley	F–E
46	Ughar Damb (gabarband)	St 31	Southern Mashkai Valley	F–E(?)
47	Malasband	St 31	Southern Mashkai Valley	H_2, B
48	Mazena Damb	St 31	Southern Mashkai Valley	G_2-G_3
49	Sohren Damb	St 31	Southern Mashkai Valley	G_2-G_2
50	Gwarjak (burials)	St 31	Southern Mashkai Valley	E(?)
51	Kalaro Damb	St 31	Southern Mashkai Valley	G_1-G_2
52	Men Damb	St 31	Southern Mashkai Valley	G_1-G_2
53	Gajar Damb	St 31	Southern Mashkai Valley	G(?)
54	Nokjo Shahdinzai Damb	St 31	Southern Mashkai Valley	G_2-G_3, E–F
55	Mehi Damb	St 31	Southern Mashkai Valley	H_2-G_3
56	Jebri Dambs (two small mounds)	St 31	Southern Mashkai Valley	H_2-G_1, J
57	Runjan Damb	St 31	Northern Mashkai Valley	G_2-G_3(?)
58	Suneri Damb	St 31	Northern Mashkai Valley	H_2-G_1, E–F, D–B
59	Gwani Kalat	St 31	Northern Mashkai Valley	H_2-G_1, E–B
60	Jawarji Kalat	St 31	Northern Mashkai Valley	H_1-G_1, E–B
61	Saka Kalat	St 31	Northern Mashkai Valley	G_1-G_3, F–E
62	Sohr Damb (Nal) (Hargreaves Site)	St 31 / Har 29	Northern Mashkai Valley	H_2-G_2
63	Shakar Khan Damb	St 31	Northern Mashkai Valley	J
64	Shari Damb	St 31	Northern Mashkai Valley	F–E
65	Lehri	St 31	Northern Mashlai Valley	F–E
66	Hamal Damb	St 31	Northern Mashkai Valley	F–E
67	Hala Damb	St 31	Northern Mashkai Valley	G_2-G_2
68	Nal Village	St 31	Northern Mashkai Valley	E, B
69	Laghor Zard (gabarbands)	St 31	Northern Mashkai Valley	?
70	Gumbat	St 31	Khuzdar area	B–A
71	Kand	St 31	Khuzdar area	B
72	Kahnak	St 31	Khuzdar area	B
73	Chimri	St 31	Khuzdar area	H_1-H_2

No.	Site	Source	Location	Period Range
Jhalawan (Kalat Division—Baluchistan) (*continued*)				
74	Miri-But	St 31	Khuzdar area	D–B
75	Geni Damb	St 31	Khuzdar area	B
76	Boluka Damb	St 31	Khuzdar area	B–A
77	Wahir I (enclosure)	St 31	Khuzdar area	F(?)
78	Wahir II	St 31	Khuzdar area	G_1–G_2
79	Belar Valley Mound	St 31 Rai 60–61	Drakalo Valley	?
80	Haji Mohammad Damb	St 31	Belar Valley	F–E
81	Inayat Shah Damb	St 31	Baghwana area (between Khuzdar and Kalat City)	F–E
82	Bit Damb or Bit Sino Damb	St 31	Baghwana area (between Khuzdar and Kalat City)	F–E
83	Natwani Damb	St 31	Baghwana area (between Khuzdar and Kalat City)	?
84	Kissu Damb	St 31	Baghwana area (between Khuzdar and Kalat City)	F–E
85	Landau Damb	St 31	Baghwana area (between Khuzdar and Kalat City)	F–E
86	Sangas Damb	St 31	Baghwana area (between Khuzdar and Kalat City)	F–E
87	Bari Damb	St 31	Baghwana area (between Khuzdar and Kalat City)	F–E, D, B
88	Radhani Damb	St 31	Baghwana area (between Khuzdar and Kalat City)	F–E
89	Londo Damb	St 31	Baghwana area (between Khuzdar and Kalat City)	F–E
90	Mugali (gabarbands)	St 31	Baghwana area (between Khuzdar and Kalat City)	?
91	Anjira	DeC 51, 59–64	Surab	J–G_2
92	Alizai	DeC 51, 59–64	Surab	F–E, D
93	Patki	DeC 51, 59–64	Surab	?
94	Gorpat	DeC 51, 59–64	Surab	I–H_1, B–A
95	Unnamed small mound	DeC 51, 59–64	Surab	?
96	Unnamed small mound	DeC 51, 59–64	Surab	?
97	Tegak	DeC 51, 59–64	Surab	?
98	Hadi	DeC 51, 59–64	Surab	F–E
99	Zari Damb	DeC 51, 59–64	Surab	H_1–G_1
100	Badu Kushtar	DeC 51, 59–64	Surab	C
101	Pir Haider Shahr	DeC 51, 59–64	Gidar	C
102	Rais Sher Mod'd	DeC 51, 59–64	Surab	H, F–E
103	Zidi	DeC 51, 59–64	Khuzdar	?
104	Reko	DeC 51, 59–64	Nur Gama	?
105	Zar Bhut	DeC 51, 59–64	Nur Gama	?
106	Kale Damb	DeC 51, 59–64	Nur Gama	F–E, C–B
107	Singen Kalat	DeC 51, 59–64	Mula River	G_1
108	Mishk	DeC 51, 59–64	Mula River	G_2
109	Jahan	DeC 51, 59–64	Mula River	H_1–G_2
110	Site near Jahan site	DeC 51, 59–64	—	H_1–G_2
111	Kuhan	DeC 51, 59–64	Mula River	F–E, C–B
112	Unnamed site near Kuhan	DeC 51, 59–64	—	F–E, C–B
113	Khul	DeC 51, 59–64	Mula River	F–E, C–B
114	Bambe	DeC 51, 59–64	Shahr Gudro	G_2
115	Unnamed site	DeC 51, 59–64	Harbub Pass	?
116	Nindo Damb (Nindowari)	Rai 60–61 DeC 64	Ornach Valley	H_2–G_2

No.	Site	Source	Location	Period Range

Jhalawan (Kalat Division—Baluchistan) (*continued*)

No.	Site	Source	Location	Period Range
117	Kinneru Damb	Rai 60–61 DeC 64	Ornach Valley	H_2–G_3, F–E
118	Kulli Damb	Rai 60–61 DeC 64	Ornach Valley	F–E
119	Sheri Damb	Rai 60–61 DeC 64	Ornach Valley	F–E, C
120	Karez Damb	Rai 60–61 DeC 64	Ornach Valley	G_1–G_3, F(?)
121	Kunar Kull	DeC 64	Ornach Valley	?
122	Unnamed site	DeC 64	Ornach Valley	?
123	Phusi Damb	Rai 60–61 DeC 64	Ornach Valley	H_1–G_3, F–E (?)
124	Jogenai Damb	St 31 Rai 60–61	Wadh Valley	F–E, B
125	Unnamed site	DeC 64	Near Kuki Damb	G_1–G_2
126	Lena Singh	DeC 64	Surab	H_1, F–E
127	Siah Damb	DeC 64	Surab	H_1–G_1
128	Zayak Mound*	Fie 55 St 31	Zayak Spring, near Jangal	G_1–G_3
129	Ander Damb	Fie 55	Surab	G_1–G_3
130	Ghuram Damb†	Fie 55	25 miles south of Kalat	H_1–G_2
131	Kapoto Damb	Fie 55	Kapoto	H_1–G_1
132	Kapoto Rock Shelter	Fie 55	Kapoto	H_1–G_1
133	Gaji Bhut	Rai 60–61	Ornach Valley	F–E, D–C
134	Ghannal Kund Damb	Rai 60–61	Ornach Valley	H_1–G_1, F–E
135	Minki Damb	Rai 60–61	Ornach Valley	F–E
136	Alam Khan Shahr	Rai 60–61	Ornach Valley	H_2–G_2
137	Kasmi Damb	Rai 60–61	Nal vicinity	H_1–G_1
138	Ala Damb	Rai 60–61	Nal vicinity	H(?), F–E
139	Surkh Damb	Rai 60–61	Nal vicinity	H_2–G_3
140	Cheshma Damb I	Rai 60–61	Nal vicinity	H_1–G_3
141	Khatti Damb	Rai 60–61	Wadh Valley	B
142	Singiot Damb	Rai 60–61	Wadh Valley	G_3
143	Wadh Thana	Rai 60–61	Wadh Valley	G_3, B
144	Bandu Damb	Rai 60–61	Wadh Valley	G_1–G_3
145	Kasmi Damb	Rai 60–61 St 31	Wadh Valley	H_1–G_1, B–A
146	Chashma Murad	Rai 60–61	Wadh Valley	H_1–G_3, F–E
147	Sork (or Sorak)	Rai 60–61 St 31	Wadh Valley	H_2–G_3, F–E
148	Guni Damb	Rai 60–61	Wadh Valley	F–E
149	Puchor Damb	Rai 60–61	Wadh Valley	H_2–G_1, F–E, B
150	Unnamed site	Rai 60–61	2 miles south of Wadh town, west of Main Road	F–E
151	Panju	St 31	Wadh Valley	H_1, F–E
152	Abdul But	St 31	Wadh Valley	G_2–G_3, A
153	Kashimi Damb	St 31	Wadh Valley	H_2–G_3, B
154	Drakalo Damb	St 31 Rai 60–61	Drakalo Valley	H_2–G_1, F–E
155	Aidu	St 31 Rai 60–61	Drakalo Valley	H_1, G_1–G_3, F–E

* In Appendix A to Field's report, F. A. Khan mentions two mounds near Jangal: Zayak Mound and Jangal. The Jangal site is not mentioned in Field's text, and it is not on any of the maps.
† Field's map No. 8 shows two sites immediately southwest of Rodinjo. These are Benn Chah and Ghuram Damb. Khan, in the appendix, apparently treats these as a single site. Stein (1931, p. 18) also records a Benn Chah site in this area. It would seem that it is not possible at this time to demonstrate which of the sites is Stein's.

No.	Site	Source	Location	Period Range
Jhalawan (Kalat Division-Baluchistan) *(continued)*				
156	Karim Dad Gatti	St 31	Drakalo Valley	$B-A(?)$
157	Kocha But	St 31	Drakalo Valley	?
158	Hassan Damb	St 31	Drakalo Valley	?
159	Makri Mas	Rai 60–61	Drakalo Valley	H_1-G_1, F–E
160	Sumr Damb	Rai 60–61	Drakalo Valley	H_2-G_2
161	Two nameless mounds	St 31	Belar Valley	B, F–E
Kharan (Baluchistan)				
1	Toji excavation assoc. with gabarbands (Pottinger Site)	St 31	Nauroz Kalat	H_1-G_1, F–E(?)
2	Pir Hassan Shah	St 31	Nauroz Kalat	G_2-G_3, F–E, C–B
3	Garuk (Fa name)	St 31	Vicinity of Besma	?
4	Mammai Damb	St 31	Vicinity of Besma	G_2-G_3
5	Kurragi Damb	St 31	Vicinity of Besma	G_2-G_3
6	Kashimi Damb	St 31	Vicinity of Besma	?
7	Taghazi Damb	St 31	Vicinity of Besma	G_3, F–E
8	Sajidi Damb (mentioned on Fa card for Taghazi Damb)	St 31	Vicinity of Besma	?
9	Pozhoi Damb	St 31	Vicinity of Besma	F–E, B
10	Zayak North	St 31	Vicinity of Zayak	H_1-G_2, F–E
11	Zayak West	St 31	Vicinity of Zayak	F–E
Las Bela (Baluchistan)				
1	LB-1 (Edith Shahr)	Fa 59–60	Southern tip of 750-foot spur; right bank of Porali near Jomon Goth	G_1-G_2
2	LB-2	Fa 59–60	On slope of hill west of LB-1	F–E
3	LB-3 (Caves Gondrani) (Corless-Thornton 1833)	Fa 59–60	Welpat	B
4	LB-4	Fa 59–60	3½ miles north of Bela	B–A
5	LB-5 (Pirkariya) (Bhit)	Fa 59–60 St 43	1½ miles northeast of Bela	F–E(?), C–B
6	LB-6	St 43 Fa 59–60	Niai Buthi, 3 miles northeast of Bela	H_2-G_2
7	LB-7	Fa 59–60	Khamkho Nal pass	F–E(?), B–A
8	LB-8	Fa 59–60	*ca.* 3 miles southeast of Bela	F–E
9	LB-9	Fa 59–60	2 miles southwest of LB-10	F–E
10	LB-10	Fa 59–60	Area above LB-1	F–E
11	LB-11	Fa 59–60	Area above LB-1	?
12	LB-12	Fa 59–60	Area above LB-1	?
13	LB-14 (Karpas Buthi?)	Fa 59–60 Rai 60–61	2½ miles northeast of LB-1, east side of Porali River	G_2-G_3, F–E(?)
14	LB-13	Fa 59–60	½ mile northwest of LB-14	G_2-G_3, F–E
15	LB-15	Fa 59–60	*ca.* 4 miles northeast of LB-13	F–E
16	LB-16	Fa 59–60	*ca.* 1 mile from LB-17	G_3, F–E
17	LB-17	Fa 59–60	*ca.* ¾ mile north of LB-13	G_2-G_3, F–E
18	LB-18	Fa 59–60	North of LB-16	F–E, B–A(?)
19	Jaroji	Rai 60–61	Welpat	G_1-G_2

No.	Site	Source	Location	Period Range
Las Bela (Baluchistan) *(continued)*				
20	Kali Kot	Rai 60–61	Northwest of Uthal	F–E(?), D–B
21	Kadr Dad Damb	Rai 60–61	Porali River	F–E
22	Khakhar Kaur	Rai 60–61	Porali River near Muridani	E–D(?)
23	Kaiara Kot	Rai 60–61	Bela	B
24	Ghulam Mohammad Goth	Rai 60–61	Near Muridani	G_2–G_3
25	Langro Damb	Rai 60–61	Porali River	F–E
26	Kanar Damb	Rai 60–61	Porali River	F–E
27	Burial Mounds	Rai 60–61	Near Mai-i-Drani	F–E(?)
28	Bala Kot	Rai 60–61	Near Sonmiani	G_3
29	Las Bela City Mound	Fa 59–60	Welpat	B–A
30	Tombs of Jains of Bela (north of Bela City)	Fa 59–60	Welpat	B–A
Makran (Baluchistan)				
1	Shahi Tump	St 31 Fie 59	Kej Valley	G_1–G_3
2	Zangian Cairns (Kambar-shor)	St 31	Kej Valley	E
3	Miri Fort	St 31 Fie 59	Kej Valley	H_1–G_3, B
4	Gushtang Damb	St 31	Kej Valley	F–E(?)
5	Kalatuk Cairns	St 31	Kej Valley	E
6	Koh-i-kalat	St 31	Kej Valley	C(?)
7	Tumpak	St 31	Kej Valley	G_3(?)
8	Karagi	St 31	Kej Valley	D–C
9	Nazarabad	St 31 Fie 59	Kej Valley	G_1–G_2
10	Dilekim	St 31	Kej Valley	E
11	Kasano Damb	St 31	Kej Valley	F–E
12	Nasirabad Cairns	St 31	Kej Valley	E
13	Haft Brat	St 31	Dasht Valley	?
14	Machuki Damb	St 31	Dasht Valley	C–B
15	Panodi	St 31	Dasht Valley	G_1–G_2
16	Sutkagan-dor (excavated 1931, 1962)	St 31 Dales 62	Dasht Valley	G_2–G_3
17	Gatti Cairns	St 31	Dasht Valley	E
18	Jiwani	St 31	Dasht Valley	E
19	Take-Dap	St 31	Dasht Valley	E
20	Mayal Chah Damb	St 31	Panjgur Oasis	G_2(?)
21	Kohna Kalat	St 31 Fie 59	Panjgur Oasis	G_3, C–B
22	Chiri Damb	St 31	Panjgur Oasis	G_3, F–E, B
23	Sari Damb	St 31	Panjgur Oasis	B
24	Serikoran Village	St 31	Panjgur Oasis	G(?)
25	Damb-i-dambi	St 31 Fie 59	Panjgur Oasis	G_3
26	Sraduk	St 31 Fie 59	Panjgur Oasis	H_2–G_3, C–B
27	Besham Damb	St 31 Fie 59	Panjgur Oasis	H_2–G_3, C–B
28	Pardan Damb (gabarbands)	St 31	Panjgur Oasis	?
29	Chorruk Damb	St 31	Panjgur Oasis	?

No.	Site	Source	Location	Period Range
Makran (Baluchistan) (*continued*)				
30	Grankan Damb	St 31	Panjgur Oasis	?
31	Khundabadan	St 31	Panjgur Oasis	C–B
32	Gar	St 31	Parom Basin	H_1
33	Pipili Kalat	St 31	Parom Basin	?
34	Diz Parom I (Fort)	St 31	Parom Basin	B–A(?)
35	Diz Parom II	St 31	Parom Basin	F–E
36	Jai Damb	St 31	Parom Basin	G_3
37	Sar Parom (Kuruzkol)	St 31	Parom Basin	G_3
38	Watuki Damb	St 31	Parom Basin	G_3, B
39	Shami Damb	St 31	Parom Basin	E, B
40	Kalatuk Damb	St 31 Fie 59	Vicinity of Nag	G_3, D
41	Nag Damb	St 31	Vicinity of Nag	G(?), B
42	Singi Kalat	St 31	Vicinity of Nag	D
43	Kargushki Damb	St 31 Fie 59	Rakshan Valley	H_1–G_2
44	Badrang Damb	St 31	Rakshan Valley	H_2–G_2
45	Gwadar Gumbaz	St 31	Gwadar	B
46	Nodiz Damb	Fie 55	1 mile west of Nodiz	G_3, C–B
47	Kalat Damb	Fie 55	Mand	G_3
48	Thale Damb	Fie 55	Hoshab	G_3
48a	Hoshab Md.	St 31	Hoshab	B–A
49	Surain Damb	Fie 55	20 miles southeast of Panjgur on Gwargo River	G_2–G_3, D–C
50	Gwargo Damb	Fie 55	20 miles southeast of Panjgur on Gwargo River	?
51	Stone Circle	Fie 55	20 miles east of Panjgur	?
52	Chiri Damb	Fie 55	20 miles east of Nag	G_3
53	Ghuram or Benn Chah	Fie 55 St 31	Panjgur	H_2–G_1
54	Sari Damb	Fie 55	18 miles west of Nag	G_1–G_3
55	Stone Circle	Fie 55	30 miles west of Nag	?
56	Stone Enclosed Cemetery	Fie 55	20 miles northeast of Nag	?
57	Nasirabad	Fie 55 St 31 (map)	Kej Valley (Nasirabad)	E, B
58	Sotka koh	Dales 60	9 miles north of Pasni	G_3
59	Ras Makabe	Unknown collector	Makran	C–B
Sind (northern sites)				
1	Jhukar	Maj 34	6 miles west of Larkana	G_3–F, D–C
2	Adatjo-daro	Maj 34	*ca.* 10 miles west of Dokri station	G_2–G_3
3	Dhamrahojo-daro	Maj 34	Near Badah	D–C
4	Lohumjo-daro	Maj 34	Near Piaro Goth Station	G_3–F
5	Pai-jo-kotrio	De&McC 49	*ca.* 30 miles north of Lake Manchhar	G_2–G_3
6	Rohel-jo-kund	De&McC 49	*ca.* 30 miles north of Lake Manchhar	G_1–G_2
7	Rajo-daro	De&McC 49	*ca.* 30 miles north of Lake Manchhar	H_2–G_3
8	Jare-jo-kalal	De&McC 49	*ca.* 30 miles north of Lake Manchhar	G_1–G_3

No.	Site	Source	Location	Period Range
Sind (northern sites) (*continued*)				
9	Nazgani-jo-kund	De&McC 49	*ca.* 30 miles north of Lake Manchhar	G_1–G_2
10	Chhuti-jo-kund	De&McC 49	*ca.* 30 miles north of Lake Manchhar	H_2–G_2
11	Alor	PA 64	Near Rohri	B
12	Kot Diji (F. A. Khan, *Pakistan Archaeology,* 1965)	PA 64	Near Sukkur	G_1(?)–G_3
13	Mohenjo-daro	—	Near Larkana	G_2–G_3, D
14	Jacobabad	PA 65	Near Jhatpat Station	E
15	Therri Bahadur Shah	PA 65	Near Jhatpat Station	G_3, D
16	Damb Buthi	Maj 34	South of Lake Manchhar	G_1–G_2
17	Bandhni	Maj 34	South of Lake Manchhar	G_1–G_2
18	Chauro	Maj 34	South of Lake Manchhar	G_1–G_2
19	Dhal	Maj 34	South of Lake Manchhar	G_2–G_3
20	Pokhran	Maj 34	Baran Nai	H_2–G_3
21	Karchat	Maj 34	Baran Nai	G_2–G_3
22	Khotras Buthi	Maj 34	Baran Nai	G_1–G_2
23	Khajur	Maj 34	Baran Nai	G_1–G_2
24	Arabjo Thana	Maj 34	Baran Nai	G_1–G_2
25	Shahjo Kotiro	Maj 34	Baran Nai	G_1–G_2
26	Ahmad Shah	Maj 34	Baran Nai	G_1–G_2
27	Othmanjo Buthi	Maj 34	Baran Nai	G_2
28	Bachani	Maj 34	Baran Nai	G_2
29	Disoi	Maj 34	Near Thano Bulla Khan	G_2
30	Unnamed mound between Shadopur and Shahpur Village	Maj 34	Between Hyderabad and Nawabshah	B
31	Unnamed mound between Shadopur and Shahpur Village	Maj 34	Between Hyderabad and Nawabshah	B
32	Unnamed mound near Shahpur Village	Maj 34	Between Hyderabad and Nawabshah	B
33	Unnamed mound near Shahpur Village	Maj 34	Between Hyderabad and Nawabshah	C–B
34	Unnamed mound near Shahpur Village	Maj 34	Between Hyderabad and Nawabshah	C–B
35	Chanhu-daro	MacK 43	*ca.* 5 miles east of Sakrand, near Nawabshah	G_3–F–E
36	Amri	Maj 34 Casal 64	Amri Station	G_1–G_3, F(?) B
37	Rati Bhiri	Maj 34	*ca.* 12 miles from Nawabshah	B
38	Bhirajio-daro	Maj 34	Near Tharushah	B
39	Unnamed mound	Maj 34	Between Moro and Naushahro	B
40	Thul Rukan	Maj 34	Near Kazi Ahmad	D
41	Daro Suta	Maj 34	Near Tando Allahyar	C–B
42	Dhakanjo-daro	Maj 34	Between Shahdapur and Sarhari Station	D
43	Batriwaro Bhiro	Maj 34	Between Shahdapur and Sarhari Station	D–C
44	Trihni (Lal Chhatlo)	Maj 34	Lake Manchhar	C–B
45	Shah Hasan	Maj 34	Lake Manchhar	C–B
46	Lohri	Maj 34	Lake Manchhar	G_1–G_3(?)
47	Lakhiyo	Maj 34	Lake Manchhar	G_2

No.	Site	Source	Location	Period Range
Sind (central sites)				
48	Jhangar	Maj 34	Lake Manchhar	F–E
49	Ghazi Shah	Maj 34	Just north of Lake Manchhar	G_1–G_2
50	Tando Rahim Khan	Maj 34	Just north of Lake Manchhar	G_1–G_2
51	Ghazishahjo-Thul (Gorandi)	Maj 34	South of Ghazi Shah	G_1–G_2, B–A
52	Naig	Maj 34	South of Ghazi Shah	G_2
53	Ali Murad	Maj 34	North of Lake Manchhar	G_1–G_2
54	Pandi Wahi	Maj 34	North of Lake Manchhar	H_2–G_2
55	Si-2	Fa 59–60	Lake Manchhar	B–A
56	Si-3	Fa 59–60	Lake Manchhar	B–A
57	Si-4	Fa 59–60	On Karachi-Sukkur rail line, about 80 miles north of Kotri	B–A
58	Gharo Bhiro	Lam 64	Nagar-Pakar	G_2–E
59	Taung	Lam 64	Hyderabad division, near near Taung	G_1–G_2
60	Qasim Kirio	PA 64	6 miles along Nawabshah-Sanghar Road	D–B
61	Bhiro Bham	PA 65	Near Bandi Station, Nawabshah	C–B
Sind (southern sites)				
62	Amilano	Maj 34	Malir River	G_2
63	Orangi	Maj 34	*ca.* 7 miles north of Karachi	A(?), G_2
64	Sasui-jo-takar (Bambor)	Maj 34	Gharo Creek	C
65	Tharro Hill Complex	Maj 34	12 miles west of Tatta	J, G_2, D, B
66	Tando Mohammad Khan	Maj 34	Tando Mohammad Khan	D–C
67	Shahkapur	Maj 34	Tando Mohammad Khan	B
68	Kakeja	Maj 34	Tando Mohammad Khan	B
69	Katbaman	Maj 34	Tando Mohammad Khan	B
70	Rarri	Maj 34	Tando Mohammad Khan	B
71	Nidamani	Maj 34	Tando Mohammad Khan	B
72	Tharri	Maj 34	Tando Mohammad Khan	B
73	Khuajo Daro	Maj 34	Near Mirpurkhas	D–C
74	Khirah	Maj 34	Near Shadipalli Station	D–C
75	Sindhri	Maj 34	Near Shadipalli Station	D–C
76	Mumalji-mari	Maj 34	Near Umarkot	D–C
77	Otjo-daro	Maj 34	Near Peeru Lishari Station	A
78	Old Badin	Maj 34, Fa 62	Near Badin	B–A
79	Kandarwaro Daro	Maj 34, Fa 62	Near Badin	B–A
80	Dodojo-mari	Maj 34	Near Badin	B–A
81	Bahumjo-bhiro	Maj 34	Between Daur and Bandhni Railroad	B
82	Hab-1	Fa 59–60	7 miles north of Diwana on Hab River	G_1–G_2
83	Si-1	Fa 59–60	5½ miles south of Gharo	B–A
84	Si-5	Fa 59–60	Near Jerruck	Middle Stone Age
85	Si-6	Fa 59–60	4½ miles west of Malir River and *ca.* 500 yards from Karachi-Thano Bulla Khan Road	G_2

No.	Site	Source	Location	Period Range
Sind (southern sites) *(continued)*				
86	Si-7	Fa 59–60	26 miles northeast of Karachi	E
87	Si-12	Fa 59–60	17 miles southwest of Thano Bulla Khan	E
88	Si-13	Fa 59–60	12 miles west of Thano Bulla Khan	E
89	Pir Manto	PA 64	10 miles north of Karachi	G_2(?)
90	Lyari River	PA 64	Near Karachi University	J
91	Nel Bazar (see also Allahdino, Majumdar, 1934)	PA 64	Near Damloti Water Works, Karachi	G_2
92	Dandhi	PA 65	On Mirpur-Patharo Road, Thatta district	B
93	Mosque (Thatta district)	PA 65	On Mirpur-Patharo Road, Thatta district	B
94	Shar Kapur	PA 65	9 miles south-southeast of Mirpur Patharo, Thatta district	B
95	Nind Kot	PA 65	14 miles south of Shah Kapur	B
96	Bamphore	PA 64	25 miles east of Karachi	E–B
97	Tatta Complex	Fa 62–63	East of Karachi	B
98	Brahminabad or Al-Mansora	Fa 62–63	North of Hyderabad	B
99	Sewan Mound	Fa 62–63		B–A
100	Damlotti Lists	Fa 62	Lists north of Damlotti Water Works, Karachi	E
101	Chaukandi Tombs	Fa 59–60 PA 56	East of Karachi	B–A
Bahawalpur				
1	Kudwala	Fie 59	See Map Fie 59	E
2	Fort Mojgarh	Fie 59	See Map Fie 59	B
3	Fort Marot	Fie 59	See Map Fie 59	E
4	Lurewala	Fie 59	See Map Fie 59	E
5	Dunkkian	Fie 59	See Map Fie 59	E
6	Fort Derwar	Fie 59	See Map Fie 59	G_3
7	Qaimpur	Fie 59	See Map Fie 59	E
8	Turewala	Fie 59	See Map Fie 59	E
9	Sulla	Fie 59	See Map Fie 59	G_3, E
10	Traikoa Thar	Fie 59	See Map Fie 59	?
11	Bhoot (Bhut)	Fie 59	See Map Fie 59	G_2–G_3
12	Pattan Manara	PA 64	?	D–C
Western Punjab				
1	Taxila	Marshall (various dates)	28 miles west of Rawalpindi	E–C
2	Biddi Site	PA	53 miles from Lahore on Lahore–Lyallpur Road	D–C
3	Six unnamed sites, vicinity of Biddi	PA 62–63	53 miles from Lahore on Lahore-Lyallpur Road	D–C
4	Harappa	Vats, etc.	Near Montgomery	G_3–F(?)
5	Sakesar	PA 64	Sargoda district	E–D
6	Sarai Kola	PA 64–67	28 miles west of Rawalpindi	G_1–G_3
7	Jolilpur	PA	Near Multan	G_1–G_2

No.	Site	Source	Location	Period Range
Northwest Frontier*				
1	Charsada	Wh 62a	10 miles northeast of Peshawar	E–D
2	Timargaha	Dani 63–67	*ca.* 75 miles north of Peshawar	F–E$_1$
3	Balambat	Dani 63–67	Near Timargaha Graves	F–E$_1$
4	Sanghao Cave (Parkho Darra)	Dani 64	Sanghao Valley	Late Stone Age, E
5	Shaikhan Dheri	Dani 65–66	22 miles north of Peshawar	E$_2$–E$_3$
6	Thana	Dani-Durrani 67	Lower Swat Valley	F–E
7	Chakdara	Dani 67	Talash	F
8	Ziarat	Dani 67	Midway between Chakdara and Timargarha	F(?)
9	Enayat Kila	Dani 67	Northwest of Khar	F–E, (?)
10	Panchpir	Dani 67	Near Hurd	F(?)
11	Pehur	Dani 67	Tarbela Dam Colony	F(?)
12	Butkara II	Antonini 63	Swat	F–E
13	Katelai I	Antonini 63	Swat	F–E
14	Loebanr I	Antonini 63	Swat	F–E
15	Butkara I	Tucci etc.	Swat	E$_3$–D

No.	Site	Source	Location	Period Range
Waziristan (Northwest Frontier)				
1	Surkh Dherai	St 29	Near Draband, Dera Ismail Khan	E–D
2	Chaduhwan	St 29	Draband, Dera Ismail Khan	E–D
3	Chicha Dherai	St 29	Draband, Dera Ismail Khan	F–D
4	Kot Azam or Luni	St 29	Near Luni, Dera Ismail Khan	?
5	Dabra	St 29	Murtaza, Dera Ismail Khan	E–D
6	Shah Zamanidherai	St 29	Near Tank	E–D
7	Lakhi Kot	St 29	Tank	C–B
8	Aba Khel	St 29	Near Tank	D–C
9	Kot Pathan	St 29	Near Tank	?
10	Kot-kat Dherai	St 29	Tank	D–C
11	Khajuri	St 29	Near Khajuri Fort, Bannu	B
12	Ark Ghundai	St 29	Near Khajuri and Bannu	D–C
13	Spinwam Ford Mound	St 29	Bannu area	B
14	Kane Wor	St 29	Shahidan Fort, near Bannu	D–C
15	Padshah Kotkai	St 29	Shahidan Fort, near Bannu	E–D
16	Zarif Khan Ghundi	St 29	Near Kach on Gomal River	E–D
17	Khidrai Kot	St 29	Near Kach on Gomal River	B
18	Mirawas Dherai	St 29	Near Gul Kach on Gomal River	?
19	Ther Dallu Rai	PA 65	30° 38′ N, 70° 30′ E	E–D
20	Bareera Mounds	PA 65	Near Fazilpur	?
21	Chah Giraz Wala	PA 65	Near Basti Baig	?
22	Ther Doogar	PA 65	Near Chah Giraz Wala	?
23	Four other unnamed sites in this district	PA 65	—	E–D

* This list (except No. 15) does not include Buddhist sites. There are at least thirty of these known and these will be added in a subsequent listing.

No.	Site	Source	Location	Period Range

Dera Ismail Khan District (Bugti Tribal Area)*

1	Kumbani Caves	Mathiesson	¼ mile east of Dera Bugti Road	?
2	Gaddu Gah Caves	Mathiesson	Kalpar	?
3	Dawrao Tul Damb	Mathiesson	1 mile east of Dera Bugti	G_1–G_2
4	Kaddour Damb	Mathiesson	South of Serani Levy Post	H_2–G_2 (?)
5	Bagh-i-kumb Damb	Mathiesson	Zin Range	J–G
6	Gand Damb	Mathiesson	5 miles northeast of Pilawagh Levy Thana	G_2–G_3
7	Unnamed damb	Mathiesson	4 miles east of Gand	G(?)
8	Iskander's Path	Mathiesson	Near Uch	B(?)

* Information on the sites of this region has been supplied by Mrs. Sylvia Mathiesson who kindly provided details on the materials found. From her description I have attempted to correlate the sites to the scheme developed for other regions. I am most grateful to her for this data.

APPENDIX G:

The Gondrani Caves of Las Bela

ANOTHER OF THE PROVOCATIVE SITES OF THE WELPAT REGION, the Gondrani Caves have been known to Westerners since 1833, when they were first reported by an English traveler, Carless-Thornton,[1] but since then they have been ignored by archaeology. The caves are for the most part located in a lateral canyon of the Kud River drainage at that point where the river leaves the mountains and enters the Las Bela plain. On both sides of the canyon the cliffs are honeycombed to a considerable height with shallow man-made caves. The local populace reports over five hundred of these, though the actual figure is probably somewhat less. The rock formation here is boulder conglomerate, and in numerous places the cliffs have collapsed, leaving only a back wall to evidence the previous cave. There is a report of painting in some caves, but search as we might, we never came across any evidence of this.

The area is rather remote, being some distance from the cultivated area. Water runs perennially in the Kud channel, and a few shepherds or wood gatherers live in one or two of the lower caves. The canyon winds tortuously, narrowing as it ascends, and caves are found for at least a mile along the way.

The typical cave would appear to have a kind of front porch, perhaps 5 to 8 feet deep and 15 feet wide. A doorway opens on a room no wider than the porch but about 20 feet deep. In some cases one or two steps in the rock lead up or down into this main room as the case may be. These walls may originally have been plastered, but most of this has fallen away. Small niches appear in some cave walls at about shoulder height, and it has been speculated that these were used for lamps. A characteristic feature of these rooms is a semicircular storage (?) area in the corner of the room. This is made up of boulders and clay and apparently came up to about waist height. In one room, small stones about fist size were laid on the floor to a height of a foot or more, forming a kind of "T" pattern.

[1] Carless-Thornton, in *Gazetter for the Las Bela District* (1910).

Access to the higher caves was very likely by ladder, since we found no stairways.

In surveying these caves we tried to reach the more inaccessible ones in hopes of getting *in situ* evidence for the original occupants. This was done because the more accessible caves showed many signs of recent use by local people. However, we were only partially successful in doing this, since special climbing equipment is required in many cases and we were not in possession of same.

Wherever we could we tested the floor of the caves, but usually at a depth of about four inches the rock floor was reached. The deposit was only dust and the remnants of wall plaster. Here and there some sherds were recovered, but these only indicate that fine wheel-made plainware and a coarse wet ware were used. A piece of an iron bit (?) was also found. A remnant of a stone grinding wheel was found in the canyon itself, but there is a singular absence of evidence at Gondrani.

Local legends ascribe the place to an ancient ruler who married a beautiful woman from another country and had trouble with a witch—a legend that is common enough in Asia and gives us no clue as to the original builders.

On the face of what evidence there is, I am inclined to date the caves as late, possibly even Islamic. For one thing, the boulder conglomerate in this area is poorly cemented and is loose and crumbly. The fact that so many of the caves are intact may indicate that they have not existed for long. Again, there is simply no evidence for classic cave users such as the Buddhists or the Hindus: no idol niches, remnants of statues, characteristic architectural features. That the caves were meant to be habitations seems clear both from their smallness and from the heterogeneity of their location, but for the moment there is no clue as to by whom or when they were occupied.

APPENDIX H:

The Archaeological Sequence in Southeastern Iran

SOME LIGHT HAS BEEN RECENTLY CAST on the southeastern Iranian region by Dr. Joseph Caldwell at Tal-i-Iblis in the Mashiz Valley of the Kerman mountains[1] and by Miss Beatrice de Cardi at Stein's old site of Bampur in Persian Baluchistan.[2]

Tal-i-Iblis has been virtually destroyed by the local population in their efforts to obtain fresh soil for their fields. Caldwell's work was thus limited; however, he has established a sequence remarkable for its earliness. The earliest level (O) had thick, coarse, soft pottery and a few prismatic flint blades dating to a little before 4000 B.C. Levels (1) and (2) are called the "Iblis Period" and seem to mark the advent of fine red-slipped pottery decorated with painted

---

[1] J. R. Caldwell, 1966.
[2] Beatrice de Cardi, "The Bampur Sequence in the 3rd Millennium B.C.," *Antiquity*, Vol. XLI (1967), pp. 33–41.

Makran	Stein Sequence	De Cardi at Bampur	Inscribed stone vessels range	Caldwell at Tal-i-Iblis
G 3 Shahi Tump Cemetery	*Bampur* stage Upper levels at Bampur, also Katskan & Kunarokaur	VI Local styles, etc.	L (?)	
Shahi Tump—upper levels	*Khurab* stage Lower levels at Bampur	V Kulli styles & Qal'ah and Shugha cultures Break style & strat	Khurab Cem D, B, E F Bii	
G 2 Shahi Tump—lower levels (below wall in section VI)	Damin Khurab Cemetery Tr A—Chah Husaini	IV 1-3, 2 & 3 reddish wares IV₁—Sh.T. V,3	Seistan link, also Mundigak IV₁ C (?)	Mashiz Period
G 1		continuity		Late Ali Abad Per. 5
H 2		III 1-4		Early Ali Abad Per. 4
H 1	*Husaini* stage	I & II		Iblis Period? 3
I	Tr B—Chah Husaini Qal'a-i-Sardugah			Iblis levels 1 & 2
				Iblis 0

geometric designs. There is also some sign of copper smelting. The pottery has typological similarities to Sialk III 1–3. Level (3) was of minor significance, since so little was found for it. Level (4) Caldwell assigns to his Early Aliabad Period. Fine buff-slipped pottery painted with geometric designs is a marker for this level. Some polychrome decoration also appears here. The painted designs are unrelated to southwestern Iran or to central Iran, and Caldwell suggests possible connection to Baluchistan. Level (4) can be dated to around 3600 B.C. Level (5), the Late Aliabad Period, continues the ceramic traditions of Level (4) with some difference in the motifs. Polychrome is also well established here. Beveled-rim bowls, common in Early Dynastic Mesopotamia up to about 2500 B.C., are found in this level, which dates to about 2860 B.C. There were other levels above (5), but these have been largely erased by modern digging. However, there is enough evidence to indicate the upper levels followed with some continuity on the earlier and marked the heaviest prehistoric settlement in the region (Mashiz).

In the Bampur area Stein had established three main groups of related material, most of it ceramic.[3] The earliest, the Husaini, was found in one of his trenches (B) at the site of Chah Husaini and on the surface of other early sites in the region (for example, Qal'a-i-Sardagah). This consists primarily of a fine painted pottery, much of it with black on red geometric designs and also some polychrome. There is a suggestion of Togau and even Nal elements in this stage.

The second group (Khurab) into which Stein's material falls is found in the higher levels of Chah Husaini (Trench A), at the site of Damin, in the lower level at the site of Bampur, and most representatively at the cemetery site of Khurab. The cemetery consists of fractional burials with complexes of fine funerary pottery which include paint-decorated wares (black on grays, buffs, and reds), some peculiar raised-banded wares, chalices, and a variety of incised stone and alabaster vessels. Some bronze has been recovered, including a fine image of a camel on the end of a staff.

The upper levels at Bampur at a few sites of the region, such as Katukan, belong to what can be called the Bampur stage. Here much of the style and type of the Khurab pottery continues, but techniques are coarser. Bull figurines occur in this stage.

De Cardi's excavations at Bampur revealed six levels. I and II are poorly known. In Level II mud-brick structures were built. The pottery was wheel-made and painted in black on cream or buff with a variety of geometric and animal motifs, the whole suggesting derivation from western Iran. Levels III and IV continue these traditions, but in III material of the type described for Seistan (p. 117) makes its appearance. In levels III and IV there are, according to de Cardi, also suggestions of a sharing of "common cultural influences" with Mundigak IV.

Level V at Bampur suggests strong new influences combining elements from southwestern Iran (Qal'ah and Shugha cultures) and the Kulli, especially in painted motifs on the ceramics. Level VI is represented by a strong local style. Whereas Caldwell's ties to the Bampur area at Tal-i-Iblis seem to be limited to a possible correlation of his levels (1) and (2) with the Husaini stage, de Cardi's work indicates that Stein's Khurab stage belongs principally with her levels IV–VI. Inscribed stone vessels also belong in this range.

The Tal-i-Iblis material with its western ties is older generally than that of

---

[3] A. Stein, *An Archaeological Reconnaissance in Northwest India and Southeast Iran*, London, 1937.

Bampur, and it can be expected that chronologically this would be the situation from region to region as settlements in the movement eastward followed in some sequence. Typologically they have similarities, but chronologically many are not contemporary. How great the lag was is still not certain. However, pottery appears to have first arrived in Baluchistan as late as the middle of the fourth millennium B.C. It would appear already to have been in use about five hundred years earlier at Tal-i-Iblis. As one comes upward in time, however, this chronological lag generally disappears.

The southeast Iranian sequence does have a direct bearing upon the situation in the Makran, the next major region of importance to the east and the geographical link to the true Indo-Iranian Borderlands. Critical here is the site of Shahi Tump, near Turbat Fort in the Kej valley. Stein's excavations at Shahi Tump revealed a cemetery of flexed burials surrounded by rather fine pottery vessels, some containing the ashes of animal bones or food offerings, bead necklaces, and a variety of copper implements, including a compartmented seal with a stud at its back, a shaft-hole axe, and a spearhead (see page 225). The vessels were usually open bowls and cups in buff or gray painted with geometric designs. The cemetery only descends about seven feet into the mound, which itself was originally a habitation site. A riddle caused by Stein's insensitive method of trenching his sites involves our lack of knowledge as to the people who lived there before the cemetery was made. The evidence would indicate that the bulk of the site was created by a people of the Khurab stage. The fact that buff figurines, a fragment of a clay cart, and a grater appear in association with the cemetery suggests that that phase was contemporary with at least one phase of the Kulli, and this is further suggested by other typological hints at de Cardi's Level V at Bampur.

Tepe Yahya

AT THE SITE of Tepe Yahya, which is located about 225 km. south of Kerman, a series of excavations have been carried on under the direction of C. C. Lamberg-Karlovsky since 1967. The site is sizable, being almost 20 meters high and 18 meters across at its base. The excavation defines six main periods in the site stratigraphy.

Period I	Sassanian	pre–400 A.D.
Period II	Achaemenian (?)	300–500 B.C.
Period III	Iron Age	500–1000 B.C.
Period IVA	Elamite (?)	2200–2500 B.C.
Period IVB	Proto-Elamite	2500–3000 B.C.
Period IVC	Proto-Elamite	3000–3400 B.C.
Period V	Yahya Culture	3400–3800 B.C.
Period VI	Coarse Ware Neolithic	3800–4500 B.C.

In terms of the sequence drawn up for Southeast Iran and the Makran (see chart at beginning of this appendix), Lamberg-Karlovsky's sequence seems to fit as follows:

Yahya

Iblis 1 & 2		V	Chah Huseini
Iblis 5 & 6	Bampur I-V	IVC	
Bampur V-VI		IVB	

Period IV Contained, among other objects, stamp and cylinder seals and sealings, steatite vessels with carved motifs common to Mesopotamia, and clay tablets with proto-Elamite writing upon them (IVC). Over a thousand pieces of steatite were found, some unworked. This suggests to the excavator that Tepe Yahya was part of an Elamite federation which had extended farther eastward than conventional conceptions of Elam's power and influence had described. Since at Tepe Yahya there is evidence for trade contact not only with Mesopotamia, whether direct or not, but also with adjacent regions such as Bampur, Kerman, and Seistan (Shahr-i-Sokhta), Lamberg-Karlovsky has put forth the theory that Yahya acted as a central place. "We . . . view Yahya as having an essentially indigenous culture which, under Elamite influence, supplied the resources it has available (steatite), while passing perishable goods on farther both east and west in a trade mechanism not directly structured by a single group but advantageous to several cultures lacking available resources."[4] One can imagine trade moving in this fashion across the Iranian plateau from cultural middleman to cultural middleman.

In terms of the Borderlands there has been some claim that several potsherds are of Nal (V) or Amri type, which would suggest some direct contact to the east. The chronological differences, however, are very great between Yahya V and the present approximation for the Nal in the Borderlands.

Shahr-i Sokhta

THE ITALIAN EXCAVATIONS at the site of Shahr-i Sokhta have considerably extended our knowledge of late prehistoric life in Seistan. The site measures some 2500 square kilometers. The excavator distinguishes three periods in the stratigraphy based primarily on changes in the mudbrick architecture, most of which appears to be of domestic type: houses divided into small rooms with fireplaces and stairways. These houses were of fair size, often more than 10 meters square, and one gains the impression that there were upper-floor living quarters and lower-floor utility rooms. Wooden beams for roofing purposes have been traced.

The material culture seems to be consistent throughout: stamp seals, clay human female and animal figurines, bone tools, wooden combs and ladles, some bronze/copper pins and knives, numerous beads, some in semi-precious stone, signs of rushing, spindle whorls, flint, and, above all, many vessels and other objects made in alabaster. The pottery, much of it painted with geometric designs (see pp. 119, 135), is familiar to the corpus of Seistan wares already known. It includes both gray wares and buff wares, and there is apparently

---

[4] C. C. Lamberg-Karlovsky, 1970, p. 80.

little distinction among them from period to period.

The impression one has of this pioneering work of the Italian mission is that it confirms the idea that Seistan was occupied at this cultural level for one main period only. There is no significant difference between either the periods defined in the stratigraphy or the character of the over forty prehistoric sites known in the region (see p. 121).

Some effort has been made to show that there were ties to other regions, in particular to Soviet Turkestan (Namazga III) and to the Kandahar area (Mundigak III-IV) and even to the Quetta Valley. In the case of the Quetta material, except for a few motifs on pottery, I am convinced that *nothing so far found anywhere in Seistan* is of Quetta type. The gray wares of Seistan are not relatives of Faiz Mohammad wares, nor are the buff wares related to either the Quetta or Kechi Beg ceramic types (see pp. 138–47). Some pottery motifs are like those of Damb Sadaat III (see fig. 34) but only in a general way. Similarly, the whole relationship of the Seistan wares to the Russian material is not precise; moreover, because so little work has been accomplished in the vast region between Seistan and Turkmenistan, there are no intermediate sites which might show the style changes attendant to diffusionary channels which might account for this lack of precision. There is, however, good ground for relating the Kandahar and Seistan regions to each other via the Helmund river, primarily because there is a clear comparative basis, not only in pottery but in beads, bronzes, figurines, and probably architecture.

Similarly, as both Tosi and Lamberg-Karlovsky have shown, there are good typological ties between Tepe Yahya and Shahr-i-Sokhta,[5] and this confirms what was previously apparent: that the Seistan settlements are culturally similar to those of Southeastern Iran and probably the Makran (see fig. 25). Whatever contact there is between the Indus Borderlands (indeed, the Indus Valley settlements themselves) and Seistan was primarily secondhand—a confirmation, perhaps, of Lamberg-Karlovsky's central place thesis.

A point of view ought to be stated here, however. I find generally that the evidence for trade in these regions is still not convincing. Lapis lazuli, for example, is found widely in the Borderlands not as a mined variety but along with jasper, carnelian, agate, rock crystal, and even onyx as an occasional raw pebble in the bed of water courses (wet or dry). Most sites of the Borderlands do produce some lapis but rarely of size or quantity. It has, however, been habitual for archaeologists to presume the existence of trade with Badakhshan or intermediate areas wherever even a modicum of lapis has been found. Only the most detailed qualitative analysis can detect the differences between Badakhshan mined lapis and that which occurs as the native indigenous product, and such analysis has not been done. Thus I am more inclined to regard settlement in places like Seistan as the product of the basic movement of sedentary life across the Iranian plateau which characterized the region over many thousands of years. Seistan could never have been an easy place to settle, vulnerable as it is to the 120-day wind in the summer and the peculiarly cold winds of the winter. The evidence at this point is certainly that late

[5] Lamberg-Karlovsky and Tosi, 1972.

prehistoric man settled here only for a limited period as if at that time there were perhaps agronomical advantages (unknown to us) that outweighed other disadvantages. Since there is so little rainfall in Seistan, flood plain agriculture had to be the basic form of agriculture, and we have no evidence that there were irrigation systems capable of tapping the waters of the Helmand on a perennial basis. The uncertainties attendant on this subsistence pattern must have limited sedentary occupation.

There is also a suggestion in the rather large houses of Shahr-i-Sokhta, in the cuprous slag deposits of the Gardan Reg area, and in the abundance of steatite everywhere in southern Seistan that some class or group of specialists —stone carvers or metal smiths, perhaps under some wealthy or powerful leader—lived in Seistan to exploit local resources. Their task ended for some reason, and they moved away as suddenly as they had come. Perhaps this is the nearest to a commercial venture that prehistoric man was ever to embark on in Seistan.[6]

A P P E N D I X   I:

Vegetation of Sind— *After* G. S. PURI*

THE DESERT IN SIND adjoins Rajputana and is closely related to the western deserts. Though not a part of India now, it is of considerable interest botanically. The flora of the Indus delta is closely related to that of Sind, but the Rajputana flora has a number of eastern species. The western deserts, being much drier than the eastern ones, have plants with pronounced xerophytic characters.

The Sind desert is in the middle of the western and eastern deserts. The western plants in Sind are *Physorhynchus, Dipterygium, Reseda, Ochradenus, Althaea, Senra, Taverniera, Alhagi, Inula, Statice, Rhazya, Periploca, Convolvulus sindicus, Linaria, Cometes, Forskahlea, Nannorhops.*

The flora of the Sind desert was divided by Sabnis (1929) into the following broad categories in accordance with the terminology of Schimper:

(1) Halophytic and semihalophytic. (4) Sand.
(2) Aquatic and semiaquatic. (5) Gravel.
(3) Kalar soil. (6) Rock.

* *Indian Forest Ecology*, Oxford Book and Stationery Co., New Delhi, 1960, Vol. I.
[6] Piperne, 1973; Tosi, 1968, 1969.

(1) Halophytic and semihalophytic species are *Ipomoea biloba, Andropogon aucheri, Calotropis procera, Salvadora oleoides, Aerua pseudo-tomentosa, Convolvulus microphyllus, Tamarix articulata, Fagonia cretica, Launaea chondriloides, Artiplex stocksii, Suaeda nudiflora, Salsola foetida,* and *Halopyrum mucronatum.*

(2) Aquatic and semiaquatic include *Nymphaea lotus, Hydrilla verticillata, Potamogeton pectinatus,* and *Scirpus littoralis.*

The semiaquatic plants along the banks of the river consist of *Capparis decidua, Portulaca oleracea,* and the species of *Tamarix, Bergia, Sida, Abutilon, Zizyphus, Indigofera, Alhagi, Rhynchosia, Acacia, Ammannia, Trianthema, Mollugo, Gnaphalium, Eclipta, Launaea, Salvadora, Calotropis, Prosopis, Leptadenia, Cressa, Lippia, Amaranthus, Aerua, Achyranthes.*

(3) Kalar soil formation has *Capparis, Bergia, Corchorus, Zygophyllum, Zizyphus, Indigofera, Alhagi, Prosopis, Acacia, Cirtullus, Trianthema, Eclipta, Launaea, Salvadora,Rhazya, Calotropis,Leptadenia, Solanum, Aerua, Achyranthes, Euphorbia, Phoenix, Panicum, Erianthus, Desmostachya,* and *Aeluropus.* Also *Capparis decidua, Zizyphus rotundifolia,* and species of *Leptadenia* and *Aerua* and *Tamarix* are found.

(4) Sand formations are found both in the plains and in dunes, the vegetation of which consists of *Capparis* and *Zizyphus.* Small groups of species of *Calotropis, Leptadenia, Crotalaria,* and occasionally *Panicum, Eragrostis, Desmostachya,* and *Tamarix* are present.

On sandy plains, associations of *Tamarix* and *Erianthus,* also *Aerua, Zizyphus, Calotropis,* etc., are found.

On sand dunes the vegetation is typically of *Capparis, Tamarix, Zygophyllum, Crotalaria, Acacia, Salvadora, Rhazya, Pentatropis, Lepadenia, Heliotropium, Lycium, Aerua, Calligonum, Pennisetum, Erianthus,* and *Desmostachya* and *Salvadora,* with or without *Euphorbia.*

At another place sand dunes have an association of the species of *Crotalaria, Capparis, Zizyphus,* and occasionally *Aerua, Leptadenia,* and *Salvadora.*

Vegetation of sandy plains consists of species of *Dipterygium, Capprais,* etc.

(5) The plants on the gravel formation are the following: *Tribulus, Sida, Trianthema, Corchorus,* and *Euphorbia.*

Climbing or twining vegetation consists of species of *Rhynchosia, Convolvulus,* and *Ipomaea.*

Plants with bushy habit form a bigger group and consist of species of *Capparis, Bergia, Eclipta, Salsola,* and *Inula.*

Among trees, species of *Zizyphus, Prosopis,* and *Cordia* are commonly found. The majority of plants belonging to this formation are found between Sehwan and Mirpurkhas.

(6) Rock formation: the Laki Range and Ganja hills are of volcanic origin and have hot springs and sulphur springs. On the Laki Range the following are found: *Corchorus, Xanthium, Eclipta, Tephrosia, Striga, Lippia, Pennisetum, Heliotropium, Zygophyllum, Daemia,* and *Aeluropus.*

Undershrubs and shrubs are represented by species of *Reseda, Pluchea, Tamarix, Alhagi, Aerua, Calotropis* and *Blepharis, Forskahlea, Zizyphus,* and *Salvadora.*

Among trees may be mentioned species of *Moringa, Dalbergia, Prospois, Cordia, Acacia, Salvadora.*

The flora on the hills has a typical western character.

Ganja hill is composed of limestones and has the following flora: *Ammannia, Cressa, Zygophyllum, Cleome, Launaea, Eclipta, Schweinfurthia, Abutilon, Calotropis, Leptadenia, Lycium, Salvadora,* and *Pentatropis.*

A P P E N D I X   J :   *Initial Steps in a Possible Decipherment of the Harappan Script—By* Shirley Blancke

AN EFFORT TO OBTAIN A MORE SPECIFIC IDEA as to the nature of the Harappan script has been under way at the American Museum of Natural History for some time. The exigencies of other work have considerably slowed up the project, but the following is an outline of the approach taken and some of the conclusions reached by myself and by co-workers, among whom Mrs. Shirley Blancke, assistant in the Department of Anthropology, is particularly noteworthy.

Initial Steps in Possible Decipherment—S. Blancke

THE CORPUS OF INSCRIPTIONS can be built up out of the Mohenjo-daro and Chanhu-daro reports. It is advisable to ignore the material from Harappa and sites in India because, for one thing, it appears that these sites are of the later phases and there may be variations and changes through evolution which would compound the complexity of this attempt, and also because we need a corpus of inscriptions to use as a test for possible decipherments.

(1) The first step is to arrange the inscriptions into a card file according to initial signs, i.e., reading from the right. The sign should be written at the upper right of the card (5 × 8). On the upper left should appear the name of the animal depicted in the body of the seal. A picture of the seal should appear on the body of the card, bibliographic reference below.

(2) The second step is to compile a sign list according to categories. Use the form set up in Marshall, 1931. However, obvious variation in drawing, i.e., stiff or incisive, must not be permitted to extend the list without clear understanding of what is being done. Where possible, clear identification of the sign should be placed in the column.

(3) Each sign in the list must be counted according to position. A table must be compiled as follows:

Sign identification	*Initial (from R)*	*Medial*	*Final*

Two character inscriptions must be given a separate listing:

Sign	*Initial*	*Final*

In cases of multiple registers, the second line must be read from left to right. *Take care to observe whether you are using a seal or a seal impression* (this should be noted on card).

In the examples of two symbols separated by multiple vertical strokes, the treatment should be to set up a separate category. It must be kept in mind that we are on fairly safe ground here in regarding multiple vertical strokes as representing numbers. Obviously numbers are used for a statement of "how many such and such." In certain forms they may be modifiers of nouns, i.e., plurals. This has to be determined by the discretion of the compiler.

Single signs, signs standing alone, should be placed in a separate category, perhaps as another column. We need to know how often a sign stands alone. This may be a clue to an ideographic usage, an abbreviation, or a purely symbolic function. The reverse depiction should be noted on the card.

5. Bracketing, underlining, or any effort to set off a given sign from the others should be noted.

6. Under no circumstances should an indistinct or uncertain representation of a sign be used in preparing the sign list or in setting forth the positioning for the table.

The Harappan Script—S. Blancke

I DECIDED THIS SUMMER that before continuing to cut apart the plates to make the card file, I would investigate a little the animals and scenes represented on the seals in relation to where the seals themselves were found, since this could be done more easily at this stage. I have not attempted to compare the inscriptions with the animal representations, as this is better done after the file is completed, I think.

Working with MacKay's tabulation of seals on pages 369–391, I listed all the seals from Area DK, Section G, by house and block number, omitting those described as coming from the street or from in between blocks. (Unfortunately, Marshall does not list this information in a convenient manner, so I decided, for time's sake, to restrict myself to MacKay's seals for the present.) I divided the seals into various categories, which are as follows: Bull, (a) with head high, (b) with head low; Mythical Bull (has trunk and tusks of an elephant); Water Buffalo; Zebu; Elephant; Lioness; Rhinoceros; seals with no pictorial device; atypical seals; and fragmentary seals (eleven categories in all).

I next plotted the seals on squared paper according to depth and house location. (I gave up plotting them by blocks, as it did not seem as if this would be of any advantage.) As a convenient way of subdividing the section into levels, I then marked in the floor levels as given by MacKay and numbered them 1 to 9 from top to bottom rather than using Marshall's arbitrary division into 3 periods, each with 3 or 4 subperiods. The depths of the floor levels are as follows (after MacKay):

(1) Owing to denudation this level is very rarely represented in the DK area. Ranges from 0.86' above to 3.2' below datum level.
(2) Doorsills and pavements average 5' below datum.
(3) Doorsills and pavements average 7' below datum.
(4) Doorsills and pavements average 9.9' below datum.
(5) Doorsills and pavements average 13' below datum.
(6) Doorsills and pavements average 15.9' below datum.
(7) Doorsills and pavements average 20.4' below datum.
(8) Approximately 24' below datum.
(9) From 24' to 30.5'.

Hopefully, these levels would represent the length of existence of a house.

Finally I totaled the seals in each of the 9 levels, but these totals cannot be taken to represent the true density of seals in the lowest levels, since MacKay dug to different depths in different areas. However, on the accompanying Chart No. 1, I have listed the total of each type of seal in each level, and for the more numerous seals, the percentage of the total in each level that they represent. There seems to be a fairly consistent pattern.

By far the most numerous seals are those depicting the bull with raised head, and these account for approximately between 50% and 70% of all the seals in each level (omitting levels 1, 8, and 9, which have too few seals to be treated satisfactorily). The largest number for any one level was 79 seals (out of a total of 121) in level 4.

The next largest category is that of seals with an inscription but no animal depicted. These make up between 19% and 23% of the total in levels 2,3,5,6, but drop to 13% in level 4 (only 15 out of 121 seals), and 4% in level 7 (3 out of 72). There is one of these seals in each of the other levels—1, 8, and 9. The other seal categories occur in only very small numbers in each level. It seems as if there is no special significance in the location of the types of seals, as they appear to be scattered randomly in different areas; nor does any one type of seal cluster in any particular house. The number of seals in one house in one level is generally from 3 to 5, which is not very many (assuming one level to be the lifetime of a house).

What were these animal symbols for? From the preponderance of bull, type (a), seals and the fact that the other types do not cluster in houses, it seems unlikely that they designate families. If this were so, one would expect a more even distribution numerically of the different types and a clustering in the houses, if not through several levels at least in one level. Could they represent calendar periods such as "the year of the bull," etc.? I think not, as again one would expect the numbers to be more evenly distributed between the different types, and there is no horizontal clustering in levels. It seems to me as if the most likely explanation is that either they represent ranks of society where the "upper crust" was comparatively few in number, e.g., ranks of priesthood designated by zebu, elephant etc., or they represent different trades whose practitioners were also comparatively few. I feel that the latter would not be inconsistent with an agrarian economy where most of the town dwellers earned their livelihoods in the fields—assuming that this is what the Harappan system was.

If, however, one of these suggestions is correct, what is the significance of the seals with no animal depicted, which constitute the second largest group? These too seem to be distributed randomly. Do the animal seals have some kind of ritual significance and the others not? Are the inscriptions spells, and do the animals merely represent different kinds of prayers or spells?

As a separate inquiry I decided to look at the atypical group of seals rather carefully to see if any of these seals seemed to have any connection with one another. I included in this group those atypical seals found in the street or between buildings in order to get a more balanced view. They can be broken down into five rough groupings:

(1) Seals with lionesses and/or a figure.
(2a) Bull seals.
(2b) Sheep-goat seals.
(2c) Water buffalo seals.
(3) Geometric seals (mostly a "swastika" design).
(4) Miscellaneous (but no elephant or zebu).

(N.B. I classed all these seals as atypical either because they represent scenes, or a single animal positioned differently, or because they are distinct from the animal seals, such as the seals with geometric design and the cylinder seals.)

The most homogeneous group (at least in subject matter if not style) is number 1, which is as follows:

Level	Seal No.	Seal	Depth (in ft.)
1		none	
2		none	
3	75	Figure with 2 lionesses	5.6
	86	Figure with 2 lionesses	5.7
	122	Figure with 2 lionesses	6.6
4	222	Seated figure with hat	8.4
	235	Seated figure with hat	8.9
5	347	"Centaur": half lioness, half hatted figure	11.0
	420	Seated hatted figure with animals	12.8
6	454	Figure with 2 lionesses	13.4
	522	Figure in tree with lioness	15.5
7		none	
8		none	
9		none	

I have included the two seals with no lioness but a figure wearing a horned hat (222,235) in this group because of the association of this figure with the lioness in seals 347 and 420. The other figures in these seals may be wearing a headdress but it is not horned. It is interesting to note that none of these seals, nor any of the seals depicting a lone lioness, occurs below level 6. The only other seals to include human figures are the water buffalo group and one rare seal (430).

The bull seals and sheep-goat seals (groups 2a and 2b) are listed in Chart 2. All of group 2b occur in level 6–8. Two seals (24, 494) depict a three-headed bull. The water buffalo group (2c) consists of only two seals but both are interesting. No. 279 (depth 9.5′, level 4) shows a man spearing a water buffalo, and no. 510 (depth 15.2′, level 6) has a water buffalo tossing people in a manner reminiscent of the Cretan bull game.

The geometric group (3) consists of nine "swastika" seals and two with circle designs. Most of them are made of faïence or pottery as follows:

		SWASTIKA			CIRCLES	
Level	Seal No.	Material	Depth (in ft.)	Seal No.	Material	Depth (in ft.)
1	—			—		
2	37	faïence	4.7	—		
	17	paste	3.6			
3	—			—		
4	172	steatite	7.8	156	steatite	7.2
5	320	steatite	10.8	—		
	383	faïence	12.1			
6	—			—		
7	550	steatite	16.4	—		
	586	faïence	17.6			
	619	faïence	18.6			
	624	pottery	19.1			
8	—			649	steatite	20.5

Found in street: 383,550,586,619,624

The miscellaneous group (4) is a catchall, as its name implies. Included in it are the cylinder seals, nos. 78, 376, 488, in levels 3, 5, and 6, respectively. The most interesting seal otherwise is no. 30 in level 2 (depth 4.4′), which appears to represent a boat. The other seals are nos. 59, 36, 73, 133, 509, 482, 604.

An incidental fact which has appeared from looking at atypical seals is that of the eight seals which depict an animal facing to the left instead of to the right, six of them occur in the bottom three levels, where there are relatively few seals. Of the other two, one is unlocalized in the top level, and the other is a poor specimen in level 3. (It is not possible to tell what the animal is, and there is no inscription.) The seals facing left are as follows:

Level	Seal No.	Animal represented
1	8	Bull
3	135	?
7	547	Bull
	554	Ibex (head turned right)
	644	Bull
8	651	Rhinoceros
	663	Water Buffalo
	673	Ibex
9	684	Rhinoceros

It seems as if above level 7 the seals were standardized to face to the right. The only other rhinoceros seal, no. 140, in level 3, which was found between blocks, faces right.

CHART NO. 1   TYPES AND TOTALS OF SEALS

Level	Bull (a)	Bull (b)	Mythical Bull	Water Buffalo	Zebu	Elephant	Lioness
1	4	0	0	0	1	0	0
2	27	1	0	0	0	1	1
3	38	4	0	0	2	2	0
4	79	4	1	1	3	5	2
5	53	9	1	0	3	1	1
6	34	3	2	0	2	3	3
7	51	0	0	1	5	2	0
8	6	0	0	1	0	1	0
9	2	0	0	0	0	0	0
TOTAL	**294**	**21**	**4**	**3**	**16**	**15**	**7**

CHART NO. 1   TYPES AND TOTALS OF SEALS

Rhinoceros	No device	Atypical	Fragmentary	Total	% of Total No Device	% of Total Bull (a)
0	1	0	0	6	—	—
0	10	6	2	48	21	56
0	15	5	2	68	23	55
0	15	6	5	121	13	66
0	22	3	9	102	22	52
0	13	6	4	70	19	49
0	3	5	5	72	4	71
1	1	3	0	13	—	—
1	1	0	0	4	—	—
2	**81**	**34**	**27**	**504**		

CHART NO 2   BREAKDOWN OF ATYPICAL BULL AND SHEEP-GOAT SEALS

Level	Sheep-Goat	Multiheaded Bull	Other Bulls
1	—	—	8 faces left 2.4'
2	—	24 three-headed 3.9'	—
3	—	—	135 faces left, bull? 6.8'
4	—	—	229 head down, raised inscription 8.4'
5	—	—	—
6	430 Ram with figures 14.9'	494 three-headed 14.8'	520 faces left, silver* 15.4'
	544 Ibex faces left, head turned right 16.5'		
7	606 faces right 18.2'	641 "star" with bull head 20.0'	644 ⎱ face left ⎰ 20.1' 547 ⎰ ⎱ 16.3'
8	670 faces right, head left 21.9'	—	
	673 Ibex faces left, long horns 22.6'		
			661 two bulls fighting 21.2'
9	—	—	—

* No. 520 appears to face left, but it is made of silver, and I believe that the actual seal has been photographed rather than an impression, so that the picture is reversed.

APPENDIX K:

Archaeological Research on the Subcontinent Since 1968

THE FOLLOWING appear to be the most important reported researches of the past six years. While certain field work, such as J. M. Casal's at Nindowari, J. Shaffer's at Said Kala, G. Dale's at Bala Kot, and my own excavations at Allahdino, are of obvious importance, they yet remain inadequately published and thus cannot be included. (This is one basis for my choice of the following researches, and it governs my estimate of others.) Nevertheless, the field teems with activity, and the problems raised here appear bound to be solved in the next decade or so. Bibliographic references can be found in the appended portion of the Bibliography. (Page numbers under the various headings refer to the sections of this book which are pertinent.)

Lower Palaeolithic
(esp. pp. 60–75)

PROBABLY THE MOST IMPORTANT STUDY of a site of the Early Stone Age in India has been carried out by G. K. Corvinus at Chirki on the Pravasa River near its junction with the Godavari.[1] Corvinus discovered what appears to be an occupation floor or series of floors lying in the depressions of the Deccan trap (i.e. the bedrock). Some of the artifact material was found in association with boulders, and some was not. It consisted of some 1510 shaped tools plus cores, flakes, and "waste." The tools divide up into types made out of cores and flakes: handaxes, picks, unifacial and bifacial choppers, cleavers, and cutting tools made on flakes. The whole points toward an Acheulean industry. Unfortunately, no evidence for type of dwelling, for hearths, or even for distinctive faunal association was found. However, in both stratigraphic position and industry typology the assemblage is clearly Early Stone Age.
    The stratigraphy:

> Gravelly slope wash
> Gravel 2 m. thick
> Early Stone Age horizon
> Deccan Trap

Middle Palaeolithic
(pp. 75–81)

LITTLE NEW EVIDENCE HAS BEEN ADDED to the study of the Middle Stone Age of the subcontinent, though there are promising studies on its chronology, ecology, and relationships to sea level of the period. Radiocarbon dating now would place the end of the period between 20,000 and 40,000 years ago.[2] The definitive study of the industries of the Middle Stone Age and of the

---

[1] Corvinus, 1973.
[2] D. P. Agrawal, R. K. Arasia, and S. Guzder, 1973.

associated problems of chronology and environment was published by Bridget Allchin in 1969.[3]

Upper Palaeolithic
(pp. 78–80, 387)

THOUGH IT IS BY NO MEANS CONCLUSIVE at this writing, there is increasing evidence that an industry equivalent to an Upper Palaeolithic elsewhere to the west was present in no small way on the subcontinent. The present position has been summarized by Bridget Allchin[4] and is outlined herewith:

N. India

Modern land surfaces (within and upon)	Microlithic industries
Silts and gravels	Blade and burin industries
Silts and gravels	Middle Stone Age industries
Old land surfaces	Early Stone Age (cleaver, chopping tools, handaxes)

This sequence is reflected in the stratigraphic situation in the Allahabad Region where a series of factory sites have been found.[5]

Factory Sites

Silts III and modern soil	Microliths and pottery
Gravel III	Blade and burin
Silts II	
Indurated gravels II	Middle Stone Age
Silts I or unconformity	
Indurated Gravels I	Early Stone Age

It is also similar in Southeastern India, where factory sites have been discovered by M. L. K. Murti near Renigunta on the coast.[6]

Southeastern India

Factory Sites near Renigunta

Modern land surfaces	Microliths
Silts and gravels	Blade and burin
Gravels	Middle Stone Age

[3] Allchin, 1969.
[4] Allchin, 1973.
[5] Sharma, 1970.
[6] Murti, 1968.

Allchin's own work in Gujarat at Visvadi, a factory site located in a fossil dune, has recovered a blade and burin industry not unlike that identified by Dani at Sanghao cave, especially in his Period I (p. 78).

Allchin has demonstrated that the Visvadi industry was present at a time of aridity in Gujarat.[7] This arid phase may be correlated with one of Dani's cool-dry phases at Sanghao (p. 78). On the grounds of analogy with such known radiocarbon-dated industries of Western Asia as that of the Baradostain, Allchin feels that the Upper Palaeolithic of India "may be expected to have a date of from 39,000 B.P. forward to as late as 20,000 or even later."[8]

Mesolithic and Microlithic Industries
(pp. 82–101) See Misra, 1973 for a summation.

REPORT OF THE DISCOVERY of so-called Microlithic sites continue unabated (see p. 101) and show that these industries were widespread from the southern Indus Valley, through Rajasthan and Gujarat, and into Central India. Radiocarbon dating indicates that these industries flourished in a post-5000 B.C. period extending up to the time of Christ.

In Western Rajasthan the habitation site of Tilwara in the Luni Valley has been excavated. The deposit is only some 50 cm. thick, but it divides into two phases: the earlier (30 cm.) consists solely of a microlithic industry which contains geometrics (lunates, triangles, trapezes); the upper phase contains wheel-made pottery and fragments of iron in addition to microliths. The microlith horizon contains what appears to be small circular houses with stone foundations 2.5 to 3 meters in diameter. There are hearths, sling balls, and grinding stones (querns and rubbers). Faunal remains include representations of animals who are usually found in grassy or open woodland terrains, such as the spotted deer, the hog deer, and the jackal; the presence of what appear to be domesticated cattle, sheep and/or goats and the pig (?) suggests an economy based on pastoralism and hunting-gathering.[9]

The site of Bagor which is located on the Kothari River, a tributary of the Banas in Mewar, is in the midst of a region rich in sites of microlithic vintage. Bagor is one of several habitation sites so far identified among these. It contains a deposit representing a continuous occupation of 1.50 m. in thickness. There are three phases within this occupation:

Phase I (the earliest, 50–80 cm. thick)—contains microliths associated with circular stone-lined huts of wattle as well as with stone-paved floors. The dead were buried with head to the west along an east-west axis. They lay in an extended position.

Phase II (30–50 cm)—microliths seem to decrease in number but there are now copper/bronze tools and handmade pottery. There is also evidence for possible digging stick weights. The dead were flexed and laid out as in Phase I but with heads to the east and accompanied by funerary furniture, including pottery and metal ornaments and tools. There is evidence that meat "offerings" were also placed in the grave.

[7] Allchin and Goudie, 1971.
[8] Allchin in Agrawal and Ghosh, 1973, p. 21.
[9] Misra, 1971a and 1971b.

Phase III (35–75 cm.)—Iron tools, wheelmade pottery, and glass beads, as well as burnt brick and stone structures, are found with a deteriorated microlithic industry. The dead are found in an extended position along a north-south axis with head to the north.

Animal bones are found in all three phases and include the hog deer, the wild boar, the barasingha (cervus duvauceli curier), the jackal, the soft-shell turtle (Lissemys punctata), the cat, the monitor lizard, and fish. Cattle and sheep-goat attest to pastoralism as at Tilwara. In terms of phase differences it appears that hunting became less important and both pastoralism and probably agriculture (Phase II and III) became more so. This is reflected somewhat in the decline in quality of the microlithic industry which initially was a finely crafted one of the geometric type with some emphasis on diminutive examples.

Bagor has produced five radiocarbon dates:

Phase I

TF-786	4480 ± 200 B.C.
TF-1007	3835 ± 130 B.C.
TF-1012	3285 ± 90 B.C.

Phase II

TF-1009	2765 ± 105 B.C.
TF-1005	2110 ± 90 B.C.
1006	

The evidence at all these sites suggests that, at least in Northwest India, microlithic-using men lived in a dry climate with open woodland, a characteristic environment.

The unpublished but ongoing work of J. Jacobson on Mesolithic cave sites near Bhopal has a basic importance since there is a strong ethnohistorical basis in his work. Its publication ought to be a major contribution to the field.

Pre-Harappan
(chapters 4, 5, 6)

A. H. DANI CARRIED OUT a series of surveys and explorations on the Gomal plain, that plain onto which debouches the Gomal River, whose valley forms one of the main passes between the Ghazni-Kandahar-Zhob regions of Afganistan and northeastern Baluchistan and the Indus River region proper. Some twenty-one sites were reported. Five of these located near Bannu are above the 1000-foot contour and are in the vicinity of the Kurram River, while the remainder lie below 1000 feet in the Tank-Dera Ismail Khan area. The five sites near Bannu were already described by Stein (Surkh Derai, Chaudhwan, Chicha Derai, Dabra, Shah Zaman Dherai) and can be assigned to cultural assemblages known to have been in existence probably from about the time of Christ to at least 500 A.D. (see page 413). In the Tank area Dani also revisited four other sites once investigated by Stein (Lakhi Kot, Aba Khel, Kot Pathan,

Kot-kat Dherai), and these can be assigned to approximately the same period as the Bannu sites (see page 413).

Dani did, however, discover eleven other sites in the Tank-Dera Ismail Khan region: Gumla, Hathala, Karam Shah, Rahman, Dherai, Hisham Dherai, Mahra Sharif, Musa Khel, Bud Ki Therai, Kot Allah-Dad, and Gomal Kalan. Of these, Gumla was chosen for limited excavation which involved sinking a trench to virgin soil with consequent limitation of results. There are six periods defined in the stratigraphy:

Period I—lying on virgin soil; contains microlithic tools, animal bones, and "community ovens."

Period II—After a gap of unknown duration there appears a bronze tool-using assemblage with new types of microliths and fine, painted wheelmade pottery; there is indication that agriculture was practiced.

Period III—A possible small gap appears after Period II, but there appear to be survivals of pottery types and designs from II. However, this period is marked by some remarkable figurines, mostly of females, generally plano-plano in cross-section (front to back) with appliqué breasts. A mudbrick wall is the only architecture. The pottery has some close resemblances to that found at Kot Diji (pp. 179–82).

Period IV—separated from Period III by a thin layer of ash and habitation debris which the excavator interprets as a mark of violence. Period IV contains much that is found in III, with the addition of objects of mature Harappan type. A podium of mudbrick was a prominent feature of the architecture.

Period V—produced grave pits and evidence for cremation burials in them. There are also horse bones and clay horse models, and the pottery suggests the possibility of some relation to Dani's Gandhara grave culture (pp. 356–57). Since the end of Period IV was violent—destroyed walls, burned material, and these grave pits are intimately associated with this "destruction" layer—Dani believes that people of Period V destroyed "Period IV cultures."[10]

Period VI is rather cursorily defined by some flexed burials with open mouths like those found elsewhere (Sarai Kola, Hathala); iron is associated with these graves.

Primarily on the basis of the sequence at Gumla, Dani was able to place the' other sites of the region into a relative sequence; this was aided by some test trenches at Hathala.

One possible interpretation would arrange the sites as follows:

Karam Shah	Gumla III–IV
Hathala	Gumla IV–VI
Rahman Dherai (the largest on the Gomal plain—1700′ x 1200′ x 15′ high)	Gumla III
Hisham Dheri	Gumla IV
Mahra Sharif	Gumla IV, VI plus Period C–B (see p. 399)
Musa Khel	Gumla III

---

[10] Dani, 1970–71, p. 30.

Bud Ki Dheri	Gumla IV (?)
Kot Allah-Dad	Period F–D (?)
Gomal Kalan	Period F–D (?)

At Jalilpur, 46 miles southwest of Harappa near to the junction of the Chenab and Ravi rivers, R. Mughal carried out limited excavations in 1971. These consisted of trenches of different sizes, one of which was sunk to virgin soil. The site measured 1400 x 1200 feet and has a height in most places of some five feet (the main trench is 56 x 60 feet) suggestive of a settlement of considerable scale. The excavator differentiates two occupational levels in some six feet of accumulation.

Jalilpur I—the earliest, consists of occupational phases characterized by the presence of thick reddish handmade pottery covered with a coarse appliqué, beads of sheet gold as well as terracotta, bone points, net-sinkers, chert blades, and many animal bones. No architectural remains were defined except for some rammed earth floors.

Jalilpur II—Wheelmade bichrome pottery of fine fabric appears in the last phase of Jalilpur I and is demonstrative of the overlap of the two main occupations. Jalilpur II consists of two structural phases, II A and II B. The architecture for both phases is of small rooms. In the earlier phase, the walls of which are a kind of pisé; in the later, of mudbrick (18″ x 9″ x 3″). The ceramics consist of globular vessels with band painted decoration; flanged vessels, some of which are painted with black designs on red; black or brown painted decoration on red wares; black and white on red; black and red painted wares, some of which are of the offering stand type and which are common

PLATE 59   *Painted pottery from the site of Jalilpur. Period II.* (Courtesy Department of Archaeology, Government of Pakistan.)

to the Harappan; there are also examples of a sandy slipped and striated ware which is well known in Northern Baluchistan. Small finds consisted of toy cart fragments, terracotta cakes, copper or bronze rods, animal figurines (especially of cattle), terracotta bracelets, shell bangles, chert blades, leaf-shaped arrowheads, grinding and pounding stones, and some fine lapis lazuli beads.[11]

Probably the most important of excavations in Pakistan has been that of Sarai Khola (p. 182). Located less than 4 kilometers southwest of Taxila, it is a small site on a hill near the Grand Trunk Road. It seems once to have consisted of two mounds, A and B, but B was washed away. The site was trenched in four seasons of excavation, and four main periods have been defined.

Period I—the lowest, produced an occupational assemblage which consisted of polished stone celts, ovoid and quadrangular in cross-section; stone scrapers and blades; and bone points. A burnished handmade red ware characterized the pottery.

Period II—even with some overlap with the pottery of Period I, that of Period II shows a distinctive change. Wheelmade painted vessels especially treated with a red wash and often decorated with dark bands were characteristic of the ceramics. There are grinding stones, and a long-blade industry seems to have been included in the stone tool repertory. Bone, shell, and terracotta are the materials for such things as bangles and points; copper rods and needles also occur. The architectural evidence is limited to six floors of rammed earth.

Period III—consists largely of a cemetery which had two phases. The site was apparently then used as a burial ground by a people who used iron for ornaments. The dead in some cases had open mouths.

Period IV—is a late occupational phase for which stone walls, hard clay floors, and hearths are evidence. The pottery is apparently mainly of storage type, but there are a number of fine and unusual clay figurines of cattle and human females, as well as terracotta bangles, beads, rattles, and balls. Semiprecious stone beads are also present.[12]

The three sites—Gumla, Jalilpur, and Sarai Khola—have great value in that they confirm the presence of pre-Harappan occupations of considerable antiquity in the Indus River Valley. Gumla I and Jalilpur I suggest that the way of life designated in the earliest levels at Kile Gul Mohammad and elsewhere (pp. 136–38) was also to be found in the lowlands of the Indus region. Furthermore, the lowest level at Sarai Khola appears to confirm the presence of the Inner Asian complex first defined at Burzahom (pp. 312–18) in the Northern Punjab. Together Gumla I and Sarai Khola I evidence a semisettled life adapted to different ecologies but sharing hunting and gathering, some pastoralism, and perhaps a modicum of agriculture.

In Gumla II–III, Jalilpur II, and Sarai Khola II we witness the establishment of fully sedentary life and both the growth and spread of villages into the northern portion of the Indus River Valley. Recently one of the most remarkable discoveries in subcontinental archaeology was made at Kalibangan (pp. 182–83): that of an intact ploughed field in pre-Harappan context there.[13]

[11] R. Mughal, 1974.
[12] Muhammad Abdul Halim, 1972; also in *Pakistan Archaeology*, No. 5, 1968, pp. 28–40; also report on skeletons of Period III in *Pakistan Archaeology*, No. 6, 1969 (Wolfram Bernard).
[13] Thapar, 1973, pp. 266–67.

PLATE 60 *Handmade pottery from the site of Sarai Khola. Nos. 1, 2, 4–7—Period I; no. 3—Period II.* (Courtesy Department of Archaeology, Government of Pakistan.)

Kalibangan is one of the Rajasthani sites (see page 182) which produced material comparable to that of the non- or pre-Harappan levels at Kot Diji (pp. 179–182). In a general way there is evidence for certain typological ties, particularly in the ceramics between Kot Diji and at least the sites of the Gomel, Jalilpur, and Rajasthani areas; and there is therefore a basis for a conception of plough agriculture as one of the firm technological foundations for this stage of sedentary life in the regions where these sites are located. At Siswal, in the upper Sarasvati valley Suraj, Bhan was able through his excavation to distinguish that the earliest phase of occupation at the site (Siswal A) compared rather neatly to Kalibangan I, the pre-Harappan occupation at the latter site. Siswal B represented both a continuance of A in a less refined form and the appearance of some classical Harappan wares along with triangular clay cakes, clay discs, flint blades, and both copper and clay bangles. This was also confirmed by his excavations at Mitathal in the same region (Mitathal I). Suraj Bhan found the Siswal material extended to some sixteen sites in Haryana and Siswal B in many parts of the Upper Sarasvati Basin. It is also known at Sarangpur close to the Siwalik foothills.[14] In the same region, by excavations at Mitathal and Daulatpur, he was able to distinguish a classical or mature Harappan occupation (Mitathal IIA) as well as a Late Harappan one (Mitathal IIB and Daulatpur I).

In Kutch the mound site of Surkotada has been excavated by J. P. Joshi. Though Harappan throughout, it appears to contain non-Harappan elements (or influences). The last period (IC) shows the presence of a ware like that of Ahar (pp. 335–50). However, in the earliest period defined there (IA) there is a ceramic type akin to that of pre-Harappan Kot Diji (and Sothi).[15]

It is apparent at this writing that each season's excavations will add to the evidence for widespread and developed village life in these regions prior to the advent of the mature Harappan culture (see p. 184). Vital to the problem of the genesis of the Harappan civilization is an understanding of the way of life of this developed sedentary existence for which there are now so many sites. This makes all the more important the development of strategies which will permit the archaeologist to understand his sites holistically. As I have remarked elsewhere, it is to be hoped that the era of the potsherd is drawing to an end and that archaeological assemblages will be related to one another by much more than simply ceramic lookalikes (see Preface to the Revised Edition).

The Harappan Civilization
(chapters 7 and 8)

LITTLE HAS BEEN ADDED to our knowledge of this civilization in the past seven years. There are now nearly 300 sites of the civilization known on both sides of the Indo-Pakistan border; most of these are small in size—that is, less than 600 feet in diameter (see pp. 241–42)—but few have been excavated. In those that have been even cursorily examined there is growing evidence that there are differences both in artifact content and style and in settlement character that suggest that the famed conformity of the Harappan civilization is not as monolithic as once was thought (see pp. 300–301).

Absolute dating continues to concern many, and there is increasing evidence that radiocarbon dating must be supplemented by other means of dating since the method has now undergone two major changes in its adjustment factors. Part of the problem lies in the lack of reliable radiocarbon dates from Mesopotamia; the Akkadian period and late Sumerian dynasties that followed it are

---

[14] Suraj Bhan, 1971–72a; 1973.
[15] J. P. Joshi, 1973, p. 177.

the only places where reasonably solid evidence exists for Harappan contacts outside the subcontinent and the Borderlands (p. 296). In spite of the long hiatus of the Kassite period in Mesopotamia and the uncertainties attendant even in the relative dating of both the Akkadian period and that of Ur III, those who would date the Harappan civilization early uphold the traditional Mesopotamian dates. The fact is that unless serious changes (and some of these are already proposed) are made in the radiocarbon adjustments, there can be no clear evidence that the Harappan civilization—in its mature phases at least—can be dated earlier than 2300 B.C.; and if we accept the radiocarbon dating as of 1970 (see also pp. 394–96), a date nearer to 1900 B.C. is in order.[16]

The Late Harappan
(chapter 8)

A CONSIDERABLE AMOUNT OF WORK has been going on, especially in India, on the definition and spread of the late Harappan. Particularly noteworthy is Joshi's work at Surkotada, already mentioned, and Gregory Possehl's as yet unpublished doctoral thesis resulting from his work in Gujarat in 1970–71. One contribution which the thesis unquestionably makes is that it demonstrates the tight interrelationships that the Harappans had both with the local ecology and with peoples of other ways of life. This is, in part, what is demonstrated at Surkotada, at Lothal, and at Rangpur (see pp. 306–7). It supports the idea that the so-called demise of the Harappan civilization was actually a matter of local adjustment to new conditions until the old style disappeared (see pp. 310–11).

Research of great interest to this question has been going on relative to the nature and place of the so-called ochre-colored ware (OCP) (see pp. 348–49). Many sites containing this ware are now known across Uttar Pradesh. Recent work has shown that :(1) the OCP is associated with the copper hoards (at Saipai, 18 km. north of Etawah Railway Station);[17] (2) that there are pottery types similar to those of Kalibangan I; (3) that some of the ceramic types associated with OCP are of Harappan character.[18] All in all, this evidence from northern India appears to demonstrate continuities of traditions rather than their disappearance.

The Malwa Cultural Complex
(pp. 342–44)

THE EXCAVATIONS AT THE SITE OF INAMGAON (the results of which are still unpublished at this date) by H. D. Sankalia, Z. D. Ansari, and M. K. Dhavalikar have given us a graphic view of the life of the mature part of this complex in its manifestation on the black cotton soil of the Deccan. Inamgaon

---

[16] For a substantive discussion of radiocarbon dating in the subcontinent, see Dales, 1973; also Sankalia, 1973.
[17] L. M. Wahal in *Puratattva* No. 5, 1971–72, pp. 12–13.
[18] R. L. Gaur, 1973; also special issue of *Puratattva*, No. 5, 1971–72.

is located in the Bhima Valley and, like its contemporary sites, Prakash in the Tapti Valley and Daimabad in the Pravara-Godavari Valley, is more than fifty acres in size. These are, of course, village sites. At Inamgaon the typical house was rectangular (5.5 cm. x 3 m.), with rainwater drains, subterranean silos, and large, probably legged, storage vessels which held cereal grains (wheat, rice, and probably sorghum). A stone and mud embankment wall surrounded the settlement and apparently was used to divert the flood waters of the nearby river.

The citizens used copper to make chisels, axes, beads, anklets, and bangles in some abundance. Their pottery was the justly famed Jorwe wares, which are of the Malwa tradition and are hard-fired, wheelmade, and often richly painted with a variety of designs.

There is evidence that this mature and flourishing Jorwe culture faded into the next period owing to a falling off of agricultural productivity caused by natural failings of weather or soil.[19]

The Later Periods
(chapter 11)

THE FRENCH WORK AT PIRAK reveals an Iron Age settlement (see footnote, p. 361) which has features akin to other Iron Age sites in the Ganges Valley, including an animal antler industry like that known at Allahapur. And, of course, the cemetery at Sarai Khola III, as well as Stacul's work in re-evaluating the graves and other complexes in Swat, gives great promise that the famous gap often called the Aryan Period will be substantially filled in the near future.[20]

[19] M. K. Dhavalikar, 1973; H. D. Sankalia, 1971.
[20] Banerjee, 1964; Casal, 1973; Stacul, 1969, 1970, 1973.

A P P E N D I X   L:

Population Estimates for Selected Sites in The Indo-Iranian Borderlands, Based on Statistics of Modern Settlement in West Pakistan

(after Fairservis, 1967)

Site	Period	Approximate Size in Feet	Square Feet	Total Number of Houses	Estimated Population
Kechi-Beg (Q14)	H-2, DS-I	210×120	25,200	35 [a]	210 [a]
Damb Sadaat (Q8)	DS-I-III	400×400	160,000	181	1,086
Mohenjo-daro [b]	Harappan	3000×2750	5,500,000	10,428	41,250
Ghazi-shah	Amri-Harappan	525×450	236,250	295	1,770
Amri	Amri-Harappan	1800×450	810,000	1,012.5	6,075
Kot Diji	Amri (Kot Dijian) Harappan	600×400	240,000	300	1,800
Lohumjo-daro	Harappan-Jhukar	900×600	540,000	675	4,050
Pir Lal Chatto	Trihni	475×420	199,500	249	1,494
Pandi Wahi	Amri	450×350	147,500	184	1,104
Chauro	Amri	500×300	150,000	187.5	1,125
Chanhu-daro (Majumdar, 1934)	Harappan	1000×700	700,000	875	4,950
Judeir-jo-daro	Harappan	1800×1500	2,700,000	3,375	20,240
Harappa, Mound E	Harappan	1200×1800	2,160,000	2,700	16,200
Harappa, granary mound	Harappan	1020×960	979,200	1,224	7,344
Harappa (Total, exclusive of "citadel")	Harappan	—	3,139,200	3,924	23,544
Harappa, "citadel"	Harappan	1800×840	1,512,000		
Malir 2	Harappan	540×420	226,800	283.5	1,701
Nal Bazar	Harappan	375×405	151,875	190	1,140
Amilano	Harappan	330×345	113,850	142	852

[a] The unit estimates are 800 square feet per person, or six people per house, in rural areas. In Q14, 180 square feet equals ¼ house, and 720 square feet equals one house; in Q8, 882 square feet equals one house. The figure of 800 square feet is the "average." (See Government of Pakistan, 1962.)

[b] Exclusive of the "citadel" and the area between it and VS, DK, and HR. As only approximately one-third of the total site has been excavated, two-thirds have been added to include the whole site as it is known from surface remains.

Bibliography

ADAMS, R. M.,
1960 "The Evolution Process in Early Civilization," *Evolution After Darwin*, S. Tax, ed., University of Chicago Press, Chicago, II, 153–168.
1962 "Agriculture and Urban Life in Early Southwestern Iran," *Science*, Vol. CXXXVI, pp. 109–122.

AGRAWAL, D. P.,
1966 "C14 Dates, Banas Culture and the Aryans," *Current Science*, Vol. XXXV, No. 5, pp. 114–117.

ALCOCK, L.,
1956 "Appendix i, The Pottery, Site Q8, Cut 1," W. A. Fairservis, Jr., "Excavations in the Quetta Valley, West Pakistan," *Anthropological Papers of the American Museum of Natural History*, Vol. XLV, Pt. 2.

ALLCHIN, B.,
1958 "The Late Stone Age of Ceylon," *Journal of the Royal Anthropological Institute of Great Britain and Ireland*, Vol. LXXXVIII, pp. 179–201.
1959 "The Indian Middle Stone Age: Some New Sites in Central and Southern India, and their Implications," *Bulletin of the Institute of Archaeology*, No. 2, pp. 1–35.
1963 "The Indian Stone Age Sequence," *Journal of the Royal Anthropological Institute of Great Britain and Ireland*, Vol. XCIII, Pt. 2, pp. 210–234.

ALLCHIN, F. R.,
1960 *Piklihal Excavations*, Andhra Pradesh Government Archaeological Series, No. 1, Hyderabad.
1961 *Utnur Excavations*, Andhra Pradesh Government Archaeological Series, No. 5, Hyderabad.
1963 *Neolithic Cattle-Keepers of South India—A Study of the Deccan Ash-mounds*, Cambridge University Press, Cambridge.

Annual Report of the Archaeological Survey of India, 1904–05
1908 Edited by the Director-General of Archaeology, Government of India, Calcutta.

441

Annual Report of the Archaeological Survey of India, 1925–26
1928 Edited by the Director-General of Archaeology, Government of India, Calcutta.

ANTONINI, C. S.,
1963 "Preliminary Notes on the Excavation of the Necropolises found in Western Pakistan," *East and West*, Vol. XIV, Nos. 1–2, pp. 13–25.

BOBEK, H.,
1953/1954 "Klima und Landschaft Irans in vor- und frühgeschichtlicher Zeit," *Geographischer Jahresbericht aus Österreich*, Vol. XXV, pp. 1–42.

BOSE, H. K., SEN, D., and RAY, G.,
1958 "Geological and Cultural Evidences of the Stone Age in Mayurbhanj," *Man in India*, Vol. XXXVIII, No. 1, pp. 53–54.

BRAIDWOOD, R. J.,
1957 *Prehistoric Man*, Chicago Natural History Museum Popular Series, Anthropology No. 37, Chicago.
1960 "The Agricultural Revolution," *Scientific American*, Vol. CCIII, No. 3, pp. 130–152.

BRAIDWOOD, R. J., and HOWE, B.,
1960 *Prehistoric Investigations in Iraqi Kurdistan*, Studies in Ancient Oriental Civilization, No. 31, Oriental Institute, University of Chicago, Chicago.

BRAIDWOOD, R. J., HOWE, B., and REED, C.,
1961 "The Iranian Prehistoric Project," *Science*, Vol. CXXXIII, pp. 2008–2010.

BRAIDWOOD, R. J., and REED, C.,
1957 "The Achievement and Early Consequences of Food-Production: A Consideration of the Archaeological and Natural-Historical Evidence," *Cold Springs Harbor Symposia on Quantitative Biology*, Vol. XXII, pp. 19–31.

BUCHANAN, B.,
1965 "A Dated 'Persian Gulf' Seal and Its Implications," *Studies in Honor of Benno Landsberger*, pp. 204–209, Chicago.

CALDWELL, J. R.,
1966 "Tal-i-Iblis—The Kerman Range and the Beginnings of Smelting," *Illinois State Museum, Preliminary Reports*, No. 7, Springfield.
1967 "Investigations at Tal-i-Iblis," *Illinois State Museum Preliminary Reports*, No. 9, Springfield.

CASAL, J. M.,
1961 *Fouilles De Mundigak*, Memoires de la Délégation Archéologique Française en Afghanistan, T. XVII, Librairie C. Klincksieck, Paris.
1964 *Fouilles d'Amri*, Publication de la Commission Des Fouilles Archéologique Fouilles du Pakistan, Librairie C. Klincksieck, Paris.

CATON-THOMPSON, G.,
1954 "Some Palaeoliths from South Arabia," *Proceedings of the Prehistoric Society for 1953*, N.S., Vol. XIX, Pt. 2, pp. 189–218.

CHHABRA, B. C.,
1956 "Ancient India and Southeast Asia," *Indo-Asian Culture*, Vol. IV, No. 3.

CHILDE, V. G.,
1957 *New Light on the Most Ancient East*, 4th ed., Grove Press Inc., New York.

COLBERT, E. H.,
1935 "Siwalik Mammals in the American Museum of Natural History," *American Philosophical Society Transcripts*, N.S., Vol. XXVI.

COLE, S.,
1963 *Prehistory of East Africa*, Macmillan, New York.

COLLIER DAVIES, C.,
1953 *An Historical Atlas of the Indian Peninsula*, Oxford University Press, Oxford.

COON, CARLTON S.,
1957 *The Seven Caves*, Knopf, New York.

COON, C., and RALPH, E. K.,
1955 "Radio-carbon Dates for Kara Kamar, Afghanistan," in *Science*, Vol. CXXII, pp. 921–922.

CUNNINGHAM, SIR ALEXANDER,
1872–1873 *Archaeological Survey of India Reports*, Vol. V.

DALES, G. F.,
1962a "A Search for Ancient Seaports," *Expedition*, Vol. IV, No. 2, pp. 2–10.
1962b "The Mythical Massacre at Mohenjo-daro," *Expedition*, Vol. VI, No. 3, pp. 36–44.
1965 "A Suggested Chronology for Afghanistan, Baluchistan, and the Indus Valley," *Chronologies in Old World Archaeology*, edited by R. W. Ehrich, University of Chicago Press, Chicago.
1966 "The Decline of the Harappans," *Scientific American*, Vol. CCXIV, No. 5, pp. 92–100.

DANI, A. H.,
1960 *Prehistory and Protohistory of Eastern India*, Firma K. L. Mukhopadhyaya, Calcutta.
1964 "Sanghao Cave Excavation, The First Season, 1963," *Ancient Pakistan*, Vol. I, pp. 1–50.
1967 "Timargarha and Gandhara Grave Culture," *Ancient Pakistan*, Vol. III, pp. 1–407.

DARLINGTON, P. J.,
1957 *Zoogeography: The Geographical Distribution of Animals*, John Wiley & Sons, Inc., New York.

DE BARYED, W. T. (ed.),
1958 *Introduction to Oriental Civilization, Sources of Indian Tradition*, Columbia University Press, New York.

DE CARDI, B.,
1951 "A New Prehistoric Ware from Baluchistan," *Iraq*, Vol. XIII, No. 2, pp. 63–75.
1959 "New Wares and Fresh Problems from Baluchistan," *Antiquity*, Vol. XXXIII, pp. 15–24.
1964 "British Expedition to Kalat, 1948 and 1957," *Pakistan Archaeology*, Vol. I, pp. 20–29.
1965 "Excavations and Reconnaissance in Kalat, West Pakistan," *Pakistan Archaeology*, Vol. 2, No. 2, pp. 86–182.
1967 "The Bampur Sequence in the 3rd Millennium B.C.," *Antiquity*, Vol. XLI, pp. 33–41.

DEO, SHANTARAM BHALCHANDRA, and ZAINUDDIN, DAWOOD ANSARI,
1965 *Chalcolithic Chandoli*, Deccan College Postgraduate and Research Institute, Poona.

DE TERRA, H.,
1937 "Cenozoic Cycles in Asia and Their Bearing on Human Prehistory," *Proceedings of the American Philosophical Society*, Vol. LXXVII, No. 3, pp. 289–308.
1939 "The Quaternary Terrace System of Southern Asia," *Geographic Review*, January.

DE TERRA, H., and DE CHARDIN, P. TEILHARD,
1936 "Observations on the Upper Siwalik Formations and Later Pleistocene Deposits in India," *American Philosophical Society Proceedings*, Vol. LXXVI, pp. 791–822.

DE TERRA, H., and PATERSON, T. T.,
1939 *Studies on the Ice Age of India and Associated Human Cultures*, Carnegie Institution of Washington Publication No. 493, Washington.

DEO, S. B., and ANSARI, Z. D.,
1965 "Chalcolithic Chandoli," Poona.

DEVA, K., and McCOWN, D. E.,
1949 "Further Exploration in Sind: 1938," *Ancient India*, No. 5, pp. 12–30.

DUPREE, L. B.,
1958 "Shamshir Ghar: historic cave site in Kandahar Province Afghanistan," *Anthropological Papers of the American Museum of Natural History*, Vol. XLVI, Pt. 2, pp. 137–312.
1963 "Deh Morasi Ghundai: A Chalcolithic Site in South-Central Afghanistan," *Anthropological Papers of the American Museum of Natural History*, Vol. L, Pt. 2, pp. 59–135.
1964 "Prehistoric Archaeological Surveys and Excavations in Afghanistan: 1959–60 and 1961–63," *Science*, Vol. CXLVI, pp. 638–640.

DURRANI, F. A.,
1964 "Stone Vases as Evidence of Connection Between Mesopotamia and the Indus Valley," *Ancient Pakistan*, Vol. I, pp. 51–96.

DYSON, R. H., JR.
1953 "Archaeology and the Domestication of Animals in the Old World," *American Anthropologist*, Vol. LV, pp. 661–673.
1965 "Problems in the Relative Chronology of Iran, 6000–2000 B.C.," *Chronologies in Old World Archaeology*, R. Ehrich, ed., University of Chicago Press, Chicago, pp. 215–256.

DYSON, R. H., JR., and YOUNG, T. C.,
1960 "The Solduz Valley, Iran: Pisdeli Tepe," *Antiquity*, Vol. XXXIV, pp. 19–28.

FAIRSERVIS, WALTER A., JR.,
1952 "Preliminary Report on the Prehistoric Archaeology of the Afghan-Baluchi Areas," *American Museum Novitates*, No. 1587, American Museum of Natural History, New York.
1956 "Excavations in the Quetta Valley, West Pakistan," *Anthropological Papers of the American Museum of Natural History*, Vol. XLV, Pt. 2, pp. 169–402.
1959 "Archaeological Surveys in the Zhob and Loralai Districts, West

Pakistan," *Anthropological Papers of the American Museum of Natural History*, Vol. XLVII, Pt. 2.

1961 "Archaeological Studies in the Seistan Basin of Southwestern Afghanistan and Eastern Iran," *Anthropological Papers of the American Museum of Natural History*, Vol. XLVIII, Pt. 1, pp. 1–128.

1967 "The Origin, Character, and Decline of an Early Civilization," *American Museum Novitates*, No. 2302, American Museum of Natural History, New York.

FIELD, H.,

1959 "An Anthropological Reconnaissance in West Pakistan, 1955," *Papers of the Peabody Museum of Archaeology and Ethnology*, Vol. LII.

FLANNERY, K. V.,

1965 "The Ecology of Early Food Production in Mesopotamia," *Science*, Vol. CXLVII, pp. 1247–1256.

FORD, J. A., and WILLEY, G. R.,

1949 "Surface Survey of the Viru Valley, Peru," *Anthropological Papers of the American Museum of Natural History*, New York, Vol. XLIII, Pt. 1, pp. 1–90.

FRASER-TYTLER, W. K.,

1950 *Afghanistan*, Oxford University Press, New York.

GADD, C. J.,

1932 "Seals of Ancient Indian Style Found at Ur," *Proceedings of the British Academy*, Vol. XVII, pp. 191–210.

GHIRSHMAN, R.,

1938–1939 *Fouilles de Sialk, près Kashan, 1933, 1934, 1937*, Musée du Louvre, Departement des Antiquités Orientales Série Archéologique, T. IV–V, Paris.

GHOSH, A.,

1953 "Fifty Years of the Archaeological Survey of India," *Ancient India* No. 9, pp. 29–52.

GHOSH, S. S., and LAL, K. R.,

1962, 1963 "Plant Remains from Lothal," S. R. Rao, "Excavations at Rangpur and Other Explorations in Gujarat," *Ancient India*, Nos. 18–19, pp. 161–177.

GORDON, D. H.,

1950 "The Stone Age Industries of the Holocene in India and Pakistan," *Ancient India*, No. 6, pp. 64–90.

1951 "Rock Engravings of Kupgallu Hill, Bellary, Madras," *Man*, No. 204, pp. 117–119.

1958 *The Prehistoric Background of Indian Culture*, Mandhuri Dhirajlal, Bombay.

GROUSSET, R.,

1939 *The Civilization of India*, Tudor Publishing Co., New York.

GUPTA, P. C. D.,

"The Excavations at Pandu Rajar Dhibi," *Bulletin of the Directorate of Archaeology, West Bengal*, No. 2, n.d.

HARGREAVES, H.,

1929 *Excavations in Baluchistan 1925, Sampur Mound, Mastung and Sohr Damb, Nal*, Memoirs of the Archaeological Survey of India, No. 35, Government of India, New Delhi.

446 / Bibliography

HEINE-GELDERN, ROBERT VON,
1936 "Archaeological Traces of the Vedic Aryans," *Journal Indian Society of Oriental Art*, Vol. IV, pp. 87–113.
1964 "Das Dravidaproblem," *Sonderabdruck aus dem Anzeiger der phil.-hist. Klasse der Österreichischen Akademie der Wissenschaften*, So. 9, Jahrgang.
HELBAEK, H.,
1960 "The Palaeoethnobotany of the Near East and Europe," R. J. Braidwood and B. How, *Prehistoric Investigations in Iraqi Kurdistan*, Studies in Ancient Oriental Civilization, No. 31, Oriental Institute, University of Chicago, Chicago, pp. 99–118.
HOLDRICH, T. H.,
1910 "The Gates of India," London.
HOLE, FRANK, and FLANNERY, KENT V.,
1962 "Excavations at Ali Kosh, Iran, 1961," *Iranica Antiqua*, Vol. II, pp. 97–148.
HUGHES-BULLER, R.
1903–1904 "Gabarbands in Baluchistan," *Annual Report of the Archaeological Survey of India*, Director-General of Archaeology, ed., Government of India, Calcutta.
Indian Archaeology, A Review, 1953–54 and 1962–63 editions, Report of the Archaeological Survey of India, Government of India, New Delhi.
Indus River Basin Studies, Division of Engineering and Applied Physics, Harvard University, Harvard Water Resources Group, Contract No. 14-08-0001-8305.
JETTMAR, K.,
1967 "An Iron Cheek-piece of a Snaffle Found at Timargarha," *Ancient Pakistan*, Vol. III, pp. 203–209.
JOSHI, R. V.,
1955 *Pleistocene Studies in the Malaprabha Basin*, Deccan College, Poona.
1961 "Stone-age Industries of the Damoh Area, Madhya Pradesh," *Ancient India*, No. 17, pp. 5–36.
1966 "Acheulian Succession in Central India," *Asian Perspectives*, Vol. VIII, No. 1, pp. 150.163.
KENYON, K.,
1957 *Digging Up Jericho*, E. Benn, London.
KHAN, F. A.,
1965 "Excavations at Kot Diji," *Pakistan Archaeology*, No. 2, pp. 11–86.
KHATRI, A. P.,
1961 "Stone Age and Pleistocene Chronology of the Narmada Valley, Central India," *Anthropos*, Vol. LVI, pp. 519–530.
1962 "Origin and Development of Series II Culture in India," *Proceedings of the Prehistoric Society*, Vol. XXVIII, pp. 191–208.
1964 "Rock Paintings of Adamgarh (Central India) and their Age," *Anthropos*, Vol. LIX, pp. 759–769.
KRAMRISH, S.,
1965 *The Art of India Through the Ages*, 3rd ed., Phaidon Press, London.
KRISHNASWAMI, V. D.,
1947 "Stone Age India," *Ancient India*, No. 3, pp. 11–57.
1953 "Progress in Prehistory," *Ancient India*, No. 9, pp. 53–79.

KRISHNASWAMI, V. D., and SOUNDARA RAJAN, K. V.,
1951 "The Lithic Tool-industries of the Singrauli Basin," *Ancient India*, No. 7, pp. 40–65.

LAL, B. B.,
1951 "Further Copper Hoards from the Gangetic Basin and a Review of the Problem," *Ancient India*, No. 7, pp. 20–40.
1954–1955 "Excavations at Hastinapura and other Explorations in the Upper Ganga and Sutlej Basins 1950–52," *Ancient India*, Nos. 10–11, pp. 5–152.
1956 "Palaeoliths from the Beas and Banganga Valleys, Punjab," *Ancient India*, No. 12, pp. 58–92.
1958 "Birbhanpur, A Microlithic Site in the Damodar Valley, West Bengal," *Ancient India*, No. 14, pp. 4–48.
1962 "A New Indus Valley Provincial Capital Discovered: Excavation at Kalibangan in Northern Rajasthan," *Illustrated London News*, March 24, pp. 454–457.
1962, 1963 "A Picture Emerges—an assessment of the Carbon-14 datings of the proto-historic cultures of the Indo-Pakistan subcontinent," *Ancient India*, Nos. 18–19, pp. 208–221.

LAL, B. B., and THAPAR, B. K.,
1967 "Excavation at Kalibangan (New Light on Indus Civilization)," *Cultural Forum*, Vol. XXXIV, pp. 78–88.

LAMBRICK, H. T.,
1964 *Sind: A General Introduction*, History of Sind, Vol. I, Sindhi Adabi Board, Hyderabad, Pakistan.

LEWIS, O.,
1958 *Village Life in Northern India; Studies in a Delhi Village*, University of Illinois Press, Urbana.

McCOWN, D. E.,
1942 *The Comparative Stratigraphy of Early Iran*, Studies in Ancient Oriental Civilization, No. 23, Oriental Institute, University of Chicago, Chicago.
1954 "The Relative Stratigraphy and Chronology of Iran," *Relative Chronologies in Old World Archaeology*, R. Ehrich, ed., University of Chicago Press, Chicago, pp. 56–68.

MACKAY, E. J. H.,
1938 *Further Excavations at Mohenjo-daro*, Government of India, New Delhi.
1943 *Chandu-daro Excavations 1935–36*, American Oriental Society, Vol. XX, Museum of Fine Arts, Boston.

MAJUMDAR, N. G.,
1934 *Explorations in Sind*, Memoirs of the Archaeological Survey of India, No. 48, Government of India.

MALIK, S. C.,
1959 *Stone Age Industries of the Bombay and Satara Districts*, University of Baroda, Archaeological Series No. 4, Poona.

MARRIOTT, M.,
1955 "Little Communities in an Indigenous Civilization," *Village India*, M. Marriott, ed., University of Chicago Press, Chicago.

MARSHALL, SIR J.,
1931 *Mohenjo-daro and the Indus Civilization*, Vol. I, Arthur Probsthain, London.
1960 *A Guide to Taxila*, Department of Archaeology in Pakistan, Cambridge University Press, Cambridge.

MASSON, V. M.,
1959 "Ancient Agricultural Cultures of Margiana," in *Materiali i Issledovaniya po Archaeologii USSR*," No. 73, Moscow.
1960 *Trudii Yushno-Turkmenistanskoi Archaeologicheskoi Komploksnoi Ekspeditsii*, Akademiya Nauk Turkmenskio SSR, Askabad, Vol. X.

MELLAART, J.,
1963 "Excavations at Catal Hüyük, 1962, Second Preliminary Report," *Anatolian Studies*, Vol. XIII, pp. 43–104.
1964 "Excavations at Catal Hüyük, 1963, Third Preliminary Report," *Anatolian Studies*, Vol. XVI, pp. 39–120.

MISRA, V. N.,
1960–1961 "Palaeolithic Culture of Western Rajputana," *The Bulletin of the Deccan College Research Institute*, Vol. XXI, pp. 85–156.

MISRA, V. N., and NAGAR, MALATI,
1961–1962 "Two Stone Age Sites on the River Chambal, Rajasthan," *Bulletin of the Deccan College Research Institute*, Vol. XXII, pp. 156–169.

MISRA, V. N., and MATE, M. S., (ed.)
1965 "Mesolithic Phase in the Prehistory of India," *Indian Prehistory: 1964*, Deccan College Postgraduate and Research Institute, Poona, pp. 57–85.

MOHAPATRA, G. C.,
1962 *The Stone Age Cultures of Orissa*, Deccan College Dissertation Series, Poona.

MOVIUS, H. L., Jr.,
1944 "Early Man and Pleistocene Stratigraphy in Southern and Eastern Asia," *Papers of the Peabody Museum of Archaeology and Ethnology*, Vol. XIX, No. 3, pp. 17–20.
1949 "The Lower Palaeolithic Cultures of Southern and Eastern Asia," *Transactions of the American Philosophical Society*, Vol. XXXVIII, Pt. 4.

NATH, BHOLA,
1963 "Animal Remains from Rangpur," in S. R. Rao, 1963.

Pakistan Archaeology, Journal of the Pakistan Department of Archaeology, 1964–1965, Nos. 1 and 2.

PEPPER, J. F., and EVERHART, G. M.,
1963 *The Indian Ocean: The Geology of Its Bordering Lands and the Configuration of Its Floor*, Department of the Interior, United States Geological Survey, Miscellaneous Geologic Investigations, Map I-380, Washington, D.C.

PERROT, JEAN,
1962 "Palestine-Syria-Cilicia," R. J. Braidwood and G. Willey, ed., *Courses Toward Urban Life*, Viking Fund Publication, Chicago.

PIGGOTT, S.,
1943 "Dating the Hissar Sequence; The Indian Evidence," *Antiquity*, Vol. XVII, No. 68, pp. 169–182.

1947 "A New Prehistoric Ceramic from Baluchistan," *Ancient India*, No. 3, pp. 131–142.

1950 *Prehistoric India*, Pelican Books, Harmondsworth, England.

PITHAWALLA, MANECK B.,

1959 *A Physical and Economic Geography of Sind*, Sindhi Adabi Board, Karachi.

POSSEHL, G. L.,

1967 "The Mohenjo-daro Floods: A Reply," *American Anthropologist*, Vol. LXIX, No. 1, pp. 32–40.

PUGLISI, S. M.,

1963 "Italian Archaeological Mission in Afghanistan. Preliminary Report on the Researches at Hazar Sum," *East and West*, N.S., Vol. XIV, Nos. 1–2, pp.3–12.

RAIKES, R. L.,

1963 "New Prehistoric Bichrome Ware from the Plains of Baluchistan," in *East and West*, Vol XIV, Nos. 1–2, pp. 56–68.

1964 "The End of the Ancient Cities of the Indus Civilization," *American Anthropologist*, Vol. LXV, No. 66, No. 2 (April), pp. 284–299.

1964b "The End of the Ancient Cities of the Indus," *American Anthropologist*, Vol. LXVI, pp. 284–299.

1965 "The Mohenjo-daro Floods," *Antiquity*, Vol. XXXIX, pp. 196–203.

RAIKES, R. L., and DYSON, R. H., Jr.,

1961 "The Prehistoric Climate of Baluchistan and the Indus Valley," *American Anthropologist*, Vol. LXIII, pp. 265–281.

RAJAN, K. V. SOUNDARA,

1961 "Quaternary pebble, core and flake cultures of India—an appraisal of the data," *Ancient India*, No. 17, pp. 68–85.

RAO, M. S. NAGARAJA,

1967 "New Evidence for Neolithic Life in India: Excavations in the Southern Deccan," *Archaeology*, Vol. XX, pp. 28–35.

RAO, M. S. NAGARAJA, and HALAHOTRA, K. C.,

1965 *The Stone Age Hill Dwellers of Tekkalakota*, Poona.

RAO, S. R.,

1962 "Further Excavations at Lothal," *Lalit Kalā*, No. 11, April.

1962, 1963 "Excavations at Rangpur and Other Explorations in Gujarat," *Ancient India*, Nos. 18–19, pp. 5–207.

1965 "Shipping and Maritime Trade of the Indus People," *Expedition*, Vol. VII, No. 3, pp. 30–37.

REDFIELD, R.,

1953 *The Primitive World and its Transformations*, Cornell University Press, Ithaca.

REED, C.,

1960 "A Review of the Archaeological Evidence on Animal Domestication in the Prehistoric Near East," R. J. Braidwood, and B. Howe, *Prehistoric Investigations in Iraqi Kurdistan*, Studies in Ancient Oriental Civilization, No. 31, Oriental Institute, University of Chicago, Chicago, pp. 119–146.

RIVERS, W. H. R.,

1906 *The Todas*, Macmillan and Co., Ltd., London.

450 / Bibliography

ROERICH, J. N.,
1930 "The Animal Style among the Nomad Tribes of Northern Tibet,"
Seminarium Kondakovianum, pp. 33–35, Prague.

ROSS, E. J.,
1946 "A Chalcolithic Site in Northern Baluchistan," *Journal of Near Eastern Studies*, Vol. V, No. 4, pp. 291–315.

ROY, S.,
1953 "Indian Archaeology from Jones to Marshall (1784–1902)," *Ancient India*, No. 9, pp. 4–29.

RYDH, HANNA,
1959 *Rang Mahal*, Papers of the Lunds Universitets Historiska Museum, Series in 4° No. 3, C. W. K. Gleerup, Lund, Sweden.

SANKALIA, H. D.,
1946 *Investigations into the Prehistoric Archaeology of Gujarat*, Baroda.
1956 "Animal Fossils and Palaeolithic Industries from the Pravara Basin at Nevasa, District Ahmadnagar," *Ancient India*, No. 12, pp. 35–52.
1963 *Prehistory and Protohistory in India and Pakistan*, University of Bombay, Bombay.
1964 "Middle Stone Age Culture in India and Pakistan," *Science*, Vol. CXLVI, pp. 365–374.
1965 *Early Stone Age in Saurashtra, Gujarat*, Diputacion Provincial de Barcelona, Instituto de Prehistoria y Archaeologia Monografias, XVI, Barcelona.

SANKALIA, H. D., and DEO, S. B.,
1955 *Report on the Excavations at Nasik and Jorwe*, Deccan College Monograph Series No. 13, Poona.

SANKALIA, H. D., and KARVE, I.,
1955 *Preliminary Report on the Third Gujarat Prehistoric Expedition*, Deccan College, Poona.

SANKALIA, H. D., SUBBARAO, B., and DEO, S. B.,
1958 *Excavations at Maheshwar and Navdatoli 1952–53*, Poona-Baroda.

SESHADRI, M.,
1956 *The Stone Using Cultures of Prehistoric and Protohistoric Mysore*, London.

SMITH, MALCOLM A.,
1931–1943 "The Fauna of British India, including Ceylon and Burma," *Reptilia and Amphibia*, Vols. I–III, Lt.-Col. J. Stephenson, ed., Taylor and Francis, London.

SOLEKI, R. S.,
1955 "Shanidar Cave, a Palaeolithic site in Northern Iraq," *Annual Report of the Board of Regents of the Smithsonian Instiution, 1954*, Publication 4190, Washington, D.C., pp. 389–425.
1963 "Prehistory in Shanidar Valley, Northern Iraq," *Science*, Vol. CXXXIX, pp. 179–193.

SOUNDARA RAJAN, K. V.,
1952 "Stone Age Industries near Giddalur, District Kurnool," *Ancient India*, No. 8, pp. 64–92.

SPATE, O. K.,
1957   *India and Pakistan*, 2nd ed., Methuen, New York.
STACUL, G.,
1966   "Preliminary Report on the Pre-Buddhist Necropolis in Swat," *East and West*, Vol. XVI, pp. 37–79.
STARR, R. F. S.,
1941   *Indus Painted Pottery*, Princeton University Press, Princeton, N.J.
STEIN, A.,
1967   *An Archaeological Reconnaissance in Northwestern India and Southeastern Iran*, London.
STEIN, Sir M. A.,
1928   *Innermost Asia. Detailed report of explorations in central Asia, Kan-Su, and eastern Iran*, Oxford University Press, London.
1929   *An Archaeological Tour in Waziristan and Northern Baluchistan*, Memoirs of the Archaeological Survey of India, No. 37, Government of India, New Delhi.
1931   *An Archaeological Tour in Gedrosia*, Memoirs of the Archaeological Survey of India, No. 43, Government of India.
SUBBARAO, B.,
1948   *Stone Age Culture of Bellary*, Deccan College Dissertation Series No. 7, Poona.
1958   *The Personality of India*, 2nd ed., University of Baroda, Archaeological Series No. 3, Poona.
TATE, G. P.,
1909   *The Frontiers of Baluchistan*, London.
1910–1912   *Seistan, Memoir on the History, Topography, Ruins and People*, 2 vols. Government of India, Calcutta.
THAPAR, B. K.,
1957   "Maski, 1954: A chalcolithic site of the southern Deccan," *Ancient India*, No. 13, Archaeological Survey of India, pp. 4–143.
1965   "Neolithic Problem in India," V. N. Misra and M. S. Mate, eds., *Indian Prehistory: 1964*, Deccan College Postgraduate and Research Institute, Poona, pp. 87–112.
1965   "Relationship of the Indian Chalcolithic Cultures with West Asia," *Indian Prehistory: 1964*, V. N. Misra and M. S. Mate, eds., Deccan College Postgraduate and Research Institute, Poona, pp. 157–176.
TODD, K. R. U.,
1939   "Palaeolothic Industries of Bombay," *Journal of the Royal Anthropological Institute of Great Britain and Ireland*, Vol. LXIX, pp. 257–272.
1950   "The Microlithic Industries of Bombay," *Ancient India*, No. 6, pp. 4–16.
VARMA, R. K.,
1965   Comment on "Mesolithic Phase in the Prehistory of India," *Indian Prehistory: 1964*, V. N. Misra and M. S. Mate, eds., Deccan College Postgraduate and Research Institute, Poona, pp. 75–76.
VATS, M. S.,
1940   *Excavations at Harappa*, Government of India, New Delhi.
VREDENBURG, E.,
1901   "A Geological Sketch of the Baluchistan Desert and a Part of Eastern Iran," *Memoirs of the Geological Survey of India*, Vol. XXXI, Pt. 2.

WADIA, D. N.,
1957   *Geology of India,* Macmillan and Co., Ltd., London.

WAINWRIGHT, G. J.,
1964   *The Pleistocene Deposits of the Lower Narbada River and an Early Stone Age Industry from the River Chambal,* University of Baroda, Archaeological Series No. 7, Poona.

WARD, L.,
1954   "The Relative Chronology of China Through the Han Period," *Relative Chronologies in Old World Archaeology,* R. W. Ehrich, ed., University of Chicago Press, Chicago, pp. 130–144.

WHEELER, Sir M.,
1947   "Harappa 1946: The Defences and Cemetery R 37," *Ancient India,* No. 3, pp. 58–130.
1959   *Early India and Pakistan,* Ancient Peoples and Places Series, Glyn Daniel, gen. ed., Frederick A. Praeger, New York.
1962a   *Charsada: A Metropolis of the Northwest Frontier,* Government of Pakistan and The British Academy, Oxford University Press.
1962b   *The Indus Civilization,* Cambridge History of India Supplementary Volume, 2nd ed., Cambridge University Press.
1968   *The Indus Civilization,* 3rd ed., Cambridge University Press, Cambridge.

WHEELER, R. E. M.,
1947–1948   "Brahmagiri and Chandravalli 1947: Megalithic and other Cultures in Mysore State," *Ancient India,* No. 4, pp. 180–311.
1950   "Five Thousand Years of Pakistan," *Royal India and Pakistan Society,* London.

WILKINSON, C. K.,
1937   "The Iranian Expedition 1936," *Bulletin of the Metropolitan Museum of Art,* Vol. XXXII.

YOUNG, T. C., and SMITH, P. E. L.,
1966   "Research in the Prehistory of Central Iran," *Science,* Vol. CLIII, pp. 386–391.

ZEUNER, F. E.,
1950   *Stone Age and Pleistocene Chronology in Gujarat,* Deccan College Monograph Series No. 6, Poona.
1952   "Microlithic Culture of Langhnaj, Gujarat," *Man,* Vol. LII, pp. 129–131.

ZEUNER, F. E., and ALLCHIN, B.,
1956   "The Microlithic Sites of Tinnevelly District, Madras State," *Ancient India,* No. 12, pp. 4–20.

Additional Bibliography of Pertinent Books Written since 1968

THE MOST IMPORTANT of the general works dealing with the archaeology of the subcontinent is the substantive, provocative, and graceful account written by Bridget and Raymond Allchin, *The Birth of Indian Civilization,* Penguin Books, Harmondsworth, 1968. N. R. Banerjee's *The Iron Age in India,* Delhi, 1964, though published in 1964, did not appear until after 1967. It forms a good account of the later periods of protohistory. J. M. Casal's *La civilisation de l'Indus et ses énigmes,* Paris, 1969, is an excellent account by one of the foremost archaeologists in the field.

Milton Singer's recent *When a Great Tradition Modernizes,* Praeger, New York, 1972, is a must for anyone who wishes to interpret Indian civilization. Two important conferences have now had their papers published and should be regarded as representative of the present state of subcontinental archaeology. These are *South Asian Archaeology,* edited by Norman Hammond, Noyes Press, New Jersey, 1973 (papers from the First International Conference of South Asian Archaeologists held in the University of Cambridge) and *Radiocarbon and Indian Archaeloogy,* edited by D. P. Agrawal and A. Ghosh, Tata Institute of Fundamental Research, Bombay, 1973.

Among the important contributions to subcontinental archaeology have been the writings of L. S. Leshnik of the Institute of South Asian Studies, University of Hiedelberg (see below). Leshnik combines a sound understanding of ethnohistory with practical knowledge of such matters as ecology and artisanship, and his various articles are of great value in the area of critical commentary especially. S. C. Malik is another whose writings bearing upon an anthropological method are worthy of attention (see below). A volume awaited with considerable interest is H. D. Sankalia's revision of his classic *Prehistory and Protohistory in India and Pakistan,* which is apparently now in press. Also of importance is D. P. Agrawal's *The Copper Bronze Age in India,* New Delhi, 1971. Agrawal is one of the leading synthesizers in Indian archaeology with a special approach made possible by his competence in physical chemistry.

AGRAWAL, D. P.; AVASIA, R. K. and GUZDER, STATIRA,
1973   "A Multidisciplinary Approach to the Quaternary Problems in Maharashtra." *Radiocarbon and Indian Archaeology,* ed. by D. P. Agrawal and A. Ghosh, Tata Institute of Fundamental Research, Bombay.
ALLCHIN, B.,
1969   "The Indian Middle Stone Age," *Bulletin of the Institute of Archaeology,* Vol. 2, pp. 1–36.
1973   "Environment, Time and Technology: The Flake Tradition and the Blade and Burin Traditions in Western India," *Radiocarbon and Indian Archaeology,* ed. by D. P. Agrawal and A. Ghosh, Tata Institute of Fundamental Research, Bombay, pp. 18–22.
1973   "Blade and Burin Industries of West Pakistan and Western India," *South Asian Archaeology,* ed. by Norman Hammond, Noyes Press, New Jersey, pp. 39–50.
ALLCHIN, B. and GOUDI, A.,
1971   "Dunes, Aridity and Early Man in Gujarat, Western India," *Man* 6 (2), pp. 248–265.
BANERJEE, N. R.,
1965   *The Iron Age in India,* Munshiram Manoharlal, Delhi.
BERNHARD, WOLFRAM,
1969   "Human Skeletal Remains from the Prehistoric Cemetery of Sarai Khola," *Pakistan Archaeology,* No. 6, ed. by M. H. Rashid, The Department of Archaeology & Museums, Karachi, pp. 100–115.

454 / Bibliography

CASAL, J. M.,
1973 "Excavation at Pirak, West Pakistan," *South Asian Archaeology*, ed. by Norman Hammond, Noyes Press, New Jersey, pp. 171–179.

CORVINUS, G. K.,
1973 "Excavations at an Acheulean Site at Chirki-on-Pravara in India," *South Asian Archaeology*, ed. by Norman Hammond, Noyes Press, New Jersey, pp. 13–28.

DALES, G. F.,
1973 "Archaeological and Radiocarbon Chronologies for Protohistoric South Asia," *South Asian Archaeology*, ed. by Norman Hammond, Noyes Press, New Jersey, pp. 157–169.

DANI, A. H.,
1970–71 "Excavations in the Gomal Valley," *Ancient Pakistan*, Vol. V.

DHAVALIKAR, M. K.,
1973 "Development and Decline of the Deccan Chalcolithic," *Radiocarbon and Indian Archaeology*, ed. by D. P. Agrawal and A. Ghosh, Tata Institute of Fundamental Research, Bombay, pp. 138–147.

GAUR, R. C.,
1973 "Lal Qila Excavation and the OCP Problem," *Radiocarbon and Indian Archaeology*, ed. by D. P. Agrawal and A. Ghosh, Tata Institute of Fundamental Research, Bombay, pp. 154–162.

HALIM, M. A.,
1972 "Excavation of Sarai Khola (Part I)," *Pakistan Archaeology*, No. 7, Karachi, pp. 23–89.

JOSHI, J. P.,
1973 "Excavation at Surkotada," *Radiocarbon and Indian Archaeology*, ed. by D. P. Agrawal and A. Ghosh, Tata Institute of Fundamental Research, Bombay, pp. 173–181.

LAMBERG-KARLOVSKY, C. C.,
1970 "Excavations at Tepe Yahya, Iran, 1967–1969, Progress Report I," Bulletin 27, American School of Prehistoric Research, Peabody Museum, Harvary University.
1971 "The Proto-Elamite Settlement at Tepe Yahya," *Iran*, Journal of the British Institute of Persian Studies, Vol. IX.

LAMBERG-KARLOVSKY, C. C. and MARTHA,
1971 "An Early City in Iran," *Scientific American*, June.

LAMBERG-KARLOVSKY, C. C. and TOSI, M.,
1972 "Tepe Yahya and Shahr-i Sokhta," *East and West*.

LESHNIK, L. S.,
1968 "The Harappan 'Port' at Lothal: Another View," *American Anthropologist*, Vol. 70, No. 5, pp. 911–22.
1973 "Land Use and Ecological factors in Prehistoric North-West India," *South Asian Archaeology*, ed. by Norman Hammond, Noyes Press, New Jersey, pp. 67–84.

MALIK, S. C.,
1968 "Indian Civilization, the Formative Period," Indian Institute of Advanced Study, Simla.

MISRA, V. N.,
1971a "Two Microlithic Sites in Rajasthan," *The Eastern Anthropologist* 24 (3), pp. 237–288.
1971b "Two Late Mesolithic Settlements in Rajasthan," *Journal of University of Poona,* 35, pp. 59–77.
1973 "Problems of Palaeo-Ecology, Palaeo-Climate and Chronology of the Microlithic Cultures of North-West India," *Radiocarbon and Indian Archaeology,* ed. by D. P. Agrawal and A. Ghosh, Tata Institute of Fundamental Research, Bombay, pp. 58–72.

MUGHAL, M. RAFIQUE. "The Early Harappan Period in the Greater Indus Valley and Northern Baluchistan." Ph.D. dissertation, University of Pennsylvania, 1970.

MUGHAL, R.,
1974 "New Evidence of the Early Harappan Culture from Jalilpur, Pakistan," *Archaeloogy,* Vol. 27, No. 2, April 1974, pp. 106–113.

MURTI, M. L. K.,
1968 "Blade and Burin Industries near Renigunta, on the South-East Coast of India," *Processings of the Prehistoric Society,* N.S., Vol. 34, pp. 83–101.

PIPERNO, MARCELLO,
1973 "Micro-drilling at Shahri-i Sokhta; the making and use of the lithic drill-heads," *South Asian Archaeology,* ed. by Norman Hammond, Noyes Press, New Jersey, pp. 119–129.

POSSEHL, GREGORY L.,
1974 "Variation and Change in the Indus Civilization: a Study of Prehistoric Gujarat with Special References to the Post Urban Harappan." Ph.D. dissertation, University of Chicago, 1974.

RAIKES, R. L.,
1968 "Archaeological Explorations in Southern Jhalawan and Las Bela," (Pakistan), Roma.

RAO, S. R.,
1973 Lothal and the Indus Civilization, Asia Publishing House, Bombay.

REDFIELD R., and SINGER, M.,
1956 "The Cultural Role of Cities," *Man in India,* Vol. 36, No. 3, July-Sept. 1956, pp. 161–194.

SANKALIA, H. D.; DEO, S. B., and ANSARI, Z. D.,
1969 *Excavations at Ahar (Tambavati),* Deccan College Postgraduate & Research Institute, Poona.
1971 *Chalcolithic Navdatoli—The Excavations at Navdatoli 1957–59,* Deccan College Research Institute and M. S. University Publication No. 2, Poona.

SANKALIA, H. D.,
1971 *Chalcolithic Navdatoli—The Excavations at Navdatoli 1957–59,* No. 6877, pp. 41–43.
1973 "Radiocarbon Dates in India, Their Consistency and Cultural Implications," *Radiocarbon and Indian Archaeology,* ed. by D. P. Agrawal and A. Ghosh, Tata Institute of Fundamental Research, Bombay, pp. 211–221.

456 / Bibliography

SHARMA, G. R.,
1968–69   *Indian Archaeology 1968–69*, pp. 78–83.

STACUL, G.,
1969   "Excavation near Ghalgai and Chronological Sequence of Proto-historical Cultures in the Swat Valley (West Pakistan)," *East and West*, XIX, pp. 44–91.
1970   "The Gray Pottery in the Swat Valley and the Indo-Iranian Connections," *East and West*, N.S. 20, pp. 87–102.
1973   "Inhumation and Cremation in North-West Pakistan at the end of the Second Millennium B.C.," *South Asian Archaeology*, ed. by Norman Hammond, Noyes Press, New Jersey, pp. 197–201.

SURAJ BHAN,
1971–72a   "Siswal—A Pre-Harappan Site in Drisadvati Valley," *Puratattva*, No. 5, pp. 44–46.
1973   "The Sequence and Spread of Prehistoric Cultures in the Upper Sarasvati Basin," *Radiocarbon and Indian Archaeology*, ed. by D. P. Agrawal and A. Ghosh, Tata Institute of Fundamental Research, Bombay, pp. 252–263.

THAPAR, B. K.,
1973   "Synthesis of the Multiple Data as obtained from Kalibangan," *Radiocarbon and Indian Archaeology*, ed. by D. P. Agrawal and A. Ghosh, Tata Institute of Fundamental Research, Bombay, pp. 264–271.

TOSI, M.,
1968   "Excavations at Shahr-i Sokhta, a Chalcolithic settlement in the Iranian Sistan, Preliminary report on the first campaign, October-December 1967," *East and West*, XVIII, pp. 9–66.
1969   "Excavations at Shahr-i-Sokhta. Preliminary report on the sceond campaign, September-December 1968," *East and West*, XIX, pp. 283–386.

WHEATLEY, PAUL,
1971   *Pivot of the Four Quarters*, Aldine.

Index